FUNDAMENTALS OF SPORT MARKETING

The Sport Management Library offers textbooks for undergraduate students. The subjects in the series reflect the content areas prescribed by the NASPE/NASSM curriculum standards for undergraduate sport management programs.

Titles in the Sport Management Library

Case Studies in Sport Marketing
Developing Successful Sport Marketing Plans
Developing Successful Sport Sponsorship Plans
Economics of Sport
Ethics in Sport Management
Financing Sport
Fundamentals of Sport Marketing (Second Edition)
Legal Aspects of Sport Entrepreneurship
Media Relations in Sport
Sport Facility Planning and Management
Sport Governance in the Global Community
Sport Management Field Experiences

Sport Management Library Titles Forthcoming

Ethics in Sport Management (2nd Edition)
Financing Sport (2nd Edition)

FUNDAMENTALS OF SPORT MARKETING

Brenda G. Pitts
GEORGIA STATE UNIVERSITY

David K. Stotlar
UNIVERSITY OF NORTHERN COLORADO

Fitness Information Technology
A Division of the International Center for Performance Excellence
262 Coliseum, WVU-PE
PO Box 6116
Morgantown, WV 26506-6116

Library of Congress Card Catalog Number: 02102472
ISBN: 1-885693-33-8

Copyeditor: Sandra Woods
Cover design: Krazy Kat Design
Developmental Editor: Geoffrey C. Fuller
Managing Editor: Jessica E. McDonald
Production Editor: Craig Hines
Proofreader: Maria denBoer
Indexer: Maria denBoer
Printed by Sheridan Books

10 9 8 7 6 5 4

Fitness Information Technology
A Division of the International Center for Performance Excellence
262 Coliseum, WVU-PE
PO Box 6116
Morgantown, WV 26506-6116 USA
800.477.4348 (toll free)
304.293.6888 (phone)
304.293.6658 (fax)
Email: fit@fitinfotech.com
Website: www.fitinfotech.com

Contents

Detailed Contents

Foreword

I had one nagging question running through my mind as I read over the second edition of *Fundamentals of Sport Marketing*, namely, Where was *this* book when I was going through school?

Once again, Dr. Pitts and Dr. Stotlar have done an outstanding job of relating the nuances of the constantly expanding, constantly evolving business of selling sports in our society. From explanations of the glitzy advertising campaigns that capture the Winter and Summer Olympics to details of strategies that help recruit sponsors for the neighborhood baseball team . . . there is something for every sports marketing professional in these pages.

Such a variety of practical information makes the second edition of this book a staple for anyone involved in marketing—the first-year student as well as the 40-year veteran of marketing wars. The book's strength stems not only from its varied subject matter, but also from the concrete examples that lend support to its well-grounded theory.

Fundamentals of Sport Marketing stands apart from its competition. Unlike some heavy-handed rehashings of marketing theory, *Fundamentals* draws liberally on actual case studies and examples to illustrate its points. It also does an outstanding job of emphasizing the need for research as one of the first steps of an effective marketing plan, which I can't recommend highly enough. Here at the Forum, we constantly field complaints from sports sponsors and advertisers who are frustrated that today's execs focus way too much on the "what" without paying attention to the "why." Heed their insights, and you'll endear yourself to corporations eager to sell their products and services to today's ever-changing consumer.

And, just as today's consumer desires are constantly evolving, so too is the sport marketing industry, and with it, this text. Readers of the first edition of *Fundamentals of Sport Marketing* will see that Dr. Pitts and Dr. Stotlar have updated the content and added new material to cover the latest innovations such as marketing via the Internet and the growth of alternative sports in our society—a society that's not limited to North America but is increasingly global. A range of examples from Major League Baseball to NASCAR enables readers of *Fundamentals* to learn the reasons and ways that savvy sports marketing professionals are looking beyond traditional borders to cultivate the untapped audience that exists in other countries. This is as it should be because at $150-billion a year and growing, the sport industry has truly become a worldwide phenomena. Why has it become so huge?

To answer that and to better learn what you need to do in order to become a part of this dynamic industry, just turn the page. It's all here, and as they say on television, " . . . it's all good!" My compliments to our authors. They continue to be in constant touch with the trends and the decision-makers that are driving our industry—we wish them a best seller!

Ron Seaver
President
The National Sports Forum

Preface

When we started our careers as professors in sport management and developed our first courses in sport marketing, there were no journals or textbooks in the field. Although this might sound as though it was a very long time ago, it was not. It was less than 20 years ago. As we developed our course lectures and materials, we used the theories and fundamentals of marketing from general business literature as the primary foundation because sport marketing is marketing applied to one industry—the sport industry. We created sport marketing language, developed terminology and definitions, and developed theories, models, and fundamentals. This is what differentiates sport marketing courses from general marketing courses. It is what distinguishes the study of sport marketing. And this, we believe, is what gives a sound basis and what distinguishes this book. Everything we have developed, as well as the other authors in the book, is based on sport marketing's foundation studies, such as, marketing, communication, athletics administration, the media, consumer behavior, sport history, internet marketing, sport sociology, sales, advertising, sport psychology, sponsorship, brand architecture, and marketing management.

In this edition, there are numerous updates to material in the first edition, and there is new material. The updates and developments in this edition are based on research and developments that have taken place since the first edition in sport marketing, sport management, the sport industry as well as the foundational areas mentioned previously. We believe the new material and sections provide the current information and tools that students need as they prepare to begin their careers in the sport industry.

In addition, all of the authors and contributors to this edition have numerous years of experience consulting and working in the industry, and of applying the theories and fundamentals of the first edition in theoretical and applied research. The result is a second edition that is the most current, contemporary, and indispensable book on sport marketing on the market.

Further, we are excited about the companion workbooks that complement the main text. Those include "Case Studies in Sport Marketing," "Developing Successful Sport Sponsorship Plans," and "Developing Successful Sport Marketing Plans." Never before has there been such a complete and comprehensive set of materials to prepare our students for their careers in sport business. We know that students in sport management today will end up in a wide variety of jobs and careers in sport business, so they will need sport marketing fundamentals that can be used in those jobs in any area of the sport industry.

Since the publication of the first edition a mere 6 years ago, there have been many changes in the sport business industry. Today, for example, the Web is a viable marketing tool for companies, NASCAR has become the most popular spectator sport, and women's sports, such as basketball and soccer, have exploded in popularity and commercial value.

In addition, there have been changes in the world that will most assuredly impact sport business. We have always stressed the study of the interrelatedness between sport and society, culture, business, and the world. After we completed the writing of this edition, the event that will most likely have the most impact on the world and thus the sport industry took place—the terrorist attacks in the United States of America in which commercial planes were hijacked and used as weapons of destruction. For the first time in decades, most sporting events were cancelled for several days as we all came to grips with what happened and tried to forecast the far reaching implications and changes that will be necessary in the sports world. The terrorists' goal, it seems, was to strike at free enterprise, democracy, capitalism, and the concept of free society. These are some of the very concepts on which sport business is built. Yet, the acts put play on hold. The temporary shut-down brought about some losses of jobs and funds. However, it will most likely bring about the development of new jobs, especially in relation to security and most likely in facility design. It impacted sport marketing immediately—for an undetermined period of time, for example, the familiar sight of small planes with attached advertising banners flowing behind them are no longer allowed to fly close to sports events.

As this book went to print, we are in wonder of what the start of this new century holds for sport business. Students in sport management will be faced with new problems to manage. This will certainly affect sport marketing efforts for a period of time. As in the first edition, in this new edition, we stress the importance of analyzing sociocultural issues and events and predicting how they influence sport business.

We also know, however, that good will prevail. The terrorists' events and words of hate have heightened the world's commitment to supporting a free, peaceful, and civilized world. Therefore, we know eventually things will return to normal and the sport business industry will once again be safe and free to develop and grow.

Acknowledgments

We first want to recognize and thank all the students who helped us gather material. Dr. Pitts specifically thanks Niki Jones, Jennifer Slattery, Chris Goodwin, Mike Smucker, Kadence Otto, and Mike Clark. We both want to thank all the students and faculty over the years who have been willing to tell us exactly what they think about the book. Students working in industry who call to tell us how they are using everything they learned and have kept the book as a guide have provided helpful suggestions for updating material. Faculty and instructors who use the book for their classes have also offered valuable feedback and suggestions.

We want to thank the Sport Management Library Editorial Board Members Joy DeSensi and Sue Ingles and the publisher and editors at FIT for their patience and persistence in the development and publication of this second edition.

Finally, Brenda thanks her family and partner, Melita, for her patience during those long hours at the laptop; and her family of Corgi girls, Korey and Resa, for their complete commitment to fun—and the knowledge that deadlines are not what's important in life. Rather, the purpose of life is to get outside and play, chase a squirrel up a tree, and find relief.

Introduction

Fundamentals of Sport Marketing, Second Edition is a textbook on the theories, fundamentals, and practical application of marketing to sport business. Our approach has been to apply sound principles of marketing to the sport industry, modify and refine, define and develop, and eventually present theories and fundamentals of sport marketing that we know work in the sport business industry.

In this book, we use the definition of sport management and sport industry as it has been defined in the field of sport management by leading scholars who have extensive experience working in both academia and industry. According to these definitions, the sport industry is broad and varied, includes the many segments of businesses that toil behind the scenes, and is not limited to the selling of sports events. Two schools of thought regarding sport management and sport industry have emerged through the development of sport management as a field of study over the last two decades. One supports the notion that sport management is limited to the study of mainstream sports events and how to market and sell those to spectators. The other supports the position that sport management is the study of all businesses that exist in the sport industry, and the sport industry is defined as all businesses and enterprises whose products are sport or recreation business related. Like no other book in the field, *Fundamentals of Sport Marketing, Second Edition* covers the diversity of sport business, not merely professional and collegiate sport. This would include, for example, sport marketing research companies, sport sponsorship management companies, sporting goods manufacturers and retailers, sports television companies, web sport enterprise, and sport tourism companies. All of these different types of companies are places where sport management and sport marketing students will be working. It is therefore incumbent upon sport management educators to prepare students with foundational knowledge that can be carried into any one of these types of companies. Therefore, our second edition is once again designed to meet these needs: sound foundational sport marketing knowledge that students can apply in any sport business.

This book is designed to introduce students to the academic and practical field of sport marketing. It provides an overview of the sport industry, sport management, and sport marketing. It further provides detailed theories, fundamentals, and practical applications about how to conduct sport marketing. In conjunction with the companion books, these books offer the most comprehensive set of sport marketing materials to date. Moreover, sport marketing professionals working in the industry could easily use these books as handbooks for sport marketing, kept on-hand for constant reference.

Scope and Organization of the Book

This book is based on the philosophy that current and future sport industry professionals should be able to apply the fundamentals of sport marketing to any sport business. Therefore, different types of sport businesses are included as examples throughout the book.

Chapter 1 presents an updated overview of contemporary sport management definitions and concepts for sport, sport industry, sport business, sport management, and sport marketing.

Written by two professors in sport management with extensive backgrounds in sport history, sport marketing, sport law, and sport management, Chapter 2 provides a thorough analysis of the commercial and business value of the sport industry since the late 1800s. This historical knowledge allows students to see the importance of history and how it can be used to predict current and future problems.

Chapter 3 introduces the student to the global characteristics of sport business and how sport and global markets merge.

Chapter 4 orients the student to the foundations of sport marketing and introduces the Sport Marketing Management Model, which provides an illustration of the elements and tasks of the practice of sport marketing.

The original chapter 5 has been split into two chapters, allowing for more information and an emphasis on the importance of sport marketing research and consumer and industry segmentation. The new chapter 5 introduces sport marketing research, its importance, as well as new examples of actual survey instruments that can be used for sport marketing research.

Chapter 6 presents the important sport marketing element of segmentation. Used to categorize and focus marketing efforts for consumer and business-to-business marketing, the importance of both consumer and industry segmentation are presented and thoroughly explained.

Chapter 7 provides the necessary tools for information management.

Chapter 8 lays the groundwork for the four Ps of marketing, each of which is the foci of chapters 9, 10, 11, and 12. Each chapter has been updated with new information from the sport business industry that arms the student with contemporary knowledge in relation to product, price, place, and promotion.

Regardless of which area of the sport industry or what type of sport business an individual is working in, at some point they will work with the media, sponsorship, and/or licensing and endorsements. Therefore, chapters 13, 14, and 15 cover these important sport marketing elements.

New to this edition is information concerning the Web. Chapter 16 specifically addresses the Web and its use as a sport marketing tool, but information concerning the Web was also added throughout the book.

The Appendices are another new and important addition to this edition. Appendix A provides a brief directory to sport businesses. Appendix B contains a directory of sport business trade organizations. Appendix C provides a directory of sport business trade publications. For nearly every specific area of sport business, there is a trade publication to which you may subscribe. Appendix D provides a directory of sport management, sport marketing, and sport law journals and their information; it also contains directories of related sport business journals, sport management associations, sport management conferences, and information about the sport management curriculum standards. Appendix E contains several examples of sport marketing academic research.

These will be helpful in finding research and locating where it is published. Finally, Appendix F contains seven different examples of research instruments commonly used in sport marketing that can be modified and used for actual research. For the first time, sport marketing instructors, students, and practitioners have actual research instruments at their fingertips. Further, each instrument is provided with a description of the topic of study, its purpose, type of instrument, methodology, and some practical uses of the data gathered by this instrument. Actual studies may be conducted using these instruments with appropriate guidance from the sport marketing course instructor.

Underlying Philosophies

Readers should note that this book includes diverse populations, such as people of various ages, genders, races, abilities, classes, sexual orientations, and cultures in order to reflect today's sport industry. We also recognize the varied nature of the industry, and we intentionally present a variety of sport businesses in discussions and as examples throughout the text. Furthermore, we have intentionally presented the material in such a way that it can be used as a practical guide to sport marketing.

Special Package: The Companion Books and Language Editions

Fundamentals of Sport Marketing, Second Edition, is part of a package of sport marketing books by the authors which, when used in conjunction with other sport marketing literature, offers a comprehensive sport marketing education. The main textbook provides the foundation of sport marketing theory and fundamentals, directories for networking and professional growth, and instruments for practical application. *Case Studies in Sport Marketing* offers situations in which students can use their new sport marketing knowledge to analyze sport businesses and possible marketing problems. Finally, *Developing Successful Sport Sponsorship Plans* and *Developing Successful Sport Marketing Plans* offer the student the opportunity to develop contracts and business plans involving sponsorship management and marketing planning. In addition, the books are being translated into languages other than English. The first translated edition of the first edition of *Fundamentals of Sport Marketing* has been translated into Chinese (2000) and is available from the publisher's Web site at www.fitinfotech.com.

Benefits to the Reader

Fundamentals of Sport Marketing was written by people with vast academic experiences, knowledge, consulting, research, and practical experience in sport marketing, both in the U.S. and in countries around the world. Some of their international experiences include speaking, working, teaching, or consulting in South Africa, The Netherlands, Spain, England, France, Singapore, Malaysia, Hong Kong, Mauritius, Australia, Zimbabwe, China, Saudi Arabia, Hungary, Greece, Italy, Germany, Korea, and Taiwan. Both primary authors are North American Society for Sport Management Research Fellow Award Recipients and recipients of the Dr. Earle F. Zeigler Scholar Award, which recognizes top scholars each year in sport management. Therefore, readers can be assured that the book is developed by years of scholarship and practical experience in sport marketing.

It is a book that can be used on the job as a handbook, guide, and reference. Since the first edition was published, students working in the industry report that they continue to use it as a handbook. The second edition builds on the foundation laid in the first edition. The second edition includes new material. Perhaps most importantly for those already in the industry, the new directories of information and research instruments in the appendix.

It is a book that we believe can be used in practically any country. Even though the examples and businesses cited are primarily North American, the theories, fundamentals, and the Pitts & Stotlar Sport Marketing Management Model (found in chapter 4) can be applied in any sport business in any country. As noted above, the first edition has been translated into Chinese, making the information and knowledge available to more countries. If you would be interested in translating the second edition in your language for your country, please let us know.

Chapter 1

The Sport Business Industry

Welcome to one of the largest industries in the United States and perhaps the world. Estimates vary on just how large it is—from $152 billion, making it the 11th largest industry, to near $300 billion, putting it among the top few. The sport business industry consists of several different segments including sports tourism, sporting goods (manufacturing and retail), sports apparel, amateur participant sports, professional sports, recreation, high school and college athletics, outdoor sports, sports businesses such as sport marketing firms, the sport sponsorship industry, and sport-governing bodies. Jobs and careers in the industry are seemingly endless and are as varied as the segments and businesses. It is an industry in which a person can often find success by linking an interest in sports with an interest in something else. For example, a person interested in shoe engineering and sports can design sports shoes as a career. A person who writes computer programs and likes sports can design programs for exercise equipment, for use in athletic training, or for gauging the air drag on race cars, speed-skating suits, or bobsleds.

Segments of the Sport Business Industry:

- Sports tourism
- Sporting goods
- Sports apparel
- Amateur participant sports
- Professional sports
- Recreation
- High school and college athletics
- Outdoor sports
- Sport marketing firms
- Sports sponsorship industry
- Sports-governing bodies

With its size, variety, and flexibility, it is no wonder that sport management is one of the fastest growing, most popular college degree programs today. Because so many students want a career in the sport business industry, many colleges and universities are adding degree programs in sport management, also called sport administration and sport business. Despite recent sport program additions, there are still too few programs and students in sport management to support the constantly growing industry. It will be several years before there are enough students trained in sport management programs to fill all of the available jobs. Until employers in the industry begin to demand employees with the appropriate sport management education, people without a sport management background or a college education will fill the positions in the sport industry. Therefore, it is important that colleges and universities continue to promote sport management education.

It is important for all students in sport management to know and understand everything about their chosen career and industry. For example, it is vital that every sport management student have an understanding of sport marketing. The student must understand sport marketing fundamentals and how they can be used in every segment of the sport industry. This knowledge will ensure the student's success in a chosen career in any segment of the sport industry.

The application of sport marketing fundamentals to the sport industry is best accomplished when the student has full knowledge and understanding of the sport business industry and its segments. It is important to understand what this industry is, how it develops, how it grows, what feeds its growth, who its consumers are, and the nature of its linkages with society and culture.

In this first chapter, the student will learn about the sport business industry. Toward this goal, it is first essential to understand the "sport industry" as it is being defined in sport management today. To do this, it is important to understand the terms *sport* and *industry* individually and also as they are defined in sport management today.

There are now over 26 million mountain bike owners compared to only 200,000 in the early 1980s.

Source: Delpy, L. (1998). An overview of sport tourism. *Journal of Vacation Marketing*, 4(1), 23–38.

Industry

An "industry," as defined by Porter (1985), is "a market in which similar or closely related products are sold to buyers" (p. 233). Some industries may contain only one product. It is more typical that an industry comprises a variety of product items sold to many existing or potential consumers who vary demographically and psychographically, and who may change in need, want, desire, or demand (Porter).

The tennis racket industry is an example of a single-product industry. Within this industry, there are different variations of tennis rackets ranging in size, color, material, and price to meet the demands of the many different consumer markets. Additionally, the tennis racket industry is part of a multi-product industry, the sporting goods industry.

The sporting goods industry is an example of an industry comprising many different but related products. It comprises all products sold as goods, equipment and apparel for use in sports, recreation, and fitness activities. This industry can be subdivided into several segments using different ways to define those segments. To see the many segments of the sporting goods industry, look inside a sporting goods store. There are departments, representative segments of the industry, for a variety of sports and activities, categorized according to their similarities such as water sports, camping activities, and soccer apparel. Keep in mind, however, that your local sporting goods store doesn't carry goods for every sport that exists. For example, to find equestrian or rodeo equipment, you would have to go to a specialty store.

Within a department, the products can be further subdivided into groups of individual sports or closely related sports. In the water sports department, for example, there are equipment, goods, accessories, and apparel for several different sports such as scuba diving, fishing, water skiing, snorkeling, and swimming. In the tennis department, you will find tennis rackets, from the single-product industry, but you will also find many other tennis products—tennis balls, shoes, socks, bags, towels, tennis ball holders, water bottles, caps, shirts, and many more. You will also find products not needed to play tennis. These are products that promote the sport of tennis such as tennis bumper stickers, key rings, jewelry, posters, and T-shirts.

Products in the Sport Industry Include:

- Participation
- Entertainment
- Equipment and apparel
- Promotional items
- Sport facilities
- Marketing research
- Management services

As you can see in the examples, an industry can be composed of one product or many products. Those products can be very closely related and similar in nature or very loosely related and not so similar. Moreover, it is important to recognize that products can be goods, services, people, places, or ideas. An industry can be composed of one of these or a combination

It is important to recognize that products can be goods, services, people, places, or ideas.

of them. Either way, the products are usually related in some way as defined by those involved in the industry.

Sport and Sport Management

Sport is defined in many different ways depending on the context in which it is used. In many fields such as sport sociology, physical education, and recreation, sport is used to denote sporting activities such as basketball, hiking, snow-boarding, and boating. Sport sociology is the study of people and sport and society. Physical education involves teaching sports to people. The term *sport*, as used in contemporary sport management and in relation to the sport business industry, is a broad concept term used to denote all people, activities, businesses, and organizations involved in producing, facilitating, promoting, or organizing any activity, experience, or business enterprise focused on fitness, recreation, sports, sports tourism, or leisure (Parks et al, 1998; Pitts, Fielding, and Miller, 1994). To classify an enterprise as a sport business, then, doesn't necessarily mean it is a business that sells sports. It might be a company in the business of sport marketing research, a sports tourism business that sells snow ski packages, a web sport company that sells Women's World Cup souvenirs via the world wide web, a sponsorship management business specializing in handling sports sponsorship packages, or a sporting goods company that manufactures mountain-climbing gear.

Sport defined:

Sport, as used in contemporary sport management and in relation to the sport business industry, is a broad concept term to denote all people, activities, businesses, and organizations involved in producing, facilitating, promoting, or organizing any sport business, activity, or experience focused on or related to fitness, recreation, sports, sports tourism, or leisure.

Notice that the title of this book is *Fundamentals of Sport Marketing* and not *Fundamentals of Sports Marketing*. Also note the use of the term *sport management* instead of *sports management*. The term *sport* has a very different meaning than *sports*. According to the North American Society for Sport Management (NASSM) (Parks and Zanger, 1990), "sports implies a collection of separate activities such as golf, soccer, hockey, volleyball, softball, and gymnastics—items in a series that can be counted" (6). This is the way most people define sports—as sports activities. This reflects primarily two things: first, exposure to sports in our schools and colleges; second, exposure to sports every day through the media. That is, what the average person sees and hears through television coverage of sports events, the sports section in the newspaper, and the sports report on TV news broadcasts is sports activities as they take place or a report of the outcome—the final score and who won. Therefore, *sports* management implies only managing sports activities. Sport, however, is a collective noun and a more all-encompassing concept. Therefore, the North American Society for Sport Management, the professional association composed of university academicians and scholars, chose the word *sport* as a term that more correctly identifies and defines the sport management field of study (Parks, Zanger, & Quarterman, 1998).

Sport Management defined:

Sport Management is the study and practice of all people, activities, businesses, or organizations involved in producing, facilitating, promoting, or organizing any sport-related business or product.

Sport management implies a much broader concept. Therefore, the contemporary definition of sport management is as follows:

Sport management is the study and practice involved in relation to all people, activities, businesses, and organizations involved in producing, facilitating, promoting, or organizing any product that is sport, fitness, and recreation related. Sport products can be goods, services, people, places, or ideas. This includes, for example, a company that manufactures sports equipment, clothing, or shoes; a person or company who offers promotion services for a sports organization; an organization charged with governing a sport; a person who represents a professional athlete as an agent; people who own and manage a sports facility; people who design and construct those sports facilities; a person who teaches golf; a company that manages the promotional merchandise and licenses for a sports event; and television companies that are involved in broadcasting sports events.

This is what *sport* means when used in the context of sport management, sport marketing, and the sport industry. It is an all-inclusive term representing every person and business involved in producing, facilitating, promoting, or organizing sports, fitness, play, leisure, or recreation activity and all related products.

The Sport Business Industry

We may now put the two words together and define the term *sport industry*. The research of Pitts et al. (1994), a study by *The Sporting News* and Wharton Econometric Forecasting Association Group (Comte and Stogel, 1990), the books of Parks, et al (1998), and a study by Meek (1997) provides descriptions of the many different products and businesses that comprise the sport industry. The products and businesses focus on sports, fitness, recreation, or leisure products. There are many different groups of consumers for these products, and they can be largely categorized as either end consumers or business consumers.

Sport Industry defined:

The sport industry is the market in which the businesses and products offered to its buyers are sport related and may be goods, services, people, places, or ideas.

Based on this research and the definitions of *sport* and *industry* presented earlier, the definition of *sport industry* follows:

The *sport industry* is the market in which the products offered to its buyers are sport, fitness, recreation, or leisure related and may be activities, goods, services, people, places, or ideas. Here are some examples of the types of products offered in the sport industry:

- Sports are products and can be offered as a participation product such as participation in a women's recreational basketball league;
- Sports can be offered as a spectatorial product (entertainment) such as the offer to watch a field hockey game, a snow-boarding competition, or the X-Games;
- Equipment and apparel are sport products needed or desired to participate in sports and fitness activities such as softball uniforms, ice-hockey pads, body-building apparel, in-line skates, and bicycle helmets;
- Promotional merchandise is a sport product used to promote a sport business, a sports league, a sports event, or fitness activity such as logo caps and shirts, fitness club shirts or towels, stadium cushions and blankets with the company logo;
- Sports facilities are sport products needed or desired for producing sport such as the construction of a new sport stadium or the remodeling of racquetball courts to accommodate wallyball; the design and the construction company for the facility are also products;

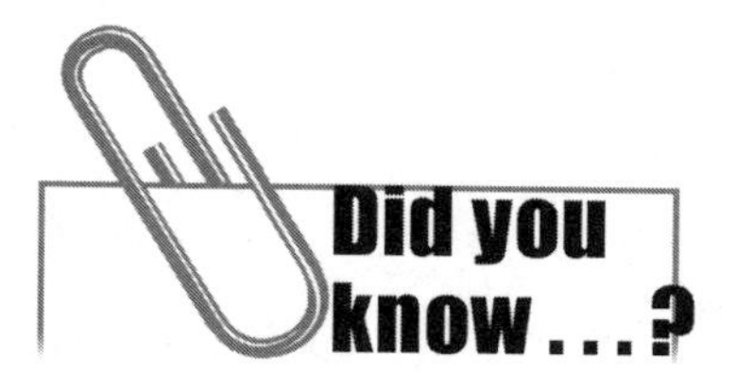

Sports is the leading spending industry for corporate sponsorship. Here are the top three:

Sports
$4.6 billion

Entertainment
$675 million

Festivals, Fairs
$578 million

Source: *IEG Sponsorship Report*, 1997

- Service businesses offer such sport products as sport marketing research, tennis racket stringing, or golf course care;
- Recreational activities are sport products sold as participation products such as mountain bicycling, hiking, camping, horseback riding, boating, cross-country skiing, sailing, and mountain climbing;
- Complete management and marketing professional services are sport products offered for a variety of markets such as the management of a large marathon, the promotion and management of a sports tourism package, or the management and marketing for an athlete; and
- Sport media businesses offer such products as magazines about specific sports such as *Runner's World* magazine and trade magazines targeted to industry business such as *The Boat Dealer*. There also are these products and companies: sports television companies, sports radio shows, and Internet sports companies.

The Size of the Sport Business Industry

The sport business industry has experienced phenomenal growth in a relatively short period. Although sports and recreational activities, events, and businesses have been around for a very long time, there has never been a period of explosive growth like the last 30 years. There are many reasons for this growth. Those are presented in the next section in this chapter. These changes represent both horizontal and vertical expansion. Horizontal growth involves addition of new markets and new products such as new sport businesses like sport marketing research firms. Vertical growth involves the growth of existing markets and products such as the explosion of girls and women in traditional sports like basketball and volleyball.

Study	Year	Size of Industry	%Growth Annual/Between		Rank
1st study	1986	$47.3 billion	—		
2nd study	1987	$50.2 billion	+6.1		23rd
3rd study	1988	$63.1 billion	+7.5		22nd
4th study	1995	$152 billion	+13.0	+141.0	11th
5th study	1999	$213 billion	+10.5	+40.1	6th

Note: The results of these five studies cannot be compared. Although each study included similar segments of the industry, they included different segments. Moreover, methodologies were not similar. However, some general conclusions can be made.

- between 1986 and 1988, the annual increase averaged +6.8%
- from 1988 to 1995, the average increase was +13%
- from 1995 to 1999, the average increase was +10.5%

Figure 1.1
Growth of the Sport Industry—1985 to 1999 According to the Findings of Five Different Studies.

Research in the first three studies was conducted by Sport Inc. and Sporting News with WEFA (Wharton Econometric Forecasting Association); the fourth study is from Meek, A. (1997). An estimate of the size and supported economic activity of the sports industry in the United States. *Sport Marketing Quarterly, 6* (4), 15–21.; the fifth study was conduced by *SportsBusiness Journal* and published in the December 20–26, 1999 issue (1999, volume 2, issue 35, pages 23–30).

A few studies have been conducted in an attempt to place a dollar value or economic impact number on the sport business industry. Although the studies were not conducted the same way and did not look at the same factors, they at least provide an estimate of the size of the industry and the various segments that have composed the industry since 1986. You may be surprised to learn that men's professional sports are not the largest segment of the industry even though there is a lot of money in some men's professional sports and some of them are the primary, and prime-time, focus of most media. However, as you will see in the figures, the largest segments of the industry are sports for the masses and sporting goods. When you give thought to what comprises these segments, then you see that it makes sense. Five studies on the size of the

The Top 50 Industries in 1987 (In billions)			
1. Real estate	$519.3	26. Paper and allied products	39.5
2. Manufacturing	479.9	27. Auto repair garages	38.9
3. Retail trade	427.4	28. Security/commodity brokers	36.7
4. Regulated Industry	408.2	29. Primary metals	36.4
5. Manufacturing (non-durable goods)	373.6	30. Lodging	35.7
6. Wholesale trade	313.0	31. Personal services	34.4
7. Health services	223.7	32. Air transportation	34.2
8. Business services	179.3	33. Petroleum and related products	33.6
9. Communications	120.9	34. Rubber and plastics	29.9
10. Radio and television	108.3	35. Educational services	29.6
11. Insurance	101.3	36. Insurance agents and brokers	28.6
12. Miscellaneous professional organizations	86.4	37. Lumber	27.7
13. Electrical machinery	85.0	38. Stone, clay, and glass	27.5
14. Banking	84.8	39. Instrument manufacturing	26.9
15. Chemicals and allied products	77.1	40. Amusement and recreation services	24.0
16. Food and kindred products	74.0	41. Apparel	22.5
17. Insurance carriers	72.7	42. Textile mills	19.9
18. Trucking and warehousing	64.2	43. Credit agencies	17.0
19. Legal services	62.3	44. Holdings and other investment firms	16.2
20. Fabricated metals	60.3	45. Tobacco	15.5
21. Printing and publishing	58.2	46. Furniture and fixtures	14.9
22. Non-auto transportation equipment	56.0	47. Miscellaneous repairs	13.9
23. SPORTS	50.2	48. Miscellaneous manufacturing	13.9
24. Motor vehicles and parts	49.9	49. Telephone and telegraph	12.7
25. Social and membership organizations	45.3	50. Transportation services	12.0

Figure 1.2
Bulk of the Sport Industry in 1987.

Source: (Comte & Stogel, 1990).

sport business industry offer an illustration of its size and segments and its growth over a decade. The first was a series of three studies about the industry in 1986, 1987, and 1988 (Comte and Stogel, 1990). A summary of the studies is presented in Figure 1.1. In this summary, we see that from 1986 to 1988 the sport industry grew an average of 6.8% yearly. This is an important figure to note when comparing the sport industry to other industries that usually average a yearly growth of one to three percent.

In the first edition of this textbook, we predicted that if the sport industry grew at the annual average rate of 6.8%, it would grow to $139 billion by 2000 and would more than double in size. We admit we were wrong. The industry is much larger than the prediction! In 1995, a study showed the sport business industry to be a $152-billion dollar industry and the 11th largest industry in the United States. That represents a 242% increase, indicating that the industry has grown almost 2½ times larger in a 10-year period. Figures 1.1, 1.2, 1.3, 1.4, and 1.5 show the information from those studies. In 1999, a

Industry	Value in billions
1. Real estate	$850.0
2. Retail trade	$639.9
3. Wholesale trade	$491.0
4. Health services	$443.4
5. Construction	$277.6
6. Business services	$275.3
7. Depository institutions	$225.9
8. Utilities	$205.3
9. Other services	$195.0
10. Telecommunications	$156.0
11. Sports	$152.0
12. Chemicals and allied products	$141.0
13. Electronics and electrical equipment	$138.5
14. Industrial machinery and equipment	$123.3
15. Insurance carriers	$115.4
16. Food and kindred products	$113.3
17. Trucking and warehousing	$100.6
18. Legal services	$100.5
19. Printing and publishing	$89.7
20. Motor vehicles and equipment	$88.7
21. Fabricated metal products	$86.0
22. Farms	$85.0
23. Security and commodity brokers	$75.6
24. Oil and gas extraction	$62.7
25. Auto repair, services, and parking	$60.5

Figure 1.3
Rank of the sport industry in 1995 compared to other industries according to the Meek study (Meek,. 1997).

Segment	1987	1988	Percent change
	(in millions)		
Leisure and participant sports	$21,599.5	$22,789.3	+5.5
Sporting goods	18,069.3	19,012.8	+5.2
Advertising	4,058.6	4,388.5	+8.1
Net take fron legal gambling	3,504.8	3,618.3	+3.2
Spectator sports receipts	3,050.0	3,240.0	+6.2
Concessions, souvenirs, novelties	2,100.0	2,348.1	+11.8
TV and radio rights fees	1,209.2	1,415.8	+17.1
Corporate sponsorships	1,012.0	1,140.0	+12.6
Golf course, ski area construction	542.3	946.9	+74.6
Sports insurance	722.0	830.0	+15.0
Magazine circulation revenues	658.6	773.0	+17.4
Royalties from licensed properties	584.0	735.0	+25.9
Athlete endorsements	520.0	585.8	+12.7
Trading cards and accessories	350.0	408.3	+16.7
Sports book purchases	241.0	330.7	+37.2
Stadium and arena construction	250.0	319.3	+27.7
U.S. Olympic Committee, NGB budgets	98.2	114.2	+16.3
Youth team fees	95.3	97.0	+1.8
Halls of fame	5.4	6.0	+11.1
Total	$58,670.2	$63,099.0	+7.5

Note: Several categories have been statistically adjusted with updated 1987 figures, which may vary from previous publication; sports insurance premiums include professional and amateur teams, and individual players, but not multi-purpose facilities.

Figure 1.4
Sport Industry Segments, 1987–88.

Source: (Comte & Stogel, 1990).

fifth study was conducted and reported by the *SportsBusiness Journal*. This study estimated the industry to be $213 billion ("The Answer," 1999). Figure 1.6 illustrates the size of the industry segments as reported in the *SportsBusiness Journal*. Figure 1.7 shows the segments of the industry that were included in the *SportsBusiness Journal* study. When you compare these studies, you can see that the *SportsBusiness Journal* study included the fewest segments of the industry. Their study was limited to organized sports that they defined as "spectator sports" and their related industries.

In Figure 1.8 are the values of wholesale sporting goods, equipment, apparel, and athletic footwear from the Sporting Goods Manufacturers Association (SGMA;1999).

Segments	Estimated Value
1. Sporting goods, footwear, apparel	$71 billion
2. Participant sports	$32 billion
3. Sports medicine	$18.5 billion
4. Construction	$11.8 billion
5. Sponsorship, endorsements, radio, TV, newspapers	$7.5 billion
6. Admissions (spectators)	$5.3 billion
7. Trading cards, video games, tapes, books, magazines	$3.5 billion
8. Concessions and souvenirs	$3.4 billion
9. Betting	$3.3 billion

Figure 1.5
Sport Industry segment sizes in 1995 according to the Meek study (Meek, A. 1997).

The SGMA constantly monitors and studies sporting goods products and participation rates. Figure 1.8 shows the results of their research for 1998 and 1999. In this report, the value of sports equipment, apparel, and footwear is $46 billion in 1999. Integral to determining the size of the sport industry is the study of individual industry segments. Although there may be some overlap, this can be used as an estimate of the size, as well as the variety, of the sport industry. Figures 1.9 and 1.10 present lists of some of the many different sport businesses in the United States and their estimated economic value. You can easily see that the sum of just a few of these segments of the sport industry exceeds the $152-billion-dollar number determined by the Meek (1997) study and perhaps the reported $324-billion-dollar size of the industry in the *SportsBusiness Journal*. Using studies and reports about all the different industry segments might be a better way to study the sport industry. Each sport management student will work in an industry segment and must continuously monitor the research about that segment as well as the entire sport industry.

	Industry	Value
1.	Real estate	$935 billion
2.	Retail trade	$713 billion
3.	Health care	$460 billion
4.	Banking	$266 billion
5.	Transportation	$256 billion
6.	Sports business	$213 billion
7.	Communications	$212 billion
8.	Public utilities	$210 billion
9.	Agriculture	$132 billion
10.	Mining	$121 billion
11.	Motor vehicles and equipment	$85 billion
12.	Motion pictures	$31 billion

Figure 1.6
Where the sport industry ranks compared to other industries in the SportsBusiness Journal study (SportsBusiness Journal, December 20–26, 1999).

This information can be found in a variety of such resources as the following:

- Industry trade publications: These include, for example, trade or business magazines, journals, newsletters, and Internet sites.
- Sport business conventions and exhibitions: These include such annual convention and trade shows as the Snow Sports Industries of America and the National Sporting Goods Association's Super Show.
- Sport management or marketing research businesses: There are numerous companies that specialize in conducting research. Some of these include Joyce Julius and Associates and Simmons Market Research Bureau.
- Local or national news publications: Much can be learned about sport industries from published articles in newspapers and magazines. Local papers carry information about local sports businesses, and national papers provide articles with a more national focus about individual sport-related businesses and whole industries. Another way to help us determine the size and especially the depth and breadth of the sport industry is to look at the factors that have affected growth and development of the industry and at what exists in the industry.

You can keep up with the latest in your industry by
- Reading trade or business magazines, journals, newsletters, and Internet sites
- Attending sport business conventions or exhibitions
- Obtaining research from sport marketing firms
- Reading local or national news publications

Factors Influencing the Growth and Development of the Sport Business Industry

The sport business industry is large and diverse. There are numerous kinds and types of businesses and organizations. Your career in the sport industry will be greatly enhanced if you understand why the industry is so large and diverse and what drives its

Spectator Sports Segment	Estimated Value	% of Total
1. Travel transportation, accommodations, meals of spectators, colleges, the 'big four' leagues, other	$44.47 billion	20.92
2. Advertising telecasts, cable, regional, print, signage, radio	$28.25 billion	13.29
3. Equipment, apparel, footwear sportswear in competition	$24.94 billion	11.73
4. Gate receipts admission, concessions, merchandise, parking	$22.56 billion	10.61
5. Team operating expenses 'big four' player salaries and operating expenses; colleges; others	$19.23 billion	9.05
6. Legal gambling wagers, horses, dogs, jai alai, internet	$18.55 billion	8.73
7. Licensed goods apparel, footwear, housewares, media, miscellaneous	$15.1 billion	7.10
8. Professional services agents, sport marketing firms, facility management, financial, legal, and insurance services	$14.03 billion	6.60
9. Media broadcast rights 'big four,' college, other, radio telecasts	$10.57 billion	5.0
10. Sponsorships events, teams, leagues, broadcasts	$5.09 billion	2.40
11. Medical treatment baseball, football, basketball, soccer, softball, other	$4.1 billion	1.93
12. Facility construction stadium, track, arena construction	$2.49 billion	1.17
13. Publications/videos magazines, videos, video games, books	$2.12 billion	1.0
14. Endorsements value of top 80 athletes and coaches	$730 million	.34
15. Internet revenue from advertising and access fees	$300 million	.14

Note: The study by the *SportsBusiness Journal* included only these few segments of the industry. The methodology included selected organized sports: those that are defined as 'spectator sports' and their related industries, as listed above. Further, the study does not reveal which sports organizations are included and which are left out. Note that this study does not include such segments as participant sports, recreational sports, or others that are listed in other figures here in chapter one (*SportsBusiness Journal*, December 20–26, 1999).

Figure 1.7

growth. To gain this understanding, it is important to understand the factors that have influenced the growth and development of the industry in the past, those that affect it currently, and those that will have an influence in the future (see Figure 1.11). The sport business professional must constantly analyze what is affecting the industry because such influences may affect the success or failure of a product or business. If the sport businessperson studies and understands how the factors affect the product or business, he or she can develop decisions and strategies that will lead to success.

SGMA RECREATION MARKET REPORT—1999

U.S. WHOLESALE VALUE OF ANNUAL MANUFACTURERS SHIPMENTS ($MM)

2000 EDITION

	1998	1999
SPORTS EQUIPMENT		
Archery	$270	280
Paintball	150	170
Total Baseball/Softball	**394**	**424**
Gloves and Mitts	104	107
Baseballs	48	50
Softballs	30	33
Bats	142	155
Batting Gloves	38	39
Protective/Other	32	40
Total Basketball	**350**	**340**
Basketballs/Accessories	220	210
Backboards	130	130
Billiards	235	245
Bowling	215	220
Total Camping	**1,620**	**1,655**
Tents	400	400
Cooler/Chests	320	340
Sleeping Bags (exc. slumber)	190	175
Jugs/Containers	115	120
Backpacks (exc. daypacks)	90	85
Other	505	535
Total Exercise	**3,370**	**3,470**
Exercise—Consumer	2.795	2.770
Treadmills	830	840
Aero gliders	300	200
Ski machines	260	200
Home gyms	240	270
Exercise cycles	190	185
Free weights	135	140
Exercise benches	125	130
Stair climbing machines	100	105
Ab machines	115	125
Other Consumer	500	575
Exercise—Institutional	575	700
Firearms and Hunting	2,068	2,100
Footballs and Sets	122	120
Total Golf	**2,665**	**2,680**
Balls	695	760
Clubs	1,470	1,395
Other	500	525
Ice Skates and Hockey	230	225
In-line roller skates only	319	225
Inline accessories	99	70
Optical goods	420	460
Racquetball	30	27
Skateboards	80	94
Scuba and Skin Diving	300	310
Snow skiing, Alpine	300	270
Snow skiing, X-Country	36	33
Snowboards	174	183
Soccer	215	210
Table tennis	19	19
Total Tennis	**215**	**225**
Balls	75	76
Racquets	95	103
Other	45	46
Volleyball (Ball, Sets)	70	65
Water sports—Ski equipment	145	125
Other water sports equipment	345	360
Fishing	950	1,000
Miscellaneous (E.g. lawn games, darts, indoor games, boxing, cricket, field hockey, gymnastics, handball, lacrosse, martial arts, paddleball, polo, rugby, sleds, toboggans, track and field, squash)	245	248
Team/Institutional (not listed above)	1,430	1,475
Total Sports Equipment	**$17,081**	**$17,328**
SPORTS APPAREL		
Socks	1,298	1,415
Sports bras	230	245
Swimwear	1,505	1,565
Sports shirts	6,255	6,620
Shorts	1,650	1,715
Ski (ex. Outerwear)	288	231
Sweat pants	1,235	1,250
Sweat shirts	1,850	1,855
Sweat suits	740	640
Parkas/Vest/Jackets (non-ski)	810	780
Team	545	525
Miscellaneous (e.g. caps and thermals)	3,084	3,173
Total Sports Apparel	**$19,490**	**$20,014**
ATHLETIC FOOTWEAR		
Running/Jogging	1,510	1,680
Basketball	1,495	1,285
Cross-training	1,495	1,385
Other non-sport (At leisure)	1.095	1,110
Walking	790	755
Other sport (golf, football, etc.)	645	665
Hiking/Outdoor	620	635
Tennis	460	490
Aerobic	230	220
Sport sandals	180	225
Baseball/Softball	115	110
Soccer	100	105
Total Athletic Footwear	**$8,735**	**$8,665**
Total Sporting Goods, Equipment, Sports Apparel, and Athletic Footwear	**$45,306**	**$46,007**
RECREATIONAL TRANSPORT		
Bicycles and Accessories	1,860	1,900
Pleasure boats and motors	6,555	7,754
Recreational vehicles (except motor homes)	6,271	7,092
Personal watercraft	709	630
Total Recreational Transport	**$15,395**	**$17,376**
Total Sports and Recreation Industries	**$60,701**	**$63,383**

Figure 1.8

This chart shows the values of sporting goods, apparel, footwear, and recreational vehicles (SGMA, 1999).

Sport business/market		Value of industry/market	Source
1.	Professional bull riding	$10 million	Fortune, June 22, 1998
2.	Sport supplement market	$1.4 billion	Fortune, June 22, 1998
3.	Oakley	$232 million	Infoseek
4.	Nike	$8.78 billion	Infoseek
5.	NBA	$1.87 billion	Infoseek
6.	Ticketmaster	$341 million	Infoseek
7.	K-Swiss	$161 million	Infoseek
8.	NHL	$1.33 billion	Infoseek
9.	Power Bar	$100 million	Infoseek
10.	WWF	$251 million	Infoseek
11.	Huber, Hunt & Nichols (build arenas)	$1.01 billion	Infoseek
12.	Topps Cards	$229 million	Infoseek
13.	Reebok	$3.22 billion	Infoseek
14.	Adidas	$5.94 billion	Infoseek
15.	NFL	$2.45 billion	Infoseek
16.	Sports Authority	$1.6 billion	Infoseek
17.	Outdoor recreation industry	$40 billion	Outdoor Rec. Col. Of Am.
18.	Snowboard industry	$2 billion	Leisure Trends Group
19.	Bicycle industry	$5 billion	Growth Cycle, Inc.
20.	Angler fishing	$38 billion	American Sportfishing Association
21.	Counterfeit golf club industry	$4 billion	U.S. Customs Service
22.	Interpublic Group of Co. (agents)	$4 billion	cnnsi.com
23.	Snowmobiling (U.S. and Canada)	$9 billion	Int. Snowmobile Man. Assoc.
24.	Sport event travel	$27 billion	Travel Ind. Assoc. of America
25.	Canadian sporting goods market	$4 billion	Industry Canada
26a.	Sport equipment	$17.35 billion	SGMA
26b.	Recreational transport	$17 billion	SGMA
26c.	Sports apparel	$19.55 billion	SGMA
26d.	Athletic footwear	$8.73 billion	SGMA
27.	Sports and recreation industry	$61.7 billion	SGMA
28.	1996 Sport fishing	$6 billion	American Sportfishing Association
29.	Snowmobiling (Wyoming)	$189.5 million	Wyoming Rec. Committee
30.	Sports tourism (1998)	$111.8 billion	Gibson, H.
31.	Sports-related corporate travel	$2.1 billion	Sports Travel Magazine
32.	Team and sports event part. travel	$6.1 billion	Sports Travel Magazine
33.	Adventure and sports fantasy travel	$62.8 billion	Sports Travel Magazine
34.	Sports sponsorship expenditure	$13.2 billion	Sports Business Daily
35.	Fishing industry (1998)	$40 billion	USA Today
36.	Athletic footwear sales (1998)	$13.8 billion	SGMA
37.	Spectator sports revenue (1996)	$66.5 billion	USA Today
38.	Stadium construction (1996)	$5 billion	SGMA
39.	Sports medicine (1996)	$64.6 billion	USA Today
40.	NASCAR (1998)	$2 billion	Fortune
41.	Sales of licensed NASCAR products (1999)	$1.13 billion	Fortune
42.	Billiards products market (1998)	$235 million	Fortune
43.	Retail slaes of sports licensed products (1998)	$71.15 billion	Sports Business Daily
44.	State of Florida sport industry	$16 billion	Florida Sports Foundation

Figure 1.9
Some examples of sport business industry segments and their values.

Event	Impact to area	Source
1. U.S. Open (tennis)	$300 million	Tennis magazine, September 1999
2. 1996 Olympics	$5.1 billion	Jeff Humphrey/ Michael Plummer
3. National girls 12 and under soccer (1997)	$750,000	Infoseek
4. 1999 Fiesta Bowl	$133 million	Arizona State University College of Business
5. Super Bowl XXXII	$295 million	Pricewaterhouse Coopers LLP
6. 1999 U.S. Open (women's golf)	$15–20 million	cnnsi.com
7. The Masters (men's golf)	$110 million	Augusta Visitors Bureau
8. Pepsi 400 (NASCAR)	$200 million	John Story, NASCAR rep.
9. Oldsmobile Classic (women's golf)	$3.3 million	Pat Baldwin
10. 1999 MLB All-Star Game	$62 million	Greater Boston Con. & Visitors Bureau
11. U.S. National Indoor Archery Championships (1997)	$400,000	Infoseek
12. Anderson Consulting World Championship of Golf	$7.6 million	Arizona Dept. of Commerce/Office of Tourism
13. 1997 Daytona 500 Speedweek	$1 billion	cbs.sportsline.com
14. Charlotte Hornets (year)	$100 million	John Connaughton, professor
15. ASA Women's Championship Slowpitch (1997)	$450,000	Infoseek
16. Senior World Series Softball (1997)	$1.8 million	Infoseek
17. U.S. Championship Gymnastics (1997)	$5 million	Infoseek
18. X-Games	$31.87 million	www.bayinsider.com
19. Witchita River Festival	$17.5 million	www.southwind.com
20. Deposit Guaranty Golf Classic Men's Golf	$8.2 million	Madison County Journal
21. National Master Swim (1997)	$640,000	Infoseek
22. 1996 Houston Livestock Show and Rodeo	$150 million	research.travel.state.tx.us
23. Police Olympic Games (1997)	$7–10 million	Infoseek
24. 1990 Goodwill Games	$150 million	research.travel.state.tx.us
25. 1993 U.S. Olympic Festival	$14.9 million	research.travel.state.tx.us
26. German Sport Holiday (1997)	$3.3 million	Infoseek
27. Texas Motor Speedway (annual)	$107 million	research.travel.state.tx.us
28. Gay Games V (1998)	$350 million	Infoseek
29. U.S. Olympic Congress (1997)	$3.2 million	Infoseek

Figure 1.10
Some examples of sport events and their values.

The factors that influence the industry are grouped into the following categories: people; sports activities and events; sporting goods; facilities, sports medicine, and fitness training; commercialization and marketing; service businesses; education; and media. Factors within these categories have been among the many causes for the growth of the industry in the past and will continue to affect growth in the future.

I. People

1. Constant Human Interest in Sport and Recreation
2. Increase in Sport Business Among Diverse Market Segments

II. Sports Activities and Events: Sports, Recreation, Fitness, Leisure, Sports Tourism

1. Constant Increase in the Number of New and Different Sport, Recreational and Fitness Activities, and Events
2. Constant Growth in the Offering of Traditional Sports
3. Constant Increase in the Number and Type of Professional Level Sport, Fitness, and Recreational Activities
4. Increase in Sports Tourism and Adventure Travel Products

III. Sporting Goods

1. Increase in Sporting Goods and Apparel Designed for the Diversity of Markets and Their Demands
2. Influence of Technology on Sport-Related Goods, Services, and Training

IV. Facilities, Sports Medicine, and Fitness Training

1. Increase in Number and Type of Sports Facilities and Events
2. Movement of Facilities From Single-Purpose to Multi-Sport and Full-Service Facilities
3. Constant Increase in the Amount and Type of Sports Medicine and Fitness Training Services

V. Commercialization and Marketing of Sport

1. Packaging of Sport as an Entertaining Product
2. Increased Marketing and Marketing Orientation of the Sport Industry
3. Increased Understanding and Knowledge of Customers of the Sport Business Industry
4. Promotion Perfection as the Goal of Sport Marketing Professionals
5. Growth of Corporate Sponsorship
6. Increased Endorsements
7. Growth in Importance of Licensing and Merchandising

VI. Sport Industry Professional Service Businesses

1. Extraordinary Growth in Service Businesses for the Sport industry

VII. The Sport Industry, Media, and Sport Media

1. Sport Industry Benefits Greatly From Mass Media Exposure
2. Sports Activities and Events as a Popular Entertainment Product
3. Constant Increase of Television and Radio Coverage
4. Increase in the Number and Variety of Magazines, Trade Magazines, and Academic Journals Devoted to Sport
5. The World Wide Web

VII. Sport Industry Education

1. Increase in Sports and Sport Business Education for Executives, Administrators, Athletes, and Other Personnel
2. Increase in Competency of Sport Management Professionals
3. Increased Prevalence of Sport Management as an Academic Discipline and as a Career

Figure 1.11
Factors That Influence the Sport Business Industry—Why the Sport Business Industry Is So Large and Diverse.

Studying the factors that influence the sport industry can reveal what types of jobs are available and help you decide on a future career.

Additionally, studying these factors can help us identify the number and types of jobs and careers in the industry. As you read about the factors listed and explained in this section, think about the number and types of jobs necessary in that area. You just might discover your future career.

I. People

People are the reason sports and the sport business industry exist. If it were not for people's interest in and demand for sports, recreation, fitness, adventure travel, and sports tourism, the industry would not survive. Sports activities, for example, do not exist until people play them. That is, a basketball game does not occur until people get together and play the sport. Further, people, at least in the United States, are fascinated with sports and recreational activities of all kinds. When people become bored with one sport, they invent a new one. Here are some factors relating to people and the sport business industry.

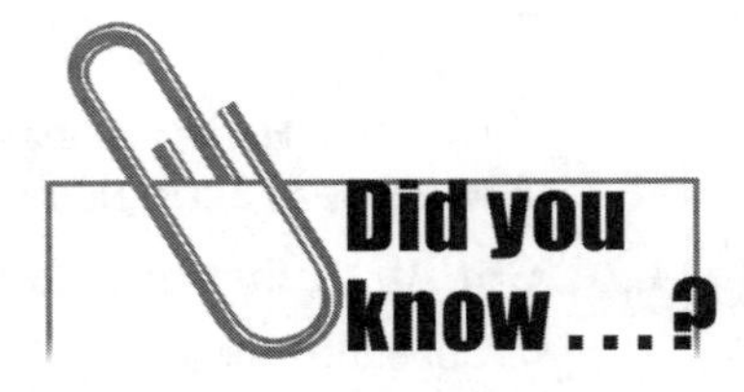

From 1993 to 1998, 98 million adults took "adventure" trips to do . . .

Off-road mountain biking (10.8 million)

Snorkeling, Scuba Diving (12.4 million)

White-water rafting, kayaking (14.8 million)

Camping (27.2 million)

Hiking (44.8 million).

Source: Travel Industry Association of America

1. Constant Human Interest in Sports and Recreation

A look at the studies presented earlier in this chapter on the size of the sport business industry shows that participant sports constitute the largest segment of the industry. People participating in sports, recreation, and fitness activities are the primary reason the sport industry exists. It is people who drive the growth of the sport industry because they are the consumers of sports, recreation, fitness, tourism, and leisure products. Millions of people in this country participate in such activities. They play, run, climb, scoot, ride, and perform numerous other skills for a variety of reasons, including, to have fun, to compete, to improve, to lose weight, to socialize, to have a good workout, and to learn a new sport. Moreover, they invent new activities. As you will learn, numerous new and different sports and activities are invented almost daily.

These millions of people spend billions of dollars to participate in sports, recreation, fitness, travel, and leisure activities annually. The majority of these dollars includes the cost of admission to the activity, which carries such labels as entrance fee, registration fee, membership fee, greens fee, and league fee. To get an idea about how much money can be spent on sports activities, try to find out how much money people in your city spend on entering and participating in some of the sports activities such as softball, basketball, and golf offered by the city parks and recreation department.

Another large portion of the dollars spent on sports is the millions spent for items needed or desired in order to participate such as equipment and apparel. For example, to play softball, the softball player needs a softball glove and a bat. This player might also want to use other products that are produced for a variety of reasons. These might be batting gloves, cap, helmet, special softball shoes, specialized socks, sunglasses, customized uniform shirts, undershirts, pants or shorts, and a customized softball bag to carry it all in. Finally, many players will want merchandise that speaks to their identity as a softball player such as funny softball T-shirts, a softball-glove key ring, and a tiny softball glove and bat to hang on the car's rearview mirror.

Moreover, this continuous interest in sports and recreation activities influences many other segments of the sport industry. Consider this: For every coed basketball league, there must be many people and products in order for that league to exist—a basketball facility, basketball officials, scorekeepers, score sheets, facility managers, facility maintenance people, facility groundskeepers, a league director, a league on-site supervisor, staff people for such jobs as paperwork, record keeping, registration and other forms, a certain number of teams registered, coaches, team managers, uniforms, shoes, socks, water bottles, towels, a coach's note pad, officials' evaluation forms, rulebooks, pens and pencils, and basketballs. There are many different companies needed to supply all of these people and to create and produce all the necessary products. Further, if the basketball league is the WNBA or the NBA, many more businesses are needed to provide additional items or services needed or desired to produce just one game. Some of those are special officials, statisticians and other specialized people, reporters, radio, television, facility security, concessions and concession stand staff, office staff, hospitality staff, promotions and promotions people, parking facilities and parking lot staff, and trophies and awards.

It is easy to see that because so many people participate in sports, fitness, and recreation activities, the sport industry is especially affected. People who participate are the primary reason the industry exists and is so large and diverse. Additionally, they are the reason that the industry has so many other segments.

2. Increase in Sport Business Among Diverse Market Segments

It is unfortunate that television executives in the past primarily chose to televise men's sports events. Doing so created the myth that only men's professional sports are serious and that they comprise the sport industry. This was reinforced by the fact that thousands of daily newspapers and newscasts report mostly men's sports activities. This daily dose further reinforces the myth that the sport industry is composed of a few men's sports. Not true! The sport business industry is a vast multibusiness and multicultural industry. It always has been and always will be. What is perhaps different is that there has been significant growth, development, and commercialization of the multitudes of sports activities and organizations that are created for and managed by the many different populations of people who live in the United States. Figure 1.12 illustrates some of the categories of different sports events.

Geographical regions	African Games Asian Games Pan American Games
Disabilities	Special Olympics Paralympics World Games for the Deaf Disabled Swimming
Religious affiliation	Maccabiah Games
Career/Profession	Police Games World Student Games Corporate Games
Sexual Orientation	The Gay Games EuroGames
Political Affiliation	Commonwealth Games
Race/National Origin	North American Indigenous Games World Games for Indigenous Peoples Cherokee Nation Youth Fitness Camp

Sources: (Preston, 1990; Pitts and Ayers, 1999; Infoseek)

Figure 1.12
Some diversity categories of sport events.

As diverse market segments such as people who are African-American, Asian-American, Jewish, Hispanic, lesbian and gay, aging, and disabled grow and emerge as viable markets, two things are happening. First, existing sports companies are targeting them and courting them as potential consumers either for existing products or potential products. Second, these people are creating their own sports companies and industries. Here are some examples:

- The National Brotherhood of Skiers Association (NBSA) for African American snow skiers has over 14,000 members. The NBSA hosts over 800 events each year. One annual event can reach an estimated economic impact of $10 million.
- The Women's World Cup was created by FIFA to meet the demands of women's soccer worldwide. After the first tournament, in 1991, tournaments have been held every 4 years. The media and fan attention has grown at an extraordinary rate since 1991; and in 1999, the number of spectators attending the matches and the number of people who watched on television broke records even for men's sports events.

- There is a gay and lesbian sports organization, business, league, or team in almost every city in the United States. These organizations offer more than 15,000 sports and recreation events each year for the lesbian and gay sports market. The events range from archery to equestrian to rodeo to snow sports to volleyball.
- Master's swimming organizations offer swimming opportunities, events, and competitions for a variety of age-groups from 20 to 90 years of age. People of different ages compete in groups of their ages only.
- The ESPN X Games were invented specifically for an age-group—18 to 34—labeled the Generation X. There are Summer and Winter X Games; and sports include skateboarding, downhill and aggressive in-line skating, bicycle stunt racing, street luge, snowboarding, snow mountain biking, and skysurfing. Started in 1995, the X Games in 1998 boasted over 400 athletes, $450,000 in prize money, 225,000 spectators 1997, and a proclaimed economic impact of $20 million (Millar 1999, Ruibal 1998).
- The Paralympic Games are Olympic-style Games designed for people with physical disabilities. Disabled Sports USA, established in 1967, offers nationwide sports programs, activities, and events to anyone with a permanent disability. Go to their website at www.dsusa.org, and find out more about this organization. Figure 1.13 shows a few of the many events offered during the year 2000.

Some of the reasons so many different groups of people are creating their own sports businesses and organizations include the following. First, in the past, the mainstream sport industry historically focused primarily on the young, white, able-bodied, heterosexual male market based on the old traditional thinking that sports were attractive only to this group. Therefore, many more sporting opportunities were developed for this market.

Huntsman Cup, Park City, Utah, Level II Ski Races
Sit Volleyball Training Camp, Chicago, Illinois
Challenge Alaska, Alyeska Resort, Girdwood, Alaska, Ski Race
Nordic World Championships, Sion, Switzerland, Nordic Race
Standing Volleyball Tournament, Toronto, Canada
6–9 Track & Field Training Camp, San Diego, California
Paralympic Trials, Cycling, Frisco, Texas
Rocky Mountain Regional Handcycle Race/Camp, Denver, Colorado
Lyons/Sambora Golf Classic, Hardyston, New Jersey

Figure 1.13
Some of the many events offered by Disabled Sports USA during the year 2000 (Source: www.dsusa.org).

Additionally, mainstream media, also historically male dominated, reported primarily on men's sports. Tiring of the discrimination and of being ignored by mainstream sports industries, many different groups of people created their own organizations, businesses, and services.

A second reason is that as populations fight for and gain civil rights, new legislation brings about increased opportunities in sport, fitness, or recreational activity. For some populations, the increase in sports opportunities has almost paralleled the fight for civil rights. The involvement of the African American population in sport, fitness, and recreation activity increased as their struggle for civil and equal rights made progress. Women and girls gained more opportunities in organized high school and collegiate athletics because of legislation aimed at stopping discrimination based on gender in educational institutions. The number of women and girls participating in sports and athletics has increased significantly since the early 1970s.

A third reason is that people like to enjoy sports activities with their friends. Typically, a person wants to be around and do activities with people they like, who have similar characteristics, who enjoy the same things, who share the same culture, and with whom they are most comfortable. It is no surprise that most groups of people with common interests organize their own sports activities and businesses. For example, the number of sport businesses, organizations, and events for the lesbian and gay population has grown at a very fast rate (Pitts, 1997, 1999). The event that exemplifies the growth of sport in the lesbian and gay population is their Olympic sporting event, the Gay Games. The Games are held every 4 years; and the number of events, participants, sponsors, and spectators has grown at an extraordinary rate. The number of participants increased 1,200% from the first Gay Games in 1982 to the fifth Gay Games in 1998. Over 14,000 athletes from over 70 countries competed in 1998. Figure 1.14 shows the growth and size of the Gay Games since 1982.

> Today's sport industry is no longer focused only on young, white, heterosexual men.

Laws and other legislation have been passed to stop discrimination against the handicapped population. The passage of the Americans with Disabilities Act of 1990 has

Gay Games Event Host Year Theme	Gay Games I San Francisco California, USA 1982 "Challenge"	Gay Games II San Francisco California, USA 1986 "Triumph"	Gay Games III Vancouver, British Columbia, Canada 1990 "Celebration"	Gay Games IV New York City New York, USA 1994 "Unity"	Gay Games V Amsterdam, The Netherlands 1998 "Friendship"	Gay Games VI Sudney, Australia 2002 "Under New Skies!"
Sports Participants	1,300	3.482	7,300	10,864	14,843	Est. 16,000
Countries Represented	12	22	28	40	78	Est. 100
Sports Events	16	17	31	31	31	30
Visitors/Spectators	50,000	75,000	200,000	1 million	800.000	Est. 1 million
Workers/Volunteers	600	1,200	3,000	7,000	3,042	Est. 7,000
Attendance: Opening Ceremonies Place Closing Ceremonies Place		(1) 20,000 Kezar Stadium (2) 30,000 Kezar Stadium		(2) 57,000 Yankee Stadium	(1) 50,000 Amsterdam Arena (1) 60,000 Amsterdam Arena	
Budget	$395,000.00	$885,000.00	$3 million	$6.5 million	$10 million	Est. $20 million
Sponsorship	Some in-kind	$210,000	$350,000	$1 million	$2.7 million	Est. $20 million
Sponsorship Sources L/G = lesbian/gay owned	Local L/G businesses	Individuals and small L/G businesses	4 major companies	5 major and 20+ minor; some L/G businesses	50 corporate, 16 foundations, 14 government. (11 are L/G)	Est. major, minor, and L/G businesses
Estimated or actual economic impact	No known reports	No known reports	Est. market report: $50 million	Est. market reports: $112–300 million	$350 million USD; from actual study	Est. $80 million AUS dollars
Press					1,000	
Number of venues: Sports Other					56 for all	

Note: (from Pitts, B.G. and Ayers, K. 1999. Economic Scale of Gay Games V. Paper presented at the annual conference of the North American Society for Sport Management. Vancouver, Canada, June, 1999. Pitts, B.G. and Sullivan, M. 1999. An Analysis of Corporate Sponsorship Recognition at Gay Games V. Paper presented at annual conference of the North American Society for Sport Management, Vancouver, Canada, June, 1999. Pitts, B.G. 1995. Leagues of their own: Growth and development of sport and sport management in the lesbian and gay population in the United States, 1970s-1990s. Paper presented at annual conference of the North American Society for Sport Management, Athens, GA, June, 1995. Pitts, B.G. 1994. Growth and development of sport in the lesbian and gay population in the United States, 1970s-1990s. Paper presented at the First International Conference of the Gay Games, New York City, NY, June, 1994).

Table 1.14
Gay Games Facts.

helped in the increased opportunities in sports and fitness activity for the handicapped and has had a significant impact on forcing the accessibility of sports facilities for the disabled (Miller, Fielding, and Pitts, 1993). The Paralympics receives major sponsorship today. In addition, there are now numerous sports organizations and equipment designers for people with disabilities.

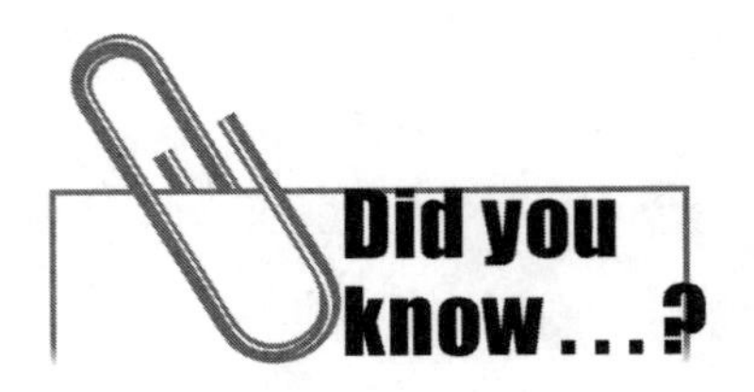

The number of registered recreational boats in the United States rose 20% from the 1980s to the 1990s: from 10 million in 1986 to 11.9 million in 1996.

Source: U.S. Coast Guard

II. Sports Activities and Events: Sports, Recreation, Fitness, Leisure, Sports Tourism

The creation, management, marketing, and production of sports, recreation, fitness, leisure, and sports tourism activities and events offer a world of opportunities to people. Many sports activities are created specifically for a particular group. For example, the popularity of the sports has led to the creation of state games such as the Bluegrass Games (Kentucky), the Sunshine State Games (Florida), and the Big Apple Games (New York). These events are multisport festivals designed for recreational athletes who live in a particular region. Figure 1.15 shows some of the many different sports and recreational activities today and the changes in participation rates over a period of time as compiled by the Sporting Goods Manufacturers Association (SGMA). Indeed, the SGMA believes that participation figures are the most important information in defining the size of a market. According to the SGMA, "sports participation defines the size, composition, and ultimately the trend of the product market and is, in effect, the 'gold standard' to which all markets eventually return" ("Sports Participation Trends," 1999, p. 4).

1. Constant Increase in the Number of New and Different Sports, Recreational, and Fitness Activities, and Events

Since the middle 1970s, the United States has experienced a consistent and fast growth in the number and type of new sport—fitness, or recreation-related activities and events—offered to a variety of sport market consumers. Consider the following examples. In the late 1970s, a seemingly new way to get fit was offered. This was called aerobics—exercising to music. Today, there must be hundreds of different kinds of aerobics offered to a wide variety of consumers. Some of these programs are soft aerobics, hard aerobics, jazzerobics, elderobics, and baby-robics.

During the past two decades, in-line skating made its way across the continent. Boogie-boarding and snow boarding were invented. Here are some others that have been created in the last 10 to 15 years: snow kayaking, parasailing, ice surfing, mountain boarding, two-person and three-person beach volleyball, skydive dancing, street luge, indoor soccer, snow biking, ice climbing, and the X-Games.

The development of new innovative sports has widened the consumer base—more options means more participants.

With this type of fast and diverse growth in inventions in sport and fitness activities comes increased participation by a wider spectrum of consumer. Whereas the traditional sport of outdoor 11-on-11 soccer played for two 45-minute halves might not interest someone, that person might be interested in trying a modified game of soccer indoor, 5-on-5, and consisting of four 12-minute quarters.

These new inventions have increased the number and types of sport-activity products offered to the consumer and have reached an increased number and type of consumer

FITNESS ACTIVITIES	1987 Benchmark	1990	1993	1998	1999	1-Year Change (1998–1999) %	12-Year Change (1987–1999) %
Aerobics (High Impact)	13,961	12,359	10,356	7,460	6,249	**-16.2**	**-55.2**
Aerobics (Low Impact)	11,888	15,950	13,418	12,774	11,585	-9.3	-2.5
Aerobics (Step)	n/a	n/a	11,502	10,784	9,503	**-11.9**	**-17.4**[2]
Aerobics (Net)	21,225	23,015	24,839	21,017	19,129	-9.0	-9.9
Other Exercises to Music	n/a	n/a	n/a	13,846	12,880	-7.0	n/a
Aquatic Exercise	n/a	n/a	n/a	6,685	5,557	**-16.9**	**-12.4**[3]
Calisthenics	n/a	n/a	n/a	30,982	27,528	**-11.1**	n/a
Fitness Bicycling	n/a	n/a	n/a	13,556	12,307	**-9.2**	n/a
Fitness Walking	27,164	37,384	36,325	36,395	35,976	-1.2	**+32.4**
Running/Jogging	37,136	35,722	34,057	34,962	34,047	-2.6	**-8.3**
Fitness Swimming	16,912	18,045	17,485	15,258	14,194	-7.0	**-16.1**
Stretching	n/a	n/a	n/a	35,114	35,278	+0.1	n/a
Yoga/Tai Chi	n/a	n/a	n/a	5,708	6,404	**+12.2**	n/a
Cardio Kickboxing	n/a	n/a	n/a	n/a	7,607	n/a	n/a
EQUIPMENT EXERCISE							
Free Weights (Net)	22,553	26,728	28,564	41,266	42,810	**+3.7**	**+89.8**
Weight/Resistance Machines	15,261	16,776	19,446	22,519	22,961	**+2.0**	**+50.5**
Home Gym Exercise	3,905	4,748	6,258	7,577	7,918	**+4.5**	**+102.8**
Abdominal Machine/Device	n/a	n/a	n/a	16,534	17,109	**+3.5**	n/a
Rowing Machine	14,481	14,639	11,263	7,485	6,269	**-16.2**	**-56.7**
Stationary Cycling	30,765	39,823	35,975	30,791	30,942	+0.5	+0.6
Treadmill Exercise	4,396	11,484	19,685	37,073	37,463	**+1.1**	**+752.2**
Stair-Climbing Machine	2,121	13,498	22,494	18,609	16,288	**-12.5**	**+667.9**
Aerobic Rider	n/a	n/a	n/a	5,868	4,165	**-29.0**	**-51.4**[3]
Elliptical Motion Trainer	n/a	n/a	n/a	3,863	5,081	**+31.5**	**+113.8**[3]
Cross-Country Ski Machine	n/a	6,390	9,792	6,870	5,921	**-13.8**	**-7.3**[1]
TEAM SPORTS							
Baseball	15,098	15,454	15,586	12,318	12,069	-2.0	**-20.1**
Basketball	35,737	39,808	42,138	42,417	39,368	**-7.2**	**+10.2**
Cheerleading	n/a	3,039	3,257	3,266	3,003	-8.1	-1.2[1]
Ice Hockey	2,393	2,762	3,204	2,915	2,385	-18.2	-0.3
Field Hockey	n/a	n/a	n/a	1,375	1,027	-25.2	n/a
Football (Touch)	20,292	20,894	21,241	17,382	16,729	-3.8	**-17.6**
Football (Tackle)	n/a	n/a	n/a	n/a	4,932	n/a	n/a
Football (Net)	n/a	n/a	n/a	n/a	18,717	n/a	n/a
Lacrosse	n/a	n/a	n/a	926	822	**-11.2**	n/a
Rugby	n/a	n/a	n/a	546	498	**-8.8**	n/a
Soccer	15,338	15,945	16,365	18,176	17,582	**-3.3**	+14.3
Softball (Regular)	n/a	n/a	n/a	19,407	17,926	**-7.6**	**-12.4**[3]
Softball (Fast-pitch)	n/a	n/a	n/a	3,702	3,214	**-13.2**	-2.3[3]
Softball (Net)	30,995	32,479	30,135	21,252	19,766	**-7.4**	**-36.2**
Vollyball (Hard Surface/Grass)	n/a	34,755	31,707	21,252	19,052	-10.4	**-45.2**
Vollyball (Beach)	n/a	11,560	13,509	10,572	9,521	**-9.9**	**-17.6**[1]
Vollyball (Net)	35,984	39,633	37,757	26,637	24,176	**-9.2**	**-32.8**
RACQUET SPORTS							
Badminton	14,793	13,559	11,908	9,936	8,884	**-10.6**	**-39.9**
Platform Tennis	n/a	n/a	n/a	352	364	+3.4	n/a
Racquetball	10,395	9,213	7,412	5,853	5,633	-3.8	**-45.8**
Squash	n/a	n/a	n/a	289	348	+20.4	n/a
Table Tennis	n/a	20,089	17,689	14,999	13,998	-6.7	-30.3[1]
Tennis	21,147	21,742	19,346	16,937	16,817	-0.7	-20.5
PERSONAL CONTACT SPORTS							
Boxing	n/a	n/a	n/a	n/a	904	n/a	n/a
Martial Arts	n/a	n/a	n/a	5,368	5,545	+3.3	n/a
Wrestling	n/a	n/a	n/a	n/a	2,546	n/a	n/a
INDOOR SPORTS							
Billiards/Pool	35,297	38,862	40,254	39,654	36,425	**-8.1**	**+3.2**
Bowling	47,823	53,537	49,022	50,593	52,577	**+3.9**	**+9.9**
Darts	n/a	n/a	n/a	21,792	19,757	**-9.3**	n/a

(continued on next page)

Figure 1.15
SGMA Sports Participation Trends
U.S. Population, 6 years or older, at least once per year (thousands). Released April 2000

Figure 1.15 (continued)

SKATING SPORTS	1987 Benchmark	1990	1993	1998	1999	1-Year Change (1998–1999) %	12-Year Change (1987–1999) %
Roller Hockey	n/a	n/a	2,323	3,876	2,853	**-26.4**	**+22.8**[2]
Roller Skating (2x2 Wheels)	n/a	27,101	24,223	14,752	12,404	**-15.9**	**-54.2**[1]
Roller Skating (Inline Wheels)	n/a	4,695	13,689	32,010	27,865	-12.9	**+493.5**[1]
Skateboarding	10,888	9,267	5,388	7,190	7,807	+8.6	-28.3
Ice Skating	n/a	n/a	n/a	18,710	17,499	-6.5	n/a
STREET SPORTS							
Stickball	n/a	n/a	n/a	423	n/a	n/a	n/a
Street Hockey	n/a	n/a	n/a	3,601	2,143	**-40.5**	n/a
OTHER RECREATIONAL ACTIVITES							
Bicycling (BMX)	n/a	n/a	n/a	n/a	3,730	n/a	n/a
Bicycling (Recreational)	n/a	n/a	n/a	54,575	56,227	**+3.0**	n/a
Fencing	n/a	n/a	n/a	527	n/a	n/a	n/a
Golf	26,261	28,945	28,610	29,961	28,216	**-5.8**	**+7.4**
Gymnastics	n/a	n/a	n/a	6,224	5,254	**-15.6**	n/a
Walking (Recreational)	n/a	n/a	n/a	80,864	84,096	**+4.0**	n/a
OUTDOORS SPORTS/ACTIVITIES OUTDOORS							
Camping (Tent)	35,232	36,915	34,772	42,677	40,803	**-4.4**	**+15.8**
Camping (Recreational Vehicle)	22,655	20,764	22,187	18,188	17,577	-3.4	**-22.4**
Camping (Net)	50,386	50,537	49,858	50,650	49,446	-2.4	-1.9
Hiking (Day)	n/a	n/a	n/a	38,629	39,235	+1.6	n/a
Hiking (Overnight)	n/a	n/a	n/a	6,821	6,421	-5.9	n/a
Hiking (Net)	n/a	n/a	n/a	40,117	40,639	+1.3	n/a
Horseback Riding	n/a	n/a	n/a	16,522	16,906	+2.3	n/a
Mountain Biking	1,512	4,146	7,408	8,611	7,849	-8.8	**+419.1**
Mountain/Rock Climbing	n/a	n/a	n/a	2,004	2,103	+4.9	n/a
Artificial Wall Climbing	n/a	n/a	n/a	4,696	4,817	+2.6	n/a
Trail Running	n/a	n/a	n/a	5,249	6,233	**+18.7**	n/a
SHOOTING SPORTS							
Archery	8,558	9,252	8,648	7,109	6,937	-2.4	**-18.9**
Hunting (Shotgun/Rifle)	25,241	23,220	23,189	16,684	16,779	+0.6	**-33.5**
Hunting (Bow)	n/a	n/a	n/a	4,,719	4,627	-1.9	n/a
Paintball	n/a	n/a	n/a	5,923	6,364	+7.4	n/a
Shooting (Sports Clays)	n/a	2,932	3,100	2,734	3,749	**+37.1**	**+27.9**
Shooting (Trap/Skeet)	5,073	n/a	n/a	3,800	4,745	**+24.9**	-6.5
Target Shooting (Rifle)	n/a	n/a	n/a	14,042	14,172	+0.9	n/a
Target Shooting (Pistol)	n/a	n/a	n/a	12,110	12,073	-0.3	n/a
Target Shooting (Net)	18,947	21,840	23,498	18,330	18,312	0	-3.4[1]
FISHING							
Fishing (Fly)	11,359	8,039	6,598	7,269	6,134	**-15.6**	**-46.0**
Fishing (Freshwater—Other)	50,500	53,207	50,198	45,807	44,452	-3.0	**-12.0**
Fishing (Saltwater)	19,646	19,087	18,490	15,671	14,807	-5.5	**-24.6**
Fishing (Net)	58,402	58,816	55,442	55,488	54,320	-2.1	**-7.0**
SNOW SPORTS							
Skiing (Cross-Country)	8,344	7,292	6,489	4,728	3,988	**-15.6**	**-52.2**
Skiing (Downhill)	17,676	18,209	17,567	14,836	13,865	-6.5	**-21.6**
Snowboarding	n/a	2,116	2,567	5,461	4,729	-13.4	**+123.5**[1]
Snowmobiling	n/a	n/a	n/a	6,492	5,490	**-15.4**	n/a
Snowshoeing	n/a	n/a	n/a	1,721	1,673	-2.8	n/a
WATER SPORTS							
Boardsailing/Windsurfing	1,145	1,025	835	1,075	624	**-41.9**	**-45.5**
Canoeing	n/a	n/a	n/a	13,615	12,785	-6.1	n/a
Kayaking	n/a	n/a	n/a	3,501	4,012	+14.6	n/a
Rafting	n/a	n/a	n/a	5,570	5,000	-10.2	n/a
Jet Skiing	n/a	n/a	n/a	11,203	9,981	-10.9	n/a
Sailing	6,368	5,981	3,918	5,902	5,327	-9.7	**-16.3**
Scuba Diving	2,433	2,615	2,306	3,448	3,095	-10.2	**+27.2**
Snorkeling	n/a	n/a	n/a	10,575	10,694	+1.3	n/a
Surfing	1,459	1,224	n/a	1,395	1,736	**+24.4**	**+19.0**
Swimming (Recreational)	n/a	n/a	n/a	94,371	95,094	+0.8	n/a
Wakeboarding	n/a	n/a	n/a	2,253	2,707	**+20.2**	n/a
Water Skiing	19,902	19,314	16,626	10,161	9,961	-2.0	**-49.9**

[1]Nine-year change [2]Six-year change [3]Two-year change [4]Small sample base—statistically insignificant change [5]New sport definition for 1999
Bold-face type indicates statistically significant change.

market segments. This kind of new product development is one key to success in competitive strategy.

2. Consistent Growth in the Offering of Traditional Sports

Even though there are a multitude of new sports activities, traditional sports haven't been set aside. Instead, there has been growth in the offerings of traditional sports and activities. In other words, if you wanted to play volleyball a few decades ago, you most likely would have had to join a YWCA, YMCA, or a local city parks and recreation league. Today, volleyball is offered by many different businesses and organizations such as multisport centers, clubs, independent organizations, individual tournaments, and even by local pubs or bars. Along the same line, soccer was a sport almost unknown in the United States just a few decades ago. Today, soccer may be found at many parks and recreation facilities, privately owned facilities, state facilities, and on the campuses of schools and colleges. It is offered to consumers of all ages. There are leagues for children who are 4 years old as well as the fast-growing leagues for the 30-something, 40-something, and 50-something year-old player.

In addition, fueling this growth are the increasing numbers of sports and recreation organizations among the many diverse populations. For example, the number and variety of sports and recreational activities and events for people with disabilities have exploded. Limited only by imagination, people with a vision or hearing impairment, for example, can participate in a multitude of sports, recreation, and fitness activities.

3. Constant Increase in the Number and Type of Professional Level Sport, Fitness, and Recreational Activities

When a new sport activity is invented, sometimes that sport will become a professional sport activity. A professional sport is one in which the participant is paid to perform or in which the participant is making a career of the activity. Consider the number and range of sport and fitness activities that are professional today: racing cars, trucks, boats, horses, dogs, and other items; Frisbee throwing; water sports such as water skiing, knee boarding, trick skiing, jet skiing, surfing, boogie-boarding, windsurfing, sailing, yachting, fishing, and other water activities; snow sports such as downhill and cross-country racing, trick skiing, ice sailing, the Iditarod, ice fishing, and others; bowling; billiards; hang gliding; aerobics competition; and body building. These have increased the number of professional sports participants as well as the number of opportunities available for the sport management and sport marketing professional in producing, facilitating, promoting, or organizing the events. In addition, such a growth in activity increases the need for sports equipment and apparel designed for the sport and participant.

4. Increase in Sports Tourism and Adventure Travel Products

Combining travel and sports is not new. Every time a person travels to another city to participate in a marathon or to go hiking in the Himalayas, this is sports tourism. Every time a group of baseball fans travels to another city to watch the World Series, this is sports tourism. When people travel to Fort Lauderdale to see the Swimming Hall of Fame or travel to tour a sports facility as if to pay homage to it, this too is sports tourism.

During the past decade, sports-tourism, sports-travel, and adventure-travel products have increased. Additionally, the number and diversity of businesses offering these products have increased. Sports tourism is a combination of sports activities and travel, either for participatory, spectatorial, or homage purposes (Gibson, Attle, and Yiannakis,1998; Pitts, 1999; Standeven and DeKnop, 1999). One report shows that sports tourism is a $111.8-billion-dollar industry in the United States (refer to Figure 1.9). Some sports businesses such as snow ski resorts rely heavily on people's willingness to travel to their place of business in order to participate in a sports activity. Others such as golf promote their resort as a golf-vacation destination even though local consumers support the resort. Some businesses are in the business of developing sports travel packages by developing a trip specifically for the purpose of participating in an activity. For example, several companies now specialize in organizing trips for hiking, camping, climbing, running, kayaking, scuba diving, and many other activities.

What is new about sports tourism is the increasing number of businesses, types of products offered, and focus on sports tourism as a developing identifiable industry.

There are now companies who specialize in putting together travel packages for the purpose of attending sports events. A few of the many sports events designed for spectatorial and entertainment purposes include the Super Bowl (a national football championship game), the Women's or Men's World Cup (the international soccer championship held every four years and requiring more than a month of time, several matches), or a local college women's or men's basketball play-off games.

In addition, people do sports-related travel not to participate in a sports activity or to watch a sports event, but to see sports-related places such as sports museums, halls of fame, arenas, stadiums, facilities, memorabilia, or monuments. In one example, companies were selling tours to Atlanta prior to the 1996 Olympic Games for people who just wanted to see the sports facilities that would be used for the Olympics. Additionally, there are people who want to visit and tour sports areas such as halls of fame to study history and see the memorabilia of big-name sports people from over the years.

Sports tourism is also an emerging field of study. There are a few textbooks such as *Sport Tourism* (1999) by Standeven and DeKnop and a journal, the *Journal of Sport Tourism*. Further, there is a special theme issue on sport tourism in the *Journal of Sport Management,* which will appear approximately in late 2002.

Spectator sports such as basketball are frequently marketed to fans.

Photo reprinted by permission of WVU Photography.

III. Sporting Goods

Sporting goods and equipment can fuel people's interest in sports and recreational activities. That is, when you browse through a sporting goods store, you may see equipment for sports that are new to you. This can sometimes catch your interest and you'll purchase that equipment and learn how to play that sport. Refer to Figures 1.8, 1.9, and 1.10 as you read this section.

1. Increase in Sporting Goods and Apparel Designed for the Diversity of Markets and Their Demands

It wasn't so long ago that all sporting goods, equipment, and services were designed and made only for the white, American, adult male participant. Today, sporting goods manufacturers are designing goods and equipment for a variety of market segments. Further, the number of companies, retail or manufacturer, owned and managed by people who are not white, American, adult males is increasing. These companies are set up to specifically design sports equipment, apparel, and services for other markets. A woman, for example, may look for running shoes made for a woman's foot instead of having to purchase a shoe made for a male and modify it to fit her feet. A child who wants to play soccer can buy soccer shoes made specifically for children. A person with only one leg can purchase specially designed snow-ski equipment.

> The sporting goods industry is one of the largest segments of the sport business industry because people must have equipment and apparel in order to participate in most sports activities.

At the same time, technology and design have influenced sports equipment and apparel. Tennis rackets are available in a variety of sizes: The grip is offered in several sizes, shapes, and materials; the racket head is offered in several sizes and materials; the string is offered in a variety of type; and the weight of the racket varies. Uniforms also come in a variety of styles, sizes, and materials. Most sports have clothing or equipment custom designed for enhancing performance. Consider the one-piece vinyl-looking suits worn in the sport of luge. The style and material are aerodynamically designed for speed.

> The sporting good industry is increasingly focused on developing products for non-traditional markets such as women, disabled athletes, and children.

Sporting goods, as well as the sport activity, are much more available, more affordable, and more accessible to more consumer segments. Historically, tennis was enjoyed exclusively by the wealthy. Today, tennis is affordable to and enjoyed by people of many income levels.

Services surrounding sport and fitness activities have expanded. Services offered in some fitness clubs include laundry service, racket stringing, golf-club cleaning, child care, concessions, restaurants, lounges, tanning beds, valet parking, and massage.

The variety of goods and services is expanding to accommodate the many diverse populations participating in sport. The demographics and psychographics of the people in the United States change almost constantly. At one time a marketer could safely assume that the greatest majority of people living in the United States were white, Christian, and heterosexual, and that a household consisted of a traditional marriage and family consisting of a woman, man, and children. In 1990, opposite-sex married couples with and without children constituted only about 55% of US households (Ball, 1989). The other 45% include people who were living alone (24%), female-headed households (12%), male-headed households (3%), people of the opposite sex living together (3%), and people of the same sex living together (2%) (Ball). Knowledge of and sensitivity to current household structure is important in decisions concerning all marketing strategies.

Sports equipment designed for the disabled is being developed more frequently today. There are softballs that emit a beeping sound. These are used in softball games for people with vision impairments. There are wheelchairs designed for speed. Materials are very lightweight, and the chair is aerodynamically designed and constructed. This wheelchair is used in basketball, running, and tennis participation, for example.

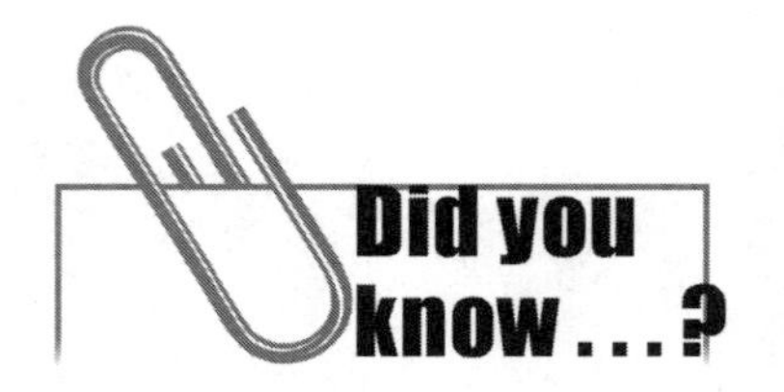

The average price paid for snow sports gear in 1998:

	Snowboarding	Alpine Skiing
Skis	—	$310
Boots	$157	$239
Bindings	$123	$141
Poles	—	$35
Snowboard	$260	—
Parkas	$122	$165
Pants	$83	$83
Total	$745	$973

Source: Snowsports Industries America

2. Influence of Technology on Sport-Related Goods, Services, and Training

The sport industry has benefited from advances in technology. Technology has influenced sports equipment, facilities, clothing, and shoes and has affected performance through sophisticated training programs. Some specific examples include computer-assisted programs in nutrition, training, skill analysis, and equipment design; and materials used in equipment, uniforms, shoes, and other gear.

IV. Facilities, Sports Medicine, and Fitness Training

Is it the facilities or an athlete's natural skill that enhances performance? If an athlete believes that a facility makes him or her perform better, is it true? Perhaps we will never know the answer to such questions. We do, however, know that what people believe can be a powerful influence on their mental or physical state. Sports facilities today are state-of-the-art and place the athlete in an ultimate surrounding for enhanced performance. In addition, many modern sports facilities are designed with the spectator in mind. At no other time in history have so many multimillion-dollar facilities been built than in the 1990s. Many are taking into consideration the many needs of and the diversity of the people who will watch the spectacle. Facilities influence and are a major segment of the sport industry.

1. Increase in the Number and Type of Sports Facilities and Events

The increased interest in sport, fitness, and recreation activity over the last few decades has influenced the number and type of facilities and events offered. Sports and fitness facilities are constantly being built to meet the demand for sports, fitness, and recreation activities, new sports, and for sports entertainment purposes. For example, a record number of football stadiums for professional teams were built in 1998. These facilities incorporate full-service communities including restaurants, shopping malls, hotels, and fitness centers.

Another factor influencing this growth in building sport facilities and offering events is money. Call any city's visitors and convention office, and they can tell you how many sports events were hosted in the city during the prior year. They can also give you an estimate of the economic impact of each of those events. Economic impact includes the money brought in to the city because of the event—money spent by the event attendees on lodging, eating, shopping, and transportation.

Realizing the money involved, many cities build sports facilities and have committees whose primary responsibility is to attract sporting events. The sporting events might include small events such as a 10k run, a car race, a three-on-three basketball tournament, a beach volleyball tournament, or a rodeo. It can also include trying to attract events as large as the Olympics.

2. Movement of Facilities From Single-purpose to Multi-Sport and Full-Service Facilities

Early sport, fitness, and recreation facilities were typically single sport or single purpose. Today, sport facilities are built with the capability to serve many purposes and to accommodate many sport events as well as nonsports events. Consider today's fitness centers. Most will have the usual weight-lifting room, sauna, and tanning beds. Further inspection will reveal large multipurpose rooms for aerobics and other activities, an indoor and outdoor pool, steam rooms, whirlpool baths, plush locker rooms and full-service dressing rooms, child-care services, restaurants, lounges, volleyball courts, racquetball courts, basketball courts, tennis courts, massage services, a pro shop, and many auxiliary services such as racket stringing, laundry services, hair dryers, shampoo, and even toothbrushes and toothpaste.

The multipurpose, multisport facility serves the modern fitness and health-minded consumer as a home away from home. Such facilities are more accessible, more convenient, and more efficient; they can accommodate the consumer's desires for something different when he or she becomes bored with one sport.

There are still some single-sport facilities built today whose primary purpose is to accommodate one sport. As examples, look at the Toronto Sky Dome, Joe Robbie Stadium in Miami, and the Super Dome in New Orleans. However, even though they were built to primarily service one or two sports, other events are staged in the facilities.

3. Constant Increase in the Amount and Types of Sports Medicine and Fitness Training Services

Regardless of status, skill, or fitness level, if an individual wants or needs medical treatment for a sports injury or professional training, it is available today like no other period of time in history. During the late 1970s and throughout the 1990s, the importance of keeping college, professional, and Olympic athletes healthy, in top physical condition, and in the game produced a need for professionals who specialized in taking care of sports injuries with an emphasis on speedy and accurate recovery and professionals who specialized in perfecting the physical. Hence, the athletic training, sports medicine, and fitness training fields of study proliferated. Today, every city has sports medicine, sports-injury rehabilitation, and fitness training clinics. It is a growing industry segment of the sport business industry. For the professional, there are degrees, certification clinics, workshops, seminars, exhibitions, conferences, magazines, newsletters, professional journals, web sites, and even consultants, all designed to support, and make money from, this growing industry.

Taking care of the athlete, regardless of level, has become big business.

Its effects on the sport business have been many, but the individuals reaping the benefits are people who participate in sports. Getting professional attention to injuries and professional training enhances an athlete's performance. Therefore, fewer sports participants have to give up participating due to an injury. Furthermore, the growth of such services is one reason for the growing numbers of people participating throughout their lifetimes, regardless of age. It is no secret that one of the fastest growing age segments in the sport industry are people 45-plus. The industry is scrambling to meet the demand, offering increasing numbers of age-group categories in most sports for those who are 50, 60, 70, 80, and even 90-plus. Indeed, for those of you reading this textbook who want to play sports forever, it is increasingly becoming possible.

V. Commercialization and Marketing of Sport

The word *commercialization* is derived from the word *commercial.* A check of any thesaurus will give you these words: business, mercantile, trade, trading, marketable, salable, vendible, wanted, advertisement, ad, plug, promo, promotion, sponsorship, and sport. Most sports and recreational activities are all these things today. The increasing commercialization and marketing of more and different sports, recreation, fitness, tourism, and leisure activities and events as well as sport-related products such as sports magazines are having a tremendous impact on the growth and development of the sport industry.

1. Packaging of Sport as an Entertainment Product

Companies with sports events for sale have done a much better job of packaging sports to attract a wide variety of consumers. Fitness centers and sports clubs have enhanced their offerings to attract and keep consumers. As you learned earlier, fitness centers have become almost a 'home-away-from-home.' Every convenience and service are offered to catch and to keep the consumer's attention.

Sports for sale as a spectatorial or entertainment product are being packaged to attract many more and a greater variety of consumers. For example, consider a minor league men's professional baseball game. The consumer is lured to the park with accommodations for tailgating (partying in the parking lot before and after a game) and offered a chance to be one of the first 2,000 people through the gate to receive a huggie (a plastic can cooler); he or she might win a brand-new truck during the seventh-inning stretch (as the result of a ticket-stub number drawing); and, for one hour after the game, a local country music band will play their hearts out while consumers two-step on the infield. What a bargain!

In another example, the Kentucky Derby offers over 70 events leading up to and surrounding the Kentucky Derby horse race. The actual race lasts only about 2 minutes, but the events surrounding the race now last about 4 weeks! The primary reason for offering the consumer more than just the sports event is to make the sports event the centerpiece of a larger event. Of course, another reason is money. Many people and businesses profit from the Kentucky Derby. Therefore, everyone cooperates in order to bring in more consumers.

2. Increased Marketing and Marketing Orientation in the Sport Business Industry

As more sport management professionals learn and then apply the fundamentals of sport marketing to the sport industry, the sport industry is treated more as a business than as a recreational interest and sport products are designed with consumer needs in mind. Maybe you have heard the expression, Give consumers what they want!

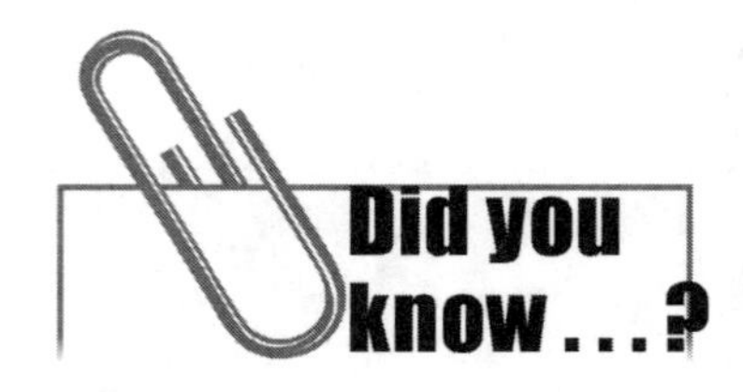

The professional spectator sports Americans expect to gain or lose in popularity over the next 30 years are

Women's Basketball
Gain: 61%
Lose: 16%
Remain the Same: 20%

Soccer
Gain: 57%
Lose: 17%
Remain the Same: 23%

Football
Gain: 38%
Lose: 11%
Remain the Same: 49%

Baseball
Gain: 32%
Lose: 21%
Remain the Same: 44%

Ice Hockey
Gain: 32%
Lose: 22%
Remain the Same: 41%

NBA
Gain: 30%
Lose: 24%
Remain the Same: 43%.

Source: *USA Today*, Feb. 9, 1999

This applies evermore to the sport industry. Take, for example, basketball rules changes specifically for entertainment value: The dunk was legalized because the fans loved it; there are TV time-outs because television's advertisers need the time for their commercials. Why isn't soccer televised in the United States on a regular basis? Because there are no time-outs in order to assure advertiser's commercials? Television officials are pressuring soccer officials to change the rules in order to make it 'TV-friendly." In other words, rules in sports are changed to make it more marketable.

3. Increased Understanding and Knowledge of Consumers of the Sport Business Industry

As you will learn in this book, there are a multitude of different products in the sport business industry and, therefore, a multitude of different consumer groups. Gone are the days when a sport business such as college men's basketball could simply offer the game and expect large crowds. Gone, too, are the days when an athlete management consulting company was the only one in existence. Because of the increased competitive structure of the industry, there are many more products from which to choose. For a sport company to thrive, therefore, it must constantly analyze the consumers. Sport management professionals are increasingly doing a much better job of studying consumer groups and meeting their demands for products.

> Decisions in the sport industry are increasingly based on consumers' desires.

Additionally, literature in sport management and sport marketing has begun to recognize that there is much more to the industry and many more types of consumers than sports participants and spectators. Therefore, sport management education materials are better preparing students for careers throughout the industry.

4. Promotion Perfection as the Goal for Sport Marketing Professionals

Many in the sport business industry have perfected the art of promotion, partially out of a desire to truly promote a product and partially out of the increasingly competitive nature of the industry. For example, there are more home fitness equipment products on the market than ever in history. In order to entice the consumer to purchase one company's product instead of the other company's product, sport marketing professionals go to great lengths to create the optimal promotional plan.

In another example, it might seem that sport marketing professionals have taken the art of promotion perhaps too far. Modern spectators of sporting events expect more than just the event. They expect to be entertained before, during, and after an event. They expect to be bombarded by advertising messages, and they expect promotional activities such as giveaway merchandise, souvenir stands, food and drink, instant replay on gigantic screens, and much, much more. At any rate, the sport marketing professional has perfected this craft.

5. Growth of Corporate Sponsorship

Sport sponsorship is estimated to be a $13.2-billion-dollar industry (refer to Figure 1.9). Sponsorship is the exchange of something for something. In its simplest form, sponsorship occurs when a company or person gives money to financially support an event, organization, or person. The return is an advertising benefit. Some exchanges can be quite complex and involve goods and services as well as funds. In exchange, the company might receive such benefits as advertising, having the event or facility named for the company, product tie-ins, on-site sales or giveaways, goods, and tickets.

Companies are heavily involved in sponsorship in the sport industry today. Because it is such a large and popular industry, companies use sponsorship primarily as an advertising tactic. Other reasons are to reach specific market segments, to increase grassroots marketing, to be associated with sports, and to do "cause" marketing.

Company sponsorship:

- promotes a caring image
- familiarizes the public with the company name
- provides relatively inexpensive advertising

Watch any racecar driver step out of her or his car. Look at the uniform, and what do you see? The uniform is covered with patches of the many companies that provided money to the racing team organization. Look at the car. It's almost impossible to see the car because it is covered with sponsor's logos.

Why do companies get involved in sponsorship? The most common reasons include the company's desires to have the public think of it as a caring company, to have the public see and remember its name, and, to use its resources wisely (in many cases, sponsorship is less expensive than other forms of advertising).

Sponsorship is a multibillion-dollar industry and growing. There are a multitude of opportunities for companies for sponsorship because there are hundreds of thousands of sports events, organizations, governing bodies, and athletes, many of which are looking for sponsorship. Sponsorship is such a large industry segment that there are conferences, trade shows, magazines, companies, and directories serving the industry.

6. Increased Endorsements

Over the last couple of decades, the use of endorsement as an advertising and promotional tool has increased. The product may or may not be a sport product. The agreement may involve a fee or goods and/or services traded for the individual's or company's time. Use of the endorser brings attention to the product by capitalizing on the popularity of the endorser. There are different categories of endorsement. The following are some examples:

- Individual endorsement: use of an athlete, coach, owner, or other individual person
- Team endorsement: use of a full team
- Full organization: use of an entire organization such as the use of the NCAA (National Collegiate Athletic Association), the NFL (National Football Association), the IOC (International Olympic Committee) or USOC (United States Olympic Committee) to endorse a product.

7. Growth in Importance of Licensing and Merchandising

Licensed merchandise is estimated to be worth $71.15 billion (refer to Figure 1.9). NASCAR, for example, reports an estimated $2 billion in licensed merchandise sales. A way to promote and to add extra income for many sports companies is to use licensing and merchandising. In the last decade, licensing and merchandising have become big business. It involves copyright protection for a company's name, logo, mark, or events and using those to create lines of souvenir merchandise. This has become so much a part of sports event that spectators at events expect to be able to purchase souvenir merchandise.

Licensing and merchandising have had a tremendous impact on the sport business industry, primarily as income boosters, but also as ways to develop brand-loyal consumers.

VI. Sport Industry Professional Service Businesses

There are a number and variety of businesses that offer such professional services as legal, sport marketing, sport finance, sport management, and consulting to the sport business industry. These have become an integral part of the industry. Some specific examples, shown in Figure 1.9, are sports medicine at $64.6 billion; Agents Interpublic Groups of Companies (agents) at $4 billion; Huber, Hunt, and Nichols (sports facility construction) at $1.01 billion; and Ticketmaster at $341 million. Most of these are business-to-business companies: Their products are sold primarily to sport businesses. You will learn more about business-to-business markets in chapter 6.

1. Extraordinary Growth in Service Businesses for the Sport Industry

Those service businesses provide legal representation, consulting, and research, marketing, and financial services. For almost every area of the industry, there are now businesses that want to provide services to help—and profit from—that part of the industry. For example, for professional athletes, there are several service businesses and consultants who want to help them with their legal, financial, licensing, sports equipment, clothing, and endorsement possibilities. These offers of help now start when athletes are still very young, even sometimes when they are still preteens. For other areas of the industry, there are service businesses. For example, if your company is a laundry detergent company and you want to know exactly how effective your $15-million racing boat sponsorship is, you can hire a sport marketing company to do the research for you.

> To match the development of the sport industry, service businesses have arisen to provide legal representation, consulting, and research, marketing, and financial services.

Moreover, although these service businesses have sprung up to offer help in the sport industry, and, of course, to profit from it as well, they have created new professions, which translates into new jobs and careers for people.

VII. The Sport Industry, Media, and Sports Media

The sport industry and the media have a relatively long history. Sports have been broadcast or reported through such media forms as television, radio, newspaper, and magazines. There are more forms of media today, and the sport business industry has benefited greatly from most of them.

Additionally, a new sport business industry segment, sports media, has emerged as a result of the popularity and growth of both media and sports as well as media technology. For instance, sports events were first televised by existing broadcasting companies. During the 1960s, a couple of hours per week might be programmed for broadcasting sports coverage. The growth in popularity of sports, fitness, and recreation gave rise to new sport media businesses such as ESPN and FOX Sports, whose exclusive programming focus was sports events and news. The continued popularity of such businesses has spawned specialization. Today, for example, there is a sports television company, the Golf Channel, that focuses only on one sport; and there are companies that focus on a region of the country such as the Sunshine Sports Network, which focuses on sports in the southeastern region of the United States. Currently, it is reported that there are 48 sports channels in the United States and that there are 235 hours of sports programming each day ("ABC Evening News," 2000).

Other forms of sport media include print media, the world wide web, film, and radio. As with television, coverage of sports came through existing companies. Later, companies whose exclusive product was sports proliferated. Today, sports print media, sport web companies, sports films, and sports radio are growing segments of the industry.

More recently, combinations of media forms have begun to redefine the sports media industry. For instance, a sports television broadcasting company that also produces sports events, sports magazines, a sports website company and sponsors a variety of sports events becomes a sports media conglomerate and can cross-market its many products. For example, the TV channel will advertise its event on TV, in its magazine, and on its website. The company can link promotional activities and fan participation activities, thus enticing the fan (consumer) to use products all produced by the same company.

1. Sport Industry Benefits of Mass Media Exposure

The advent of television and certainly the broadcasting of sports on television have had a tremendous impact on the growth of the sport industry. Through television, people are exposed to a variety of sports and sport events. The demand for sport on television gave way to advertising dollars for the networks and for the sport enterprise as well. The exposure has influenced the awareness of sport, the popularity of sport, and the participation in sport.

Television has also created new sport business opportunities and a new sport industry segment has taken off—TV sports. Gone are the days when people were limited to watching a few select sports events on national broadcasting channels sandwiched between all sorts of other programming. Today, numerous sports channels offer the consumer the chance to watch sports and recreational events 24 hours a day, 7 days a week. Fueling this increase is target marketing. Sports channels are being created to meet the desires of target markets. For example, for those avid golfers, there is the golf channel, and for women's sports fans, there is the women's sports channel.

> Exposure to TV, the radio, and the Internet has increased popular interest in sports and the sport industry.

These sports channels are having profound effects on the sport industry. Not only are they an enormous industry segment creating millions of jobs, but they also introduce, educate, and entertain millions of consumers each day.

They have launched two more industry segments: nonsports companies that use televised sports events for advertising their products and sports created for TV. In the first instance, which is sometimes called "marketing through sports," many companies pay millions of dollars to advertise during televised sports events, or to sponsor the event, to reach certain markets. In the second instance, sports, fitness, and other recreational

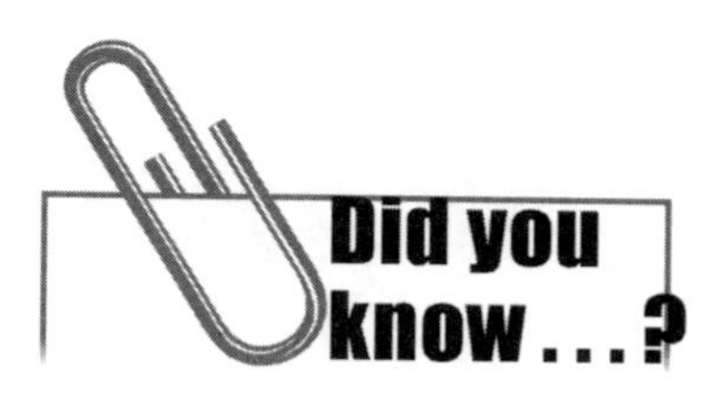

Among the largest metro areas, San Francisco has the largest percent of adults who have health/exercise club memberships: 20%

Source: *USA Today*

activities and events are invented specifically for television. For example, ESPN2 created the X-Games as a television sports event commodity.

Another mass media outlet includes print media such as newspapers. No other industry enjoys its own separate section in nearly every newspaper worldwide. Reading about sports and recreation increases the awareness of sport and the desire to participate in sports and recreation.

The Internet, which is revolutionizing business and the way people shop, interact, and communicate, has also had an enormous impact in the sport industry. There are already numerous sport businesses and other opportunities on the web. To find some of them, simply go to any search engine and type in "sports" or "sport business" as the subject. In one example, www.CBSsportsline.com is a company created specifically to be a web company. It offers information and is a sports shopping mall.

2. Sports Activities and Events as a Popular Entertainment Product

As presented earlier, many sports and recreation activities and events have become very popular events. This makes them great products for media. Some of the American culture is built around using sports activities and events as entertainment. For example, a family can use the fact that one of their children participates in mountain biking as an excuse to get a long weekend vacation and family outing for the event. In another example, tailgating has become an American phenomenon, and some have turned it into an art form. The SBJ study, shown in Figures 1.6 and 1.7, focused on spectator sports and estimated the value of that industry and its segments.

This entertainment value of a sports activity or event makes the event a great media event. For example, live television coverage of the Kentucky Derby begins at 6:00 A.M. on the day of the race, a 2-minute sports event usually run at around 4:30 P.M. However, television crews and reporters are at every possible spot on the track and talk with many different people: inside and outside the track, at the stables, at the corporate tent areas, up in Millionaires Row, on the infield, in the trailers with the jockeys, and at the gates to interview people as they arrive. The media know this event has become a major entertainment event, and they are there to cover it all the way.

3. Constant Increase in Television and Radio Coverage

Coverage of sport activities and events on television and radio is big business. Most major and minor broadcasting companies compete for the rights to broadcast events, large and small, traditional and contemporary. In addition, there are several sports broadcasting companies whose full-time coverage is sports activities and events. It has been estimated that there is 235 hours of sports programming in a 24-hour period on 48 sports channels ("ABC Evening News," 2000). This constant and growing coverage of sports, recreation, and fitness events has helped increase the popularity of sports.

4. Increase in the Number and Variety of Magazines, Trade Magazines, and Academic Journals Devoted to Sport

Walk into any local bookstore and go to the magazine section. How many magazines can you count that are sports, fitness, health, leisure, travel, and recreation magazines? If the activity exists, there is or soon will be a magazine for it. The variety includes boating, sailing, in-line skating, fishing, flying, running, walking, adventure travel, camping, hiking, mountain biking, four-wheeling, canoeing, water sports, and snow sports.

What are the purposes of the magazines? What purposes do they serve for the consumer? They expose the consumer to a sport. They educate, encourage, and support participating in the sport or becoming a spectator of the sport. They serve as a source of information and as a resource for networking. They serve as a catalogue of sport equipment and apparel and therefore offer to the manufacturers a source of advertising directly to a target market. Of course, there also is a profit to be made for the publishers. This industry segment grows steadily every year. As new sports appear and as new markets emerge, sports entrepreneurs bring magazines onto the market and fuel the popularity. *SportsBusiness Journal* reported that this industry is a _multibillion-dollar industry. Advertising in sports magazines, for instance, is estimated at $9.21 billion (Morris, 1999).

Trade magazines are primarily for people in the various careers and trades in the sport business industry. For example, there are magazines that provide boating industry information, market data, and business strategies for the owner and manager of a boat dealership. For the sports tourism company, there are sports travel magazines and, for snow sports businesses, there are snow sports business magazines such as *WinterSport Business* and *Snowboarding Business*. Additionally, there are annual convention and trade shows for many businesses such as the annual sporting goods manufacturers trade show held annually in Atlanta and the snow sports industries trade show held annually in Las Vegas.

> The plethora of magazines devoted to particular sports not only promotes awareness of specific sports, but also provides education, encouragement, and support for the sport's participants.

This proliferation of information has influenced both the popularity and growth of participation in sport-, fitness-, and recreation-oriented activity and the effectiveness of the sport business. As people read about, hear about, or see sports, they are more inclined to become involved. As sport businesses study and learn more about their business and industry segment, they more effectively manage and market their business. Both groups reap great benefits.

5. The World Wide Web

As yet another media outlet, the web has had an impact on the sport industry in an instantaneous way. The web is now a major business force, creating a way for communication and conducting sports businesses in an instant. It joins the sport business industry, what we call e-sport business, as another new product and part of the burgeoning sport business industry. For existing companies, the web serves as a new way to distribute the sport product to the consumer. Further, the web is now a place of business for new sports businesses that exist only as web companies.

VIII. Sport Industry Education

Where there is an industry, there is a need for appropriately educated individuals. The vastness and diversity of segments, jobs, and careers in the sport business industry have led to a constant increase in the number and type of educational opportunities. From certifications to doctoral degrees, education for the sport industry professional can't grow fast enough.

1. Increase in Sports and Sport Business Education for Executives, Administrators, Athletes, and Other Personnel

There are several categories of sport education. There are people who want to learn how to play sports, games, and other activities. Some want to learn how to officiate, coach, or train athletes. Some want to learn how to organize and manage sporting enterprises. Others want to learn how to produce or promote sports events. When people desire something, it is usually (eventually) offered for sale. Today's consumer is offered an abundance of sports and/or sport business educational opportunities that range from rock-climbing lessons and biking instruction to sport business CEO workshops and coaching clinics. In addition, there are meetings and clinics to educate officials. A vast array of books, videos, and magazines offers lessons, suggestions, hints, and tips for improving performance. All of these products have positively affected the sport industry. The opportunities help educate people who are already working in the industry and people who want to work in the industry.

> Sport education is directed towards
> - Participants
> - Officials, coaches, trainers, producers, and promoters of sports events
> - Producers and promoters of sports events

2. Increase in Competency of Sport Management Professionals

Although sport management is still a new field of study when compared to most other disciplines, it is having a positive influence on the level of competency of sport management professionals in the sport industry. The number of undergraduate, graduate, and doctoral programs of study in sport management continues to increase in the United States, Canada, and around the world. In 1993, the members of the North American Society approved curriculum standards for Sport Management, and in 1994, an approval process began, headed by a joint committee called the Sport Management Program Review Council of NASPE-NASSM (Fielding, Pitts, and Miller, 1991; Parks and Zanger, 1990). As students complete degrees in sport management, they will fill the jobs in the sport industry. Eventually, there will be more employees and executives in the sport industry who have a sport management degree than those who do not. As appropriately educated sport administrators begin to manage in the sport industry, they will have a positive effect on the industry.

3. Increased Prevalence of Sport Management as an Academic Discipline and a Career

Sport management is growing as an academic discipline. In the United States alone, there are approximately 220 undergraduate programs, 100 master's degree programs, and 7 doctoral programs. The growth of sport management academic programs is creating jobs for those interested in education and research and the sport business industry. Today, there are more sport management faculty than ever before.

With the growth in the number of programs comes growth in sport management as an academic discipline, and an academic discipline must have a scholarly body of knowledge. Today, the body of knowledge in sport management is larger than ever before. For example, there are now over a dozen sport management academic journals; these include five journals devoted to sport law, the *Journal of Sport Management*, the *International Journal of Sport Management*, the *European Sport Management Review*, the *Sport Management Review* (Australia), the *Sport Marketing Quarterly*, the *International Journal of Sports Marketing and Sponsorship*, the *Cyber Journal of Sport*

Marketing, and the *Journal of Sports Economics*. Additionally, there are closely related journals such as the *Journal of Vacation Marketing*, the *Journal of Sport and Social Issues*, and the *Journal of Sport Tourism*. There is a scholarly society in North America, the North American Society for Sport Management, and some in other countries such as the Sport Management Association of Australia and New Zealand, the European Society for Sport Management, and the Taiwan Association for Sport Management. Each of these associations holds annual conferences during which numerous academic papers are presented. See appendix for more information.

The Organization of the Sport Industry

You should have a good start on understanding the depth and breadth of the sport industry. As you have read in the preceding sections, the industry is quite large and varied. It is so large and diverse that it is necessary to organize what exists in the industry to make it easier to study and easier to understand everything that might be included in the industry.

Consider an experiment in determining exactly everything—sport activity, sport business, and all related products—that is included in this super-large industry. Do this by developing a list. You could get organized by creating categories. The categories could contain products in the industry that have commonalities such as categories of sporting goods and equipment, clothing, shoes, sport activities, sport marketing companies, and fitness centers. Of course, trying to list everything in the United States would be practically impossible. You would end up with an enormous list. So let's start with your hometown. Consider some resources that will help you such as the yellow pages and copies of your local newspaper. List all the YMCAs and YWCAs and what each one offers. Write down every activity, service, good, league, tournament, and other products offered at the Ys. Now list city recreation offices and everything offered. List the fitness centers and health clubs and everything offered. Develop a list of youth sport organizations and everything offered. Add to your list sporting goods outlets (hunting, fishing, general), golf courses and driving ranges, sports clubs, recreation centers, company recreation and fitness centers, sports magazines, newspapers, books, videos, television shows, local college athletics departments, professional sports teams, church-affiliated sports or fitness centers, water-sport outlets and marinas, sailing clubs, snow-ski outlets and clubs, bowling centers, tennis centers, running clubs and events, and everything related to sport.

How many pages do you have so far? You should have several even if you live in a very small town. You may not have realized just how much you are surrounded by sport and sport-related products.

Now multiply the number of items on your list by the number of towns and cities in your state. Remember, the lists will grow longer as population and city size increase. Now you have an idea of the size of the sport business industry in your town and in your state and of the many different companies in that industry.

All of these businesses can be categorized to help you make sense of such a large and diverse industry. One method is *industry segmentation*. In a study by Pitts, et al. (1994), a model for categorizing and segmenting the industry into product function was developed. Figure 1.16 illustrates that model. It shows that the industry can be categorized into three industry segments: sport performance, sport production, and sport promotion. Their theory is that every product and business in the sport business

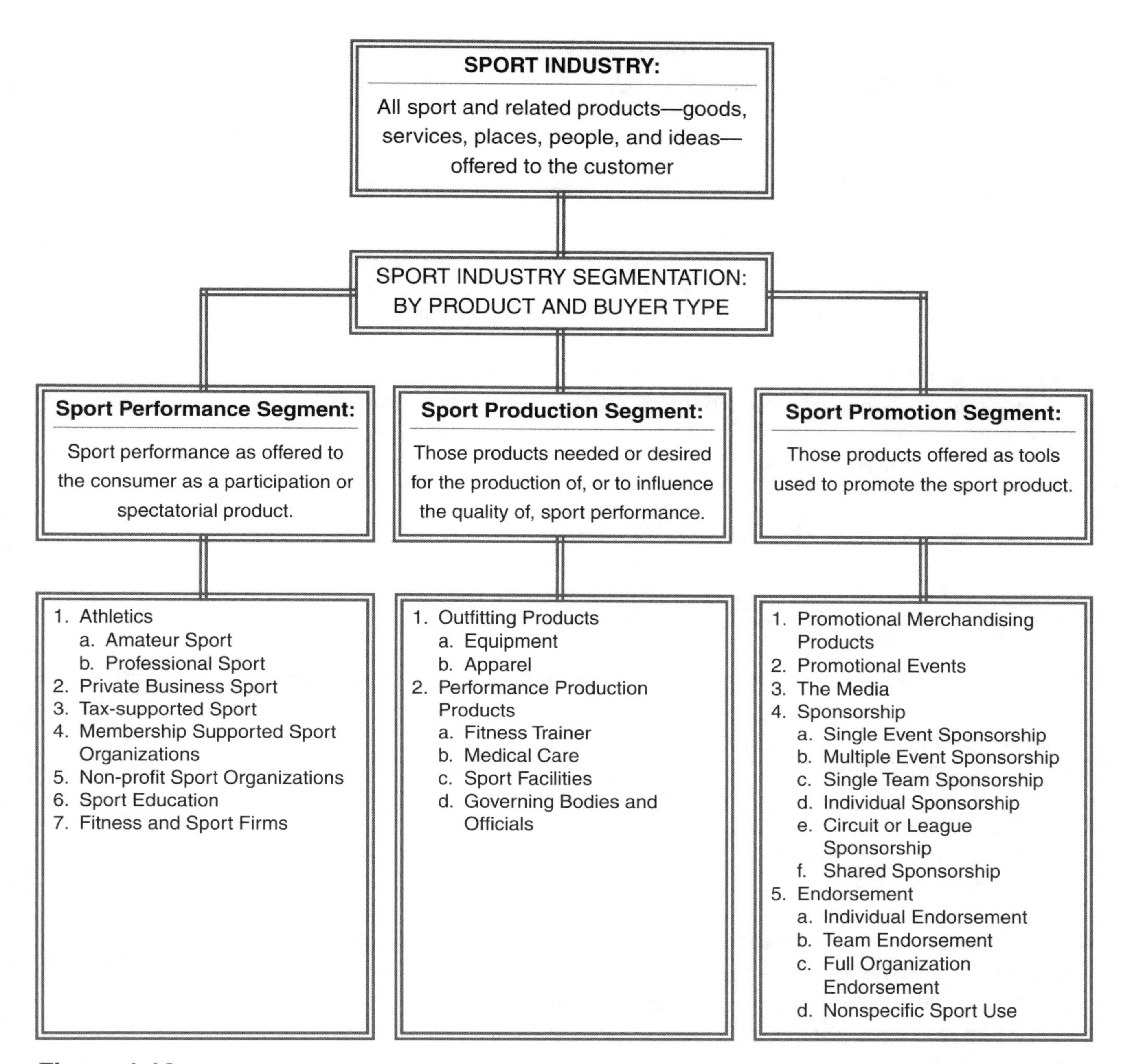

Figure 1.16
The Sport Industry Segment Model (Pitts, Fielding and Miller, 1994).

industry falls into one of these three segments. This kind of research can help the sport management and sport marketing professional better understand their products and their consumers, and therefore enhance their decisions regarding their particular sport business. For example, if your business manufactures tennis rackets, this product falls into the sport production segment in the Pitts, Fielding, and Miller model. That is, a tennis racket is a product needed or desired for the production of or to influence the quality of sport performance. To play tennis, one must have a tennis racket. There are, however, a great variety of tennis rackets, and they vary by color, material, grip size, weight, head size and configuration, and string. As a player increases skill level, the player might desire a custom-made racket in order to try to enhance performance. Your tennis racket company, then, might consider manufacturing a line of rackets that range from the inexpensive one-size-for-all racket to a customized for the individual and usually very expensive racket. Your knowledge of this product segment, sport industry segment, purposes of the racket, and your consumer greatly enhances your decision making. You will learn more about segmentation in chapter 7.

Chapter Summary

The student in sport management and in sport marketing must develop an understanding of the sport business industry, sport management, and sport marketing. An industry is a market containing similar products. Some industries contain only one product. The sport industry contains many. The sport industry is a market in which the products offered to its buyers are sport, fitness, recreation or leisure related; these products may be activities, goods, services, people, places, or ideas. The sport industry is a very large, very broad, and very diverse industry. Its products serve a very large and very diverse base of consumers. Studies have created categories or industry segments as a way of organizing the sport industry in order to better define and understand it.

Many factors have affected and will affect the sport industry. Some had an impact in the growth and development of the industry. Some will continue to have an effect on the industry. The sport management and sport marketing person should constantly monitor these factors and others in order to develop educated decisions and strategies.

Questions for Study

1. What is the sport business industry? Give some examples.
2. Describe the size of the sport industry in dollars.
3. What is sport management?
4. What is the North American Society for Sport Management?
5. What are the many factors that influence the growth and development of the sport industry? Give examples and explain how each factor influences the industry. Why is it important to know this?

Learning Activities

1. Create a list of sport industry businesses, organizations, clubs, and other enterprises in your city or community. Categorize everything according to the three sport industry segments created by the Pitts, Fielding and Miller (1994) model: sport performance, sport production, and sport promotion.
2. For each item on your list, list the jobs within each.
3. For each item on your list, list the sport products offered to the consumer.
4. Write to the North American Society for Sport Management and ask for information about the organization.
5. Subscribe to sport management-related journals such as the *Journal of Sport Management, Sport Marketing Quarterly*, and the *Seton Hall Journal of Sport Law.* Read and summarize the studies you find in the journals. Describe how sport management and sport marketing professionals can use the information.
6. With a group, create a list of 10 very different products offered in the industry. Determine which industry segment of the Pitts, Fielding and Miller model each product falls into and why.

Chapter 2

Historical Eras in Sport Marketing

Hillerich & Bradsby's Marketing Plan

In 1921, Hillerich & Bradsby Co. (H & B), producer of the Louisville Slugger baseball bat, became the industrial leader in baseball bat production. H & B's market position resulted from the implementation of a market plan. The market plan included an analysis of external forces (macromarketing) that were beyond the control of H & B. H & B's reaction to these external forces resulted in decisions about their product, place, price, and promotion (micromarketing). An analysis of H & B's market plan informs readers about the elements of sport marketing and functions as an introduction to sport marketing's historical development.

External Forces (Macromarketing)

Ten external forces influenced H & B's market decisions. These forces are briefly outlined below.

1. *Increased market size.* The youth baseball bat market began to grow in 1912 and rapidly expanded after 1919. After World War I, the adult baseball bat market also expanded.
2. *Market growth rate.* The market growth rate increased after 1919 because of youth market expansion and the return of soldiers from World War I.
3. *Industrial profitability.* The sporting goods industry in general and the baseball bat industry in particular experienced high profits in the years immediately before and after World War I. This led to the emergence of new entrants like Hilton Collins and Wilson Sporting Goods.
4. *Government policy change.* Beginning in 1919, the US government imposed a 10% tax on all sporting goods sales. This tax gave buyers greater power over producers. Not wishing to lose sales, some manufacturers elected to absorb the tax. Other companies attached the extra 10% cost to the selling price and attempted to maintain sales through advertising and promotions. Overall, the 10% tax increased competition among baseball bat producers.
5. *Resource availability.* Between 1919 and 1923, there was a shortage of second-growth ash wood. This caused baseball bat manufacturers to scramble to line up supplies. It also influenced a search for alternative material to make baseball bats.

6. *Technological change.* The cork-centered baseball, introduced by Reach and Co. in 1909, gradually changed the emphasis in baseball from base hits to home runs. With the advent of home-run hitters like Babe Ruth, the emphasis on bat weights changed from heavy to light. (The problem with lightweight ash bats was breakage.) Technological innovations in the early 1920s made lightweight bats stronger and more resistant to breaking. Successful companies used warranties to alert buyers about their new break-resistant bats.
7. *Economies of scope.* Strategic fits among related businesses offered competitive advantages. The amalgamation of Wright and Ditson with Victor Sporting Goods and the acquisition of Chicago Sporting Goods and Sell Sporting Goods by Thomas E. Wilson Company allowed these companies to reduce costs and gain competitive advantage. Much of the competitive advantage was gained through market-related fits. Wilson Company, for example, combined sales forces, used the same brand names, advertised related products in the same advertisements, and coordinated delivery and shipping. Wilson also realized operating and management benefits.
8. *Economies of scale.* Economies of scale existed in bat production, in distribution, and in raw material purchase.
9. *Buyer preferences for differentiated products.* Baseball bat purchasers wanted special bats, bats that increased prowess or linked the buyer to a special player.
10. *National economy.* A depression swept through the American economy during 1920 and 1921. Sporting goods manufacturers believed that the depression actually increased sales because of forced leisure.

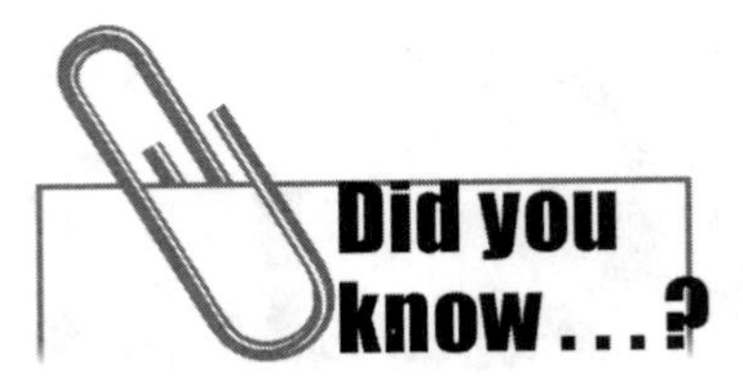

The 2,483 subscribers who answered a survey by *Sports Travel* magazine on August 3, 1998, were in the business of

Entertainment and sports events booking agents (642)

Corporate incentive travel planners (1,067)

Corporate sponsors of sports (1,301)

College athletic departments and professional teams (1,482)

Sports market travel agencies (1,795)

Sports governing bodies, organizations, associations, and alumni groups (1,911).

Source: Sports Travel Magazine. Presentation given at the sports tourism conference. George Washington University, Washington DC, 1998.

Internal Responses (Micromarketing)

H & B's response to the external forces listed above involved micromarketing decisions about product, place, price, and promotion. External forces influenced more than one micro decision area. H & B's micromarketing decisions are briefly outlined below.

1. *Product.* Product development at H & B was a response to market size and growth. H & B introduced its first autograph model Louisville Slugger in 1905. It was an exact replica of the bat used by Honus Wagner and was intended only for the adult market. With the growth and expansion of the youth market, H & B introduced the autograph model junior slugger in 1915. The large market-growth rate that occurred after 1919 induced H & B to produce a variety of autograph models in a variety of lengths and weights to appeal to different segments of the baseball bat market. (This decision was also influenced by changes in buyer preferences. Customers wanted autograph models of their favorite players.) The technological changes that brought about the "lively ball" also influenced H & B. In 1921, H & B introduced the new "powerized" Louisville Slugger, a lighter, stronger bat that resisted breakage. The "powerized" bat was marketed with warranties and appealed to the new class of baseball home-run hitters. During this same period, H & B became aware of the necessity of economies of scale. Consequently, H & B increased production capacity and efficiency through a series of changes that permitted them to increase production capacity to 10,000 bats a day by 1923.

2. *Place*. H & B's largest competitors, Spalding, Wilson, Draper and Maynard, Goldstein, and Rawlings, benefited from economies of scope. Economies of scope permitted better distribution and greater customer contact. To combat these advantages, H & B increased the size of its sales force in order to increase contact with independent retailers. Although H & B continued to sell through jobbers, the company began a direct sale to retailer policy in 1919.

3. *Price*. H & B's pricing policy was a response to the 10% sporting goods tax, resource availability, and a concern for the continuance of industrial profitability. H & B emphasized vertical price maintenance. They wanted Louisville Slugger bats sold at recommended prices by jobbers and retailers. (H & B saw this policy as necessary to maintain profitability in the face of the increased competition from chain stores and mail-order houses. The cost of ash wood and the 10% sales tax also influenced their policy.) H & B also considered economies of scale in setting prices. H & B was able to cut production and distribution costs through economies of scale. H & B's pricing policy passed these savings along to customers in the form of lower prices. Buyer preferences for special bats also influenced H & B's pricing policy. H & B realized that customers were willing to pay higher prices for differentiated products like autograph model baseball bats.

4. *Promotion*. H & B desired to increase market share in an expanding baseball bat market. The company was also concerned about industry profitability. Promotional decisions were based upon these concerns and were also responses to economies of scope that competitors employed. The need to differentiate products to meet buyer preferences further influenced H & B's promotional decisions. H & B expanded advertising and sales promotions. In 1919, the company began an integrated advertising and promotion campaign that included popular and trade magazine advertisements, a promotional pamphlet, and an advertising slogan. These decisions were prompted by a desire to increase market share in an expanding baseball bat market. H & B's advertising and sales promotional decisions were also a method of combating economies of scope employed by larger companies. In addition, H & B's decision to employ economies of scale emphasized the need for a unified promotional campaign. Finally, because customers preferred differentiated products, H & B needed an effective method for informing potential buyers about the special bats produced by the company.

A competitive marketing plan must consider external forces that affect the whole industry and develop internal responses that enable the company to get and keep customers.

H & B's market plan considered external forces (macromarketing) and developed internal responses (micromarketing) to either utilize or combat the external forces outlined under macromarketing. H & B's marketing plan was a competitive strategy. The plan used H & B's resources to manipulate product, place, price, and promotion in response to influences beyond the company's direct control. These influences were in effect large aggregates that affected the national economy in general and the baseball bat industry in particular. H & B's market plan began with an analysis of the whole industry: market size, market growth rate, industrial profitability, government policy, resource availability, technological change, economies of scope and scale, buyer preferences, and national economy. H & B analyzed how the purposes and resources of the company interacted with the contingencies imposed upon it by external forces. H & B's marketing plan sought to capitalize on the industry's opportunities and the company's strengths while mitigating industry threats and company weaknesses. For example, when H & B developed the autograph model junior slugger, they assumed the new product would be attractive to members of the growing youth market (Miller, Fielding and Pitts, 1993).

Historical Eras in Sport Marketing

Sport marketing consists of two interrelated concepts. The first concept considers sport marketing at the macro level. Sport marketing at the macro level considers external forces that affect the industry as a whole. It analyzes these forces in an attempt to develop a competitive advantage. The second concept defines sport marketing at the micro level. It includes a set of activities performed by the company in an attempt to get and to keep customers. Typically, this set of marketing activities includes anticipating needs; determining what products are to be made; developing and designing products for sale; packaging; pricing; developing credit and collection policies; determining transportation and storage needs; deciding when and how products are to be advertised and sold; and planning after-sale services, warranties, and product disposal (McCarthy and Perreault, 1984).

Sport marketing evolved over time. Its history is an account of how individuals and companies attempted to solve marketing problems. H & B's marketing plan was an attempt to solve marketing problems. It benefited from techniques, traditions, and knowledge that had developed in sport marketing during the 19th and early 20th centuries. The marketing plan was, of course, solely H & B's. Further, it was positioned in time. The company's macromarketing analysis dealt with external forces that existed in the years immediately following World War I. The company's micromarketing responses depended upon resources and abilities that existed at that same point in time. Later, H & B's marketing plans and marketing plans developed by other companies also were attempts to solve marketing problems that existed at a specific point in time.

The history of sport marketing is a history of both continuity and change over time. The continuity part involves the linkage of macro opportunities and threats with micro reactions. All companies, regardless of historical date, dealt with external forces and developed internal responses in an attempt to achieve a competitive advantage. Their success or failure depended upon their ability to understand external forces and use resources to respond effectively. What changed over time was the nature, extent, and power of both external forces and internal resources with which companies responded. The development of sport marketing was influenced by changes in market size, market growth rate, industry profitability, government policy, resource availability, technological change, economies of scope and scale, buyer preferences, and national economy as well as company responses to these external forces, and the manipulation of product, place, price, and promotion.

The discussion that follows will develop a brief outline of the history of sport marketing in the United States. The major focus will be on change over time. However, continuity, the linkage of macro concerns with micro solutions, will form the basic structure of the discussion. The discussion will be limited to only two aspects of the sport industry. Spectator sports in the form of college athletics and professional sport will be included. The sporting goods industry will be the second aspect of the sport industry discussed.

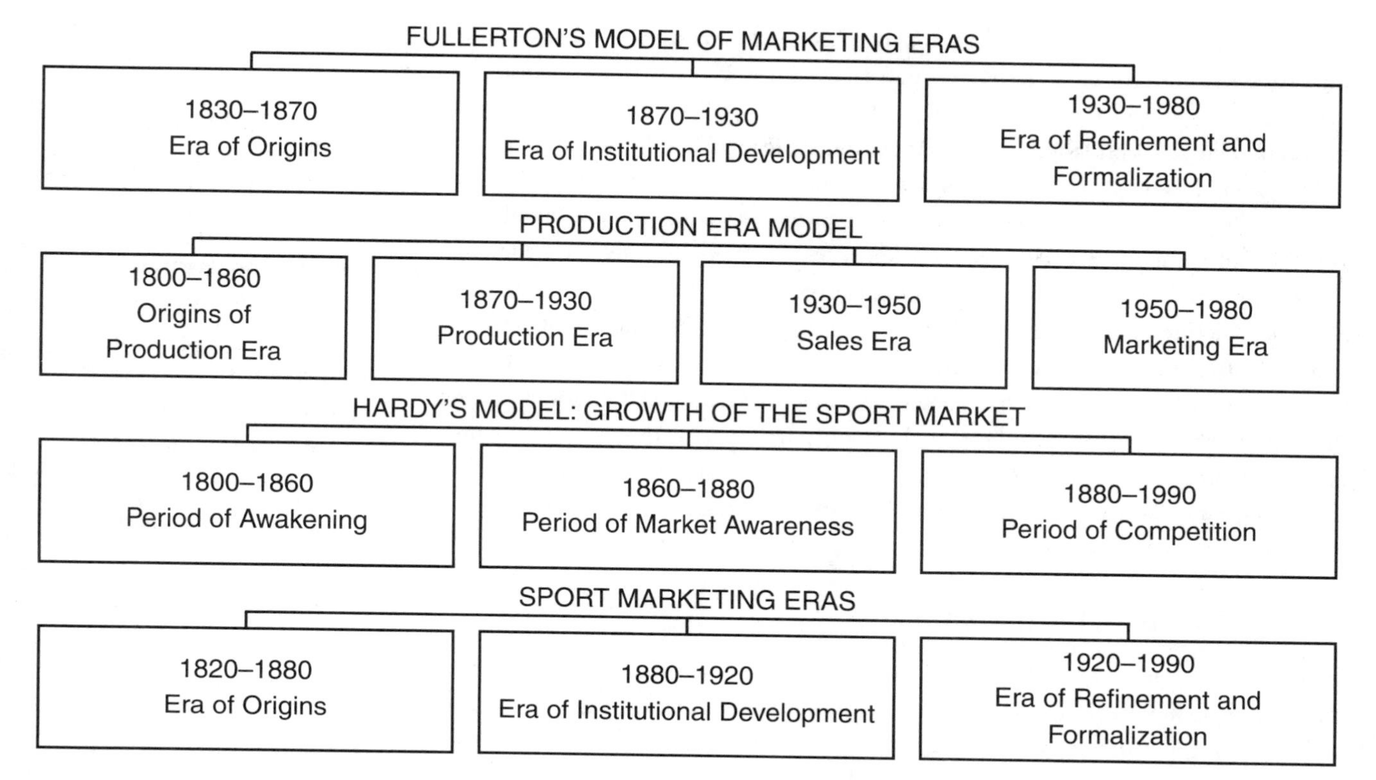

Figure 2.1
Marketing Era Models.

Based upon historical models developed by Fullerton (1988) and Hardy (1990), the history of American sport marketing will be divided into three broad contrasting periods:

1. The Era of Origins: 1820–1880
2. The Era of Institutional Development: 1880–1920
3. The Era of Refinement and Formalization: 1920–1990 (Figure 2.1).

Only the first two of these eras will be discussed. The major emphasis will be placed upon the second era, The Era of Institutional Development, because during this era, all the elements of modern marketing were developed and refined. The third era, The Era of Refinement and Formalization, will be summarized, highlighting the changes in external forces that influenced refinements in marketing techniques. The general characteristics of the first two eras will be discussed and examples of sport marketing within each era presented.

> It wasn't until after 1880 that marketing considerations such as consumer preferences, societal needs, and supply and demand began to influence product development.

Within this brief historical outline of sport marketing, we contend that all the micro and macro concepts associated with modern sport marketing evolved between 1880 and 1920. During these years, micromarketing functions such as product planning, product development, and product management gradually emerged. Other marketing functions such as distribution, pricing, and promotion also evolved. Prior to 1880, product development proceeded with little regard to buyer demand and other marketing elements.

After 1880, marketing considerations influenced product development. Macro marketing considerations evolved with micro concerns. Producers considered competition and demand and were concerned about overproduction. General economic conditions influenced micro decisions about sport contests and sport products. Society's needs, aspirations, and objectives affected the development of sporting goods products as well as influenced decisions about athletic opportunities at the amateur and professional levels. By 1920, all the fundamentals of modern sport marketing were established. Developments after 1920 were refinements. Sport marketing adjusted to new technologies such as motion pictures, radio, television, and computers. Sport marketing activities existed before 1880. Attempts to market harness racing, horse racing, pedestrianism, boxing, billiards, baseball, and a variety sport equipment occurred before 1880. However, sport marketing before 1880 was confined to isolated sport events and local circumstance. Sport entrepreneurs copied marketing techniques that had proven successful in selling other nonsport products or services. Some modern marketing activities were employed, but there was no systematic linkage of activities and no marketing plan.

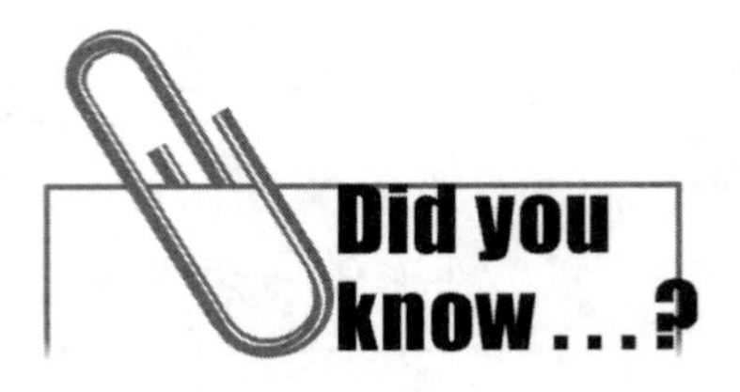

In 1997, 13 million Americans aged 55 and over who participated on a frequent basis in some type of sport, fitness, or outdoor activity—a 25% increase over 1987.

Source: SGMA. *1999 State of the Industry Report.*

The Era of Origins: 1820–1880

Sport marketing micro activities existed before 1880. William Fuller's tactics in promoting boxing in Charleston, South Carolina during 1824 are an early example. Fuller enticed paying customers to his "Extravaganza of Fun, Frolic, Fashion, and Flash" through newspaper advertisements and handbills that announced theater plays, boxing, and fire works (Wignall, 1924, p. 209). Boxing promotions in the 1840s and 1850s followed similar tactics with more elaboration. Although boxing was illegal, individual boxers still promoted bouts through newspapers, issuing challenges and setting stakes. Newspapers reported about the local and ethnic rivalries that added meaning and increased interest in the fight. Estimates of the amount of money wagered on the outcome both measured and increased interest. To avoid police interference, newspapers seldom informed readers about exact fight locations. Instead, fans were directed to a meeting place or a transportation site. Excursion tickets were purchased, and fans traveled by boat or rail to the secret fight site. Word of mouth was also used to direct customers to the fight location (Adelman, 1986; Gorn, 1986; Reiss 1989).

Michael Phelan's promotion of billiards and billiard tables during the 1850s and 1860s marked a significant advance over earlier boxing promotions. Phelan began his billiard career in 1846 as the proprietor of the Arcade Billiard Saloon in New York City. Like earlier boxing promoters, Phelan used the *Spirit of the Times*, a national circulation newspaper, to challenge British champion John Roberts to a $500-per-match, home-and-home series in 1850.

Phelan's challenge served two promotional functions. First, it helped to promote Phelan's book, *Billiards Without Masters*. Phelan included in the challenge the fact that he was writing a book about billiards. Second, the challenge functioned to promote Phelan as America's foremost billiard player (Adelman, 1986). When Phelan went into business with Hugh Collender to produce billiard tables in 1854, he promoted himself as the American champion who manufactured billiard tables. Phelan promoted business by suggesting that an American championship tournament be organized among the leading billiard players. In 1856, Phelan began publication of the *Billiard Cue*, the first billiard periodical in America (Adelman, 1986; see Endnote 1). He also played in several challenge matches defeating opponents and proclaiming the merits of his billiard tables. Phelan's challenges were published in newspapers and contained specifications about the equipment to be used: "The balls to be played with are to be 2$^3/_8$ in. in diameter, and the game to be played on a true and correct cushion table" (Betts, 1974, p. 42). A "true and correct cushion table" could mean only a Phelan table because Phelan held the patent for the India rubber cushion (Betts; see Endnote 2). Phelan retired from active challenge play in 1863 but remained the sport's leading figure. In 1865 he helped organize the American Billiard Players Association. Throughout his career Phelan used his influence and reputation to advance the sale of his billiard equipment. Phelan and Collender were the leading manufacturers of billiard tables until Collender joined with Brunswick and Blake in 1884 (Adelman, 1986).

Although the examples of Fuller and Phelan have much in common, there are important differences. The differences link the development of sport and the development of sport marketing. Fuller attempted to sell boxing along with other forms of entertainment. In 1824 boxing was not only illegal but also not very popular. Boxing became more popular during the 1840s and 1850s. During these decades, large numbers of Irish immigrants came to American cities like New York and Boston. They became part of what Adelman (1986), Polsky (1969), Rader (1990), Reiss (1989), Somers (1972), and have termed the male bachelor subculture. This bachelor subculture formed the basis of the sporting fraternity (Reiss). In 1824, when Fuller attempted to sell boxing in Charleston, this sporting fraternity did not exist in large numbers. Only five percent of the total population lived in cities (Chudacoff, 1981). Fuller and other early boxing promoters marketed a varied product (excursions, trips, and frolics). Price was unannounced or part of a package (transportation or, in Fuller's case, theater plays and fireworks). Place was hidden or hard to reach. Promotions included newspapers and handbills but relied heavily upon word of mouth among a small sporting fraternity whose membership was, quite possibly, unknown to Fuller.

In contrast, Phelan was very much aware of the male bachelor subculture that existed in 1850. The sporting fraternity had grown considerably between 1820 and 1850. This was particularly true of billiard players. In the 1820s only 16 tables existed in all of New York City. By 1850 the number of tables had increased to over 400 (Phelan, 1850). By the late 1840s the poolroom had emerged as a major locus of the bachelor subculture (Polsky, 1969). Urban population growth, particularly in respect to males between the ages of 18 and 35, provided recruits for the sporting fraternity in cities like New York, Boston, Chicago, Philadelphia, New Orleans, and Detroit. Phelan attempted to market billiard equipment to a growing sporting fraternity and the proprietors of poolrooms and taverns who catered to this fraternity.

Phelan either knew or assumed that the market for billiard equipment extended beyond New York City to other large cities. His hyped challenges to other billiard players, his attempts to organize national tournaments, his attempts to be declared national champion, his publication of the *Billiard Cue*, and his leadership in the organization of the American Billiard Players Association all helped extend the popularity of billiards (Adelman, 1986). They were also marketing tools that functioned in two important ways. First, they helped connect Phelan's name with the billiard equipment he and his partner, Hugh Collender, produced. The basic message was that Michael Phelan, the best billiard player in America, made the best billiard equipment (Adelman, 1986; see Endnote 3). Phelan and Collender were not the only billiard manufacturers in America. There were at least four others in New York City. More important, Phelan and Collender were contending with two very successful Cincinnati companies. Julius Balke's Great Western Billiard Manufactory was well established by 1854 when Phelan and Collender began production. Brunswick had been producing billiard tables in Cincinnati since 1845 and had established a second factory in Chicago by 1848. By 1854, when Phelan and Collender began production, Brunswick had established a branch office in New Orleans. By the middle 1860s Brunswick had sales offices in 10 cities in the United States and Canada (Kogan, 1985). Phelan and Collender needed name recognition in order to contend with these larger more successful companies. Second, Phelan and Collender needed the name recognition to contend with newer companies entering the field. Because of the growing popularity of billiards, other manufacturing companies began to produce billiard equipment. Phelan used his influence and well-established reputation as a billiard player to block the entry of these new companies. By 1869 the fight for the biggest share of the billiard market was down to three companies: Brunswick, Blake (Great Western Billiard Manufactory), and Phelan and Collender (Kogan).

External forces limited Fuller's success in marketing boxing but aided Phelan's marketing of billiard equipment. As already noted, Phelan dealt with a much larger market than Fuller did and had the additional advantage of large market growth (see Endnote 4). Phelan had several other advantages. First, unlike boxing in the 1820s, there was no government policy against billiards (see Endnote 5). Second, technological changes influenced billiard table production. The development of the band power saw for cutting slate increased resource availability and made large production of slate-bed tables possible. Phelan's patent on the India rubber cushion improved billiard tables, allowing for a more exciting style of play (Adelman, 1986; Kogan, 1985). These technological changes, combined with Phelan's influence through rule committees on the standardization of billiard equipment, permitted Phelan to influence buyer preferences for differentiated products (see Endnote 6).

Whether or not Phelan can be classified as a "key innovator" in sport marketing, particularly in the sense that Hardy (1986) intended in his groundbreaking essay, "Entrepreneurs, Organizations, and the Sport Marketplace: Subjects in Search of Historians," is debatable. However, Phelan's actions were a prelude to a more thorough development of micromarketing techniques during the 1865 to 1870 baseball fad.

The commercialization of baseball began with the charging of an admission fee for a series of all-star matches between New York and Brooklyn played at the Fashion Course in 1858 (Goldstein, 1989). After this example, clubs charged occasional admission fees under the guise of prize matches, "benefits" for players, and money raised for charities (Goldstein). By 1862 the charging of admission had become firmly established as a method to meet expenses and to pay players (Rader, 1990). By the end of the Civil War, baseball players demanded a share of the gate receipts and baseball became openly professional (Adelman, 1986; Kirsch, 1989; Seymour, 1989; Voigt, 1983).

The commercialization of baseball brought with it a more thorough development of micromarketing techniques.

The commercialization of baseball brought with it a more thorough development of micromarketing techniques. Descriptions of baseball as a product were designed to attract customers. Baseball was entertainment. It was skilled action, filled with drama and excitement. Baseball was scientific play by popular players and stars. Teams represented towns, neighborhoods, and cities. Games were intensely competitive rivalries or cham-

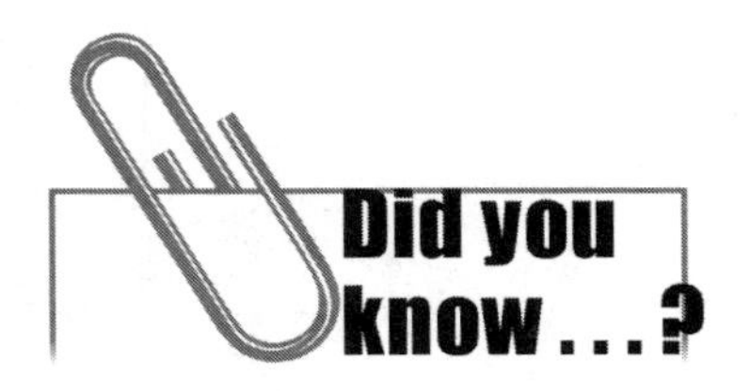

More than 3.7 million people went snowboarding in 1998.

Source: Snow Sports Industries America

pionships where victory meant supremacy and bragging rights. These elements describe the baseball product that appeared in newspapers, weekly journals, and special baseball publications (Adelman, 1986; Goldstein, 1989; Kirsch, 1989).

The micromarketing elements of place and price were influenced by macro elements including the emergence of large commercial and industrial cities. The commercialization of baseball began in New York City. It spread to other large urban, industrial cities: Boston, Philadelphia, Baltimore, and Washington on the eastern seaboard; Chicago, Detroit, and St Louis in the Midwest; New Orleans in the South, and San Francisco on the West Coast. These urban centers shared common features that influenced the marketing of baseball. The economic impact was most important. Nonmanual laborers experienced improved standards of living and more discretionary time. There was a concomitant growth in the popularity of baseball (Adelman, 1986; Freedman, 1978; Goldstein; Kirsch). Industrialization gave rise to a growing pool of semiskilled and unskilled workers who worked long hours at low pay. The physical growth of cities and the increase in population influenced land use. Inner-city play space declined; baseball fields moved outside of the urban core either near middle-class neighborhoods or along transportation routes (Hardy, 1982; Reiss, 1989). In 1862 baseball clubs charged 10 cents admission. By 1865 this had been raised to 50 cents. Some promoters argued that the increase was necessary to support a higher level of play. Other promoters argued that the increase was necessary to keep rowdies out (Adelman, 1986). Both explanations are plausible. Baseball micromarketers catered to a middle-class audience.

Baseball promotions involved a variety of techniques between 1865 and 1870. Tours functioned in two ways. First, they expanded the market by further popularizing the game. Second, tours served to increase the recognition and prestige of particular teams. The Cincinnati Red Stockings' 1869 tour, for example, accelerated the growth of baseball but also brought fame to the Red Stockings as they completed an undefeated season with lopsided victories in the San Francisco area (Barney, 1978; Kirsch, 1989). Baseball tournaments and championships relied upon urban boosterism and resulted in similar, though not always positive, publicity. Most championship matches were contrived. They consisted of a three-game series with the winner claiming to be champion. Players from both teams received a share of the gate receipts. Rumors of second games' being lost on purpose to permit a third game and larger gate receipts were common (Adelman, 1986; Kirsch, 1989).

Local newspapers, national sporting journals (Wilkes's *Spirit of the Times* and *The New York Clipper*), and special baseball publications (Beadle's *Dime Baseball Player* and *The Ball Player's Chronicle*) promoted baseball in a number of ways. They announced baseball games, tours, tournaments, all-star contests, and championship games. They also provided statistical reviews of games and seasons. Writers emphasized baseball's drama and excitement. Newspapers promoted the representational nature of baseball teams, linking victory to local prestige and superiority and connecting team success to local pride (Adelman, 1986; Kirsch, 1989). By stressing the health and moral aspects of baseball, local and national writers also helped legitimate the game (Adelman, 1986; see Endnote 7). Baseball's propagandists further promoted baseball by declaring it America's National Pastime (Kirsch).

During the Era of Origins (1820–1880), micromarketing decisions gradually became more sophisticated in response to the growth and greater impact of external forces.

The examples of William Fuller, Michael Phelan, and the baseball promoters during the late 1860s demonstrate the evolution of sport marketing in respect to micro decisions and macro forces as well as the continuity of the interaction of external forces with internal marketing decisions (see Endnote 8). Fuller's decisions about product, price, place, and promotion were framed by external forces that he could not manipulate or use to gain much of a competitive advantage. Fuller, of course, had few competitors. Phelan faced heavy competition. His micromarketing decisions attempted to manipulate external forces such as market size, market growth, and technology to gain a competitive advantage over other billiard equipment manufacturers. Like Phelan, early baseball promoters made decisions about product, price, place, and promotion based upon market size and market growth. Baseball promoters took advantage of the increase in per capita and discretionary time. Micromarketing decisions in baseball also took advantage of technological advances in transportation, communication, and publishing. Fuller's micromarketing decisions were fairly simple. He had few competitors, and the external forces he dealt with were few in number and local in nature. Forty years later, baseball promoters faced a more complex market. There were many more competitors. External forces were greater in number and far more extensive. Micromarketing decisions were more sophisticated because they had to be. During the next 60 years, external forces would continue to expand, and micromarketing responses would become more complex.

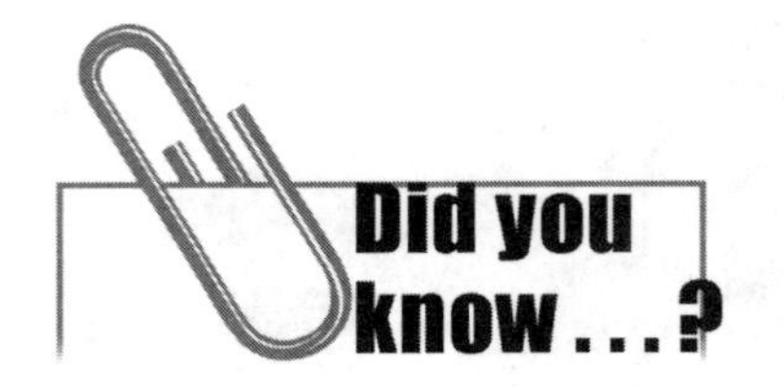

The number of athletes (aged 50 and over) competing in the 1999 Senior Summer Games was 12,000.

Source: *Amy Love's Real Sports Magazine*

The Era of Institutionalized Development: 1880–1920

The Era of Institutionalized Development built upon the Era of Origins. Micromarketing functions expanded to combat or take advantage of new and more powerful external forces. Product considerations, little more than reactions to anticipated demand during the Era of Origins, expanded to included strategic planning, development, and management. During the period of Institutionalized Development, sport products were branded and trademarked. Packaging to identify brand and enhance appeal became a standard practice. Sport products were graded in an attempt to expand demand by segmenting products by price ranges and by allowing consumers to better judge quality from grade. Many products also became standardized to meet the requirements of sport-governing bodies and rules committees. Sport products were designed by experts to improve performance; autographed by renowned players to signify quality; and styled by shape, color, and texture to enhance appeal. Market analysis to determine customer needs, estimate market potential, and study competition began at the turn of the century. By 1920 large companies like A.G. Spalding and Brothers and Thomas E. Wilson had their own marketing departments (see Endnote 9).

Distribution activities and initiatives changed between 1880 and 1920. Producer-owned "branch houses," begun in the 1860s by companies like Brunswick, became widespread after 1900 as companies took over wholesale and retail functions in order to circumvent antitrust laws and control distribution (see Endnote 10). Many sporting goods companies used historical inventory trends to guide ordering and developed connections between inventory and market analysis. Sporting goods manufacturers also increased contact with independent retailers and chain stores. In order to compete with other manufacturers, a manufacturer was required to provide financial assistance to retailers in the areas of advertising, market research, window displays, and equipment demonstration (Fullerton, 1988).

During the Era of Institutional Development, price became an important part of the marketing plan. Before 1880, pricing had been largely a matter of guesswork or negotiation rather than a major factor in the marketing plan. Sporting goods manufacturers, for example, advocated vertical price maintenance for two reasons. First, it was a way to control perceived consumer quality. Second, it was a way to enlarge distribution channels by allowing the small retailer to compete with the large distributor who was engaged in significant price gauging. Manufacturers believed that price was too important a part of marketing to be left outside the control of the producer. Without vertical price maintenance, marketing plans that relied upon grading or market plus pricing (pricing that reflected the psychic value of trademark) were worthless (Fullerton, 1988).

After 1880, sporting goods manufacturers and sport promoters began to develop the relationships between product quality and price and market segmentation and sales.

Promotional activities expanded in volume and intensity between 1880 and 1920 and became more highly organized. Prior to 1880 Phelan and the early baseball promoters demonstrated how to use newspapers, journals, special publications, tours, championships, and popular players to induce customers to buy tickets and products. These kinds of activities increased after 1880. Advertising, for example, expanded enormously. During the 1890s many sporting goods manufacturers hired professional advertising agencies to handle ad campaigns, and at least four sporting goods manufactures were among the top 25 national advertisers. Before 1920 all the larger sporting goods manufacturers had marketing departments responsible for developing and integrating promotional campaigns. Sporting goods producers assumed the role of communicating with customers and attempted to build awareness and appeal for their products. Company sales forces became an integral part of promotions during the period. Equipped with displays, advertising, direct-mail follow-ups, advertising and sales advice, and technical knowledge about products, company salesmen visited jobbers and retailers to promote company products. By 1920 nearly all medium and large firms had their own sales forces (Fullerton, 1988).

External forces made the above changes in marketing necessary. Market growth in terms of increased population was tremendous between 1880 and 1920. During each decade between 1880 and 1920, the population increased by more than 10 million. Annual immigration reached peaks of over 800,000 in the early 1880s and 1910 and seldom fell below 200,000 annually (Higgs, 1971). The population increased from slightly over 50 million in 1880 to well over 100 million by 1920 (US Department of Commerce, 1976). The increased population was marked by two important trends. The first trend was a migration from the settled areas in the East to the less populated sections of the West (Paulin, 1932). The second trend was a steady movement from rural to urban areas. In 1880 28% of the American population lived in cities of 2,500 or over. By 1920 this figure had climbed to 51% (Legergott, 1946; US Department of Commerce). Considered together, the two trends describe a market that was continually expanding and at the same time a market that was becoming more and more concentrated within urban environments as it spread west.

Population expansion and concentration were accompanied by a significant increase in discretionary money. With the exception of the depression years during the 1890s, yearly earnings of non-farm employees increased at a rapid rate between 1880 and 1920. The cost of living decreased during the 1880s and 1890s. The increase in the cost of living during the first decade of the 20th century was overshadowed by a much larger increase in yearly earnings. Only during the latter part of the second decade, when the impact of the European War (World War I) began to be felt, were cost of living increases greater that increases in yearly income.

As Figure 2.2 demonstrates, Americans had more money to spend during the period between 1880 and 1920 (Borden, 1942; Legergott, 1946). Indeed, as Murphy and Zellner (1959) have argued, during the three decades preceding World War I, the levels of income for various sectors of the work force "did not deviate greatly from those to which they aspired" (p. 402). According to Norris (1990), much of the public complaint against the rising cost of living near the end of the second decade of the 20th century was "conditioned by the experience of over two generations with a rising standard of living" (pp. 10–11).

	Yearly Earnings	% Increase/ Decrease	CPI	% Increase/ Decrease	Difference YE-CPI
1880	386		97.8		
1890	475	+23.0%	91.5	-6.0%	+29.0%
1900	483	+1.7%	84.3	-7.9%	+9.6%
1910	634	+31.0%	94.7	+12.3%	+18.7%
1912	657	+3.6%	97.2	+2.6%	+1.0%
1914	696	+5.9%	100.0	+2.9%	+3.0%
1916	706	+1.4%	108.7	+8.7%	-7.3%
1917	805	+14.0%	127.7	+17.0%	-3.0%
1918	1041	+29.0%	150.0	+17.0%	+12.0%
1919	1174	+12.8%	172.5	+15.0%	-2.2%
1920	1343	+14.2%	199.7	+15.8%	-1.6%

Source: Davis, L.E., Easterlin, R.A., and Parker, W.N. (Eds.). (1972). American economic growth. Harper & Row: New York, p.212.

Figure 2.2
Comparison of Annual Earnings and Consumer Price Index.

Sport benefited from these developments. Industry profitability increased during each decade between 1880 and 1920. Numerous studies document the increased popularity of sport (Betts, 1974; Lucas and Smith, 1978; Mrozek, 1983; Rader, 1990). To meet the demand for sporting goods products, established companies in related industries began to produce sporting goods products while new manufacturing companies also evolved.

Improvements in the standard of living and an increase in spending money made sport increasingly available among Americans.

Figure 2.3 documents the growth of new companies. In 1879 only 86 companies manufactured goods categorized as sporting and athletic goods (see Endnote 11). By 1921 the number of manufacturing companies had risen to 152. During this same period, the aggregate value of manufactured products increased from slightly over $1.5 million in 1879 to over $34.7 million in 1921 (US Department of Commerce, 1924).

Technological changes influenced the distribution and the production of sporting goods. The railroad brought about a revolution in distribution. By 1880 over 70,000 miles of railroad track were in operation. The overland transport network, including both east-west and north-south trunk lines, was completed during the 1880s. By

	Number of Manufacturers	Number of Workers Employed	Value of Product
1879	86	1401	1,556,258
1889	136	2008	2,709,449
1899	143	2225	3,628,496
1909	180	5321	11,291,552[1]
1919	188	6412	25,335,063[1]
1921	152	7063	34,711,174[1]

[1]includes production values of establishment in other industries that produced sport equipment.
Department of Commerce: Bureau of Census (1921). Biennial Census of Manufacturers. P. 1242.

Figure 2.3
Sporting and Athletic Goods Manufacturers.

1900 over 200,000 miles of track were in use. This increased to over 250,000 by 1920. Most small cities, villages, and even hamlets in the nation had railroad service by 1920 (Chandler, 1977). Increased mileage meant increased service. The railroad provided fast, dependable, and inexpensive transportation for manufactured products. It made possible economics of scale in regards to distribution (Chandler). One reflection of the increased importance of the railroad in distribution was the rise in tons of freight shipped. Freight carried by the railroad increased from 338 million tons in 1880 to 2,002 million tons in 1914 (Frickey, 1947). Sporting goods were a part of the freight transported by rail.

The revolution in distribution made possible by the railroad was also influenced by the telegraph and the telephone. The telegraph followed the railroad, relying upon the same rights-of-way. Where the railroad provided fast, regular, dependable, all-weather transportation, the telegraph made possible fast, regular, dependable, all-weather communication (Chandler, 1977). The railroad and the telegraph combined made the traveling salesman not only possible, but also essential. Increased competition influenced manufacturing companies, jobbers, and wholesalers to communicate directly with retailers in an attempt to gain a competitive advantage. This was particularly true for bicycle manufacturers during the 1890s and sporting goods and athletic goods manufacturers after the turn of the century. The telephone began commercial operations in the 1880s. Initially, it was used almost totally for local communication. With the development of long-distance lines in the 1890s, faster, almost instantaneous communication became possible, and the telephone emerged as an important business tool (Chandler).

Technological changes influenced the production of certain kinds of sporting goods. Most sport equipment manufactured during the Era of Institutional Development was labor intensive. The prerequisites for mass production of sporting equipment did not exist (Hounshell, 1984). However, some progress towards mass production was made in certain segments of the industry. Bicycle manufacturers developed and applied techniques such as drop forging, straight-machining, nickel plating, brazing, and sheet steel stamping to bicycle production. Bicycle manufacturers like the Pope Manufacturing Company and the Western Wheel Works used quantitative models, gauging systems, rational jigs, fixtures, special purpose machines and sequencing to improve the quality and the quantity of bicycle production. Assembly was the greatest production problem. Despite improvements in all other areas of production, assembly remained very labor intensive (Hounshell). Producers of golf and tennis balls, like B.F. Goodrich, used technology to improve products and speed production (see Endnote 12). A. J. Reach used sequenced machines to produce baseballs during the late 1890s (*Sporting Goods Dealer*, 1899). The automatic lathe and the automatic sander speeded up the production of baseball bats (*Sporting Goods Dealer*, 1906a). In each of the above examples, technology improved quality and permitted larger product quantities. However, none of the above examples eliminated the need for extensive labor in the production of sport equipment.

Spectators' involvement is a major contributor to the atmosphere of any sporting event.

Photo reprinted by permission of WVU Photography.

The advent of the 10-cent magazine between 1885 and 1905 added another external force for sport marketers to use and contend with. Lower priced magazines were made possible by technological improvements in the printing press (Isaacs, 1931) and by an increased use of advertising to lower cost to readers (Norris, 1990). The passage of the Postal Act of 1879, which granted favorable mailing rates and privileges to journals and magazines, helped to increase market size (Norris, 1990). In 1885 only four general magazines with a circulation of over 1,000 existed. Each was priced at either 25 cents or 35 cents per copy. By 1905 there were 20 general-purpose magazines catering to a middle-class market. All but four of these magazines sold for 10 or 15 cents. The aggregate circulation of these middle-class magazines was over five and a half million (Mott, 1957).

Cheaper prices recruited millions of new readers and advertising dollars. The new magazines were intended to make money primarily from advertising (Norris, 1990). The formula for success of these magazines aimed at the growing middle class—mass circulation and low unit cost of production—proved attractive to advertisers. *The Saturday Evening Post* is a good example. The *Post* was taken over by Louisa Knapp Curtis in 1897 when it was almost defunct. Advertising revenue during the first 2 years was low. By 1900 advertising revenue reached $159,300. By 1905 advertising revenues were greater than one million dollars. Advertising revenues were $5 million in 1910 when circulation reached one million. In 1917 the *Post*'s circulation exceeded 1.8 million, and advertising revenues were over $16 million (Wood, 1949). Sporting goods manufacturers were very much a part of the advertising revolution. By 1898, 11 of the top 150 national advertisers were sporting goods firms, and sporting goods advertising made up 10% of all national advertising (Presbrey, 1929). Sporting goods

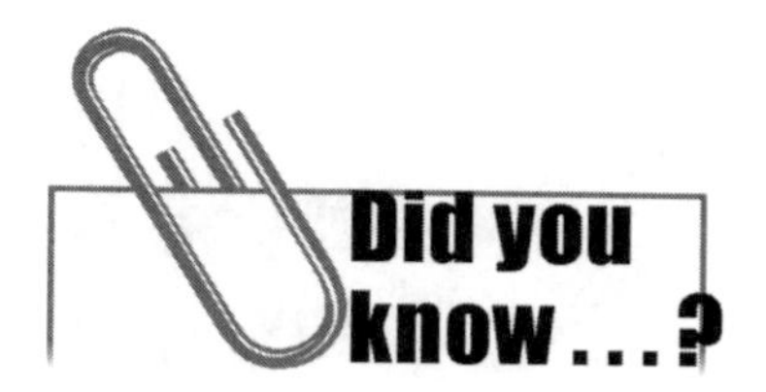

The top five organized sporting events included on trips of 50 miles or more taken in the past 5 years:

Baseball/Softball (33.7 million travelers)
Football (30.3 million travelers)
Basketball (18.8 million travelers)
Auto racing (15.0 million travelers)
Golf tournament (11.1 million travelers)

Source: Travel Industry Association of America

manufacturers continued to emphasize advertising throughout the Era of Institutional Development (see Endnote 13).

The increased production capacity of manufacturers, the revolution in distribution and communication, and the revolution in advertising made economies of scale possible and necessary. High-volume producers achieved competitive advantage by lowering the cost of per-unit production (Hounshell, 1984). High-volume distribution extended the advantage by lowering the cost per unit for shipping goods (Bucklin, 1972). High-volume advertising lowered the cost per ad and influenced wholesale and retail turnover rates (Norris, 1990). Sporting goods manufacturers expanded plant size and updated equipment, beginning in the 1890s and continuing for the next three decades, in an attempt to achieve economies of scale (see Endnote 14).

Economies of scale influenced economies of scope and vice versa. Once a firm had reached sufficient size to engage in economies of scale, it often found that it could not simply produce goods and achieve competitive advantage. Economies of scope became an attractive alternative. Companies achieved economies of scope in one of two ways. First, some companies pursued economies of scope through vertical growth. This vertical integration strategy was usually forward into marketing, but some companies integrated backward into owning their own raw materials. Second, an alternative strategy involved horizontal growth. Horizontal integration was achieved when companies that produced similar products or product lines joined to form a combination of their interests. Occasionally, horizontal integration led to vertical integration. Economies of scope provided strategic benefits. They permitted greater utilization of economies of scale in production, distribution, and advertising.

With few exceptions, sporting goods manufacturers were not involved in economies of scope until after the first decade of the 20th century. The sport industry was not part of what Glenn Porter (1973), in *The Rise of Big Business*, termed the, "Great Merger Wave," which took place between 1895 and 1905. A.G. Spalding and Brothers began vertical integration in the late 1870s with the acquisition of Wilkins Manufacturing Company (Levine, 1985). A decade later Spalding initiated a horizontal integration strategy with the acquisition of Peck and Snyder and, in the early 1890s, acquired Wright and Ditson and A.J. Reach and Company (Van Pelt, 1946). As the 20th century began, several sporting goods companies chose not to engage in economies of scope but joined to enact barriers to entry and control the market, thereby achieving advantages related to economies of scope. These amalgamations included the Bicycle Trust (1899), the Ammunition Trust (1901) and the Bicycle Bell Trust (1904; see Endnote 15).

Economies of scope became common after the creation of Thomas E. Wilson Company in 1913. The Wilson Company, bolstered by an enormous amount of money from its meat-packing business, moved quickly into both horizontal and vertical integration in an attempt to gain a competitive advantage over A.G. Spalding and Brothers (Ashland Personnel, 1916; see Endnote 16). Spalding responded by purchasing the Victor Sporting Goods Company through its subsidiary Wright and Ditson (*Sporting Goods Dealer*, 1918; see Endnote 17). The period ended with a flurry of amalgamations as other sporting goods companies attempted to compete.

Successful sporting goods companies during the Period of Institutional Development reacted to and used external forces to achieve a competitive advantage. In this process of reaction and utilization, sporting goods companies relied upon internal resources to manipulate micromarketing techniques (promotion, product, place, and price) to gain competitive advantage. The best single example of how successful companies used internal resources to combat or manipulate external forces to achieve a competitive advantage is the A.G. Spalding and Brothers Company. Spalding began in 1876 with a capital of $3,800. Profits for the first 10 months amounted to $1,083 (see Endnote 18). In 1920 Spalding's net income was $1,172,910, and the company was capitalized at $7 million ("Spalding Increases Capital Stock," 1922).

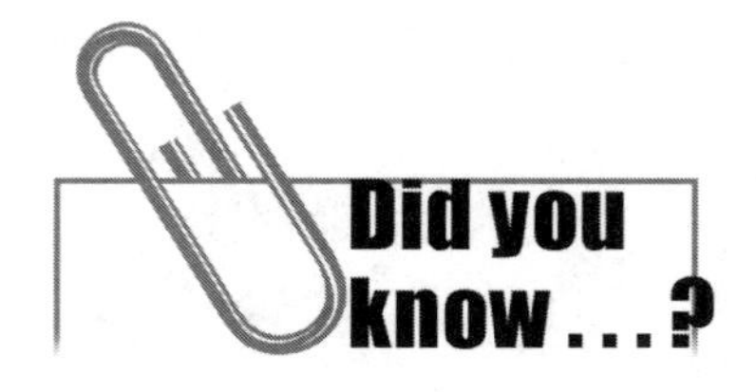

Females control 60% of U.S. wealth and influence, account for a majority of sport apparel purchases, and make more than 80% of all purchases.

Source: 1999 SGMA State of the Industry Report

In November of 1915 the leaders of A.G. Spalding and Brothers discussed the reasons for their success with the editorial staff of the *Sporting Goods Dealer* ("Reasons for Spalding Success," 1915). First, Spalding resources, " great aggregations of capital," allowed the company to operate economies of scale and scope ("Reasons for Spalding Success," p.41). Spalding operated 15 large factories in the United States. The Chicopee plant, for example, had four and one-half acres of floor space (*Sporting Goods Dealer*, 1911). Spalding manufactured on a large scale. Spalding also operated 35 branch stores that performed retail and wholesale functions (*Sporting Goods Dealer*, 1918). Spalding's vertical integration was considered a second major factor influencing company success. A third reason was Spalding's organizational structure and management. Marketing decisions, for example, were made and coordinated by top management. These decisions were passed on to factories and branch stores by vice presidents. Factories and branch stores followed these directives but were operated as separate units by career-oriented middle managers. The marketing strategy functioned to coordinate production, distribution, and sales. Spalding recruited and trained middle managers and provided career-ladder opportunities for advancement within the organization. Top management visited branch stores and factories to provide direction and ideas. In the words of one Spalding manager, "it is the system that works" ("Reasons for Spalding Success," p. 49). The system provided for a "uniformity and regularity of everything," a fourth reason cited for Spalding success. A fifth reason given for Spalding success was the variety of merchandise sold under the Spalding brand name ("Reasons for Spalding Success").

The expansion of the Spalding product line took place gradually and was a reaction to external forces. Spalding began as a small retail store in 1876. The company sold only baseball equipment, and their largest customer was the Chicago White Sox Baseball Club ("J. Walter Spalding Original Ledger," 1947; *Sporting Goods Dealer*, 1908; see Endnote 19). Encouraged by the growing market for other forms of athletic goods, Spalding expanded his product line in 1878 (*Sporting Goods Dealer*, 1907). A year later Spalding purchased an interest in the Wilkins Manufacturing Company, which produced ice skates, fishing equipment, baseball bats and croquet equipment (Levine, 1985). To "insure the quality of goods," Spalding bought out Wilkins in 1881 and established the policy of manufacturing all Spalding trade mark goods (Levine; *Sporting Goods Dealer*, 1908, p. 11). Throughout the 1880s Spalding responded to market opportunities by expanding the number of products manufactured by the company. In 1886, for example, Spalding began manufacturing footballs because the market growth of football in colleges and high schools insured financial success (Levine; *Sporting Goods Dealer*, 1906b; see Endnote 20). Product expansion continued in the 1890s with the acquisition of A. J. Reach and Co. (1889), Peck and Snyder (1889), Wright and Ditson (1891), Lamb Manufacturing Company (1893), St Lawrence River Skiff and Canoe Company (1895), and the George Barnard Company (1896) (Levine; Van Pelt, 1946). These purchases permitted Spalding and Brothers to expand its policy of insuring quality by producing their own trademark goods ("Andrew Peck Pioneer," 1916; Levine; Van Pelt; see Endnote 21). The new acquisitions also allowed Spalding and Brothers to more effectively tap into expanding markets in baseball, ice skating, tennis, bicycles, golf, boating, and athletic and sportsman's wear. By the turn of the century, Spalding was manufacturing bowling balls, protective football equipment, tackling dummies, bathing suits, table tennis equipment, and gymnasium lockers, all to meet the growing market demand for sporting goods products (*Sporting Goods Dealer*, 1900a,b,c,; 1902a,b,c). Spalding continued to expand their product lines throughout the period. By 1920 the company owned 15 factories in the United States, 4 in England and 2 in Canada (*Sporting Goods Dealer*, 1918). A. G. Spalding and Brothers produced a greater variety of products than any other company in the United States. The gradual expansion of product lines was a reaction to opportunities created by market growth.

Spalding reacted to opportunities created by market growth with promotions that targeted specific populations. Promotional efforts began as soon as the company was formed. Spalding spent $483.51 on advertising over the first 10 months, approximately 4% of the company's total sales (see Endnote 22). Spalding acquired the right to publish the "official" book for the National League. At the same time he published *Spalding's Official Baseball Guide*. Both books promoted the Spalding name and advertised Spalding products (Hardy, 1990; Levine, 1985; see Endnote 23). Both books promoted baseball. *Spalding's Official Baseball Guide*, for example, included league rules and constitution, records, descriptions of the past season's play, playing instructions, and history (Hardy, 1990). As early as 1878 Spalding held a contract to provide the National League with the Official Ball. Spalding had wrestled the contract away from L. H. Mann of Boston by agreeing to pay the National League a dollar a dozen for the privilege of supplying free balls (Hardy, 1990; Levine). Official guides and official balls were great promotional tools. Spalding knew that his target audience would never play major league ball. He understood that his audience desired to use what the professionals used because in their minds it signified the best (Levine). Spalding marketed other "official balls" for football, basketball, polo, soccer, and volleyball as well as "official" boxing gloves and the "official" discus (*Sporting Goods Dealer*, 1900d, 1906a). Spalding added guides for a variety of other sports when the market appeared favorable (*Sporting Goods Dealer*, 1899a,b). A. G. Spalding and Brothers was among the first companies to promote sales through packaging. It was among the first to develop general catalogs and to use seasonal catalogs. It was among the first to develop a national sales force. It was among the first to target specific markets through the use of grading techniques (*Sporting Goods Dealer*, 1899a,b). It was among the first companies to target the youth market (*Sporting Goods Dealer*, 1901a, 1923; see Endnote 24).

Spalding not only reacted to opportunities created by market growth, but the company also influenced market growth (Hardy, 1990; Levine, 1985; M. Porter, 1985). A. G. Spalding realized that the key to market growth was increased sport participation. Spalding's promotional efforts were designed not just to sell Spalding products but also to expand the sport market by enlisting new participants. The Spalding Library of American Sports, inaugurated in 1885, was designed to educate future participants (Levine, 1985). Changed to "Spalding's Athletic Library" when James E. Sullivan became managing editor in 1892, by the turn of the century the Library contained over 300 separate titles on sport and physical activity. By 1916 the series listed 16 separate groups of activities arranged by activity. Spalding claimed that it was "the greatest educational series on athletic and physical training subjects that has ever been compiled" (Levine, 1985, pp. 82, 162; see Endnote 25). The Spalding Athletic Library taught readers about sport, provided instruction from experts, presented the benefits of participation, and encouraged activity. Spalding also promoted sport by organizing tours, organizing contests, donating trophies, participating in sport shows, establishing instructional schools, sponsoring professional teams, supporting the Olympic movement, and providing expert advice for facility construction (Levine; *Sporting Goods Dealer*, 1899b, 1901a, 1902a, 1905, 1907). These activities promoted sport participation, which influenced market growth and also helped to sell Spalding products.

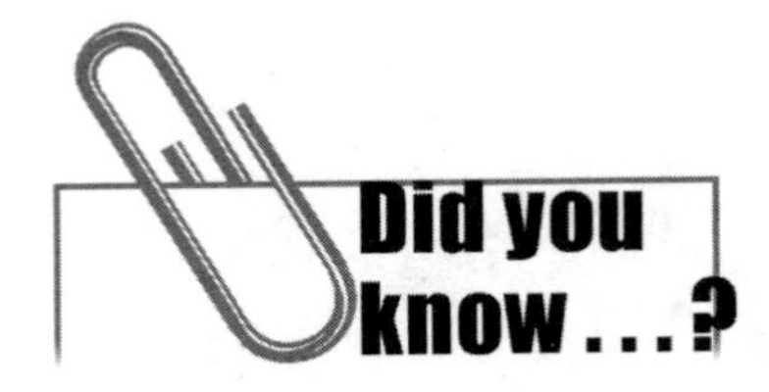

- More girls and women are playing football.
- The Women's Professional League started in 1999.
- An estimated 800 girls play football at the high school level.
- The International Women's Flag Football League has over 1,000 members.

Source: *Amy Love's Real Sports Magazine*

Spalding's product development and product diversity and Spalding's promotional efforts were key factors in the company's success (*Sporting Goods Dealer*, 1908). Equally important was Spalding's vertical integration into wholesale and the expansion of its retail operation into a national system of branch stores (*Sporting Goods Dealer*, 1918). Backward integration into distribution began in 1884 when Spalding opened a wholesale store in New York City. Expansion to New York was prompted by two considerations. First, establishing a wholesale house in New York would more effectively serve east coast retailers. The move meant that Spalding products could be displayed in a place far more accessible to eastern retailers ("Julian W. Curtiss," 1928; "New Gotham," 1924; see Endnote 26). Second, the New York operation was also a distribution center. Spalding goods were displayed on the first floor, and products were stored on the remaining four floors. This permitted Spalding to ship goods to eastern retailers far more effectively ("Julian W. Curtiss"; see Endnote 27). Spalding continued the policy of creating wholesale/distribution centers during the next two and one-half decades. By 1909 the company had 20 such centers in the United States and one each in Canada and England (*Sporting Goods Dealer*, 1909).

Spalding's development of retail branch stores occurred much more slowly. Spalding opened a retail store in New York in 1885. Boston and Philadelphia stores were opened in the early 1890s. The push for retail outlets occurred after the turn of the century (*Sporting Goods Dealer*, 1927). Three divisions were formed, one in the East, another in the West, and later one on the Pacific coast to coordinate activities and services (*Sporting Goods Dealer*, 1927). The development of retail branch stores was prompted by three considerations. First, Spalding saw the opportunity to increase sales. Company stores would sell all kinds of equipment manufactured by other companies but would more effectively push Spalding products (*Sporting Goods Dealer*, 1902a). The Spalding name and trademark would be displayed on the storefront, and Spalding products could be seen in the store windows. Second, the company believed that it could more effectively serve its customers by establishing a retail chain (*Sporting Goods Dealer*, 1927). Company leaders believed that branch stores would ensure quick shipment of goods. Store managers would be more aware of customer needs and would alert Spalding distribution centers about those needs in a timely fashion.

Finally, it appears that Spalding was concerned about price maintenance. In 1899 Spalding established a policy of dealing directly with retailers. Spalding would sell to everyone at the same price in exchange for the assurance that the retailer would sell Spalding products at prices determined by the firm (Levine, 1985). According to Levine, Spalding thought the policy would "increase business, stabilize market situations and eliminate price-cutting" (Levine, p. 83). The policy appeared to be a huge success. Six months after its inception, Walter Spalding "told a *Sporting News* reporter that 'there had been a wonderful increase in their athletic business' and that price-cutting had virtually ended" (Levine, p. 84). The movement into retail branch stores 3 years later was prompted, at least in part, by the success of the 1899 policy. It appears that Spalding Company leaders like Julian Curtiss and C.S. Lincoln believed that retail store owners were maintaining Spalding prices but were discounting comparable goods of other sporting goods manufacturers. This practice hurt the sale of top-grade Spalding products (*Sporting Goods Dealer*, 1923; see Endnote 28). The only way to combat such practices was to control the retail outlets where the goods were sold (Van Pelt, 1946; see Endnote 29). Spalding moved into the development of retail branch stores so that they could control prices at those stores (see Endnote 30).

Very little is known about Spalding and Brothers' price policies. The company began in 1876 with a cash sales policy (Hardy, 1990). This was continued until 1893. During that year Spalding established a credit policy to improve bicycle sales. There is no evidence that Spalding extended the credit policy to other Spalding products until after the turn of the century. Spalding advertisements to dealers are silent about the possibilities for discounts or terms. Spalding's traveling salesmen could have handled these matters. When Spalding moved into the mass market during 1884, they established a grading policy. A decade later they advertised 18 different grades of bats and 15 grades of baseball. Prices for baseballs ranged from 5 cents to $1.25 (Levine, 1985; *Sporting Goods Dealer*, 1901a). Claiming that the company actually lost money on high-quality goods for the youth market, Spalding adjusted prices on these products (*Sporting Goods Dealer*, 1923). Spalding and Brothers' concern for price maintenance, discussed briefly above, continued throughout the period of institutional development. Other than the 1899 sales policy and the suggested connection between retail branch stores and price maintenance, little is known about Spalding pricing policies.

Producer Activities	Yes	Percent	No	Percent	Undetermined	Percent
Trademarks	430	84%	86	16%		
Packaging	293	57%	223	43%		
Grading and Standardization	325	63%	191	37%		
Segmentation (by price)	235	45%	281	55%		
Market Analysis	94	18%	181	35%	241	47%
Product Design	353	68%	160	31%	3	1%
Branch House	45	9%	471	91%		
Producer Owned Retail Stores	19	4%	497	96%		
Direct Sales to Consumer	191	37%	325	63%		
Cooperation with Independent Retailer	288	56%	228	44%		
Price Maintenance	71	14%	445	86%		
Co. Sales Force	317	61%	199	39%		
National Advertising	335	65%	181	35%		
Advertising Agency	102	20%	221	43%	193	37%

Figure 2.4
Sporting Goods Industry 1899–1905 (N = 516).

A. G. Spalding and Brothers were not the only sporting goods manufacturers to apply micromarketing techniques as a response to external forces. Spalding's attempts to achieve a competitive advantage were copied by other companies. Figure 2.4 documents the use of micromarketing techniques by a large number of sporting goods manufacturers to gain a competitive advantage or to establish a barrier to entry.

Figure 2.4 is an adaptation of Fullerton's (1988) "How Modern Is Modern Marketing?" The left-hand column lists 14 producer activities. These producer activities correspond to specific micromarketing functions. Trademarks, packaging, grading and standardization, segmentation, market analysis, and product design are product micromarketing activities. Producer-owned branch houses, producer-owned retail stores, direct sales to customers and contacts with independent retailers are distribution functions. Price maintenance is a price micromarketing activity. Company sales forces and national advertising are promotional activities (Fullerton, 1988). The "yes" column in Figure 2.4 lists the number of sporting goods companies that employed the technique. This column is followed by a percentage column. The "no" column in Figure 2.4 lists the number of companies that did not use the micromarketing technique. This column is followed by a percentage. For example, 430 sporting goods producers, or 84% of the sample, used trademarks. Eighty-six sporting goods producers—16% of the sample—did not use trademarks. The "Undetermined" column in Figure 2.4 lists the number of companies in the sample for which data about the marketing activity do not exist. This column is followed by a percentage. For example, under number 5, market analysis, there were 241 companies in the sample for which we could not determine whether market analysis was applied or not. This constituted 47% of the total sample.

Category	Number
General Manufacturer	28
Arms and Ammo	104
Bicycles	138
Fishing Equipment	60
Boats and Equipment	43
Skating	13
Golf	41
Gymnastics and Exercise	13
Billiards and Bowling	11
Uniforms and Sport Clothing	27
Boxing	15
Tennis	8
Baseball	25
Basketball	3
Football	13

Figure 2.5
Categories of Sporting Goods Manufacturers

Figure 2.5 divides the sample into specific categories of sporting goods manufacturers. The data for Figures 2.4 and 2.5 was gathered from company histories, trade magazines, and advertisements and includes only those companies that existed between 1899 and 1905. The sample included 516 companies that manufactured products for the sporting goods market. Some companies made products for other markets. For example, many companies classified under Arms and Ammo also manufactured products for the military. Twenty-eight companies produced a variety of sporting products. To avoid confusion, these companies are classified as General Manufacturers. A. G. Spalding and Brothers, for example, manufactured a variety of sport equipment products. Rather than list the Spalding company several times under each separate heading, it is listed only once, under General Manufacturers.

Figure 2.6 illustrates the extremes within the sport industry. It follows an abbreviated format of Figure 2.4 and adds some key examples. Figure 2.6 suggests that certain categories of sporting goods manufacturers were far more advanced than others in the use of micromarketing techniques. As Figure 2.6 documents, general manufacturers of sporting goods and arms and ammo producers used micromarketing techniques to a greater extent than did golf and tennis equipment manufacturers. The two extremes portrayed in Figure 2.6 have two important implications for the development of sport marketing. First, participation in tennis and golf was not as great as participation in

Producer Activities	General MFG Sp. Good		Arm & Ammo		Golf		Tennis		Key Examples
	Yes	No	Yes	No	Yes	No	Yes	No	
1. Trademarks	24	4	70	0	16	25	6	2	Chicago Sporting Goods Peter's Cartridge
2. Packaging	18	10	69	1	12	29	6	2	Spalding & Bros. Peter's Cartridge
3. Grading and Standardization	27	1	68	2	22	19	5	3	Remington Arms Co. A.J. Reach
4. Segmentation	25	3	58	12	6	35	2	6	A.J. Reach Daisy Mfg. Remington
5. Market Analysis	14	2	38	12	5	28	2	1	D&M McClean Arms Co. Wright & Division
6. Product Designed by Specialist	25	3	70	0	16	25	4	4	Goldsmith & Sons Ted Kennedy
7. Producer Owned Branch Houses	11	17	20	50	2	39	1	7	Spalding Hazard Powder B.F. Goodrich
8. Producer Owned Retail Stores	13	15	0	70	1	40	0	8	Spalding & Bros. BGI
9. Direct Sale to Consumer	20	8	32	38	5	36	0	8	Patrick Bros. Crandel & Stone
10. Contact Independent Retailer—Chain Store	21	7	65	5	10	31	8	0	BGI Winchester
11. Price Maintenance	7	4	26	7	0	41	0	8	Spalding & Bros. Iver Johnson
12. Company Sales Force	20	8	68	2	12	29	8	0	Wright & Ditson A.J. Reach
13. National Advertising	21	3	67	3	11	30	5	3	Winchester Rawlings Goldsmith
14. Advertising Agency or Specialist	19	5	31	7	4	32	2	1	Chicago Sport Goods Spalding & Bros. D&M

Table 2.6
Extremes Within the Industry: 1899–1905.

hunting. The market was not as large. Competition was not as keen, and barriers to entry were not as great. There were many more manufacturers of arms and ammo than there were of golf or tennis equipment. Manufacturers of golf and tennis equipment did not need to rely upon micromarketing techniques to the same extent that producers of arms and ammo did. Second, the general manufacturers of sporting goods and the arms and ammo producers were much larger companies than the producers of golf and tennis equipment. In each instance, the key examples listed in the right-hand column of Figure 2.6 were large companies. They had the internal resources to combat or use external forces through micromarketing activities.

During the Era of Institutional Development (1880–1920), sporting goods manufacturers developed and refined micromarketing techniques in response to new and powerful external forces. Innovators like A. G. Spalding and Brothers introduced new micromarketing activities to the sporting goods industry. Other companies copied and further refined these techniques. By 1920 all the elements of what Fullerton has called modern marketing existed in the sporting goods industry (Fullerton, 1988). What followed during the Era of Refinement and Formalization (1930–1980) was refinement, further development, and formalization of already established micromarketing techniques as sporting goods companies reacted to new opportunities and challenges made possible by external forces.

The Era of Refinement and Formalization: 1920–1990

During the last 70 years, sport marketing has continued to develop along lines established during the Era of Institutional Development. External forces have played important roles in this development. The increased popularity and diversification of sport interests have increased market size. Sport fads have periodically increased market growth rates. Industry profitability has fluctuated through turbulent periods like the depressions of the 1930s and the early 1990s and the prosperous times of the 1950s and 1960s. Government policies have also influenced sport marketing. The National Industrial Recovery Act (1933) placed restrictions on sporting goods manufacturers but also influenced the development of fair trade practices, particularly when connected to the Robinson Packman Act of 1936. Miller-Tydings (1937) and the Consumer Goods Pricing Act (1975) influenced the pricing practices of sporting goods companies. More recently the North American Free Trade Agreement (1993) and the Brady Bill (1994) will influence how sporting goods companies do business. Technological changes have influenced both how and from what materials sporting goods are made. New materials such as plastics, fiberglass, aluminum alloys, spandex threads, and graphite have improved athletic performances and altered athletic styles. At the same time these new materials have made possible the development of special machines to mass-produce sport equipment. Economies of scale have been made possible by new materials and new manufacturing techniques, new and more economic forms of transportation, and new and more effective forms of communication. Modern marketers have the use of many specialized trade journals, radio, television, computers, and fax machines to convey and receive information. The increased opportunities for economies of scale have influenced preferences for economies of scope. Prior to 1920 economies of scope led to amalgamation and consolidation within a domestic sport industry. Today economies of scope include leverage buyouts, global competition, and offshore industries.

Questions for Study

1. Identify three ways in which sport marketers contributed to a growing sport market between 1820 and 1880.
2. What problems did Fuller encounter when attempting to market boxing in the early 1820s?
3. Were advertisements used to market the game of baseball in the 1860s significantly different from the modern advertisements used to market baseball?
4. List 10 characteristics associated with the Era of Institutionalized Development and elaborate on their significance.
5. By what year did most all medium and large sporting goods companies have their own sales force?

6. During what stage of the product life cycle does the sporting goods industry occupy between 1880 and 1920? Defend your answer.
7. Elaborate on the contribution the railroad, telegraph, and telephone provided to sport marketing.
8. Elaborate on the impact of technology during the Era of Institutional Development.
9. How does a competitor's advertising help to sell sport? Elaborate.
10. Elaborate on how both economies of scale and economies of scope can facilitate marketing efforts.
11. How did vertical integration facilitate Spalding's marketing efforts?
12. Identify the five reasons attributed to Spalding's success in the 1920s. Why were these factors important to Spalding's success?
13. Spalding has a significant learning curve advantage. Explain.

Endnotes

1. *The Billiard Cue* was a four-page monthly. It went out of print in 1874. The exact contents of the periodical are unknown. Doubtless it promoted Phelan and his billiard products.
2. Phelan developed the India rubber cushion in 1854. Phelan also held a patent on a machine that made standardized billiard balls.
3. Adelman (1986)points out that other manufacturers, who were not "crack players," took issue with Phelan's claim.
4. Phelan did of course try to increase market size. According to Adelman (1986), he was very successful.
5. Although poolrooms were always opposed by middle-class morality (Polsky, 1969, pp. 6, 12).
6. Phelan did not deal with economies of scope or scale. Brunswick's absorptions of Blake in 1869 and Phelan and Collender in 1879 are examples of economies of scope.
7. This relationship is developed extremely well in respect to football in Oriard (1993).
8. These examples are not intended to be exhaustive. Struna's (1981) development of the North-South horse races is an excellent study. For an excellent study of harness racing, see Adelman (1981). Gorn (1986) is the best single source for the study of early boxing promoters. In the sporting goods industry, accounts of the early development of marketing techniques exist for several companies. See for example, "B.F. Meek and Sons—Bluegrass Reel," *Sporting Goods Dealer* (March, 1911); "E.K. Tryon Company," *Sporting Goods Dealer* (May, 1908; February, 1911; March, 1911).
9. Our development of this section follows Fullerton (1988) and Hardy (1990).
10. Branch houses combined warehouses with selling offices and allowed a company to sell and distribute its goods directly to retailers.
11. Sporting goods included the following: fishing equipment, oars and paddles, gun accessories (such as gun cases and shell boxes), toboggans and skis, bows and arrows. The manufacture of firearms and ammunition was classified as separate industries. Athletic goods included baseball equipment, basketball supplies, boxing, bowling, cricket, exercisers, football, golf, gymnasium goods, hockey, skates, tennis, playground apparatus, circus apparatus, and similar commodities (US Department of Commerce, 1924).
12. B.F. Goodrich produced the Haskell Golf Ball. See *Sporting Goods Dealer* (September, 1927) for a discussion and description of the manufacturing process.
13. Presbrey (1929) maintains that companies within the industry continued to advertise at equal or greater rates after 1898, but comparisons between 1891 figures and 1928 figures are impossible due to the tremendous increase in journal advertising space.
14. In nearly every issue from 1898 through 1920, the *Sporting Goods Dealer* published announcements by manufacturing companies about plant expansions. In almost every instance, the reason for expansion was to meet the growing demand and to lower costs to customers.
15. When people spoke of trusts around the turn of the century, they were usually referring to companies that were engaged in horizontal integration (G. Porter, 1973). None of the trusts survived. The Bicycle Trust was bankrupted by 1905, the Bicycle Bell Trust collapsed in 1906, and the Ammunition Trust was struck down by the courts in 1908.
16. Wilson purchased Ashland Manufacturing Company (1913), Sell Sporting Goods (1917), the Chicago Specialty Shoe Company (1919), Chicago Sporting Goods Company (1919), National Baseball Manufacturing Company (1922), and Western Sporting Goods Company (1925). In 1917 it opened its first retail store in Chicago. The original name of the sporting

goods company was Ashland Manufacturing Company. It was changed to Thomas E. Wilson Company in 1917. Wilson continued to expand by purchasing other companies during the 1930s and 1940s (*Sporting Goods Dealer*, 1964).

17. This amalgamation also included Roper Brothers Company of Massachusetts and the Whitney Sporting Goods Company of Denver. Spalding and Brothers was not named in the article.
18. Levine (1985) reports that $800 came from Harriet Spalding, the mother of A.G. and Walter Spalding. Hardy (1990), using the records of the Dunn Collection, reports the initial capital at $2,500. Our figures are taken from "J. Walter Spalding Original Ledger," p. 5, which shows a $400 contribution from each brother and a $3,000 loan. A Photostat copy of parts of the ledger can be found in *Sporting Goods Dealer* (June, 1947, pp. 128–9).
19. "J. Walter Spalding, Original Ledger," pp. 138, 173, 176, and 203, lists accounts for Reach and Johnson, Pop Anson, Field Lieber and Company (later Marshall Fields), Peck and Snyder, Hibbard Spencer and Company, and Good Year.
20. By 1886 Spalding dealt with tennis equipment, baseball equipment, gymnasium supplies, fishing tackle, guns, bicycles, and general athletic furnishings.
21. A.J. Reach produced Spalding baseballs and gloves; Peck and Snyder produced Spalding ice skates and became a major distribution center for Spalding products in the east. Wright and Ditson produced tennis rackets, and the Lamb Manufacturing Company made bicycles. When Spalding began the production of golf clubs in 1893 and golf balls in 1896, these products were made by the Lamb Manufacturing Company. The St. Lawrence River Skiff and Canoe Company manufactured boats, canoes, and accessories. The George Barnard Company was the largest manufacturer of athletic sportsman's wear in the world.
22. "J. Walter Spalding, Ledger Book" (no page number, page labeled "Profit and Loss"). Spalding sold $12,088 during the first 10 months.
23. Levine documents Spalding's attempts to expand the circulation of Spalding's Official Baseball Guide. Spalding claimed a circulation of 40,000 by 1884. Hardy provides an insightful analysis of Spalding chicanery in passing off his guide as the "official" National League guidebook. *Spalding's Official Baseball Guide* especially promoted Spalding products.
24. C.S. Lincoln claimed that targeting the youth market was one of the reasons for Spalding's success.
25. Levine reports that Spalding published guides for "every sport imaginable." Spalding also published the official publications of the YMCA, the Public School Athletic League, the National Association of Amateur Oarsmen, and other special publications.
26. Julian Curtiss, vice president of Spalding and Brothers, believed that the importance of the wholesale operation in New York was that it cut travel time required of eastern retailers when they visited Spalding. Curtis believed that the store increased eastern sales.
27. Curtiss believed that this created additional sales for Spalding because it allowed goods to reach the customer more quickly and influenced retailers to reorder.
28. Lincoln, vice president of Spalding, believed that the policy forced retailers to sell lower-priced grades of Spalding goods in order to compete with other companies. This detracted from the sale of high-quality Spalding products.
29. Significantly, Spalding phased out its retail branch stores when it became possible to maintain prices through state legislation in the late 1930s. Another factor that influenced Spalding policy in the late 1930s was the existence of sporting goods trade organizations that helped maintain prices.
30. Spalding could not, of course, control prices at retail stores that the company did not own.

Chapter 3

The Global Market for the Sport Industry

Globalization is not coming—it is here. The NBA, NFL, Nike, Reebok, and nearly every major sport enterprise in the United States are doing business in a global environment. Yeh and Li (1998) noted that "the globalized economy has imposed a great challenge on sport management professionals to develop an understanding of issues associated with the globalization of sport, and accordingly come up with appropriate coping strategies" (p. 32). As a multinational corporation, Nike cornered 32% of the worldwide market in athletic footwear, bringing in over $9 billion in annual sales. Reebok, second in the market with a 15% market share, was able to capture $3.5 billion in sales (Koranteng, 1998). In total, the United States exported $2.43 billion in sporting goods in 1997 and imported $7.9 billion (Sporting Goods Manufacturers Association, 1998). As you can see, sport is a global marketplace.

The purpose of this chapter is to enable sport marketers to think in international and global terms. It is not intended to provide the forum for billion-dollar multinational corporations. Although many lessons and examples can be learned from such companies, you do not have to play in their league to learn from their experiences. Therefore, this chapter has been written with the following objectives in mind: (a) to provide information about the global marketplace for the sport marketer, (b) to identify information and knowledge necessary for entry into a global market, and (c) to present a context for thinking about marketing internationally.

The globalized economy has imposed a great challenge on sport management professionals to develop an understanding of issues associated with the globalization of sport.

According to Pride and Ferrell (1997), fewer than 10% of small-to-midsize companies participate in global marketing and trade, but 70% express an interest in international sales. Thus, it seems only natural that many businesses have limited knowledge of international trade. This information void may contribute to a reluctance to begin examining global aspects of the sport industry.

Traditional concepts of import and export arise when international markets are mentioned, yet these are not the only factors in a global approach. It will become increasingly necessary to view all of the corporate resources, finance, manufacturing, distribution, retailing, and human resource management, from a global perspective.

As Americans have experienced, much of our sport equipment is manufactured abroad, but have we truly examined foreign markets for the sale of our products and services? Are there markets where our products or services could dominate? Could mergers and cooperative agreements provide increased revenue and markets for US and foreign companies?

With these questions in mind, it becomes necessary to investigate the global market in more detail. Although the global marketplace is ever changing, the areas presented below may provide some knowledge and insight for international market exploration.

The Global Business Structure

The structure of the international business environment is complex. Business schools offer complete courses in international business, and some graduate programs are designed with international commerce as their focus of study. Following is an overview for the sport marketing professional of the key topics in the area.

Several avenues are available for entering international markets. The Internet and the world wide web certainly provide opportunities for engaging in international commerce. However, because individual consumers are burdened with clearing items through customs and paying duty on goods (over $400 for goods imported into the United States), this option is not widespread or prevalent in the sport industry

The easiest and least complicated avenue available for entering international markets is exporting. This practice depends on either corporate or agency interest in domestic products. For example, a sporting goods company in Argentina may contact your firm about the possibility of purchasing in-line skates from your company for export. You would simply supply them with the product, and they would deal with the issues of duties and tariffs to import the items into Argentina. The benefits are easy to see. Your outlay of capital is negligible, and you are not overburdened with customs procedures. Perhaps the only modifications that you would need to make would be in package labeling or modifications in color to satisfy local appeal. On the other hand, exporting in this manner depends on the emergence of demand, as opposed to activating demand (Pride and Ferrell, 1997).

Exporting provides the easiest avenue for international marketing.

In some instances, trading companies can more actively identify markets and move your products more effectively into international channels. Trading companies typically purchase goods in one country and then resell them in various international markets. Again, the advantage for you is that the risks and capital outlay are minimal. If the products don't sell, the trading company absorbs the loss.

The Four Steps in the US Customs Process:

1. Filing of the appropriate entry documents
2. Inspection and classification of the goods
3. Preliminary declaration of value
4. Final determination of duty and payment

(Tuller, 1991, p. 332)

The formation of *joint ventures* and *strategic alliances* are two additional forms of penetrating international markets prevalent in the sport industry. These marketing techniques involve a greater level of risk and the commitment of more corporate resources.

Joint ventures are characterized by partnering with a corporation residing in the target nation. This practice has been successfully implemented in the athletic footwear industry. Major US shoe companies have formed partnerships with Asian factories to dedicate portions of their factory space or a percentage of their production-line time to produce shoes. Pride and Ferrell (1997) noted significant growth in the implementation of strategic alliances in the late 1990s.

What differentiates strategic alliances from joint ventures is that in the formation of a strategic alliance, partners "often retain their distinct identities, and each brings a distinctive competence to the union" (Pride and Ferrell, 1997, p. 93). Thus, a Korean golf-equipment manufacturing group could receive much needed capital for expansion and engineering innovation from a US sporting goods company. The US firm would obtain high-quality products manufactured at labor and material costs far lower than it could have secured domestically.

Direct ownership is the final alternative to entering a foreign market. In this instance, the domestic company commits significant resources to build a factory and corporate office and hire a local work force to manufacture goods and distribute them within the market. Because of the level of capital required and the tremendous risk involved, few sport firms are willing to select this strategy. Regardless of the structure selected for international marketing, a thorough understanding of the business environment is required. Additional topics presented below provide information that should prove useful.

International Economics and Finance

Gaining a working understanding of world banking and finance is essential for sport marketers. Most Americans are accustomed to dealing with commercial banks through such services as deposits, loans, and checking accounts. In the United States, commercial banks are widespread and need only a license to operate. However, most industrialized nations have a system controlled by a central national bank. For the sport entrepreneur, two choices exist: You can deal with the central bank of the host country, or you can deal with a foreign branch of an American bank.

American banks may have familiar-sounding names and executives who understand the American way, but overall, foreign banks have fewer restrictions and less regulation than do American banks. For that reason, "foreign banks are generally easier to deal with, cheaper, and less inclined to hassle the customer, than their American counterparts" (Tuller, 1991, p. 214).

In selecting a bank for foreign business activities, the size of the bank is not as important as are the services it can provide. Managers should look specifically for banking institutions that can

1. Move money from banks in one country to banks in another through wire transfer.
2. Handle export financing through personnel in their internal department.
3. Arrange for collections and payments in various currencies.
4. Process foreign currency through exchange conversion at the lowest possible rate.
5. Issue and process letters of credit to guarantee payments and collections from clients.

A common nightmare for sport marketers is foreign currency. If the only experience you have in dealing with foreign currency is exchanging your dollars for pesos on your Mexican vacation, you are in for an education. Not all international monetary units are the same with regard to exchange and convertibility. The term *hard currency* has generally been defined as a unit of monetary value readily convertible to other units. In international business transactions, the US dollar, the Japanese yen, the English pound, and the Euro are all convertible with one another at established rates of exchange. However, because of fluctuating exchange rates, variance in financial backing, and government stability, not all world currencies are equally acceptable.

Problems can easily result in situations where the standard payment method has not been well conceived. Suppose you close a deal to provide 100,000 baseball bats at 6,750 Venezuelan Bolivars each ($1.00 US = 577 Bolivars). Once the shipment arrives, payment is required within 30 days. However, because of inflation within the country, the value of the payment may be less than expected at the time of delivery to your account in Caracas. The international monetary system may have devalued the Bolivar against the dollar. The result could be that you would actually lose money on your deal. In another example, the Golf Channel began negotiating with Taiwanese television officials in 1998 to supply 24-hour programming. However, when "the Taiwanese dollar plunged, the deal fell apart" (Mullen, E. 1998, p. 46).

Did you know . . . ?

The estimated size of the U.S. billiards products market was $235 million in 1998, a 5% increase over 1997.

Source: 1999 SGMA State of the Industry Report

This same situation can also wreak havoc with international employees. If agreements for salary were negotiated in local currency, employees might find that their standard of living deteriorates considerably with inflation or devaluation. On the other hand, if they contracted to be paid in US dollars and the local currency decreased in its value against the dollar, they could have expanded their buying power immensely. Precisely this situation occurred with the Asian Games in Bangkok during 1998. In an 8-month period, the Thai *baht* dropped in value against the US dollar by more than 54%. However, because most of the expenses incurred by the organizers were in *baht* and their income from sponsors was in US dollars, the event and revenues were protected. Most international corporations have contractual language that addresses this issue. When possible, avoid taking foreign currency in payment for an account.

In dealing with the problems of international currency, many companies use countertrade agreements. These agreements are similar to barter in which products and services are exchanged for other products or services that can be resold to another party for hard currency. According to Tuller (1991), "countertrade is probably the best guarded secrets in international trade" (p. 263).

To avoid a common sport marketer's nightmare, don't take foreign currency in payment for an account and consider using countertrade agreements.

One multinational sport corporation, ProServ, encountered a situation such as this in negotiating with Eastern European backers for a professional tennis tournament. Although the promoters wanted television production and coverage of the event, they did not have any hard currency with which to pay. However, a German firm was located that needed to make a series of payments for their employees in the local currency, and ProServ agreed to make the payment for the German firm, which would in turn pay ProServ in deutsche Marks (Briner, 1992).

Finally, Tuller (1991) recommends the following guidelines for using the global banking system:

1. The education process—Get up to speed in internal finance as soon as possible. Take a college course in international finance. Spend some time with the head of the international department of a regional bank.

2. Read, read, read—The fastest way to learn about global banking and develop a global financial mentality is to read everything available on the subject.

3. Choosing a commercial bank—Determine which local bank has an international department. Interview the department manager.

4. Experiment—Open a foreign bank account. Transfer small amounts back and forth. Incorporate exchange rate variances in forecasts—even if you have to use fictitious entries.

5. Conquer the "big boy" syndrome—The more a person investigates global banking the more one realizes it is not just for the "big boys." (p. 221)

Trade Regulations

Since the industrialization after World War II, the General Agreement on Tariffs and Trade (GATT) has governed much of international trade. Through this accord, member nations agree to certain practices involving international commerce. Although it may be beneficial for sport marketers to review this agreement, relatively few of the member countries meticulously follow its bylaws. Many countries in the world continue to establish and enforce trade agreements and tariffs that protect their products and restrict competition. However, the success of GATT agreements between the 124 participating nations has reduced the average tariff on manufactured items from 45% to 5% (Pride and Ferrell,1997).

Examples of trade regulation affecting sports organizations are numerous. In 1994, the United States, Mexico, and Canada entered into the North American Free Trade Agreement (NAFTA), which reduced and eliminated many previously imposed tariffs. By 2009, almost all tariffs between these nations will have disappeared. If you had been contemplating creating a product to compete with a Canadian firm, the price differentials pre- and postlegislation could have been substantially affected. However, lifting trade regulations has provided greater access to Canada's more affluent population and has increased trade from the United States by 50% since NAFTA's inception. Although many consumers in Mexico are less affluent than those in either the United States or Canada, trade between the United States and Mexico was enhanced because of a strong desire for US-made products. US firms were also able to redirect manufacturing to Mexico, where the costs of labor have traditionally been much lower. In the manufacture of sporting goods, this labor market may prove attractive in business relocation and product sourcing. As will be discussed later, the practice of using cheap labor to produce US consumer goods has created considerable controversy in some segments of the sport industry. NAFTA could also have an impact on the export of products where previous tariffs may have priced US goods too high for some consumers; thus, additional markets for US sporting goods and equipment companies could be more accessible (Pride and Ferrell,1997).

Free-trade agreements could also affect sport-related corporations in terms of liability costs. In the last 20 years, many sporting goods corporations relocated to foreign countries because of the growing cost of equipment-related liability in the United States. If import tariffs were eliminated between the United States and the manufacturer's host country, some corporations might be able to realize greater profit margins by relocating to a foreign manufacturing site.

Specifically in Europe, the formation and liberalization that took place with the European Union (EU) in 1992 also brought many challenges and opportunities in sport. This event had dramatic effects on the sport industry. One example surfaced in Formula One (auto racing), where officials in charge of regulating antitrust situations across the European Union have challenged F1 authorities' restrictive television contracts. One of the main issues pertains to whether or not sport is a business and subject to regulation (Stewart, 1999).

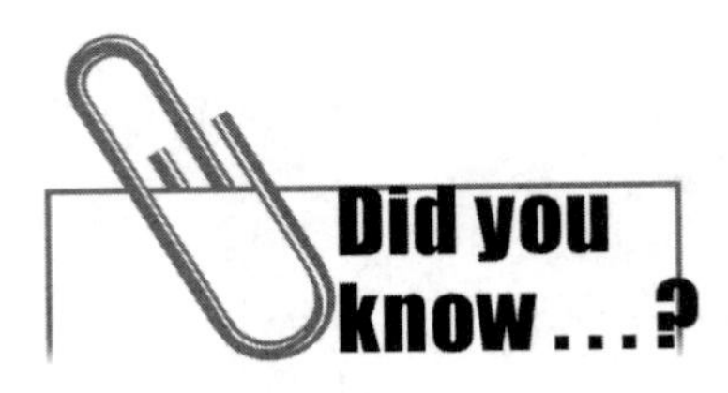

Between 1987 and 1997, sales of fitness equipment increased 63%.

Source: 1999 SGMA State of the Industry Report

Prior to the unification of the EU, sport marketers who desired to do business in Europe had a multitude of rules and regulations specific to each country. However, with consolidation in many key business areas, the bureaucracy of transacting business in Europe has been standardized, if not reduced. The introduction of a standard currency, the Euro, also helped with international transactions. Although not all member countries adopted the Euro as domestic currency, inter-European and international trade was calculated in Euros.

In sport marketing, we must be careful not to become too restricted in our perceptions. Although EU regulations may allow for more standardized products to be sold, the sport marketer should not automatically conclude that European consumers have similarly homogeneous needs and desires. Specific demographic and psychographic research will continue to be required. As an example, the spread of income across the richest EU member nations to the poorest has been as high as 138%. EU markets have become more accessible, but not significantly more similar (Quelch, Buzzell, and Salama, 1990).

A primary concern for professional sport organizations is the free movement of labor. Both the Single Europe Act of 1986 and Article 48 of the 1957 Treaty of Rome stated that residents of member States have the right to work and live in other member States and that a free movement of goods, services, persons, and capital must be ensured. In European sports, this meant a free and open market for all athletes within the sports teams of the EU. The general effect of free trade in professional sports remains unclear. Meetings of the EU Committee for the Development of Sport in 1992 produced legislation that limited the number of "foreign" players to three per team (*Sports Information Bulletin*, 1992). It may be that bidding wars for the top players will cause salaries to escalate substantially, or quite possibly, supply and demand may equalize player earnings across Europe.

Another area of concern has been in sports equipment. Manufacturers in England had previously been required to follow one set of product safety codes whereas those in France have had another. These and other issues related to sport and commerce are continually being clarified.

The general strategy predicted for companies in the EU will be that as new markets open, price-cutting is likely to be a popular move to increase initial market share. New products will also be used as development will have been made less costly through standardization. New products will also help attract consumers who may have been previously unfamiliar with a company's product line. Experts have also postulated that distribution of goods will also be facilitated because regulations covering truck transport (accounting for 80% of EU goods) will be reduced and border clearances will be considerably faster (Quelch, Buzzell, and Salama, 1990). The EU unification therefore brought serious issues to light for sports professionals and sporting goods companies.

Other areas of the world also offer opportunities for sport-related businesses. In Saudi Arabia, the United States Sports Academy, an American college located in Alabama, has conducted business affairs since the mid 1970s, at one point having over 500 employees in the region. However, by modifying regulations in the 1980s, the Saudi government changed the rules for calculating taxes and income for foreign corporations. Excellent planning by the CEO provided for the formation of a locally held corporation to take over the sport and recreation services once provided by the United States Sports Academy. By seeking local executives and changing the business structure of the venture, the United States Sports Academy was able to continue effectively to do business with the country.

Free-trade zones also provide interesting opportunities for sport marketers. These zones are regulated by government agencies in host countries. In the United States, such zones allow for the manufacture and/or assembly for goods that are not intended for national consumption. Thus, you could import parts for gymnastics equipment from Asia, assemble them in a Colorado free-trade zone, and ship them to Europe without paying customs duties. Similar situations have also been developed in foreign nations. On a recent trip to Taiwan, a sport executive planned to purchase a high-quality set of golf clubs that he had discovered were manufactured in Taiwan. Figuring that he could find a great bargain, he began to search for his prized clubs. Much to his surprise, he learned that they were manufactured in Taiwan, but they were produced for "export only." Yes, they could be purchased in Taiwan, but only when reimported from the United States. With twice the shipping expense, the clubs were cheaper in the United States.

International Marketing Structure

The structure of international marketing in contrast to that of domestic sport enterprises contains more similarities than differences. Tuller (1991) reports that the main concepts of selling directly to consumers or selling through agents are indeed the same. Other traditional marketing activities contained in this book are also required in global marketing efforts. The process is similar, but the information and sources will be significantly different.

Differences come in the format that facilitates transactions. Terms such as *foreign trading corporations* and *export management companies* are unique to international business. Sport marketers who choose to compete in the global market will invariably learn to deal with these terms and to work effectively with foreign distributors.

Probably the most difficult aspect of foreign trade is customs. If you are dealing in sports goods and products, successfully negotiating the customs system is key to your success. If you are importing goods into the United States that have been manufactured overseas, you will be required to clear the goods through customs at their port of entry. Kapoor and McKay (1971) also cite factors that differentiate international marketing from domestic. There appears to be greater government regulation in foreign markets and consequently a greater need for feedback and control. In addition, more data are needed for marketing decisions because of the cultural differences that exist. Many marketing decisions are made in US sport organization, because of a knowledge of sport in our

> The formation of the EU is expected to have significant effects on the sport industry such as a decrease in prices and increased ease of distribution as restrictions are lifted and a potential for either the elevation or equalization of player salaries.

societal context. This knowledge simply does not exist for US sport managers making decisions in foreign countries. To offset this problem, most organizations will enlist the assistance of national experts from the target nation.

These experts can also be helpful in communicating value differences between cultures. For example, US and German executives typically value punctuality and promptness, whereas in other cultures a 10:00 A.M. meeting simply means sometime in the morning. It is not that executives in other cultures are being rude; punctuality is just not important in their value system. International managers must learn to respect the value systems of others, not merely tolerate them.

Another difference in international marketing is that in many countries, government-owned business can compete with privately held companies. For instance, you may own a sport concession management business similar to Aramark in the United States. Aramark has a variety of contracts with professional and collegiate stadiums around the country to supply concession and management services. However, in some foreign countries, government-owned corporations may be granted exclusive rights to public stadiums. Another complication could be government subsidies to local corporations. Either of these practices would severely restrict the ability of a successful US company to compete in that market.

The Global Sports Structure

A precursor to involvement in international sport management is a thorough understanding of the global sport environment. The framework for comprehension begins in the United States with the recognition that the United States Olympic Committee (USOC) is chartered by Congress to oversee amateur sport in the country. This encompasses all sports that are in the Olympic and Pan-American Games. Sports that fall outside those parameters may hold membership with the USOC, but are not governed by them. Professional and collegiate sports in the United States are self-governing through private voluntary associations such as the major league offices and the National Collegiate Athletic Association.

In the international sports environment, the International Olympic Committee (IOC) maintains authority over the Olympic Games and regional Olympic-style competitions (Pan-American Games, Asian Games, etc.). It is only these multi-sport competitions where the IOC retains control. The IOC manages and markets these events internationally. The Olympic Partners (TOP) sponsorship program includes multinational corporations such as Coca Cola (USA), Panasonic (Japan), and Samsung (Korea).

> The best source for a study of the global sport environment is Chalip and Thoma's book entitled *Sport Governance in the Global Community* (1993).

Each specific sport is governed by an international federation for that sport. Track-and-field is a member of the International Amateur Athletic Federation; basketball has its International Amateur Basketball Federation; and each sport maintains an affiliation with its International Federation (IF). These federations work very closely with the IOC in staging the Olympics, but have as their main purpose setting rules and regulations for their sports and conducting the world championships in their sport on a yearly basis.

The organizations are also linked through National Governing Bodies (NGB). Each IF designates an NGB in each country to organize and govern a specific sport within national borders. This NGB must be recognized by its national Olympic committee (i.e., USOC). As such, the NGBs work with the IFs for rules and regulations dealing within a one-sport setting, yet for Olympic competition, the NGBs work with their national Olympic committee to ensure participation in the Olympic Games. Several corporations have secured official supplier contracts through positive relationships developed with Olympic-governing bodies. This status was effective in invigorating product sales. As a sport marketer, it is imperative that you become well versed in the relationships between each of these groups and tune into the political dynamics of the world sport community.

Global Market Selection and Identification

Global markets can seem overwhelming if viewed as a whole. Only when they are dissected and analyzed individually can the sport marketer make wise marketing decisions. Market conditions vary considerably in different countries, and thus, the sport industry exhibits varying growth rates. For instance, the global growth rate for the industry was projected to be 12% for the athletic footwear market, yet the US rate was 5% whereas the projected growth of the Asian market was 36%. These data indicated that average yearly per capita spending on athletic footwear in the United States was $30.88 at wholesale; Japanese consumers spent $10.36, whereas the Chinese market figures indicated spending of only $0.02 (but remember, the Chinese market is 1.2 billion). Collectively, the global market was set to expand from $18.2 billion in 1997 to $25.2 billion in 2000 ("From the Field," 1997). For any single company like Nike, the percentage of company profit derived from international sales can run as high as 37% (Himelstein, 1997). Fortunately for the sport marketer, there are a variety of ways to investigate foreign markets.

Contrary to what you may think, your tax dollars really do provide services for you and other American citizens. The US government is one of the best sources of information on foreign markets. As an example, the US Information Agency managed the US Pavilion at the 1992 World Expo in Seville, Spain. During the run of the Expo, one American sport or fitness activity was presented every day for the 50,000 (per day) visitors. This created excellent opportunities for American firms to demonstrate their products and services to worldwide consumers. Information and contacts obtained through the United States Information Agency offices can be invaluable in developing a network of sport professionals.

> For information on foreign markets, consult the US Information Agency, the US Agency for International Development, or other agencies in the Department of State.

Other government offices in the Department of State also have reams of information about foreign economies, information that is available at little or no cost. Consideration also should be given to contacting the US Agency for International Development, which has as its main purpose improving trade with developing countries.

Interestingly, most foreign governments are also attempting to attract US business and have personnel at their embassy to accommodate your needs. Brief meetings or telephone conversations with their staff are often beneficial during the early stages of project development. Other sources for international marketing contacts can be made through international trade associations, economic development councils at the state or local level, and international trade shows. With a little digging, even small sport companies can obtain quality information for entering the global marketplace.

Key issues according to Tuller (1991) include whether a market economy exists or one that is government controlled, the existing market demand, growth, and competitive forces, US government trade policies, and the local government policies toward trade with the United States. Each factor should be evaluated, and the decision regarding market entry should be based on a thorough analysis

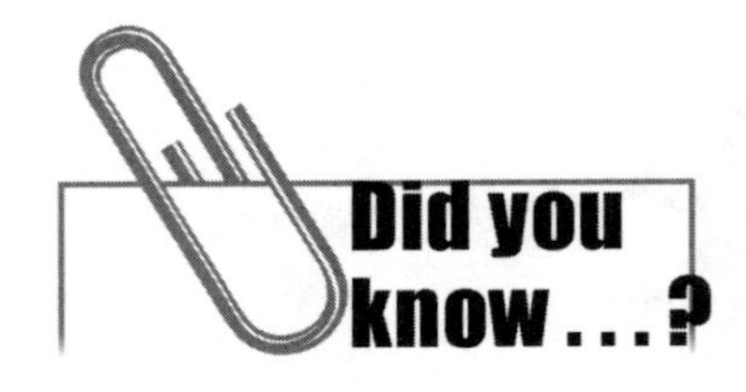

Retail sales of sports-licensed products in the United States and Canada totaled over $71 billion in 1998.

Source: 1999 SGMA State of the Industry Report

Pride and Ferrell (1997, p. 83) noted that "before a company enters a foreign market, it must thoroughly analyze the environment." Similar to marketing to domestic customers, marketers must evaluate cultural, social, technological, political, and economic forces in target regions. Considerable attention over the past 15 years has been focused in varying degrees on Japan, the Pacific Rim, Europe, South America, and developing nations throughout the world. In no particular order, a discussion of several of these markets follows.

Japan and Asia

Why, you might ask, has this section been called Japan and Asia? Isn't Japan part of Asia? Yes, from a geographical perspective, but not from a marketing point of view. For many years Japan has presented an obstacle to American sport marketers. With the endless debate over Japan's high tariffs, complex system of distribution and sales, and governmental reluctance to encourage foreign business activity, sport marketers have not generally been successful. The climate has appeared positive for them with a stable hard currency and an attractive market size. Yet, many have taken the approach of trying to sell the Japanese on American products. Sports marketers might find better results if they concentrated more on the needs of the consumer rather than the products and services their company needs to sell.

In his presentation *Development and Structural Changes in Sport Business in Japan*, Harada (1993) indicated that the sport market in Japan rose from $25 billion in 1982 to $50 billion in 1992. As with the general economy in Japan in the early 1990s, some slow growth was seen as a result of the recession. "Nevertheless, as lifestyles change in Japan, people should be showing greater interest in lifetime sports activities and thus sports business on the whole should see an increase in market scale" (Harada, 1993, p. 4)

Asia, as a geographic and social region, is extremely diverse. Social and political conditions affecting sport vary considerably from predominantly Muslim nations such as Malaysia to the socialist ideology in the People's Republic of China. China, with a population in excess of 1 billion people (22% of the world population), has commanded considerable attention from sport marketers.

According to Jizhong (1997), "China's sport market is still at its initial stage. We are carefully developing it so that it will smoothly reach maturity" (p. 2). Estimates reveal that in 2000, China will import $1 trillion in products from the international market, making it the world's largest consumer market. Some of the nations are newly industrialized (Singapore, South Korea, Taiwan) and can provide active, growing markets for both consumption and production of sports products, whereas other nations are still in the stages of economic development. Entry into the sports markets of Japan and Asia will demand considerable study and analysis, but the rewards can be immense.

Eastern and Western Europe

Considerable attention has already been given to Western Europe. The dynamic changes with the formation of the European Union have in some ways helped sport marketers and in other ways hindered their success. A unified Western European market has allowed a much freer access to markets than was previously available, yet the increased competitiveness of EU companies has also increased competition. The generally held view is that in most sport industry segments, the opportunities are still limited and extremely competitive.

Eastern Europe, on the other hand, may provide more opportunities. With pent-up consumer demand and a reduction of government controls, sport purchasing and sponsorship avenues may proliferate. However, some of the problems that sport marketers will encounter include the lack of hard currency and unstable governments. It is also important to realize that sport expenditures are often considered luxuries and are made with discretionary funds. These funds may be limited in the Eastern European communities well into the next decade.

Specifically, the situation in Hungary was reported by Dénes and Misovicz (1993). Their research indicated several phenomena that may be similar in other parts of Eastern Europe. In Hungary, the demise of socialist rule in the early 1990s meant that the sport economy changed as well. Previously, the government had subsidized, yet with the political changes, governmental resources were allocated to other parts of the economy. Ticket prices for sports events rose with inflation that impacted the economy, yet few citizens could afford to attend, instead diverting their income to cover the costs of food and shelter. In addition, many workers took on second jobs to generate funds necessary for maintaining an acceptable lifestyle. The market for leisure sports products, once supplied by the government, had all but disappeared (Dénes and Misovicz,1993).

The Caribbean and Central and South America

In 1983 the US government passed a law that made trade with the Caribbean nations both more accessible and more lucrative. The Caribbean Basin Initiative (CBI) was designed to increase trade and assist in the economic development of this region. The 1989 report indicated that recreational items and sporting goods were some of the products that had benefited the most from this legislation (Tuller, 1991). The business climate in the area has been enhanced through this Act, and sport marketers should examine the possibility of taking advantage of the benefits extended through the CBI Act. These include tax breaks and the elimination or reduction of import duties. In addition, special financing programs are available for start-up companies. Of special note is the fact that many of these nations also have special agreements with European nations for importing and exporting goods and services. Therefore, it may behoove the sport marketer to investigate the range of possibilities of operating out of the Caribbean.

> Sport marketers can take advantage of special conditions in the Caribbean, including tax breaks and the reduction of import duties.

Central America presents several points of interest. With the previously discussed free trade possibilities, manufacturing potential exists in the sports goods industry. Depending on the economic and political fortunes of the area, additional consumer demand for both goods and services may also exist.

South America has been under the shadow of its severe debt crisis for the past two decades. As mentioned in the section on international economics and finance, triple-digit inflation and hard-currency issues will hamper sports entrepreneurs in South America. The sport marketer should realize that the public interest in sport is considerably high in much of the region and that considerable potential exists in numerous market segments.

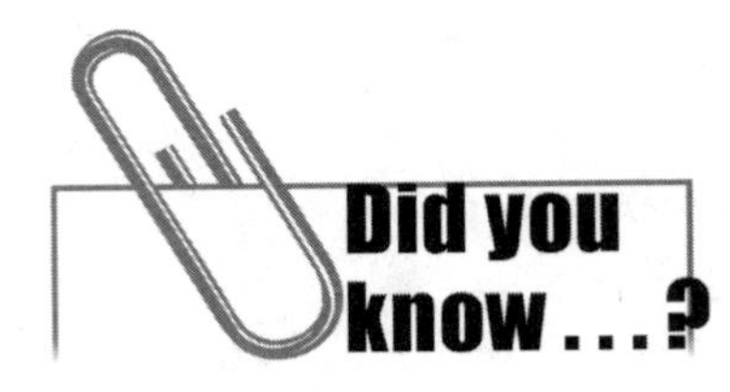

In 1998, sales of athletic shoes were

46% women's shoes

41% men's shoes.

Source: *The Sports Business Daily*, March 24, 1999.

Conducting business in the Caribbean and Central and South America has positive attributes, but only if the sport marketer is able to cope effectively with the business and political idiosyncrasies of the region.

Africa

As diverse as Central and South America, the African market is understood by few American companies (Tuller, 1991). Generally, the continent consists of Muslim North Africa, Central, East and West Africa, with South Africa presenting a special case of its own. Sports activities in North Africa are, in line with traditional Muslim view, predominantly male and rooted in tradition. For American sport managers to conduct business here demands an understanding of the culture and the emphasis on sport. Within that context, the markets are available to US representatives.

West Africa has, for the most part, put political upheaval behind and is entering an era in which sport market development is possible. Of specific importance will be sport equipment and supplies as well as sport services in coaching and sport management. However, many of these markets offer limited growth potential. As recent as 1990, the product advertised in the window of a sporting goods store was a pair of adidas Rome running shoes, popular in the United States in the early 1970s. Central Africa has yet to achieve the stability conducive to market entry. This will of course be an area to watch for future growth and development in sport.

In South Africa, enough wealth exists for any multinational corporation to flourish. However, because of past economic and political practices, a two-tiered economic market exists. For the sport marketer, both segments offer possibilities. With the political changes in the country in the early 1990s, the lower class was provided greater access to sport and recreational facilities. This created immense demand for sports equipment. Corporate sponsorship and financing for sport activities also created an atmosphere conducive to a growth market. Another factor in favor of expansion into South Africa is the abundance of well-educated and effective sport management personnel. These have been most apparent in South Africa's hosting major international sports events in rugby and auto racing.

As with other regions in the world, the problems of soft currency and political instability will restrict many African sport-marketing opportunities. Yet, with attention to these factors and a careful study of the market, sports marketers can successfully meet the demands of these consumers.

International Sport Marketing Personnel

The selection of well-trained and experienced personnel is essential. Tuller (1991) indicated that trying to enter global markets without the expertise of someone experienced in international trade is a common error made by American executives: "To try and arrange financing, market products, or negotiate contracts with foreign customers without assistance from internationally experienced management personnel will always lead to disaster" (p. 12).

The selection of personnel for managing foreign markets or for heading up foreign units is affected by several criteria. Among those found to be most important were proven domestic marketing ability, foreign national status, prior international training, and a strong desire for global involvement. Personnel training can be performed through a variety of different methods. Some corporations conduct in-house training sessions using the expertise and experience of their existing staff. Some corporations handle the training through their foreign offices. Both of these methods have proven to be successful in the sports environment. Outside resources have also been retained for the training process. This method is often expensive, but without internal expertise, it is essential.

It is imperative that personnel be educated for cultural sensitivity prior to their involvement in international affairs.

Speer (1999) indicated that the main difficulty experienced by foreign market managers was adapting to cultural diversity. Research has indicated that adaptability to foreign cultures is equal in importance to marketing skills developed in a domestic position.

Adaptation to Cultural Diversity

Sport business personnel have a common bond with sport executives in other nations through their athletic experiences; however, culture variations on appropriate business and sport etiquette can sabotage chances for success. The successful sport marketer needs to have a clear understanding of the dos and don'ts of foreign culture. What follows are some national and international customs in business relations.

Before traveling and dealing with international executives, be sure to review the special characteristics of your host nation.

Touching. In much of North America, touching is acceptable between friends, but overt touching of casual acquaintances in a business setting is not tolerated. The local custom in many Latin countries allows for hugs following an introduction. In the Middle East, on the other hand, you may find two men walking down the street holding hands to signify their friendship (Axtell, 1991).

Review and understand the following issues about your host nation before traveling and dealing with international executives.

- Touching
- Relationships between males and females
- Drinking
- Gifts
- Time and schedules
- Business etiquette

Relationships between males and females. Women have for many years played increasing roles in the conduct of sport business in the United States. Many women serve as CEOs of major sport corporations, sport marketing firms, and professional team franchises. Yet, in other parts of the world, women may not be accepted in business meetings. Because we believe in equality of the sexes does not mean that everyone in the world does. Your firm must make a decision whether to do business with countries that have different beliefs about the role of women in business relations and follow a strategy that will produce the best business results.

Drinking. The easiest rule for drinking is to follow the lead of the host. If the host orders a drink, you are welcome to imbibe. Be cautious about bringing alcoholic gifts for your host. Even though you are from the South, possession of a fifth of Southern

Comfort will land you in prison in almost any Islamic nation. On the opposite end of the spectrum, refusing a glass of wine in France or a cup of sake in Japan will be considered rude. One experience at the International Olympic Academy in Greece found that the Russian delegation's vodka was one of the most cherished barter items between participants—worth at least five Olympic pins.

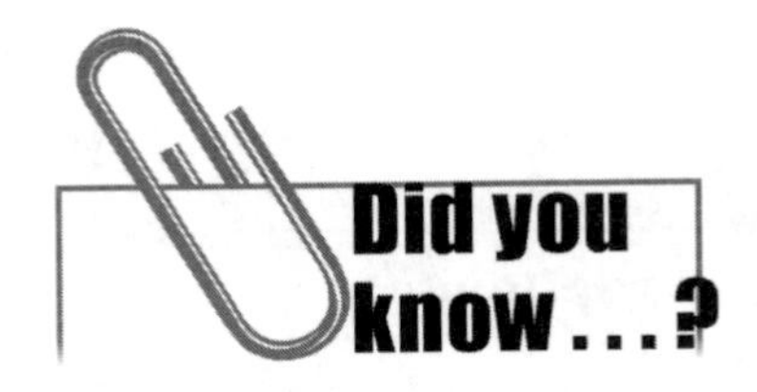

NASCAR is now a $2-billion industry.

Source: *The Sports Business Daily*, March 24, 1999.

Gifts. Exchanging gifts is a custom that is more prevalent in other countries than it is in the United States. In fact, in the 1970s the US government passed the Foreign Corrupt Practices Act to curtail bribes and kickbacks (Tuller, 1991). The line is very vague as to what constitutes a payoff and what is a generous gift (Speer, 1999). Most sport marketers will face difficulty in this area. Try to learn ahead of time from a confidante or fellow sportsperson the tradition and local custom. A good practice is to carry small company pins or souvenirs and to graciously accept similar extensions from your host.

Time and schedules. In many parts of the world, time is a relative concept. This is especially true in many Latin countries and in the Middle East. Both of the authors of this text have conducted sport-marketing seminars around the globe and can attest to this phenomenon. In Malaysia, an 8:00 A.M. meeting means in the morning, yet just across the bridge in Singapore, you had better be there at 7:30 to get a seat. One style is not right or wrong; it is just different. It is also important that everyone be clear on how dates are written. The US military writes dates with the day first, then the month and year (i.e., 7 June 1999). This does not create confusion until it appears as 7/6/02. Much of the world uses the same style as does the US military, so when placing the order for the delivery of your tennis rackets, be specific.

Business etiquette. Every country will have its unique protocol for conducting business. In England, you had better wear a jacket and tie for your initial business meeting; however, try that in Manila, and you will not only roast but will also look like a fool in the process. The mix of business attire and casual sports clothing is something that should be explored carefully; it never hurts to ask. Careful determination should also be made in deciding when and where to talk business. In England, work is work and play is play. Don't confuse the two. However, in many other countries, the best deals are put together on the golf course. You should also be perceptive about special interrelationships. In England, you seat the most important person to your right, British military custom. In South Africa, you rise to greet your Afrikaner guest, but don't when meeting a Zulu guest; according to tribal custom, such a movement is confrontational. In South Africa and other parts of southern Africa, sports marketers and event organizers have experienced problems from a simple question, "Do you understand this proposal?" When the answer was "yes," all matters seemed settled. Only later was it determined that all was not well. The polite answer to the question was "yes." To answer "no" would imply that you had not explained it well and be considered insulting. Better initial questions would have been "What is your understanding?" or "Do we have an agreement on these points?" Similarly, in negotiating with Japanese executives, "We'll consider it" means "no" (Morrison, Conaway, and Borden, 1994).

The integration of international marketing into the domestic corporate culture is also of great importance. Depending on the size and nature of the international versus the domestic market, jealousies and conflicts can arise if executives are not adamant in clarifying the priority of both global and national marketing activities (Tuller, 1991). The selection and training of international sport executives encompass many different considerations. They often involve difficult and awkward adaptations to normal business practices. However, if you invest the time, the results can be rewarding.

Specifics of International Sport Marketing

The expansion of professional and amateur sports internationally has been well recognized in the sport-marketing arena. "Faced with a maturing US sports market, the [professional] leagues have looked overseas" (Ozanian and Taub, 1992, p. 49). One of the first professional sport organizations to recognize the global demand for its product was the National Basketball Association. From a historical standpoint, professional boxing has had worldwide events for many years, but these have been primarily single events. Professional baseball had early opportunities to restructure and include demand in Asia and Latin America, but decided that such a move was not in its best interests. The NBA, on the other hand, has viewed international markets from an entirely different perspective.

In recognition of the 200 million people around the world who participate in basketball, the NBA embarked on a global marketing campaign in 1989. Games played in Europe and Asia spawned a growth in NBA television rights of 30% per year with the sales of licensed goods growing at twice that rate. The NBA sold licensed products in more than 100 countries in 1998. Based heavily on the success of the 1992 US Olympic (read that, NBA) basketball team, the NBA commissioner recognized the global nature of basketball and positioned the league to capitalize on the phenomenon (Ober, 1992). For the 1997–98 season, the NBA provided 11,700 hours of international television programming in 14 languages to over 195 countries. Total reach of the NBA was 600 million households worldwide (National Basketball Association [NBA], 1998).

As the NBA has stressed global marketing, basketball equipment manufactures have followed suit. Nike, Reebok, Converse, and Spalding all saw tremendous growth in global sales of basketballs and basketball shoes in conjunction with NBA positioning. In the early 1990s, shoe sales were in the neighborhood of $40 million per company, an increase of 300% from the mid-1980s (Stotlar, 1989). In Europe alone, NBA licensing revenues reached $68 million in 1998 (NBA, 1998).

The sport of soccer (football, in the international community) is the most popular sport on television across the globe. The worldwide cumulative audience for the 1998 World Cup was over 36 billion. This popularity has affected the sport industry in many ways. Many of the world's top teams have been able to secure sponsorship from multinational corporations. Nike sponsors the perennial power, Brazil, whereas Adidas sponsors Germany. Within the European league, teams like Manchester United attract a global audience and annually earn several million dollars from licensing rights fees.

It should also be noted that global demographics are significantly different from those in the United States. The United States has an aging population, yet in much of the developing world, the population is considerably younger and becoming even younger. An amazing 70% of the world's consumers abide in developing countries. With respect to the example above, children tend to buy shoes more frequently than adults do, which contributes many of the marketing decisions for sporting goods manufactures.

"The international reach of the fitness business is also noteworthy. Overseas clubs call on US fitness experts to fashion American-style clubs that meet the demands of style-conscious clientele" (Holland, 1992, p40.). The depth of the market is such that International Fitness Association of America (IDEA) has representatives in 70 foreign countries.

World tournaments and international events are at the center of many international marketing activities. Because the recognition and value of international events grew considerably in the 1980s and 1990s, most television agreements, sponsorship contracts, and licensing programs have necessarily become international. Without attention to these details, sport marketers could find themselves in the same situation as Nike during the 1992 Olympic Games when another company in Spain had registered the word *Nike*, thereby complicating the US firm's marketing efforts.

Trends for the Future

As the United States and many leading economic powers evolve as information societies and reduce their strength in manufacturing, the licensing of sport manufacturing technology and professional services will be a major growth area in the sport industry. Sporting goods companies and sport consultants will protect products through extensive licensing and manufacturing agreements and will issue "covenants not to compete" to ensure the protection of their intellectual properties. The result will be a greater emphasis on strategic alliances, mergers, and joint ventures than has existed in the past.

Sport marketers will begin to think more of international demographics in the development of products and services in the sport industry. Pan-European consumers will begin to develop more similarities than differences as EU markets mature. Around the world, the newly industrialized nations will begin to demand more sport-related products and services, and new markets will emerge. However, friction between the countries that supply the cheap labor for sporting goods production and those that consume the goods will continue. Cause-related sport marketing will also make favorable impressions on consumers. These humanistic trends must be incorporated in the operation of all sport organizations in the global environment.

> Companies that can communicate their concern for global problems through the delivery of the sport products and services will be more highly valued than will those who ignore this social component.

With the developments outlined in this chapter and evidence in the professional literature, there will undoubtedly be a greater need for internationally trained and educated sport managers. Professionals in the area and aspiring sport managers should become well versed in international sports affairs. This training will open a vast new job market and should provide an array of exciting experiences.

Chapter Summary

The purpose of this chapter was to provide information about the global marketplace for the sport marketer. It is clear that sport is a major component in the global economy and that sport marketers must be prepared to work in this environment. Specific skills and knowledge regarding the international banking system, world sport structure, and the application of marketing principles in specific cultural contexts are necessary to succeed in international markets, and sport marketers must obtain the requisite training. Furthermore, Pride and Ferrell (1997) noted that marketers must "customize marketing mixes according to cultural, regional and national differences"(p. 81). The global sport marketplace provides a wealth of opportunities for corporations and organizations that commit to spending the time for market research and flexibility in market perception.

Questions for Study

1. Diagram the relationship of the International Olympic Committee to a specific International Federation. Include a discussion of how each functions with the United States Olympic Committee and a national governing body in the United States.
2. What are the keys to successful banking in international sport marketing?
3. How does marketing a sport product internationally differ from marketing the same product in the United States?

Learning Activities

1. Investigate opening a Swiss bank account. It could be a lot of fun and a great conversation topic among friends.
2. How would you handle the following situation? You had just completed a consulting project negotiating sponsorship deals for the Lithuanian National Basketball team and were due to be paid $10,000 in US dollars. At the last minute, you were informed that they could pay you only in the local currency. What is that currency? How much of it would you get? Would you accept payment in that form, and if not, what would be an alternative?

Professional Associations and Organizations

United States Information Agency
301 4th Street SW
Washington, DC 20547

International Events Group
640 N. LaSalle, Suite 6000
Chicago, IL 60610-37777
www.sponsorship.com
1-800-834-4850

Suggested Readings

Axtell, R. E. (1991). *Gestures: The do's and taboos of body language around the world.* New York: John Wiley and Sons.

Chalip, L., and Thoma, J. (1993). *Sport governance in the global community.* Morgantown, WV: Fitness Information Technologies.

Morrison, T., Conaway, W., and Borden, G. (1994). *Kiss, bow, or shake hands.* Holbrook, MA: Bob Adams, Inc.

Tuller, L. W. (1991). *Going global.* Homewood, IL: Business One Irwin.

Chapter 4

Sport Marketing Theory

Sport Marketing

Welcome to the world of sport marketing! Many people think that marketing is advertising. That's because advertising is the promotional element of sport marketing. However, advertising is only one element of many marketing activities that a sport business does. *Sport marketing* is the process of designing and implementing activities for the production, pricing, promotion, and distribution of a sport product to satisfy the needs or desires of consumers and to achieve the company's objectives. It is a complex and dynamic part of every sport business.

With any definition, it is first important to understand the components of the definition and how the definition was developed. This definition is derived primarily from sport marketing theory, which is built on fundamentals of marketing, marketing theory, sport business industry knowledge, and the sport marketing and sport management bodies of knowledge. Although sport marketing textbooks and courses are new, sport marketing is not. Sport businesses have been practicing sport marketing for as long as they have been selling sport products. What is new about sport marketing is the development of sport marketing as a field of study. Sport marketing involves marketing fundamentals applied in one industry, the sport business industry. The development of sport marketing fundamentals is therefore based on basic marketing principles. The practice and activities of sport marketing are also based on the basic marketing activities, but are modified and adapted to one sport business in one industry. Therefore, sport marketing is based on its primary and parent discipline—marketing. However, it is not enough that students who will work in the sport business industry take only marketing classes in a business school. Those students will learn basic marketing principles, but will not learn sport marketing, that is, the principles and fundamentals of marketing as they have been modified and adapted to the sport business industry. Hence, it is imperative that a sport management student's college education to be primarily in sport management courses.

Sport marketing defined:

The process of designing and implementing activities for the production, pricing, promotion, and distribution of a sport or sport business product to satisfy the needs or desires of consumers and to achieve the company's objectives.

Sport marketing is the most important function of a sport business. This is because the sport marketing activities define the business. It is also because the growth of the sport industry is phenomenal and shows no signs of slowing. It has grown from the

23rd largest industry in the United States to the 11th largest industry in a short period of 10 years. Growth means there are increasing numbers of sport companies and products. Each sport product or company is competition. The concept of competition in business is the idea that a sport business is competing against another business to win the consumer's dollar. Winning in business means staying in business at a successful level. Success is defined by the sport company and is usually measured by achieving the company's objectives.

Companies in the sport industry have plenty of competitors. A sport company today must employ sport marketing as a significant business function of the company to the extent that every facet of the company is guided by the sport marketing concept. It is the function that guides the sport business toward identifying the products that consumers need or desire, that identifies and analyzes competitors, that develops pricing strategies, that develops the promotional strategies to be used for the company's products in order to get the consumer to the product, and that identifies how to get the product to the consumer.

To more completely understand sport marketing, let's look at its base—marketing. After that, let's study the theory and fundamentals of sport marketing.

Marketing Defined

Marketing is a business process that developed along with the development and growth of business. Bartels (1988) wrote that marketing is the element that "revolutionized the economy of the country and gradually affected the whole world" (p. 1). The word *marketing* comes from the word *market,* which means a group of buyers and sellers (producers and consumers) negotiating the terms of exchange for something. Buyers are consumers, and there are many different categories of consumers as you will learn later in the book. Sellers can be manufacturers, producers, retailers, promoters, and wholesalers. Negotiation takes many such forms as deciding to buy or not to buy simply based on a nonnegotiable price, making offers and counteroffers until agreement is reached, and determining a fair or satisfactory exchange. Terms can involve negotiating over delivery and acceptance, warranty, aftersales service, payment methods, and promises of quality. The exchange can involve many such factors as delivery, terms of payment or trade, and transaction. Finally, the word *something* in the definition usually involves the trade of something (money) for something (a tennis racket) that could be goods, services, ideas, benefits, perks, deeds, and, of course, money. One example of the market at work is a flea market. Of course, a flea market is not a place where fleas are sold! It is an area, or a marketplace, where sellers bring their wares and buyers come to shop. At a flea market, it is expected that buyers and sellers will haggle in the exchange process to trade something for something else. Usually, in this setting, the buyer and seller negotiate over the worth, or value, of a good. The seller has established a price, but the buyer will offer a different price based on the buyer's belief of the good's value—or to try to get the good at below a fair market price. Buyer and seller negotiate until some exchange agreement is reached.

> Marketing is the study of people and what they buy, how much they will pay, where they want to purchase a product, and how they are affected by promotional tactics and messages.

In another example, the value of goods in a sporting goods store is set using pricing strategies. The buyer typically enters the store and decides whether or not to purchase the good at its "sticker" price (the price placed on the good by a little sticker). Usually

The fan's team flag is a product of sport marketing.
Photo reprinted by permission of WVU Photography.

there is no negotiating between buyer and seller like the kind of bargaining we find in a flea market. However, the buyer can send a message to the seller about price by making the decision to buy or not to buy. If a product is not selling, the company must determine why. If the company discovers the product does not sell because too many consumers think the price is too high, the company can relay this important information to the producer. The producer now has to analyze the situation and make a decision about what to do about the price. It's not a simple decision of lowering the price because perhaps the price is high because of the high cost to manufacture the item.

Marketing as a business activity developed and evolved primarily from the study of people and what they buy, how much they will pay, where they want to purchase a product, and how they are affected by promotional tactics and messages. Additionally, the elements, functions, principles, and theories of marketing were also developed through the study of many other factors such as industrial production expansion, inventions of new products, the study of human behavior (sociology and psychology), population studies, education and income studies, and studies of new and diverse markets. As a response to these and other factors, a market-driven economy developed. This meant that businesses paid increasing amounts of attention to consumers and studied what the consumer needed or wanted (Bartels, 1988).

The sport marketer must be able to recognize and analyze a business's environments, determine their effects, and make strategic decisions that will enhance the success of the sport business.

Today's marketing concepts evolved from a simple to a more complex and broad concept of marketing. It draws from the social sciences and is more than merely a business activity. Businesses exist in a variety of environments such as political, social, and economic environments that constantly provide opportunities and threats for a business. Although marketing is a business function that should be a significant part of every business, the functions of marketing should be a critical part of every department within the business. Companies faced with the challenge of achieving profitable growth in an environment of intense competition, product proliferation, and escalating costs must make marketing a priority function throughout the company. Marketing must be a total company effort, and the company therefore should develop a marketing orientation—that is, every task and decision of the company should be a reflection of its marketing plan.

The company's every task and decision should be a reflection of its marketing plan.

The marketing orientation, or concept, is a philosophy concerning the way a company should be managed. It consists of three requirements (Cravens and Woodruff, 1983):

1. Examine people's needs and wants as the basis of deciding what the business (or economy) will do.
2. Select the best way to meet the consumer's needs that are targeted by the firm.
3. Achieve the organization's performance objectives by meeting the consumers' needs satisfactorily.

In short, the company must study what the consumer wants and provide it. Although this seems like an easy rule to follow, there are many functions that must be performed and receive critical analysis and proper management in order for successful marketing decisions to be developed. It is not an easy task to identify what someone wants or needs and then to provide it. The human being is a complex organism affected by a remarkable variety of influencing factors. Although the marketer might discover what the consumer wants today, that desire may be different tomorrow.

Complicating the task of producing what the consumer wants is the company's capacity to manufacture it, distribute it, and offer it. In addition, the company must consider its values and objectives and if it can ethically offer the products. Therefore, careful management of the marketing functions and critical analysis before decision making can increase the company's chances for success. The incorporation of a marketing management strategy is critical.

Sport Marketing Fundamentals and Theory

Theory can be defined as "a system of assumptions, accepted principles, and rules of procedure devised to analyze, predict, or explain a set of phenomena" (*Webster's*, 1978). Theory is built from a foundation of research and knowledge and may be tested through research and application. Research can be defined as a systematic and organized investigation. When the research is complete, the results may be used in a variety of ways, some of which are to add to one's knowledge or a body of knowledge solutions for problems and to discover answers to specific questions.

Sport marketing is a new field of study. It does not yet contain a substantial body of knowledge when compared to many other fields of study. However, the body of knowledge is growing. Sport marketing is very new when compared to fields of study like law,

narrow focus, exclusive: ⟷	broad, inclusive, contemporary
Marketing sports and events to two groups of consumers: participants and spectators.	Using sport marketing fundamentals in any business that is part of the sport business industry.
Definition is based on concept of selling and promoting sports activities and events.	Definition is based on the broad concept of contemporary sport management and the industry.

Figure 4.1
The two different concepts of sport marketing being used today.

Paricipation Sports
Spectatorial Sports Events
Sporting Goods
Sports Media—Print
Sports Media—Broadcast
Sports Media—Electronic
Sponsorship
Athlete Management
Sports Tourism and Travel: for participation or spectatorial
Facility and Venue Design and Construction
Licensing and Merchandising
Sport Marketing Research
Web Sport Business
Sport Law Firms
Sport Event Management
Sports Medicine
Sports Governing Organizations
Advertising
Endorsement Management

Figure 4.2
Some segments of the sport business industry.

education, management, medicine, or marketing. For example, this textbook is one of only five textbooks about the fundamentals of sport marketing. In addition, there are two research journals for sport marketing, the *Sport Marketing Quarterly* and the *International Journal of Sports Marketing and Sponsorship*. Finally, sport marketing is just beginning to be considered a singular academic discipline.

Although sport marketing is becoming an academic discipline, academicians have not yet agreed on what sport marketing is (see Figure 4.1). They are divided into two camps. Some believe that sport marketing involves just the selling of sports events to two groups of consumers: sports participants and sports spectators. These groups use the terminology of "sports" marketing, or, the marketing of sports. Others believe that sport marketing is closely related to the contemporary definition of sport management and the sport industry. That is, sport management is the study of management and business principles in the sport industry. The *sport industry*, as defined by research, (Clay, 1995; Meek, 1997; Parks, Zanger, and Quarterman, 1998; Pitts, Fielding, and Miller, 1994), includes all businesses offering any sport, recreation, fitness, tourism, and leisure-related product (See Figure 4.2). Those include such companies as a sport marketing research firm, a sport facility design and construction company, a sporting goods manufacturing company, a web-based sport collectables company, a sport licensing and merchandising business, a sport law firm, a sporting goods retail business, an athlete management company, and a sport governance organization as well as companies that sell participation such as a golf resort and companies that sell sports events as entertainment such as the LPGA. Therefore, many different sport business companies offer many different products, which means there are many different consumer segments. It is the contemporary definitions of sport marketing and the sport business industry that we have used to define sport marketing, to develop our theory of sport marketing, and to develop our sport marketing management model.

Although sport marketing is a developing field of study, this does not mean that marketing has never been used in the sport industry. As pointed out in chapter two, marketing practices and principles have been used in the sport industry throughout history and are still being used today. Sport marketers have drawn from and continue to draw from marketing and a variety of fields of study. In addition, academicians and practitioners are hard at work conducting research in sport marketing as is evidenced by the studies published in a variety of research journals and trade magazines. Further, this book adds to the young but growing body of knowledge in sport marketing. As marketing principles are applied to the sport industry, they are modified as necessary. As marketing strategies and models in the sport industry are studied and research is published, the body of knowledge will be developed. As higher education responds to the needs of the sport industry, textbooks, courses, and curriculum in sport marketing will be developed. Each will add to the development of the body of knowledge and to sport marketing as a field of study and will serve as the foundation of a theory of sport marketing.

Sport marketing knowledge is developing from the following fields:

Sport studies:

sport management
sport sociology
sport psychology
leisure management
recreation administration
legal aspects of sport
sports tourism
sports information

Business:

marketing
economics
finance
business law
consumer behavior

Communications:

journalism
public relations
media studies
advertising
broadcasting

Social sciences:

human relations
cultural studies
population studies
labor market studies

Technology:

e-commerce
Web business and marketing

The theory of sport marketing is still developmental and constantly evolving. These theories and fundamentals should be used as conceptual frameworks for research. To study the developing theory of sport marketing, we must study the foundation from which it is being built. Foundation refers to the basis on which something stands or is supported. Foundation is research, fundamentals, principles, and theories. The foundation of sport marketing knowledge is being built primarily from five broad fields of study: sport studies, business administration studies, social science studies, technology, and communications (see Figure 4.3).

Within each broad field of study are specific or specialized areas of study from which sport marketing is developing its body of knowledge. Within sport studies, these specializations include sport management, sport sociology, sport psychology, leisure management, recreation administration, legal aspects of sport, sports tourism, and sports information. Within business, the specializations include marketing, economics, finance, business law, and consumer behavior. In communications, the areas include journalism, public relations, media studies, advertising, and broadcasting. The areas in the social sciences include human relations, cultural studies, population studies, and labor market studies. Technology includes E-commerce and web business and marketing.

Figure 4.4 presents a list of some areas of study in sport marketing today. As an example of how academicians and practitioners in sport marketing are using other fields of study to develop the theories in sport marketing, let us consider how the social sciences may be used. Yiannakis (1989) suggested that sport marketing could be strengthened through the study and application of sport sociology. In a study of sport sociology literature, Yiannakis suggested that sport sociology could make significant contributions to sport marketing and management in the following ways:

1. Conceptualization, design, and implementation of good market research;
2. Instrument development;
3. Interpretation of the findings by grounding both a priori and post hoc explanations in existing knowledge bases;

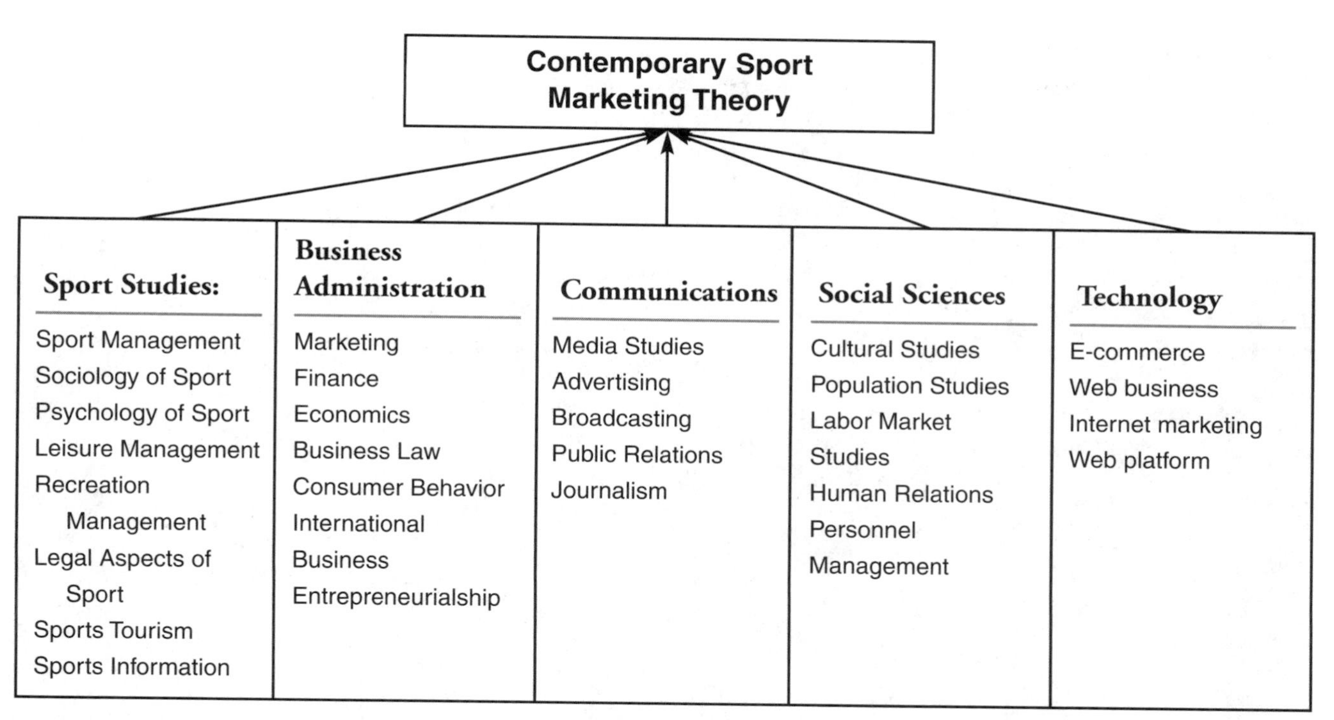

Figure 4.3
Contemporary sport marketing theory. These fields of study are serving as the foundation and framework to build the fundamentals of sport marketing.

sponsorship analysis
spectatorial sport
sporting goods
licensing and merchandising
consumer market identification and analysis
web sport business
sport law
sport event management
economic impact
sports tourism impact
sporting goods consumption
commercialization
trends
financial analysis

Figure 4.4
Examples of areas of study in sport business management.

4. Advertising effectiveness by providing essential information bases, especially in the area of lifestyle characteristics;
5. Development of a general marketing information base (target market characteristics);
6. Exploration and identification of new markets; and
7. Introduction of social science orientation to the enterprise.

Yiannakis stated that this involves

> an appreciation of the interactive nature of system forces in the marketing environment and their impact on consumer preferences, underlying patterns and trends and their potential impact on consumer buying readiness, cultural differences and their influence on purchasing decisions, and the role that sport plays in society in terms of influencing values and attitudes, shaping tastes, providing role models, creating new fashions and the like (105).

Another author, Kates (1998), agrees that research and theory in sport marketing literature can be greatly enhanced by using each other's theory, methods, and insights. Kates writes that "some scholarly work within consumer research has focused upon the study of subcultures" in sport, and that this work is providing "theoretical frameworks and substantive findings regarding the enculturation of people into a new set of norms and values while interacting with others." "By linking these discourses, new marketing tactics can be formulated." Kates concludes that "bringing the discourses of consumer behavior,

By reading stories in the classroom, this college athlete provides children with a positive role model.
Photo reprinted by permission of WVU Photography.

sport sociology, and sport marketing together, new research agendas and new marketing insights will result" (p. 29).

Critical analysis and research of the many different groups of such consumers in the sport industry as the African-American sport market (Armstrong, 1998), the Hispanic sport market (McCarthy, 1998), the gay and lesbian sport market (Pitts, 1998, 1999), and the Generation X sport market (Shoham, Rose, Kropp, and Kahle, 1997) can provide a sport business with the knowledge and understanding needed in today's constantly increasing diverse industry. As a matter of fact, there are vast numbers of sport businesses developed and owned by these markets that offer sport products specifically for these markets, as we learned in chapter 1. This new knowledge and understanding can then be used to formulate successful marketing strategies. Therefore, the theories existing in those fields must be used in sport marketing and in studying the sport industry; these theories should continue to be used in the development of a sport marketing theory.

The Sport Marketing Management Model

Sport marketing is a process. A process is a continuous cycle. Therefore, marketing is a function that never ends. The *sport marketing management model* is an illustration of the elements and process of sport marketing. It should serve as a guide for the marketer for managing the company's marketing functions. Figure 4.5 illustrates the model. The model illustrates the elements of marketing, the succession of elements and functions, the process of managing, and the interdependency of the elements. This chapter will present an overview of the model, sport marketing management, each element, and the process. Subsequent chapters discuss in detail each sport marketing element.

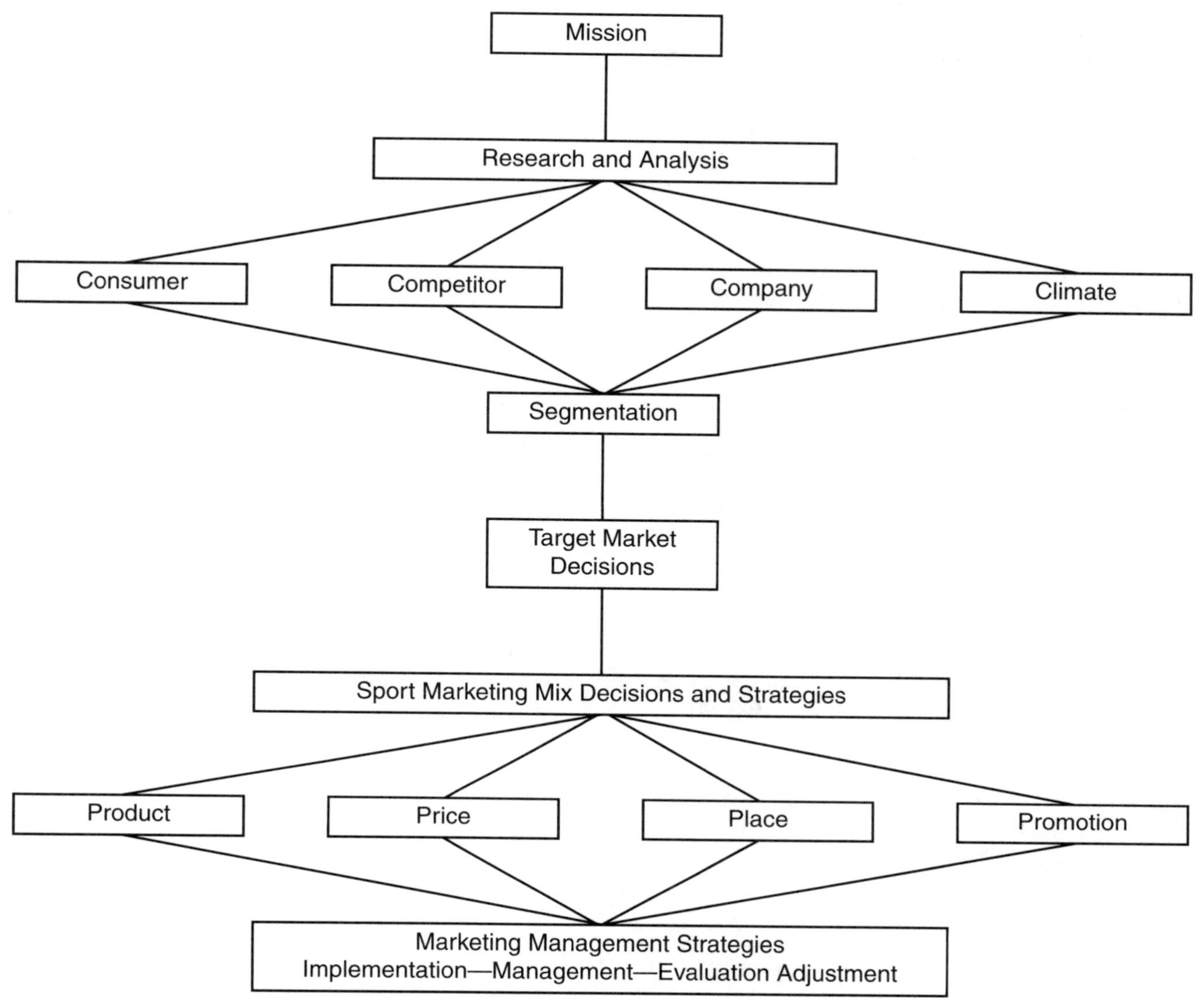

Figure 4.5
The Sport Marketing Management Model.

The Sport Company's Mission and Objectives

Every business exists for a purpose. Each company strives to stay consistent with its purpose in order to greatly enhance its chances for success. The company's purpose may be found in its stated mission. For example, an intercollegiate athletics program's mission may be "to provide athletic participation opportunities for the college student." In another example, a city parks and recreation department's mission might be "to provide the means for leisure pursuit for the city's population." The company will offer products with the intention of meeting the company's mission. The mission, then, is the reason it exists.

> Understanding the company's mission and its current status enables the sport marketer to make key decisions and formulate strategies.

All marketing activities must begin with a clear understanding of the company's mission and the company's current situation. The stated mission must be accompanied by the company's objectives. The objectives provide specific and concrete direction whereas the mission statement often may be broad and ambiguous. The objectives should state the exact directions management wants for the company. For example, whereas the mission of the college athletics department is to provide athletic participation opportunities for the college student, its objectives will be detailed concerning specifically what the athletic department wants to try to achieve within a given period of time. One such objective might be the following: to win a national championship in track-and-field within 5 years. The direction is established in the objective, and the college will implement programs and strategies that will most likely achieve the stated objective.

In another example, a professional women's basketball league may have an objective to increase consumer awareness of its existence and to increase attendance by 20% by the end of the regular season. The marketer must now make decisions and implement strategies that will take the league toward attaining the stated objective.

Sport Marketing Research and Analysis

Chapters 5, 6, and 7 cover the details of sport marketing research and managing this information. Information gained from marketing research is a significant element when forming decisions and strategies for the marketing mix. Research will provide vital information in the four key areas the marketer studies that we call the 4 Cs: the consumer, the competitor, the company, and the climate.

We exist in a world that seems small because communication systems and transportation are phenomenal. The amount of information produced and disseminated through communication systems is massive. In fact, the last decade has been labeled the Information Era. Moreover, we are currently in a time that is literally changing the entire face of business. The one factor responsible for this is the world wide web. Emerging business on the web has acquired several names, including e-commerce (the e stands for electronic), e-business, web-based business, and web malling. It has created a new mode of delivery for business. We can, if we wish, do everything from working to shopping for necessities and never leave the chair in front of the computer.

The marketer must achieve the ability to conduct research, obtain information, analyze the results of research and the data gathered, envision uses for the information, and formulate strategic decisions based on the research and information. In addition, the marketer must have or create a system to manage the information and research.

Sport marketing research is a system of gathering and analyzing information. What types of data and how data are gathered is specifically organized and determined by what question is in need of answering. For example, if the company's product isn't selling, the question becomes, Why isn't this product selling? Research is then designed to gather and analyze data to try to answer this question.

An MIS, or Marketing Information System, enables businesses to handle vast amounts of information by collecting, storing, and retrieving it.

The sport marketer will need the information gained through research to formulate decisions and strategies concerning every aspect of the company and its marketing plan. Marketing research usually focuses on one problem. At the same time, broad databases may be established and maintained concerning specific aspects of the company or the company's consumer markets and competitors.

Consumer:	demographics psychographics lifestyle geodemographics purchase behavior
Competition:	the industry and marketplace product differentiation pricing strategies financial strategies positioning promotion strategies
Company:	mission and objectives financial strength production product management pricing objectives and strategies distribution strategies promotion strategies
Climate:	economic legal social and cultural political ethical trends technological education community corporate

Figure 4.6
The 4 Cs: what the sport business needs to study.

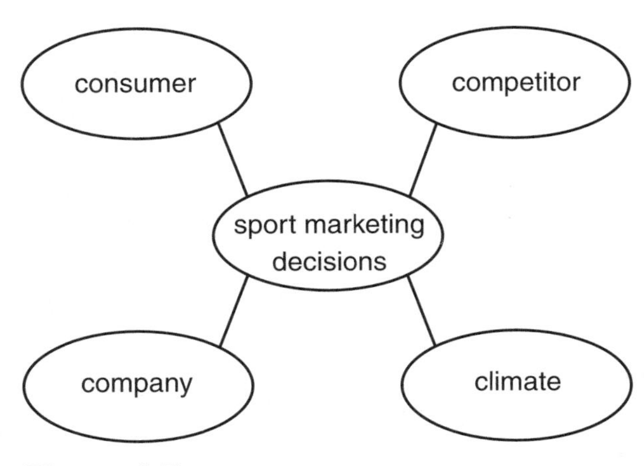

Figure 4.7
The 4 Cs: affecting sport marketing strategies.

The massive amount of information requires a sophisticated information management system. This is usually called a *marketing information system*, or MIS. The purpose of the MIS is to collect, store, and retrieve specific information.

An MIS can be as simple as a few index cards or as complex as a state-of-the-art computer system. Some of the determining factors include the company's capability for funding a system, the amount and type of information to be managed, and the ways in which the marketer will need to use the information.

The Four Cs: Consumer, Competitor, Company, and Climate

Everyone in a sport business must possess vast knowledge about many different things. These factors have direct and indirect influence on the company that must be used or referred to when making decisions and developing strategies. The sport business should develop a way to constantly study and analyze them. Most all of these can be categorized into four categories: the consumer, the competitor, the company, and the climate. Figures 4.6 and 4.7 presents the 4 Cs and their variables that the sport business should constantly study. The following are brief descriptions of each. Thorough details of each are presented in later chapters.

The Consumer

The sport marketer needs to know and understand the people (consumers) who need or want the company's products (see Figure 4.8). This is called *consumer analysis*. With this knowledge the marketer may make educated strategic decisions for the company that will position the company for success.

It is also important to identify potential consumers. These are consumers the company might want to attract. For example, you are the owner of a soccer club. You currently offer soccer leagues for two age divisions: 29 and under, and 30 and over. You should consider offering other age divisions as well because you are in the unique position to create a product for a new consumer. That is, you could create a 40-and-over division. All of your 30-and-over players will turn 40 one day. They will probably want to continue to play soccer, but they might not want to continue to play against younger players.

> Knowledge of your consumers will guide you and your sport business in making important decisions about product, price, distribution, and promotion.

The sport marketer must constantly study and analyze existing consumers and the potential for new consumers. This will afford the sport marketer the knowledge to develop new products, change existing products, set new goals, and make other strategic decisions for the company.

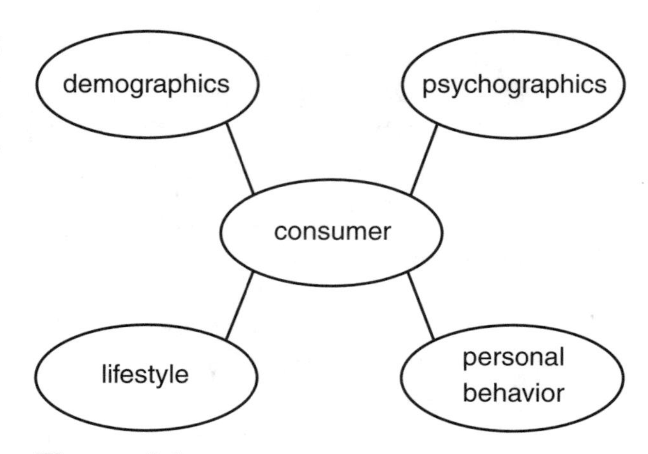

Figure 4.8
The consumer and its factors that affect sport marketing strategies.

The Competitor

Studying the competitor involves studying closely related competitors and the particular industry of the business (see Figure 4.9). That is, although it is imperative that you constantly study closely related competitors, it is just as important that you study and understand what is happening in your industry. This is called *competitor analysis,* and it also involves *industry analysis*. For example, let's say that your company is a sport marketing research business. It is important for you to study sport marketing research companies that sell the same products. At the same time, it is important for you to study what's happening in the sport marketing research company industry to help you make decisions.

> Knowing your competitors and being aware of events in the industry enable you to improve your own business.

The information about consumers must be analyzed along with information about the competitors. As stated earlier, every business operates in a variety of environments and not in a vacuum. What other businesses are doing will affect your business. The sport marketer must continuously study and analyze the competition to gain an understanding of what competitors are doing, what they are capable of doing, and how these activities might impact upon your business. With this information the marketer will be able to change existing strategies, if needed, and formulate new strategies.

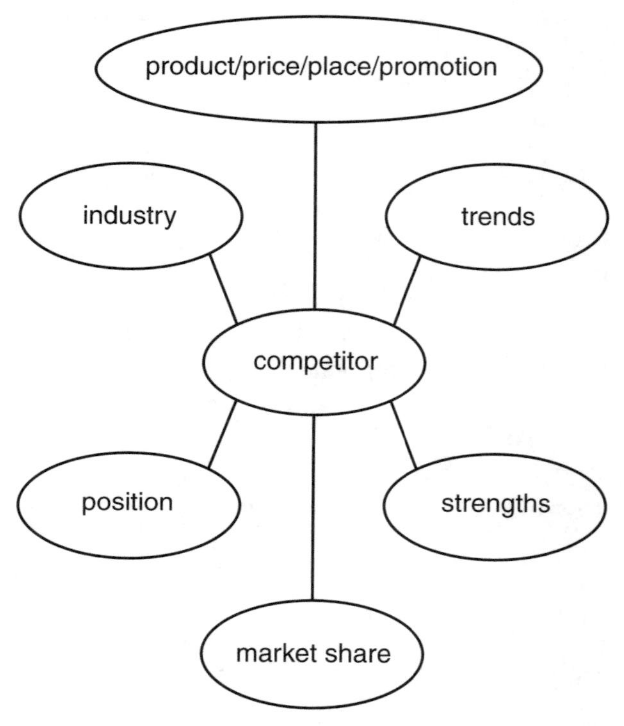

Figure 4.9
The competitor and its factors that affect sport marketing strategies.

The Company

The study of your own company is vital to success. One example of a method of company study is a SWOT analysis. SWOT is an acronym for Strengths, Weaknesses, Opportunities, and Threats. Other criteria that should be considered are mission and objectives, financial strength, production, product management, pricing objectives and strategies, distribution strategies, and promotion strategies (see Figure 4.10). Further, these many factors can be compared to competitors.

The information is useful is informing most decisions concerning almost every move the company is considering making. For example, you wouldn't plan to buy another company unless you had a strong financial position, could absorb the other company under current company structure, and could take over the operation of the other company. In another example, your company might be considering entering a market with a product new to the company. A complete analysis of the barriers to entry, competitors, and whether or not your company can afford such a move is vital to this decision.

Figure 4.10
The company and its factors that affect sport marketing strategies.

The Climate

An important responsibility of the sport business management team is to analyze the climate (see Figure 4.11). *Climate*, also referred to as environment or atmosphere, refers to the current situational factors in a society that can affect the sport business. These include economic, social and cultural, political, ethical, trends, technological, community, education, corporate, and legal aspects of society. With an analysis of each of these in specific relation to its effects on the sport business, the sport marketer must determine how each can influence the company (Gauws, 1997). For example, today there is heightened sensitivity toward civil rights and humanity and thus not offending groups of people. Therefore, titles, names, and logos of some sport businesses have been challenged in relation to their offensiveness to groups. For instance, some sports team's logos that were considered to be offensive and degrading to particular groups of people have been changed.

The economic climate. The state of the economy could impact the sport company. The sport marketer must analyze the current economic situation and determine its effect on the company. There may be opportunities for success and, on the other hand, the possibility for financial disaster for the company. For example, how did the Great Flood of 1993 affect tourism in St. Louis and specifically spectatorship and gate receipt revenue at Major League Baseball games? How much of a financial impact did the flood have on the parks and recreation industry, and how will a specific recreation area be affected?

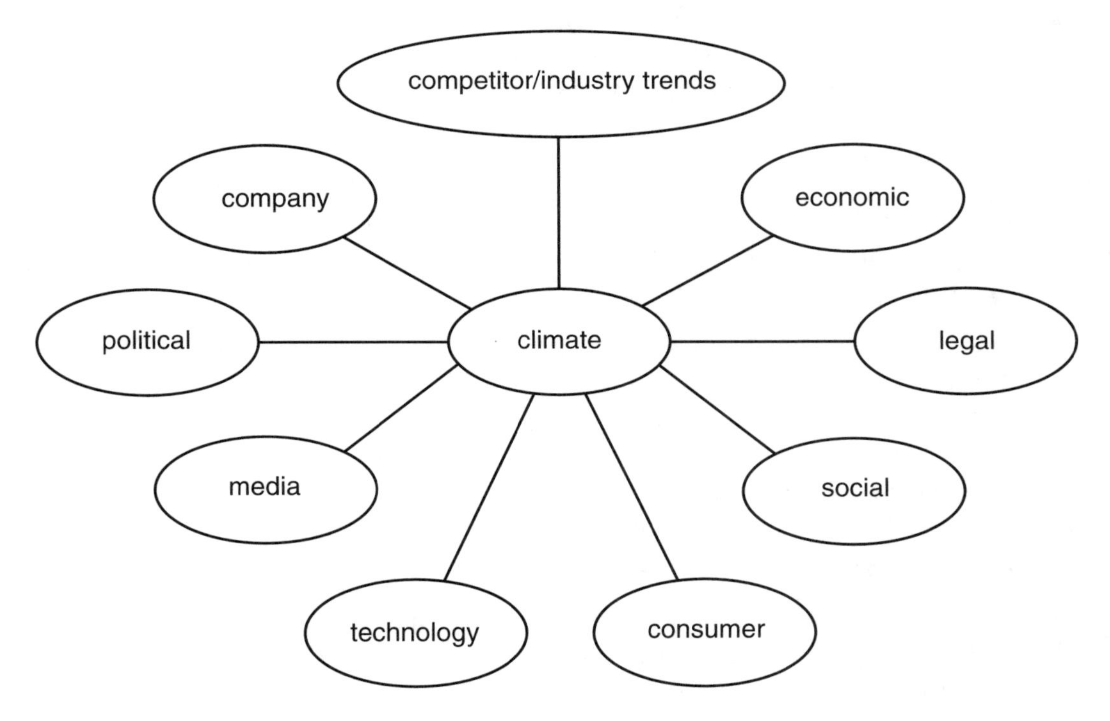

Figure 4.11
The climate and its factors that affect sport marketing strategies.

The social and cultural climate. Cultural and social traditions and attitudes may affect your company. The sport marketer must grasp the social and cultural structures within which the company exists as well as those that exist within the company and analyze the effects on the company and the effects of the company on society. Some examples include (a) public pressure on private golf clubs that have only white members to allow others and (b) sport organizations such as professional fishing groups that do not allow women. Present and future social issues may affect your company.

The political climate. This consists of individuals and organizations that strive to establish tolerance or intolerance within the public sphere for specific business practices. For example, those private golf clubs that do not allow women to reserve tee times on Saturday mornings are under pressure to change that practice. In another example, collegiate athletic programs are under pressure to change many aspects concerning women in athletics such as the number of opportunities to participate, which directly affects the number of sports offered, the number of scholarships offered, and the number of coaching and other staff positions directly involved with the women's athletic program.

The legal climate. "When all else fails, sue." This seems to be the most popular way of handling issues today. However, it has resulted in a great variety of local, state, and federal legislation to protect the consumer. It is important that the sport business knows and understands laws, how they apply to specific products or segments of the sport industry, and how legislation may be used to reveal opportunities and threats for the sport business.

The ethical climate. Society, culture, and business develop certain ethical mores that influence life and business. The ethical climate in the United States was studied intensely during President Clinton's impeachment investigation. People and businesses questioned and discussed their ethical philosophies. The current ethical guidelines will influence the sport business. The marketer needs to know how this is occurring in order to develop strategies.

Taking advantage of trends can be beneficial to sport businesses, especially if the trend becomes commonplace and exists long-term.

Trends. Trends can affect the sport business in many ways. We cannot determine if a trend is simply a trend and will be short-lived, or if a trend will become the next commonplace and institutionalized phenomenon. For an example of the influence a trend can have on an industry, just remember that aerobics was once considered a passing trend.

The technological climate. Technology has tremendous effects on the sport business world in many ways. The rise of electronic commerce has reshaped business and marketing. Advances in materials for facility construction, equipment design, and even sports clothing have significant influences on the sport business industry. The sport marketing specialist must study these advances, determine how best to utilize them to maximize success, and capitalize on the competitive advantages they can bring.

The educational climate. The education of sport marketing professionals influences the business world. Imagine a world in which higher education, or any education for that matter, did not exist. It would be stagnant. Education is vital to the sport business industry. Because every segment of the industry constantly grows more complex, education is necessary to prepare individuals for those challenges. The sport business

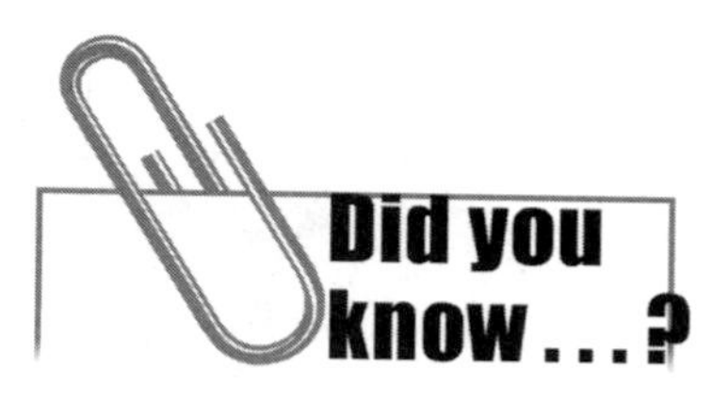

These are the states with the most Alpine ski areas:

New York (54)
Michigan (40)
Wisconsin (38)
Pennsylvania (34)
California (32)

Source: National Ski Areas Association

industry should work with sport management education to ensure professors are teaching future industry workers exactly what they need to know to be successful on the job.

Educators in sport management have sport management curriculum standards that were designed based on the minimum knowledge every sport management student should have to go into any career in the industry. The sport management educator should make every effort to design curriculum modeled on the standards and to attempt to achieve program approval.

Sport management education is proliferating. Every year there is an increase in the number of colleges and universities starting programs in sport management. Unfortunately, most programs have only one or two faculty members, and many times, these faculty members are expected to teach outside of sport management while managing the entire sport management program. There is a critical need for sport management faculty in general, candidates from doctoral programs designed to appropriately prepare them exclusively for sport management education, and those who are working exclusively in sport management. Moreover, there is a critical need for sport businesses to get involved with sport management education and support the efforts of sport management faculty. Indeed, it will be the sport business that benefits.

One day, there just might be colleges or schools of sport business, just as there are colleges of education or business. There will be full departments based on the curriculum content areas such as sport marketing, sport finance, and sport law. The halls will be lined with nicely framed plaques showing sport businesses that have endowed faculty positions, research centers, and department chairs.

The community climate. The local community within which the sport company resides will influence the company. Each area has different climates in relation to economic, legal, environmental, and cultural issues, for example. The sport business in that community must understand the community climate and how it will influence the business. All of these can have influences on the sport business. With that knowledge, the company can make educated decisions regarding its business in the community. For example, one person wanted to start a company with a driving range and lights for nighttime practice. However, people in the residential area that surrounded the new driving range complained that the huge lights would detract from their property values and quality of life. The future driving-range owner ignored the residents and installed the range and the lights. This led the residents to file a formal complaint with the city. The city investigated and sided with the residents. The driving-range owner was only allowed to use the lights one night a week, every other week. The owner learned a hard and expensive lesson. The lights cost several hundred thousand dollars to purchase and install, and it will be many years before the owner will recoup the costs. In addition, the local newspaper ran several stories about the disagreement, and the owner appeared to be insensitive to the needs and desires of the residents, resulting in negative publicity for the company.

The corporate climate. Each company develops what is called its "corporate climate" and is influenced by a regional or national corporate climate. This involves both trendy corporate factors and those that take on a long-time personality. Typically, top administration establishes both the spoken and unspoken rules or limitations and philosophy that govern the way a company conducts business and how it treats its employees. This makes employees believe they must follow the rules in order to stay with the company. Moreover, it creates an atmosphere for business in which an entire industry will operate. For example, it has become corporate practice for large companies to set up manufacturing plants in countries outside the United States because wages are extremely low compared to wages in the United States. This practice has backfired in that Americans have criticized those companies for exporting American jobs and for supporting poor and uncivil working conditions in poverty-stricken countries. In certain situations, the consequences of this can be boycotting of the company's products, negative press, and a tarnished reputation. These consequences can sometimes be devastating to the company.

In another example, sexual harassment is a corporate climate no longer tolerated, at least by law. This is not to say that sexual harassment does not continue to take place—it does. However, the issue has been so very well pressed that many corporations have stiff penalties for any employee who is found to be sexually harassing another employee.

The sport business must become aware of corporate climates, how they affect their company, and how the company can make corrections or utilize them to company advantage.

Sport businesses must be aware of the climate in which they operate. For example, the corporate practice of establishing plants in foreign countries to take advantage of the relatively low wages has faced heavy criticism by Americans who object to exporting American jobs and to condoning poor and inhumane working conditions in underdeveloped countries. Business practices should not be undertaken without considering their potential effects on other aspects of the business.

In summary, the sport marketer needs to study and understand the many climates in which the company works and how each affects the company. This knowledge will guide the sport marketer in developing marketing decisions and strategies.

Segmenting, Targeting, and Positioning

Segmenting, targeting, and positioning are essential for every sport business. Without these, the sport business puts itself in serious jeopardy of failing. Segmenting, targeting and positioning enable the sport business to develop strategies appropriate to different sets of consumers. *Segmenting*, also called *segmentation*, is differentiating groups of consumers based on unique characteristics. Through segmentation, the company identifies and understands the common characteristics of the consumers in that segment and can determine how to address their unique demands. *Targeting*, also called *target marketing*, is the selection of consumer segments (also called target markets) for which selective marketing-mix strategies are developed. *Positioning* is the way a company uses its marketing mix to influence the consumer's perception of a product. Such moves may influence what the consumer thinks about the product's quality, value, status, convenience, and many other factors.

The process of segmentation varies. Segmenting strategies can include the division of consumers by, for example, buyer identification, salespeople, purchase location, time of purchase, purchase quantity, product design, product bundling, product tie-ins, and pricing. Other strategies include those that identify consumer segments by sets of demographics, psychographics, and lifestyle. Typically, consumer segments are labeled for identification and definition. Some examples of labeled segments with which you might be familiar include the baby boomers, the senior market, the Generation X market, and the women's market. Some industry segments of the sport industry identify consumer segments according to loyalty. Some examples of these are the hard-core fan, soccer hooligans, and the occasional fan. Some labeled consumer

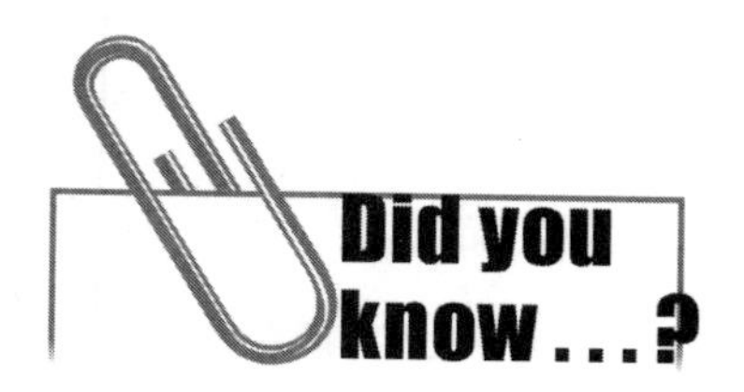

Adults aged 20–29 rank these activities as “getting cooler”:

Golf
(76%)

Mountain biking
(67%)

Snowboarding
58%)

WNBA
(57%)

M.L.S
(48%)

Source: *USA Today*

segments in the participant sports segment of the industry include, for example, the thrill-seeker, the adventurer, the competitor, the weekend warrior, the elite athlete, and the recreational participant

Segmentation is used in identifying and understanding the different business segments in the sport industry. These are called *industry segments*. Industry segmentation is used to better identify, define, and understand the common characteristics of those businesses within that industry segment and to help with competitor analysis and competitive advantage strategies. The sport industry can be segmented in several different ways. One example is segmenting the industry by type of business. One industry segmentation study shows the industry segmented into three segments: sport performance, sport production, and sport promotion (Pitts, Fielding, and Miller, 1994). In this model, all sport businesses that are in the business of marketing, promotions, merchandising, and the media are categorized into the sport promotion industry segment. You and your sport business would study this segment, analyzing its strengths and weaknesses, and develop competitive strategies.

A sport business must identify its industry segment in order to formulate marketing objectives and long-term company goals. This knowledge allows it to make better decisions about product, price, place, and promotion and to determine positioning strategies.

Target market decisions. Segmentation is used to identify categories, or markets, of consumers and competitors. There can be many segments. The marketer must direct the company in deciding which segments the company is capable of serving. The segments chosen become the company’s target markets. A target market is a segment of consumers who are homogeneous and who have purchasing power and the willingness to buy. Target markets should be the basis for all marketing strategies. It is the target market for which a product is produced and offered, a specific price is determined, where to offer the product is selected, and promotion strategies are formulated. Here are a few examples of target marketing:

1. The Women’s Basketball Hall of Fame opened in the spring of 1999 (“The Herstory of Basketball,” 1999). The target market is the large and growing women’s basketball market. The Hall of Fame is in Knoxville, Tennessee, which is where the hugely successful and popular University of Tennessee women’s basketball team and Coach Pat Summitt reside. Speaking to the market, the advertisement for the hall of fame uses the slogan “Honor the Past. Celebrate the Present. Promote the Future.”

2. Condé Nast spends $40 million to publish the monthly *Condé Nast Sports for Women* magazine, first launched in 1997. The target market is sportswomen. The product is sports publications (Fahri, 1997).

3. In 1998, the *Sports Business Journal* launched its first issue. Targeting sport business industry management people and sport management educators, the *SportsBusiness Journal* joins the sports industry publications industry segment with an emphasis on trade and business.

4. Targeting high school athletes who want help to find college scholarships, the company SportsStar Marketing, Inc. has opened offices in 6 more states (“Coast to Coast,” 1999). The product is a scholarship finding and matching service.

5. The Federation of Gay Games' primary target market is the lesbian and gay sports market around the world. The product is sports participation. The most recent event was Gay Games V, held in August, 1998 in Amsterdam, The Netherlands (Pitts and Ayers, 1999). The event hosted 14,843 athletes from 78 countries in 31 sports, had an estimated 1 million spectators, and an economic impact of $350-plus million.

6. Several snow ski companies in Colorado host special weekend festivals targeting the Hispanic population.

7. Targeting collectors of the phenomenal Beanie Baby beanbag critters, Major League Baseball saw the most successful increase in attendance with this promotion (King, 1998). Stating that baseball fans are more interested in giveaway items that they can use or that have value, the Beanie Baby giveaways produced an average increase of 37.4% per game, the largest increase of any promotion held at the parks during the 1998 season.

In these examples the products were planned and produced specifically for a particular group of consumers—a target market. It is the target market that informs decisions concerning the marketing process, especially the marketing mix.

Sport Marketing Mix Strategies

The *marketing mix* is the strategic combination of the product, price, place, and promotion elements (see Figure 4.12). These elements are typically called the *4 Ps of marketing*. Decisions and strategies for each are important for the marketer. Information for making educated decisions involving the four Ps comes from your marketing research involving primarily the four Cs—consumer, competitor, company, and climate. A critical decision and one of the greatest challenges for the sport business is how to strategically combine the four Ps to best satisfy the consumer, meet company objectives, enhance market position, and enhance competitive advantages.

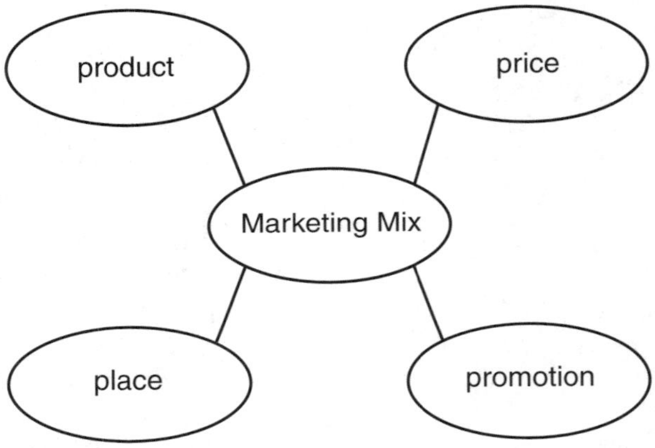

product
price
Marketing Mix
place
promotion

Figure 4.12
The Marketing Mix: The Four P's.

Market position, also called *positioning*, refers to the way a company uses its marketing mix to influence the consumer's perception of a product. Such moves may influence what the consumer thinks about the product's quality and what the consumer is getting for the money, features not found on another similar product, status, convenience, and many other factors.

Product

The centerpiece of a marketing mix is the product. The product should be understood as a concept and not simply as a singular item. A sport product is any good, service, person, place, or idea with tangible or intangible attributes that satisfy consumer sport-, fitness-, or recreation-related needs or desires. The consumer is looking for functions and benefits. The product is the satisfaction agent for those. The product is something that will satisfy something that the consumer needs or wants. Price, place, and promotion strategies are designed specifically for the product in order to increase the probability that the product will sell.

The sport company must constantly study the consumer in order to discover what the consumer wants or needs. The result could mean developing a new product or changing an existing product in some way. The sport business must use information concerning the competition in making these decisions. For example, if the mechanic for the sailing club discovers that the sailing club members are not buying sailboat hardware at the club's shop because they cannot get what they need, the prices are higher than at other stores, and the quality is not as good, the mechanic should tell the marketer. The marketer may decide to survey the members to get more information. If the research supports what the mechanic said, the marketer must determine if action is needed. In this case, the marketer should consider further research to determine what hardware the members need and find out what prices the other stores are using and if higher quality products are available and can be sold at a specific price level.

> The sport business must study the consumer and the competition in order to move its product into line with current trends, wants, and needs.

The sport marketer will make many critical decisions concerning the sport company's products. One such decision involves the number and types of products to offer. This is called *product mix*, the complete set of all products that the sport company offers. A sport company will determine what is, or will be, the right combination of products for the company. Product management involves tracking the sales of each product to determine if sales are increasing, maintaining, or decreasing. An analysis will provide the sport marketer with knowledge to make adjustments to specific products or to terminate a product.

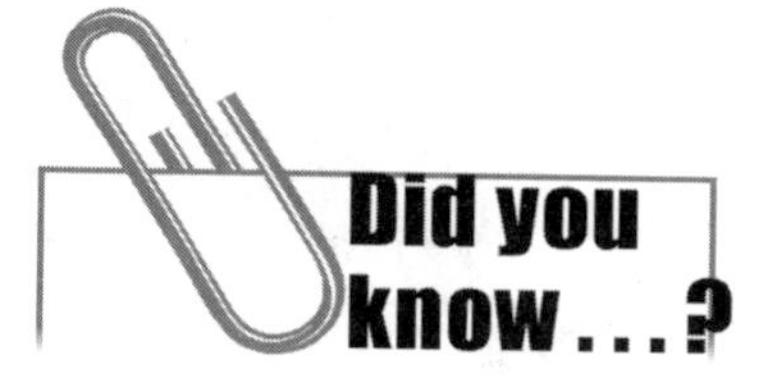

Eight percent of American adults are scuba divers who have spent a combined $640 million on equipment.

Source: Gallup and Leisure Trends for Diving Equipment and Marketing Association

The decisions concerning the company's products are important for the company. The product is the company. Any changes, additions, or deletions will have specific effects on the company. It is the sport marketer's job to try to forecast the effects and initiate only those changes that could have positive results for the company and the consumer.

Price

Price is the exchange of something for something—that is, one item of value for another item of value. The price of something can have a tremendous effect on a consumer. The consumer's decision to buy something can be affected by many factors. Some of those factors include what the consumer can afford to pay, if what the consumer gets for the money is of value, if the consumer thinks she or he is getting "a good deal," friends' attitudes, family influences, how the product compares to another similar product in terms of features and other factors, and the product's warranty and extended services.

Setting the price for a product is a very important decision for the sport marketer because price affects the product's success, status quo for the product, and the consumer's perception toward the product. The decision should be based on many factors such as knowledge of the consumer and what the consumer will pay, cost to the company to produce and offer the product, profit-making strategies of the company, the competition's prices, and supply and demand within the product market. Although chapter 11 is a detailed chapter on price and pricing strategies, here is one example of how setting prices works.

In Center City, USA, there exists one indoor soccer complex, Soccer City, Inc. The city's population is 600,000, and soccer leagues, both recreational and in the schools, are full and growing. Soccer City opened 5 years ago, and its facility includes one indoor soccer court enclosed by a giant net, a concession bar, and a tiny soccer equipment and apparel store (rented space to a local soccer store). Soccer City enjoys a monopoly on indoor soccer. As the popularity of soccer has grown and proliferated in the city, so has indoor soccer. It offers a place to play soccer during the winter months, which are the off-season in all outdoor soccer venues. The demand is high. All leagues offered fill quickly even though the price has gone sky high. The adult league fees are $400 for an 8-week session of 1 game per week. The high school and youth fees are even higher. The fees for these teams are per person. The high school players will pay $75 per person for an 8-week session of 1 game a week. Although most of the players complain of the high fees, leagues are always full.

Within the year, a new indoor soccer facility will open, Pele's Palace. The CEO of Pele's Palace has a choice to make concerning prices. Pele's Palace could charge lower fees compared to Soccer City and probably win quite a few of Soccer City's customers. A second choice is this: Pele's Palace could charge the same fees as Soccer City because it has been established that those prices are what consumers will pay for indoor soccer. Which would you do? Which is better for the company? Which is best for the consumer? Are there any other pricing strategies you could consider? How much does the product (indoor soccer) cost the company to produce and how will this affect your pricing decisions?

As you can see from the example above, pricing a product is not a simple matter. It involves many factors and critical analysis of those factors before determining marketing mix strategies.

Place

Place is where and how a company gets a product from its production or origination point to a place where the targeted consumer can have access to it. Remember that sport industry products include people, places, goods, services, and ideas. Goods that are typically manufactured in a factory must be transported from the factory to the market. Some products such as services must be delivered to the marketplace to the consumer in a different way. Sports activities are very different because a sports event does not exist until a person manufactures it—that is, basketball is an intangible and doesn't exist until someone plays basketball. It is a product like a play in a theater or a live concert by Tina Turner or Ricky Martin that is manufactured and consumed simultaneously. In a sports event, the consumer is the participant. The consumer has paid for the product, softball, for example, but does not take possession of it until the consumer actually creates it, or plays softball. In this example, the consumer will probably have to go to a softball field on a given day at a given time to get what was bought. Getting this type of product to the consumer is different from transporting a good from a factory to the marketplace and requires the sport marketer to make specific decisions.

Place, or distribution as it is also called, requires knowledge of type of product, how best to get that product to the consumer, or how to get the consumer to the product, efficient and effective distribution channels, packaging, and other factors. Analysis will lead to better decisions. Chapter 9 details the marketing mix variable place.

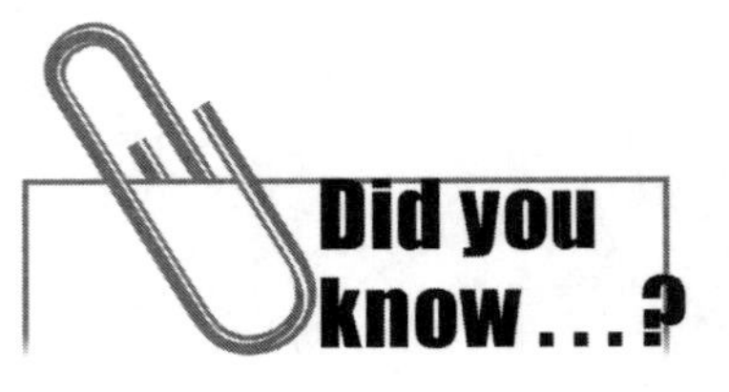

The average price paid for a tennis racket in different countries (in U.S. dollars) in 1998 was

Germany	$170.11
Japan	$153.05
Chile	$144.14
USA	$99.00
France	$95.80
Australia	$91.40
Czech Republic	$68.94

Source: World Tennis Association

Promotion

Promotion is what the general public thinks is marketing. That is because the promotions are what the public sees. More specifically, promotions are especially designed to get a person's attention. Advertising, one category of promotion, comes in the forms of TV commercials, radio commercials and announcements, advertisements in magazines, in books, in movie theaters, in video movie rentals, on billboards on every highway, on the sides of buses, trucks and cars, signs on tops and sides of buildings, signs on athletic fields, stadia, arenas, and uniforms. In other words, it is everywhere. People are surrounded by advertising.

Sport businesses lure people to sporting events by incorporating special promotional events, sometimes called promos. Consider these examples: a Leanne Rimes concert the day before a NASCAR race event; a gift such as a coffee mug for the first 2,000 people through the gates; a gift such as a 45-inch television given away at the halftime break at the local college women's basketball game; and the appearance of a sport superstar who will sign autographs after the game. These are just a few of the many promotional methods that sport marketing people use to get the attention of the consumer.

A marketer's message should grab people's attention, educate or convey a message, and entice people to purchase.

It is no wonder then that the general public thinks that marketing is promotion and promotion is advertising. Promotion, however, involves more than creating advertisements and inventing special events. As you will see in chapters 12, 13, 14, 15, and 16, promotion is multifaceted.

Promotion is the process of promoting. Promoting means raising awareness. Therefore, a simple definition of promotion is: the process of making people aware of something. The process may involve a variety of methods of gaining the attention of potential consumers in order to tell them something and/or to educate them about something. In addition, once the marketer has the consumer's attention, the marketer must keep it long enough to get a message across. Usually the message contains information about a product or a business. The marketer's purpose for promotion is to encourage the person to purchase the product. Therefore, the message must be developed in such a way that it serves three functions: First, it gets the attention of people; second, it gets across a message or educates the people; and third, it tempts the people to purchase the product.

The promotion may be any one or more of a variety of promotional methods and strategies. The sport marketer may choose any one or a combination of promotional methods and strategies.

The promotional message and strategies are put together to speak to a specific kind of person—a market segment. The sport marketer uses research data about the consumer and the competition to create strategies and the promotional message.

Promotional methods may include

- direct-mail advertising
- radio and television advertising
- local newspaper or nationally circulated magazine advertising
- billboards advertising
- special limited-time sales
- special financing
- special customer services
- the use of specific colors on a product or its package
- the use of a concert in conjunction with a sporting event
- offering a variety of product packages at various prices
- product giveaways during an event

Marketing Management Strategies: Implementation, Management, and Evaluation

The sport business must have a system for managing the process of sport marketing. This system includes the implementation, management, and evaluation of all sport marketing components. Management is a multidimensional step that involves setting objectives for the sport marketing strategy, developing the sport marketing plan, selecting and managing sport marketing personnel, establishing a financial plan, establishing and managing an organizational structure, establishing and overseeing deadlines and scheduling, acting as the liaison between sport marketing personnel and top management, and coordinating all sport marketing functions.

The development of the sport marketing plan is an important task. Strategic planning functions to strengthen relationships between sport marketing and other management functional areas in the company. The sport marketing plan is the written, established plan of action for the company or for an element (or product) of the company. It drives the company.

The plan contains the marketing objectives, identified target markets, financial strategies, and details of the marketing mix strategies. The marketing plan can be written for a single sport product, a group of products, a new promotional strategy, or the entire sport company.

The sport marketing management model, illustrated in Figure 4.5, is a graphic representation of most of the components of a marketing plan and should be used as a guide in the development of a plan.

The sport marketing plan should not be taken lightly. It requires time, research, and critical analysis. It should be the culmination of this effort during which every possible task, angle, financial analysis, and every function of the company and the product have been thoroughly studied and analyzed. The final plan should reflect informed decision making and strategy formulation. Refer to the new companion workbook, *Developing Successful Sport Marketing Plans* (Stotlar, 2001) for detailed help in developing a sport marketing plan.

Implementation involves establishing a system for planning and managing the implementation of the sport company's marketing strategies. Evaluation involves establishing a system for analyzing marketing strategies to determine if the strategies are accomplishing the established objectives.

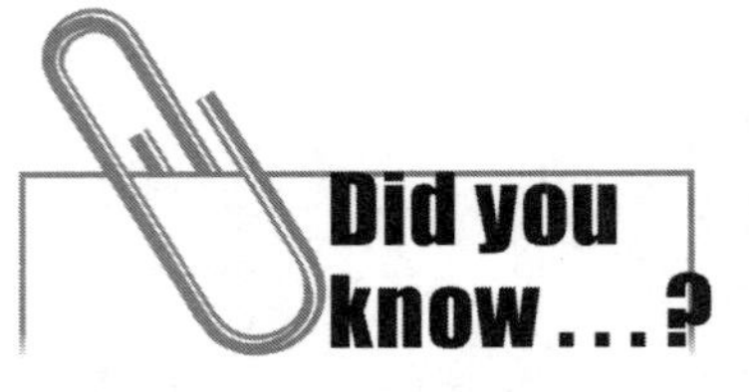

The U.S. Census Bureau projects growth in the number of Americans aged 85 and older:

Year: 2030
85-plus population: 8.1 million
% of U.S. population: 2.4%

Year: 2050
85-plus population: 18 million
% of U.S. population: 4.6%

Source: U.S. Census Bureau

Chapter Summary

In this chapter we presented the concept of sport marketing theory, defined sport marketing, presented the sport marketing management model, and briefly discussed the components of the model. Subsequent chapters will provide specific details, methods, and strategies of each component. We encourage you to refer to the sport marketing management model (Figure 4.5) throughout your study and practice of sport marketing. It will remind you of the total picture of marketing and where each component fits.

Theory is built from a foundation of research and knowledge. Sport marketing theory is in the process of being developed as it is a new field of study when compared to many other fields of study. To study the developing theory of sport marketing, one must study the foundation from which it is being built. The foundation of sport marketing is being built from several fields of study.

Sport marketing is the process of designing and implementing activities for producing, pricing, promoting, and distributing a sport product to satisfy the needs or desires of consumers and to achieve the company's objectives. Sport marketing is one of many management functions. It has become, however, one of the most important functions because the sport industry continues to grow at a phenomenal rate. The growth means competition and the sport industry is a highly competitive industry.

The sport marketing management model illustrates the elements of sport marketing, the succession of elements and functions, the process of managing, and the interdependency of the elements. The model should be used as a guide for the sport management or sport marketing professional.

Questions for Study

1. What is theory?
2. What is marketing?
3. What is sport marketing?
4. What is sport marketing theory? What fields of study serve as the foundation of sport marketing fundamentals and theory? What are some of the areas of research in sport marketing?
5. What is the sport marketing management model? What are the components of the model? Define and describe each one.
6. What are the research journals for the field of sport marketing?
7. What are the different climates within which a sport business exists? Describe each one and how it affects the business.

Learning Activities

1. (a) Select a list of people who work in the sport industry in different types of sport businesses across the United States. Interview them about sport marketing at their company. Ask them what their theory of sport marketing is. (b) Now do the same with college professors of sport marketing. Interview them about teaching sport marketing. Ask them what their theory of sport marketing is. (c) Compare and analyze your results. Give a presentation in class.
2. Go to the university library and check out textbooks in marketing. Look for the definitions, fundamentals, and theory of marketing. Compare these to the definition, fundamentals, and theory of sport marketing in this book. Analyze your results. Give a presentation in class.
3. Take this book to some people who work in the industry. Ask them to look at the sport marketing management model and to tell you if it matches the marketing activities they perform (or someone performs) in the company. Compile their answers. Give a presentation in class.

Further Reading

Most basic fundamentals of marketing textbooks

Gouws, J. S. (1997). *Sport management theory and practice.* Pretoria, South Africa: Sigma Press.

Shilbury, D., Quick, S., and Westerbeek, H. (1998). *Strategic sport marketing.* St Leonards, NSW Australia: Allen and Unwin.

Chapter 5

Sport Marketing Research

Overview

As you learned in the sport marketing theory chapter, research is the foundation of all sport marketing and sport business activity. All decisions in a company should be made based on the information and knowledge gained from research. Good information that is timely, accurate, interactive, flexible, and accessible is the lifeblood of the sport company. Among many other reasons, good research can help maximize a company's sales, identify future product and market opportunities, identify potential threats to the company, provide information for understanding consumers, help in the advertising development process, provide consumer feedback on product improvements, and assist in determining prices. Good research helps answer key questions such as the following:

- What are the emerging consumer markets that our company could begin to target?
- Can our company get into e-commerce, create a Web-site store, and sell our logo merchandise through the Web site?
- What new product can our company produce for a new consumer market?
- What do consumers like and dislike about our new sports facility?
- How can we upgrade our manufacturing process without having to add too much to the price of our product?
- Which sport businesses could benefit from our sport marketing research services?
- Do spectators at a major sporting event recognize that our company, having spent over $12 million, is a major sponsor for this event? Will they be more likely to buy our product because of our sponsorship?
- How does our company compare to others regarding employee benefits?
- Why are some consumers protesting our new advertising campaign? What do we need to do now?
- What is the hottest, newest sport? Can our company be involved in some way?
- If the national weather offices are predicting a warm winter, how can our snow ski resort lessen the potential financial damages and make up potentially low profits?
- What are the largest markets today, and how will they change in 10 years? How can our company plan for the change?

- What is the true economic impact of our marathon and 10K?
- How are consumers perceiving our new promotional gimmicks?
- Who are our competitors? Where are they? What is their market share? How do their products and prices compare to ours?

At first glance, the questions seem like common, simple questions. But, try this: start with the first question and develop a thorough answer. How would you answer this question? What kind of information do you need? Does this information already exist? If so, where can you get this information? Will the information be accurate? Will it be current? Is it specific to your company, your product, and your part of the industry?

If it doesn't already exist, how can you collect the information you need? Do you need to conduct a study? What kind of study? What kind of measurement instrument do you need? Does an instrument already exist, or do you need to develop one? Will the instrument collect the right kind of information? Will it be accurate?

Will the information be useful when it is collected, or will you need to manipulate it somehow? How do you analyze the information you collected? Will your analysis be accurate for your needs?

How will you be able to use the information for the company? Won't you need to now study the company with the new information and determine how it will work within the company?

After doing this little exercise, you can see how what appears to be a simple question must be treated with a professional, organized, and calculated approach. That professional approach is research.

In this chapter you will learn what sport marketing research is, how sport marketing research is conducted, and how it is used in the analysis and development of marketing decisions and strategies in the sport industry. In chapter 6 you will learn how sport marketing research is the basis for segmentation, target marketing, and positioning, and in chapter 7 you will learn how to manage all of this information gathered through research.

Sport Marketing Research

Sport marketing research is the process of planning, collecting, and analyzing data (a) to gain relevant information or solve a problem to enhance decisions in the sport business exchange process and (b) to enhance the body of knowledge in sport marketing as a field of study. In the first instance—to gain information or solve a problem—research is a fundamental tool for the sport company to obtain information or solve a problem. Information is necessary for formulating decisions concerning the sport company's financial aspects, product development, pricing strategies, distribution strategies, promotional strategies, and all other functions and operations within the company. This information comes from research.

In the second instance—to enhance the body of knowledge in sport marketing—research is conducted to add to and further the level of knowledge about a topic in sport marketing. This type of research is typically developed based on a conceptual framework. That is, it should be based on theory. This textbook, for instance, is based

Sport Marketing Research:

is the process of planning, collecting, and analyzing data to (1) gain relevant information needed or solves a problem to inform decision in the sport business; and, (2) to enhance the body of knowledge in sport marketing as a field of study.

on the theories of marketing as they apply to the sport industry. Research tests theories and forwards the body of knowledge. Theories lead to the development or improvement of practice. Research can be applied. Both theoretical and applied research can help answer questions, solve problems, test theories, or lead to new ideas for theories or practices. In the end, theory leads to practice, and practice leads to theory. For instance, the information and theories in this book are what you, the student, will need to know in order to practice sport marketing on your job—hence the bridge between theory and practice.

Sport marketing research can range from a very simple task to a complex and time-consuming job. Figure 5.1 illustrates the sport marketing research continuum. The type of research conducted is based on what information is needed. For instance, if the sport marketer of an indoor soccer club needs to know the addresses of current consumers in order to send direct-mail promotional flyers, the information may be gathered easily from membership application forms. If the publisher of a wakeboarding sports magazine wants to know what's happening in the sport, the company can read and study information published in industry trade publications. At the other end of the continuum, if the management of the LPGA (Ladies Professional Golf Association) needs to know how many people are attending each event, who they are, and why they attend, a study will need to be designed and conducted over a long period of time in order to collect the appropriate data.

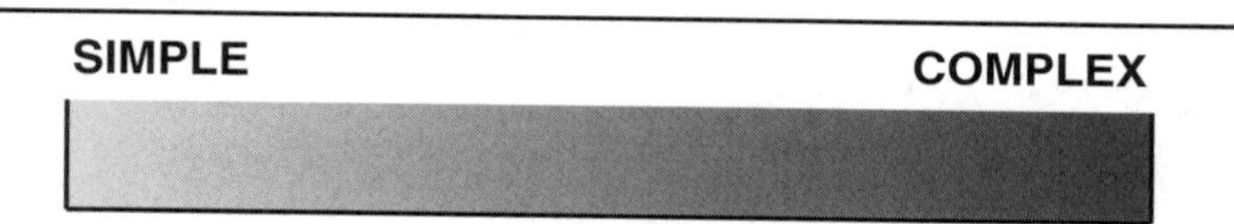

Examples:

Simple—Reading a newspaper, magazine, or sport management journal.
Results: learn about a new sport business opening; a new technology being used in sporting equipment; a study on the demographics of fans of the LPGA.

Complex—The design and conduct of a study that involves, for example, (a) a new metal for a new softball bat, (b) a longitudinal study of children with disabilities in sports activities to determine their sports activity choices in adulthood, or (c) a study of arena advertising to determine its effects on spectators over a long period of time.

Figure 5.1
Sport Marketing Research Continuum.

Research conducted by sport management academicians and scholars can also range from rather simple methods to more formal and complex methods. The appendix at the end of this book contains examples of research conducted by academicians that enhances the body of knowledge in sport marketing and can be used by the sport business executive. For instance, many academicians—professors—have worked as consultants to sport businesses and conducted research for them. This research is used by the sport business. Some research is published in journals such as those presented in Figure 5.2 and in an appendix at the back of the book. Some research is presented at academic conferences such as the annual conference of the North American Society for Sport Management (NASSM), the Sport Management Association of Australia and New Zealand (SMAANZ), the Sport Management Council of the National Association for Sport and Physical Education, the Society for the Study of Legal Aspects of Sport and Physical Activity (SSLASPA), and the European Association for Sport Management (EASM). Often, summaries (abstracts) of these research presentations are published in the conference proceedings of the association.

Sport Management	Sport Studies	Business Administration
Sport Marketing Quarterly	*Journal of Sport Behavior*	*International Journal of Advertising*
Journal of Sport Management	*Journal of Sport History*	*Journal of the Academy of Marketing Science*
Cyber Journal of Sport Marketing	*Journal of Sport and Social Issues*	*Journal of Advertising*
Sport Management Review	*International Sports Journal*	*Journal of Advertising Research*
*European Sport Management Quarterly**	*Women in Sport and Physical Activity*	*Journal of Consumer Marketing*
Journal of Legal Aspects of Sport and Physical Activity	*Sociology of Sport Journal*	*Journal of Consumer Research*
Seton Hall Journal of Sports Law		*Journal of Marketing Science*
Journal of Sports Marketing and Sponsorship		
NASSM Abstracts		

Note: Contact information can be found in the appendix. **European Sport Management Quarterly* is a new title as of April, 2001. The original title is *European Journal for Sport Management.*

Figure 5.2
Examples of academic research journals.

Purposes of Sport Marketing Research

Why do we need to do research? What are the purposes of research? Without research and analysis, decisions and strategies can be risky. When a decision is not based on real and accurate information gained from research, the sport company risks making a wrong decision. Wrong decisions can adversely affect the company. Therefore, decisions should be based on information and knowledge gained from research.

Some of the purposes of sport marketing research can be found in a definition of marketing adopted by the American Marketing Association (AMA). This definition states that

> marketing research links the consumer, customer, and public to the marketer through information—information used to identify and define marketing opportunities and problems; generate, refine, and evaluate marketing actions; monitor marketing performance; and improve understanding of marketing as a process. Marketing research specifies the information required to address these issues; designs the methods for collecting information; manages and implements the data collection process; analyzes the results; and communicates the findings and their implications. ("New Marketing," 1987, p. 1).

Using the AMA definition, let us apply it to the sport industry and identify some of the purposes for sport marketing research.

To Form a Link Between the Consumer in the Sport Industry and the Sport Company

The marketers and managers within the sport company can use the information about the consumer to get to know existing and potential consumers and what they want. The consumer receives messages from the sport company that it is trying to meet the consumer's needs. The following are examples of how this works.

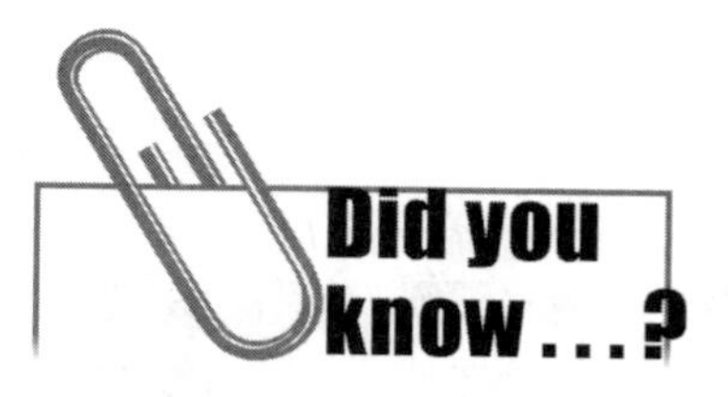

The percentage of U.S. golfers aged 5–17 rose 3% from 1991 to 1997, from 10.6% to 13.6%. In 1998, that number shot up to 29%.

Source: National Golf Foundation

The National Handicapped Sports Association (NHSA) organized to meet the needs of a growing population that wants to be involved in sports activities (National Handicapped Sports, 1993). NHSA was established in 1967 and is a "national, nonprofit educational association dedicated to providing year-round sports and recreation activities for people of all ages and abilities, including people with orthopedic, spinal cord, neuromuscular and visual impairments" (p. 4). The organization tracks the numbers of people with disabilities who want sports activities and encourages the development of programs to meet the needs of the consumer. Without the research, NHSA would not have the information it needs to understand its consumer or offer to its consumer what the consumer needs.

The SnowSports Industries America Top Line Retail Audit studied the market for snow sports equipment in 1998 (Carpenter, 1999). Among the findings were the following: Sales of short skis grew 176% between August and December; overall snowsport equipment and apparel sales were down 2.9%; total sales within specialty stores were down 2.8% to $910 million; and chain store sales were down 3.1% to $311 million. Some sport equipment sales increased: New shaped alpine skis were up 10% although traditional shaped alpine skis were down 29% and considered "beyond dead." In addition, one might think that the highly popular snowboarding would overshadow slumping sales in other winter sports. However, research shows that the snowboard equipment market is oversupplied, and manufacturing companies are pulling back. The snow-sports magazines are also subject to oversupply. For instance, there were 11 snowboard magazines in 1995. Now there are only 3 (Byrd, 1999).

Sports magazine businesses are finding that they are being forced to reconsider how they report sports news. The emergence of the Web has created a world in which news from the other side of the globe can be instantly reported by posting the story via the Web. This raises the question, Why purchase a magazine whose news has already been on the Web for a week or more?

> One way to use the increased availability of media to the consumer is to create a media package that offers a variety of ways to access the information and then cross-promote and sell all the parts.

One answer has been to create a media package for the consumer. That is, offer a Web site, magazine, newspaper, direct-mail newsletter, membership, and television network in a package. Then, cross-promote and cross-sell everything. For instance, ESPN is doing this. They use the television arm to promote the Web site and the magazine, use the Web site to promote the magazine and the television programs, and use the newspaper to promote the Web site, magazine, and television channel (Liberman, 1999).

The link between the consumer and the company is the consumer's need or desire for something. That is, the company must know and understand what the consumer needs or desires in order to create products that will meet those needs and desires. To know the consumer requires research and constant monitoring. To do this research, the company must have contact with the consumer. This contact is done through formal research methods such as surveys and interviews and informal methods such as conversations and spending time together. In these ways, the company can learn about the consumer and can then make better decisions in relation to product, price, place, and promotion.

To Identify and Define Marketing Opportunities, Problems, and Threats

A *marketing opportunity* is a chance for a sport company to capitalize on a new idea or new product, move to a new location, gain a specific consumer market, take advantage of a financial management technique, or engage in other activity that will most likely prove a positive activity for the company. A *marketing problem* occurs when something is not quite right in the company. A *marketing threat* is usually more serious for the company. It means that something could have a serious adverse affect on the company. Only through research that the sport marketer will discover opportunities, problems, or threats for the company. Let us consider some examples.

A Marketing Opportunity:
is a chance for a sport company to capitalize on something that will most likely be positive for the company.

A Marketing Problem:
occurs when something is not quite right.

A Marketing Threat:
occurs when something will most likely have a negative effect on the sport company.

Customized soccer. Through interviews and casual conversations, both of which are types of research, a soccer league player, Pam Reeves, discovers there is no summer soccer league for women in Louisville, Kentucky, and that there is a group who want to play in the summer (Pitts, 1993). This is a marketing opportunity: Here is a group of consumers who want something that does not exist. In further interviews—more research—Reeves gathers information about what type of league the women would like. Some of the data gathered included the following information:

1. Consumers wanted a shorter-than-regulation game. A regulation game is two 45-minute halves, or 1½ hours of running. In the summer months in Louisville, the average temperature is hot, and the humidity is very high, which makes it very uncomfortable. A game that lasts around an hour with breaks would be desirable.
2. They wanted teams to consist of fewer players than regulation. Regulation requires 11 players on the field. Fewer players would allow the teams to be flexible in recruiting players and not have to worry about getting enough to show up. The summer months are used for holidays and vacations, which means that many players will be absent from games. It is easier to find 10 players who will commit to a team in the summer than for 16 to 18 players commit to a game every week.
3. They wanted the game to be fun and not as structured as the highly competitive and structured fall and spring leagues.
4. They wanted the games to be held in the evening when it is not as hot as during the day.

Using the information gathered, Reeves invented a game and started the league. The new game is played on a small field 70 yards long and 40 yards wide, whereas a regulation field is 110 yards long and 60 yards wide. The new game is a 7-on-7 game with a goalie. Hence, Reeves named the league "Seven-Up Soccer." (There are actually 8 players, but Seven-Up Soccer is a catchy name.) Pam incorporated a "you must have fun" rule to create an atmosphere of lightness and sportswomanship. To keep the price down, Reeves uses no officials. This is probably the most unusual and interesting aspect of the product: There are no officials; hence, every player can officiate. Any player can make a call when there is an infraction of a rule or a foul has occurred. This was the toughest part of the game for the players to get used to because, in a regular game, part of a team's game strategy is to figure out which violations and infractions

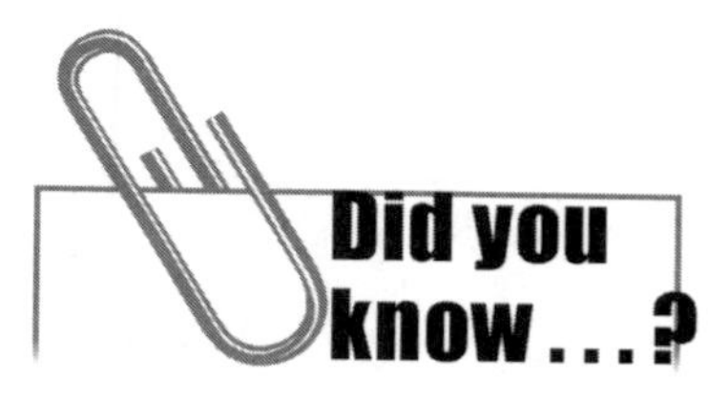

The average total spent on new exercise equipment for a home gym is $473.

Source: Target Management for Fitness Products Council

the official will catch and to work around that. When everyone can officiate, a player cannot get away with anything. This results in a very clean and almost foul-free game.

In the first year, the league was offered on a Sunday evening. However, teams had problems with players showing up because they were gone on summer vacation. After more research, the league was offered on a Wednesday evening the following year. Wednesday was selected because it is the night most players were available from other summer activities such as softball and vacations.

Most of the rules developed were based on the summer heat factor and include unlimited substitutions at any time, including when play is taking place; and the game consists of four 12-minute quarters with 1 minute between quarters and 2 minutes at halftime. The first rule allows the player to get off the field to rest and cool down at any time during play. The second rule keeps the game short and includes breaks for rest, water, and cooling.

In the first year of the league, there were three teams. Four years later, there were ten teams, and Reeves has plans to extend the league to two women's divisions and is considering offering a coed or a men's division.

Through research, Reeves discovered a marketing opportunity. With continuous research, she changed and molded the product to meet the consumer's needs and has a successful product.

Fitness foe. Research can reveal threats. Let us consider fitness centers as an example. Today there are fitness centers everywhere. During the 1970s and 1980s when the number of fitness centers was growing rapidly, the increase was a problem and a threat to the few existing fitness centers. For example, if the Downtown Fitness Center (DFC) is the only fitness center within a 20-mile radius, the DFC feels safe, knowing that competition is at least 20 miles away. When the owner of the DFC discovers through research that three companies are making plans to open within the 20-mile radius, the owner becomes aware of a threat to the DFC. With this information, the owner is in a position to do something so that the new fitness centers will have either no effect or minimal effect on the DFC's business. Without the research effort, however, the owner of the DFC never would have known that competition was about to increase substantially.

Baseball bargains. Stacy Travandi is a sales representative for a large baseball bat manufacturing company. The professional baseball leagues, which currently allow only wood bats, are considering allowing bats made of other materials. Spectator attendance has been slowly declining in the last 4 years, and leaders in the baseball leagues believe that bats made of other materials will result in more hits, and thus more excitement for fans, and thus increased attendance. There are currently 12 professional baseball leagues in this particular country—4 men's leagues, 4 women's leagues, and 4 minor leagues. Changing the bat-material rule could have significant impact on the bat manufacturing companies, especially those companies whose sole product is wood bats and who sell only to the professional leagues.

Stacy's company, the Acme Baseball Bat Company, manufactures bats from two materials: wood and aluminum. The wood bats are all produced on machines that individually produce bats one at a time according to the specifications of each player who orders bats. The aluminum bats are mass produced in a factory in another country and shipped. The aluminum bats, however, are children's bats and much smaller than an adult's bat. The Acme company started producing these bats as promotional items—autograph models of some of the professional players. Children using these bats choose according to the name. For example, a child whose favorite professional players include Kelly Powers, Mike Star, and Jay Jay Homer can use the aluminum bats named for the players and dream of becoming that player one day.

Stacy figures that it ought to be easy for the company to make the transition and stay in business if the leagues decide to allow bats of materials other than wood because the company already makes bats out of materials other than wood. So, Stacy proposes this idea to the company's top administration. Stacy is assigned to research the idea.

Stacy makes a trip to the aluminum bat factory to talk to the director and discovers that their aluminum-bat-making machines will not make bats large enough for an adult. The company would have to purchase all new machines. Stacy's research into this leads to the discovery that each new machine, along with reconfiguring the existing factory, will cost $1.2 million. There would also be additional expenses including personnel, extra space, and numerous overhead costs. Further research reveals that the company would have to have a factory with 30 of these machines in order to produce enough bats to sell to be efficient and cost-effective.

After presenting the research to the company's top administration, it is determined that the cost of start-up and production is a problem—one that will require major, long-term commitment from the company in order to effectively produce this new bat. The administration also decides that the problem warrants further research, especially because they are the only wood bat company that already produces bats of other materials. However, more research is needed regarding how many companies currently produce adult-size bats of other materials that could more quickly meet the professional players' demands and perhaps corner the market.

> Research can reveal marketing opportunities, potential threats to businesses, and the work involved in the development of a new product.

In this situation, start-up costs to enter a product market present a problem for this company. Unless further research is conducted, it is not known if a cost-effective solution might be found.

To Generate, Refine, Evaluate, and Monitor Marketing Actions

Marketing actions include such actions as determining the company's products and all of their characteristics, determining pricing strategies, developing promotional methods, and deciding on distribution. Research is needed in order to first generate and design those actions. Decisions about what product to offer and how to offer it can only be made after the research is conducted. Once those decisions and actions are in place, they should be monitored constantly in order to evaluate effectiveness and performance. The following situation illustrates one way this works.

To Market: A New Era in Sponsorship Marketing

It is no secret that the average spectator of many professional sports is being squeezed out of the prime seating areas of the sports venue. But who would have predicted that spectators would cease to be the prime target of sponsorship advertising? A growing trend in some professional sports, where sponsorship is a form of advertising, is busi-

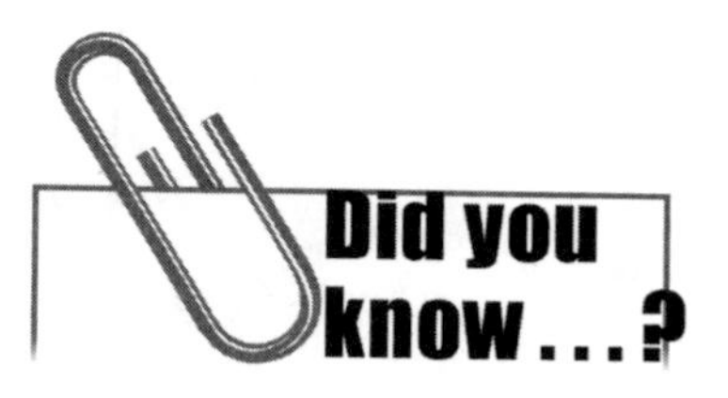

The chief financial officers at large corporations say their favorite leisure activity other than being with friends/family is

Golf (21%)
Reading (14%)
Team sports (10%)
Working out (9%)
Movies (9%)
Adventure Sports (9%)

Source: Accountemps

ness-to-business sponsors (Owens, 1999). That is, corporate sponsors whose products are only manufactured for and sold to other companies are targeting businesses with their advertising rather than spectators. The trend is not hard to spot. For example, which fans recognize the consumer products being touted by a chemical company such as Dupont? Only those who either work for or do business with Dupont. Dupont doesn't need the fans to recognize their product—their target is corporate. Constant research involving trends of consumers of many professional sports reveals the changing nature: the number of corporations that purchase box seats and tickets and also purchase (rent) the pricey spaces around the sports venue for a corporate party tent is increasing. The tent space is, of course, an extra cost and can range from a small amount to hundreds of thousands of dollars. The increasing number of corporate consumers is causing sponsors to take notice. Companies who had never been sponsors for sports events are taking advantage of the opportunity to market to a target audience. Although most sponsors are still producers of consumer products, a growing number of companies whose consumers are businesses are getting involved. For instance, in NASCAR, many sponsors are not companies whose consumers are end consumers—they are retailers. That is, businesses who do business with other businesses. A sponsor in NASCAR can spend $8 million annually to support a race car and team. That sponsor will most likely spend another $8 million for promoting the sponsorship and using it to entertain and enhance business with clients and potential clients.

Many events now have enormous areas in which to create hospitality villages for sponsors. Although the average fan at the event may wander through the village and benefit from promotional giveaways or drawings, the village exists for the corporate sponsor executives and their business partners. The sponsors' focus is on the businesses that buy their products in huge quantities. In other words, a train shipment of sales is worth much more than an individual sale to one consumer. The retailers and wholesalers are being courted for their attention and their wallets.

Constant research and monitoring of the existing and potential consumer and their needs and desires are the only ways the sport marketing professional can discover these needs and desires and then plan to meet them. In this instance, sports event executives should study the changing needs of current sponsors in order to serve them best. This will require changes in the product offered—the sponsorship deal, sponsor's needs, and sponsors' areas—in order to meet the desires of the new market—the business-to-business sponsorship.

To Monitor Marketing Performance

Every sport business must determine if its marketing efforts are performing according to the established goals. That is, if one goal of a particular marketing effort was to increase brand awareness, how can the sport business determine if that goal was met? Of course, the answer is research. The sport marketing professional can use brand-awareness research tools to determine if consumers are aware of and recognize the company's brand.

As you will learn throughout this textbook, there are many different marketing efforts. For promotion, for instance, there are numerous promotional methods. Some are advertising in newspapers, television commercials, promotional giveaways, licensed promotional merchandise, and sponsorship promotions. All of these efforts should be monitored—studied—in order to determine if they are working and if they are meeting the objectives set for them.

It's my turn. In a study of the WNBA's marketing tag line "We Got Next!" researchers found that only a small number of fans know what the phrase actually means (Shoenfelt, Maue, and Hatcher, 1999). The researchers studied basketball spectators and a generic group of undergraduate students and found that more basketball spectators than students had watched a WNBA game and could link the tag line to the WNBA. However, very few of both groups knew the meaning of the phrase. The phrase is one used in basketball pick-up situations where players or groups line up for their time in the game or on the court. The phrase essentially means that the speaker is the next in line. The WNBA wanted to convey to the basketball world to move over, it's time for the women to shine. The slogan also refers to the season scheduling. The NBA season is played "first," and the WNBA season is "next."

If the WNBA now knows that its consumers don't really know what the phrase means, they can make some decisions to effect a change. For instance, they could mount a campaign to attempt to educate consumers as to the meaning of the phrase, or the WNBA could decide to develop a new phrase.

To Improve Understanding of Marketing as a Process

A process can be the routine execution of a method. To understand marketing as a process, research can provide answers to questions concerning why and how the process works. For instance, the sport marketing academic journals, the *Sport Marketing Quarterly* and the *Cyber Journal for Sport Marketing*, provide outlets for the publication of sport marketing research conducted by people in both the academic and practitioner worlds of sport management. All of the studies and other materials published add to improving our understanding of sport marketing and its process. Figure 5.2 provides a representative list of sport marketing, sport management, sport law, sport studies, and business administration journals in which sport marketing research can be found. Examples of this type of research are presented in the appendix at the end of the book. These are brief summaries of the research. You should find the source and read the full study to gain a full understanding of the research. In addition, all of the information presented in the "Sport Business Fact Book: Did You Know . . . " boxes throughout this book are examples of bits of information discovered through research.

The new knowledge and understanding gained through research leads to theory. Theory is the basis of sport marketing practice and therefore of this textbook and others on sport marketing. Table 5.3 is a list of the sport marketing textbooks available. The material in the field of sport marketing has changed and been enhanced over the last 10 years because of the research both in the academic field and in the industry. As new and more research is conducted, it adds to the body of knowledge helping it grow and mature. As this happens, it is

Sports Marketing: Competitive Strategies for Sports. (1994). Christine Brooks. Englewood Cliffs, NJ: Prentice-Hall.

Sport Marketing. (2000). Second Edition. Mullin, Hardy, & Sutton. Champaign, IL: Human Kinetics.

Fundamentals of Sport Marketing. First Edition. (1996). Pitts & Stotlar. Morgantown, WV: Fitness Information Technology.

Fundamentals of Sport Marketing. Second Edition. (2002). Pitts & Stotlar. Morgantown, WV: Fitness Information Technology.

Fundamentals of Sport Marketing. Chinese Edition. (2001). Pitts & Stotlar. Morgantown, WV: Fitness Information Technology.

Sport Marketing: Managing the Exchange Process. (1999). Milne & McDonald. Sudbury, MA: Jones & Bartlett.

Sports Marketing: A Strategic Perspective. (1999). Matthew Shank. Upper Saddle River, NJ: Prentice Hall.

Case Studies in Sport Marketing 91998). Brenda Pitts. Morgantown, WV: Fitness Information Technology.

Strategic Sport Marketing. (1998). Shilbury, Quick, & Westerbeek. St. Leonards, NSW, Australia: Allen & Unwin.

Cases in Sport Marketing. (1999). McDonald & Milne. Sudbury, MA: Jones & Bartlett.

Developing Successful Sport Sponsorship Plans (2001). David Stotlar. Morgantown, WV: Fitness Information Technology (a workbook).

Developing Successful Sport Marketing Plans. (2001). David Stotlar. Morgantown, WV: Fitness Information Technology (a workbook).

Figure 5.3
Sport Marketing textbooks

Consumer classification data and sponsorship effect that were measured in the nine papers.

1. Sponsored property consumer profile
   - demographics
   - buying habits
   - image of sponsored property
   - attitude towards sponsorship
   - attitude towards sponsors
   - perception of sponsored property symbols
   - size
   - frequency of sponsored property consumption
   - perception of fit between sponsor and the sponsored property
2. Exposure

   amount of exposure
   - number of people who were exposed to the sponsor's message
   - number of seconds signage was on TV
   - number of mm of print (newspapers, magazines)
3. Effects on consumer

   on awareness
   - Unaided awareness (compared with competitors)
   - aided awareness (compared with competitors)
   - share of voice/mind—% of total mentions compared with other sponsors/non-sponsors
   - recall by viewing weight—i.e., by frequency of exposure
   - signage recall
   - high- versus low-profile brands share of voice analysis
   - awarenss of current and past sponsor
   - association of sponsor with the sport generally (i.e. soccer, rugby)
   - association of sponsor with the sponsored property (i.e., World Cup)
   - change in share of voice/mind (compared with competitors)
   - change in recall (compared with non-sponsors)

   on image/attitude towards the company
   - degree of image change (compared with non-sponsors)
   - effect on company image (compared with non-sponsors)
   - effect on product image (compared with non-sponsors)
   - general image of sponsor (compared with non-sponsors)
   - on attitudes among business decision maker (compared with non-sponsors)
   - on employee satisfaction

   on behavior
   - effect on brand preference (compared with non-sponsors)
   - rate of growth of brand preference (compared with non-sponsors)
   - on buying intentions
4. Multimedia effects
   - synergy with other communication mediums
   - relative value return of sponsorship versus advertising
   - awarenss by means of message—advertising, sponsorship, product placement, spot advertising
   - relative ability of sponsorship isolated from other communication efforts

Figure 5.4
Sport marketing research (Brooks, 1998).

the student and the practitioner in the industry who will benefit from the information. For instance, Table 5.4 presents research from nine studies on sport sponsorship. The figure summarizes the type of consumer information studied and the sponsorship effects that were measured in the research. Students, practitioners, and educators can benefit from this information, which can be used, for example, in designing sponsorship studies.

To Analyze and Understand the Sport Company, Its Industry, and Its Competition

Within this should be the typical journalist's questions: who, what, when, where, why, and how. The sport marketer should seek to understand the answers to these questions concerning the sport company, its consumers, its competitors, and the climate—the 4 Cs discussed throughout this text. Examples of the many questions the sport marketing professional should constantly ask and monitor are shown in Figure 5.5. Marketing decisions and strategies should be formulated based on real information and an accurate understanding of the company, the consumer, the competition, and the climate. Again, making uneducated and uninformed decisions is risky. Consider the information presented in Figure 5.6, which is the results of research by the Sporting Goods Manufacturers Association (SGMA). The SGMA surveyed sporting goods manufacturers and asked them to rank sports perceived to be the hottest sports activities for 1999. Notice how the rank for some sports has risen and the rank for others has fallen. How would you analyze this information? If you perceived that in-line skating and roller hockey were fast-growing, hot new sports, and that golf is boring and just an old, slow person's sport, how do you explain the information revealed in this research? Try to answer the following questions by analyzing the information from the various positions:

- If you are a sporting goods retailer, how would you view this information in relation to your specific business?

- If you are a soccer ball manufacturer's sales representative, how do you think this information would affect your product and company?
- If you work for a computer company and you are head of a team to seek sports activities events for sponsorship possibilities, how would you use this information?

	CONSUMER	COMPANY	COMPETITOR	CLIMATE
WHO ...	... are our consumers? ... consumes the competitor's products? ... could become our next 1,000 consumers?	... works for us? ... is making key decisions?	... is our competitor?	... can influence the economy, law, etc.?
WHAT ...	... do our consumers like/dislike? ... are they willing to pay?	... does our company do? ... can our company do? ... is our financial status?	... does our competitor do? ... is their advertising like? ... is their financial status? ... are their prices?	... is the future of our economy? ... are the laws that affect my company?
WHEN ...	... does the consumer want this product? ... can the consumer pay? ... should we advertise?	... can our company offer a product? ... does the company need to be paid? ... should the company advertise?	... does the competitor offer its products?	... do the new laws go into effect?
WHERE ...	... are our existing consumers? ... are our potential consumers?	... is our company located?	... is the competitor located?	... will the economic setbacks hit hardest?
WHY ...	... does the consumer want a product? ... does the consumer want to pay a particular price?	... does our company offer this service? ... doesn't our company offer this service?	... does the competitor offer a particular service?	... is the economy hit hardest in this area?
HOW ...	... can the consumer use this product? ... can the consumer pay for this product?	... can our company offer a product? ... does our company track sales of its products?	... do we compare with our competitor? ... are we different? ... does our competitor offer the product?	... will the economy be in three years? ... will the new law affect my company?

Figure 5.5
Questions for the sport marketer.

In another example of research from the SGMA, Figure 5.7 shows data concerning which types of retail outlets hold market shares for sales of athletic footwear. If you had the perception that sporting goods stores sold the most athletic shoes, this data should change your mind. The data show that department stores sell the most shoes. With this information, consider the following question: Your company manufactures tennis, soccer, softball, basketball, and running shoes. What types of retail outlets will you target for the sale of your shoes?

Right away, you can see that even a simple survey can reveal interesting and sometimes surprising information and that the information will be viewed and analyzed

	1995	1996	1997	1998	1999	2000
Soccer	2	3	2	1	1	1
Golf	7	5	4	2	2	3
Baseball	–	–	–	–	2	5
Basketball	4	4	3	3	4	6
Exercise/Fitness	–	–	–	8	5	2
Roller hockey	3	2	4	5	6	–
Softball	–	–	–	7	6	4
Fitness walking	–	–	–	8	8	7
In-line skating	–	1	1	4	9	–
Snowboarding	–	7	7	–	–	8

Sporting Goods Manufacturers Association. Website: www.sportlink.com

Figure 5.6
Hottest Activities Rating.

	1993	1994	1995	1996	1997	1998
Department stores	22.0	22.8	22.3	22.2	21.5	21.5
Athletic footwear	21.9	19.5	18.9	20.0	19.4	19.9
Discount stores	14.0	15.9	16.2	14.7	14.8	14.4
Sporting goods	12.9	12.7	12.5	12.6	13.2	13.2
Family shoes stores	11.8	10.7	9.7	9.8	9.2	8.8

Sporting Goods Manufacturers Association. Website: www.sportlink.com

Figure 5.7
Athletic footwear retail outlet market share (by percent).

differently depending on the type of company that is studying the research. Each one of the different companies can use the information provided, but each needs it for different reasons. The new knowledge could affect the company. Therefore, the information must be considered in the company's planning.

A Basic Process for Designing Research

There are some specific models and methods for research design and activity. Figure 5.8 illustrates a basic process for designing sport marketing research. This illustration outlines the process and a series of questions to guide the sport marketer through the process.

Step 1: Define the Objective or Problem

The first step is to define the objective of the project or specify the problem. What does the company need to know? What is the problem? Refer to the list of questions at the beginning of the chapter. Defining the objective or problem can be as simple as knowing the question. Once the objective or problem has been identified, the development of the research will be guided by what is needed.

Step 2: Locate Existing Relevant Data

The second step is to locate information that might answer your question or solve your problem. If this can be done, there might be no need to conduct further research. That is, if you can find information that is accurate, specific, and timely enough to address the objective or solve the problem, then this might be as far as you will need to go. If not, then further research is needed.

Determine what information you need and where it might be available. Typically, information is available in two sources: primary and secondary. *Primary sources* include those sources from which information is gathered directly. Gathering information about your consumers directly from your consumers is using the primary source—the consumer.

Secondary sources are those that contain information that is already compiled or published. A marketing report purchased from a sport marketing firm is a secondary source. The information comes to you secondhand. There are several secondary sources available to the sport marketer.

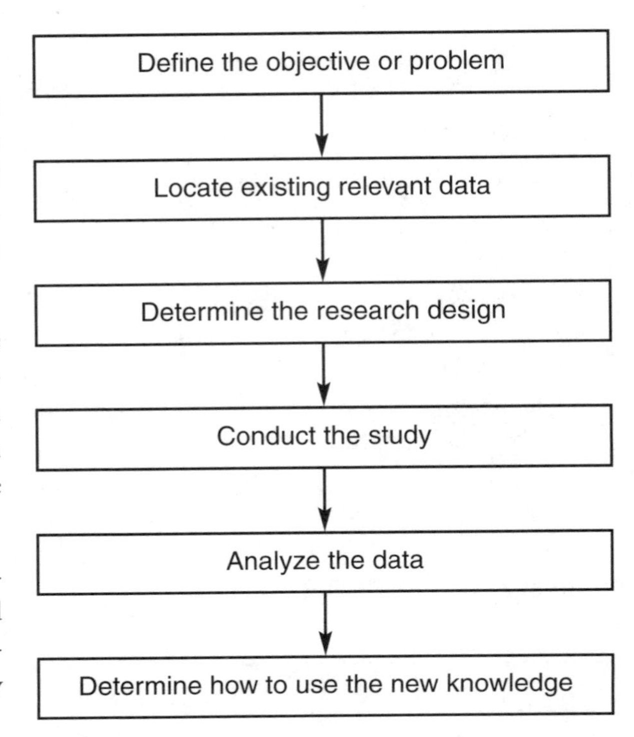

Figure 5.8
A basic process for designing sport marketing research.

Primary Sources: are those sources from which information is gathered directly.

Secondary Sources: are sources that contain information that someone else compiled and reported, published, or collected.

Determine the Kind of Information Needed

Typically, most information needs fall into the 4 Cs categories as previously discussed in chapter 4—the consumer, competitor, company, and climate. For each one of these areas, there are numerous elements that must be studied. The following are descriptions of some of the kinds of information needed concerning each of the 4 Cs and the most common types of research methods used to study them.

The consumer. The sport business must know and understand its consumers and potential consumers. Chapter 6 presents specific information needed concerning the consumer and how that information is analyzed and used. Kinds of information studied include

- demographics such as age, gender, disabilities, sexual orientation, income, ethnicity, and education;
- psychographics such as lifestyle preferences, favorite color, household, employment, purchase behavior, brand preferences, class, culture, reference groups, personality characteristics;
- consumer behavior such as consumer values, lifestyles, perceptions, purchase decisions, purchase decision process, problem recognition, perceived value, postpurchase behavior, and factors affecting purchase involvement level; and
- business consumer segments such as producers, retailers, service providers, resellers, governments, vendors, business-to-business buying behavior.

The competitor. Studying the competition is necessary in order to ascertain what your competitors doing and how those actions will possibly affect your own company.

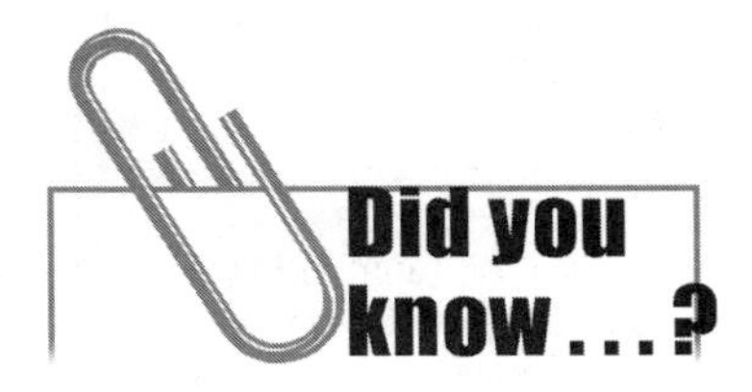

The five most popular names for U.S. golf facilities are

- Riverside
- Rolling Hills
- Lakeview
- Hillcrest
- Lakeside.

Source: National Golf Foundation

Additionally, thorough knowledge of the competition can reveal much information that might be helpful. That is, one company can learn from another company's successes. Sometimes, those successes have to do with hitting on a promotional idea that becomes popular. For example, the use of animals in advertising has been rising in popularity. Who could argue that the Taco Bell dog isn't one of the most highly recognized animals in advertising? Sometimes these popular advertising themes take on a life of their own. The popularity of the Taco Bell dog spawned a full complement of licensed merchandise.

Study of the competition includes study of an industry segment and the industry as a whole. In an industry as enormous as the sport industry, it is essential to remember that oftentimes, one industry segment can affect another. This requires industry analysis. Sometimes this research can be found in industry trade magazines. It is important to read and study these publications because they record and reveal what's happening in an industry.

The company. Monitoring and studying your own company is essential to making decisions regarding every area of the company. This type of research conducted depends on what is needed to know. For instance, a general overall study of the company can be done with a SWOT (Strengths, Weaknesses, Opportunities, Threats) analysis. Using a SWOT analysis, the company can attempt to critically and objectively determine its strengths and weaknesses, for example, and use this information for strategic planning.

The climate. Those environmental considerations as outlined and discussed in chapter 4 that must be studied, both internally and externally, include economic factors, the social and cultural climate, and corporate, political, legal, and ethical climates. For instance, it is important to know what is happening in the economy. The economy can affect everyone, and sport businesses are not excluded.

Sources of Information and How to Get Them

There are two categories of information sources: primary and secondary. As you learned before, *primary information* is information collected directly from the consumer via personal interview, phone surveys, or consumer questionnaires. *Secondary sources* are those sources from which you may obtain information that has been reported, published, or collected. There are also internal and external sources of information. *Internal sources* are those sources inside the sport company. *External sources* are those sources outside the sport company. There are primary internal and external sources, and there are secondary internal and external sources. A *primary internal source* is an interview conducted with one of the sport company's employees. A *primary external source* is an interview conducted with consumers. A *secondary internal source* is a report by one of the departments in the company. A *secondary external source* is a report issued by the United States Census Bureau.

Primary sources are those sources from which you collect the information directly. That is, when you collect data directly from your consumers, that is primary information. To do this, you design a study for the collection of data. Designing a study is presented in the next section.

Here are some ideas on where to find secondary information. You can collect a wide array of information from the local government offices and other nonprofit agencies.

1) Sports Participation in 1998: Series I and Series II
These publications present participation research on the following 63 sports and activities: aerobic exercising, archery (target), backpacking/wilderness camping, badminton, baseball, basketball, bicycle riding, billiards/pool, boating (motor/power), bowling, calisthenics, camping (vacation/overnight), canoeing, cheerleading, climbing (mountain and artificial wall), dart throwing, exercise walking, exercising with equipment, fishing (fresh water), fishing (salt water), football (tackle and touch), golf, handball, hiking, hockey (ice), horseback riding, horseshoe pitching, hunting (bow and arrow; firearms), ice and figure skating, kayaking/rafting, kick boxing, martial arts, miniature golf, mountain biking (on- and off-road), muzzleloading, racquetball, roller skating (traditional 22 wheels and in-line wheels), rugby, running;/jogging, sailing, scuba (open water), skateboarding, skiing (alpine and cross country), snorkeling, snowboarding, soccer, softball, step aerobics, surfboarding, swimming, table tennis, target shooting, tennis, volleyball, waterskiing, windsurfing, and work-out at club.

The report offers demographic data including, for example, gender, age, gender by age, household income, education, head of household female, and head of household male.

2) Sports Participation in 1998: Lifestyle Demographics
This report offers research using the LifeCycle segmentation system developed by NPD Research to analyze sports participation in the continuum from affluent singles to seniors. Households are classified into different life stages using demographic criteria and focuses on 34 sports. Households are classified into 5 segments, with each segment divided into two or more subgroups including: Affluent Singles; Low/Middle Income Singles; Double Income/No Kids (DINKS); Working Parents; Single Parents; Affluent Traditional Families; Low/Middle Income Traditional Families; Affluent Empty Nesters; Low/Middle Income Empty Nesters; Single Active Seniors; Married Active Seniors; 75+ Seniors.

3) The Sporting Goods Market in 1999.
This report contains research involving 100,000 U.S. households and an analysis of consumer purchases of sports equipment and footwear. The footwear section includes 20 styles of footwear and the equipment section reports retail sales for 1998 and 1999 for specific products in more than 20 sport categories. Purchase demographics include annual household income, age and gender of major user, education of household head, and region of the country. There is a 10-year history of sales which allows for analysis of long-term trends. There's also place-of-purchase data which allows for analysis of distribution channels.

4) Sports Equipment Expenditures in 1998.
This research provides estimates of total dollar equipment expenditures per household for selected sports and establishes correlations between participation and purchases. Percentage of total household (HH) expenditures are reported for dollar ranges such as $50–99, $250–499, and $750-plus. Data are reported by demographics such as female HH head age, male HH head age, female HH head education, male HH head education, HH income, market size, and census regions.

5) Team Licensed and Sports Clothing Diary
For clothing, consumer diaries are recognized as producing accurate information. This report includes research on a variety of sports clothing, such as fleecewear, shirts, jackets, t-shirts, caps, shorts, swimsuits, socks, sports bras, and thermal underwear. The research reports total dollars spent, total units purchased, and average cost per unit. Other research includes channels of distribution covered, price point distribution, and licensed and logo products according to a variety of sports categories.

Source: NSGA—National Sporting Goods Association, 1699 Wall Street, Mt. Prospect, IL 60056; Website: www.nsga.org.

Figure 5.9
Some of the types of research offered.

Some of these are the local chamber of commerce, department of health, city planning and zoning offices, city census offices, local colleges and universities, and local real estate or homebuilding offices.

Trade or industry-specific associations also can provide information. For almost every career, there is a professional association. Many of these associations track demographic and other data concerning their industry. The National Sporting Goods Association, for example, tracks sporting goods sales and sports participation and publishes the information. Figures 5.9 and 5.10 present a few of these. More are listed in appendixes B and C.

Professional associations are another source of information. For example, the American College of Sports Medicine (ACSM) is a professional association for a variety of professionals and practitioners in areas such as sports medicine, athletic training, orthopedic medicine, and exercise physiology. The ACSM tracks and collects information about these areas. There are two outlets for the information: (a) annual conferences and meetings and (b) newsletters and journals. Appendix B contains a list of some sport business trade associations.

1) *Bicycle Retailer and Industry News* offers news and features about the bicycle industry for retailers, manufacturers, and distributors of equipment, bike-wear, and accessories.
   Frequency: 18 times per year
   Circulation: 12,000
   Phone: 505.988.5099
   To Subscribe: 800.554.7470
2) *Fly Fishing Retailer* focuses on the health, development, and success of the fly fishing industry. Covers issues, details information, and bring them into focus for retailers, manufacturers, and raw-goods suppliers for this marketplace.
   Frequency: 5 times per year
   Circulation: 4,900
   Website: fly-fishing-retailer.com
   Phone: 949.376.8135
   To Subscribe: 949.376.8135
3) *Golf Retailer* is a business-to-business publication focusing on off-course golf retailing. Covers in-depth market news and analyzes one of the fastest growing segments of the golf market.
   Frequency: 8 times per year
   Circulation: 12,000
   Website: golfretailer.com
   Phone: 212.714.1300
   To subscribe: 800.833.0159
4) *Health and Fitness Business News* focuses on bringing industry management late breaking reports on merger, acquisitions, line extension, distribution shifts, hirings/firings, financial disclosures, and more.
   Frequency: 24 times per year
   Phone 212.714.1300
   To subscribe: 800.950.1314
5) *Inside Sporting Goods* is a electronic and fax newsletter providing sporting goods industry with current news and information concerning the market.
   Frequency: 48 times per year
   Phone: 212.714.1300
   To subscribe: 800.833.0159
6) *Sporting Goods Business* has been published for more than 30 years. SGB covers and analyzes the sporting goods business.
   Frequency: 18 times per year
   Circulation: 26,500
   Website: sgblink.com
   Phone: 212.714.1300
   To Subscribe: 800.255.2824
7) *Outdoor Retailer* focuses on specialty sports retailers of backpacking, mountaineering, camping, hiking, climbing, cross-country skiing, paddling, mountain biking, adventure travel, snowboarding, snowshoeing, and related clothing.
   Frequency: 12 times per year
   Circulation: 16,100
   Website: outdoorbiz.com
   Phone: 800.486.2701
   To subscribe: 800.255.2824

Source: Miller Freeman, One Penn Plaza, New York, NY, 10119-1198. Lisa Rudnick. www..mfisports.com

Figure 5.10
A few examples of industry trade publications: Marketplace Research Resources (see also appendix).

Publications are another source of information and consist of, for example, magazines, newsletters, newspapers, reports, and journals. Some of these sources are available on newsstands, some in bookstores, some by subscription, and others by membership in an organization. Consider, for example, the many sports magazines. To get an idea of how many there are, walk into any bookstore and look at the magazine section. On average, the section will contain over 50% sports and sport-related magazines. Each magazine holds information about that sport and its participants, equipment manufacturers, retailers, and other types of information. *Boating World* magazine, for example, publishes water sports participation data. *Golf World* magazine even publishes stock information (see any issue)! Appendix C at the back of the book contains a list of some sport business trade publications.

Step 3: Determine the Research Design

If the information collected cannot answer your questions, then you will need to conduct further research and collect primary data. You have several research methods from which to choose. However, specific ones must be selected and matched to specific research needs. This must be done to be sure you are conducting the right type of research in order to collect the right data.

Determining the research design includes identifying the right research method and determining the right sampling procedures. The following sections describe these procedures.

Sport Marketing Research Methods

A research method is a procedure, usually an established and tested one. That is, several research methodologies have been developed, tested, and perfected through the years. These methods have higher degrees of reliability and validity. *Reliability* is a measure of the level of consistency of the method. That is, will the method and the results it produces be consistent? *Validity* is a measure of the level of correctness of the method. That is, does the method actually test what it claims it will test? The higher the reliability and validity of a method, the more accurate the resulting data will be.

The research method a sport business or organization selects depends on the purpose of the research. Research methodology is determined by the research question or need. In some instances, research is conducted to enhance understanding and knowledge. That type of research is called *basic* research. In other instances, research is done try to solve a practical problem. That is called *applied* research. Sport businesses typically conduct both basic and applied research, depending on need. Most businesses, however, more often conduct applied research because of their need to solve problems, answer questions, develop solutions, create products, test promotional strategies, increase sales, and address other practical needs.

Examples of the more commonly used sport marketing research methods include the following:

- *Survey research.* The most popular technique used for gathering primary data is survey research. In this method, a researcher interacts with people to obtain information such as facts, attitudes, perceptions, and opinions. Some of the forms of the survey research include personal interviews, mall-intercept interviews, telephone interviews, focus groups, mail surveys, and Web surveys. Sample surveys and questionnaires are given in appendix F. The survey can be in a printed form, or it can be done in interview format. Either way, development of a list of interview questions or the survey questionnaire is essential to the research. All survey research requires that the questionnaires be consistent so that each person in the study will be asked the same series of questions. Questionnaires consist of three types of questions: closed ended, open ended, and scaled response. *Closed-ended questions* require the respondent to make a selection from a limited list of responses such as a multiple-choice exam. *Open-ended questions* ask the respondent to give an answer in essay form. *Scaled-response questions* require the respondent to select from a range of usually intensive related answers such as most to least, higher to lower, strongly agree to strongly disagree. Closed-ended and scaled-response questionnaires are used most often. They are easier to analyze, but they are also more objective in nature. In contrast, open-ended responses are subject to the researcher's interpretation.
- *Observation research.* Observation research calls for observing people's behavior. This type of study is usually conducted when a company wants to determine buyer behavior. It is also used in studying consumer's reactions to products.
- *Scientific research.* Research of a more formal and involved nature is typically labeled scientific research. It includes, for example, laboratory research for new product development such as the study and testing of new materials for sport apparel, research to design and increase the aerodynamics of a racing bike or a racing wheelchair, and physiological studies of elite athletes to improve a sport technique for enhancing performance.

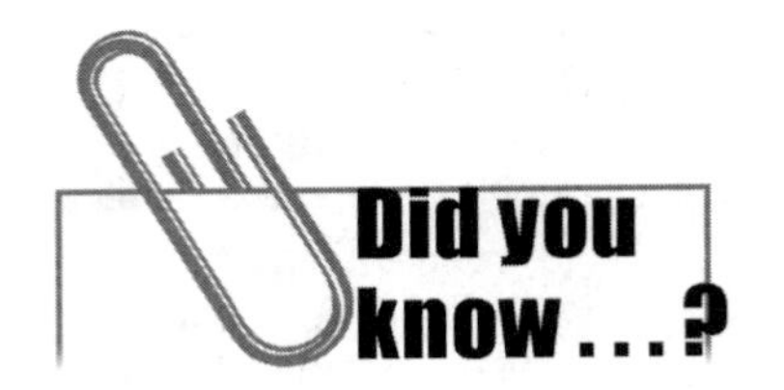

The top five live events that NFL fans say they prefer to attend when they are not watching their sport of choice:

Other pro sport events (44%)

Night club (23%)

Rock concert (16%)

Other musical concert (14%)

Comedy club (11%)

Source: USA DATA, Inc.

Sampling Procedures

A research sample is a representative group of people from a whole population. For instance, if there are 2 million people in a city from which you would like to collect data, you could try to collect the data from all 2 million or select a sample of the population from which to collect. The sample could be 1,000 people of the total population.

To do this, the population must be identified first. This is the group from which the sample will be drawn. The researcher must also decide what kind of sample to select. That is, the researcher can choose a random sample or a convenience sample. A *random sample* is a way to select the members of a sample so that every member of the population has an equal chance of being selected. For example, if you want to survey a population of 20,000 season ticket holders but don't have the time or money to survey every one, you can use random sampling to get a smaller group. You can select the sample number to be 400. Then you can select every 50th person listed on an alphabetical list of all season ticket holders. Thus, you obtain a random sample. A *convenience sample* comes from using respondents who are convenient, or readily available/accessible to the researcher.

A convenience sample allows the researcher to use nearby or established contacts to glean information.

For instance, if you elect to use a convenience sample of the season ticket holders, you select a sample because of its convenience for you. One way to do this is to assume that all people seated in luxury boxes are season ticket holders. They are easily available and convenient for you to access. You simply distribute surveys to all the people seated in the luxury boxes.

Most sampling procedures have weaknesses. It is therefore important to know what these are and to analyze the data within those limitations. Refer to research design books in order to determine the best sampling method for your work.

Step 4: Conduct the Study

Plans must now be made for conducting the study. The research design selected will usually call for procedures on conducting the study and collecting the data. The plans for conducting the study should include logistical procedures such as time frames, dates, times, places, and people involved. The plans should also include arrangements for collecting the data and storing it. For example, if the study is a study on sponsorship recall, this type of research methodology calls for the survey/interview technique. Usually, a mall-intercept approach is used. The researcher stays in one area and approaches people wandering by to participate in the study. Researchers must obtain permission to conduct surveys from the site management, decide how many surveys and researchers will be needed at the study site, determine what materials will be needed, and decide what to do with the completed surveys.

Step 5: Analyze the Data

The fifth step is to analyze the data. In other words, ask the question "What does this information mean?" The purpose of data analysis is to interpret the information and draw some conclusions. Of course, the data analytical methods will have already been decided when the research method is chosen because the data must be collected in a specific way according to data-analysis methodologies.

Make use of fresh perspectives by asking for input on the data you collect from other people in the business.

Interpretation of the data can consist of running the data through statistical procedures. If the data collected are numerical, some simple statistics applied to the data may help. Ask others in the company to study the information and tell you what they see. Compare the information to other similar studies and look for similarities and differences. Another idea is to take the information to a research expert such as a sport marketing professor who conducts research, a sport marketing research company, or a general marketing research company.

Step 6: Determine How to Use the New Knowledge

The final step is to determine how you can apply the new knowledge to the business. The information may be used according to why you needed the information in the beginning. Why did you need the information? If you needed the information to understand why your indoor tennis club is losing consumers during June and July, the new information will help you decide what you need to do to retain consumers during these months. Let us say that the reason the club loses consumers in June and July is that they go to play tennis on outdoor courts so that they can be outside during the summer. What can you do? Your club has no outdoor courts. Can you afford to build outdoor courts? If not, is there another way to compete with the outdoor courts? In the next chapter, there are several examples of consumer research and how the information from the research can be used.

Chapter Summary

Research is a very important tool for the sport business. Every sport marketing person should know how to conduct research. The sport business needs information that is accurate, timely, interactive, and flexible in order to enhance success. Information and new knowledge come from research. This information is used in formulating decisions and strategies in the sport marketing elements.

Questions for Study

1. What is sport marketing research? Why is it important?
2. What are the purposes of sport marketing research?
3. List and describe some types of sport marketing research.
4. What are the sources of information? Give examples of each.
5. What are the primary areas of sport marketing research? Give examples of each.

Learning Activities

1. Interview people in a variety of sport businesses, organizations, or other enterprises in your city or community and ask them what kind of marketing research they conduct and why.
2. Identify at least 10 different places you could obtain existing information in your city or community. Go to the places and research the types of information available at these places. Create a notebook of these resources and save this material for the future.
3. With a group of other students, and with the supervision of your instructor, develop a research study to determine sponsorship recognition (see appendix F). Conduct the study during a local sports event. Analyze the results and present your analysis to the class.
4. See appendix F. With the supervision of your instructor, design a study using one of the examples of surveys, conduct the study, analyze the results, determine how the information can be used by the sport business, and share the results with the class and the business.

Chapter 6

Segmentation, Targeting, and Positioning in Sport Business

Overview

The world population reached 6 billion in 1999 (Population Reference Bureau, 2000). It will only take about 13 years for the next billion people to arrive. Yet, although the number of people is incredible, the world is growing smaller in many respects. In relation to communications, travel, movement, news, and culture, for instance, the world's peoples meet, exchange ideas, influence each other, and become changed forever. There are advantages and disadvantages to merging peoples and cultures. For instance, as one measure of diversity, there are about 6,000 languages spoken around the world today (National Geographic, 1999). Yet, as people and cultures merge, it is predicted that that number could drop to 3,000 by the year 2100. However, the fact remains, we live in an ever-growing multicultural society, but one that is merging, mixing, and changing.

Just when marketing gurus thought they had the mass marketing theories and models completed and working well, the world started changing. Today, with ever increasing numbers of populations and cultures in any given country, a marketing professional must constantly monitor the population, known in business language as *consumers*.

The United States is undergoing a transformation from a primarily mono-cultural society to a multicultural one. The total population of the United States is predicted to increase from 276 million in 2000 to 404 million in 2050 (Population Reference Bureau, 2000). During the 1980s, 1990s, and at the start of the new millennium, the country has been shifting from a society dominated and controlled by whites to a society characterized by several more groups, particularly Black, Asian, Hispanic, lesbian and gay, Jewish, disabled, and Native American. It is predicted that the white population will drop to 64% of the population by 2020. The Hispanic population is expected to realize the greatest growth from 10% to 15%, whereas the African-American population will grow from 12% to 14%, the Asian-American population will grow from 4% to 7%, and the lesbian and gay population will continue to be about 10% of all populations (U.S. Census Bureau 2000).

Because of these new emerging markets, businesses are using new marketing tactics such as relationship marketing, cause marketing, niche marketing, and e-marketing to communicate with them. *Relationship marketing* is the attempt to development a relationship with the consumer by trying to be more to the consumer than just a company from whom the consumer buys products. *Cause marketing* is the development of marketing tactics designed to recognize and support the cause of a group or organization. *Niche marketing* is targeting specific niches, or groups, that no other company targets. *E-marketing* is the attempt to reach a market through electronic media, specifically, the web. As groups proliferate and cultures emerge, marketing professionals will need to stay knowledgeable about the changes and continue to develop marketing strategies to ensure success.

New marketing strategies are emerging to keep pace with the changing demographics in the US.

Sport marketing professionals in the sport business industry are in the same boat. It is not an industry existing in a vacuum as though untouched by the outside world. As the point was made in chapter 1, the sport business industry is as multicultural as any population. Therefore, sport marketing professionals must continuously monitor growth and changes in consumers and develop sport marketing strategies to enhance success.

As the population and its many different groups proliferate, the importance of and need for segmentation, targeting, and positioning increase. Segmentation is the marketer's tool to make sense of these numerous and various groups of people in order to make changes in product, price, distribution, or promotion strategies. Targeting, positioning, and brand awareness management are ways to determine a specific consumer segment to attract.

Segmentation

Segmentation is the division of a whole into parts. Putting things in order helps arrange them so that we can make sense of them. It helps make order out of chaos. For example, products in a sporting goods retail store are arranged by categories: Tennis goods are found in the tennis department; soccer goods are found in the soccer department; boating equipment is found in the water sports department; and sports shoes are all found in the shoe department. The purposes for doing this are to make it easy for customers to find something, to make it easy for workers to stock the shelves, and to groups that are similar in a practical manner. This categorization is a method of segmentation—the division of a whole into relatively similar segments.

In sport business, the work of segmentation is done primarily in two broad areas: the industry and the consumer market. The industry is divided and grouped in a number of ways to make practical order of it. The consumer market is divided and grouped in a number of ways to study consumers, to reach them, and to meet their needs, wants, and desires. The division of a consumer market into relatively homogeneous segments is *sport consumer market segmentation.* The division of the sport industry into relatively homogeneous segments is *sport industry segmentation.*

Segmentation of the consumer market allows sport businesses to understand and target specific groups that share characteristics and behaviors.

Sport consumer market segmentation involves consumer analysis. Consumer analysis is the process of studying a total market or population and dividing the population into groups that have similar characteristics.

In Sport Business:

segmentation involves dividing and grouping consumers and the industry into relatively similar segments for varying purposes.

Sport Consumer Market Segmentation:

the division of total markets into relatively homogeneous segments.

Sport Industry Segmentation:

the division of the sport industry into relatively homogeneous segments.

Sport companies want to know and understand the people who purchase their products, and companies also want to learn about the people who do not purchase their products. These data help the sport marketing professional make decisions concerning the company's product, price, distribution, and promotional strategies. You will learn more about consumer segmentation in the section titled "Sport Consumer Market Segmentation."

Sport industry segmentation involves industry analysis (also called competitive analysis). Industry segmentation is the process of studying an industry to divide it into industry segments that have similar characteristics. The sport marketing professional uses this information to analyze the segments, analyze which segment the company is in, and develop decisions and strategies for the sport company based on the knowledge about the industry segments. You will learn more about industry segmentation in the section entitled *Sport Industry Segmentation.*

Sport Consumer Market Segmentation

The Importance of Market Segmentation

Until the 1960s, few companies practiced market segmentation. Most of the country, up until the 1960s, consisted of a fairly homogeneous population that could be described easily—historical patriarchal family structure of white heterosexual male, wife, three children, a dog and a cat; the man worked outside the home, the wife worked only at home as a housewife.

Segmentation:

is the first step toward understanding consumer groups, determining target markets, and informing marketing mix and positioning strategies.

Since that time, and especially today, the population is very different. Businesses must constantly monitor consumers to determine marketing mix strategies. Today's population is distinctively different in relation to race, ethnicity, or national origin as evidenced by consumer groups of Hispanic Americans, Asian Americans, Latin Americans, Irish Americans, and African Americans. The population also comprises numerous different groups of people with different characteristics such as age, gender, race, ethnicity, religion, disability, national origin, sexual orientation, household status, lifestyle characteristics, cultural factors, social factors, class, income, education, and attitudes. For instance, today we hear about groups called the baby boomers, the Silver Fox market, the Pink Market, Generation Y, yuppies, guppies, Generation X, the Lost Generation, and DINKS.

Segmentation is the first step toward understanding consumer groups, determining target markets, and informing marketing mix and positioning strategies. The determination of target markets is essential to the business. Target markets are those specific groups of consumers for whom the company produces its products and to whom the company tries to sell its products.

Purposes of Segmentation

The primary purpose of market segmentation is specialization. Using consumer market analysis and segmentation, the sport company can select one or more consumer market segments on which to concentrate and specialize in meeting the segment's needs. Products, prices, services, advertising, and other promotional methods are developed for specific consumer market segments and with the competition in mind.

> Industry analysis and segmentation can reveal how a company compares to the competition or determine if it can compete in a particular segment. This allows the company to concentrate its efforts on particular segments and thus use its resources most efficiently.

Take a look at the information in Table 6.1, and think about how just these few data are going to affect how we market a product to the world and the United States today, in 10 years, and in 20 years. Businesses must mon-

Table 6.1
Some Population Information (sources: Hodgkinson, 1992; *National Geographic*, 1999; The New Face, 1993).

- In 2010, four states (New York, California, Florida, and Texas) will have approximately one-third of the nation's youth. More than 50% of them will be "minority." This means that the new minority will be white.
- The population of the United States is aging rapidly. In 1992 there were 30 million people over the age of 65. In 2020 that number is expected to be 65 million. Most of them will have one year of retirement for every year of work.
- Children under the age of 18, who were 34% of the population in 1970, will be only 25% of the population is 2010.
- In 1990 the population of the United States was 76% Anglo, 12% Black, 9% Latino, and 3% Asian. It is estimated that by 2050, the population will be 52% Anglo, 16% Black, 22% Latino, and 10% Asian.
- There are more than 100 languages spoken in the school systems of New York City, Chicago, Los Angeles, and Fairfax County, Virginia.
- Ethnic minority shoppers, predominantly African Americans, Asians, and Hispanics, spent $600 billion in 1992. This is an increase of 18% since 1990. By the year 2010, minority populations may account for more than 30% of the economy.
- Over 32% of the Asian American households earn an income of $50,000 or more. That is contrasted with 29& of Caucasian households.
- Sixty-four percent of Asian American families are linked to the Internet, compared to 33% of all U.S. families.
- Africa's population will increase from 13% of the world's population in 2000 to 16% by 2025 and 20% by 2050.
- During the same time, Europe's population will decrease from 12% to 7% by 2050. Asia's population will decrease from 61% today to 58% by 2050.
- India's population reached 1 billion on May 11, 2000. One third of its population is under 15 years of age.
- USA ranks third largest in population in 2000 at 276 million and is expected to rank third in 2050 with a population of 404 million.

itor the many new, changing, or emerging population segments. More and more businesses are redesigning their products, prices, and promotional methods for the new markets. In pursuit of these markets, many companies are relying less on traditional forms of mass marketing and more on specialized media (cable-specific television, ethnic-centered magazines, and specific-topic magazines).

Companies in the sport industry are also paying attention. As pointed out in chapter 1, there are sports, events, sporting goods, and other sport products and types of sport management and marketing companies specifically designed for and offering products to the many different markets. Targeting specific populations is the future of marketing in sport business.

Targeting specific populations is the future of marketing in sport business.

As the years have gone by, businesses in the United States have changed. There are many more industries than ever before, and the new ones are different. The newest industries are high technology such as computers, electronics, cable TV, and space study. Some other new industries are in human services such as travel agencies, consulting, therapy, management services, and fitness consulting. All are consumer driven—developed to meet the needs of new consumer segments.

The sport industry has grown partially because most of the newest segments, which may be the fastest growing segments, are consumer driven. Take, for example, sporting goods and equipment. There are such a variety of people participating in sports activities that equipment is becoming more customized. Golf clubs come in a variety of sizes, weights, materials, colors, and lengths. Tennis rackets are also offered in a variety of sizes, weights, materials, and other factors. Clothing comes in a variety of sizes, styles, and colors. Sport shoes are offered in a variety of sizes, sport-specific styles, and materials. Camping equipment is varied based on consumer preferences, geography, and types of camping. There is a booming variety of water-sports goods and equipment: The air-jet engine is revolutionizing the boat industry; for powerboat enthusiasts, there is a constant new variety of water toys such as the knee board; the ski seat; the skurfer; single, double, and triple-person tubes; the ski board; and barefoot skiing equipment. It is apparent that the new equipment is popular because any Saturday on any lake reveals that people using these new toys outnumber traditional water skiers by four to one.

The sport industry is growing to meet new consumer needs and to provide new support and services.

Sports and other activities, sport organizations, and sport businesses developed and designed by and for specific consumer segments are a fast-growing area of the sport industry. As pointed out in chapter 1, many populations in the United States are very busy developing sport organizations, businesses, clubs, leagues, Olympics, and facilities specifically for their population.

Another growing area in the sport business industry includes those sport businesses whose products are service and support. Some of those services include such products as consulting, management, legal work, financial management, research, and marketing services. Here are some examples. If you are a professional athlete and you desire legal and financial help, there are individuals and companies that provide them. If your sport business wants research on why sales of its product are decreasing, there are companies that will do this work. If your business wants to know if it should put a newly designed hockey stick on the market, there are companies that will study this for you. If your company wants to find a sponsor for a beach volleyball event, there are companies that specialize in sport sponsorship management. They will not only find a sponsor, but they also will negotiate the contract and manage the entire process.

Important Market Segmentation Criteria

Sport marketing professionals use segmentation for several reasons. Segmentation helps identify groups of consumers with similar characteristics and purchase behaviors. Segmentation provides the sport marketing professional with valuable information that guides marketing mix decisions and strategies specifically customized for the consumer group. Segments can be of any size and mix of characteristics. To be useful, however, segmentation methods should produce segments that meet certain criteria. The most useful criteria include identifiability, substantiality, accessibility, and responsiveness (see Table 6.2).

Table 6.2 **Important segmentation criteria.**
Identifiability: segments must be identifiable and measurable.
Substantiality: segments must be of a size large enough to justify marketing mix attention.
Accessibility: segments must be reachable with the customized marketing mix.
Responsiveness: segments must respond to a marketing mix customized to that segment.

Identifiability

Segments must be identifiable and measurable. For instance, it is fairly easy to identify segments using different ages in a high school population. However, the segment must also be measurable in its response to a marketing mix. That is, the group and number of high school 15 to 18-year-olds are identifiable and measurable. Say we want to know how many will attend all the high school's football games. We must find a way to measure that segment so that it is both identified and measured. Otherwise, we will have trouble determining if that segment is worth developing a marketing mix for.

Further, each market segment should be homogeneous within. That is, those within a segment should be as similar as possible. Segments should be heterogeneous between groups. That is, a segment should be distinguishably different from all others. These guidelines help the marketer determine like and different characteristics within and between segments.

Substantiality

Segments must be large enough to justify marketing mix customization and attention. Otherwise, the time and money spent on the marketing mix may never realize a return on investment or a profit. On the other hand, a population can be segmented using so many variables that each segment contains only one individual. The sport marketing professional must determine if and when the segment is large enough to justify customizing a marketing mix.

Accessibility

Segments must be reachable with the customized marketing mix. Some segments are easy to reach, and others are hard to reach. For instance, hard-core baseball fans are easy to reach because they watch a lot of baseball. Therefore, we know where to find them and how to market to them. On the other hand, full-time RVers are hard to reach because they do not live at permanent addresses. An RVer is a person who has purchased an RV, or recreational vehicle, also known as a camper trailer. A full-time RVer is a person (or a couple) who has sold everything in order to live full time in the RV. These people are constantly traveling, camping at RV parks, and enjoying life as RVers.

Responsiveness

Segments must respond to a marketing mix customized to it. Otherwise, there's no use having the customized marketing mix. If the segment does not respond to the customized product, price, distribution, or promotion efforts, maybe that segment need not be considered as a separate segment anymore.

Bases for Segmentation

Sport marketing professionals use bases or variables to divide a total market into segments. These are characteristics that are divided into several categories. The choice of bases is crucial because an inappropriate group of bases will not be successful in relation to response to marketing mix. The key is to identify bases that produce a right mix of identifiability, measurability, substantiality, accessibility, and responsiveness in that segment.

> The object of market segmentation is to develop useful data about a particular group. Segmentation using one base selects members from a group that share a particular characteristic, while multiple base segmentation selects for a variety of characteristics. The latter method is increasingly popular as the culture becomes more multi-faceted.

Markets can be segmented using one or more bases. For example, a segment can be created using just gender. WNBA season-ticket holders can be segmented by gender. Markets can be segmented using multiple bases. For example, the WNBA ticket holders can be segmented into groups by gender, age, income, race, household status, zip code, favorite color, favorite movie, and so forth. The disadvantage of using multiple-base segmentation for this market is that it will create too many segments that are small in number and will probably not be of a substantial size to justify a customized marketing mix for each group. However, today's trend is toward the use of more bases rather than fewer because of the multicultural, multifaceted population: More segments want their differences recognized. As mentioned earlier in this chapter, this trend has led to the development and increased use of relationship, cause, and niche marketing tactics. After all, these marketing strategies meet the most basic of marketing fundamentals—give the customers what they want.

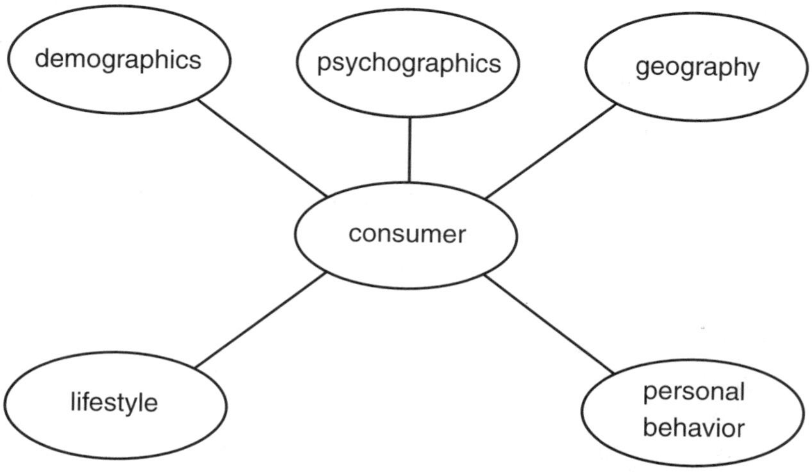

Figure 6.1
Bases for segmentation.

In the sport industry, companies commonly use one or more of the following five bases to segment markets: demographics, psychographics, geography, purchase behavior, and product use and benefits sought (see Figure 6.1). Within each base are several individual characteristics or variables that must be considered. A more detailed description of these bases follows.

Demographic Segmentation

Demographics are those data about a person that might be called hard-core data. That is, it is information that is not necessarily changeable such as age, education level, and income. Table 6.3 illustrates some of the many demographic variables. Demographic segmentation is used commonly in sport business. As you can see in Table 6.3, demographic information includes basic information about a person that can present a partial picture of the personality and characteristics of that person. Using a few examples from sport marketing research, Tables 6.4 and 6.5 show the demographics of the people who participated in those studies. Note that each example shows some of the commonly used demographical data such as gender, age, ethnicity, sexual orientation, income, and education. By analyzing these data, the sport marketing professional can describe the consumers in these studies and use this information to help with decision making in marketing strategies. Discussion of some of the primary demographic segments is presented here.

Age

Two things are happening in the sport business industry in relation to age segmentation. First, increasingly, current businesses in the sport industry are recognizing a

Table 6.3
Some demographics and typical breakdowns.

Typical Demographics	Some Typical Breakdowns
Age	under 12; adolescent; teen; 18–24; 25–29; 30–34; 35–39; 40–44; 45–49; 50–54; 55–59; 60–64; 65+; 18–24; 25–39; 40–54; 55–69
Gender	female; male
Household status	single; married/partner; divorced
Income: individual or household	under $10,000; $10,000–20,000; $20,000–30,000. $30,000–40,000; $40,000–50,000; $50,000–60,000; $60,000–75,000; $75,000–100,000
Occupation	clerical; sales; craftsman; technical; manager; professional; official; teacher
Education	grade school; some high school; high school; some college; college; graduate work; doctoral
Race	White, Black, Asian, Hispanic
Nationality	American, French, German
Social class	lower-lower; upper-lower; lower-middle; middle; upper-middle; lower-upper; upper; super-rich
Religion	Catholic, Jewish, Protestant, other

Table 6.4
Example of demographics from a study (Zhang, Pease, Hui and Michand, 1995).

Variables	Category	N	%	Cumulative %
Household income	above $200,000	59	6.9	100.0
	$150,000–199,000	37	4.3	93.1
	$100,000–149,000	101	11.7	88.8
	$80,000–99,000	131	15.2	77.1
	$60,000–79,000	151	17.5	61.9
	$40,000–59,000	168	19.5	44.4
	$20,000–39,000	147	17.1	24.9
	below $20,000	67	7.8	7.8
Gender	Male	533	61.9	100.0
	Female	328	37.1	37.1
Ethnicity	Caucasian	617	71.7	100.0
	Hispanic	103	12.0	28.3
	African American	62	7.2	16.3
	Asian	23	2.7	9.1
	Others	46	6.4	6.4
Marital Status	Married	460	53.5	100.0
	Single	291	33.8	46.5
	Divorced	46	5.3	12.7
	Widowed	14	1.6	7.4
	Others	50	5.8	5.8
Education	College Graduate	270	31.4	100.0
	High School Graduate	189	22.0	68.7
	Advanced Degree	129	15.0	46.7
	School Student	114	13.2	31.7
	College Student	73	8.5	18.5
	Others	86	10.0	10.0
Occupation	Professional	207	24.0	100.0
	Management	141	16.4	76.0
	Sales	75	8.7	59.6
	Technical	59	6.9	50.9
	Education	59	6.9	44.0
	Skilled Worker	39	4.5	37.1

Descriptive Statistics for the Demographic Variables (N = 861)

greater variety of age segments as serious consumers of a variety of products in the industry. Second, new companies and organizations have been started whose sole focus and product is age-specific segmentation.

In the first instance, numerous existing sport businesses and organizations that offer sports activities and other sport-related products are recognizing more age-groups as consumers and offering an increasing variety of products for those markets. The age-groups range from the very young to the very old. Soccer organizations are offering leagues for age segments that range from the under-5-years-old division to the age 50-plus division. In tennis, some tournaments offer age divisions such as the women's 60, 70, and 80 national clay court championships (United States Tennis Association, 1999). Swimming and track-and-field are two sports in which age, used as age-group divisions or leagues, is offered as an age-related product. More recently, however, those age-groups now include higher age brackets and are typically called the master's divisions. More sports organizations and businesses are doing the same.

Table 6.5
Example of demographics from a study (Pitts, 1998).

Variables	Category	N	%
Gender	Female	104	57.1%
	Male	77	42.3%
	Transgender	1	.5%
Age	25–34	96	52.7%
	35–44	55	30.2%
	45–54	19	10.4%
	55–plus	3	1.6%
	18–24	8	4.4%
	under 18	1	.5%
Sexual orientation	lesbian/gay	167	91.8%
	heterosexual	11	6.0%
	bisexual	4	2.2%
Citizenship	United States	148	81.3%
	other	34	18.7%
Income level	$31,000–$45,000	50	27.5%
	$21,000–$30,000	43	23.6%
	under $20,000	40	22.0%
	$46,000–$60,000	21	11.5%
	$61,000–$75,000	11	6.0%
	$100,000 plus	11	6.0%
	$76,000–$100,000	6	3.3%
Education level	undergraduate degree	87	47.8%
	graduate degree	44	24.2%
	high school diploma	33	18.1%
	terminal degree	18	9.9%
Gay Games involvement	athlete	87	47.8%
	spectator	81	44.5%
	worker	9	5.0%
	other	5	2.7%

Study Participant Demographics Data (each set listed in descending order).

In the second instance, more recently, a number of sports businesses and organizations have begun whose sole focus and products are age-groups, primarily for the upper ages. For instance, annually, there is a senior's softball national championship with age divisions of 50–54, 55–59, 60–64, 65–69, and 70-plus. The PGA offers the Senior Tour, and more recently announced was the Women's Senior Golf Tour by The Jane Blalock Co. of Boston (Broughton, 2001).

Gender

In the past, most spectator sports were a few men's professional sports whose owners and marketers promoted to the male market. Today, however, with an incredible 235 hours of sports programming in a 24-hour period on 48 sports television channels, and with more sports and other fitness and recreational activities televised or offered otherwise at an entertainment event, the sports spectator market has grown exponentially (ABC News, 2000). The sports spectators are no longer only males.

In addition, it's not just a few men's sports that we see on television anymore. The number of women's sports and mixed-gender sports, some of which are setting records for spectatorship, is increasing. For instance, Table 6.6 provides several notes of numbers of spectatorship for women's sports in 1999.

In sports offered as a participant product, it is also a gender-bending period. Women's participation in sports, fitness and recreational activities is at an all-time high and shows no signs of slowing. Table 6.7 presents some facts about women's participation in sports.

Table 6.6
Women's Sports Spectatorship

- In 1998, the Women's Tennis Association Tour set an on-site attendance record, topping 3.6 million
- ESPN scored a 4.3 rating (3.24 million households) for its coverage of the 1999 NCAA Women's National Basketball championship
- ABC Sports estimates that 40 million viewers watched the Women's World Cup final, eclipsing all previous records for television viewership of a soccer game in the U.S. It drew more than double the 6.9 rating of the 1998 Men's World Cup.
- The NBA took 29 seasons to average 10,000 fans per game; the WNBA did that in two.
- An all-time high of more than 7 million fans attended college women's basketball games in 1997–98. That was the 17th consecutive year of increased attendance.
- HBO Sports increased its ration of women's to men's 1999 Wimbledon coverage to 60-40 to satisfy a viewer demand for women's matches. The tournament ratings increased 18% to 1.9 from a 1.6 in 1997.
- More than 650,000 tickets were sold to the 1999 Women's World Cup tournament. The final match drew a women's sports record of 90,185 to the Rose Bowl stadium.

Table 6.7
Women's Participation (Women's Sports Foundation, 1999).

- Over 43 million women play sports each year
- Over 11 million women age 18–34 play sports 2+ times each week
- More women—20.4 million—are frequent exercisers than men; 15.5 million
- 80% of women identified as key leaders in Fortune 500 companies participated in sports during their childhood
- The number of women who golf in the U.S. has increased 5.7 million; 40% of beginning golfers are women
- During the 1990s, the number of girls who played on high school teams increased by 31%
- The number of women of college teams increased 38% in the 1990s

Table 6.8
Women's Consumerism and Commercial Value in the Sport Industry (Women's Sports Foundations, 1999).

- More than 50% of the time, women make the decision to purchase sports products
- Women make up 70% of all purchases of NFL licensed merchandise
- In the $14.3 billion dollar athletic footwear market, the women's segment makes up 41% ($6.09 billion), the men's 45% ($6.68 billion) and the children's 12% ($1.71 billion)
- Corporate sponsorship of women's sports has more than doubled from $285 million in 1992 to $600 million in 1997
- The 11 sponsors of the 1999 Women's World Cup paid $44 million for sponsorship
- 85% of females and 47% of males feel it is very important for corporations to sponsor and support women's sports
- 59% of females and 27% of males feel better about purchasing products or services from a company that sponsored/supported women's sports.

The women's market is being felt across the sport industry in a number of ways. For example, Table 6.8 illustrates several instances. As girls and women have become serious participants, athletes, spectators, managers, owners, manufacturers, and consumers in a variety of ways in the sport industry, their consumerism and commercial value have risen dramatically.

Disability

Disability, or handicap, no longer restricts an individual's access to, or participation in, sports, fitness, recreation, or leisure activities or in sport business. The Paralympics, World Games for the Deaf, U.S. National Wheelchair Games, National Wheelchair Basketball Association Championships, and Special Olympics are some of the events that have been leaders in paving the way for the full participation in sport and sport business of people with disabilities. In addition, the Americans with Disabilities Act has helped open the door for many more opportunities in the sport industry for people with disabilities.

In today's changing industry, specialized sporting equipment has been the norm.

Photo reprinted by permission of WVU Photography.

Disability sport is defined as "sport that has been designed for or specifically practiced by athletes with disabilities" (DePauw and Gavron, 1995, p. 6). These sports competitions are not as new as many of us think. For example, the First International Silent Games was held in 1924. The First U.S. National Wheelchair Games were held in 1957. The First International Games for Disabled were held in 1960. Many well-known marathons such as the Boston Marathon have wheelchair divisions, the first of which was established in the 1970s.

Many sports, fitness, recreational, and leisure activities today are modified in relation to rules and equipment to an individual or group according to disability. For example, for people with vision impairments to play softball, there is a softball with a chime inside so that the players can utilize their sense of hearing to compensate. In track, people with vision impairments use their hands to follow a string around the course or track. In water skiing, people with leg impairments have water skis modified so that the skier can sit on the skis. These are just a few of the numerous adjustments made to activities and equipment so that people with disabilities can participate.

Race and Ethnicity

Some groups in the United States can have a single characteristic that places them in one market—race or ethnicity. People who are of Hispanic origin might all be categorized into the Hispanic market segment. People who are Asian might all be categorized into the Asian market segment. These segments, and a few others, are increasing as a proportion of the population in the United States while the proportion of whites is declining. These segments are also increasingly exercising their consumer and com-

Table 6.9
Strategies for sport marketers about the Black sports consumer market (Armstrong, 1998).

Key Findings about Black Consumers	Strategies for Sport Marketers
1. The Black consumer market is a challenging segment with many cultural nuances that influence their thoughts and behaviors.	Involve individuals with expertise in the Black consumer market in the designing of marketing strategies.
2. Black consumers have unique media consumption patterns.	Use Black media outlets (particularly Black radio) to promote events.
3. Blacks respond more favorably to culturally based approaches of marketing communications.	Advertisements and promotional messages should contain a theme and content that offer a reference point for Black audiences.
4. Blacks often seek a means of identifying with organizations as they decide whether or not to support their business.	Engage in activities that allow Blacks to find a self-reference link to identify with the organization.
5. Black consumers often have an allegiance to patronize Black businesses.	Conduct business with Black vendors to provide organizational needs, and involve them as corporate sponsors.
6. Black consumers often seek a cultural experience in their leisure activities.	Amend the product/service with extensions that are culturally salient to Black consumers.
7. Black consumers are socially conscious individuals.	Demonstrate a respect for the Black community through socially responsible/cause-related marketing.
8. Black consumers may have personal and structural difficulty accessing the existing channels of distribution.	Distribute tickets through outlets that are easily accessible to Black consumers. Also, find creative ways of exposing the product to the Black communities.
9. Sport behaviors are often a result of socialization occurring during childhood.	Invest in programs to include Black youth to nurture their involvement.
10. Just as any other community, the Black community also has opinion leaders.	Form a support group of Black constituents from various realms of the community to serve as staff multipliers.

mercial value as sport businesses target them and as they create their own sport businesses and organizations to serve their sporting demands.

Articles appearing in the *Sport Marketing Quarterly* offer good advice concerning marketing to the African American and Hispanic American sports markets. Tables 6.9 and 6.10 illustrate the points from those articles. Sport businesses wanting to target these segments

Table 6.10
Strategies for sport marketers about the Hispanic sports consumer market (McCarthy, 1998).

1. The Hispanic market is a rapidly growing market.
2. The Hispanic population is young.
3. Hispanics tend to locate in urban areas.
4. The market is financially stable.
5. Advertising in the Spanish language is more effective than advertising in the English language.
6. Hispanic culture provides a basis for successful marketing strategies.
7. Community marketing strategies are effective means of penetrating the market.
8. Using cultural icons of the Hispanic community is an effective means of marketing.
9. Successful spokespersons tend to be "average-looking" Hispanic people.

would use this information to develop marketing mix strategies. With these segments, it would also be wise marketing to use cause-and-relationship marketing strategies.

Sexual Orientation

The lesbian and gay population comprises approximately 10% of the population, or 27.5 million. It is estimated that almost half, or 11–13 million, people who are gay or lesbian participate in sports, recreation, leisure, and fitness activities and that this market spends an estimated minimum average of $2,000 each per year, or a total estimated $22 billion in the sport industry (Pitts, 1997, 1999a; Simmons Market Research Bureau, 1996). Of course, those numbers might be higher or lower if more accurate research were conducted.

Table 6.11
Strategies to Reach the Gay and Lesbian Sports Market (Source: Pitts, 1999b).

1. Your company must become a "gay friendly/lesbian friendly" company. This will gain the attention and establish the trust of the lesbian and gay market.
2. Become a member of the IGTA (International Gay Travel Association) and be sure the IGTA logo is displayed in your ads.
3. Develop a strategy specific to the lesbian and gay population.
4. Use market-specific advertising, imagery, and direct marketing copy.
5. Select appropriate media.
6. Stay informed about the dynamic gay and lesbian market in general, and the gay sports industries and market specifically.
7. Form partnerships with local, national, and international lesbian/gay sports organizations and governing bodies.
8. Support gay/lesbian rights organizations and causes.
9. Be sure your company offers equal employment benefits for your lesbian and gay employers.
10. Sponsor lesbian/gay sports events.

Similar to race or ethnic segments, the lesbian and gay sport market also have organized and started their own sport businesses. It is estimated that there are approximately between 3,000 and 15,000 sports events each year organized by, and targeted primarily to, the gay and lesbian market.

Like other groups, the lesbian and gay sport segment has its own Olympics-like event—the Gay Games, held every 4 years. The Gay Games is an incredible success, having grown at a rate of 275% since the first held in 1982 (Pitts 1999b). Table 1.14 in chapter 1 presents some interesting facts about the Gay Games.

After identifying this market, the sport business should then develop marketing mix strategies customized for it. Further, it would be a good idea to develop relationship and cause marketing strategies similar to those suggested for race and ethnic segments. Table 6.11 presents a list of 10 strategies that a company might consider.

Income

Income is divided into two categories: disposable income and discretionary income. *Disposable* income is all money, after taxes, at your disposal. *Discretionary* income is all money, after necessities, to be used at your discretion. Of course, it is discretionary income that sport marketing professionals study. The national average expenditure on recreational activity is now about 8% (Kelly and Warnick, 1999). Therefore, if a per-

PERSONAL INCOME:

DISPOSABLE INCOME—
money, after taxes, at your disposal

DISCRETIONARY INCOME—
money, after necessities, to be used at your discretion

Table 6.12
Average price paid at specialty stores (Snow Sports Industries America).

Equipment	Snowboard	Alpine
Skis	—	$310
Boots	$157	$239
Bindings	$123	$141
Poles	—	$35
Snowboard	$260	—
Parkas	$122	$165
Pants	$83	$83

son's discretionary income is $30,000, then the average amount of actual dollars spent for recreational and leisure activity is about $2,400. As the amount of income increases, so does the amount spent on recreational activity: An income of $50,000 yields about $4,000; an income of $75,000 yields about $6,000; and an income of $100,000 yields about $8,000.

Income has long been a demographic used readily in the sport industry. For instance, to which income segment do sports such as polo, sailing, yachting, scuba, snow skiing, and golf seem to be targeted? Although more income groups can afford golf today, there are still many golf clubs to which only the wealthy can belong. Figure 6.2 illustrates the income demographics of snowboarders and skiers. As you can see, the largest segments are those whose household incomes are in the $50,000 to 74,000 and $75,000-and-over categories. Table 6.12 illustrates how much money is spent on snowboard and ski equipment. As you can see, these are not inexpensive sports.

Table 6.13 illustrates how consumer market information is used to determine which subsegments within a market primarily constitute the segment. In this example, we can see that the segment

Table 6.13
The snowboard consumer market breakdown (Snow Sports Industries America).

	Kids (Ages 7–11)	The Core (Men 14–24)	The Employed (24 or older)	Women (All ages)	Beginners (all ages)
Growth Trendline	Modest	Substantial	Substantial	Modest	Moderate
Percent of Snowboard Population*	17%	56%	30%	24%	45%
Buying power	$3.47 million *(30% more than in skiing)*	$9.5 million *(200% more than in skiing)*	$6.6 million	unknown	unknown *(but believed to be significant)*

*Some overlap doesn't add up to 100 percent.

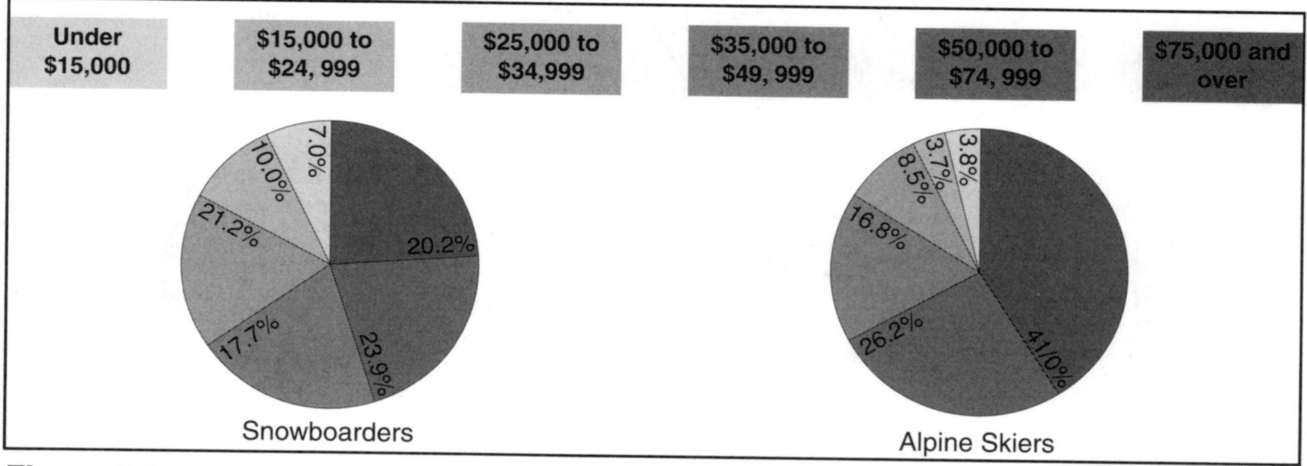

Figure 6.2
Household income of snowboarders and skiers (Snow Sports Industries of America).

labeled "The Core" is the largest segment—56%—of all snowboarders and that it accounts for $9.5 million in buying power whereas "Beginners" are close at 45%. A sport marketing professional working in the snow-sports industry segment would use this information to make decisions on product, pricing, and promotion and in establishing competitive strategies.

> Sport marketing research reveals interesting information about people's lifestyles, life cycles, or life courses that can be used to determine markets and develop market strategies.

Lifestyle, Life Cycle, and Life Course

Earlier in this chapter we mentioned different lifestyle segments identified in the U.S. population, such as the baby boomers. For each identifiable segment, there are specific demographic and psychographic information concerning life course variables such as household characteristics concerning marriage or domestic partnership, divorce, and children.

Other marketing information presents life-cycle information as actual cycles as though moving from point A to point B. For example, Figures 6.3 and 6.4 illustrate some of the possible life situations in one's life cycle.

Sport marketing professionals should monitor such demographics pertaining to their existing markets and potential markets. In today's world, it is a mistake to assume that everyone's life cycle follows the old traditional route of young-single, married, married-with-children, and retired. For instance, in establishing membership categories,

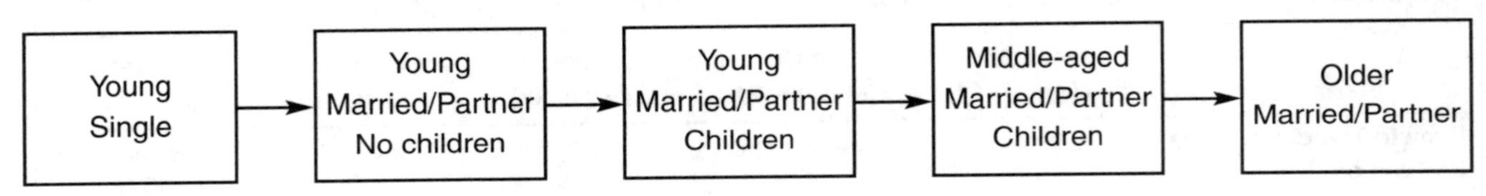

Figure 6.3
Some other possible life situations during a life cycle.

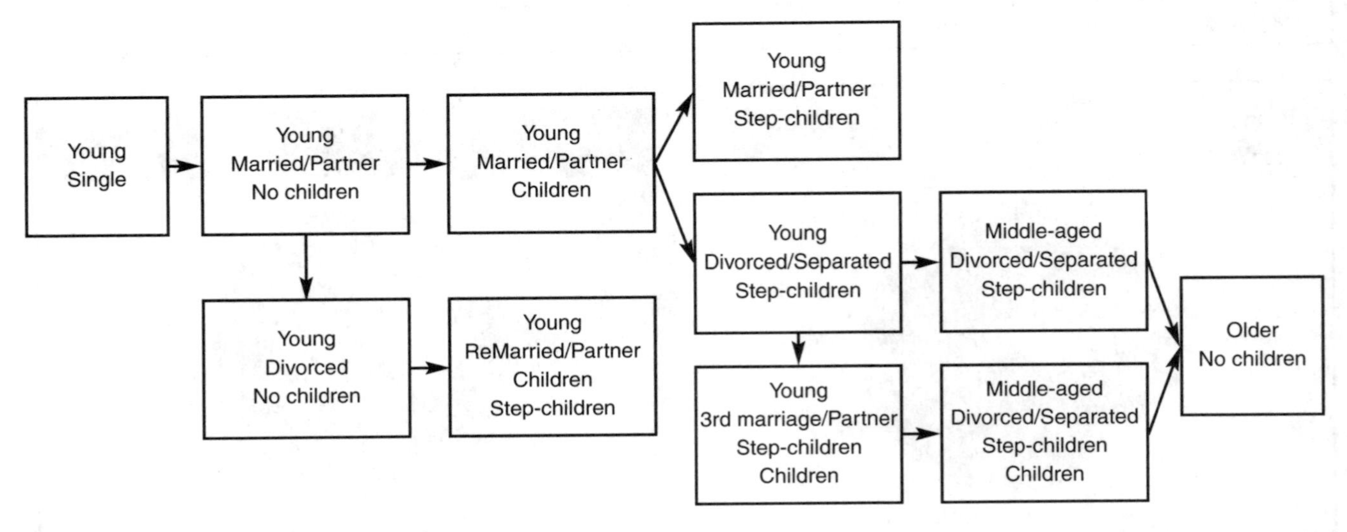

Figure 6.3
A few of many possible life situations during a life cycle.

most fitness center and sports club businesses are moving away from the old traditional categories of "single" and "family" to more contemporary categories of "individual" and "household." In those businesses that might continue to use "family" designations, for instance, the definition is contemporary, and the member is given full control to define the family group. For example, the traditional definition of "family" was "married man, wife, and children." Today's definition includes several variations in order to be inclusive and more accurately reflect today's family groups.

Psychographic Segmentation

Demographic information is a good start in describing and developing segmentation strategies, but demographics don't paint the full picture. Personality characteristics, favorite color, motivation factors, desires, attitude, and beliefs are some of the many other types of information that describe and define a person. These are called psychographics. Partially deriving from the word *psychological*, psychographic information is psychologically related characteristics about a person. Table 6.14 presents a list of several psychographic variables. Note that many of these kinds of information are psychological and preference based such as favorite color, favorite drink, prestige, happiness, and beliefs. Thus, they are subject to change as circumstances and situations in a person's life changes. For example, the way a people spend leisure time can change when they become a parent. At the most basic level of psychographic information are basic human needs, wants, and desires. As Maslow's hierarchy of needs shows, in Table 6.15 , people are driven by particular needs at certain times (Maslow, 1954). The most basic human needs are physiological—the needs for food, water, sleep, and shelter. These needs must be satisfied first because they are necessary for survival. Recent sports drink advertising, for example, attempts to appeal to the need to survive and thrive while participating in sports events.

Table 6.14
Some psychological factors used in segmentation (Walthorn, 1979; Liebert & Splegler. 1978; Kelly & Warnick, 1999).

Personality: values, beliefs, habits
Physiological: food, drink, sleep, shelter
Psychological: affiliation, beauty, belonging, curiosity, esteem, independence, love, motive
Lifestyle: household style, parent style, importance of life comfort, culture, financial resources, occupation and education, community
Desire for: acceptance, achievement, comfort, fame, happiness, identification, prestige
Freedom from: anxiety, depression, discomfort, fear, harm, pain, sadness

Table 6.15
Maslow's Hierarchy of Needs (1954).

Self-actualization Needs self-fulfillment, self-expression
Esteem Needs self-esteem, self-respect, recognition
Social Needs love, appreciation, fun, belonging
Safety Needs security, freedom from pain
Physiological Needs food, water, shelter

Safety needs are second and include the need for security and protection and freedom from fear, pain, discomfort, ridicule, and harm. Sport marketing professionals often attempt to exploit the human's fear for safety and freedom from pain, for instance, by attempting to show, in ads, potential harming effects if certain actions are not taken. For example, an ad showing bones of extreme osteoporosis in someone who has not been active versus the healthy bones of someone who is active is an attempt to play on fear.

The human's social needs are commonly exploited in advertising. These include such needs and desires as love, acceptance, achievement, prestige, recognition, respect, satisfaction, appreciation, happiness, identification, sensual experiences, and status. Many sport marketers use these in a variety of ways to reach consumers. These can be seen in, for example, such advertisements as promotions for encouraging tailgating activities at sporting events such as football games, car races, and boat races. The ad for a softball bat that tells readers that the bat will make them the envy of the team and will give them more home runs is attempting to appeal to the need and desire for prestige and status, in the first instance, and achievement and satisfaction, in the second instance.

Esteem needs are those that include self-esteem and external esteem, or respect from one's group. These needs include self-respect and a sense of accomplishment, for instance.

The highest human need is self-actualization, which involves reaching a point in life where the person believes he or she should be. This includes self-development, self-fulfillment, self-expression, self-identification, and self-realization. To reach this need, the marketer attempts to speak directly to the individual about her or himself. Typically, in these ads you will find such phrases as "you've reached that point in life where you've accomplished everything you wanted" or "you've made it; now you can sit back and enjoy the good life." These tend to be directed more often at the mature markets.

Typically, psychographic information is categorized in three areas: personality, motives, and lifestyle. Personality characteristics are those traits, attitudes, and behaviors that make us "who we are." Many sport products are marketed on the basis of personality segments. In one area of the sport industry in which sporting events are marketed to spectators as consumers, this is most noticeable. The NFL markets primarily to certain male segments based on personality characteristics. Typically, those commercials show male groups with distinct personality characteristics such as the "serious couch potato fan," or "the crazy painted in-the-stands fan." The WNBA markets primarily to certain female personality segments. With slogans such as "We got next," the WNBA is attempting to reach those girls and women whose attitude toward male basketball players and fans is, Okay. You've had your time. Move over, now. It's our turn.

Motives are those needs or desires that give humans a need for action, or motivation. Fitness center advertising usually always centers on motivation. In those ads are slogans and phrases such as "Summer's coming—can you fit into your bikini?" or "Body check—how do you look in the mirror naked?" These phrases are meant to motivate the human into wanting to get into great shape.

In a study to look at motivations of sports participants and sports spectators, Milne and McDonald (1999) categorized motivation variables and Maslow's hierarchy of needs. Table 6.16 presents those motivational factors along with a brief description of each. In studying these, it is easy to see how a sport marketer could use them to segment consumers and to develop successful promotional campaigns in a number of sport industry businesses. For instance, people who exercise at a fitness center might be categorized in a "physical fitness" segment. This would be used as part of the message, slogans, or tag lines in advertising for fitness centers. In another example, those

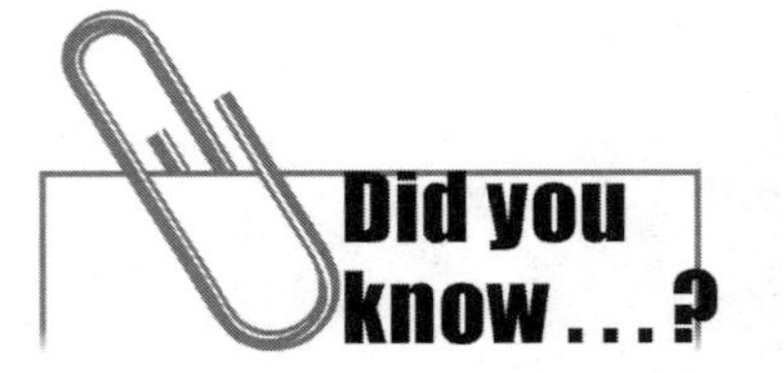

Kids under 18 were asked what they preferred over the Internet for fun. Their answers:

Playing sports (90%)

Watching movies (79%)

Spending time with friends (55%)

Talking on the phone (26%)

Watching television (8%)

Reading (2%)

Source: Jupiter Communications *1997 Online Kids Report*

Table 6.16
Sport Participation Motivation Factors (Source: Milne & McDonald, 1999)

Physical Fitness—desire to being in good physical condition and improving health
Risk Taking—desire to participate in risky, thrilling, and extreme activities
Stress Reduction—desire to reduce anxiety, apprehension, fear, and tension
Aggression—desire to inflict aversive stimulus on another person, either in an attempt to reduce or increase aggressive levels
Affiliation—desire to be connected to associated with something; confirms sense of identity
Social Facilitation—desire to be with others who enjoy the same activity
Self-Esteem—desire to enhance one's positive regard of self
Competition—desire to enter into a rivalry, or contest with another, usually as a test of skill
Achievement—desire to accomplish a specific goal
Skill Mastery—desire to positively enhance performance
Aesthetics—desire to be near or part of the beauty, grace, artistry, and creative expression of sport
Value Development—desire to develop values such as loyalty and honesty through sport
Self Actualization—desire to fulfill potential

who participate in an eco-challenge competition might be categorized into the "achievement" segment. This need to achieve would then be used by the sport marketer in promotions to enter and participate in the event.

Lifestyle, life-cycle, and life-course factors are those characteristics concerning life situations. Although also used as a demographic, and described earlier in this chapter, lifestyle characteristics can be viewed as preferences and, as such, can be considered beliefs and attitudes.

Table 6.17
VALS 2 Psychographic Segments.

Actualizers—people who are successful, sophisticated, active, leader-oriented, have high self-esteem and abundant resources, growth-oriented; seek to develop, explore, and express; and have a cultivated taste for the finer things in life.
Fulfillers—people who are mature, satisfied, reflective, comfortable, value order, knowledge, and responsibility; are well-educated, well-informed, professionally employed; tend to be conservative, are practical consumers, concerned about value, quality, and durability.
Believers—people who are conservative, conventional, traditional about family, church, community, and country; conservative and predictable consumers.
Achievers—people who are success-oriented in work and play, value control, live conventional lives, conservative, respect authority; favor established goods that demonstrate success.
Strivers—people who are self-defined, seek motivation and approval from the world around them, easily bored, impulsive, believe money means success, emulate those who have more possessions.
Experiencers—people who are young, vital, impulsive, enthusiastic, seek excitement and variety; dislike authority and conformity; avid consumers especially on clothing, fast food, movies, music, and videos.
Makers—people who are practical, down-to-earth, value self-sufficiency, traditional in family, work, and play.
Strugglers—people who are poor, ill educated, low skilled, lack social bonds, live for the moment, immediate satisfaction and gratification; are cautious consumers.

Psychographic segmentation can include individual variables or can be combined with other variables in order to more accurately describe market segments. One such system, offered by Stanford Research International, is called VALS—Values and Lifestyles program (VALS 2, 1990). This system categorizes consumers by their values, beliefs, and lifestyles. Table 6.17 presents the segments as developed by VALS. When this system is studied, it's easy to see how many different consumer groups in the sport industry can be segmented into these categories. For instance, those who participate in risky sports such as skydiving might be segmented into the "Experiencers" segment. Those who participate in polo might be categorized into the "Actualizers" segment. Then, using this kind of psychographic information, the sport marketer can develop promotional and advertising campaigns that have a higher chance of success.

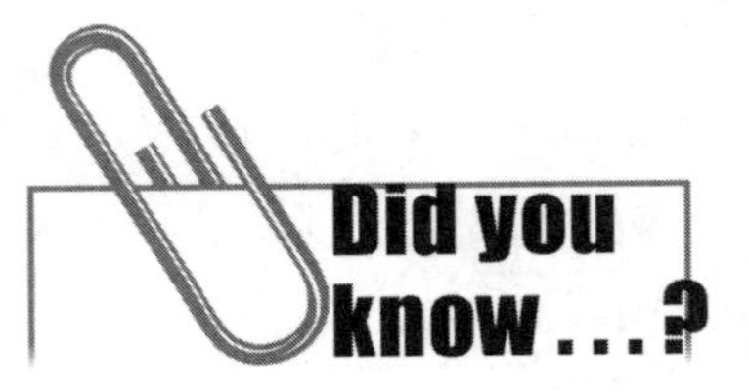

The top five participatory sports (played at least one time in the past year):

Bowling (52.2 million)
Freshwater fishing (45.9 million)
Basketball (45.6 million)
Billiards/Pool (44.5 million)
Free weights (42.8 million)

Source: American Sports Data, Inc.

Geographic and Geodemographic Segmentation

Geographic segmentation involves dividing or describing a population according to geographic regions or areas. Geodemographic segmentation involves using demographics, psychographics, and lifestyle information to segment a geographic region.

The United States can be segmented according to purely geographic lines. The simplest division is North, South, East, and West. Beyond that, however, geodemographic segments can be developed. For instance, there are segments with such labels as Westerner, Texan, New Yorker, Midwesterner, Yankee, Snowbird, and Southerner. Truthful or not, descriptions of people who live in these areas have been developed.

In sport business, there are sports that must take place in northern climates and sports that are better suited for southern climates. Snow skiing and water skiing are examples. This also means that a company whose products are either snow skis and equipment or water skis and equipment will want to distribute them primarily to those regions closest to where those sports take place—hence, geographic-segment marketing decisions.

Combining demographics and geography, most cities have areas that are segmented by income. There are neighborhoods and subdivisions in which the lower classes cluster and in which the upper classes cluster. This information could be used, for instance, in determining where to locate a private membership, high-priced golf and tennis country club.

Geographic segmentation is used to make distinctions between local, regional, national, and international markets or market segments. A sport company might be more successful at a local level than at a national level. On the other hand, a different sport business might be developed to compete specifically at the national or international level.

In another way in many sports, sport marketers have developed levels of competition based on geographic regions to which participants strive. Within a sport, such as boat racing, a team must first complete or win local events, then regional competitions, in order to compete at the national race. In softball, as sponsored by ASA, for example, in order to be able to compete in the national championship, a team must first win at the local, state, and regional levels.

Table 6.18
A typical consumer decision-making process.

All are affected and influenced by personal and social factors.

- **Step 1**—Problem Recognition
- **Step 2**—Information Search
- **Step 3**—Evaluation of Alternatives
- **Step 4**—Purchase
- **Step 5**—Postpurchase Behavior

Purchase Behavior Segmentation

Consumers approach purchasing products based on a number of influencing factors. An obvious one is income: a wealthy person might have little regard for the price of a set of golf clubs, whereas a lower-middle-class person will probably seek to buy a set of golf clubs on the secondary market. Income will also affect where and when each consumer shops. The wealthy person is likely to purchase at the country club's pro shop or directly from the manufacturer, whereas the other person will seek clubs through secondary outlets such as yard sales, ads in bargain paper classifieds, or previously owned sports equipment sporting goods stores.

Many other influencing factors, of which most are demographics, psychographics, geography, location, and product use, affect a person's purchasing behaviors. These factors affect the consumer's decision-making process toward a purchase—a step-by-step process used when buying products. The typical process involves problem recognition, information search, evaluation of alternatives, purchase, and postpurchase behavior (see Table 6.18).

One area of study in sport marketing that helps the sport marketer understand consumers is in the area of participant satisfaction and is based on the question of why people participate in sports activities. Gaining an understanding of why people participate in a sports activity helps the sport marketer develop marketing strategies aimed at attracting new consumers and keeping current consumers.

A growing area of study within sport marketing concerning consumer behavior involves the study of spectators. Most of this research involves studying the factors that affect the spectator's decision to attend the event. In a study of why people attend NBA (National Basketball Association) games, researchers studied 14 factors categorized into four groups (Zhang et al 1995). Table 6.19 presents the information from that study. You can see that the factors listed have to do with promotions, facts about the teams involved in the event, and the game schedule.

Many other factors influence the purchase behavior of spectators of sports events. Tables 6.20, 6.21, 6.22, and 6.23 present information from studies on factors that influence the purchase behavior of spectators for

Table 6.19
Promotion, teams, and schedule factors that affect the consumer's decision to attend NBA games.
(Source: Zhang, Pease, Hui & Michaud, 1995).

Direction: Please rate the following variables that may have generally influenced you on making decisions to attend the NBA games. Please circle only one answer (5 = very much, 4 = much, 3 = somewhat, 2 = a little, 1 = none).

Item	Rating	Loading
Game Promotion (6 items)		
1. advertising	5 4 3 2 1	.86
2. publicity	5 4 3 2 1	.84
3. direct mail and notification	5 4 3 2 1	.76
4. good seats	5 4 3 2 1	.66
5. giveaway/prize	5 4 3 2 1	.56
6. ticket discount	5 4 3 2 1	.45
Home Team (4 items)		
7. win/loss records	5 4 3 2 1	.88
8. league standing	5 4 3 2 1	.87
9. superstars	5 4 3 2 1	.54
10. overall team performance	5 4 3 2 1	.46
Opposing Team		
11. overall team performance	5 4 3 2 1	.90
12. superstar	5 4 3 2 1	.88
Schedule Convenience (2 items)		
13. game time (evening)	5 4 3 2 1	.44
21. day of week (weekend)	5 4 3 2 1	.40

Solution of Factor Analysis by Principal Component Extraction and Orthogonal Rotation (*N* = 861)

Table 6.20
Level of involvement of other factors that affect the consumer's decision to attend soccer games.
(Source: Nakazawa, Mahony, Funk & Hirakawa, 1999).

	Total	Preboom	Boom	Postboom
Favorite team				
Don't have	11.5%	8.2%	6.7%	26.9%
Have	88.5%	91.8%	93.3%	73.1%***
Favorite player				
Don't have	34.7%	31.1%	31.0%	47.7%
Have	65.3%	68.9%	69.0%	52.3%***
Understanding rules				
Well	24.8%	45.6%	19.7%	13.1%
Enough	57.7%	49.8%	63.0%	53.7%
A little	15.5%	3.7%	16.5%	26.7%
Not at all	2.0%	0.9%	0.7%	6.6%***
Experience of soccer				
Don't have	64.2%	43.9%	70.0%	73.6%
Have	35.8%	56.1%	30.0%	26.4%***
When decide to go				
Day of game	5.2%	6.1%	3.8%	7.0%
Before day of game and after pregame	20.1%	17.3%	17.5%	29.4%
Before previous session	74.7%	76.6%	78.7%	63.7%
How to get information (M.A.)				
Newspaper	19.7%	24.0%	21.1%	11.3%***
TV/Radio	8.7%	8.7%	9.6%	6.4%
Soccer magazines	25.5%	31.5%	27.6%	14.0%***
General magazines	7.2%	6.7%	6.6%	9.5%
Friends/Acquaintances	23.4%	18.3%	19.2%	39.4%***
Posters	4.3%	3.8%	5.3%	2.4%**
Club newsletters	29.1%	31.0%	34.7%	13.5%
Others	19.3%	18.0%	19.3%	21.3%
How to get tickets				
Purchase tickets in advance	57.8%	56.3%	62.4%	48.3%
Purchase tickets at stadium	9.0%	11.0%	7.6%	10.0%
Purchase with package tour	1.8%	1.7%	2.0%	1.5%
Receive as a gift	21.1%	19.9%	17.9%	29.8%
Others	10.3%	11.1%	10.0%	10.3%***

	Total	Preboom	Boom	Postboom
How to purchase tickets				
Through ticketing agency	37.1%	34.1%	35.6%	46.5%
Through supporter's clubs	39.2%	40.9%	43.0%	25.0%
At game	11.3%	14.0%	9.3%	13.3%
Others	12.3%	11.0%	12.0%	15.2%***
Transportation time (min.)				
Mean	75.0	73.9	74.3	78.1
SD	52.4	52.8	52.8	51.2
Size of party				
Go alone	13.0%	17.4%	11.8%	10.7%
Go in a pair	52.6%	50.0%	52.8%	55.4%
3 persons	12.8%	12.6%	13.5%	10.7%
4 persons	12.4%	8.9%	14.0%	12.8%
More	9.2%	11.1%	7.8%	10.4%***
Who to go with				
Friends	36.6%	39.9%	35.5%	36.6%
Work Friends	10.6%	10.5%	9.9%	12.8%
Social contract	4.8%	5.6%	4.0%	6.1%
Family/Relatives	42.8%	37.9%	46.6%	37.4%
Others	5.2%	6.1%	4.1%	7.1%***
Belonging to supporter clubs				
I am a member	45.0%	50.7%	50.1%	19.2%
I want to be	17.0%	14.6%	17.1%	20.7%
I do NOT want to be	37.9%	34.7%	32.7%	60.1%***
Frequency of attendance (games)				
Mean	4.4	6.0%	5.1	1.7***
SD	5.3	6.0%	5.2	3.3
Watching games on TV				
Often	67.0%	77.9%	71.2%	44.4%
Sometimes	25.7%	19.3%	23.3%	38.4%
Seldom	4.6%	2.0%	3.8%	9.4%
Almost never	2.7%	0.7%	1.7%	7.7%***
Watch other sports				
Don't	56.2%	36.9%	47.8%	41.4%
Do	43.8%	63.1%	52.2%	58.6%

Notes: *$p < .05$, **$p < .01$, ***$p < .001$

soccer, golf, and ice hockey events. Figure 6.5 presents a compilation of all of several factors from sport marketing studies (Lu, 2000). As you can see, there are many factors that play a part in the consumer's decision-making process concerning whether or not to attend an event. The sport marketing professional can use this type of purchase-behavior information to develop or modify marketing mix strategies.

When compared to other types of products, sports events present a complex sport business problem for the sport management and marketing professional. This is perhaps unique in the universe of selling products. It is certainly different from factors that influence the purchase behavior and decision-making process of a consumer's decision to purchase such products as laundry detergent, a DVD movie, or property. Yet, selling sports events is similar to such products as a Broadway play, a circus, or a trip to Disney World. These are all entertainment products, and sports events fall into this category of product. Therefore, sport marketing professionals working for sport businesses selling sports event can use research and information from studies in entertainment.

Table 6.21
Entertainment options that affect the consumer's decision to attend a minor league hockey game (Source: Zhang, Smith, Pease & Jambor, 1997).

Entertainment Option	% of Response to the Likert Scale					Mean	*SD*
	1	2	3	4	5		
Professional & Amateur Sports							
Attend pro football games	44	26	16	6	7	2.7	2.5
Attend pro indoor soccer games	83	8	5	2	2	1.4	3.0
Attend pro basketball games	31	27	22	11	9	2.4	1.3
Attend pro baseball games	23	26	25	15	11	2.6	1.3
Attend intercollegiate games	40	21	18	10	11	2.3	1.4
Attend other sport shows	25	23	32	13	8	2.0	1.3
Recreational Participation							
Play recreational sports	16	15	24	18	27	3.3	1.6
Work out/Exercise	11	16	23	21	29	3.4	1.4
Travel	8	13	27	24	28	3.5	1.3
Arts							
Attend concerts	18	27	27	16	12	2.8	1.4
Attend movies	7	15	26	26	26	3.5	1.8
Television							
Watch sports on TV	7	11	17	25	41	3.9	1.6
Watch nonsports programs on TV	5	12	21	25	38	3.8	1.2
Dining and Night Clubs							
Attend bars/restaurants	8	7	20	28	37	3.8	1.3
Attend night clubs	35	23	18	12	12	2.5	2.5

*1 = Never; 2 = Occasionally; 3 = Sometimes; 4 = Often; 5 = Always

Table 6.22
Factors that affect the consumer's decision to attend a golf event as a spectator (Source: Lascu, Giese, Toolan, Guehring & Mercer, 1995).

Number of Professional Tournaments Attended (Past 5 years)	0	1	2–5	6–10	Over 10
	22.3%	8%	50.3%	12.6%	6.9%
	n = 39	n = 14	n = 88	n = 22	n = 12

Number of Professional Tournaments Viewed on Television (Past year)	0	1	2–5	6–10	Over 10
	1.7%	2.9%	14%	18.3%	62.3%
	n = 3	n = 5	n = 26	n = 32	n = 109

Years of Golf Played	Under 10	11–20	21–30	31–40	41–50	Unknown
	50%	21%	12%	9%	4%	4%
	n = 88	n = 37	n = 21	n = 15	n = 7	n = 7

Rounds of Golf Per Year	0	1–10	11–25	Over 25	Unknown
	13.7%	17.1%	18.3%	50.3%	.6%
	n = 24	n = 30	n = 32	n = 88	n = 1

Table 6.23
Level of involvement factors that affect a consumer's decision to attend a golf tournament
(Source: Lascu, Giese, Toolan, Guehring & Mercer, 1995).

Variable	Involvement Low	Involvement High	t-Value	Prob.
Motivation for Attendance				
Proximity to golfers	3.99	4.39	140.94	.017
Live action	4.36	4.70	132.41	.007
Fitness motivation	3.07	3.44	138.73	.070
Personal love of golf	3.79	4.67	117.46	.000
Support for charity	3.47	3.93	139.98	.016
Golfing tips	3.07	3.86	135.44	.000
Excitement of the final round	3.78	4.33	140.00	.002
Promotions associated with event	2.49	3.10	133.65	.004
The company of friends	3.35	3.89	140.95	.005
Exposure to advertisements	2.45	2.95	136.31	.022
Ticket value	2.60	3.03	138.07	.055
Excitement of first two rounds	2.47	3.25	125.66	.001
Commitment to Golf				
Golf tournaments attended	2.45	3.07	142.41	.001
Golf tournaments watched	4.08	4.60	127.32	.001
Rounds of golf played	2.58	3.57	125.34	.000
Number years playing golf	11.75	17.92	138.65	.007
Golf Digest	.37	.56	142.74	.025
Use of golf for business	.19	.33	137.92	.053
Money spent last year	1.40	3.14	132.91	.003
Likelihood of attending similar event	4.04	4.72	101.22	.000
Ability to identify Cellular One as a sponsor	.14	.04	115.97	.045

Step 1: Problem recognition. Do you feel thirsty after your soccer game? Did you break your softball bat? Does your sport company need research? These questions describe situations you might find yourself in often. In order to solve the problem, you first must recognize it. Therefore, you have learned that you will get thirsty at your soccer game and so will determine that you need a sports drink to take to the game. You need a new softball bat because you broke the one you have. Your sport business needs to know how consumers think about the new stadium, so you might determine that you need to hire a sport marketing consulting firm to do this research and solve the problem. All of these are situations in which a problem has been recognized. The need for a solution develops.

Step 2: Information search. The first step toward finding a solution is seeking information to help develop the best solution. A person will consider such factors as money available, time available, and memory. These are internal factors that influence the knowledge or decision to purchase a particular product. Other variables that will influence this decision are external factors. External factors include information that a person receives from friends, family, advertising, and sales people.

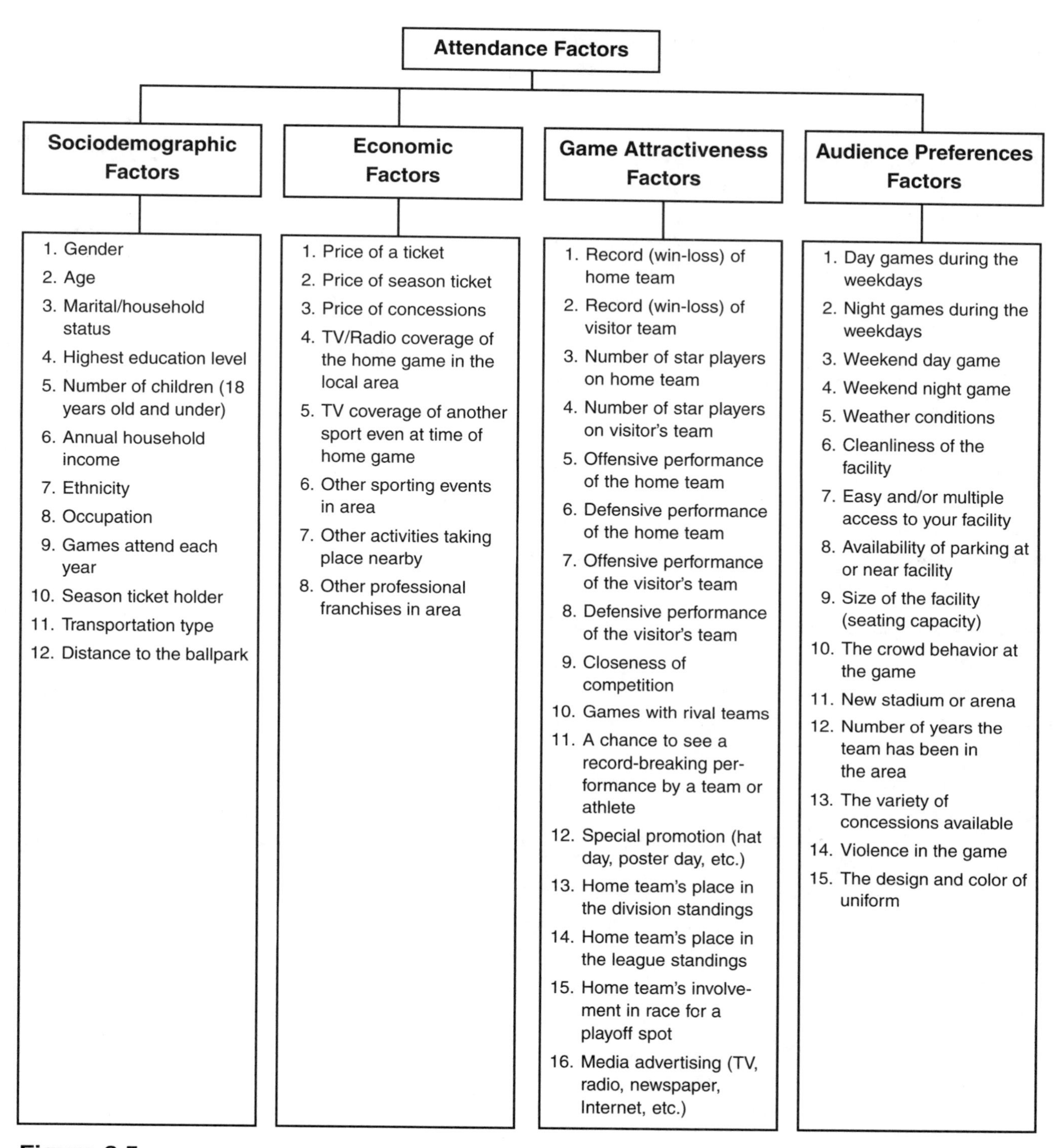

Figure 6.5
Compilation of factors that affect attendance. (Source: Lu, 2000)

An information search can occur internally, externally, or both. The type of product needed or desired and its uses and functions will influence the extent to which the consumer uses internal, external or both factors. Additionally, price can have a fairly significant influence. As presented in the price chapter, the price of a product can affect consumers in a number of ways such as influencing the consumer's willingness to spend, expectation of quality and performance, and postpurchase anxiety or comfort.

The type of product and its uses and functions will trigger an internal or external search, or both. For example, athletic tape needed to wrap a sprained ankle is a necessity. Most people are not trained in sports medicine. Most retail stores such as Walgreen's and Eckerd's carry only one or two brands, and they are practically identical to the general consumer. Therefore, there is very little, if any, information needed to make this purchase. However, if the consumer is considering purchasing a boat for skiing and other water sports, the consumer is much more likely to employ a majority of external information search. The purchase of a boat requires some knowledge of the following: how you will use the boat (product uses and functions); how often you will use the boat; where the boat will be used; what size boat you need or want; how many people you expect to have on board on a typical outing; the activities you plan while on the boat and using the boat; the kind of towing vehicle you have; will you have to tow (trailer) the boat for each use; how far you will have to trailer the boat; the kind of terrain you will have to cover in trailering the boat; the amenities you want or need in the boat such as stereo, toilet, water, built-in cooler, kitchen, built-in wet bar, and trolling motor; the kind of engine you want, outboard, inboard, stern drive, or jet drive; the kind of water sports equipment you want or need—skis, kneeboard, skurfer, wakeboard, tubes, or barefoot skiing equipment; and the kind of safety equipment do you want or need. As you can see, to purchase a boat, a consumer will need to collect much information that will help answer those questions and many more.

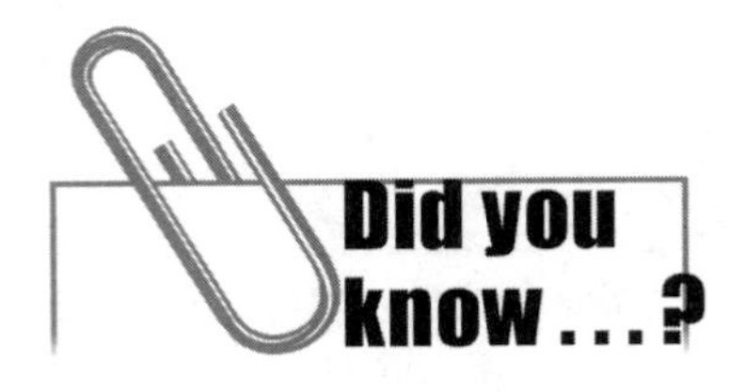

The average cost of a family-of-four NHL outing (including parking, tickets, food, and souvenirs) in 1999 was $238.87.

Source: USA Today

Consumers with prior knowledge or experience with a product are less needy of external information searches. They will rely primarily on the knowledge gained from the experience with the product from the previous purchase.

Steps 3 and 4: Evaluation of alternatives and purchase. After collecting information concerning the targeted product, the consumer will consider all alternatives, develop a set of criteria, weigh advantages and disadvantages, consider internal and external information again, and then begin to narrow decision to finalist products. Again, as you can see in Tables 6.20, 6.21, 6.22, and 6.23, there can be many factors to consider. Some of those factors are alternative products. If the product is attending and watching a sports event, you can see in the example in Table 6.21 that there are a number of alternative things to do that compete for the consumer's attention or purchase.

Consumers who already know about or have experience with a product require a salesperson who can speak knowledgeably about the product and answer more detailed questions.

Step 5: Postpurchase behavior. Your consumer may exhibit postpurchase behavior. This involves how the consumer feels and what the consumer thinks about the purchase and whether or not the consumer is satisfied or dissatisfied in regard to the consumer's expectations about how the product is performing. In other words, if the consumer went into the purchase with a certain set of expectations (product uses and benefits) and those expectations are being met, then the consumer will probably be satisfied and feel comfortable with the purchase. If, however, the product does not perform to the consumer's expectations, then the consumer will probably be dissatisfied and feel uncomfortable about the purchase. For example, if a consumer buys tickets to a Super Bowl game and expects to have an enjoyable experience with a game that is exciting and close, yet the game turns out to be a large margin-of-victory game, then the consumer would be dissatisfied with the purchase. If, however, a consumer bought tickets to the final of the 1998 Women's World Cup, was a United States team fan, and expected to find a fair-sized crowd and an exciting game, that consumer was probably happily surprised to find that the U.S. team won the World Cup, crowd numbers were well above anyone's expectations, and the game was an exceptionally exciting game. This consumer will conclude that the purchase was above expectation and will be satisfied.

Sport businesses must avoid over-broad promises about their products to ensure that consumers receive what they expect.

Post-purchase behavior is another area of concern for any sport business and should be considered as part of the company's customer service department.

Sport business management and marketing professionals must take care not to promise too much in a product, lest that product does not meet the claims made and thus adds to the consumer's dissatisfaction with the product. Too much post-purchase dissatisfaction can lead to the development of a negative image for the company. Consider, for example, the image problem facing several professional men's sports today in relation to some public opinion that the players are overpaid and get away with anything, that the league is a haven for criminals and encourages violence, and thus that the games are not worth watching and certainly should be hidden from youth. Sport marketing professionals are making attempts to counter some of these claims in order to maintain a supportive consumer base.

Product Use and Benefits Segmentation

A consumer needs a product in order to satisfy a need or desire. Therefore, the product is the tool for the consumer to perform certain functions and realize certain benefits. A softball bat is a tool for the player to hit the ball, but a well-selected bat is what the player chooses in looking to improve hitting percentage, have more control, get more home runs, and enhance status among teammates and fans. A fitness center provides the potential for the consumer to get in shape, become physically fit, enhance health, lower blood pressure, control weight, meet people, sweat, grow stronger, lose those holiday-gained pounds, be a part of the cool crowd, fit into certain clothes, and/or get ready for the swimsuit season. As a matter of fact, the sport marketer uses these exact words in advertising for these products. Knowing how the consumer wants to use the product, the functions the consumer expects the product to perform, and the benefits the consumer expects to receive from the product is important for the sport marketing professional in developing marketing mix strategies that are well informed. This enhances the chances for success.

A Consumer Needs:

a product in order to satisfy a need or desire. Therefore, the product is the tool for the consumer to perform certain functions and realize certain benefits.

Product usage information can be used in a number of ways in the marketing mix. For example, there is a theory called the 80-20 rule. This means that 20% of all consumers generate 80% of consumption. This can be seen in fitness centers, for example, where a small group of consumers (about 20%) are responsible for the core (about 80%) of the consumption of the product. The rest of the consumers do not use the facility as much or as often. Sport marketing professionals have developed categories for these kinds of groups. Some of those include heavy users, medium users, light users, and nonusers; high involvement and low involvement; hard-core fan and fan; and high loyalty, spurious loyalty, latent loyalty, and low loyalty. These kinds of segmentation categories can be used by the sport marketing professional to study consumers and develop appropriate marketing strategies. The information presented in

Tables 6.22 and 6.23 is from a study on sports participation and its influence on sports spectators. That is, the researchers were studying the relationship between a person's involvement as a participant in a sport and his or her involvement as a spectator of that sport. In general, the researchers found that high-involvement consumers—those who participate more frequently in the sport—are more likely to attend more of the sport's events in person, watch more on TV, pay more attention to activities offered at the live event, pay more attention to promotions associated with the event, and such consumers are more capable of correctly identifying the event sponsors (Lascu et al 1995).

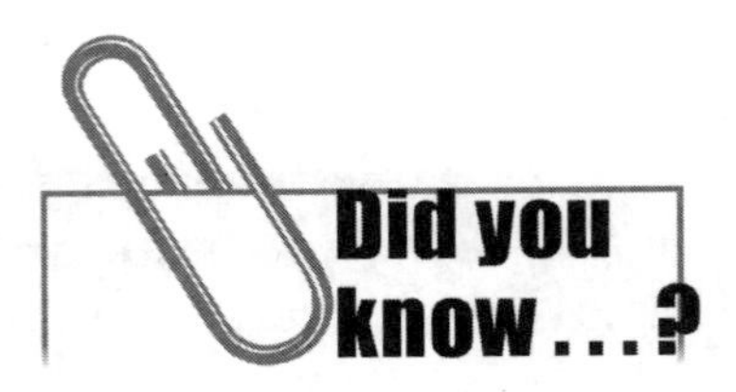

The three highest endorsed golfers in 1998:

Tiger Woods ($28 million)
Arnold Palmer ($20 million)
Greg Norman ($14 million)

Source: *Sports Business Journal*

Business Consumer Segmentation

If your business produces products for businesses, then your consumers are business consumers. Business-to-business marketing involves the marketing of products to individuals and organizations for purposes other than personal consumption (Lamb, Hair, and McDaniel, 1996). These consumers acquire products and services for purposes of manufacturing, production, resale, operations, enhancement of a company's position, or other business-related reason. For example, if your company manufactures T-shirts to sell directly to a licensing and merchandising company for a sports event such as the national rodeo, then your consumers are business consumers. If your company conducts studies of sponsorship advertising and its effects for companies who are the sponsors or the companies who manage the event, then your consumers are business consumers.

Segmenting and targeting business consumers are similar to segmenting end consumers (those who purchase products for personal consumption). Business consumer segmentation involves categorizing into groups with similar characteristics. Most business consumers can be categorized into the following groups: manufacturers, resellers, sports-governing bodies, institutions, and media sports enterprises. Manufacturers are those businesses that purchase products that are used to manufacture or produce products or that are used for the daily operations of the company. For example, Hillerich & Bradsby Co. (H & B) is a producer of baseball bats and ice-hockey equipment. To manufacture these, H & B must purchase materials such as wood and plastics. Therefore, H & B is a business consumer. H & B also sells primarily to business consumers. Such companies as sporting goods retailers, distributors, and wholesalers who purchase H & Bs products such as their bats and golf clubs do so for resale purposes. Therefore, H and B must study, segment, and target business consumers.

Resellers include those businesses that purchase products for the purpose of reselling them for a profit. Sporting goods retail stores, for instance, are resellers: They purchase many products from many different companies in order to resell them for profit. Another example includes promotion and sponsorship management companies. For instance, a company that consults and manages sponsorship contracts must purchase signs for signage from a sign manufacturer. Therefore, they are a business consumer. Also, their products are targeted primarily to business consumers—those companies who want their sponsorship management products. In another example, a college licensing and merchandising company is a business-to-business company and therefore both a business consumer and a company that targets business consumers. This type of company will purchase merchandise from manufacturers and producers and sell them to their business customers.

Governing bodies include numerous organizations whose business is to govern various sports, recreational, and leisure activities, events, and organizations as well as equipment and facilities. The International Olympic Committee, for instance, governs everything involved in the Olympics enterprises. Its business-to-business product is primarily to stage, or produce (sell), a multisports event to end consumers, yet its transactions involve primarily selling the rights to broadcast the event to media sports enterprises such as TV and radio, rights to produce the event to a host organization, and sponsorship products to sponsorship companies. Thus, the IOC practically never directly sells the event to the end consumer.

Institutions are usually nonprofit entities that include such organizations as schools, colleges and universities, faith-based sports clubs, city sports commissions, sports foundations, youth sports organizations, and city sports and recreation offices. They purchase such business products as facilities, office equipment and supplies, sporting goods, equipment, apparel, and promotional merchandise.

Media sports enterprises are those for-profit businesses that seek to broadcast, or distribute, sports events, sports-related shows, sports news, and sports-related material via media such as television, radio, magazines, video, DVD, and the Web. Sports events broadcast on TV and radio are a common product. As pointed out earlier in this chapter, there are 235 hours of sports programming every 24 hours on 48 sports channels. Although many sports magazines, video, DVD, and Web products target end consumers, the companies that manufacture these products must transact with several businesses to purchase such products as the rights to the sports event for publications purposes, paper, videotapes, DVD disks, Internet Web-site providers, and satellite distribution companies. Some of these companies also target businesses consumers with some of their products. For instance, trade publications are targeted to businesses.

Bases for Business Consumer Segmentation

Business consumer segmentation variables are a little different from end consumer variables. Whereas end consumer bases focus on human characteristics, business consumer bases must include business characteristics. Although it will be humans who make particular purchase decisions for the company, the company most likely has purchase criteria or policies that the buyer must follow. The following are brief descriptions of bases for business consumer segmentation (from Lamb, Hair, and McDaniel, 1996).

Sport Business Consumers:

Manufacturers
Resellers
Sports Governing Bodies
Institutions
Media Sports Enterprises

Geographic location. As presented earlier in this chapter, consumers can be segmented according to geographic location variables. Common variables using simply geographic locations include local, state, and region. For instance, often various regions of the United States are known for certain sports: The West is associated with rodeo events; coastal regions are associated with ocean-related sports; the Rockies areas are associated with winter sports and mountain-climbing sports; certain states such as Tennessee are known as basketball states, and certain states such as Texas are known as football states. Companies that sell to industries that are concentrated geographically would benefit by locating close to those markets. For instance, surfboard companies will enhance efforts if they locate in coastal areas. In another example, sports agents might enhance efforts if they locate in large city areas that can sustain several professional and semiprofessional sports organizations.

Customer type. Segmenting by type of customer has benefits because the seller can concentrate marketing mix strategies. For instance, manufacturers of sports equipment can focus on retail stores, specialty stores, or distributors. Thus, marketing mix strategies would be developed specifically to one or more of these.

Customer size. This base is similar to segmenting end consumers based on product usage such as heavy, medium, and light. This base involves volume. Your company might decide that its best strategy is to target those companies that purchase in large volume only.

Product use. Many products can be used in different ways, especially raw materials such as wood, plastics, and steel. How your customers will be using these products will determine how much they buy and other criteria. For instance, if a golf club manufacturer produces steel shafts, then the company will probably need to purchase a particular type of steel and a certain amount of steel. In another example, if a licensing company needs T-shirts for a very large sports event, such as the Kentucky Derby, then their use of the product for a once-a-year event will affect their purchase.

Purchase criteria. A company might purchase based on specific criteria such as price, quality, reputation, or delivery. If your company can deliver what the company needs when they need it, then you might want to use this as a reason to target this company.

Did you know . . . ?

The first all-sports radio station debuted in 1987 (WFAN, NY), and in 1996, there were 156 sports radio stations.

Source: USA Today

Industry Segmentation

Industry segmentation is the process of dividing or categorizing an industry into logical and/or similar parts, or industry segments. It involves industry analysis—the study of an industry. The sport marketing professional needs to know and understand the whole sport industry and, more specifically, its segments. This will help in determining where an individual sport business fits into a particular segment and into the whole industry. It helps in determining how events in the industry, or in a segment, will affect an individual sport business. This knowledge will help in marketing strategy.

Understanding the entire sport industry and its segments allows the sport marketing professional to determine where to position the business in the industry and what type of competitive strategy is needed.

Industry segmentation may be conducted in a manner similar to consumer segmentation: one whole group divided into categories of smaller groups based on homogeneous characteristics. The primary purpose for industry segmentation is competitive strategy formulation. Other reasons include to identify marketing opportunities and threats within a specific segment, to develop an appropriate marketing mix, and to inform resource allocation (Pitts, Fielding, and Miller, 1994).

Bases for Industry Segmentation

Segmenting an industry is typically done primarily using two variables: products and buyers. An industry can comprise one product and one buyer. More typically, an industry segment comprises multiple similar products and buyers. The following are some of the ways the sport business industry has been segmented.

The sport industry is divided into numerous segments by sports. The circle in Figure 6.6 illustrates all of the sports in the sport business industry. Inside are some of the numerous segments divided by sports. Often the industry is mentioned according to "the basketball industry," "the softball industry," or "the running industry." Each segment is illustrative of everything that relates to a particular sport. For basketball, that would include basketball spectator sports, recreational sports, and equipment. If you work for a sport business that manufactures basketballs, you could consider your business as part of the basketball industry segment. Therefore, you would want to monitor every other manufacturer in this segment as well as basketball participation (consumer) rates. This information would help in strategizing.

Figure 6.7 is an illustration of the Pitts et al. (1994) sport industry segmentation model, which categorizes the whole industry according to product function. Figure 6.8 shows the full model. If your company offers products whose function is promotion, then your company is categorized into the sport promotion segment. In this segment, you would want to monitor your competitors and all consumers of these products. This knowledge will help will competitive strategy development.

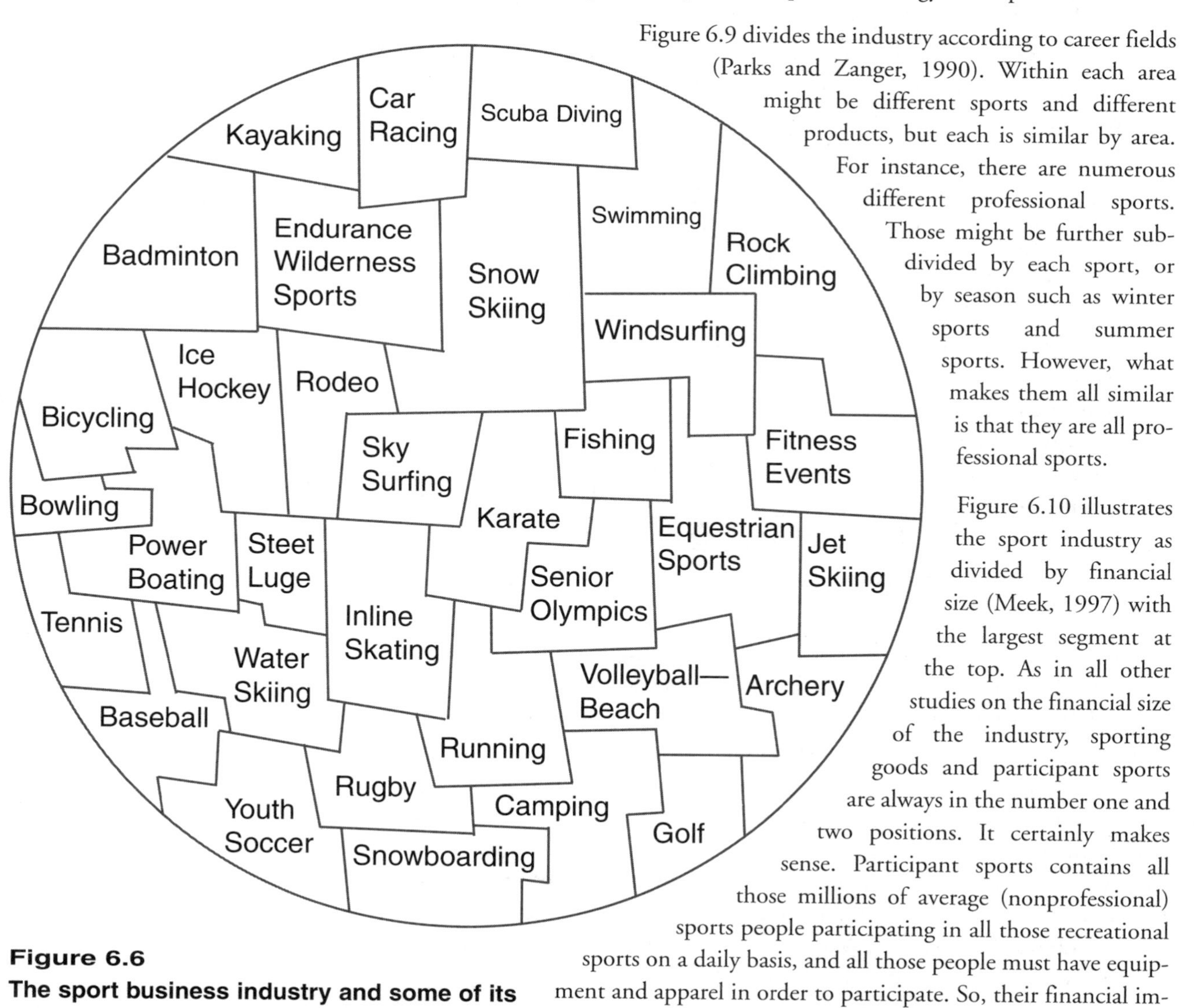

Figure 6.6
The sport business industry and some of its numerous segments as divided by sports.

Figure 6.9 divides the industry according to career fields (Parks and Zanger, 1990). Within each area might be different sports and different products, but each is similar by area. For instance, there are numerous different professional sports. Those might be further subdivided by each sport, or by season such as winter sports and summer sports. However, what makes them all similar is that they are all professional sports.

Figure 6.10 illustrates the sport industry as divided by financial size (Meek, 1997) with the largest segment at the top. As in all other studies on the financial size of the industry, sporting goods and participant sports are always in the number one and two positions. It certainly makes sense. Participant sports contains all those millions of average (nonprofessional) sports people participating in all those recreational sports on a daily basis, and all those people must have equipment and apparel in order to participate. So, their financial importance should come as no surprise.

Other methods include segmenting the industry by product. For example, baseball bat manufacturers study the "baseball bat industry"; athletic shoe manufacturers study the "athletic shoe industry"; golf course construction companies study the "golf course industry"; and a boat manufacturer studies the "boat-building industry." Each company needs to know what is going on in its specific area.

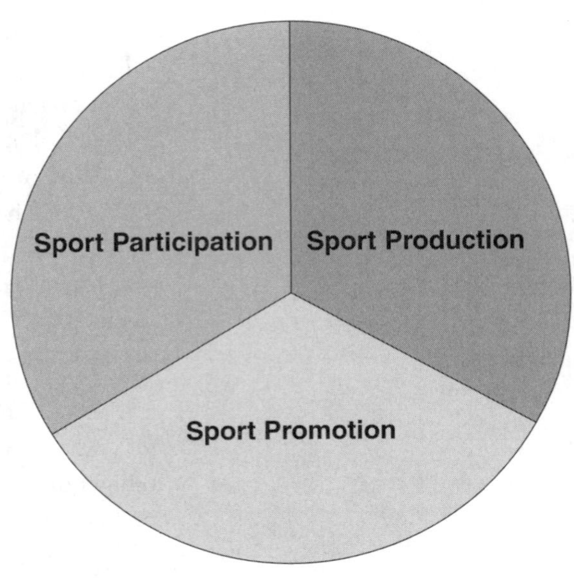

Figure 6.7
The sport industry and its segments as divided by product function in the Pitts, Fielding & Miller Sport Industry Segmentation Model (1994).

Industry Segmentation Information

Industry segment information is readily available. Appendixes B and C offer information on sport business trade organizations and trade publications. *Trade* refers to a particular vocation, skill, knowledge area, profession, or business type. These businesses and publications offer information regarding industry information, research, and market events. The following is an excerpt from a book titled *Recreation Trends and Markets* (Kelly and Warnick, 1999). This book offers information on several sports segments in relation to its trends, markets, and future projections of growth. This kind of information would be important to someone working in the water sports industry, particularly the surfing industry segment.

> Surfing, unlike swimming, is a niche activity with specific locations. Dedicated surfers, however, travel to those locations at least on vacations. Trend data are available only since 1991.
>
> General Trends: Surfing is a niche activity that has grown somewhat in the 1990s from a very small base. The 1991 rate of 0.8 percent (of the population) has about doubled with a high of 2.2 percent in 1994 and a most recent 1.5 percent in 1996. In general, only about 2 percent of the adult population ever surfs. This yields about 3 million surfers age 18 and over and 60 million participation days. Of these, about 40 percent are frequent and 30 to 50 percent, infrequent. Surfing seems to be divided between the committed and those who do a little, perhaps on vacations. Wet suit technology and board improvements have extended the season for frequent participants.
>
> Market identification: in 1995 there was little gender difference, 2 percent male to 1.7 percent female. The rate of 2-plus percent is steady to age 45 and then drops to 1.6 percent age 45 to 54, 1 percent age 55 to 64, and a surprising increase to 1.6 percent for those 65 and older. These figures suggest that many surfers do no fit the image of bronzed young males running high surfs in Hawaiian competitions. The more inclusive types of boogie boards and body surfing are included in the survey reports. Education level does not discriminate and income only slightly. There are, of course, 30 percent more singles than the married. Surfing would appear to be divided between the "big wave" elite and the more inclusive "play in the wave" participants.

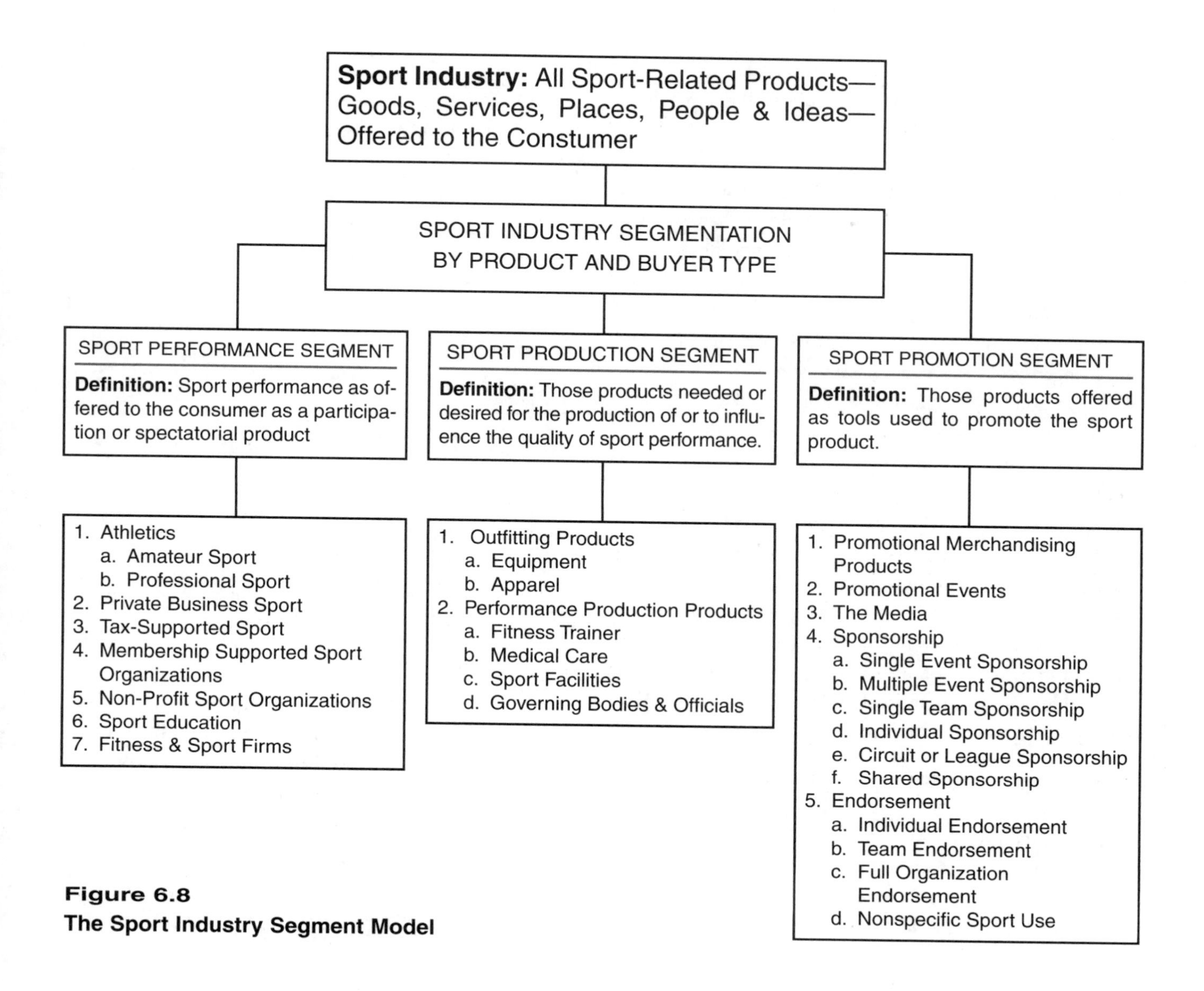

Figure 6.8
The Sport Industry Segment Model

Growth markets: Growth is most probable among the occasional vacation surfers who travel to coastal resorts with moderate waves and equipment. There may also by carryover from the growing sport of snowboarding with seasonal rhythms.

Established markets: The core remains the young surfers on the West coast and in Hawaii. The secondary market comprises those who vacation there and in other coastal locations.

Low markets: Those who lack access to surfing conditions are, of course, a low market, that is, inland regions and many coastal areas as well.

Projections: overall participation may increase slightly related to resort vacations. The core of "big wave" surfers, however, will not grow unless snowboarding brings in a modest number of crossover surfers." (pp. 137–138)

In another example, boat manufacturers and retail sellers would be very interested in a new boat manufacturing breakthrough. *Trailer Boats* magazine is well-known in the boating industry for its technical information. In an article in the December 2000 issue (Bourdon, 2000), it was revealed that a company has invented a new way to build the boat's hull using a new virtual engineered composites (VEC) technology. The VEC system produces a complete hull in a closed mold. Through the process, there is no materials waste, the complete hull stringer system floor is molded in, aluminum plates are bonded in, and the deck is manufactured in the same way. The molding takes two people only minutes to prepare and 35 minutes to mold, and it is 93% cured. Compare that to the conventional method, which takes eight or more people to produce a hull, with a curing time of 12 hours or more. Further, the molds can be changed in less than an hour, which offers significant flexibility during the manufacturing process. Moreover, the new VEC hull is so precise that it can be finished with a robotic router, has significantly fewer instances of hull thickness variations, and hull weight varies less than a pound. Additionally, the company is offering a lifetime warranty on the hull.

Consulting
Sport Marketing
Sports Club Management
Sports Information
Intercollegiate Sports
Physical Fitness
Athletic Training and Sports Medicine
Campus Recreation
Community Sports
Facility Management
Professional Sport
Aquatics Management
Entrepreneurship
Sports Journalism

Figure 6.9
The sport business industry as divided by career fields (Source: Parks, Zanger, and Quarterman, 1998).

A sport marketing professional in the boat business will need to know this information. This revolutionary manufacturing process will most likely influence the entire boat manufacturing industry. Competitors will be forced to study the new process and determine if their company will need to purchase the new technology or develop something similar in order to compete.

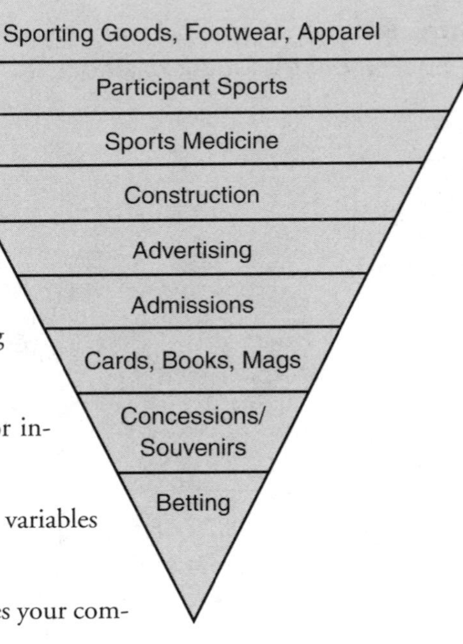

Figure 6.10
The Sport Business Industry as Divided by Economic Size According to Meek (1996)

The Segmentation Process

Now that we know what characteristics to use in segmenting markets and an industry, let's look at a simple step-by-step process in segmenting a market. Table 6.24 illustrates the steps in such a process. Remember that the primary purpose of segmentation is to understand specific groups of consumers or an industry segment to inform marketing mix strategies.

Step 1. Select a market or industry. Determine which set of consumers or industries your company wants to consider and study.

Step 2. Select one or more segmentation bases. Determine which bases and variables your company wants to use.

Step 3. Select specific variables. Within the bases, determine which variables your company wants to consider.

Step 4. Analyze the segment. Study, analyze, and determine conclusions about the segment(s) chosen. Which will be most beneficial to the company?

Step 5. Select one or more target markets. Determine which specific market or industry segment your company wants to target.

Step 6. Develop appropriate marketing mix strategies. Develop marketing mix strategies based on your information about the target market(s) or industry segment.

Target Market(s) Selection Strategies

From the segments, your company will select which one or more to target. These become the company's target markets or industry segments. These groups are the ones for which the company will develop specific marketing mix strategies. The following are typical target market strategies (from Lamb et al., 1996).

Table 6.24
A Typical Segmentation Process.

Step 1—Select a market or industry
Step 2—Select one or more segmentation bases
Step 3—Select specific variables
Step 4—Analyze the segment
Step 5—Select one or more target markets
Step 6—Develop appropriate marketing mix strategies

When segments are very similar to each other, an undifferentiated targeting strategy—much like mass marketing—may be used, whereby all consumers receive the same marketing treatment.

Undifferentiated targeting strategy involves making no distinctions between any of the segments. Therefore, this is similar to mass marketing. This approach will work if the segments are so similar in characteristics that a distinct differentiation cannot be made. Marketing mix strategies will concentrate on the entire market.

Niche targeting strategy involves the selection of one segment on which to focus. Typically, niche marketing will work if the company is the only one selling the only product to its consumers. This strategy will be successful as long as the situation stays the same. However, once another company begins to offer the product, your targeting strategy will be changing.

Multisegment targeting strategy involves the selection of two or more segments to target. Usually, this strategy can be the most successful in terms of efficiency and effectiveness. Even if there is very little difference between segments, people feel special when showered with attention.

Positioning the Sport Business

Position is what a consumer thinks about a product in comparison to other products. Positioning refers to the development of specific marketing-mix elements to influence the consumer's perception of a product, brand, or company. For instance, a consumer might think that the golf clubs made by the Red Brand Company are better than those made by the Blue Brand Company because the Red Brand clubs are lighter, stronger, give more control, give more distance, and are higher quality clubs because they are more expensive. The Red Brand Company's product carries a particular place, or position, in the consumer's thinking.

The consumer could have developed this perception with no input. However, it might be more likely that the marketing tactics and strategies of the Red Brand Company influenced the consumer. For instance, the Red Brand Company can use the phrase "lighter, stronger, longer" so much in all of its advertising that the consumer can be influenced by the words.

Positioning assumes that a consumer will compare products produced by different companies and could be influenced by the company's positioning tactics. Of course, if a product has been positioned to target a specific market, then that market will be more readily influenced because it already possesses the demographics and other segment variables to which the product was customized. For example, if a golf club company wants to target a wealthy segment and position the club to be the club for the wealthy, then the consumers in this segment are more likely to be influenced by the marketing mix strategies and are more likely to be attracted to that club.

Positioning establishes the image of a product or company and becomes the consumer's base of reference when deciding which company's product to purchase.

Positioning is a critical element for the sport marketing professional. Most sport businesses have more than one market. Many products therefore have more than one market, and some products have more than one function (use). The sport business must develop the image of the product that it wants the consumer to hold concerning that product. If there is more than one consumer market for a product, and if the product has more than one function, then the sport business must develop a position for each market and each function. The following steps outline a simple process for developing a positioning strategy for a product (see Table 6.25).

Table 6.25
A Simple Positioning Process

Step 1—Identify the target market's product attribute preferences
Step 2—Identify current positioning strategy
Step 3—Analyze current position and the market's preferred product attributes
Step 4—Determine a positioning strategy

Step 1. Identify the target market's attribute preferences. A market wants or needs a product for a specific function—the attributes of the product (refer to the product chapter for further study). Study the market for those attributes. If the product and its consumer market are known, study the current market. If the product is new and the consumer market is not yet known, determine the potential consumer market.

Step 2. Identify current positioning strategy. How is the company currently positioning the product? How do competitors position their product? Typically, positioning can be found in the advertising for a product because advertising is where the company communicates to a market. So look there first.

Step 3. Analyze current position and the market's preferred product attributes. Study the current positioning strategy and the consumer market's preferred product attributes, and determine if they match. If the positioning strategy matches the consumer market's preferred product attributes, then the current positioning strategy is a match. If the current positioning strategy and the consumer market's preferred product attributes do not match, then it may be time to reposition the product.

Step 4. Determine a positioning strategy. Using the research collected in steps 1, 2, and 3, determine a positioning strategy to meet the consumer market's preferred product attributes.

Positioning statements. Table 6.26 presents some examples for positioning statements for one product to target different consumer markets. Note how the statements for each different consumer market are specific to that market's preferred product functions.

Chapter Summary

With constantly changing markets and industries, the sport marketing professional must constantly monitor and develop marketing mix strategies that will be beneficial for the company. Segmentation involves the study of markets and industries to divide

Table 6.26
Examples of Positioning Strategies Based on Multiple Markets

Sample 1: Manufacturer of personal watercrafts (commonly known as jet skis).	**Sample 2:** An indoor soccer arena and club.
Overall: We offer a fantastic line of personal watercrafts. We have PWCs of all sizes, for ever need, or for fun. No company has more variety. *Business market*: Our line of working PWCs are all you need for emergency, rescue, or waterway control. Our PWCs are built tough to give you more years of service and dependability, ready to serve in the line of duty when you need them. Traditionally or custom rigged, your company can have a fleet of the most rugged and dependable PWCs on the water today. *Recreational market:* The (name) is built with your fun in mind! No company offers the variety of PWC that we do. No matter what your fun requirements, we've got the PWC for you—fun, fast, and safe.	*Overall:* We offer the most flexible indoor soccer facility for any of your needs—practice, fun, or competition—our arena can serve your every need. *Business market:* We offer the best practice facility for soccer or field hockey in the area. Just call and talk to our friendly staff today and schedule your practice. And if you need the coaching room, just let us know! We have a fully equipped coaching room just waiting for you and your team—the place where you can plan your winning strategy. *Recreational market:* The best soccer fun in town! Looking to play indoor soccer for fun? Or is your team looking for some serious competition? We have both! Every session includes recreational and competitive divisions. We also have age-group divisions from under 16 to 40 plus. Register your team today—the next league starts soon.

a whole into parts in order to develop customized marketing mix strategies. In the sport industry, sport marketing professionals study primarily two broad categories: sport consumer markets made up of end consumers and business consumers, and the sport industry, made up of a variety of industry segments.

Segmentation is the first step toward understanding consumer groups, determining target markets, and informing marketing mix and positioning strategies. Segmentation bases and variables are used to segment a consumer market or an industry. The choice of bases and variables is crucial because an inappropriate group of bases will not be successful in relation to responding to a marketing mix.

Target marketing involves the development of marketing mix strategies customized for one or more target markets or industry segments. These groups are the ones for which the company will develop specialized marketing-mix elements, strategies, and promotional campaigns.

Positioning involves communicating to the consumer what the company wants the consumer to think about the product. It is a critical element in marketing because it positions the product, or company, with a particular image about the product's functions in the consumer's mind.

Questions for Study

1. Describe how the population of your country has changed over the last 25 years and how it is going to change in the next 25 years. How will this affect the sport business industry?
2. What types of marketing strategies are sport businesses using more often for emerging markets? Describe each one and how they work.
3. What are segmentation, sport consumer market segmentation, and sport industry segmentation?
4. What are bases for segmentation? Describe how they are used.
5. What is target marketing? Describe how to determine one or more target markets for a sport business.
6. What is positioning? Describe how to develop a positioning strategy for a product and a consumer market.

Learning Activities

1. Using students in your class, conduct a study of demographics, psychographics, and other segmentation bases and variables using sporting goods as a basis. What did you learn about the class? How could this information be used if your company is a sporting goods retail company?
2. Write down a sports product that you purchased recently, one that is sold by more than one company. Create two columns. Label one column "My Buy" and the other column "Didn't Buy." In the "My Buy" column, create a list of all of the reasons you bought the product. In the "Didn't Buy" column, create a list of all of the reasons you did not buy the product from other companies. On another sheet, try to consider all the information you gathered to help you decide on your purchase and list them (family, friends, advertising). Write down all the things the people told you or that you remember from the advertising. Now compare all your notes and see if there is a relationship between any of them. Why do you think you found a relationship between, for example, the reasons you bought the product from a specific company and the company's advertising for that product?
3. With a group, determine a way to segment the sport industry. First, determine a reason for segmenting the industry such as pretending that your group is a television broadcasting company that focuses on extreme sports events. Develop bases for segmentation. Determine an appropriate marketing mix strategy for your company.
4. Pretend that your company is a team of the WNBA. You want to increase spectator attendance numbers for each game, but you also want to increase the number of games that many of your fans attend during a season. Develop a list of the factors that have an influence on attendance and design a study that will answer the questions you have for your fans.
5. Identify some different sport businesses such as a manufacturer and a sport facility. Identify different consumer markets for the products. Develop positioning statements for each consumer market.

Chapter 7

Marketing Information Systems

The growth and expansion of information that sports organizations generate daily are staggering. The major problem is that our thinking and skills have not been developed to accommodate this tremendous onslaught of data. It has been estimated that sport managers spend 80% of their time on information transactions (Horine, 1995). This phenomenon demands the development of systematic methods to process the abundance of information that is available and use it in marketing our sports products and services.

> Marketing information systems—known as MIS, CIS, and IAM—deal with large amounts of information and are essential to the success of your sport organization or company.

Marketing information systems are about information management. They have been referred to by many names—marketing information systems (MIS), computer information systems (CIS), and information asset management (IAM). Although no one title is singularly appropriate, the development and use of systems that can manage information for your sport organization or company is essential. Mullin (1985) said, "The MIS provides the link between the market and the marketer, and it is therefore the lifeline of marketing" (p. 210).

Marketing information systems are generally characterized as a collection of data that are utilized by management in the operation and development of marketing programs and market-related decisions. In past decades, former coaches and athletes have managed many sport organizations. Marketing and management decisions were often intuitive judgements rather than logical choices based on data. The time has long passed when organizations can remain competitive in today's environment with yesterday's decision style. Successful sport marketers must develop skills and abilities to interact with technology in making data-based decision for marketing their products and services.

Vavra (1992) noted that each contact that a company has with customers represents an opportunity to acquire customer information. Examples of these interactions include warranty cards, coupon redemption, and credit applications.

> MIS allows companies to establish channels of communication in order to maintain a relationship with consumers. These relationships allow marketers to increase consumer loyalty and thus encourage repeat purchases.

Advances in technology have enhanced corporate utilization of information. Typically, this information is used to develop a customer database. Vavra (1994) identified several benefits that this information can provide for marketers. First, the information allows marketers to access basic customer information such as name and address, information that could facilitate direct marketing. More important, these data open channels of communication through which marketers can establish and maintain a relationship with consumers. Through these relationships, marketers are able to increase consumer loyalty and thus encourage repeat purchases (Javalgi and Moberg, 1997). Most sport executives realize that repeat purchasers are essential in inducing a higher lifetime value from each customer.

Sports organizations have access to a considerable amount of information on their customers. Some use it; some do not. Mullin, Hardy, and Sutton (1993) indicated that much of the information available to the sport marketer is either lost or not retrievable. Therefore, the purpose of this chapter is to assist sport marketers in the development and utilization of an effective marketing information system.

Obtaining Information

The first step in building an effective marketing information system is to collect or generate useful data. But, you may ask, where do you obtain the data? Traditionally, sports organizations have not been as sophisticated as many other business operations in collecting and using marketing data, so it is important to improve in this area of operations. Managers of sport organizations receive various kinds of information from within their organization and from other sources with which they must interact on an ongoing basis (Stotlar, 1987). These must be clearly identified and will become the main sources for sport marketing data.

Sources of MIS data are typically identified as being either primary or secondary (Mullin et al., 1993, Mullin, 1985; Stotlar, 1989). Primary research is research conducted with, or collected directly from, your customers. Sports organizations can, through automation, keep very accurate records of all their clients, all people doing business with the organization. This includes both those who have purchased from the organization and those from whom the organization buys goods and services (Stotlar, 1989).

> The most popular methods for primary data collection for sports organizations are direct-mail surveys, telephone interviews, and personal interviews.

Health and fitness clubs have access to considerable amounts of information about their clients. They all filled out application forms that included not only their name and address, but also typically their occupation and income. Many clubs also have an extended system that can track the programs and equipment used in the club by each member and can generate reports detailing individual and club usage. This information can be quite useful to the market manager in tracking renewals and future marketing campaigns.

The University of Northern Colorado Athletic Department implemented an MIS in 1991 to better track the students attending athletic contests. Prior to implementation, students would just show their ID to access gate entrance; however, with the new system, the ID was scanned at the entry gate. The athletic department now had current and reliable information on student attendance. These data were used successfully to push forward plans to locate a new stadium closer to the main student housing areas. These data could also be cross-referenced with basketball attendance to see if the consumers were the same or different, and appropriate marketing efforts could then be initiated. As a side benefit, former students who had been accustomed to flashing their out-of-date IDs and proceeding through the gate were stopped and referred to the ticket window.

The forms these exercisers filled out when they joined give the gym owners much useful demographic information.

Photo reprinted by permission of WVU Photography.

Another innovative method for collecting marketing and consumer information was introduced at Colorado ski resorts in 1993. Several of the major ski resorts implemented computerized systems from validating and tracking skiers. The systems included scanners located at all lift locations across the resort. When skiers lined up for transport up the mountain, the lift operators scanned their lift tickets or season passes. Information collected through the process could then be analyzed and evaluated by resort managers. Specific information that would be valuable would be the types of terrain skied by the most skiers, the frequency and duration of runs, and the typical ski pattern for the majority of skiers on the mountain. These data could also be tabulated from week to week throughout the season, and individual reports could be generated for season-pass holders. One interesting advantage of the system was discovered in 1998 when two young skiers were reported lost at the end of a day skiing. Resort personnel were able to use the scanned data to locate the last ski lift accessed by the skiers, and a rescue was launched in the most likely areas where the boys would have skied. One boy was rescued though the other unfortunately died. However, the rescue of the lone survivor would most likely not have been successful without MIS data.

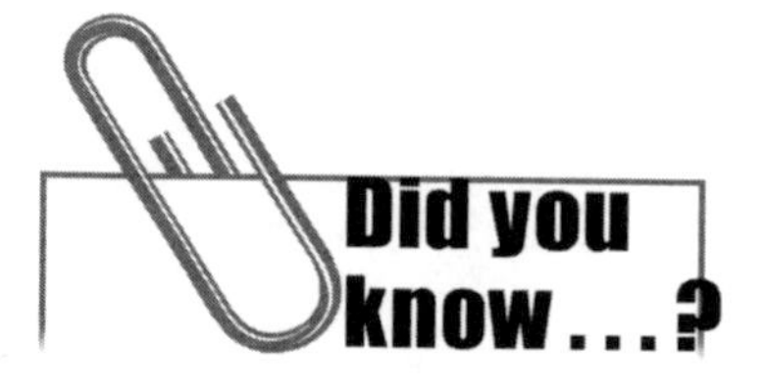

Large golf ranges (50 or more tees) sell a median of 30,000 buckets of balls each year.

Source: National Golf Foundation

The most popular methods for primary data collection for sports organizations are direct-mail surveys, telephone interviews, and personal interviews. Data generated through client questionnaires or surveys can be valuable sources of information about customers' attitudes toward your products and services, as well as short-term demand trends (Stotlar, 1989). Primary data can also enhance a sound quality-control system by eliciting feedback to be used in refining product and service offerings.

Primary data collection can also take the form of pilot testing and product experiments. Those companies that manufacture sporting goods are continuously involved in this type of research, specifically in product development.

Unfortunately, many sport organizations discard valuable consumer information. Mullin (1985), a marketing executive with different Major League Baseball teams, said that some "baseball franchises that make it to the playoffs throw away the names and addresses of unfilled ticket applications, when these individuals clearly should be added to the mailing list" (p. 205). Spoelstra (1997) also found that when he joined the front office of the NBA New Jersey Nets, they were throwing away valuable data. When customers called the Nets to obtain an copy of the season schedule, the ticket office staff simply grabbed an envelope, wrote down the caller's name and address, and mailed the schedule. Because these people had expressed an interest in the Nets' product, Spoelstra felt that their names should be placed into an MIS for additional direct-mail marketing.

A similar oversight in many organizations is failure to record information when clients pay by check. These people may not be regular customers, and they could be included on special mailings designed to attract new business. This technique is often used with fitness clubs when guests of current members register at the front desk. The office staff is trained to enter the visitors' names into a "prospects" file that can be used in future marketing activities.

In the late 1990s, many sport organization began to realize the value of collecting information and designed programs similar to the airline industry's frequent flyer programs. One of the first teams to initiate such a program was the San Diego Padres of MLB. In 1996 the Padres introduced the Compadres Club. In their first year of operations, they signed up 90,000 members. Forty-six percent of the club members increased their game attendance over the previous season. Other clubs (Anaheim Angels, Mighty Ducks of Anaheim, San Francisco Giants) quickly followed the model established by the Padres.

The three models of consumer loyalty programs are the points and prizes model, the plateaus, perks, and prizes model, and the membership program model.

Barlow (1992) detailed three models of consumer loyalty programs. The first model is the points and prizes model. As you would expect, consumers earn points for purchases and eventually achieve point levels appropriate for prize redemption. A second, more structured model allows customers to continually accumulate points for awards. When specified point levels are attained, predetermined awards are distributed. The plateaus, perks, and prizes model has proven successful in numerous business segments. The third and least complicated loyalty program is the membership program. Customers are encouraged to join a corporate club that entitles them to special benefits and discounts. This model has been used as the basis of many sport fan clubs.

The Padres, and with some variation the other professional teams noted above, adopted the plateaus, perks, and prizes model. Padre fans were encouraged to join the Compadres club by completing a club application. Huang (1999) investigated the types of data collected by these teams through their application forms. He found that the teams collected vast amounts of consumer information, more information than did other business-sector loyalty programs. The data collected included personal data, demographic background, and purchase behavior. The personal information requested included name, address, phone and fax numbers, and date of birth. The demographic variables encompassed gender, age, marital status, ethnicity, number of children, education, household income, and occupation. In addition, some information was collected regarding the customers' lifestyle interests. Finally, application forms requested data relating to the applicants' purchase behavior. Factors such as where tickets were purchased, previous and future purchases, seating location, and media influences were also recorded. Collectively, these data would be of significant benefit to sport marketers.

Sport organizations are also consumers; therefore, every supplier to the organization should also be considered as a potential consumer. A wide variety of products and services are purchased by your organization and represent another possible marketing opportunity. These companies could be contacted for ticket purchases, product donations, and sponsorship opportunities (Stotlar, 1989).

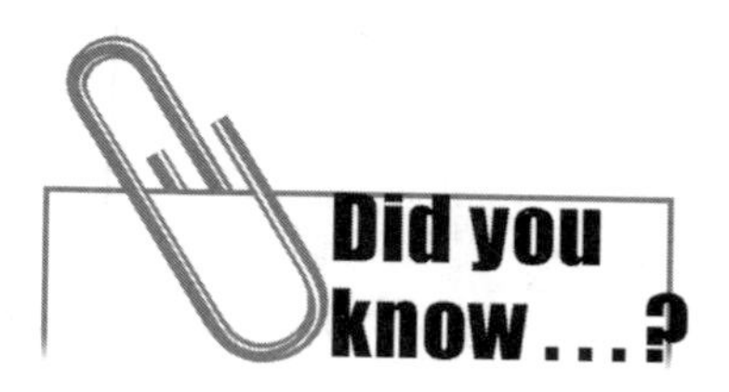

Tourist visits to U.S. national parks rose from 237.1 million in 1986 to 265.8 million in 1996.

Source: National Park Service

Secondary research is characterized by the fact that it is not conducted directly by the sport organization. According to Shaw (1991) "the information-vending business grosses $15 billion in the USA and is the fastest growing area of the information business in marketing information" (p. 38).

Several major companies are in the business of market research, including sport market research. A considerable amount of data can be obtained from these organizations, which collect and publish data about the sport industry.

Probably the most comprehensive data are available through Simmons Market Research Bureau, which produces volumes of marketing research for all industries, including sports and fitness. Their data are presented in a variety of areas, and an entire volume is devoted to sports and leisure. Sport marketers will be most interested in the data on sports participation, attendance at sporting events and sports equipment sales. Simmons details consumers by age, income, geographical location, occupation, education, marital status, and size of family. Access to Simmons Market Research Bureau is available at most public libraries.

Professional and trade associations also publish information that is crucial for sport marketers. For example, the Sporting Goods Manufacturers Association conducted a study of 10,000 children aged 10–18 regarding their participation, attitudes, and opinions surrounding sport. These data would be quite valuable in defining both market size and potential for sport retailers. The International Health, Racquet and Sportsclub Association (IHRSA) conducts an annual analysis of the fitness and exercise club industry. These data would certainly be helpful to fitness clubs in designing and correctly positioning their products and services. For example, IHRSA data indicated that for all health and fitness centers in the United States, average revenues per club member was $678 per year. The mean revenue per square foot of floor space was $43 whereas revenue for tennis-only facilities was $63 per square foot. These data would be essential when assessing operating efficiency of your business. They would also be critical in making decisions regarding which business sector to enter (International Health, Racquet and Sportsclub Association, 1998)

Manufacturers have become very ingenious in ways to build MIS data. For example, Nike placed a hand-tag on their Air Jordan youth apparel. This tag was an application form to join the Air Jordan Flight Club. Membership in the club included a poster, membership card, and special T-shirt, but most important, Nike obtained the name, address, and phone number of a young sports consumer.

The sources for information are almost unlimited, but finding the information takes a little time, imagination, and effort. A national governing body could easily access information from sporting goods retailers concerning who purchased related equipment specific to their sport. These names could in turn be entered into a database and included in future membership or marketing efforts.

Sport manufacturers and sport organizations must collect market data, and with this abundance of data, the sport marketing professional needs a marketing information system to supply managers with the necessary data for making informed decisions. The accuracy and availability of marketing data are vital for sports organizations because their fans, clients, participants, and consumers change rapidly (Mullin et al., 1993). Therefore, the MIS must be designed to store, retrieve, and assimilate the data in meaningful ways.

Designing Information Systems

The MIS does not make decisions, but merely makes information available quickly, accurately, and in a form that marketers can interpret. Refer to the model of marketing information systems for sport organizations presented in Figure 7.1. It should be noted that although not every MIS is computer based, the microcomputer and an MIS function well together. The advantages of a microcomputer-based MIS are that information can be retrieved much faster than through traditional methods and that computers are more accurate than manual methods (Stotlar, 1987).

Marketing information systems must be integrated so that fragmented data can be fused into composite pictures of individual consumers and specific sport markets (Shaw, 1991). It is imperative that when sport marketers are required to make decisions, they make informed decisions based on the best and most current information. All sport marketers can make decisions, but the success of the marketing decision often depends on the quality of the information on which it is based (Stotlar, 1987). It is the function of the MIS to provide that information.

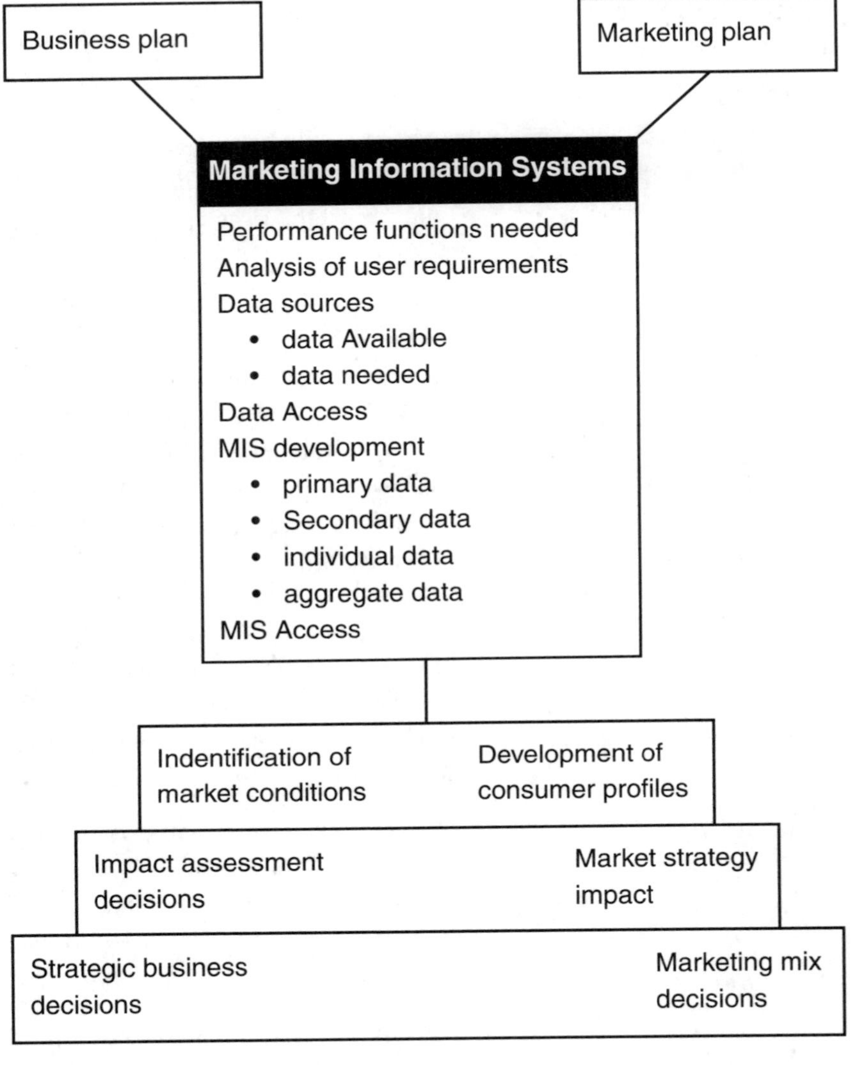

Figure 7.1
Integration of marketing information system for sport organizations.

Mullin (1985) was one of the early sport marketers to recognize the value of a well-managed MIS. He indicated that "the full value of an MIS is realized only when data from various sources are integrated into a common database" (p. 207). Mullin (1985) and Grantham, Patton, York, and Winick (1998) describe the essential characteristics of an effective sport marketing database as follows:

1. A protocol must be established to collect data needed for the system.
2. It must be linked to a central processing unit. An organization needs to have all of its data located in one centralized system.
3. Storage capacity must be planned into the system through a thorough analysis of anticipated data volume and characteristics.
4. The various databases (consumer files, accounting records, sales records, etc.) need to be fully integrated so that the data from one source can be contrasted and/or combined with data from another source.

5. The data must be retrievable in a form that the sport marketer can use for decision making.

6. Control mechanisms should be designed into the system to facilitate data security.

Maintaining Data Security

Two distinct types of security problems accompany the use of microcomputers. The first problem involves the software used to perform the various tasks. Because the information on the software program and the information that has been entered by the staff are stored on a disk, the characteristics of that disk are important. Almost all microcomputers use combinations of zip drives and CD-ROMs. Larger computers will use removable hard drives and other storage systems. Although storage disks are relatively durable, they can be erased through exposure to any magnetic object. This totally destroys any information on the disk, program, and/or files. Disks have also been known to "crash" on their own. Therefore, one of the most important aspects of data security is "backing up." This involves making a duplicate of all programs and information stored on disks. This may seem like much work, but the penalty for failing to back up work is that someone must reenter all of the information that was lost.

> Watch for two potential security problems with using microcomputers to help manage data—the erasure of a disk's content upon exposure to magnets or general disk failure and the availability of data to unqualified people.

The second problem regarding security involves access to restricted information. Sport organizations consider their marketing information confidential. It is important that this information be reserved for viewing only by appropriate people. This restricted access is often accomplished through the password system. The user must enter a predetermined password to gain access to MIS files. New developments in security are constantly evolving. Systems that evaluate the user's eye geometry are currently being used in some corporations. These security measures are also quite important when any unauthorized access could cause severe problems for the organization.

Getting the System to Work

Two common mistakes are often made in the application of computers in sport organizations. First, managers buy a computer with the idea that a job will be found for it to do. Second, the people who will be using the computer are often not involved in the testing and purchase of the system (Danziger, 1985; Stotlar, 1987). On many occasions, a well-intentioned administrator has purchased a computer to assist staff, only to discover that the computer will not perform the functions that the staff needs it to perform. The computer and the software should be purchased with specific requirements in mind, and the staff should be involved in the decision from the very beginning of the process.

Two basic types of programs are available, custom programs and commercial "off-the-shelf" business applications. Commercial software packages are readily available to create and manage marketing information, and they can handle the majority of information storage and retrieval needs of sport marketers. Each program has unique strengths and weaknesses, and many of them will let you create custom forms for storing and retrieving your marketing information. Another advantage is that many office workers will be familiar with the operation of the more well-known software programs.

In the event that your organization has special needs, you may need to have a software program written especially for your applications. Although these programs will fit your needs, they are generally expensive, and any future modification that is required will often mandate hiring the same person (or company) that designed the original program. It goes without saying that this situation would not leave you in the best market position.

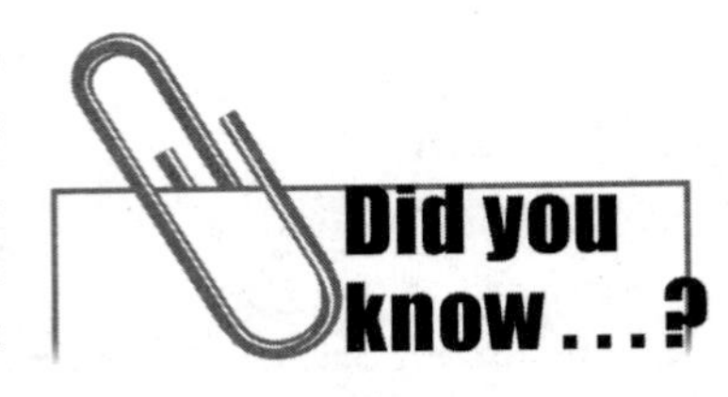

Eighty-six percent of Americans say they exercise, and 41% say they exercise regularly. The reasons:

Stay healthy (65%)
Lose weight (18%)
Have fun (10%)
Look good (7%)

Source: USA Today

A commercial database usually allows for individualized category ("field") names to be developed by the end user. The computer manages pieces of information by these "fields;" therefore, each piece of information by which the marketer may wish to sort, list, or search must have its own field, so it is important for the sport marketer to carefully review the ability of the program to handle files by fields. When considering either a custom-programmed package or a commercial one that allows for individualized fields for each file, the sport marketer must determine the exact information that will be needed.

Many commercial programs have companion software that will allow you to create and move information from one application to another. Thus, a marketing director in a fitness center could have a memo written on the word processor, have the MIS select the addresses of all members who had not been in for a workout in the past month, and merge the mailing list with the memo.

Considerable attention has thus far been devoted to the various tasks and programs for the accomplishment of those tasks. One more type of program must be addressed: the integrated database-graphics programs. These programs can also combine word processing, graphics, spreadsheets, database, and telecommunication. Use of this software facilitates sales reports, market projects, and communication with both clients and staff. This enables the user to purchase one piece of software that will do just about everything. Integrated software is more expensive, but the convenience of a "one-system" package is often worth the expense.

A well-designed database system can also perform many standard business tasks. Some MIS applications can perform accounts-receivable functions such as preparation of invoices, maintenance of customer accounts, and production of sales and other reports. In sports organizations, this function is often applied to ticket sales or membership payments. The accounts-payable segment of the program would generally enjoy a wider application through the organization detailing all vendors with whom business is transacted. The features that often appear in this function are purchase-order control, invoice processing, check writing and control, cash-requirement forecasting, and vendor-information analysis (Falk, 1983). Programs may be designed for specific accounting and data management, but a truly integrated MIS can be adapted for a variety of uses in sport marketing activities.

In the sport setting, these features may surpass the needs and desires of the average sport marketer, but they should be fully compatible with the associated needs of the entire sport organization. The business computer industry has expanded so fast in the past decade that it is difficult to believe that a commercially available package cannot be found that could meet all of your MIS needs.

Working With the System

It should also be pointed out that an MIS cannot be expected to solve problems efficiently as soon as the computer comes out of the box. It takes about 40 hours for a person to become fully acquainted with the operation of any hardware system and about 20 hours to be become familiar with a specific software package (Danziger, 1985). According to Shaw (1991), an MIS must be designed "with a view to the people who will use them, and with an understanding of how the business in which they work operates. [An MIS] must deliver the right information to the right people at the right time" (p. 60).

With the right system, access to the information is quick, and updating the material is much simpler than with conventional methods. Printouts of data should be available by any combination of factors selected by the sport marketer. This will allow for effective sales and market planning.

Producing Results

The point of marketing research and data analysis is to better identify segments of the market that are most likely to purchase your goods and services. The individual pieces of data in your MIS can tell you who bought what and when. However important that may be, what you really want to know is who will buy what and when. This is the aspect of sport marketing called *forecasting*. Forecasting is a distinct advantage provided by computerized MIS systems.

Exactly what is forecasting and why is it necessary? Forecasting is the ability of the market manager to see how the future will be affected by anticipated or hypothetical decisions, the playing of "what if?" This can be very beneficial to sport marketers because hypothetical figures can be entered into the MIS for such items as sponsorship revenues, ticket prices, or membership fees. The program could then be manipulated to perform calculations detailing the financial and market consequences of those decisions.

> The main goal of conducting marketing research and analyzing data is to determine who will buy what goods and when.

Although MIS information is entered into the system piecemeal, sports marketers need to be able to look at that organization's data as a whole. There is a need for aggregate information to develop business and general marketing strategies, yet there is also a demand for synthesizing data to project individual consumer profiles. Sport marketers must clearly see the macro and micro perspectives of their consumer base. Therefore, both individual and aggregate information is needed for intelligent marketing mix decisions.

Chapter Summary

All sport organizations deal with consumers, and consumer information is ideally suited to the storage and retrieval capabilities of the MIS. Having discovered the broad range of application for an MIS, it should be clear that marketing information systems will not immediately make a poor sport marketer competent or an inefficient sales person good, but it is a tool that can be used by skilled employees and managers to assist in the performance of sport marketing tasks and decision making. Typical information contained in MIS files would include the consumer's name, address, age, occupation, and purchasing activity. It is precisely this type of information that is particularly well suited to MIS and a computer-managed database because of the need to continually update and change entries. Sport marketers can combine these data with other information in the corporation database to facilitate decisions on target markets and consumer profiles. Remember that the quality of your decisions is reflective of the quality of the information upon which they were based.

Questions for Study

1. What are the essential characteristics of a well-designed marketing information system?
2. What MIS sources would be available for an intercollegiate athletic program, and how would you go about setting up an MIS?

Learning Activities

1. Select your favorite sport and consult a copy of Simmons Market Research Bureau. See where you fit in the demographic segments presented.
2. Take a trip to your local fitness center or health club, and inquire about the types of information they have on their clients. Also look at their application form if they are uncooperative with your first request.

Professional Associations and Organizations

Sporting Goods Manufacturers Association
200 Castlewood Drive
North Palm Beach, FL 33408

Suggested Readings

Poppel, H. L., and Goldstein, B. *Information technology*. New York: McGraw-Hill Book Company.

Shaw, R. (1991). *Computer-aided marketing and selling*. London: Reed International Books.

Chapter 8

The Marketing Mix and the Sport Industry

Overview

This chapter presents a brief overview of a significant element of the sport marketing management model called the marketing mix. The marketing mix is crucial because it defines the sport business, and much of the sport marketer's time is spent on various functions within the marketing mix.

The marketing mix comprises four elements: product, price, place, and promotion. In this chapter we will define the marketing mix, present a description of its place in the sport marketing management model, present a brief description of each of the elements of the marketing mix, and describe how the elements are combined to create the marketing mix for the sport company.

The Marketing Mix

The *marketing mix* is the strategic combination (mix) of four elements called the 4 Ps. These are product, price, place, and promotion. At the heart of the decision-making process are the research and knowledge gained about the consumer, the competition, the company, and the climate (see chapters 5, 6, and 7). All factors must be given careful attention. If the sport marketer ignores one or the other, this increases the chances of making wrong decisions (Schnaars, 1991).

The development of the marketing mix involves determining the optimal combination of product, price, promotion, and place. Reaching the optimal combination depends on developing and manipulating each of the 4 Ps until each one is right for a particular product—and for the business. For the business, "optimal" means the combination that sells—meets consumer needs. There are many variables of each of the 4 Ps that can be manipulated by the sport marketer. They are manipulated for meeting the consumer's desires or needs or for competitive strategy, according to what the company can do, and within ethical, political, economical, and legal constraints and considerations.

> Creation of the marketing mix involves the process of discovering or developing the right combination of product, price, place, and promotion.

The 4 Cs—consumer, competitor, company, and climate—constantly change, and therefore require constant monitoring and research. When any one of these elements changes, it can have an impact on one or all of the 4 Ps. The change has the potential to be positive or negative. This could be considered an opportunity or a threat to the company. The important thing is that you know about the change, can study it and its possible consequences—opportunities or threats—and can make decisions necessary to optimize or minimize those consequences.

Marketing Mix:

the strategic combination of product, price, place, and promotion decisions and strategies.

Marketing Mix Elements:

The 4 Ps
- Product
- Price
- Place
- Promotion

Product. The product is what the sport company is trying to sell. The challenge is to produce the *right* product for the consumer. Products can be goods, services, people, places, and ideas. There are many products in the sport industry. There are many consumers and competitors also. As you learned in chapters 5, 6, and 7, the sport marketer must analyze the consumers to understand exactly what the consumer wants and analyze its competitors to learn what already exists in the market. As you will learn in chapter 9, the process for developing the right product can be very involved.

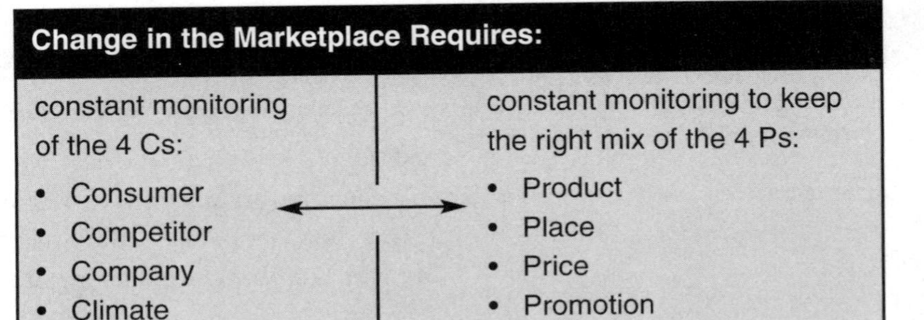

The product can be manipulated, or differentiated as it is called in marketing. A tennis racket may be produced with a new shape or a new color. The sport center can offer new divisions in a volleyball league based on age, gender, or skill level. The same sport center could offer a new form of volleyball by simply changing some rules, court size, or number of players. As an example, there is now beach volleyball that can be played in a 2-player, 3-player, or 4-player format.

Price. Price is the exchange value of a product. The challenge for the sport marketer is to determine the *right* price for the consumer. The price of a product can be manipulated many ways. Promotional pricing can be used: 2-for-1 tickets to the game or 2-for-1 memberships to the fitness club, special sale prices on sports clothing for special times such as holidays, special sale prices on sporting goods equipment for seasonal sports, or price breaks as the quantity purchased increases. There are also long-term price-planning strategies that the sport marketer can use. Refer to chapter 10 for details of price as a marketing mix element.

Place. Place is the process of getting the sport product to the consumer. It is also called distribution: distributing the sport product to the consumer. The sport marketer will analyze the types of distribution methods available and select those that will deliver the product to the right place. The right place means: where the consumer is, shops, or will travel to. There are two types of distribution in the sport industry because of the types of products offered. *Hard goods* are those products that must go from a manufacturing plant to a retail outlet and therefore involve the kind of distribution in which moving products is involved. There also are products that cannot be moved in the sport industry. For example, a basketball game is not a product that can be moved to a retail outlet and sold. The consumer must go to the place in which the game will be played (manufactured) in order to consume it.

If the consumer believes that a product is overpriced or even underpriced, there is a good chance that the consumer will not purchase the product.

One way to promote a sporting event is to build the reputation of the team's mascot.

Photo reprinted by permission of WVU Photography.

The distribution (place) of a product can be changed. One can now purchase tickets to various sporting events through many different ticket outlets because they are distributed through many outlets. Sport facilities are becoming a one-stop-shopping facility: many new ones include hotels, shopping malls, and other attractions including fitness centers and amusements parks. Sport sold as a spectator product can change other factors in the way it is distributed to the consumer. For example, there are over 60 official Kentucky Derby Festival events prior to the actual Derby race, a sporting event that lasts about 2 minutes! Refer to chapter 11 for the detailed information about distribution.

Promotion. Promotion is the element of marketing that the general public thinks IS marketing. That's because promotion is the element that the general public sees and relates to as marketing. Promotion includes advertising and other promotional methods. These are designed to attract the consumer's attention. Therefore, the consumer believes that promotion is all that marketing is about.

There are many promotional methods and tricks available for the sport marketer to use, and there are some used in the sport industry that are rarely used in other industries. In one extreme example of trying to get the attention of the consumer and the media, when the first Super Bowl (at that time it was called the AFL-NFL World Championship Game) of the National Football League (NFL) was played in 1966, organizers were so worried that the event would be ignored by the nation, they planned to create interest by staging a kidnapping of the silver trophy (Carucci, 1994)! Promotional methods include television commercials, print advertisements in magazines, direct-mail advertising, promotional pricing, "giveaways" at sports events, and press guides. See chapters 12, 13, 14, 15, and 16 for the detailed information concerning promotion in the sport industry.

> Though the public is often under the impression that promotion is strictly advertising, it is actually a process—the goal is to create enough interest in a product to convince a consumer to purchase it.

All of the marketing mix elements are manipulated by the sport marketer for two reasons: first, to stay in business and, second, to be successful. The only way to do this is to offer products that will sell, at a price that will be paid, offered through a place where they can be bought, and made attractive to the consumer. In other words, the sport marketer needs to develop the right product at the right price offered at the right place and promote it with the right methods.

The sport business professional uses the elements to develop the optimal combination for target markets and in response to changes in the market. It is the responsibility of the sport marketer to control and manage the marketing mix. Although each of the elements is developed through a specific planning process, they are not planned in a vacuum. The elements are interrelated. As such, all decisions regarding one element must be done in conjunction with decisions regarding all other elements.

> Research is the foundation upon which all marketing decisions are made.

In addition, decisions concerning the elements in the marketing mix must be made in relation to what the consumer wants, compared to what the competitor has, considered for its fit for the company and considered against legal, ethical, social, cultural, and political climates.

The Interrelationship of the Elements

The marketing mix elements are interrelated. This means that each element affects the others. The sport business professional must develop the optimal combination. Decisions should be made based on the information gained in the marketing research.

The consumer is looking for the right product, at just the right price, and that can be purchased at the right location. As you will learn in chapter 9, the consumer does not arbitrarily buy products—the consumer is looking for something to satisfy a need or desire. From that perspective, the product and everything about the product take on characteristics beyond the intended function of the product. This notion must be understood by the sport businessperson and used during the development of a marketing mix. For example, let's look at a consumer who wants a new pair of running shoes.

The consumer's existing shoes are not quite worn out, but this consumer is becoming a "serious runner." A serious runner is a different person than a "recreational runner" and therefore has different product needs and beliefs about those needs. This runner believes that the shoes must be thought of in the running community as "serious-runner" shoes. This is in marketing terms what can be described as a consumer who is image conscious, perhaps brand loyal, has high product knowledge, wants to fulfill a desire, and price is not really a factor. The sport marketer, having studied the running market, understands the serious-runner consumer and recognizes what this particular consumer wants. Therefore, the sport marketer will produce a serious-runner shoe, and most likely, price will be no factor. The shoe will be advertised in serious-runner publications only, and the advertisements will carry the message and image that this shoe is only for the serious runner. In addition, the shoe will be sold only through serious-runner stores. This will add to the notion that the shoes are for serious runners only.

> Consumer purchases are not arbitrarily—the consumer is looking for a product that satisfies a need or desire.

In this example, the sport marketer studied and understands this particular consumer. A product is produced specifically for this consumer; the price is set at what the consumer is willing to pay; the promotional methods imply the type of product for this particular type of consumer; and the product is offered for sale in specific places. This process and the decisions about the combination of the four elements are indicative of the interrelationship and impact of the elements.

The Marketing Mix Strategy in the Sport Industry

The primary strategy for the sport business in designing a marketing mix is to customize the marketing mix for a specific consumer market until the optimal mix is found. As the sport marketer identifies consumer market segments and selects target markets, the marketing mix elements are designed specifically for the consumer. For example, if the sport marketer determines from research that the typical consumer of memberships in fitness centers is female, aged between 28 and 46, single, with one child; an income range of $32,000 to $98,000; an education level of at least a bachelor's degree; and favorite sport and fitness activities of weight training, working out on the stair climbing machine, aerobics, tennis, and volleyball, then the sport marketer can design the product—a fitness and sport center—for the consumer, price it for the consumer, develop promotional methods designed to attract the consumer, and place the facility in an area of the city in which a high percentage of those types of consumers live.

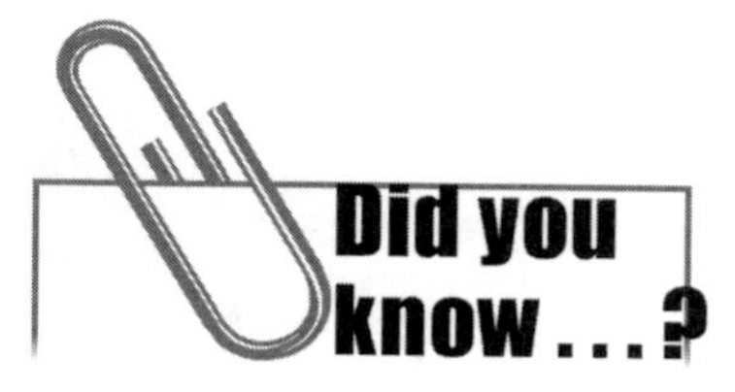

A third of adults took an historical or cultural trip in 1999:

Washington, DC (61%)

Hawaii (53%)

Alaska (48%)

Source: Travel Industry Association of America

Also affecting the decision to open a fitness center is information concerning the industry and the competition. For example, if a fitness center already exists that offers exactly what the consumer wants, at the desired price, and in the right location, the sport marketer must determine if it will be feasible to open a fitness center. If reports of the fitness industry nationwide show that fitness center membership purchase is increasing, how does this compare to the local fitness industry?

In addition, the marketing mix should change as markets change. You have learned earlier in this chapter that the product, price, place, and promotional methods can be manipulated. Here is where the constant research is needed. If it has been eight years since your company conducted any marketing research, the decisions and strategies are riskier as every year goes by.

A good example of the kind of constant research a company should do is the research done on the baby boomer market. This is most likely a market you've heard about because they are mentioned in relation to practically everything in this country, from politics to retirement to toys to sports utility vehicles (SUVs). The baby boomer market has been given responsibility for making or breaking the success of many products, companies, and even whole industries, some of which are the fitness industry and the SUV industry.

Other examples of groups you have most likely heard about are the X-Generation, Techies, and Dead Heads. Each of these is a market—a group of people (consumers) with some like characteristics or interests. They are studied and monitored constantly because their purchasing decisions and product needs and desires affect a company's marketing mix.

The information gained from research should be current. Therefore, research should be an ongoing process within the company. With a flow of current and accurate information, the sport marketer's decisions and strategies for the marketing mix can be much more successful.

Chapter Summary

The marketing mix is the strategic combination of four elements: product, price, place, and promotion. It is the component of the sport marketing management model on which the sport marketer will spend a great percentage of time. It is a crucial element because it involves decisions and strategies concerning the product, price, place, and promotion. The marketing mix is designed based on information concerning the consumer, the competition, the company, and the climate. Chapters 9 through 16 are devoted to the 4 Ps and detail the intricate functions within each element.

Chapter 9

The Product in the Sport Industry

Product Defined

People seek to satisfy needs or desires. To do this, they seek goods, services, people, places, and ideas—products. It could be said that people do not buy products. They are looking for something that will satisfy specific needs, wants, or desires. Products perform as the satisfaction agent. Consider the following examples:

1. A softball player *desires* to improve hitting and enhance batting average. The player will search for the product that will fulfill those desires: the right bat. What the person *wants* is to hit better and to attain a better batting average. The bat is the implement that might meet the consumer's desires.
2. Someone wants to lose weight and get into shape. This person decides that the product to fulfill those desires is a fitness center. In order to get into the fitness center, the individual must purchase the opportunity to do so: a fitness center membership. The fitness center is offered as the opportunity for the person to fulfill those desires: the place to exercise.
3. A bicycle manufacturing company wants to increase sales and reach more markets. After much research, the company executive determines that the Internet would be a good choice as an outlet store for sales. The Internet is the product for this company—it will purchase an Internet site and hire someone to design and manage the Web site. The bicycle company has sought services to meet needs.
4. While someone is playing tennis, the strings of the tennis racket snap. This person wants to continue playing tennis. In order to fulfill that desire, the racket's strings must be replaced. The service of stringing the racket provides the opportunity for the racket to be repaired so that the individual can fulfill the desire to once again play tennis.

These examples serve to partially explain why and how a person purchases a product—people are actually purchasing functions and benefits. The product is the satisfaction agent for those functions and benefits.

Product:

should be understood as a concept and must be used as an umbrella term that includes goods, services, people, places, and ideas with tangible or intangible attributes.

A definition of product should represent the breadth of the term. Therefore, *product* should be understood as a *concept* and must be used as an umbrella term that includes goods, services, people, places, and ideas with tangible or intangible attributes. The softball player wants the softball bat for what it will *do*, what function it will fulfill, and not that it is simply a softball bat.

A sport marketer should strive to understand exactly *what* the consumer wants in order to offer just that. As stated before, products provide benefits and fulfill functions. For instance, a fitness center is a "place" that provides the opportunity to fulfill desires for fitness, weight loss, socializing, fun, relaxation and other benefits. In the example of replacing the broken tennis racket strings, the consumer gets both a "service" and a "good" new string and the job (service) of putting the strings on the racket. The bicycle company's needs to increase sales and reach new markets were fulfilled by the Internet site.

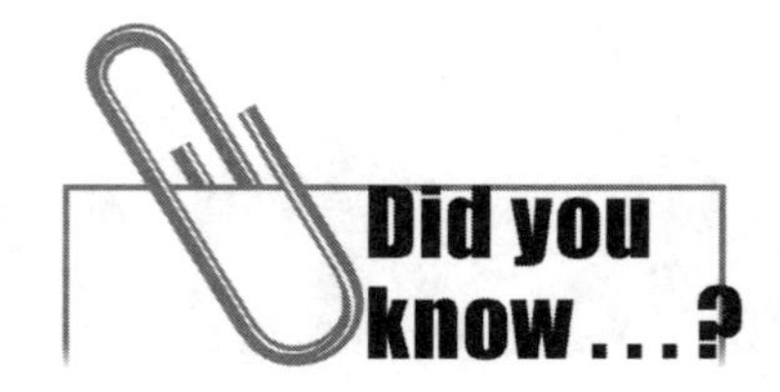

NBA games are broadcast to 190 countries.

Source: Infoseek

Benefits of products include intangibles such as guarantee of quality. The consumer purchases a product with the company's promise of "satisfaction or your money back." The seller is promising that the product will satisfy the consumer's desires or needs. If satisfaction is not realized, whether real or perceived, the consumer may return to the seller, who will give the consumer a refund or satisfy the consumer in some other way. For example, the tennis racket stringing was guaranteed. If the strings were to break, the consumer may return to the company, which will resolve the situation.

The fitness center example is somewhat different. The fitness center may guarantee satisfaction. In this case, satisfaction may be measurable only by the consumer's perception. This is different from the tennis racket stringing. If the strings break, the materials or the service was faulty. If the fitness center consumer is not losing weight and getting into shape, at least according to the consumer's definitions, where does the fault lie—with the consumer or the center? In this situation, the consumer must perform—exercise—in order for the product—weight loss and fitness—to work. The fitness center can only provide the opportunity—*place*—and the means (exercising equipment, classes, and other). Hence, if the consumer does not perform, there will most likely be no weight loss or fitness gain. In this case, is there an obvious opportunity for consumer satisfaction and a money-back guarantee? For instance, a fitness center in Arizona offered a 30-day money-back guarantee. However, the offer was based on an agreement between the club and the consumer: The consumer promised to attend three times a week for a 4-week period and included fitness goals. This resulted in only 3 of 3,000 members asking for a refund.

Toward developing an understanding of a *concept* of product, let's first consider some definitions of product from a variety of marketing textbooks.

> A product is everything, both favorable and unfavorable, that one receives in an exchange. It is a complexity of tangible and intangible attributes, including functional, social, and psychological utilities or benefits. (Pride and Ferrell, 1991, p. 240)

> A product is a bundle of physical, service, and symbolic attributes designed to enhance consumer want satisfaction. (Boone and Kurtz, 1989, p. 271)

A tangible product is a concrete, physical object while an intangible product is indefinite. To buy a baseball is to receive a tangible product; to attend a baseball game is to receive an intangible product.

> A product is a set of tangible and intangible attributes, including packaging, color, price, quality, and brand, plus the services and reputation of the seller.

> A product may be a tangible good, service, place, person, or idea. (Stanton, Etzel, and Walker, 1991, p. 168–169)

Ticketmaster has approximately 2,900 outlets in nine countries and sells more than 70 million tickets a year.

Source: Infoseek

> A product is "the sum of the physical, psychological, and sociological satisfactions that the buyer derives from purchase, ownership, and consumption" and includes "accessories, packaging, and service." (Tarpey, Donnelly, and Peter, 1979)

There are words common to most of the definitions. It is important in reaching an understanding of the concept of product to first understand these terms.

Tangible and intangible. A tangible product is something that is concrete, definite, discernible, and material. It is a physical object. A softball bat is a tangible product. It physically exists. An intangible product is something that is indefinite, indiscernible, indistinguishable, and imperceptible. It is not a physical object. When the broken tennis racket strings need to be repaired, the task of replacing the strings is an intangible product, in this example, a service. Further, a tangible object is involved in this purchase. The consumer gets new strings, a tangible product, and the broken strings are replaced, an intangible product.

Professional sport events provides us with examples of intangible products. A professional men's basketball game is an intangible product. One can only watch the game. Benefits realized include entertainment, socializing, fun, and a number of other personal satisfactions.

It is important that sport marketing decision makers understand the concepts of tangible and intangible. This knowledge guides decisions concerning product strategies and influences other marketing variables as well.

Utility and benefits. "Utility may be defined as the attribute in an item that makes it capable of satisfying human wants" (Stanton, Etzel and Walker, 1991, p. 16). There are four types of utility: form, time, place, and ownership (possession). *Form utility* is the production of a product—using raw materials to create finished products. *Time utility* is getting a product to the consumer *when* the consumer wants it. *Place utility* is getting the product to the consumer *where* the consumer shops. *Ownership utility* is the ability to transfer ownership or possession of a product from seller to buyer (Boone and Kurtz, 1989).

A product's utility is its ability to satisfy a consumer's need. Four aspects of this include the product's form, time, place, and ownership.

Four Types of Utility

Form—using raw materials to produce a product

Time—making a product available when the consumer wants it

Place—getting the product to the venues where the consumer shops

Ownership—transferring ownership or possession of a product from seller to buyer

Using our previous examples, let's consider utility. The consumer who wants a specific softball bat (form utility) to improve batting average wants the bat *before* the softball season begins (time utility), *from* a reputable sporting goods store *close to* where the consumer lives (ownership and place utilities). The sport marketer's job is to produce the bat from specific raw materials (form utility), get it on the market in advance of softball season (time utility), and in reputable sporting goods stores and other outlets (ownership and place utilities). It is only when the sport marketer completely understands the consumer's specific needs—what, when, how, why—that the marketer may make informed decisions concerning form, time, place and ownership utilities.

For the bicycle company that needs the Internet site to increase sales and reach new markets, every utility is met. The company is getting its Web site through which to sell their products; they are getting it when—immediately—they need it; they are getting it from a well-known and respected company (an Internet service company); and they are getting it close to where they want it—the Web manager they hired works in the main office suite.

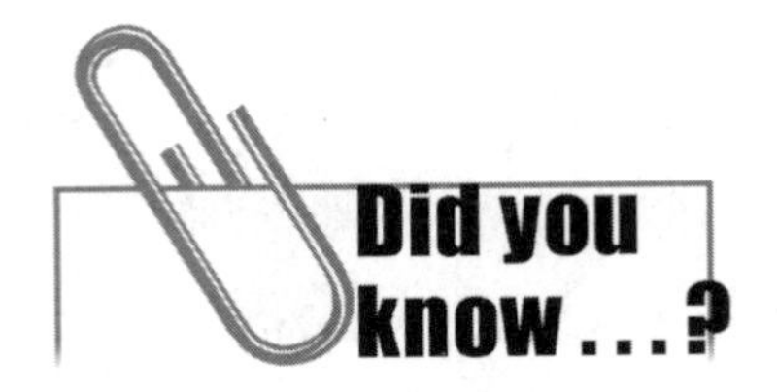

The WWF produces 12 pay-per-view shows and approximately 200 live events a year.

Source: Infoseek

The *benefits* of a product are everything the consumer derives from the product. In other words, benefits may include functions of the product and intangible benefits such as status, quality, durability, cost effectiveness and others. For example, the consumer who wants to improve batting average expects that the selected bat will improve batting average. The sport marketer, based on an understanding of what the softball player wants, promotes the bat as a bat that will give the player a better batting average. Promotion messages such as "this bat has a bigger sweet spot," "the only bat for champions," or "the home-run hitter's dream bat" are strong suggestions to the consumer that this bat will give the consumer what he or she wants, a better batting average.

You should now have a good understanding of product. It is not simply a good or a service. It is something that functions in some capacity and fulfills a consumer's desire or need. The sport marketer must know what the consumer wants the product to do—benefits—and guide the company toward meeting those demands—utility. The sport company produces a product *after* learning what the consumer wants.

Sport Product Defined

There is a vast array of products in the sport industry. Based on the definition presented in chapter 1, we recognize the sport industry as broad and comprised of industry segments such as fitness management, recreation and professional sports, any product that fulfills the sport, fitness, or recreation-related needs or desires of a consumer is considered a sport product. This requires a broad concept definition of sport product. Drawing on the definition of sport and the sport industry in chapter 1 and the general definitions of product in this chapter, the definition of sport product is "any good, service, person, place, or idea with tangible or intangible attributes that satisfy consumer sport, fitness, or recreation related needs or desires."

Sport Product:

Any good, service, person, place, or idea with tangible or intangible attributes that satisfy consumer sport, fitness, or recreation related needs or desires.

Return to chapter 1 and reread the section on what exists in the sport industry. Using our definition of sport product, those are all sport products offered to fulfill consumer sport-related needs or desires. With so many sport products in this industry, it is necessary for the sport marketer to identify differing consumer needs and desires in order to create and offer products that will fulfill those needs and desires. The most common method is product classification.

Sport Product Classifications

An initial step in developing products is to determine what type(s) of product(s) to offer. This task involves studying a particular product category, also known as a product market or an industry segment. The reasons for studying product categories or segments are similar to the reasons for studying and segmenting consumers. A thorough understanding of your product, its benefits and functions, and its utilities, along

A product category is a group of products that are either exactly alike or have homogeneous characteristics. Studying these categories enables marketers to fully understand and market their product.

with understanding the same about your competitor's product, is critical to product management. Constant study of your product and all products like it will guide decisions concerning product development or diversification, pricing strategies, distribution tactics, and promotional strategies.

This information provides the basis for the sport company to define its product(s), make decisions concerning opportunities or threats, develop appropriate marketing plans, develop a successful product mix, and determine the right time for product differentiation and deletion.

One method of classifying products is based on the consumer. In this method, products are traditionally classified in two very broad categories: consumer products and business products. *Consumer products* are those products offered to the final consumer for personal or household use (Evans and Berman, 1987). *Business products* are those products offered to businesses or organizations for use in the production of other goods and services, to operate a business, or for resale to other consumers (Stanton et al., 1991).

The sport industry offers a wide diversity of products targeted to both business consumers and end consumers. In each category, products can be either goods, services, people, places, or ideas. In relation to service products, they can be classified into one of three categories: rented-goods service, owned-goods service, and non-goods service

A *rented-goods service* is the renting of a product for a period of time. Some examples in the sport industry include the following: a fitness center rents a fitness video to

Water skis are one type of rented-goods service.
Photo reprinted by permission of WVU Photography.

clients; a tennis center rents tennis rackets to members; a tennis center rents court time; a park near a lake rents a jet ski on an hourly basis; a snow ski resort rents skis for a day or a week; a marina rents a houseboat for a weekend or for a week.

Owned-goods services include those services to repair or alter something that the consumer owns. Some examples of owned-goods services in the sport industry are replacing broken strings on your tennis racket; getting your golf clubs cleaned at the club; getting numbers, names, and logos put on your softball uniform; having your boat's engine repaired; getting your wheelchair repaired in order to play in your wheelchair basketball game.

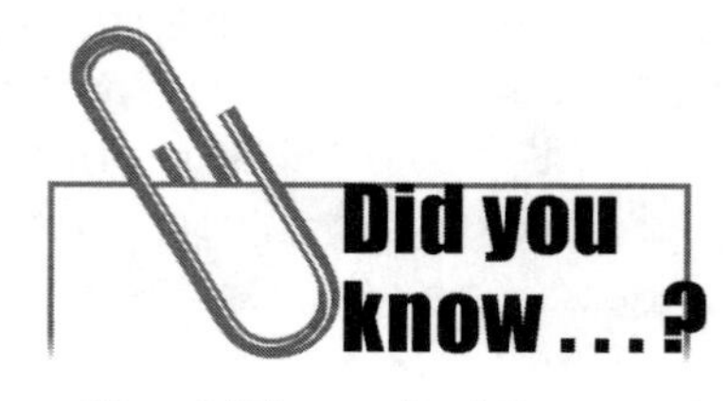

The NFL sealed the most expensive sports TV rights ever, awarding TV contracts to ABC, ESPN, CBS, and FOX for nearly $18 billion.

Source: Infoseek

Nongoods services do not involve a good at all. This category includes personal services offered by the seller. In the sport industry some examples are tennis lessons, golf lessons, or summer basketball camp; a fitness center offers childcare service on site. This category also includes those services offered by sport management or sport marketing companies that specialize in managing and/or marketing a sporting event for you. For example, you hire a sport marketing company to market and manage every aspect of a large marathon in your city.

Business products. Business products in the sport industry are those products offered to sport businesses for use in the manufacture of sport products, to operate a sport business or for resale. Hillerich & Bradsby, manufacturers of the famous Louisville Slugger bats, purchases wood as a material used to make wood baseball bats (Pitts and Fielding, 1987). Consider the following variety of other types of business products offered to business consumers:

- A golf club manufacturer purchases graphite and other materials to produce golf clubs.
- A running shoe company purchases a variety of rubber, leather, and other materials in order to make running shoes.
- A bicycle manufacturer purchases aluminum to use in the manufacture of lightweight bicycles.
- A sport sponsorship management company purchases research services in order to help analyze sponsorship effectiveness.

If the sport marketer understands these types of classifications, the marketer will understand consumer type and what the consumer is looking for. Another method used in marketing to classify products is industry segmentation.

Industry Segmentation

Industry segmentation is another method used by marketers to classify products and buyers. *Industry segmentation* is defined by Porter (1985) as the division of an industry into subunits (industry segments) for purposes of developing competitive strategy. An *industry segment* is a combination of a product variety and a group of consumers who purchase it (Porter).

Some industries contain just one product. More typically, an industry contains a variety of product items sold to many existing or potential consumers who vary in many ways. The sport industry contains a wide variety of products offered to a great variety of consumers—final and business. Trying to keep up with every product in the sport industry would be practically impossible. It becomes important and even necessary that the sport marketer focus on a section or segment of the total industry. This guides the sport marketer in the identification of marketing opportunities and threats within a specific prod-

Industry segmentation is the division of an industry into industry segments in order to develop a competitive strategy. The sport industry can be divided into the sport performance segment, the sport production segment, and the sport promotion segment.

uct market and the development of an appropriate marketing mix (Day, Shocker and Srivastava, 1979; McCarthy and Perreault, 1984; Porter, 1985).

The sport industry segmentation model (Pitts, Fielding and Miller, 1994; presented in Figure 9.1) is a unique study of products in the sport industry. The authors used a portion of the Porter (1985) model for industry segmentation and used product function and buyer types in segmenting the sport industry. Three sport product industry segments were identified. These are the sport performance segment, sport production segment, and sport promotion segment. The information is important to the sport marketer in developing an understanding of the product segment within the sport industry in which the company's product(s) fits, identifying and monitoring the competition, and determining product management strategies (Figure 9.2).

The *sport performance industry segment* consists of sport performance as a product. Sport performance is offered to the consumer in two ways: as a participation product and as a spectatorial product. Each of these may even be considered separate segments

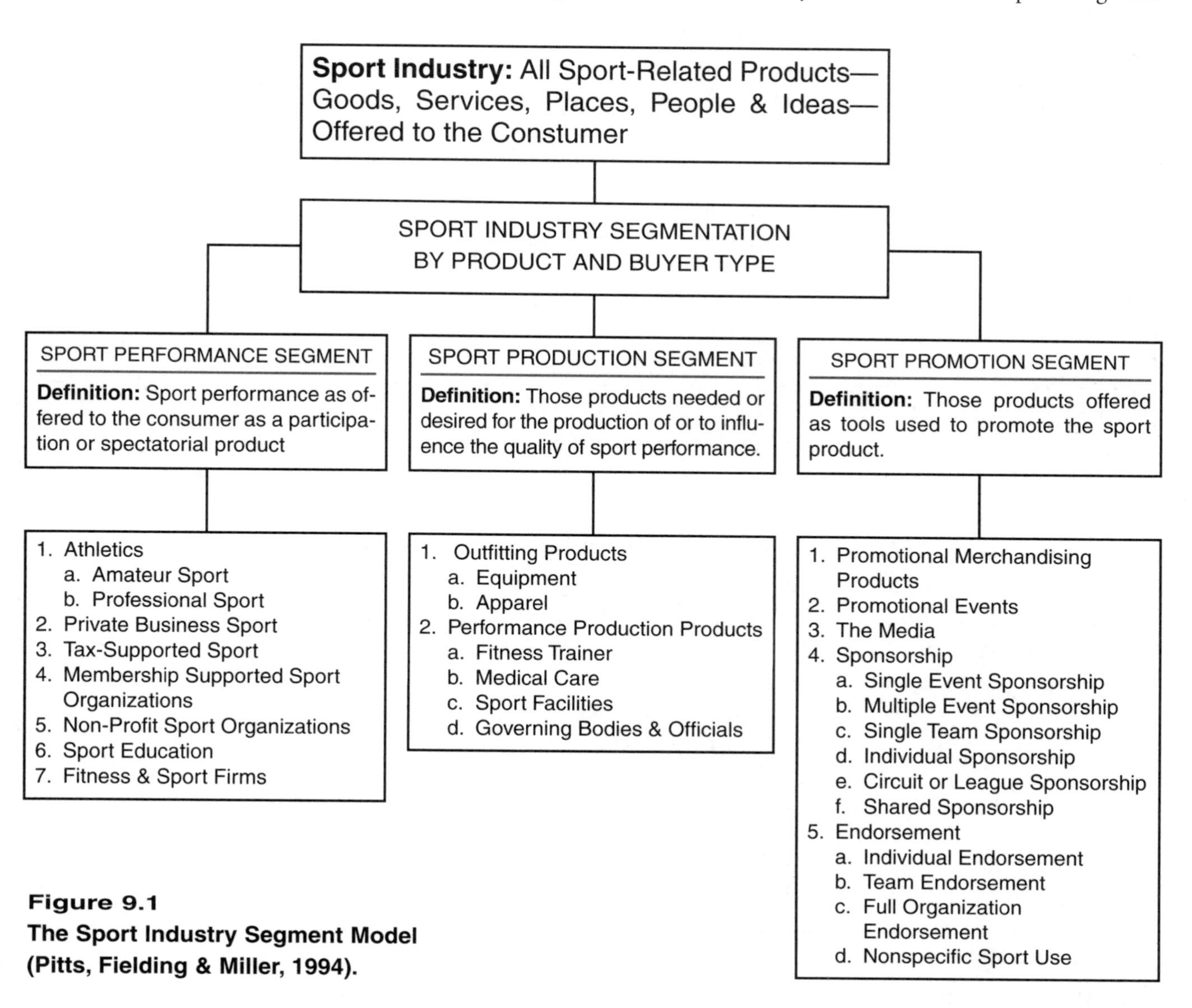

Figure 9.1
The Sport Industry Segment Model (Pitts, Fielding & Miller, 1994).

as the marketing of participation and spectatorial products is different. However, they were placed in one category due to their similarities in function and benefit. Functions and benefits include working out, stress management, fun, activity, competition, and entertainment. Examples include basketball, hiking, boating, swimming, jogging, camping, Frisbee throwing, martial arts, and many, many more. These activities are offered in a variety of settings, to a variety of consumer markets, and in a variety of formats (a tournament, a league, a one-day event, a single event, a weekend event, lessons, clinics, seminars, and many more). Figure 9.3 shows some examples of the variety of sport performance segment products.

1. To understand the company's product
2. To identify and monitor competitors.
3. To determine product management strategies.

Figure 9.2
Three Reasons for Understanding Sport Industry Segments.

SPORT PERFORMANCE INDUSTRY SEGMENT		
	PARTICIPATION	SPECTATORIAL
EXAMPLES OF SETTING	Collegiate athletics Pro sports Recreational leagues	Collegiate athletics Pro sports Recreational leagues
FORMAT	League Event Tournament Lessons Clinic Rehabilitation Seminar Camp Lab Olympics Matches	Games/matches/meets/contest
MARKETS	By age groups By gender and mixed By race By disability By sexual orientation By religion By skill level	By age groups By gender Special groups such as Girls or Boys clubs By race
FUNCTIONS AND BENEFITS	Fun Fitness gain Skill development Knowledge gain Weight loss Competition Stress management Entertainment Rehabilitative	Entertainment Fun Stress management Activity Support

Figure 9.3
Products in the Sport Performance Industry Segment (Pitts, Fielding & Miller, 1994).

1. Sport-specific equipment
2. Safety and protective equipment
3. Apparel: Clothing, shoes
4. Facility:
5. Performance enhancing products
   - personal fitness trainer
   - fitness equipment
   - sports medicine care
   - equipment and supplies
   - coaches
   - other staff
6. Governing organizations:
   - rules committees
   - officials: referees, umpires
   - governing associations
   - statisticians
   - scorekeepers, announcers, and other officials

Figure 9.4
The Sport Production Industry Segment Examples (Pitts, Fielding & Miller, 1994).

As a spectatorial product, sport performance is offered primarily in two ways: attendance at a sport event and spectating via television or video. Sport spectating has changed dramatically over the last few decades. The spectator is offered plush skyboxes, restaurants, and even a hotel in the sport facility; entertainment before, during, and after the event; and even spectator participation events during the sport event. These have become an integral part of the sport event spectator's package.

The *sport production industry segment* is defined as including those products necessary or desired to produce or to influence the quality of sport performance. Most sport participation requires specific equipment and apparel before it can be properly performed. The equipment and apparel afford the production of the sport performance. Further, in an effort to enhance performance, specific products or services may be desired. This creates a demand for a variety of products and product quality for the production of sport and to enhance the quality of performance. For example, Venus Williams can probably play tennis with any tennis racket. However, she prefers custom-designed rackets in order to enhance performance. She also purchases a number of other products that influence her tennis performance such as a personal fitness trainer, weight training equipment, a sports medicine

1. **Promotional Merchandise:** Merchandise with a logo, might include caps, cups, key chains, bumper stickers, decals, mugs, hats, t-shirts, dress shirts, ties, napkins, sweaters, jackets, clocks, shorts, sweat shirts and pants, blankets, stadium seats, pencil holders, stationary holders, pens and pencils, checks.
2. **Promotional Events:** Offering an event or activity along with a main sport event to bring attention to the product. Examples include holding a Beach Boys concert after a Major League Baseball game; offering a golf tournament to promote pre-game, half-time, and post-game events that surround the Super Bowl.
3. **The Media:** The media provide vast exposure for some segments of the sport industry. Sport marketers negotiate with television, radio, and print media for coverage of sporting events. The coverage promotes the sport event.
4. **Sponsorship:** Sponsorship is a two-way promotional tool. The sponsorship company provides funding for a sport event, which is a form of advertising for the company. Sport marketers use the funding to produce and manage the event. The company providing funding gains exposure and promotional benefits. Examples: Almost all college football bowl games have sponsors; many of the women's and men's professional golf tournaments have sponsors; the auto racing industry is practically driven by sponsors; the Olympics, Special Olympics, Gay Games, and Maccabiah Games all have sponsors.
5. **Endorsement:** Similar to sponsorship, endorsement is also a two-way promotional tool in the sport industry. Some examples: Mary Lou Retton's picture on Wheaties cereal boxes suggests her endorsement of that product; Michael Jordan's endorsement of Nike products.

Figure 9.5
The Sport Promotion Industry Segment Examples (Pitts, Fielding & Miller, 1994).

person and sports medicine equipment and supplies, and a professional tennis coach. Figure 9.4 presents examples of products in the sport production industry segment.

The *sport promotion industry segment* is defined as those products used in the promotion of sport industry products. Refer to Figure 9.5 for examples of products in the sport promotion industry segment. For example, college women's basketball can exist without promotion. However, it is enhanced, promoted, and in some situations, partially funded by promotional tactics. The competitors in all segments of the industry use a variety of promotional products and techniques. This creates a demand for promotional products, events, methods, and people who specialize in promotion, marketing, public relations, and other related areas.

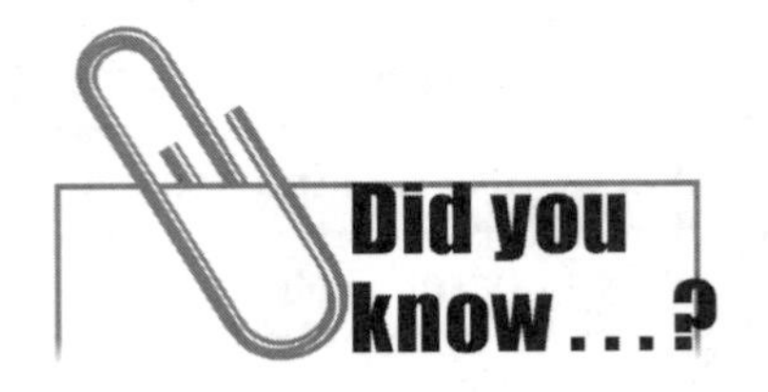

Gatorade saw its revenues climb by $837 million after signing Michael Jordan as an endorser.

Source: *Fortune*, June 22, 1998

With a thorough understanding of the sport company's product, the sport marketer increases chances for successful sport product management strategies. However, sport products come and go. Sometimes, the product can be labeled a fad. In other cases, the product was simply not a good idea. If the sport marketer can identify the success level of a product, decisions can be determined that may save the life of the product or, at a minimum, save the company. This product analysis is called the *product life cycle*.

The Sport Product Life Cycle

Just as people go through changes and stages throughout their lifetime, so do products. A person is born and then goes through childhood, adolescence, teenage years, young adulthood, adulthood, middle age, the senior citizen stage, and eventually death. A product begins life as an idea. It is then introduced onto the market, experiences a period of growth, a time of maturity, and even will decline and be taken off the market. One major difference between the person's stages and the product's stages is this: The person's stages may be measured using years of age. Death is certain. Although a product's stages may be measured using several factors, some of which are sales and profits, the amount of time in each stage can vary markedly. For example, a human's life span is estimated at approximately 74 years whereas a product's time on the market can range from just a few short days to hundreds of years (for example, religion).

> Studying, understanding, and managing products and their life cycle stages can have considerable influence on the success of a company.

The product life cycle is a concept popularized by Levitt in 1965 (Levitt, 1965). It is a way to define and understand a product's sales, profits, consumer markets, product markets, and marketing strategies from its inception until it is removed from the market. Studying your company's products and understanding the product life cycle stage in which each product qualifies is imperative to planning marketing strategies. Through research, it is now known that (a) product lives are shorter now than in the past; (b) higher investment is now required for new products; (c) the marketer may use the product life cycle to adjust marketing strategies; and (d) the marketer may strategically establish a more successful product mix in relation to the product life cycle concept—planning to establish products in each stage of the cycle so that, as one product declines, another product is introduced. As an example, let's look at fitness centers.

In the 1960s and early 1970s, fitness centers were known as health spas. The typical spa offered only a few products: a small weight room, a small pool, rolling machines, and locker rooms with a sauna and steam room. Typically, no exercise classes were offered as the "instructors" were hired only to look good and sell memberships. With the "fitness boom" of the late 1970s, a new crop of fitness centers sprang onto the market, and existing spas found themselves in the decline stage of the product life cycle. The new health-conscious consumer wanted more, and the new companies jumped into the fitness product market and offered much more in their facilities. Some of the existing spas changed, but some did not. Those that did not eventually lost out to the new multipurpose fitness centers.

Today's fitness centers offer a much greater product mix. In most, you will find a very large weight room, large pool, indoor running track, and a variety of exercise classes such as aerobics classes, swimming or pool exercise classes, fitness and nutrition classes. There will usually be a few sports such as tennis, racquetball, wallyball, volleyball, and basketball. The locker rooms are large, clean and airy with a full service of towels, shampoo, hair dryers, toothbrushes and toothpaste, and deodorants as well as plush carpeting, beautiful lockers, big-screen television sets complete with a VCR for your convenience in viewing specific videotape programs also supplied by the center. In addition, you will probably find nice, large whirlpool baths, saunas, and steam rooms. There will be a number of other services such as a childcare service—sometimes a child-size fitness center itself, laundry service, full clothing services, sporting goods and apparel shops, restaurant and lounge, and a small business office area complete with phone, computer, fax and copy machines so you can carry out business functions while at the center.

Stages of the Product Life Cycle

The stages of the product life cycle are introduction, growth, maturity, and decline. The stages are shown in Figure 9.6. Sport management executives or marketers must be able to recognize in which stage of the product life cycle a product is at any given time. This determination will affect marketing strategy decisions.

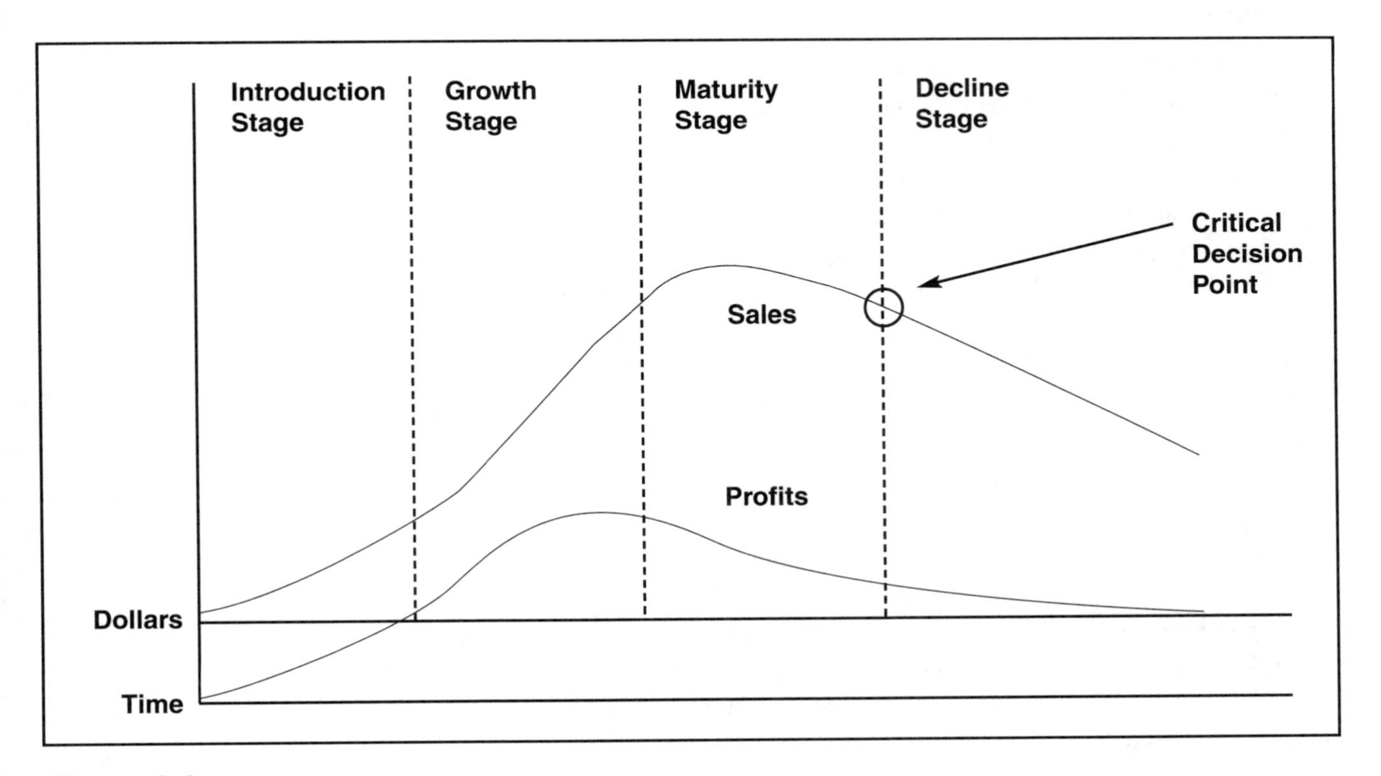

Figure 9.6
The product life cycle stages.

The *introduction stage* is the period when a sport product is put on the market (offered to the consumer) for the first time. During this time, it is most likely that no one knows the product exists. The sport marketer must promote aggressively to make distributors and consumers aware of the product. Typically, sales are practically zero and profits are negative. The sport company has invested in manufacturing and promoting the product but has not begun to receive profits from sales. The product that is offered is one that probably went through many stages of refinement such as idea generation, research and development, test marketing, and pilot trials. Investment during this period, for some products, may reach into the millions of dollars.

Product promotions stress information about a product, as well as its features and, perhaps most important, what it does for the consumer.

As Figure 9.6 indicates, sales are low and losses of profits are common. There is also a high percentage of product failure during this stage. The sport company may have the marketing research showing that there is a market for this product, but when the product finally hits the marketplace, many things could have happened: The market may be no longer interested; consumer needs or wants may have changed; or another company was first to the market and has established share. The sport company must promote aggressively during this stage to create demand for the product.

As demand for the sport product begins to develop and the product begins to sell, it enters the next stage in the product life cycle, *the growth stage*. As Figure 9.6 indicates, it is during this stage when sales and profits rapidly and steadily increase. Although sales and profits may soar, the company may still be in danger. It is during this stage that competitors will enter the product market with identical or similar products. This competition will drive prices down, and profits will decline. Aggressive pricing promotions, adjustments in costs, legal action against imitators, and other marketing strategies will help to stabilize profits.

After the bumpy road, the sport product may finally reach *the maturity stage*. It may have found a steady place in the market. However, during this stage, there still are many competitors, and this keeps prices low, which keeps sales and profits down. It is also during this period that the product has been changed enough to finally meet the consumer's needs. Differences among competing products diminish. It is at this point, however, that companies will begin to promote any difference in their product that they believe will gain some market advantage. Usually, pricing wars begin and continue until one or more companies are driven out of the particular product market. Critical marketing decisions must be made at this point.

By the time a product reaches the maturity stage, all the companies producing it have most likely discovered the successful product, price, and other marketing strategies that keep the product selling.

During *the decline stage*, sales fall rapidly. There may be many reasons, some of which are new products on the market, a shift in trend, or new technology. Now the sport marketer is faced with the decision of terminating production of the sport product or making changes, sometimes drastic, to revive it. Of course, the sport marketer may also wait and see which companies drop out of the market. This can be a successful strategy because if a large number drop out, your company may become one of a few making the product and the cycle can be stopped. This tactic is risky as always when one plays a wait-and-see game.

	PARTICIPANT SPORT ACTIVITY	SPORTING EQUIPMENT/CLOTHING	SPORT OFFERED AS ENTERTAINMNENT (SPECTATOR PRODUCT)
INTRODUCTION STAGE	• snowboarding	• graphite composite softball bats	• men's professional soccer • women's professional boxing
GROWTH STAGE	• rollerblading	• rollerblades (in-line skates)	• women's and men's professional beach volleyball • women's collegiate basketball • women's professional golf
MATURITY STAGE	• softball • volleyball	• aluminum softball bats • spandex clothing	• men's professional baseball, basketball, and football
DECLINE STAGE	• racquetball • boating • field hockey	• single-gear bicycle	

Figure 9.7
Examples of some sport products in the product life cycle stages.

It must be understood that the length of each stage can vary for any given product. The challenge to the sport marketer is to be able to recognize each product's life cycle stage and make marketing decisions accordingly. For example, let's say that you are the manager/marketer for a multisport club. You are experiencing an unusual, sharp decline in participants in the adult tennis leagues. Upon investigation, you find that most of those clients are now playing tennis at a different club because it is now offering childcare services any time it is open. You are faced with a decision: Change what you offer or lose consumers to another company. Figure 9.7 shows a variety of examples of sport products in various product life-cycle stages.

The Product Mix and Product Management

Product management and product mix are critical elements of a sport company's business plan and marketing strategy. It is the sale of products and services that makes a company successful or may bring about failure.

Product mix is the complete set of all products that the sport company offers to the consumer. It consists of all of the company's product lines and all related services. A collegiate athletic program offers 12 women's and men's sports and promotional merchandise. A sporting goods manufacturer offers 10 different sport equipment products. The local fitness center offers a variety of fitness and sport-related products, which includes a full range of exercise classes, tennis classes and leagues, volleyball leagues, swimming classes and open swim time, a clothing and sporting goods shop, childcare services, equipment repair, laundry service, towel service, a restaurant and lounge, and many others.

SPORT COMPANY	Product Assortment (Mix)	Product Line	Product Items Offered in the Product Line
FITNESS CENTER	fitness weight loss restaurant and lounge aerobics weight training tanning massage testing-fitness; cholesterol sports leagues: tennis volleyball swimming pro shop	aerobics classes	low impact aerobics kid aerobics elderrobics advanced aerobics
		weight training	body building free weight training sport-specific strength events
		tennis	classes beginner's league intermediate league advanced leagues club tourney
COLLEGE ATHLETICS	women's sports men's sports	women's individual sports	track field swimming cross country tennis
		women's team sports	basketball volleyball soccer
SPORTING GOODS MANUFACTURER	golf equipment tennis equipment	golf	golf clubs: 4 different sets golf balls golf umbrellas
		tennis	tennis rackets tennis string tennis balls tennis ball retriever

Figure 9.8
Examples of Product Mix, Lines, and Items in the Sport Industry.

The product mix may be measured by its product lines and items. A *product line* is a set of closely related products. For example, as Figure 9.8 shows, a fitness center offers fitness, sport, clothing, and equipment as four of its product lines. Within each product line, there are product items. A *product item* is a specific product within a product line. Aerobics classes are a product item in the fitness center's fitness product line. Tennis, volleyball, and swimming are product lines. Each of these may consist of a variety of classes, leagues and other items. In another example, a sporting goods manufacturer offers three product lines: softball equipment, baseball equipment, and tennis equipment. The softball equipment line consists of a variety of items: bats, gloves, batting gloves, softballs, and equipment bags. In a different example, a professional women's golf league offers two lines: golf spectation and souvenir merchandise.

The product mix of a sport company may be described by its width, depth, and consistency. The fitness center has a narrow width for it offers product lines that are primarily of a fitness or sport nature. There are a wide variety of products offered within each product line, which means that the fitness center may be described as having depth. For example, the tennis line contains the following items: (a) classes: classes for age-groups of 5–7 years old, 8–12, 13–15, 16–18, 19–21, 22–25, 26–30, and in 5-year increments after 30; (b) classes for skill levels: beginner, intermediate, and advanced; (c) individual instruction; (d) leagues consisting of the following categories: skill groups ranging from beginner through advanced and within each are categories for women, men, and coed singles, women, men, and coed doubles (see Figure 9.9). There may most likely be other items such as special clinics or seminars, league tournaments, special tournaments, and competition with another center. The fitness center would be considered consistent as its product mix is focused on products of a similar nature.

The product mix has three aspects:

Width is the number of product lines offered.

Depth is the number of items within a line.

Consistency refers to the similarity of product lines.

1. Classes Segmented By:	Age Groups Skill Levels
2. Instruction:	Individual Lessons Lessons for Double Play
3. Leagues Segmented By:	Skill Levels: beginners to advanced Gender: women's, men's, mixed
4. Clinics, Seminars:	for coaching, for individuals, for play strategy, for rules knowledge
5. Tournaments:	—Intramural —Extramural

Figure 9.9
The Center's Tennis Line.

Product management presents a major challenge for the sport company. Products are what your company produces, if the company is a manufacturer, or what your company selects and buys, if your company is a wholesaler or retailer, in order to fulfill needs and desires of consumers. Effective management of the product is crucial to success. The remaining sections of this chapter are devoted to product management strategies.

Product management involves deciding which products to offer, what type of a product line to carry, when to keep or delete a product, when to add new products, and other product management strategies. In marketing terms, this includes management of the product life cycle, positioning of the product, new product development, product diversification, line extension, product identification, and product deletion. Decisions concerning these areas make up *product mix strategies.*

Product positioning involves trying to position a product appropriately in the market. A product's position is the image or perception that the consumer holds about the product's attributes, quality, uses and other functions as these compare to other similar products. As was pointed out in the opening paragraphs of this chapter, a consumer does not simply purchase a product. The consumer is looking to satisfy needs or desires. Products perform as the satisfaction agent.

Consumer perceptions are measured through marketing research. The research will show what the consumer thinks about a product and how it compares to another company's product. This information is important in making changes to the product or to the image of the product.

New product development as a strategy is the addition of a new product to a company's product line. There are many reasons a company might consider developing a new product including a need to stimulate sales, a desire to capture a new consumer need, a desire to improve the company's reputation, or a desire to expand.

New products are a constant event in the sport industry. In chapter 1, we discussed many factors that have positively influenced the growth and development of the sport industry. Some of those factors are the consistent offering of new sports, new activities, new leagues, new sport organizations for all populations, and new sport equipment. There are, perhaps, more sport equipment and clothing products than sports when considering that most sport activities require a few pieces of equipment, special clothing, and footwear for each participant.

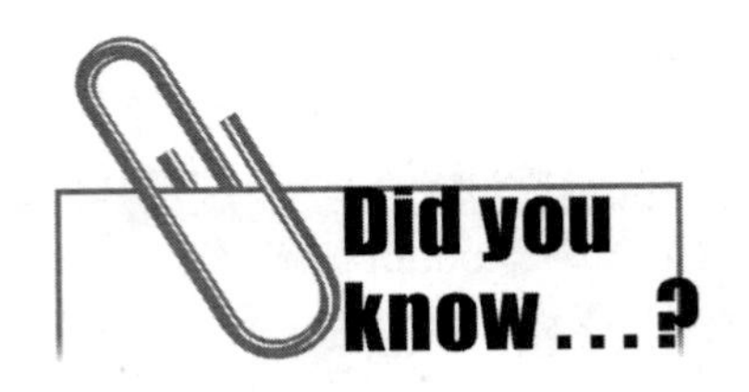

The sports supplement market was a $1.4-billion industry in 1997.

Source: *Fortune*, June 22, 1998

In the sport industry, it can be quite confusing when trying to determine which comes first: the sport or the equipment. In some cases, ideas for a new sport develop first. James Naismith developed some rules for a new sport and used a soccer ball. That sport today is basketball and requires very different equipment than was first used.

Every year the Sporting Goods Manufacturers Association (SGMA) stages its annual super show of sporting goods, apparel, shoes, and equipment. Thousands of sporting goods manufacturers and businesses are involved. They bring their most current products for show. People attending are buyers for retailers, wholesalers, distributors, and resellers.

Of course, not every new product introduced is successful. As a matter of fact, most new products fail. The failure rate is estimated to range between 33 and 90%. Companies spend tremendous amounts of money during the process to get a new product to the market. There are many elements involved in new product development. Some ideas require years of research, which can involve scientists, technology, testing, manufacture of the new product, and promotion. However, with all the money and time invested in producing the new product, there is no guarantee that the product will sell.

There are some common reasons that new product offerings fail. The primary reason is failure to match the product to the consumer's needs. If the product will not do what the consumer wants, the consumer will not buy it. Further, this may be the result of poor consumer research, the company's failure to stick to what it does best, and failure to provide a better product at a better value than the competition (Peter and Donnelly, 1991).

Good product management and planning can increase your chances of new product success. As was pointed out in the chapter on research and earlier in this chapter, information and research are primary keys in making decisions.

As pointed out earlier, there are many reasons a company offers a new product. Sometimes, a new product isn't a brand-new product. It is a product that has been modified as a means of offering a differentiated product or an improved product. For example, consider the variety of aerobics type classes offered today. Some examples are hard aerobics, soft aerobics, water aerobics, elderobics, jazzercise, and step aerobics. All of these are not brand-new products. Rather, they are variations of the original aerobics product. In another example, arena football (football played in a small, indoor field with fewer players and a variety of rule modifications) might be considered a brand-new product because it is different from the original football sport. However, arena football is a variation of the original product. It is marketed as a different product—different from the regular 11-player game.

How many ways might one offer a new product? There are at least nine (Peter and Donnelly, 1991). Following are the nine ways with examples in the sport industry (also see Figure 9.10).

1. *A product that performs an entirely new function.* When the snowmobile was introduced, it performed a new function: motorized transportation across snow-covered areas in a small personal-sized vehicle.

1. A product that performs an entirely new function.
2. A product that offers improved performance of an existing function.
3. A product that offers a new application of an existing one.
4. A product that offers additional functions over an existing product.
5. When an existing product is offered to a new consumer market.
6. Offering a lower cost on a product can attract new buyers.
7. A product offered as "upgraded" or an existing product integrated into another product.
8. A downgraded product or the use of less expensive parts or components in the manufacturing process.
9. A restyled product.

Figure 9.10
Nine Ways to Offer a New Product (Peter & Donnelly, 1991).

2. *A product that offers improved performance of an existing function.* As an example, consider the introduction of new materials for wheelchairs. Aluminum and other composite materials offer the possibility for wheelchairs to be light and durable. This provides wheelchair athletes the capability to enhance performance in athletic feats.

3. *A product that offers a new application of an existing one.* Personal watercrafts (more commonly known as the jet ski) were first introduced to be used as recreational vehicles: new toys for play on the water. Today, personal watercrafts are used by police, emergency water rescue services, and coast guard operations for law enforcement, safety, and rescue functions.

4. *A product that offers additional functions over an existing product.* In one example, a fitness center may offer more sports and services than does another fitness center, thereby offering more functions to the consumer. In another example, weight-training equipment, one product is a single unit that allows the consumer to perform up to 12 exercises whereas another product is a single unit that offers only one exercise.

5. *An existing product that is offered to a new consumer market.* This may be done either by repositioning the product or offering the product in new markets (market development). In an example of the latter, the National Football League (NFL) is trying to gain market development by offering its product—football games—in European and Asian countries.

6. *A product that can attract new buyers with lower prices.* When a new material is used for golf clubs, the existing clubs may be offered at a lower cost. Softball bats are offered in a wide range of prices. A fitness center may offer special priced memberships to first-time consumers for a limited period of time.

7. *A product that is offered as "upgraded" or an existing product that is integrated into another product.* In one example, fitness centers offer a variety of possibilities for "upgrading" a consumer's membership. The consumer may purchase one level of membership with the possibility of upgrading it to another level. In another example, computers have been integrated into a variety of sport equipment as a method of upgrading the equipment. Playing a round of golf indoor in a small room is possible with the use of a computerized golf course system. Through the use of video, screens, displays, sensors and other equipment, the consumer uses real golf clubs and golf balls to play a round of 9 or 18 holes of golf without stepping a foot outdoors.

8. *A product that has been downgraded or that uses less expensive parts or components in its manufacture.* Many sporting goods and equipment manufacturers use plastics and other less expensive materials, parts, or components in their products. This changes the cost to produce the product and is sometimes promoted to the consumer as "new low price" or "we pass the savings on to the consumer" item.

9. *A restyled product.* Examples include the almost annual changes in sport clothing, running shoes, and other sporting equipment.

In another approach to offering new products, Ansoff (1965) developed *growth vectors,* which are used by most businesses today (see Figure 9.11). These are product strategies involving present or new consumer markets and present or new products, and they include market penetration, market development, new product development, and product diversification. *Market penetration* is a strategy in which a company tries to sell more of its present products to its present consumer markets. *Market development* is a strategy in which a company tries to sell its present products to new consumer markets. *New product development* is the creation of new products. *Product diversification* is a strategy in which new products are added in an attempt to meet the needs of new consumer markets.

Markets	Products	
	Present	New
Present	Market Penetration	Product Development
New	Market Development	Diversification

Figure 9.11
Growth Vector Components (Ansoff, 1965),

New Product Development Planning and Process

How does a sport company organize for new product development? The type of company and the products it offers will influence the eventual organization, planning, and process the company will use to develop new products. A fitness center that offers a variety of products must make a decision concerning the addition of new products such as new sports, fitness activities, or even new tennis clothing in the pro shop. A tennis racket manufacturer will study the possibility and feasibility of manufacturing a new tennis racket. These are different types of companies: One is a manufacturer and the other a retailer. However, each must have and manage a new product development process. The process will involve hours, sometimes years, of analyzing information concerning factors such as consumer markets and product markets, cost of producing the product, cost to the consumer, capability of the company to produce the product, distribution possibilities and cost, as well as promotion possibilities and cost.

Consider another and very different example—the National Basketball Association (NBA). For the NBA, a new product might be an additional team in the league or a modification of the rules of the game of basketball. The addition of a new team to the league requires analyzing consumer markets and product markets, production (start-up) costs, price (ticket prices) to the consumer, and many other decision factors. Modifying, adding, or deleting rules can change the game—the product—dramatically.

There have been many modifications to the game of basketball since it was invented. Some of those changes were instituted specifically to make the game more attractive to the consumer. For example, dunking was not allowed until the late 1970s primarily for safety reasons: Rims and backboards were not made for dunking and would break. Another reason was that the dunk was not considered to be a skill. A stiff penalty was levied against a player who dunked either during the warm-up period before a game or during a game: The player was ejected from the game. Dunking became a tactic. Coaches realized that a dunk motivated the team and excited the crowd. Specific players were instructed to dunk at key moments: during the warm-up period before the game or during the game. It wasn't long before coaches, athletic directors, and others involved in selling the game realized that the crowds loved to see someone dunk the ball. Soon the rules were changed, and rims and backboards were modified to be safe for dunking. The dunk changed the game. Today there are even slam-dunking contests with large amounts of money, prizes, and titles involved.

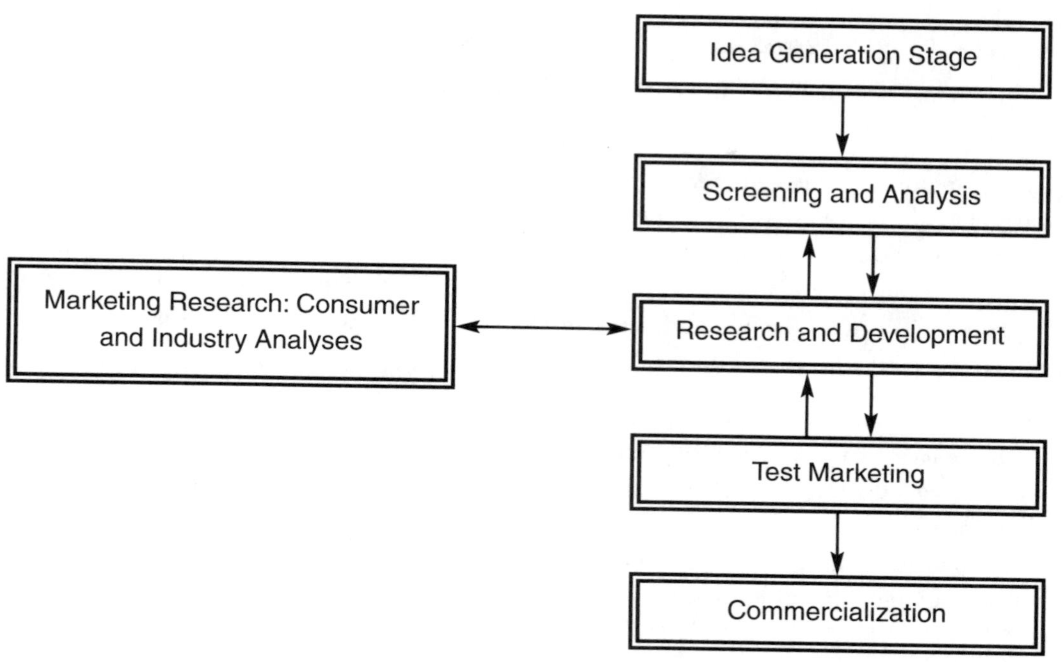

Figure 9.12
Stages in New Product Development Process.

Stages in the New Product Development Process

There are some common stages in the new product development process within most companies. These are idea generation, screening and analysis, product research and development, test marketing, and commercialization (Boone and Kurtz, 1989; Peter and Donnelly, 1991; Stanton et al., 1991). Figure 9.12 represents the stages within a new product development process a sport company might utilize.

Idea generation should utilize information obtained through marketing research concerning the consumer and product markets.

The *idea generation stage* involves generating ideas for new products, product modification, or other types of product change ideas. Ideas may come from a multitude of sources. If the company has the resources, it may contain a product research and development department, commonly known around the company the "R and D" department. It is the responsibility of the "R and D" people to generate product ideas, research them, and present feasible product ideas to company management. In other companies, product ideas must originate from various employees. In either situation, the company management must create an atmosphere that supports idea generation. Some companies offer incentives for those employees whose ideas eventually result in a successful product. Eventually, a decision will be made to take the next step and study the feasibility of a product.

The next stage is *product screening and analysis*. This involves determining the feasibility of a product. This process includes determining if the company can market a product profitably, if the product fits with the company's mission, if the company has all the necessary resources or technology, or if it might be beneficial to form partnerships with other companies. Based on the conclusions drawn from the research, a decision will be made, and the product could move into the next stage.

In the *product research and development stage*, product ideas with potential are converted. The type of product and its conceived functions determine the type of testing. If the product is a tangible item, a model can be produced. The model will undergo a number of tests in an effort to develop the best possible product.

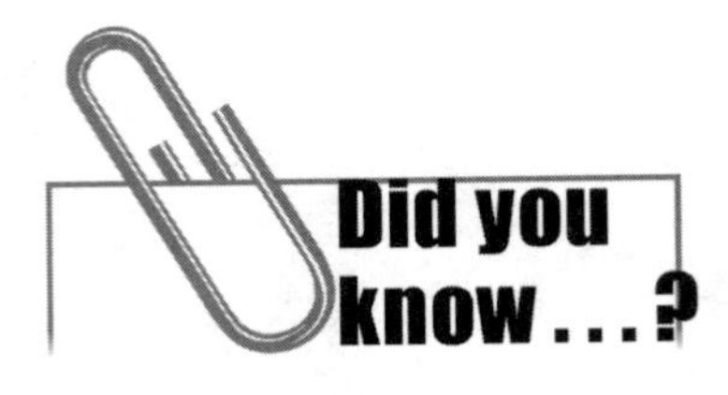

You can buy a Zamboni on-line at SportSite.com for $100,000.

Source: *Fortune*, June 8, 1998

Type of product requires further discussion here because there are many different types of products in the sport industry. Remember our definition of product earlier in the chapter. Product is a concept that includes goods, services, people, places and ideas. Also, remember that consumers are looking for a specific function—what the product will do. With this in mind, let's consider examples of each type of product and how it may be developed through testing.

Tangible good. Softball bats provide a good example. The research and development department in a bat manufacturing company is considering the idea that aluminum might be a good material for bats. The purpose or function of a bat is to hit a softball. However, what the softball player wants is a bat that will hit a softball farther, consistently, and with control. The question, then, the company should consider is this: Will an aluminum bat meet those needs? Other questions are

- Can aluminum bats be made?
- What kind of aluminum can be used?
- How much will it cost the company?
- What kind of machinery and other equipment are needed to construct an aluminum bat?
- Where might the company get the aluminum?
- Will the aluminum bat function?
- How can it be tested?
- What will the consumer think about the idea of an aluminum bat?
- Will the consumer accept—and purchase—a bat made of metal instead of wood?
- Are any other companies considering making aluminum bats? If not, can this company possibly be the first with this product?

If most of these questions can be answered positively, the company's next move is to produce some bats made of aluminum and test them in the company's laboratories. A variety of aluminum would be used in a variety of models. The bats would be put through a battery of tests. The company could also test the models by providing them to some softball players, teams, and/or leagues. The company would follow the players throughout the league and receive feedback from them. The information is used to make changes in the bat until reaching a point at which the players seem to be satisfied with the performance of one or more models. Further test marketing would include placing the bat on the market in a region and waiting for the results. If specific outcomes are reached, the company would consider going into full-time production, getting the bats into more markets, and going into full promotion status.

Service product. The testing of a service product could follow the following process. A fitness instructor at a fitness center overhears customers discussing why the center does not offer childcare services. The customers say that they would come to the center more often if they did not have to spend the extra amount of time, effort, and money finding a sitter. The instructor thinks offering child care might be a good idea and takes it to the center's manager. The manager also thinks it might be a good idea and organizes a committee, headed by the instructor, to study the idea. The committee, after studying the idea and surveying their members, concludes that the center has the space needed and could charge a small fee to cover the addition of an employee to manage the childcare center, and that the fitness center ought to offer the service for at least six months to test the idea.

Person. What might a company do if the company's products are people? As an example, consider a sport marketing and management company that specializes in managing and promoting professional athletes. The company's task is to try to find the best contracts and jobs for the athletes. The company uses the athletic and personal characteristics of the athlete as selling points. When the company considers the addition of a new product (adding another athlete) to its line of products (athletes already under contract), it will research many factors. Some of these factors are popularity of the individual, consumer markets (the variety and extent of demand for the athlete), cost to the company, and possible profitability. Further, the company might add the athlete for a one-year trial basis (test marketing).

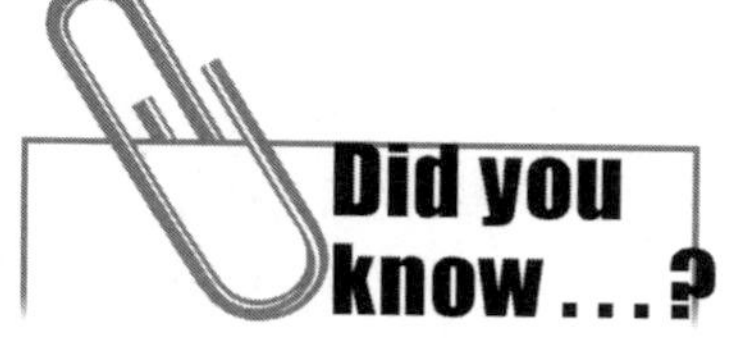

Total prize money awarded by sponsors in the Professional Bull Riders Tour in 1998 was $4.5 million, up 1,800% from the first season in 1994.

Source:: *Fortune*, July 6, 1998

Place. When the product is a place, research and development are contingent on factors such as the type of place (facility) and whether or not it exists. Let's look at an example of a facility that does not exist. The local state university has announced that it would like to have a new facility to house the women's and men's basketball and volleyball teams. The programs are very successful and have been nationally ranked in the top 25 for over eight years. The existing facility was built in 1936. The process for determining the feasibility of this product can be very complicated. The university is a state-supported institution, which means that tax dollars are involved. The process might include the development of a committee to study the idea. The committee needs to gather information such as facility needs, the cost of such a facility, if resources exist or where the university might obtain the resources, if space (land) is available and obtainable, ticket price structure, who will use the facility, how many ways the facility might be used, expenses involved, consumer surveys, and other. This will involve working with contractors, architects, the state education department, state government, and many other agencies and individuals. The committee could perform all the research or hire a marketing company to do the work. In this type of situation, the university usually hires a marketing company to do the research. Be careful to hire a marketing company with experience in the sport industry and with specific experience in sport facilities and sport facility research.

When the testing is complete and test results yield information, conclusions may be drawn about the product. The information from the research will guide decisions pertaining to moving to the next stage.

The *test marketing stage* is the next step in the new product development process. Test marketing involves selecting a specific market area in which to offer the product. It is usually offered with a specialized marketing campaign. The primary reason for test marketing is to determine how the product performs in a real market. In selecting the test market area, some factors to consider are size, control of selected promotional media, cost, the consumer markets, and the product markets.

A sports wheelchair manufacturing company has developed a wheelchair for basketball. The company offers the chairs in two large cities (test markets). The company's plan is to promote the wheelchairs in the two cities for a one-year period. If the wheelchair sells well in the two test markets, the company will expand to additional large city areas.

You may decide to skip this stage because it can be very expensive. The decision to skip test marketing should be based on the conclusion that the new product has a very high possibility of selling and success.

The final stage is *commercialization.* Full marketing strategies are planned, and the entire company gets ready to make the necessary adjustments for the new product. Complete business and marketing plans are developed, implementation plans are identified, plans for production are developed, personnel considerations are established, and promotional efforts are determined. The product is finished and goes on the market.

Each sport company should organize its new product development process and attempt to manage the process for success. Management must remember, however, the high rate of unsuccessful new products and make a commitment to support the investment necessary for new product development.

Product Identification

Product identification involves establishing an identity for your product through the use of some identifying device. The primary purpose of product identification is to differentiate your product from other relatively homogeneous products. It may also be used as a strategy to increase the strength of the company or product image, to establish or to use an established reputation, and to facilitate market and product development strategies.

The most commonly used methods of product identification are branding and packaging. Branding is accomplished through the use of a brand, brand name, or trademark. A *brand* is a name, symbol, term, and/or design intended for the identification of the products of a seller. It may consist of any combination of a name, word, letter, number, design, symbol, and color. A *brand name* is the word, letter, or number that can be vocalized. The symbol, design or coloring is the *brand mark.* It can be recognized by sight and not expressed vocally. For example, the brand mark of NIKE includes the word NIKE and a mark that looks like a well-rounded checkmark. NIKE calls it a "swoosh." One would never know that the symbol actually has an identifying name, however, until looking into Nike's legal papers that describe the NIKE brand name and mark. It is at this point that the brand name and mark may become what is commonly called a *trademark.* The trademark is essentially a legal term. It is a brand that has legal protection; that is, it is protected from being used by other companies (see chapter 15). Why would a company want to use another company's trademark instead of developing its own identity? The reason is to confuse and trick the consumer. The consumer purchases the product thinking that the product is from a well-known company. What the consumer actually purchased is a copy—an imitation of another company's product. These products have become known as "the clones." For example, the consumer sees a mark that looks like the NIKE swoosh on a pair of sneakers. The consumer purchases the product because the price is very low

> The establishment of a brand—a name, symbol, term, or design that represents a product—is important because it allows the idea of a product to exist in a consumer's mind even when the product itself isn't visible.

(compared to the price for the real NIKE product) and believes it is a deal too good to pass. In reality, the consumer purchased an imitation product.

Success in branding lies in selecting a good brand name and mark. The company should select something short, easy to pronounce and spell, suggests something about the product, and is unique. Other factors to be considered are ethics, market segments, and current events. A company can do harm to its image and its product if its brand name or mark is insensitive to cultures, populations, or specific current events. For example, in 1993 Converse intended to release a basketball shoe called the "Run 'N Gun" until community groups in Boston, where Converse is located, protested the implications of the name. The name is derived from a basketball term used to describe a specific type of play. The protesting groups, however, pointed out that in today's society the word *gun* means a gun. Further, youths have actually been robbed and even murdered for their clothing and popular name brand shoes. Converse recognized its responsibility to young people, the impending bad press, and the possibility of a boycott and decided to change the name of the shoe. (Its new name is "Run 'N Slam") (Moore, 1993).

Consumers react to branding on three levels: brand recognition, brand preference, and brand insistence. Companies aim for brand insistence, the level at which consumers will buy only their brand and no other.

There are three levels through which a consumer might progress in relation to branding. In the first level, brand recognition, a consumer is only aware of the existence of a particular brand. At the second level, brand preference, the consumer has developed a preference for a specific brand and will select it for purchase over other brands. At the third level, brand insistence, the consumer will purchase only a specified brand. It is, of course, the third level that is the goal of most companies. This level, however, is difficult to achieve due to the speed at which competitors can enter the market.

Packaging is the activity of enclosing a product. It involves designing and enclosing the product in some type of package or container in an attempt to differentiate the product from others. In addition, the package should protect the product, should be a convenient size, easy to open, attractive so that it can be used as a promotional tool, and honest. Although the sport marketer has many decisions to make concerning packaging, information guiding these decisions must also include consumer data. Because design and package costs are included in the final price of the product to the consumer, the marketer must know the price that a consumer is willing to pay for the product. Final decisions on packaging usually mean compromise when final cost becomes a major factor.

It is important to remember that sport event packaging includes not only the product or services themselves, but also certain elements of presentation such as the cleanliness of facilities, the attitude of the staff, and the amount of attention paid to the consumer during the event.

In the sport industry, there are products for which packaging takes on a slightly different meaning. Sport marketers have developed a way to "package" sporting activity events in an attempt to make the event more attractive to a greater diversity of consumer segments. Packaging a sport event involves enveloping the event with an array of activities, benefits, and products. In one example, sport marketers trying to sell season tickets to collegiate women's basketball games create a variety of ticket packages. The lowest cost season-ticket package might contain just the tickets and nothing else. The highest cost ticket package might include VIP valet parking, no parking fee, seats on or near the 50-yard line, admission to a pregame and half-time reception, admission to a postgame party with the coach, and admission to the end-of-the-year banquet.

One of the shortest events in sport is surrounded by a month of activities. The event is a racing event over a distance of one mile and a quarter ("Derby winners 1875 to 1992, " 1993). The race lasts just a few seconds over two minutes. The event is the Kentucky Derby—a horse race. The Derby's first race was in 1875, and since that time, it has grown to a major money sport event with an attendance of over 120,000 (McMasters, 1993). In 1971, there were 12 events and activities surrounding the Derby (Harris, 1993). In 1993, there were 63 official Kentucky Derby Festival events and activities and countless unofficial events, parties, socials, and other activities. Of the 63 events, 12 were sports events. These included the following:

- the Derby Festival Budweiser $1 Million Dollar Hole-In-One Golf Contest
- the Derby Festival Thunderball University of Louisville Spring Scrimmage
- the Derby Festival Miller Lite Volleyball Classic (sand volleyball)
- the McDonald's Derby Festival Basketball Classic Night of the Future Stars
- the Derby Festival Great Balloon Race
- the 20th Annual Derby Festival miniMarathon
- the 20th Derby Festival Bodybuilding Extravaganza
- the 20th McDonald's Derby Festival Basketball Classic
- the 13th Derby Festival American Life Soccer Tournament
- the Derby Festival Bass Classic
- the Derby Festival USAC Midget Auto Races
- the Derby Festival Fightmaster Golf Tournament for Exceptional Children
- the Derby Festival Miller Lite Pro Beach Volleyball Exhibition
- the Derby Festival Pro-Am Golf Tournament
- the Derby Festival Great Steamboat Race.

The Kentucky Derby race is held every year on the first Saturday in May. The official Kentucky Derby Festival events and activities in 1993 were held beginning on April 7, and the last event was held on May 14. The events surround the Derby race providing a multitude of activity and entertainment for the consumer. Hence, the Kentucky Derby is a packaged sports event.

Sport event packaging goes beyond events and activities to include often-overlooked factors such as facility cleanliness, friendliness of workers and staff, and prompt attention to a variety of consumer needs while attending the event. Everything included in the package is designed to create an atmosphere in which the consumer believes that she or he is getting plenty more than just viewing the event.

Product Deletion

For most products, the time will arrive when it no longer is fulfilling a need or desire for a consumer. The sport marketer must be able to identify that time and make the decision to eliminate the product. The decision should be based on an analysis of the product's situation: sales and sales trends, profits trends, cost analysis, and product life cycle stage. There are also indirect factors to be considered such as the effect of eliminating a product on the company and employees, the effect of eliminating a product on other companies, and the effect of eliminating a product on the consumer.

If the sport company has decided to eliminate a product, there are some techniques that may be used in order to decrease the many effects that its elimination could have. For example, the product could be *phased out* over a period of time. This will allow everyone involved in the production of the product and the consumer to begin to make the transition toward the day that the product is no longer offered.

Chapter Summary

Products are the company. Products provide benefits and fulfill functions. The sport consumer looks for products that will satisfy specific needs or desires. In the sport industry there is a vast array of products. Product needs to be understood as a concept because a product involves tangible and intangible characteristics.

The wide variety of sport products available to the consumer in the sport industry requires some method of classification. Product classification typically involves an analysis of the consumer and, in particular, consumer needs and desires. It is the function of the product for the consumer that is the reason for its existence.

The product life cycle is a concept that must be understood by the sport marketer. Product management strategies are influenced by the stages in which the company's products might be categorized in the product life cycle. Product mix and product development strategies are also influenced.

New product development is important to the sport marketer as new products are a constant event in the sport industry. When the sport marketer understands the industry segment in which the company's products exist, informed decisions and strategies may guide the company to the successful addition of a new product.

The sport company must establish an identity for the product through product identification. This can include branding and packaging. Packaging is the activity of enclosing a product. There are some products in the sport industry that require a different kind of packaging—surrounding the product with an array of other products, activities, and events.

Product deletion is also a sport management and marketer's responsibility. A time will come when a product will no longer fulfill the needs or desires of the consumer. At this critical point, a decision must be made concerning the elimination of the product.

Questions for Study

1. What is a product? What is a sport product? List examples of sport products.
2. Why do people purchase sport products?
3. Define these terms: form utility, time utility, place utility, and ownership utility. Give an example of each.
4. What is product classification?
5. What is the product life cycle? What are the stages in the product life cycle?
6. Give examples of sport products in each product life cycle.
7. Why is it important for the sport marketer to know in which stage of the product life cycle each of the sport company's products may be categorized?
8. What is the product mix? Why is it important?
9. How many ways might a sport company offer a new product?
10. What is the new product development planning process? What are the stages?
11. What is product identification? Why is it important? How is it used in the sport industry?

Learning Activities

1. Using the definition of sport product in this chapter, create a list of 10 sport products for each of the categories: goods, services, people, places, and ideas.
2. Using the Pitts, Fielding, and Miller Sport Industry Segmentation segments, list products offered to consumers and business consumers in your city or community.
3. Determine in which stage each of the products you listed in number 2 fall onto the product lifecycle.
4. Interview some of the sport businesses, organizations, or other enterprises in your city or community and ask about new product development and new product research and development.
5. Conduct a class study of product identification. Show company brand names or logos on overhead transparencies and ask students to try to identify each.
6. To study how today's sports events are packaged, attend a small sporting event and a large sporting event. Take a notebook. Make a list of everything involved and surrounded the events: parking, pre-event events (such as, pre-game shows), and other activities and services offered.

Chapter 10

Pricing Strategies for the Sport Industry

What do I get for my money? This is a question asked by consumers everywhere. What consumers pay for something and what they believe they get for their money varies from one consumer to another. As an example, let's consider a conversation between two individuals about two boats. Consumer A believes that Boat #1 is the better buy because the boat has more features and instruments than Boat #2 has. Consumer B believes that Boat #2 is a better buy because the engine has more horsepower. Consumer A points out that the price of Boat #1 is slightly lower than the price of Boat #2. Consumer B replies that the reason is that Boat #2 has a larger engine and engines are expensive. Consumer A argues that Boat #1 has more safety features such as a built-in automatic fire extinguisher in the engine compartment. Consumer B argues that Boat #2 has a good-looking color combination and that a more powerful engine is necessary to produce the speed and power needed when pulling water skiers. Consumer A states that water skiing isn't fun anymore and everyone's favorite toys are tubes and kneeboards.

This discussion can go on for hours, days, or even weeks. Which consumer is right? Both are right insofar as each is willing to pay a particular price for what each believes is the best buy. Which one is the best buy? The consumer defines "best buy" according to needs and desires. In addition, the definition will change from situation to situation and from product to product.

Determining the price of a product in the sport business industry is the sport marketing mix element decision most difficult to determine. The sport marketer must consider that price is perhaps the most sensitive element of a product for the consumer. The price, from the consumer's perspective, is the amount of money the consumer must sacrifice for a product. In addition, money is relative. Every consumer has a unique amount of money to spend and only a specific amount to spend for sport products. Further, many other factors affect the consumer's decision to buy. These and other factors that affect the determination of price, pricing objectives, pricing methods, and pricing strategies will be discussed in this chapter.

We will first define price, consider it as a concept, and look at the many ways it is presented to the consumer. Second, we will discuss the 4 Cs and their relationship to affecting price determination. Third, we present the concept of elasticity of demand.

Statistics show that people using tubes and other new water toys far outnumber traditional water skiers.

Photo reprinted by permission of WVU Photography.

Fourth, we present a discussion on determining pricing objectives for the sport business. Finally, we present pricing methods and strategies that can be used in the sport industry.

Price

Simply stated, price is something a consumer exchanges for products. There are two terms to understand in these definitions: exchange and value. *Exchange* is the trading of something for something. The form of exchange may be money, services, or other forms for the exchange of products from the seller to the buyer. A long time ago, the first system of exchange was bartering, or trading. If you wanted corn, you might expect to trade wheat for it. If you wanted a little boat, you might have to trade a couple of cows for it. Eventually, something called money became the trading means of choice. Today, currency is the most common means in the process of exchange used by the consumer to obtain wanted or needed products.

Value is not an easy term to define. One definition states that value is a "quantitative measure of the worth of a product" (Stanton, Etzel, and Walker, 1991). Where do we begin to determine the quantitative worth of a product? In the above example of trading, or bartering, a couple of cows for a boat, the individuals involved negotiate over the exchange. If the individual wanting the boat—the buyer—believes that two cows are too much to trade for the boat, that means that two cows are worth more than the boat. The individual with the boat—the seller—believes that the boat is worth two cows. The bartering, or negotiating, will continue until an agreement can be reached. If an agreement cannot be reached, we can conclude that the buyer believed that the VALUE of the boat was not worth two cows. The buyer might decide to not make the trade. The seller has lost a deal.

> Price is the exchange value of a good or service and fluctuates according to its exchange value in the marketplace, or its market value.

Price:

is the exchange value of something.

Value:

is the quantitative measure of the worth of a product.

Perceived Value:

is what the consumer thinks something is worth.

This is exactly what takes place in today's marketplace. The buyers and sellers negotiate over price. Negotiation takes place in more than one form—verbal and nonverbal. For example, negotiation over some products might be realized through nonverbal communication when the consumer decides not to purchase a particular product because of the price. This can force the seller to set a different price—or face no sales. In the negotiation over some other products such as cars or boats, verbal negotiation takes place. The buyer and seller negotiate until an agreement can be reached. As a matter of fact, negotiation over price is expected for some products in the United States. In some other countries, negotiation over prices, sometimes called bargaining or haggling, is expected and part of the culture. For example, anyone who has been to certain cities in Mexico will agree that negotiation is commonplace among the street vendors. If the buyer does not haggle over the price and pays the asking price, the buyer is considered foolish and an easy target by the seller. The seller will pass the word to other vendors. Some vendors consider the buyer rude if the buyer does not negotiate, and other vendors are insulted if the buyer does not negotiate.

There can be many factors involved in the determination of value, and it can have several meanings. This is because each individual involved in determining the value of a product has a unique perspective. For example, let's revisit the opening discussion of this chapter concerning the two consumers discussing two boats. Each individual holds attitudes, preferences, values and beliefs, a certain amount of expendable money, an amount of money each thinks should be spent on a boat, and other ideas that will affect what each believes ought to be the price, or value, of the boat. In other words, many factors besides price affect the establishment of the value of a product. Hence, we can suggest that price is a reflection of value.

Price is presented to the consumer in a number of ways, and this is also true in the sport industry. One reason for this is to give identification to the product through the price title. Another reason is to soften the blow: Other words are easier on the ear than the word *price*. Take a look at the following examples of words used in place of the word *price* that can be found in the sport industry:

- A licensing fee is the price a sports apparel company pays a university for the right to sell a T-shirt with the university's logo on it.
- The ticket charge is the price you pay to enter a facility and watch a basketball game.
- Membership fee is the price you pay to use a fitness center's facilities.
- Admission is the price you pay to enter the water sports park.
- Rental is the price you pay to use a water tube at the water sports park.
- A league fee is the price your softball team must pay to play in a softball league.
- A sponsorship fee is the price the local bank pays to be the sponsor of a Special Olympics event. (What the bank gets for its money is advertising and goodwill exposure.)

- Registration fee is the price you pay for your daughter to attend the summer basketball camp.
- A signing bonus is part of the price a professional basketball team pays to assure the services of a player.
- A salary is the price a professional baseball team pays for the services of coaches and players.
- Commission is the extra bonus-oriented price a sports marketing company would pay its sales people for their services.
- Shipping and handling is the price a sporting goods company pays to have its products moved from one place to another.
- The purse is the price a professional golf organization pays the golfers who place in money-winning finishes in a tournament.
- A bid is your offered price for an item at a sport art collection auction.
- An endorsement fee is the price a sport shoe company pays to have a famous athlete like Mia Hamm or Brandi Chastain state that she endorses—believes in, favors, prefers, and supports—the products of that company.
- Broadcasting rights is the price a television station company pays to televise the local women's volleyball match.
- A consulting fee is the price a company pays a sport marketing research company to analyze the effectiveness of their sponsorship of a sports event.
- A franchise fee is the price an organization or individual pays to enter a team in a professional sports league.

These are some of the terms used in place of the word *price* in various segments of the sport industry. The words give definition and identification to the product. This creative use of language is also part of the company's promotional efforts: Price is used as a promotional tool. This illustrates the inter-relatedness of marketing mix elements.

Price can be a complex element of marketing for the sport marketer. Figure 10.1 is a model for developing pricing decisions and strategies. Each of the parts of the model will be discussed in the following sections of the chapter.

The Four Cs of Price Determination

The sport marketer must consider a multitude of factors. However, most of these factors can be organized in order to consider them in a manageable manner. They fall primarily into four categories: the consumer, the competitor, the company, and the climate (environment). Each of the four Cs, in relation to pricing, is presented here with a brief description.

The Consumer

Although the price for something is a sensitive factor for the consumer, the consumer considers much more than the price in making a purchase decision. The consumer also considers factors such as product quality, warranty, company service agreement, refund policy, the consumer's image and reputation, and product bargain. Each factor

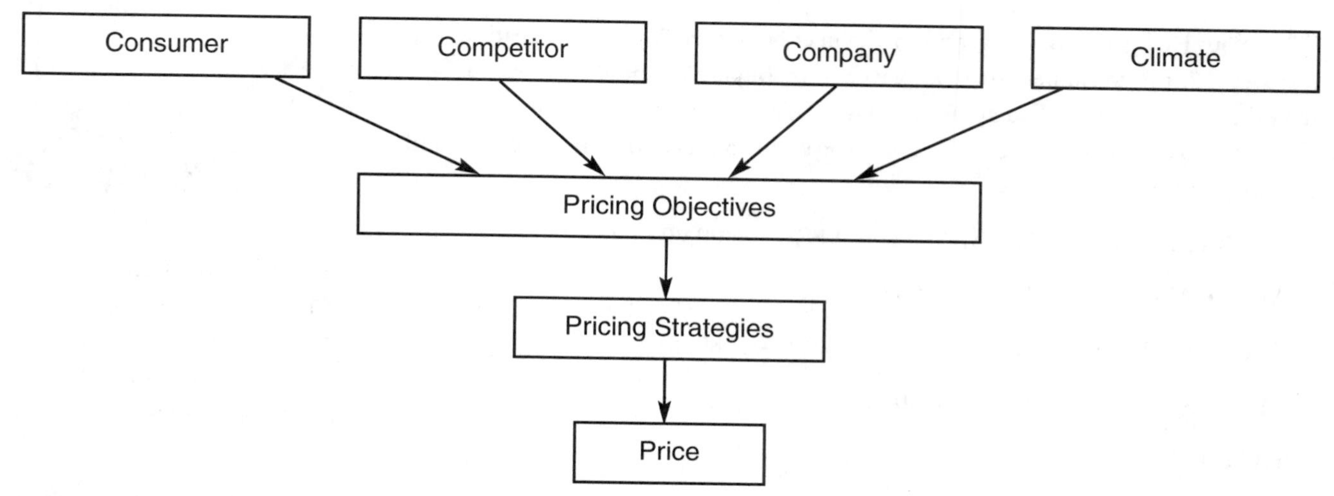

Figure 10.1
Developing an Effective Pricing Strategy.

is weighed in the consumer's analysis according to what the consumer will obtain of each one for the price. For example, if the consumer is considering the purchase of a fitness center membership, he or she will consider services included in the membership package. Because this package costs more than another, how many services are included, and will the consumer use them?

In addition to the factors mentioned, the consumer's buying decision is also affected by the decision-making pathway to reach conclusion. Along the path, the consumer's decision process could be affected by the opinions of friends, family members, a significant other, and salespeople. The consumer could also be affected by age, income, education, geographic location, race, sexual orientation, and gender. Other factors include the consumer's personality, favorite activity, religion, and lifestyle. In addition, some consumers will research a product and its price to inform the decision to be made. There is information available through consumer product reports, product research labs, and government and private product testing organizations.

The study of the consumer's consideration of price is an element of a specialized field of study called consumer behavior. We recommend that the sport marketer read extensively in this area.

The Competitor

There is another factor the sport business cannot ignore: the competitor. More specifically, the sport marketer cannot ignore the competitor's prices and pricing strategies. When determining the price to place on a product, you should give serious consideration to the price in the marketplace—prices being used by the competitors. For example, let's say that you are planning to build and manage an indoor soccer facility. Presently, there are three indoor soccer facilities in the same city. You decide, without investigating the competitor's prices, that you will establish the price, or league fee, for two of your products as follows:

1. Women's advanced league—$400.00
2. Men's advanced league—$400.00

When your facility opens, you get no entries in either league. Upon investigation, you discover that the consumers—soccer players—are buying the product—playing—at the other three facilities. You approach some of the players to ask why and find that they believe your price is too high. You investigate the prices of the other facilities and find the following:

FACILITY A: WOMEN'S ADVANCED FEE—$300.00

MEN'S ADVANCED FEE —$300.00

FACILITY B: WOMEN'S ADVANCED FEE—$280.00

MEN'S ADVANCED FEE —$300.00

FACILITY C: WOMEN'S ADVANCED FEE—$295.00

MEN'S ADVANCED FEE—$295.00

The amount that the consumers of indoor soccer are willing to pay has been established. The consumers have been paying a specific amount for soccer for quite a few years, and they are not willing to pay more.

Finally, you decide that there is a simple solution. You will set the price below your competitors' prices. You set the fee at $100.00 for each of the leagues. This time, a couple of teams register and pay the $100.00, but there are not enough teams to fill the eight slots needed. Therefore, you have to cancel them and return the money to those who had registered.

Once again, you investigate by talking to the consumers. This time you discover that the consumers thought that the price you set was some kind of a hoax with plenty of other hidden charges that would eventually add up to the $400.00 you originally wanted to charge. In addition, some of them tell you that they were concerned with what they would get for only $100.00. In other words, they think that $100.00 is a very low price to pay for soccer and that they will not get a quality product.

This situation reflects two factors in price consideration: first, the consumer's perception of the value for a product; second, careful analysis of the competitor's prices.

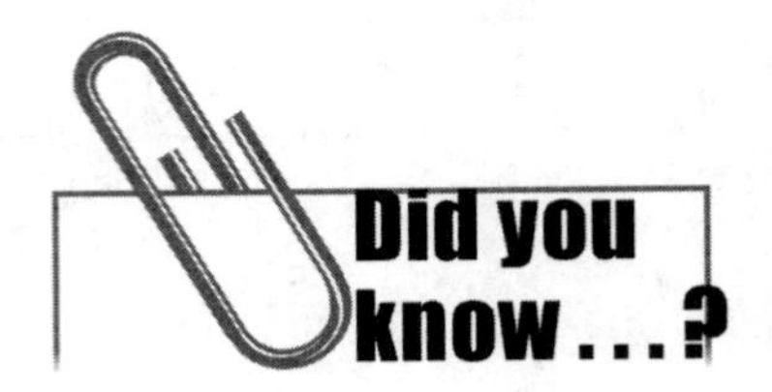

The average MLB ticket in 1999 cost $14.91, up 72.6% since 1991. The most and least expensive average tickets:

Boston
($24.05)

Minnesota
($8.46)

Source: Team Marketing Report

The Company

Another important piece of the puzzle is your company. What are the factors in your sport company that will affect setting the price of a product? Some of these are materials, equipment, rent or mortgage payment, payroll costs, maintenance, renovation, promotion, and dividends to stockholders. If the company is a manufacturer, it cannot put a price on a product that does not, at a minimum, cover the cost of producing the product. If it is a retailer or wholesaler, the price must at least cover the purchase of the product.

The type of sport company will also affect price determination. Generally, there are two types—nonprofit and for-profit. Nonprofit sport companies include those that are supported by government funding such as community recreation facilities and nonprofit sport companies supported by membership fees such as a YMCA. Usually, these are tax-exempt. For-profit sport companies are the opposite—companies owned by individuals, groups, or large conglomerates that do not receive government funding support and are not tax-exempt.

There is a difference in the costs associated with producing similar products in nonprofit and for-profit enterprises. For example, a nonprofit community fitness center receives a variety of tax breaks. Therefore, the total cost of producing the sport product is less than is the total cost for a for-profit fitness center. This allows the nonprofit sport company to set decidedly lower prices for the same products that the for-profit sport company offers. Hence, for-profit sport company owners complain that this is unfair competition (Berrett, Slack, and Whitson, 1993).

Nonprofit sport enterprises gave special attention to raising prices, however, in the early 1990s. The reason was decreasing government and charitable funding. As the budgets of state governments struggled during the early 1990s, the proportion of funding to recreation and sport facilities decreased. Nonprofit companies reported a decrease in charitable giving in the early 1990s due to the recession and the change in tax laws governing charitable giving—less of a given amount is deductible on a person's income tax calculations. As a result, some companies implemented higher fees. As government changes tax laws and these changes affect charitable giving, the sport marketing professional must become aware of these changes and how they will affect their business.

Raising fees will affect consumers and the companies. It will be up to the sport marketer to analyze carefully and estimate the effects of higher prices. As you will learn later in this chapter, the company might lose some consumers if prices are increased, but may make a greater profit.

The Climate

The climate includes those factors that are primarily external and that the sport marketer cannot directly control. These include factors such as laws pertaining to pricing, government regulations, the political climate, the economic situation, and local public attitude.

The economy can have perhaps the most direct effect on the sport company's pricing strategies. For example, the early 1990s in the United States were labeled the "Age of Disinflation" (Farrell and Schiller, 1993). America was in the grips of recession involving high unemployment rates, which slow economic growth. Even with interest rates at their lowest since the late 1970s, consumer spending was very low. When consumers are not buying, the consumer price rate—known as inflation—falls. Therefore, if a company cannot raise prices to cover costs and company objectives, it is forced to change pricing strategies.

The sport marketer cannot afford to develop something referred to as "tunnel vision." Tunnel vision means that the person has stopped paying attention to or studying all factors affecting a situation and has become lazy or egotistical, paying attention to only one or a few factors. The sport marketer must constantly study all factors involved in order to make educated decisions.

Elasticity of Demand

The sport marketer must understand a marketing concept called the elasticity of demand. Here is a simple definition: changes in the market (sales) when there is a change in price. *Elasticity* is a measure of how consumers react—consumer sensitivity—to changes in price. The following questions can help you understand this concept:

1. What will happen if we raise the price of a sport product? If fewer consumers purchase the product, how many is "fewer"? How will that affect revenue, profit, and sales?
2. What will happen if we decrease prices? Will more consumers purchase the products? How will this affect revenue, profit, and sales?
3. Is there any guarantee that any change in price will result in a change in consumer purchase pattern?

The sport marketer can answer these questions only through estimation or experimentation. The sport marketer can attempt to estimate what will happen when a change is made to the price. The following example illustrates the concept of estimating elasticity of demand.

Wet'n'Wild Water Sports Park

The cost of admission to the Wet'n'Wild Water Sports Park is $8.00 for a full day pass. If the price is increased to $10.00, our first analysis is that there will probably be an immediate drop in attendance. This drop may level off, and the final effects will be minimal when we consider this situation over a long period and if the increase in revenues from sales equals or is greater than current revenue from sales.

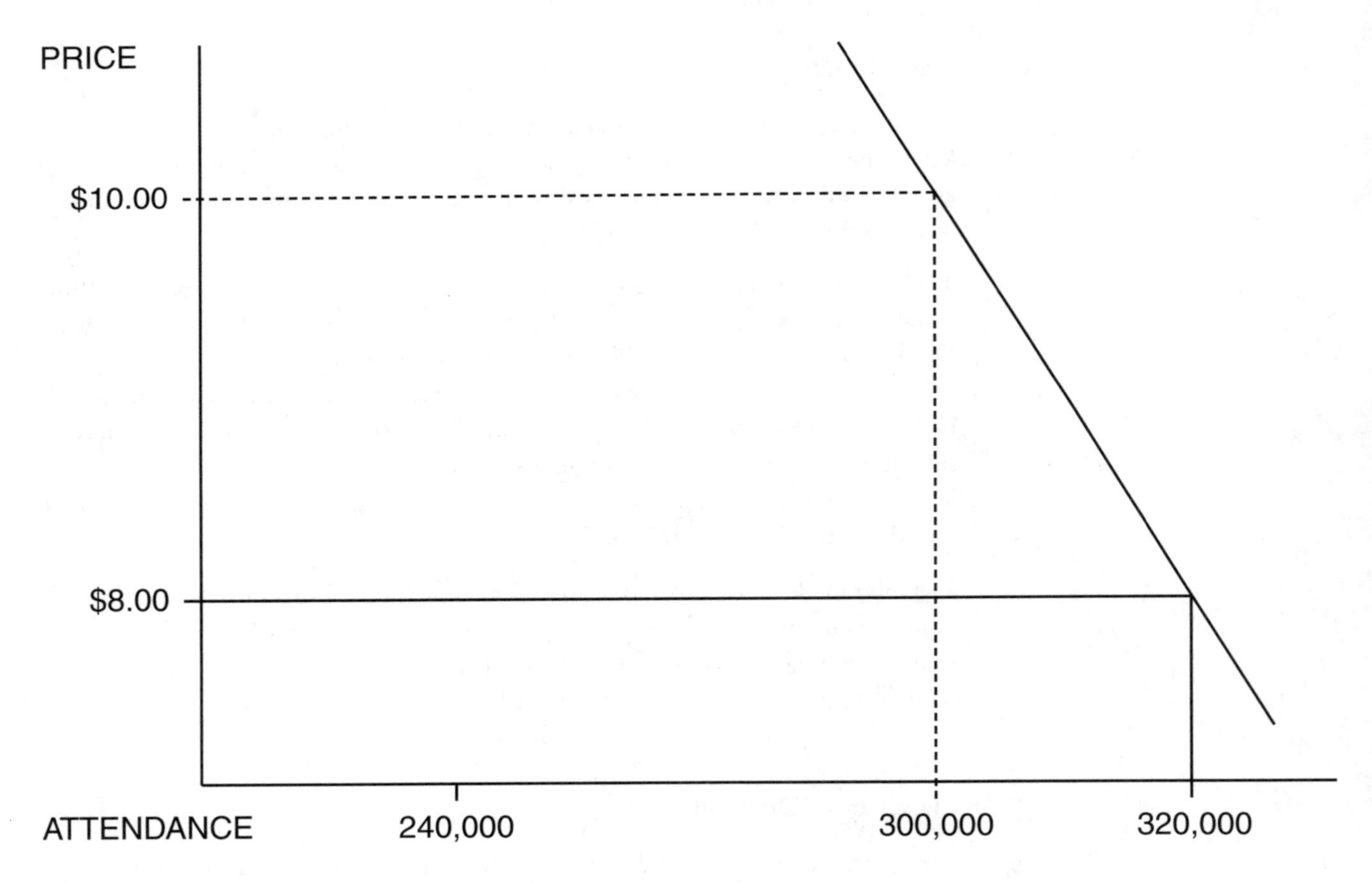

Figure 10.2
Elasticity of Demand at the Wet'n'Wild Water Sports Park. This situation is considered relatively inelastic.

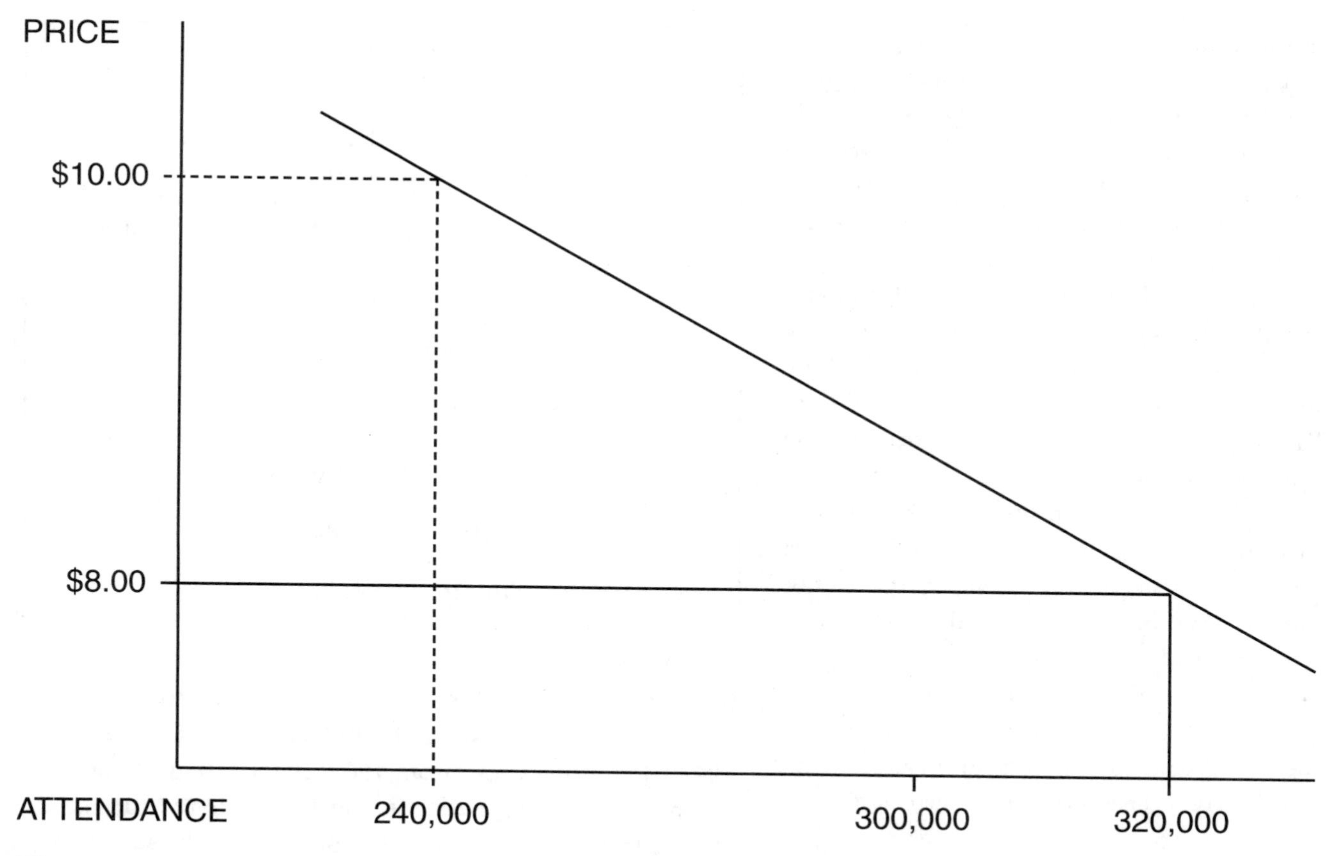

Figure 10.3
Elasticity of Demand at the Wet'n'Wild Water Sports Park. This situation is considered relatively elastic.

If the attendance number decreases, we can conclude that the demand for this product is relatively inelastic. Refer to Figure 10.2 in which the graph illustrates the two-dollar increase and attendance figures. The graph shows that although the attendance number decreased from 320,000 to 300,000, total revenue increased from $2,560,000 to $3,000,000—an increase of $440,000, although there was a decrease of 20,000 buyers. This means that this situation is relatively inelastic because the change in price results in a parallel change in revenue (DeBrock, 1991; Stanton et al., 1991).

Figure 10.3 illustrates the estimate of what could happen if there were a drastic change in consumers. If the number of buyers drops from 320,000 to 240,000—a difference of 80,000 buyers—and this decrease results in a loss in revenue, demand is relatively elastic: A change in price causes an opposite change in revenue (Stotlar, 1993; Walsh, 1986). The higher price and fewer buyers resulted in a $160,000 decrease in revenue.

Determinants of Elasticity

What causes elasticity and inelasticity of demand? First, consider the situation at the beginning of the chapter: the consumers comparing two boats. Many factors affect their decision to buy. One factor is what they would "expect" to pay for a specific boat with a specific set of features. This "expected price" is what the consumer thinks the product is worth (R. E. McCarville, Crompton, and Sell, 1993). The expected price usually is one somewhere within a range of prices with relative minimum and maximum limits: a price most frequently charged, price for similar products, price of the brand usually purchased, or the price last paid (Winer, 1988). For example, the consumer might expect to pay between $100 and $300 for a one-year membership in a fitness center because that is the range of prices for that product in today's market. In another example, a consumer might believe that a fair price for a new pair of running shoes is "not over 80 dollars." If a consumer has "shopped around," this means that the consumer has compared prices of a product at two or more places. This is also precisely what the sport marketer should do. As one means of estimating setting a price, shop around—compare prices of the same or a comparable product. If the product seems to sell well within a specific range of prices, this is a fairly accurate estimate of "expected price," or what the consumer expects to pay and is paying. Some of the other factors that affect elasticity are presented in Figure 10.4. They are discussed here next.

product necessity or luxury
product substitute availability
frequency of purchase
proportion of income available for a specific product
economy
brand loyalty
competition (quantity and quality)
quality of the product
product specialization
time frame of demand

Figure 10.4
Some Factors That Affect Elasticity of Demand (Sources: Boone & Kurtz, 1989; Burnson & Shelby, 1993; Howard & Crompton, 1980; Pajak, 1990; Peter & Donnelly, 1991; Raju, Srinivasan & Lal, 1990; Stotlar, 1993; Stotlar & Bronzan, 1987; Stotlar & Johnson, 1989; and Tarpey, Donnelly & Peter, 1979).

Necessity or luxury product. Price can be relatively inelastic if the product is a necessity and elastic if it is a luxury. For example, football pads are a necessity, and there are no substitutes. Therefore, the buyers must pay the set prices. On the other hand, going on a sports adventure trip is a luxury, and there are plenty of substitutes. Therefore, prices must be set specific to consumer markets because the consumer does not have to spend money for a trip.

Product Substitutability. Have you ever seen or heard these advertising words: "There is NO substitute," "Accept no substitute," or "No other product compares"? The availability of substitutes for products can have a strong affect on elasticity. Those sport products or other products that can meet the consumer's needs, wants, or desires are direct competition for the consumer dollar. In research on recreation and leisure, *substitutability* has been defined as "an interchangeability among activities in satisfying participants' motives, needs and preferences" (Hendee and Burdge, 1974). More recently, Brunson and Shelby (1993) offered the following definition:

> The term recreation substitutability refers to the interchangeability of recreation experiences such that acceptably equivalent outcomes can be achieved by varying one or more of the following: the timing of the experience, the means of gaining access, the setting, and the activity. (p. 69)

Using this definition, the sport marketer must study two factors: what the consumer is looking for and the potential substitutes for their product. With this knowledge the sport marketer can incorporate pricing and other marketing-mix strategies to try to keep the consumer from selecting the substitute.

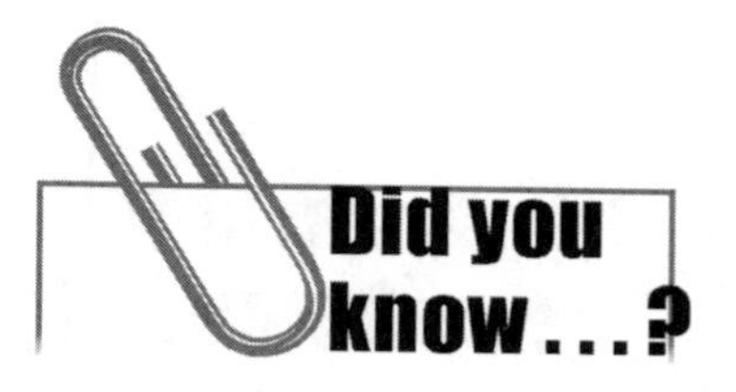

The number of PGA tour millionaires (in prize money) tripled between 1994 and 1997 from 6 to 18.

Source: USA Today

Frequency of purchase. The frequency with which the consumer must purchase a product affects elasticity of demand. Frequency can be linked to necessity. For example, if a consumer has a consistent need for athletic tape to stock the sports medicine clinic, pricing strategies can be set according to the frequency of purchase. In another example, if the sport product is such that there is a very low frequency of purchase such as the need for a sport marketing study on building a new student recreation center for the university, price will likely be much higher.

Income. An individual's income limits the amount of money a consumer has available to spend on discretionary products after all the bills are paid. As income increases, the percent of income a consumer has to use for food and bills decreases. This means that the percent of income available for discretionary purposes increases. An individual with a lower income spends a larger percentage on food and bills and is therefore left with a smaller percentage for discretionary spending. For example, consumer A's take-home income is $25,000 and consumer B's take-home income is $50,000. Both use approximately 40% of their income for necessities such as mortgage, food, vehicles, insurance, utilities, phone, and cable TV. Forty percent of each income is

$\$25{,}000.00 \times 40\% = \$10{,}000$

$\$50{,}000.00 \times 40\% = \$20{,}000.$

Now calculate how much money each consumer has left for discretionary spending:

$25,000–$10,000 = $15,000 or $1,250 per month

$50,000–$20,000 = $30,000 or $2,500 per month.

Consumer B has more discretionary income than consumer A has even though each uses the same percentage of income for necessities.

The economy. The economy affects elasticity of demand. For example, how does recession impact consumer spending and setting prices? As stated earlier in this chapter, the early 1990s were labeled the "Age of Disinflation" (Farrell and Schiller, 1993). Inflation is the rising price level measured in percentages over a period of time, usually annually. Inflation in the United States reached double-digit proportions in the late 1970s and early 1980s and eventually reached 13.6% in 1980. Between 1990 and 1993, the inflation rate has decreased from an annual 5.4% to a 1993 rate of 2.7%. Forcing this period of "disinflation" were recessionary factors such as high unemployment, slow economic growth, increased fierce global competition, and worldwide overcapacity. What this means to the sport marketer is that when the consumer has less money to spend due to unemployment or is spending less money for reasons due to the fear of losing employment, the company will begin to feel the effects. The sport marketer must either redesign pricing strategies or implement significantly radical ones.

Changes in market demand are important to the sport marketer because they affect consumer spending patterns.

On the other hand, sports activities seem to be sustained as compared to many other product markets during times of recession. It seems that Americans love their sports, recreation, and fitness activities, and they are more willing to forego the purchase of a washer and dryer in order to continue participating in their favorite activity. Moreover, these activities are thought to be therapeutic and stress-relief activities, adding to justification for not giving them up.

Brand loyalty. A consumer can become brand-loyal, meaning that the consumer will purchase only products of a certain brand. As an example, Consumer A believes the running shoes of the Smith Company are the best and only shoe that fits everything the consumer is looking for in a running shoe and, more important, that the Smith Company is the only company that the consumer has come to believe in. The consumer will buy the shoes and probably other products from the Smith Company. Consumer B will buy running shoes from any company as long as they fit and the price is right. In this example, Consumer A is loyal to one brand.

In 1997, there were 24 events over a period of 6 months in 14 states with over $4 million total prize money on the AVP Tour.

Source: volleyball.org

Most companies strive to create brand loyalty within its consumers. It will even use this as part of its advertising. Have you ever seen or heard the advertising slogans presented here: "Our customers always come back" and "Once a S ______ customer, always a S ______ customer"?

Brand loyalty applies to the sport industry in another unique way: something called the "hard-core fan." A hard-core fan is someone who picks and supports a particular team, or sport, and will stick with it through good times and bad. For example, a hard-core fan of a university basketball team whose college colors are gold and white may be heard to exclaim, "My blood runs gold!"

The competition. The prices of products of the competition will affect elasticity of demand. Sometimes "price wars" evolve between two or more companies or between companies within an entire industry. For example, the fitness center industry experienced such phenomenal growth in the late 1970s and throughout the 1980s that the market became saturated with fitness centers. Almost all fitness centers offered the same set of products to the consumer. Therefore, the only difference between centers was the price. If the manager of a fitness center wanted to stay in business, prices had to be lowered—some prices were below the cost of the product.

To be able to make educated decisions and to set marketing strategies that will compete best with the competition, the sport marketer must study the competition's prices and pricing strategies.

Product quality. A sport product's quality will affect consumer purchasing and hence elasticity of demand. If the consumer knows, or even suspects, that a sport product is of poor quality, demand will be relatively elastic. Thus, if prices are increased, the consumer simply will not buy, believing that the product is not worth the increase.

Product specialization. The specialization of a sport product will affect elasticity of demand. For example, a softball player must use a softball glove to participate in softball. A softball glove is a specialized sport product. There are over 30 million estimated softball participants over the age of 6 in the United States today. All of them must have this specialized piece of sport equipment to participate in softball. Therefore, the consumer (the softball participant) will purchase this product because it is the only product to perform the function he or she needs. However, there are many softball glove manufacturers and retailers. The consumer has a wide range of choice. This keeps the price down.

Time frame of demand. Another factor affecting elasticity of demand is the time frame of demand: the amount of time a consumer has or is willing to take in the process of making a purchase. Following are three examples. If a soccer player needs athletic tape to wrap an ankle before a game and forgot to purchase the tape in plenty of time before the day and time of the game, the player will be under pressure and will pay almost any price for the tape. The player must stop at the closest store to purchase the tape and does not have time to shop around for the best price. In another example, consider the consumer who wants to buy a new softball bat. This individual currently owns a bat and is fairly satisfied with it. The new bat purchase is a consideration for the future. Therefore, this consumer is under no time pressure to purchase and can shop around for exactly what she wants and for the price she wants. In another example, a college athlete is pursued by several athlete-agents trying to persuade the athlete to retain their services if and when the athlete ever wants or needs an agent. The athlete can be under great time constraints as the senior year approaches.

Pricing Objectives for the Sport Business

One of the most fundamental management skills necessary for positively affecting success is setting objectives. Objectives give direction to determining the price and pricing strategies. Pricing objectives should derive from the established marketing objectives that were established in line with the sport company's objectives and mission. A question the sport marketer must always ask first is "What results does the company expect to occur as a result of the price?" The objectives should be clear, forthright, quantitative, realistic, and achievable; and they should establish vision for the future. Figure 10.5 shows some examples of a variety of pricing objectives categorized by type based on the 4 Cs.

Consumer	Competition	Company	Climate
• price sensitivity • purchase decision • fairness • image • maximize opportunity • targeted markets	• meet competitive prices • be price leader • stabilize the market • discourage entrants to the market	• image • cost • efficient use • return on investment • profit margin • increase market share • survival • growth	• legal restraints • sensitivity

Figure 10.5
Pricing Objectives Categorized by the 4Cs.

Objectives are general aspirations toward which all marketing activities are directed. An objective is declared; then goals are formulated to meet the objectives. Objectives are open-ended statements. Goals are concrete and usually quantitative; goals have specific timelines. Further, company objectives and goals often involve more marketing elements such as promotion and production than pricing. For example, if a running-shoe manufacturer has an objective to become the largest market shareholder, then more than pricing strategies will be involved.

The sport marketer and management of the sport company have the responsibility for establishing the pricing objectives. Each objective has potential positive and negative consequences for the company and its consumers. The sport marketer and all of management must analyze the consequences and make decisions based on this knowledge and on the direction in which they want the company to go. Once they have identified the objectives, the next step is to plan the methods and strategies that have the best potential in achieving the objectives.

Pricing Methods and Strategies for the Sport Business

After you have established pricing objectives, the next step in setting prices for your sport products is deciding on specific methods and strategies. In this section we will present some common pricing methods and strategies that may be used in the sport industry with a brief description of each.

Going-rate pricing (also called status quo pricing). This method is applied when the company wants to keep prices at the going rate—the average price of your competitors for same or equivalent products. For example, if you were working with a fitness center, a check of all membership prices charged at fitness centers will be used to determine the going rate.

A strategy is a detailed plan of action by which an individual or company intends to reach objectives and goals.

Demand-oriented pricing. Using this pricing method, the sport marketer ascertains the price that potential customers are willing to pay for a particular product. The price that potential customers are willing to pay can be determined through using consumer surveys or studying the competition.

Price discrimination. In this pricing method, different prices are charged for the same sport products (Berrett et al., 1993; Walsh, 1986). This method uses consumer demographics and other factors. For example, sport companies use variables such as the following:

- Age—senior citizen discounts; under-12 prices
- Income—a sliding-scale pricing method according to income
- Facility use—peak prices for peak-use times
- Corporate rate—skyboxes sold to companies for luxury suites at the arena.

Peak-load and off-load pricing. This is the method of charging different prices for the same products demanded at different points in time. It is very similar to demand-oriented pricing. The peak-load method involves charging higher prices during times when product sales will have a peak time. For instance, the primary selling time for softball bats is in March, April, and May just prior to softball season. Prices for softball bats during this period will be a little higher than they will be during December and January.

Off-peak pricing involves setting prices lower during off-load times. Some fitness centers use this method. Because the high-use times are those times just before work (6:30–7:30 A.M.), lunch hour, and just after work (5:00–6:30 P.M.), fitness center management wants to encourage more use during the low-use times by offering price incentives. For example, the center can offer a membership discount price to those who promise to use the center between those high-use times.

Seasonal pricing. This pricing strategy is used when a sport product is affected by the seasons and usually relies on specific seasons. Snow ski resorts charge higher prices during winter when there is plenty of snow and skiers want to go skiing. Lower prices are charged during summer months. During the summer, houseboat rental fees are almost twice the amount charged during winter.

Average cost pricing. This method utilizes the following formula (Howard and Crompton, 1980):

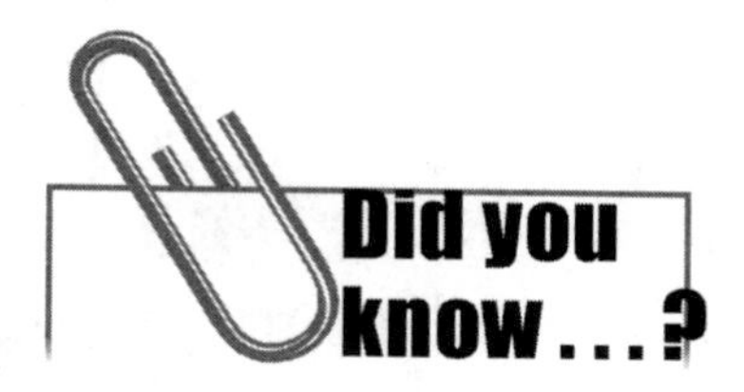

The three highest paid positions in baseball in 1997 were:

First base ($3.7 million)

Designated hitter ($3.6 million)

Outfielder ($2.4 million)

Source: Major League Baseball Players Association

Average Cost Price = Average Fixed Cost + Average Variable Cost

where

Average Fixed Cost = Total Fixed Costs / Number of Participants

and

Average Variable Cost = Total variable Costs / Number of Participants.

The first step in average cost pricing is to determine which fixed costs and variable costs you will use in the formula. Fixed costs are those expenses within the sport company that are constant such as mortgage or rent, payroll, utilities, and phones. Variable costs are expenses such as short-term loan payments, temporary staff, short-term facility rental, and equipment purchases or rental. Once these have been determined, the formula can be used. Howard and Crompton (1980) give the following example:

IF Total Fixed Costs = $1,000

Total Variable Costs = $500

Projected Number of Participants = 100

THEN the Average Cost Price (ACP) = $1,000 / 100 + 500 / 100

THUS ACP = $15.

Penetration pricing. This pricing strategy is used when the sport company wants to penetrate a market by using price as a primary marketing tactic. Prices are relatively lower than other prices for the same products on the market. Penetration pricing is typically used as a first-time offering of a product. For example, a sport marketing company will be opening for business. They decide their pricing strategy will be penetration pricing. To try to secure consumers, they set prices for their services much lower than those of other companies. The company must use a promotion message that speaks to product quality. You'll remember we discussed the problem of setting price too low. Once the product achieves some market recognition, prices can be slowly increased over a period of time.

Cost-plus pricing. In this pricing method, the price of the sport product is based on the cost of the product plus a desired profit (Stanton et al., 1991). If the cost to produce one game of indoor soccer is $70, the price for a game will be $40 plus any amount of profit desired. Therefore, if the indoor soccer facility wants to make $60 of profit from each game, the price of one game will be $100. This will be multiplied by the number of games in a league round of play (usually 8–10 games). If there are 10 teams in the league and the schedule is a round-robin schedule, each team plays each other team once, a schedule that gives each team nine games. Apply the round-robin formula for determining how many games will be played (Byl, 1990):

N × (N-1) / 2 = Total Number of Games*

(*N is number of entries)

In this example we find that 10 × 9/2 = 45 games.

Hence, there will be 45 games in the league. If the price per game is established at $100, the total price for all 45 games is $4,500.

Your next step is to determine what to charge each team. The common method is to charge a league fee: Divide the $4,500 by the number of teams entering. Thus, $4,500 / 10 = $450. At this point in the formula, each team will pay a league fee of $450. Now add the "plus" amount to the $450. This amount can be any amount needed or desired, provided, of course, that the "plus" amount won't put the price out of reach for the consumer. The "plus" amount can be added according to goals and objectives for the company. For example, the company wants to start saving for the purchase of some equipment and wants to be able to purchase the equipment at the end of 2 years. Use the cost of the equipment divided over 2 years and divided among all teams in all leagues in all sports to determine the "plus" amount to add to the cost.

Clemson University alumni had the highest average salaries in the 1997–1998 season in the NBA at $6.25 million.

Source: Sports Business Journal

Break-even analysis. This method for pricing is determined through an analysis of costs and revenue, more specifically, when the costs of producing the product equal the revenue taken from the sales of the product (Pride and Ferrell, 1991). If Central College sold $200,000 worth of tickets to its sports events and the events cost the college $200,000 to produce, the college broke even. In this example, however, Central College didn't make any profit. Break-even analysis will determine how many tickets need to be sold at what price to first break even, and every ticket after that point is profit.

To use break-even pricing effectively, the sport marketer first determines the break-even point for a product using several different prices. This allows the sport marketer to determine total costs and revenue for each price being considered. Figure 10.6 illustrates this method using different prices for tickets to Central College's events.

Short-term pricing methods. The many short-term pricing methods all involve selling a product at a discounted rate for a limited period of time.

Product line pricing. This method involves setting specific price minimums and maximums for each product line (Boone and Kurtz, 1989). Acme Tennis Racket Company can carry three lines of rackets differentiated by price: the $500 line, the $300 line, and the $100 line.

Ticket Price	Quantity to Sell	Revenue	Event Cost	Breakeven Point (Units that must be sold to break even)
$2.00	100,000	$200,000.00	$200,000.00	100,000
$5.00	40,000	$200,000.00	$200,000.00	40,000
$7.50	26,666	$200,000.00	$200,000.00	26,666
$10.00	20,000	$200,000.00	$200,000.00	20,000
$15.00	13,333	$200,000.00	$200,000.00	13,333

If Central College sports events average 200 paying attendees and there are 100 events, the total number of paying attendees to all events is 20,000. The breakeven price is $10.00 and the breakeven point is 20,000. Thus, if the ticket price is set at $10.00, Central must get 20,000 paying attendees to break even. In this example, Central will not make any profit at $10.00 per ticket. Central should consider raising the price to make a profit. At $15.00 per ticket, with 20,000 paying attendees, Central will profit $100,000.00.

Figure 10.6
Calculating the breakeven point using different prices.

Short-term pricing methods:

- Quantity discounts (the more you buy, the lower the price per unit)
- Special sales
- Allowances
- Rebates
- Clearance sales
- Promotional sales

Single price. This method involves setting just one price for everything the company offers.

Secondary market pricing. This method involves determining the secondary market value of an item and establishing price. For example, the popularity and growth of the Play It Again, Sports store is proof that there is a desire and a market for previously owned sports equipment. The management of the store established the value (price) of each item based on its condition and what it might sell for.

Chapter Summary

In this chapter we outlined and discussed pricing for the sport marketer. We discussed the broad conceptual definitions of price, exchange, and value. We looked at the 4 Cs of price determination and discussed each one in relation to its effect on price and the pricing strategy. We discussed the concept of elasticity of demand and its effect on price. The determinants of the elasticity of demand were presented. Last, we looked at several pricing objectives, methods, and strategies that can be used by the sport marketer.

The decision-making process for pricing for the sport marketer is not an easy one. Before establishing the price for a sport product, sport marketers must consider, study, and understand many factors. The sport marketer will be making educated decisions and decisions that will have increased positive potential when all factors have been analyzed and the pricing decisions are based on research.

Questions for Study

1. How does the consumer perceive "price"?
2. Discuss the concept of price.
3. List some examples of words used in place of the word *price* that can be found in the sport industry. Explain why these words are used.
4. What are the 4 Cs of price consideration? Discuss each and give examples.
5. Discuss the concept of the elasticity of demand.
6. List some examples of pricing objectives for sport.
7. List and describe some pricing strategies for the sport industry.

Learning Activities

1. Identify sport businesses, organizations, or other enterprises and their products in your city or community that use these pricing strategies: going-rate pricing, demand-oriented pricing, price discrimination, seasonal pricing, short-term pricing, and product line pricing.
2. Identify in your city or community some of the sport businesses, organizations, or other enterprises that use the price titles as presented in this chapter such as licensing fee, admission, and purse.

Chapter 11

Marketing Channels and Distribution Decisions in the Sport Industry

Overview

A sport business has to get its product to the consumer, or, in some instances, get the consumer to the product. This is called *distribution* (also called *place*). There are many different ways this can be done. For example, there are tangible and intangible products, and each has to be delivered or transported in unique ways. There are many categories of consumers such as the end consumer and the business consumer. Some distribution channels work best for different types of consumer, and there are different marketing channels with different costs involved. For example, the cost to ship one product in one package for next-day delivery for one consumer is much more expensive than the cost of shipping a large truckload of thousands of the product with a three-week delivery period to a retail store.

> The best method of distribution is contingent upon the type of product as well as other factors such as cost, time, laws, and promotional possibilities.

In this chapter you will learn about distribution in the sport industry, the role of distribution in marketing strategy, the selection of a distribution network, and the types of distribution intermediaries available for moving sport industry products.

Distribution Defined

The sport business must determine how to get its products from the manufacturer or producer to the consumer. Distribution involves identifying distribution channels or intermediaries and determining the cost of distribution, the best distribution process for a specific product, and the distribution intensity. The distribution system is contingent on the type of product, the best interests of the sport company, the consumers, and other factors.

> Distribution is the process of getting the product to the consumer.

A *distribution system*, also called a *marketing channel*, is the methods and channels used in delivering products from producer to consumer. An *intermediary* is an individual or organization through which products move from producer to consumer.

Distribution and Marketing Channel Decisions in the Sport Industry

Distribution decisions in the sport industry depend on the type of product and consumer, among many other factors. In this section, you will learn about five different types of products in the sport industry and the kinds of distribution channels typically used for them. Those five product types are sports activities, sport goods, sport services, sports entertainment, and sport media. Refer to Figure 11.1.

A Distribution System:

is the methods and channels used in delivering products from producer to consumer.

An Intermediary:

is an individual or organization through which products move from producer to consumer.

Product Type	Consumer Type	Product Examples	Distribution Type	Channel Examples
Sports Activities	End Consumers: Sports Participants	events & activities, such as leagues, tournaments, meets, races	Direct	Producer/Provider: Sports Complex or Organization
Sport Business Goods: 1. Sporting Goods 2. Business Goods 3. Promotional Goods	1. End Consumers, such as sports participants. 2. Business Consumers 3. End Consumers: fans, participants	1. bowling ball, snow bike 2. astroturf 3. logo t-shirt; keychain	1. Complex 2. Direct 3. Complex	1. sporting goods retailer 2. direct sales: business-to-business 3. retailers, vendors
Sports Business Services: 1. sporting 2. business	1. End Consumers: sports participants 2. Business Consumers: corporations	1. racket stringing 2. marketing research; sponsorship management	1. Direct 2. Direct	1. Producer—a person set up in a pro shop 2. Producer: business-to-business
Sports Entertainment: Spectator Sports	Two Types: 1. End Consumers: sports spectators 2. Business Consumers: corporations	WNBA, NASCAR, Olympics, X-Games, American Gladiators, PGA/LPGA, NFL	1. Complex 2. Direct	1. ticket retailers and brokers 2. direct sales
Media: 1. Sports Magazine 2. E-sports business 3. Industry Trade Magazine	1 & 2. End Consumers, readers of sports information 3. Business Consumers: retailers, producers, advertisers	1. Snow Boarding Magazine, Outdoors, Runner's World 2. CBS Sportsline 3. Sporting Goods Business, WinterSport Business, Sportstyle	1. Direct & Complex 2. Direct 3. Direct	1. subscription; retail stores 2. online 3. subscription

Figure 11.1
Examples of Distribution and Channel Types Based on Consumer and Product Types

Product Types

Sports Activities

Sports activities are participation products such as participation in basketball, bowling, scuba, hiking, sky diving, running, weight training, sailing, water skiing, golf, and snow-boarding. The consumers of these products are people who want to participate in these activities. Numerous sports, fitness, recreation, leisure, and sports tourism activities are offered to millions of different consumers today. Participatory sports activities are the largest segment of the sport business industry in the United States.

The sport industry is driven by consumers who want to participate in or watch sports.

Photo reprinted by permission of WVU Photography.

The activities are offered—packaged—to the consumer in a number of ways such as leagues, tournaments, championships, races, meets, regattas, outings, and adventure travel packages. These are further delineated by using a number of different demographical, psychographical, or lifestyle segment elements to customize the events for different target markets. For example, softball may be offered by gender, age, skill level, company, sexual orientation, religion, race or ethnicity, geographic region, and climate.

Consumers of sports activities are end consumers, although there can be some business-to-business transactions surrounding the activity such as sponsorship. The type of distribution for these products is direct: from producer to consumer. Examples of producers include city parks and recreation departments that offer basketball leagues; a privately owned sports complex that offers snow skiing; a sports organization that offers a roller hockey tournament; and a sports club that offers yachting tournaments, sailing races, or scuba outings. The exchange is directly from producer to consumer.

Sport Business Goods

These are tangible goods such as sports equipment and apparel, artificial turf, facilities, and trophies. This type of product must be manufactured or produced in factories, shops, or plants and must be transported from the factory to a place where the consumer can purchase the good. Consumers include both end consumers and business consumers, depending on the product. As you can see in Figure 11.1, some of these kinds of goods include sporting goods, business goods, and promotional goods.

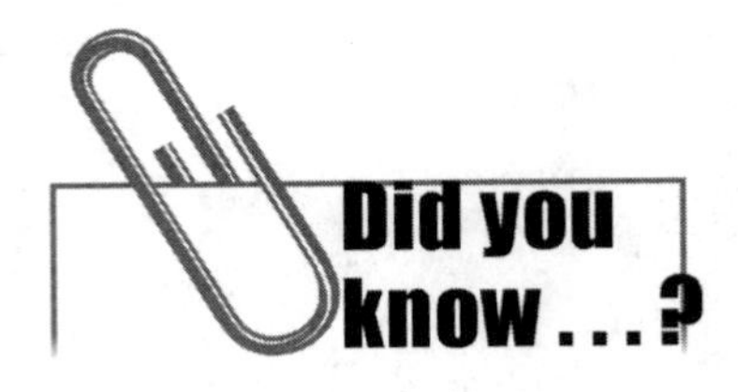

Anglers spent $5.2 billion on motorboats during 1996, $2 billion of which was for bass boats.

Source: 1996 US Economic Impact of Sport Fishing in the U.S., American Sportfishing Association

The distribution system for these products will be either direct or complex, depending on the product type. Most sports equipment, for example, is manufactured in a factory and must be transported from that factory to where the consumers can purchase the product. For example, snowboards are manufactured in a factory in Delaware. Snowboard consumers are in several states and towns. Therefore, the snowboards must be transported from Delaware to places where the consumers can obtain them. Typically, snowboards are sold in sporting goods retail stores. The manufacturer must decide how to move the snowboards from Delaware to the stores. There are many marketing channel options available such as transporting by truck, plane, or train. Usually, some combination is required.

Sport Business Services

Many of those millions of sports participants are going to need their sports equipment cleaned, repaired, and/or maintained. This, of course, sustains a fairly large industry segment of services such as tennis racket stringing, golf club cleaning, pool maintenance, and equipment repair. For these products, which are primarily intangibles, the distribution is usually a direct exchange. For example, a tennis player with a racket in need of new strings and stringing takes the racket to a person who can perform this service.

> The cleaning, repair, and maintenance of sports equipment alone makes up an important part of the sport service industry.

Other products are business service products. These consumers are business consumers. Therefore, typically the exchange is a business-to-business exchange (refer to chapter 6 for details on business consumers). For example, a sport company needing sponsorship management services will work directly with the provider of these services.

Sports Entertainment

Some sports events are produced and sold as entertainment products. In the United States, some sports events such as the American Gladiators and the X-Games have been created specifically as entertainment products, and some sports events such as college athletics were slowly developed as entertainment products. Consumers of sports as an entertainment product include both end and business consumers. End consumers are those who are typically called "spectators." Spectators go to the event to watch the event and be entertained. Business consumers can be one of two types: those corporations that purchase the box seating (skyboxes or corporate luxury boxes) or those companies that purchase advertising, sponsorship, or other similar space at the event.

> The development of sports as an entertainment product is a fast-growing segment of the sport business industry.

Distribution depends on the type of consumer. Distribution to end consumers usually occurs through a complex system of ticket retailers and brokers. Sales to the corporate business are usually direct.

Sport Media

Some examples of sport media are sports magazines (print), electronic sports businesses (Web-based businesses), and industry trade magazines. The consumers of these can be either end or business consumers. Consumers of sports magazines are end consumers: those who want to see and read about sports, fitness, and recreation activity. Distribution can be either complex or direct. For industry trade magazines, however, the more typical distribution is direct.

There are a number of Web-based sports businesses today. These businesses use one distribution channel—the Web—as a point of purchase. However, the delivery of the actual product requires transporting the product to the consumer. In many cases, the product is shipped through a company such as Federal Express directly to the consumer.

Distribution of Products

Tangible products are physical objects. Most are manufactured in mass quantities at a factory and must be moved—distributed—to a place of purchase—retailer or wholesaler. For example, running shoes are manufactured in a factory and must be moved to a retailer to be sold.

Intangible products are not physical objects and include products such as services, places, and ideas. In addition, entertainment is included in this category. Most intangible products are not produced until ordered by the consumer. In a fitness center in which laundry services are offered, the consumer must order the service, then simply leave dirty laundry in a bag in a certain spot. The center will perform the service and return the clean laundry to the locker area.

Entertainment, however, is scheduled for a specific date, time, and place and the consumer must be available at that time and be able to go to the place where the event is offered. A basketball game, for example, can be offered as an entertainment product. The game will be scheduled at a specific date and time and in a sports facility. To consume the product, the consumer must travel to the facility and watch the game. In addition, the game is not produced, or manufactured, until the players play the game. Therefore, the consumer must be present when the game is played.

Another significant difference between the tangible running-shoe product and the intangible laundry service or basketball game is something called shelf life. The running-gear product has a long shelf life—it is manufactured and can exist for quite a long period of time until sold. The laundry service has a long shelf life. The service is produced and then awaits the consumer to take possession. The basketball game, however, has no shelf life. The game cannot be manufactured and put on the shelf until a consumer purchases it. As a matter of fact, the game is not manufactured until the players play the game. In other words, the game is simultaneously manufactured and consumed.

Shelf life is the amount of time that a product can remain in a good and consumable condition after being manufactured.

The game must be consumed at the same moment it is being produced. If not, it is not consumed and perishes. That game will never be manufactured again. There is, however, through the use of video and audiotape, a secondary product that the consumer may purchase to watch the game: videotapes of the game sold to the consumer.

Because of the perishable shelf life of spectator sports events, today's spectator sports marketers take great pains to increase what consumers receive for the amount of time and money spent at the game. Hence, most spectator sports events offer a variety of sideshows, concessions, services, souvenirs, and rewards in the form of door prizes or fourth-quarter drawings.

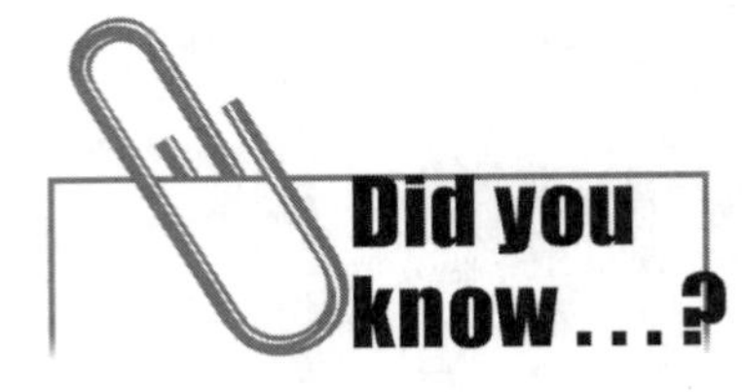

The top three states in terms of numbers of adult anglers:

Florida (2.9 million)

California (2.7 million)

Texas (2.6 million)

Source: 1996 US Economic Impact of Sport Fishing in the U.S., American Sportfishing Association

In a different sport product, some providers of participation sports are offering the consumer more than participation for their money and time. To attract more runners, management and marketers of many marathons and 10K runs offer much more than just the race itself. Many offer the consumer t-shirts, concessions, pasta dinners, door prizes, rewards for every entrant and every person who crosses the finish line, child care services, changing and shower services, medical care services, insurance, souvenirs, and photographs of the runner crossing the finish line. Some of these are included in the price of entry, and some are sold separately.

For some types of products in the sport industry, *how* and *when* the product is packaged and offered to the consumer are important parts of distribution. Almost all running events are held on Saturday mornings. Professional football games are held on Saturday, Sunday, or Monday evenings. Softball leagues are offered during the summer months and on weekday evenings. The local college women's and men's basketball games are played in evening slots. These are important elements of distribution called time, place, and possession utility. These are described in detail in the following section.

Time, Place, and Possession Utility Through Distribution

Distribution offers time, place, and possession utility to the consumer. The product must be accessible to the consumer, when it is needed, in the desired form. For example, a softball player needs to be able to purchase a softball bat before the season starts, usually in the summer; to buy the bat close to home; and to take possession of it when wanted.

Time utility is getting the product to the consumer when the consumer wants it. *Place utility* is getting the product to the consumer where the consumer wants it. *Possession utility* is creating possession of the product for the consumer (Boone and Kurtz, 1989). The distribution system is the channel through which the producer gets the product to the consumer when, where, and how the consumer wants it. For example, women's basketball fans want women's basketball at prime times (evenings, weekend evenings, prime-time slots such as seven or eight P.M.), in a great facility (in the same arena used by the men's team), and on a major broadcasting station (the major broadcasting networks, not the hard-to-find stations), and they want season tickets (giving them rights to specific seats for the entire season instead of "admission-at-the-door and no reserved seating"). Spectator sports marketers are listening, and more women's basketball is being offered in prime-time slots on major broadcasting stations, and presold tickets and season tickets are being offered. This offers the product to the consumer when, where, and how the consumer wants it.

In another example, a manufacturer of sporting goods must distribute the goods to places where the consumer is most likely to purchase the goods. For example, Hillerich & Bradsby Co., manufacturer of the famous Louisville Slugger baseball and softball bats, has a manufacturing plant in Louisville, Kentucky. Their bats, however, are sold around the world. Therefore, H & B must decide on a method, or more than one method, to move the bats from the plant to places around the world where the consumer is most likely to purchase them. Those places are usually sporting goods retail stores and department stores with a sporting goods department. Some of the methods involved in moving the goods include moving them by truck, plane, ship, or train.

The Distribution System

The truck, plane, ship, and train mentioned above are examples of distribution intermediaries. Others include wholesalers, retailers, agents, brokers, distributors, sales agents, and shippers. *Distribution intermediaries* are those individuals or organizations through which products are moved from producer to consumer. They are the links through which products move on the route from manufacturer to consumer. The sport business management, as part of the overall marketing plan for a product, should have decided before a product is manufactured which intermediaries will be best for the company, the product, and the consumer. The determination of distribution intermediaries is a part of the development of a distribution plan (Evans and Berman, 1987).

Types of Distribution Intermediaries

There is a variety of distribution intermediaries available to the sport marketer. Some of these are listed and briefly described here.

Wholesaler—a company that buys goods in large quantities specifically to resell to retailers or final consumers (Peter and Donnelly, 1993).

Retailer—a company that buys goods to resell to consumers (Peter and Donnelly, 1993).

E-tailer—an electronic retail store.

Agent—a person or a company who "moves" products (facilitates the sale) by taking orders for a buyer and placing the order with the producer (Boone and Kurtz, 1992).

Mail order—a company that buys direct from a manufacturer or producer and offers the products through a catalog or electronic system (Cravens and Woodruff, 1986).

Distributor—a wholesale intermediary (Peter and Donnelly, 1993).

The distribution plan is called the distribution system (also sometimes called a distribution network, distribution channel, or marketing channel). The *distribution system* is the system developed for moving products from producer to consumer (Peter and Donnelly, 1993).

How does one construct a distribution system? There are many different systems because there are many types of companies, many different types of products, and many different consumers with different needs. The distribution system selected must be one that is effective and efficient for the manufacturer or producer, the intermediaries, the product, the company, and the consumers. In addition, the company must give serious consideration to the environment. The management must not be fooled into thinking that the fastest or most economical method for moving products is also automatically environmentally friendly. A question a sport marketer or sport management executive will always face is one of ethics: If something is good for the company, is it okay for the environment, and is it ethical to proceed?

A distribution system can range from direct (also called simple) to complex. A *direct distribution system* is one in which only the manufacturer and the consumer are involved as depicted in Figures 11.2 and 11.3. In a direct system, the sport product moves from the manufacturer or producer directly to the consumer. There is no intermediary involved. A few examples include the following:

1. A sport sponsorship management company that sells services directly to a client,
2. A tennis pro who sells lessons directly to a student,
3. A sport facility construction company that sells directly to a college athletic department,
4. A city parks and recreation department that sells basketball leagues directly to teams, and
5. A professional football championship game that sells directly to the spectator.

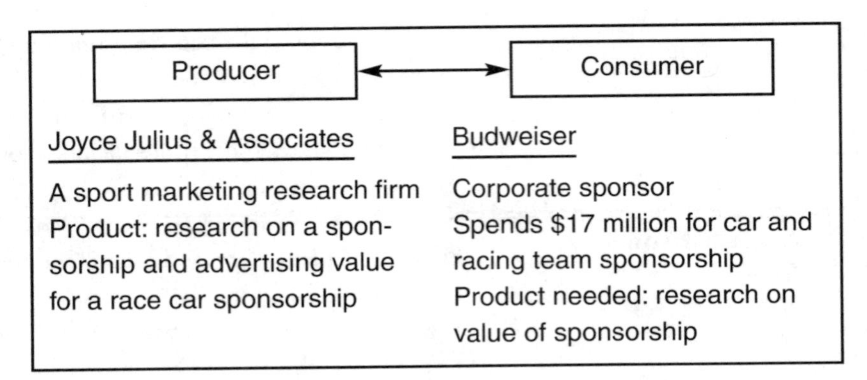

Figure 11.2
Example of a direct distribution transaction, from producer to consumer. This is a business-to-business transaction. The consumer is a business consumer.

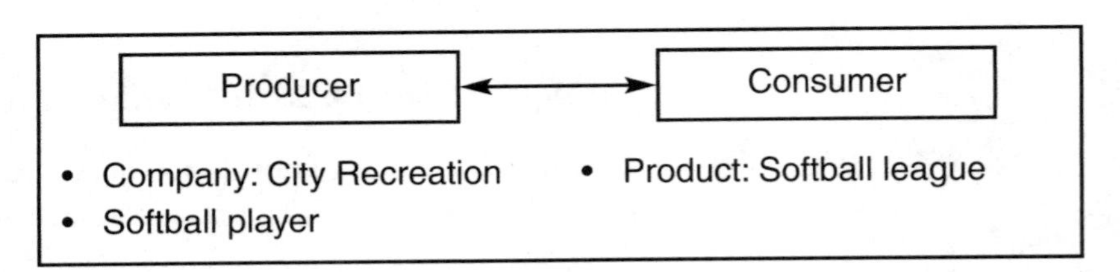

Figure 11.3
Another example of a direct distribution transaction. Here, though, the consumer is the end-consumer.

A *complex distribution system* is one in which one or more intermediaries are involved in the movement of the sport product from the producer to the consumer. Examples of routes of a complex system are illustrated in Figure 11.4. In one network, the product moves from the producer to an agent to a retailer and then to the consumer. In another network, the product moves from the producer to a distributor to a retailer and then to the consumer. In a third network, the product moves to a wholesaler and then to the consumer.

In most instances in which intermediaries are involved, the final price of the product to the consumer is higher—hence, the popularity of a phenomenon called the "outlet store" or "factory-direct" store. No intermediaries are involved, which keeps the cost of moving the sport product very low. This equivocates to a lower price to the final consumer and an increased profit margin for the manufacturer. When intermediaries are involved, the price of the product to the final consumer is driven up. For example,

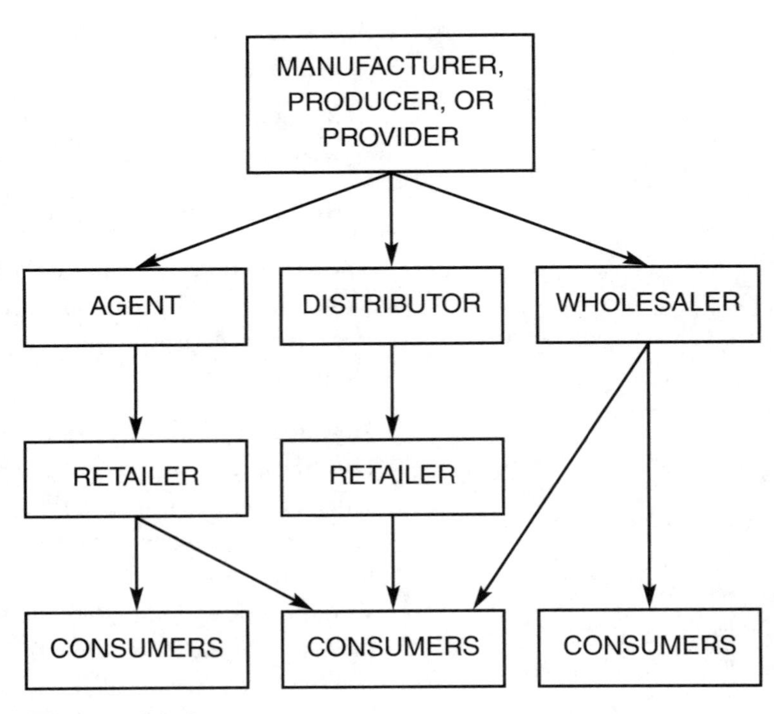

Figure 11.4
A complex distribution system in the sport industry.

Cost to Manufacture Bat	3.75
Packaging	1.25
Shipping Charges to Distributor	.50
Other Expenses Such as Advertising	3.50
Manufacturer's Total Cost	9.00
Manufacturer's Profit Margin	+3.50
Manufacturer's Price to Distributor	12.50
Shipping Charges to Retailer	.50
Other Expenses	.50
Distributor's Cost	13.50
Distributor's Profit Margin	+5.00
Distributor's Price to Retailer	18.50
Retailer's Expenses	2.00
Retailer's Profit Margin	+19.45
Retailer's Price to Consumer	$39.95

Figure 11.5
Example of a sport product's increasing cost as it moves through a distribution system.

the manufacturer sells the sport product to a distributor who sells it to a retailer who sells it to the final consumer. Each entity involved must make a profit. Therefore, an aluminum softball bat that costs $3.75 to manufacture will be sold to the consumer for $39.95. Figure 11.5 illustrates this process and what happens to the price of the product along the way to the consumer.

However, intermediaries are necessary for many products. Although the costs of intermediaries drive up the final price of the product, many products would not be available to consumers if intermediaries did not exist. For example, it is not practical for a consumer who lives in Central City, Michigan, to travel to a running-shoe manufacturing plant in another country to purchase needed running shoes. Therefore, the manufacturer must move the product from the factory to Central City. To hold down cost, the manufacturer sells many products to retail stores in Central City. The running shoes are transported as part of a large shipment of goods to the stores in the city. To get the running shoes, the consumer simply shops at one of several sporting goods and shoes stores in the city. Figure 11.6 illustrates how many manufacturers use these intermediaries to distribute products, to reduce the number of transactions between consumers and manufacturers, and to increase effective and efficient transportation of goods from producer to consumer.

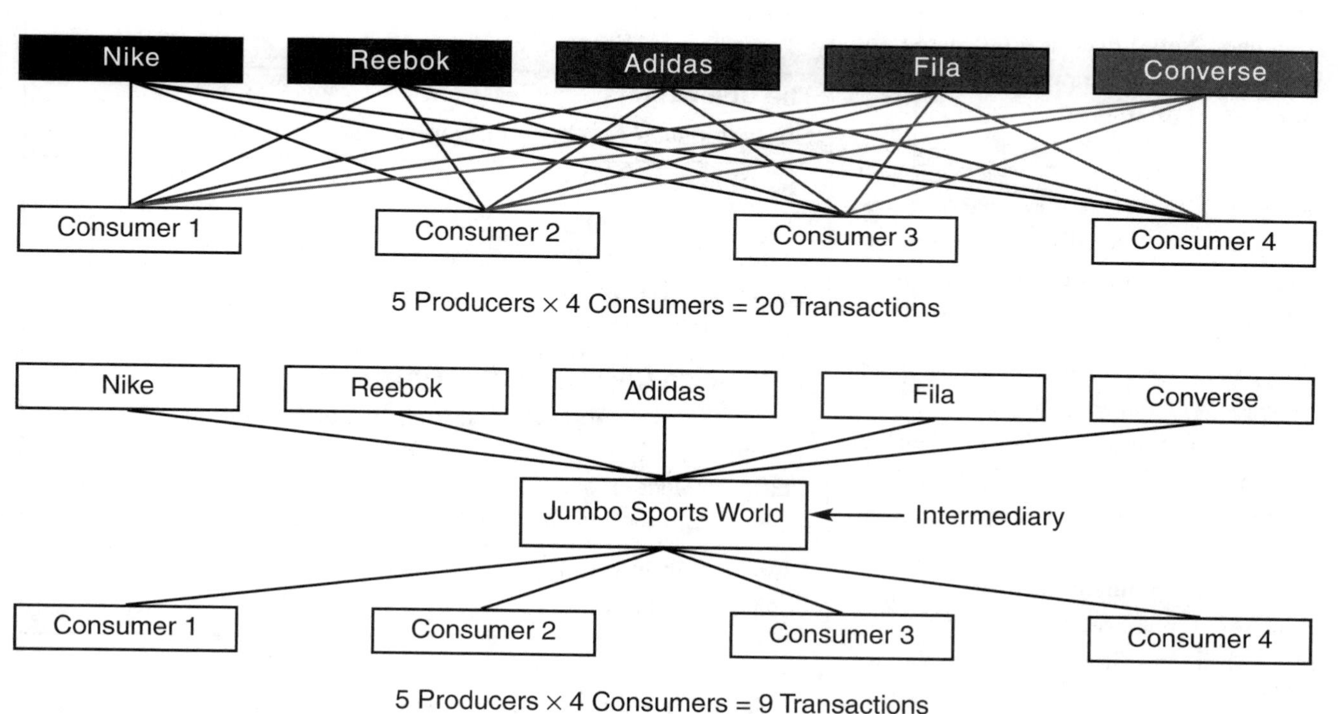

Figure 11.6
How an Intermediary Reduces the Number of Required Transactions.

Selection of a Distribution System

At first glance, the task of selecting a distribution system might seem overwhelming because there are so many options. However, if the sport marketer will first consider the factors that will affect the final selection, this will help guide the sport marketer's decision-making process.

An important element to remember is that the distribution system should be consumer driven. After all, it is the consumer who will purchase the product. Therefore, the product should be offered to the consumer when, where, and how the consumer wants it—time, place and possession utility. One idea is to begin with the consumers of the product and trace the path from the consumer to the manufacturer.

> The considerations of the consumer should be the deciding factor in the selection of a distribution system.

Another important question to consider is which distribution options are available to you. Some sport marketers spend hours creating and designing elaborate distribution systems only to discover that intermediaries do not exist or will not serve their needs.

Factors Affecting Selection

The many factors that affect the final selection of a distribution system, or channel, are presented in Figure 11.7. It is important that the sport marketer analyze each factor, how each one is interrelated to others, and how the distribution system considered fits with the overall marketing objectives. Notice that the 4 Cs come into play again in distribution with the important element of product.

The Consumer
Characteristics: number, geographical location
Needs: purchase behavior, when needed, how needed, where needed
Psychographic Characteristics: promotion

The Sport Company
Strengths: financial, location, availability of distribution options and weaknesses

The Sport Product
Type of Product: tangible, intangible, shelf life, packaging and shipping requirements

The Competitors
Characteristics: number, geographic location, distribution methods

The Climate
Legal: laws, regulations, policy
Political: who is in office; what is "politically correct & incorrect"
Economic: cost, inflation, and other economic factors
Ethical: rights, issues, and other ethical considerations

Distribution Channels/Intermediaries
Availability of Channels: what intermediaries exist and are available to you?
Characteristics: types, location, cost, strengths and weaknesses, acceptance of product, ability to handle product

Distribution Intensity
Positioning the product

Figure 11.7
Factors to consider in the selection of a distribution system. [Adapted from Evans & Berman(1987), Boone & Kurtz (1992), Cravens & Woodruff (1986), and Peter & Donnelly (1993).]

The consumer. Consumers want a product when, how, and where they need or desire it. This must be studied and understood by the sport company in order to know when, how, and where to distribute products.

The sport company. Position of the sport company will influence distribution. For example, the company might not be able to afford the higher-priced distribution channels or intermediaries and would have to select less expensive ones. The location of the company might be a barrier. If the company is in a city with no airport, distribution intermediaries will be limited to other forms of transportation.

The sport product. The type of product will influence how it is distributed. Shelf life, for example, is the amount of time a product can last before it loses quality. Of course, most of us know that fresh vegetables must be consumed before rotting, but what about sport products? What products are there that have a long shelf life or a short shelf life? Here is an example of each. A Super Bowl game has a short shelf life. The game must be consumed at the moment it is produced. A basketball has a long shelf life. It can remain in a sporting goods store for a long time until consumed.

Products that are goods and products that are services require different distribution channels. A good is usually transported from producer to consumer through intermediaries. A service is usually sold directly to the consumer without the use of intermediaries.

A company should study what its competitors are doing before making any sort of business decision.

The competition. Unless the sport company has the only product of its kind, the sport company has competitors. To stay in business, the company must take the competitors into consideration when making most all business decisions. This information could help with ideas or could shed light on why the competitor always gets its product to the consumer first.

The climate. Laws, politics, economic situation, ethical considerations, and environmental concern will all have an influence on decisions about distribution. These should be constantly monitored so that the information gained can be used in determining distribution systems.

Determining Distribution Intensity

One of the elements of distribution on which the sport marketer must decide is the intensity of the distribution of the product. The degree of distribution intensity will affect sales of the product and is linked to positioning the product. *Distribution intensity* is the amount of distribution selected for a particular sport product. Distribution intensity ranges from intensive to exclusive and is contingent on most of the same factors that affect the sport marketer's decisions on distribution channels. Figure 11.8 illustrates the range of intensity.

	INTENSIVE	SELECTIVE	EXCLUSIVE
WHERE DISTRIBUTED:	everywhere possible	a few places	a few select places
EXAMPLES: Basketball Game	• TV & cable channels • radio taped for later broadcast • taped for sale in-person	• in-person • only one TV channel • two radio stations	• in-person • only one TV channel
Softball Bats	• every sporting goods outlet possible • stores and department stores	• only half of all sporting goods stores	• only one select sporting goods store

Figure 11.8
Continuum of Distribution Intensity and Some Sport Product Examples.

The type of distribution intensity selected becomes part of the advertising message to the consumer primarily to let the consumer know where the product is available and to establish status quo for the product or company. An advertising message used to let the consumer know might be "widely available" or "available at all local sporting goods stores."

Intensive distribution. If the sport marketer chooses an intensive distribution strategy, then the product will be offered in as many places as possible. In the examples given in Figure 11.8, softball bats would be offered everywhere possible: all sporting goods stores, pro shops, department stores with sporting goods departments, and other outlets. A basketball game would be offered through as many outlets as possible: many television channels, many radio stations, in-person viewing, taped-for-later broadcast, and videotaped for later sale.

Selective distribution. If the sport marketer chooses a selective distribution strategy, the product will be offered in a limited amount of places. The softball bats will be offered only in sporting goods stores. The basketball game will be offered through one local television station, one local radio station, and in-person viewing.

Exclusive distribution. With exclusive distribution as a strategy, the sport marketer will offer the product in one or a small number of outlets. The softball bats will be offered in only one sporting goods store. The basketball game will be offered only through one television station or in-person viewing.

Another factor affecting the decision on distribution intensity is advertising dollars. In intensive distribution, much of the advertising effort falls with the place of distribution. In exclusive distribution, much of the advertising effort lies with the producer, although the outlet selected can claim to be the exclusive outlet for the product.

Another factor is image. Exclusive distribution creates an image of prestige. The advertising message will sometimes include the words "available only at S_____'s Sporting Goods."

Exclusive distribution also allows for price increases. If your company is the only company with a product that has high demand, you can take advantage of the situation and assign higher prices than normal. For example, some television broadcasting companies pay for the rights to exclusively broadcast certain sports events. In this situation, the broadcasting company can increase the cost of advertising during the event. In some cases, the broadcast can go to a pay-per-view status in which consumers must pay specifically to view that particular event on television.

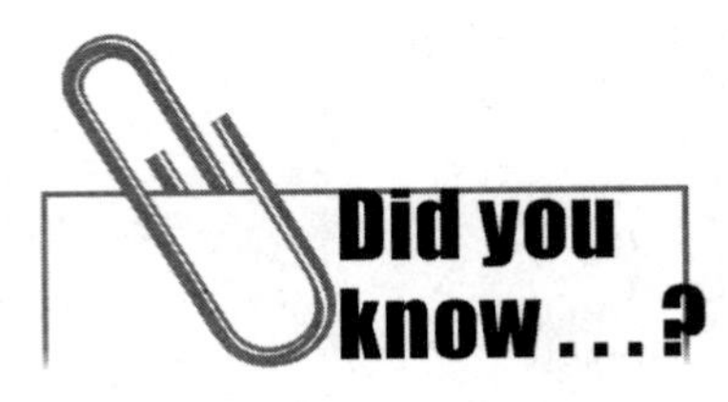

The five largest sports publications ranked by circulation in the United States:

Gameday Magazine
3.3 million

Sports Illustrated
3.28 million

Touchdown Illustrated
2.68 million

Field and Stream
1.75 million

Golf Digest
1.54 million

Source: *Street and Smith's Sports Business Journal* research and *The Standard Periodical Directory* (21st ed.), 1998

Exclusivity drives up demand, which in turn drives up prices.

Chapter Summary

The sport business must decide how to get the product to the consumer through the selection of a distribution system. The selection process is affected by many factors including the consumer, the company, the product, product positioning, the climate, and distribution systems available to the sport company. Distribution intensity will determine how extensively the product will be made available to the consumers. Some distribution channels work best for different types of consumers. Each distribution channel has unique costs involved that should be given serious consideration in the selection process.

There are many different products in the sport business industry. Distribution decisions depend on the type of product, the consumer, the company, the climate, and the competitor, among other factors. The ultimate decision is to find the most appropriate way to get the product to the consumer, or the consumer to the product, when and how the consumer needs it, and in a way that meets the company's objectives.

Questions for Study

1. What is distribution?
2. Describe the different kinds of distribution in the sport industry.
3. What are distribution intermediaries? Give some examples.
4. What is a distribution system? Give some examples of systems in the sport industry.
5. What are the factors that affect the selection of a distribution system?
6. What is distribution intensity? Why is it linked to promotion and positioning the product? Give some examples of each type.
7. What are some examples of different types of products found in the sport business industry? Develop what you think would be some appropriate distribution channels for these products.

Learning Activities

1. List some sport products offered in your city or community. Create a distribution system for each. Research the real costs of your systems. Give a presentation in class.

Chapter 12

Promotion in the Sport Industry

People will not buy a product if they do not know it exists. The purpose of promotion is to tell people about a product. It is such an important variable that companies have been formed for the sole purpose of selling promotional products. Promotion is also critical for the service sector. According to Delpy, (2000) "event organizers can no longer just open their gates and expect spectators to attend" (p. 8). Similarly, few clients will just "drop by" a sport massage business without prompting.

Promotion is a critical part of the marketing mix for a sport company.

So many companies have been formed for the purpose of providing promotional support to sport organizations that "sport promotion" is considered an industry. There are marketing firms and sport marketing firms, advertising firms, agents who specialize in promoting sports people or teams, and companies that specialize in producing promotional products such as logo t-shirts, bags, cups, mugs, hats, towels, key chains, watches, jackets, flags, banners, trinkets, and drink coolers. Further, within the promotion industry there is specialization. One company, Multi-Ad Services (www.multi-ad.com) in Illinois specializes in the production of media guides, newsletters, scorecards, game programs, brochures/catalogs, and logo design. If you need inflatable displays, there's a company for that too. IDG (Inflatable Design Group, www.inflatabledesigngroup.com) created a 25-foot inflated Spalding Basketball for a WNBA promotion. Other products have included many of the inflatable play structures, all with customized team logos, used around the stadium for children.

There are also companies that specialize in manufacturing products that will be sold to companies that specialize in printing logos, trademarks, team names, or other images on the products that a sport organization may desire. One such company, Logo Athletic (www.logoathletic.com), originated in 1968 to capitalize on consumer demand for licensed sports wear. Their licensed products included all of the professional leagues, multiple NCAA institutions, the Indianapolis Motor Speedway, and other properties, all produced through their Logo 7 and Logo Athletic brands. In addition, approximately 15% of their business resulted from proprietary items created for the sole use and distribution of the client. Ultimately, when the licensed-goods market collapsed, Log Athletic declared bankruptcy.

There are companies that specialize in managing the logos, licensing, and merchandising for sport properties (Pitts, Fielding, and Miller, 1994). For example, the Collegiate Licensing Company represents a prestigious base of universities, bowls, and athletic conferences (Battle, Bailey, and Siegal, 1991; Bhonslay, 1999b; Conklin, 1999). One of their tasks is to develop a base of licensees and retail outlets to successfully market licensed products. Their efforts are intended to target consumers of collegiate products and facilitate their purchase of licensed products. They also assist the marketing directors of their member institutions with establishing goals and marketing strategy.

As in other industries because it is the communication tool of the industry, promotion is a very important element in the sport industry. Again, people will not buy a product if they do not know it exists. In the sport industry, promotional communication is used to inform, educate, remind, and persuade people.

Promotion and Sport Promotion Defined

From a general marketing perspective, Boone and Kurtz (1992) define promotion as the function of informing, persuading, and influencing the consumer's purchase decision. Another definition indicates that promotion is "any form of communication used to inform, persuade, or remind people about an organization's goods, services, image, ideas, community involvement, or impact on society" (Evans and Berman, 1987).

The word *promotion* brings many concepts to mind—some good, some bad. Promotions include all corporate activities aimed at influencing consumers' purchasing attitudes and behaviors (Boone and Kurtz (1992). (However, to some, promotions have come to mean some shady practice where misrepresentation and inaccuracy are used to sway the public into unwanted or unnecessary purchases.) In a sport marketing perspective, promotion applied to the sport industry is defined as "the function of informing or influencing people about the sport company's products, community involvement, or image." In this definition the many segments of people to whom the sport company promotes are a significant factor when developing promotion strategies. The sport company promotes to the end consumer, the business consumer, the general community, the business community, and the media. To inform means that the sport company wants to tell them something. To influence means that the sport company wants a specific action from the person. Usually the final action wanted is a purchase action.

According to Ries and Trout (1986), consumers screen and reject a considerable amount of the product and marketing information delivered via traditional communication sources. Thus, consumers may not be conscious of wants until their wants are stimulated by the sport marketer through an array of well-selected and designed promotional activities. Creating new concepts and ideas about consumer desires as well as products or services to fulfill them is difficult; therefore, sports marketers must be proficient in their promotional strategy to move the consumer to purchase.

One innovative idea was set in place at the 57th St. Niketown in New York City. The store encompasses virtual reality, sport memorabilia, and computerization. Shoe sizing is not performed with the standard Brannock device. Instead, just put your foot on the NGAGE digital sizing system, and the computer prepares a 3-D image of your foot. Although the true benefit of this new system is yet unproven, it has shown to be an effective promotion and convinces consumers that Nike is on the cutting edge of technology.

> It is incumbent on the marketer to develop communications that are socially responsible and ethically sound.

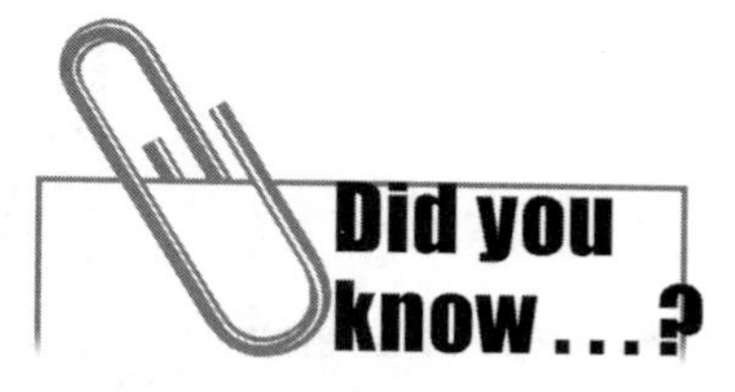

The Coca-Cola Co. is the national soft drink sponsor for the NFL for about $4 million a year.

Source: *The Sporting News*, May 22, 1998

Promotions are an integral part of all communication efforts. One of the objectives of promotion is the acquisition and retention of public acceptance of an idea, product, or service. This can be accomplished through effective communication with consumers. The general literature on communication theory suggests that there are four essential ingredients in promotional communication: the sender, the message, the medium, and the receiver. For messages to convey clear and succinct meanings, the sender must accurately create the message and put it in an appropriate media form. When the receivers encounter a message, it must be decoded and interpreted. Interpretation of the message is influenced by the receiver's emotional status, perceptions of the sender, and cultural disposition, among other factors. The people to whom the sport company will communicate are existing and potential consumers. In addition, the sport company communicates to the general community, the business community, and the media. As a result, sport marketers use promotional communications to influence or change the attitudes, opinions, and behavior of consumers in the sport industry.

For example, many sport companies want the general community to know that they care about the community. One way this is accomplished is through the financial support of local children's recreation leagues. Companies often select a billboard in the community to disseminate the message. Companies may choose to have a message emblazoned on the billboard such as "We care. We are the proud supporter of the Central Children's Sports Leagues. —Southland Sporting Goods—where your family shops for all your sporting needs." Companies may use more than one method to reach the audience. They may choose to post signs around the children's ballpark, send flyers through direct mail to everyone in the community, and hold a special sale in recognition of their involvement in the children's leagues. Each company must decide which methods will be most effective in gaining the attention of its audience and imparting the message.

Rationale for Promotion

There are other reasons for promotion because there are a variety of different messages a sport company wants to communicate to the people about its product or company. Effective promotions can facilitate a variety of marketing functions.

Promotion establishes an image. The sport marketer has a reason for being in business and a mission for the company. The company was designed based on a specific market segment. Therefore, the sport marketer wants to communicate to the consumer and the community a specific image. According to Ries and Trout (1986), a company's image is the sum of beliefs, ideas, and impressions held by consumers about the company and its products. The image may be luxury, prestige, convenience, cost savings, one-stop shopping, or creativity. The message of the promotion will communicate the company's image. For example, if the company is a marina and the objective of the marina is primarily to service and house large, expensive yachts, the promotional mix and message should communicate luxury and prestige. The marina's name might be "Class One Yacht Club." The communication through promotional methods such as advertising might be a slogan like "Your home is our home at Class One Yacht Club" or "Yachting is your luxury and your luxury is our business." Through the name of the company and the communication message in the slogan, the consumer is told that this marina is for the upper-class consumer who owns a yacht and that this company will take care of consumers in the fashion to which they are accustomed.

Promotion can reposition the image of a faltering product. For example, personal watercraft (PWCs), more commonly known as jet skis, have begun to develop a poor reputation because of the loud noise level of the engine, the recklessness of the drivers, the increase in accidents, and the increase in numbers invading previously quiet water areas without PWCs. The Personal Watercraft Industries Association (PWIA) and several PWC manufacturers have rallied to create a variety of promotional methods they hope will facilitate control of the reputation and turn it around. Their activities are directed at the end consumer, manufacturers, PWC rental businesses, and state and local water-governance organizations. Some of their activities include educational programs on safety (posters, videocassettes, brochures), research to decrease the noise produced by the PWC, rescue and education loan programs in which manufacturers lend PWCs to area Coast Guard offices or rescue units for their use and lend PWCs to lake and beach lifeguard stations for rescue operations (Holland, Pybas, and Sanders, 1992). The cooperative promotional effort is to change the reputation of the PWC in order to positively affect sales.

If a product has gained a poor reputation, the sport marketer can use effective promotions to reverse consumers' image of the product.

Promotion creates awareness for new products. As stated earlier, if people do not know your product exists, they will not buy it. If the sport company is planning to release a new product, no one will know unless the company implements an appropriate approach. Various sport companies orchestrate product launches using celebrity endorsers and press conferences. Many times, these promotional activities are coordinated through sport trade shows. An array of methods is integrated to publicize the offering.

Promotion alerts the consumer to sales. The consumer will not know that the company will be having a sale unless the company tells them. The sport marketer must identify promotional methods and design a communication message that will tell the consumer about the sale: dates, times, type of sale, purpose of sale, and any other information the consumer might need. If your company is a sporting goods retail store and you are planning a Thanksgiving sale, you must create the promotion to tell the consumer. Another important factor is your decision on when and where to promote. For example, your Thanksgiving sale will be the Friday, Saturday, and Sunday after Thanksgiving. Perhaps the best promotion is an advertisement in the local newspaper, and the best time to run the ad is in the Sunday paper before Thanksgiving.

Promotion tells the consumer where your business is located. Although this sounds like a simple message, and it is, it is very important. If the information is provided, the consumer does not have to spend extra time trying to find the business. This communication is usually handled within the promotion as a map depicting the location or as directions to the business. Sometimes a business will refer to a well-known landmark as a locater. For example, a well-known landmark in the city of Louisville, Kentucky, is the Water Tower—an historic city waterworks facility situated on the Ohio River. Businesses in the area use the Water Tower as a locater. A boat retailer's advertisements include the words "next to the Water Tower." A restaurant uses the same words. An indoor soccer facility uses the wording "located close to the Water Tower." The purpose of the message in the promotion is to establish the location of the business. For Web-based companies, clearly presenting the Internet address serves the same purpose.

Promotion Planning

Figure 12.1 illustrates the steps to be taken in promotion planning. Promotion planning is the process of developing all aspects of the company's communication effort. Many factors should be considered that will affect decisions concerning the promotion elements of the company's marketing mix. Some of these factors are the consumer, the competitor, money and other resources, product life cycle, and mission and objectives of the sport company. The following sections discuss the steps in the promotion planning process.

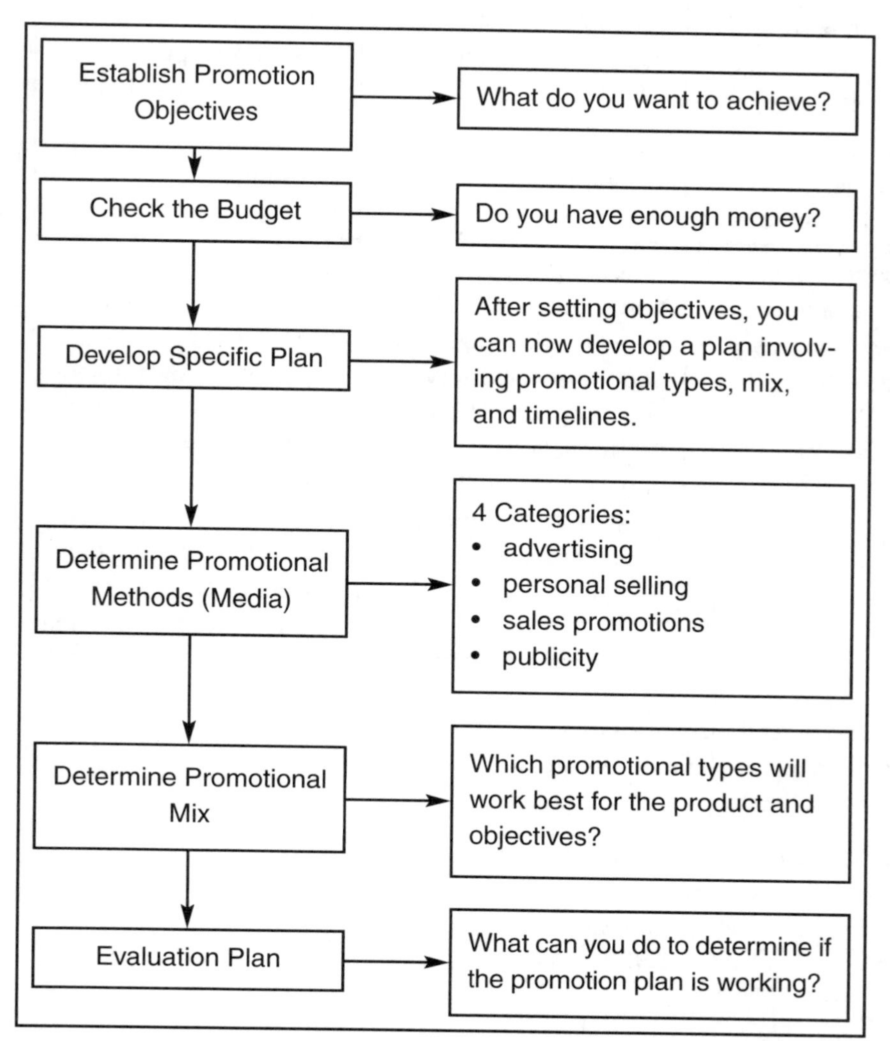

Figure 12.1
Promotional Planning Model.

Set Promotion Objectives

In the promotion planning process, the first step is to establish promotion objectives. The establishment of promotion objectives is based on this question: What does your company want to achieve through promotion? The promotion objectives should emerge from the marketing objectives, which should emanate from the company objectives.

Promotion objectives are statements that specify exact results desired by the company. They are based on what the company wants to accomplish. Usually the objectives are demand oriented, education oriented, or image oriented. The overall objective is to affect behavior, knowledge, or attitude. Each promotional action selected must be based on the objectives of the promotion. Therefore, a sport company should select the specific type of promotion, or form of communication, based on carefully crafted objectives. Table 12.1 illustrates these objective types, purpose, outcome desired, message, and an example of each.

> Consider the following when designing promotion goals:
> - stage of product life cycle
> - reasons for considering a promotion plan
> - available resources

If the sport company wants to affect behavior, demand-oriented objectives will be established. The behavior that the company wants to affect is purchase behavior. The company wants the consumer to purchase its products and wants to persuade the consumer to do so. With this as an objective, the company must design a promotional method and message that persuade the consumer to buy.

If the company wants to educate or inform the consumer about something, education-oriented objectives are developed. Usually, the company wants to educate the consumer

Table 12.1
Sport Promotion Objective Types.

TYPES OF OBJECTIVES:	DEMAND	EDUCATION	IMAGE
PURPOSE	To affect behavior	To affect knowledge	To affect attitude or perception
OUTCOME DESIRED	Consumer purchases the company's product	To educate or inform the consumer about the company or its products	Consumer thinks of company in specific terms: good, positive, brilliant, creative, fun, serious, etc.
MESSAGE	• persuasive • demand oriented	• informative • reminder	• informative • persuasive
EXAMPLE	A sport shoe manufacturer uses a famous male basketball player to persuade the consumer to buy its shoes.	A new sport marketing firm is opening. It places an ad in a local business paper that tells story of company, what it does, its products and services, where it is located, and its hours of business.	A women's professional golf association uses TV and billboard ads to tell about its disadvantaged-youth golf-with-the-pros day held once a year. The association and the players pay for the youth to spend a day with the players golfing and participating in other events.

about something about the company, its products, services, or other information. Typical information includes the location of the company, information on sales taking place and the company's offerings, or details about the company's products.

If the sport company wants to affect attitude or perception, it will develop image-oriented objectives. The company wants to assist consumers' formation of positive attitudes toward the company and its products. Marketers must strive to ensure a consistent image across all promotions.

Review the Budget and Other Resources

During the process of developing the objectives, it would be very wise for the sport marketer to know how much money is available for promotion and whether the company has other necessary resources available. This information will certainly have an impact on decisions made for promotional planning. Some promotional methods are expensive whereas others are inexpensive, and still others are free. Television advertising can be very expensive. On the other hand, staging an open house is relatively inexpensive. Realistically, the sport marketer must determine if there are enough money and other resources to pay for and follow through with the promotional methods selected.

Idealistically, the sport marketer must determine what promotional methods are available that are most effective for the objectives set.

A promotion plan of action should include

- promotional objectives
- a budget
- personnel assignments
- promotional mix strategies
- a schedule with deadlines and time lines
- an evaluation plan

The primary components of promotion in the sport industry include advertising, publicity and public relations, personal selling, and sales promotion. These components exist in conjunction with each other and can be used by the marketer in consort or separately to accomplish marketing and sales objectives.

After checking the budget and other resources needed for the promotional methods selected, you must develop a detailed plan of action that involves selecting the most appropriate and effective promotional types, determine a promotional mix, and develop an evaluation plan.

Utilize Promotional Methods

As noted above, there are four general categories of promotional methods: advertising, publicity, personal selling, and sales promotions. Table 12.2 illustrates the four categories and specific promotional methods available for the sport marketer in each category.

Table 12.2
Four Categories of Promotion Methods and Some Examples.

ADVERTISING	PERSONAL SELLING	SALES PROMOTIONS	PUBLICITY
• newspaper ad • magazine ad • television • radio ad • direct mail • billboard ad • ads on buses, grocery carts, walls, etc. • sponsorship • merchandising • the logo	• sales force • public speaking	• telemarketing • price • point of purchase display • newsletter • giveaways • target market specials • sponsorship • special events • open house day dinner, parties, etc. • exhibitions • merchandising	• press conference • press release • articles in local or other newspaper • coverage on TV or radio

Advertising. Hiebing and Cooper (1990) define advertising as a message that informs and persuades consumers through paid media. We are all aware of effective and ineffective advertising. Think for a minute about ads that you have seen and enjoyed, but from which you cannot remember the product; in contrast, other ads immediately bring a specific product to mind. All advertising firms plan for success, but it is not always achieved. Consider the short-lived Reebok campaign of "U.B.U." and Nike's long-running "Just Do It" advertising.

Advertising is a controlled medium. That is, the message delivered to the consumer is carefully crafted and controlled by the organization so that its content consists of only information that the organization wishes the consumer to receive. However, because the company controls advertising, its credibility with consumers may be low.

In sport, advertising can take many forms. There is advertising of sport products and services and advertising through sports events. The advertising of sport products and services is a multimillion-dollar industry. In 1996, the NBA Phoenix Suns created an advertising campaign to attract women as fans. Their ads featured seven of their female executives with the following copy: "Hiring women managers at the Phoenix Suns is more than just good PR. . . . It's good ticket operations, good advertising, good media relations. Good business (Phoenix Suns, 1996)."

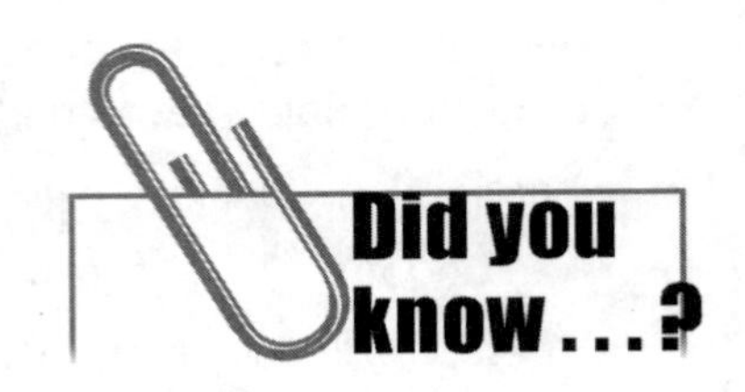

Hiking in the United States grew 94% to nearly 50 million participants between 1983 and 1995.

Source: Outdoor Recreation Coalition of America

Advertising through sport is also a sizable segment of the industry. According to Stotlar (1993), the cost of sport advertising approaches $5 billion per year. Much of that total is spent by companies that use sport events and publications for advertising non-sport products. A primary motive for this activity is that sports present a wholesome image and a wide demographic profile from which specific segments can be targeted.

Advertising through sports events can also take the form of a sponsorship, as will be detailed in chapter 14. Research on sponsorship through stadium advertising (Branvold, 1992; Stotlar and Johnson, 1989) has shown that it is an effective media purchase.

A popular advertising-related promotional activity conducted by many sport organizations is the trade-out, the process by which a sport organization gives something of value (complimentary seats, stadium advertising space, program ads) to the media in exchange for advertising space or airtime for use in promotional activities.

Promotional trade-out programs within the university segment seek to do two things: increase the attendance at athletic events and increase overall support of the school's programs. Radio seems to be a viable choice as one of the media selected for trade-out campaigns. Many sport organizations trade out radio time for tickets at a cash-value ratio of about 4 to 1 favoring the organization (Spoelstra, 1997). Using coveted football or basketball tickets as barter, some universities have negotiated deals with major TV markets. Newspaper and billboard space can also be included in this strategy. This area presents a variety of issues. Many media sources always quote "full rate card" prices in the negotiations. On the other hand, the sport organizations occasionally inflate the prices printed on tickets that are included in trade-out and sponsor packages.

Some universities use TV and radio networks to blanket their region including critical consumer areas in adjoining regions. During the summer and early fall, tapes can be made by players and coaches discussing their upcoming season. In this setting, you need to make sure that all of your activities are in compliance with collegiate rules. These plans have been particularly successful in encouraging advertisers who have rejected more traditional appeals for direct advertising. Additional coverage of this topic is in chapter 14 in dealing with leveraged media sponsorships.

Publicity. Publicity, although not identical to advertising, is often considered in discussion of the topic. Hiebing and Cooper (1990) indicate that publicity differs from advertising in that, although it informs and affects consumer attitudes, it is free. This includes the promotion or communication that comes from being mentioned in a magazine or being the subject of an article in the local newspaper. The disadvantage of publicity is that the company usually has no control over the content. This means that if the local paper wants to write an article about your company, the reporter can write almost anything.

Publicity is any form of unpaid promotion.

Some sport companies try to influence the kind of publicity they believe will be developed and offered to the public. For example, most university athletic departments

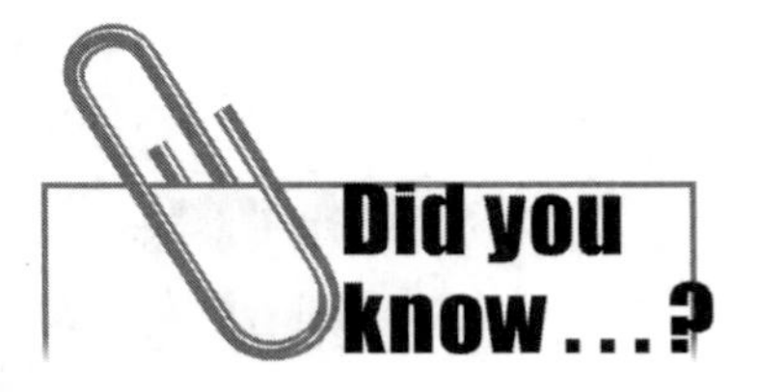

Over 57 million Americans participate in bicycling, representing an estimated $5-billion industry.

Source: Outdoor Recreation Coalition of America

will stage a press day to which they invite reporters, journalists, and sports broadcasters. They are encouraged to interview and photograph the athletes and coaches. Packets of material are offered to each individual. The packets contain information about the athletes and coaches, such as their records in high school, past season's records, highlights, hometown information, human-interest information, and expectations for the upcoming season. There will also be plenty to eat and drink. The purpose of press day is to treat the press positively in the hope that the press will return the favor through their stories, reports, articles, and broadcasts. The treatment doesn't stop here. At every sport event during the season there is a special room for the press. The pressroom will again contain packets of information, pictures, and current statistics about the season.

Most college athletic departments employ a full-time person, typically called a sports information director, to coordinate and manage the press and public relations activities for the college. The sports information director, called the SID, will have a staff ranging from one work-study student to a corps of employees, including an assistant SID, graduate assistants, secretaries, and several work-study students. It is the job of the sports information office to manage all of the public relations, media relations, and publicity activities for the athletic office. This office develops the media guides, manages press day and the pressroom, develops the press packets, and makes available up-to-the-minute statistics and general information. Although these activities are sales promotion activities, the target market includes the media, and the activities are designed to influence attitude and perception.

Many other sport enterprises also engage in media relations activities in an attempt to garner positive publicity. Most often these are managed by the public relations staff or marketing managers. Specifically, retail sporting goods companies engage in many of these strategies. Reebok's running division seeks to maintain close trade relations with leading running-enthusiast magazines like *Runner's World.* Rohm (1997) reported that Reebok's objectives are to "ensure critical editorial coverage and proper running-product reviews" (p. 22). This does bring to question some ethical issues with regard to advertising. It has been hypothesized that some magazine advertisers put a considerable amount of pressure on trade publications to provide favorable reviews or risk losing their advertising revenues.

Because publicity comes from a third, presumably neutral party, it is more credibile than advertising.

Publicity is one of the most important factors in designing promotional methods. As with advertising, the primary objective of publicity is to draw attention to a product, an organization, or an event. However, because publicity comes from a third, presumably neutral party, its credibility is greater than that of advertising (Stotlar, 1993).

However, sport marketers should realize that publicity alone will not sell tickets, raise funds, win supporters, retain members, or sell merchandise. Nevertheless, publicity can be helpful in conveying ideas to people so that these ends can be more easily attained.

Publicity efforts should be planned with these guidelines in mind:

1. Too much publicity can be poor public relations, because often at a given point, people tend to react negatively to excessive publicity.
2. The amount of publicity absorbed is important, not the amount printed.

3. The amount of publicity disseminated does not necessarily equal the amount used.
4. The nature of the publicity eventually tends to reveal the character of the institution or department it seeks to promote, for better or worse.
5. Some publicity an institution or department receives originates from outside sources.
6. All promotional activities do not result in publicity.

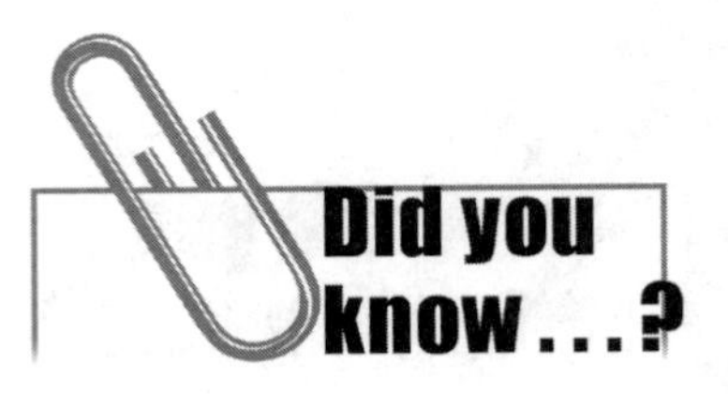

Kayaks were the hottest paddle-sport purchase in 1996 and, combined with canoes, totaled $99.1 million in sales.

Source: Outdoor Recreation Coalition of America

A successful publicity program depends on the development of an effective plan. This plan should incorporate the following elements:

1. Identification of publicity needs,
2. Recognition of appropriate media sources,
3. Development of goals for each source,
4. Creation of a specific methodology for targeted sources,
5. Implementation through selected promotional materials, and
6. Assessment of publicity outcomes.

Although the primary objective of publicity is to draw attention to a person, organization, or event, sometimes attention is directed to the sport organization in negative situations. Accusations, accidents, and indiscretions can occur in any sports organization, and unfavorable publicity often results. One of the worst mistakes that a public relations practitioner can make is to give additional publicity to bad news by attempting to deny or explain the problem (Helitzer, 1995). In one-to-one communication, a dialogue can exist and a general conclusion as to the truth can be reached. However, mass media do not operate on a one-to-one basis. It is certain that only part of the audience that saw or heard the original story will hear or see the rebuttal. Thus, the part of the audience who received only the rebuttal will begin to seek additional information and add impetus to the "crisis." Furthermore, those who received only the original story remain unaffected by the rebuttal.

Sport marketers should not draw extra attention to negative publicity by trying to explain or excuse it.

Personal selling. Personal selling is defined as an oral presentation with potential customers for the express purpose of making a sale. Commitment to personal selling as opportunity is one of the keys to effectiveness. There is an understanding among those in sales that communicating how a product or service can benefit the consumer is paramount. Within this approach is the belief that without the salesperson, consumers would not be capable of realizing the benefits of consumption and that personal selling therefore is the most important aspect in the promotional mix.

You may not personally adhere to that philosophy, but there are many in personal selling who do. They see their role as providing the link between the organization and consumers, so that consumers' lives may be enhanced by the product or service to which they were introduced.

Personal selling is direct promotion between the seller and a potential consumer (Peter and Donnelly, 1991). The initial stage of personal selling has been termed the *approach phase*, "creating a favorable impression and building rapport with potential

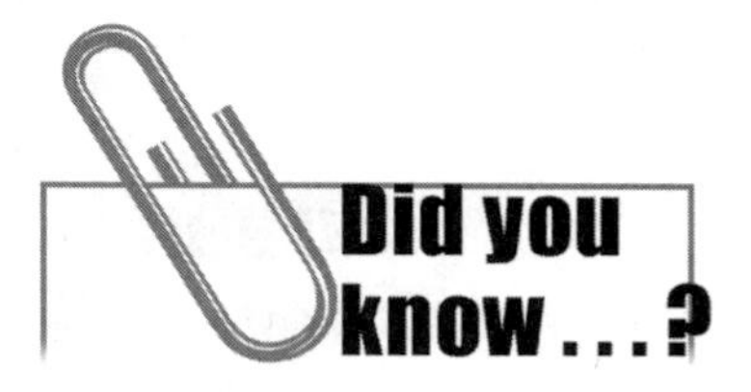

1996 retail sales in the outdoor recreation industry were estimated at $4.7 billion, up $400 million from 1995.

Source: Outdoor Recreation Coalition of America

clients" that sets the stage for all subsequent interaction between the salesperson and the prospective customer (Pride and Ferrell, 1997, p. 446). Several authors (Miller, Shaad, Burch, and Turner, 1999; Pride and Ferrell, 1997) have noted the importance of establishing a relationship with the consumers before activating sales-related dialog. Personal selling also includes selling face-to-face as well as via the telephone, videoconferences, and interactive computer links (Boone and Kurtz, 1992; Miller et. al.). In addition, today there is selling through television. Consider those television channels dedicated to bringing into your home hundreds of thousands of products. Professional salespeople host these, and a simple phone call to the company completes the purchase of any product offered on the show. Personal selling is a major element in the sport industry. There are salespeople in the sporting goods stores, salespeople for sports apparel manufacturing companies to sell their products to retailers, promoters whose job is to sell a sporting event to television and sponsors, telemarketers whose job is to sell tickets for the team, and salespeople whose job is to sell advertising space in the Super Bowl program. In the sport industry, individuals who are not trained as salespeople also become salespeople. For example, in college men's basketball, the players and coaches become salespeople for the program. They are scheduled to speak at local banquets and other activities. The coach usually has a local show aired once a week, and the coach usually is hired by local businesses as a "pitch person" in advertisements for their products.

Success in personal selling depends heavily on locating potential consumers (Miller et al., 1999; Pride and Ferrell, 1997). Connor (1981) said that "if you can master one skill in selling, become a master prospector. It will guarantee your future success" (p. 14). What exactly is prospecting? It is building a viable portfolio of potential clients and customers that positions the salesperson for work. Just as many executives go to the office, the person in sales consults the prospects' database. The question arises, just how do you go about creating a client base with potential customers? For the sport marketer, this often leads to the marketing information system discussed in chapter 7. You should also remember the traditional 80–20 business adage where 80% of your sales usually result from 20% of your customers.

A substantial amount of interaction with consumers occurs through the Internet. Although an entire chapter has been devoted to this topic, some discussion is warranted here. The Internet serves as an effective communication tool for interacting directly with consumers. Although a bit atypical from personal selling in that the consumers search for the company, rather than vice versa, the promotional methods most closely resemble personal selling. Some have argued that websites are simply advertising offered through an alternative media; however, because customers can almost always engage immediately in purchasing products or services, this characterization does not fit.

Tucker (1997) noted that the Internet is "a useful part of today's marketing and communication mix" (p. 29). He noted that for fitness clubs, the Internet provides excellent opportunities to promote club services, sell merchandise, and communicate with existing members. In particular, the Internet was effective in publicizing "up-to-date information on club events" (Tucker, p. 29). Sport organizations are also using websites for promotional activities. The Snow Industries Association, the Outdoor Recreation Coalition of America, and the Sporting Goods Manufacturers Association are among the organizations that use the Internet to gain name recognition and explain organizational services. Some professional sports teams use their websites to communicate with fan clubs. Through this medium they typically offer special deals to club members and occasionally run trivia contests and other interactive activities.

Ski resorts have also begun to use the Internet for promotional activities. This method seems to be particularly effective in this industry. Because snow conditions change quite literally overnight, resorts are quick to promote fresh snow and great skiing conditions via the Internet. In market research from Vail (Colorado), marketers found that 30% of their customers preferred the Internet as a source for gathering information about the resort (Gonzalez, 1998).

The Internet offers other promotional advantages over advertising. The mere fact that it is the consumer who seeks the information is powerful. Research has indicated that only 6% of upscale, highly educated consumers (exactly those using the Internet) do not trust advertising a credible source for product information ("10 Steps," 1998). The objective is almost always to develop meaningful relationships with customers that enhance overall company sales.

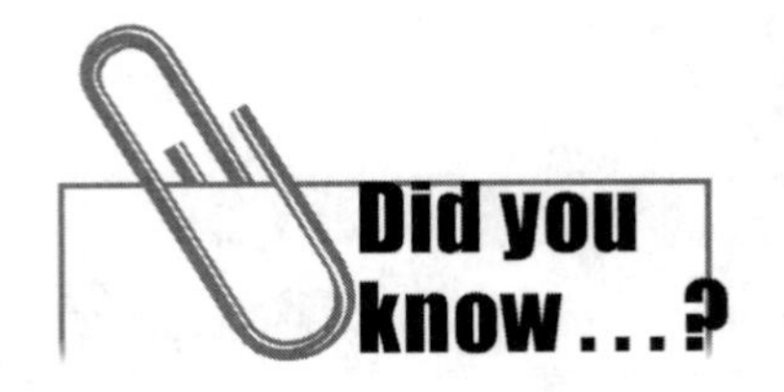

Hiking footwear accounted for approximately $374 million in sales in 1996 whereas outerwear generated $552 million.

Source: Outdoor Recreation Coalition of America

Sales promotion. The term *sales promotion* has been characterized as "a catch-all for all communication instruments that do not fit into advertising, personal selling or publicity categories" (van Waterschoot and Van den Bulte, 1992, p. 87). In their review of contemporary definitions, van Waterschoot and Van den Bulte indicate that sales promotions are activities of short duration that are intended to move consumers to an immediate exchange. Sales promotions often consist of those promotional activities other than advertising, publicity, or personal selling; and they are designed to affect consumer attitude or behavior. Some sales promotions include telemarketing, price promotions, point-of-purchase display, newsletter, giveaways, sponsorship, merchandising, and special events.

In the sport industry, several examples exist that can be categorized as sales promotions. Point-of-purchase displays are particularly effective. In retail sporting goods stores, displays of products are often used to tie the product with previous advertising. The phrase "as seen on TV" should be familiar to most sports consumers. Point-of-purchase displays can also initiate recall of sponsorship. A cardboard cutout of Lindsey Davenport in front of the tennis racket section could stimulate the consumer's memory of Davenport's recent victory and move the consumer to purchase the racket that sponsors her tournament play.

Trade shows have also been effective sales promotions for sporting goods companies. The Sporting Goods Manufacturers Association has conducted a nationwide trade show for many years with the express intent of motivating large-scale retail chains to order merchandise "hot off the line." The International Health and Racquet Sportsclubs Association (IHRSA) has organized and run trade shows in the fitness industry for many years with great success. Many club managers place orders directly at these shows because they have been able to compare equipment from different companies firsthand and, based upon what they see, initiate the purchase. As you can see, that makes this type of activity crucial to marketing success.

Discount coupons have been a popular promotion for many years. McCarville, Flood, and Froats (1998) noted that over 7 billion coupons per year were redeemed in the United States. Coupon popularity has been attributed to four factors: "(a) the monetary (or discount) effect, (b) the advertising effect (the coupons provide the consumer with product information), (c) a reminding effect (they enhance awareness through repeated exposure to the coupon), and (d) a utility effect (satisfaction is gained through the redemption process" (p. 54).

Sports organizations can also serve the sales promotions of nonsport businesses through incentives. Situations in which purchasers receive free tickets to a sporting event with the purchase of a particular item may move that person to purchase. Store appearances of a sport celebrity at point of purchase can also stimulate immediate sales.

Although sales promotions have been referred to as a "catchall" category, they strike at the heart of marketing, consummating the exchange. Sales promotions must be incorporated with other elements in the promotional mix.

Determine the Promotional Mix

After establishing the promotion objectives, developing the budget, and considering promotional methods that will work best for the company, product, and consumer, the sport marketer must determine its promotional mix. The promotional mix is the combination of promotional methods that will help the sport company meet its objectives in the most effective way. It is rare that a sport company will use only one method—for example, a college athletic program use only direct mail, a sport marketing company use only journal advertising, a sporting goods retailer use only newspaper advertising, or the Special Olympics use only merchandising. It is more typical and much more effective for the company to use a mixture of these methods.

1. A different function for each method
2. The company
3. Stage of product life cycle
4. Access to promotional methods
5. Channels of distribution
6. Target markets
7. The competition
8. Geographic dispersement of the consumer market
9. The product
10. Push or pull strategy
11. Laws
12. Sport company resources

Figure 12.2
Factors Affecting Decision on Promotional Mix.

The decisions about which methods to use are contingent on many factors. Figure 12.2 illustrates many of the factors that affect the decision on promotional mix. Each of these is discussed briefly here.

Each promotional method serves a different function (Evans and Berman, 1987). Advertising on television can reach a large number of consumers, but it is expensive. Publicity can reach a large number of consumers but cannot be controlled by the company. Personal selling is effective if the salesperson is knowledgeable and influential, but it serves a very small number of consumers. Sales promotions are effective in different ways, depending on the type of sales promotion. Each sales promotion attracts a different consumer and a different number of consumers.

The company will affect the promotional mix (Evans and Berman, 1987). Some promotional methods fit some companies better than others do. Giveaways and Scout nights (sales promotions) are more effective for a minor league professional league baseball team than for a sport marketing company. Direct mail may be more effective for the New York Marathon than for the Super Bowl.

The stage of product life cycle will affect decisions concerning the promotional mix (Bradbury, 1990; Stanton, Etzel, and Walker, 1991). During the introductory stage, the company should aggressively promote the product. This means that the promotion budget will need to be extensive. During the growth stage, sales will increase. This means that revenue will increase. Promotional methods and aggressiveness will change, and money put into promotion will typically decrease. In the maturity stage, the pace of sales may slow and will eventually plateau. During this stage, however, the product is established, and promotional objectives and methods change. If a product is approaching the decline stage, promotional objectives and methods must change to avoid disaster. If the product is allowed to continue in this direction, eventually all sales will cease. Typically, promotional objectives and methods become more aggressive, and sometimes the product is repositioned and treated like a new product.

Access to promotional methods will affect which methods the sport company is able to use (Evans and Berman, 1987). Some methods may not be accessible to the sport company. Some of the factors that affect accessibility include the following:

1. Budget: Sometimes there is no money or not enough money for the objectives the sport company wants to accomplish. For example, advertising on television is more expensive than advertising in the local newspaper.
2. Location of the promotional method: The promotional method may not be accessible within the defined geographical location, or the method may not reach a particular geographical segment that the sport company needs to reach.
3. Requirements: The promotional method may have requirements that the sport company cannot meet.

Channels of distribution will impact decisions on the promotional methods used (Evans and Berman, 1987). Managers of specific channels may have requirements that the sport company cannot or will not support. Based on their marketing experiences, many marketing managers often favor specific channels of distribution.

In one example, signage—a form of advertising in a stadium or arena—is an effective promotional method for many companies (Stotlar and Johnson, 1989). Although most of the companies using signage are not sport companies, some are. Signage has as its roots outdoor billboards. However, whereas a billboard has space and location limitations, and captures the attention of the consumer for a few seconds as the consumer drives by, a sign in a stadium is in front of the consumer as long as the event lasts, which can range from 1 to 5 hours. That amounts to a lot of impression time.

Impression time is the length of time an ad or message is displayed within the consumer's line of vision.

During an event such as the Indy 500, which lasts approximately 5 hours, signage can make a significant impact on impression time. The Indy 500 event is televised and attracts a large viewership. The signage is everywhere, including on the cars and the drivers' suits and helmets (Ruff, 1992a,b). The spectator attending the event is surrounded by the signage, and the consumer watching the event on television also will be impacted with the advertising. As the camera captures and focuses on a specific car, the television viewer will see the advertising on the car. As the camera follows the cars around the track, various signs come in and out of view. As the research shows, nearly 70% of spectators could correctly identify advertising seen during an event (Stotlar and Johnson).

Impression time was also created at the dramatic conclusion of the 1999 Women's World Cup soccer match when the U.S.A.'s Brandi Chastain ripped off her jersey in

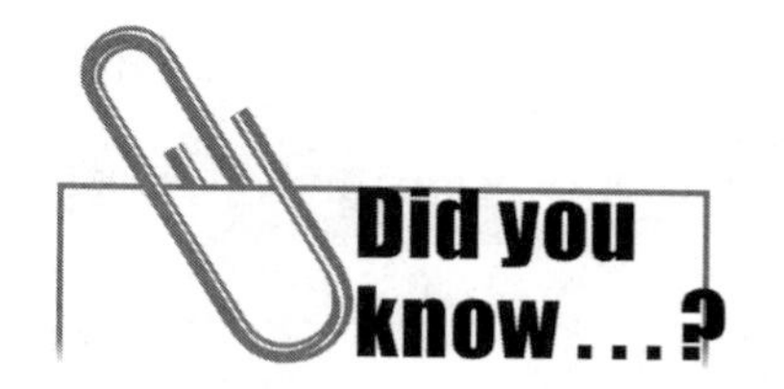

The 1999 Women's World Cup final drew 90,185 fans, far surpassing the record attendance for a women's sporting event.

Source: Cyber Soccer Association/Soccer Sport

celebration after scoring the winning goal. This act displayed her Nike sports top. Nike immediately began negotiating for video footage and still photos. According to one expert, "that ten second piece of film is all Nike needs to sell more sports bras than it can produce" (Wells and Oldenburg, 1999, p. 1A).

Target markets of the sport company will influence promotional methods. The promotional methods will need to be effective for each target market identified by the sport company. Target market factors to consider include geographic location and size as well as the associated demographic and psychographic characteristics. Some promotional method factors to consider are listed below in the form of questions:

1. Which method will catch the attention of the market? Only sport marketing consumer research can answer this question. A true understanding of the consumer will guide the sport marketer to decisions concerning the method to which the consumer will positively react.
2. What kind of message will attract the consumer, and will the consumer be able to understand it? Again, consumer research will guide the sport marketer to the answer to this question. The sport marketer should develop the promotional message so that the consumer can relate to it and understand it. In other words, the sport marketer should consider writing the advertising message in the consumer's language.
3. Can the promotional method reach the intended target market? If a sport magazine is being considered as an advertising medium, does the target market subscribe to the magazine? For example, the Gay Games uses promotional methods that reach its specific target market: the lesbian and gay population around the world. Some of these methods are direct mail using mailing lists of prior Games participants and from lesbian and gay magazine publishers; merchandising advertisements in mail-order catalogs such as Shocking Gray; and advertising in lesbian and gay targeted magazines such as *The Advocate, Deneuve*, and *Out*.

The competitor will affect the promotional method selected for the sport company. Although the promotional methods must be selected and designed for the consumer, equal attention must be given to the competitor (Schnaars, 1991). Promotional methods selected can impact sport marketing strategies with gained market share, the outmaneuvering of a competitor in a specific area such as price, market penetration, and advertising message.

The sport company must spend time gaining an understanding of the consumer and what the consumer wants while simultaneously studying the competitors.

Geographic dispersal of the consumer market will affect the promotional methods selected. Personal selling may be best for localized markets. However, as the location of the sport company's consumers spreads geographically, the company will have to consider promotional methods that will reach the consumers.

The product and its elements will affect the promotional methods selected. The type of product and the characteristics and elements of the product will impact the method and message of promotion. Some of the characteristics include product type (good, service, person, place, idea), customized versus standardized, differentiation, quality, features, performance, design, and product life-cycle stage.

The decision to use a push or a pull promotion strategy will affect the promotional method used (Cravens and Woodruff, 1986; Peter and Donnelly, 1991). The objective of both strategies is to get the product into the consumer's hands. A *push strategy* involves trying to move the product into the channels of distribution and encouraging sellers to increase sales volumes. The strategy usually involves offering a variety of awards and enticements to the channelers. Many sporting goods manufacturers use this strategy. A company will offer incentives or price breaks to a wholesaler or retailer that increases sales volume. A *pull strategy* involves strong promotion directed toward the end consumer in order to affect the consumer's demand for the product. The consumer's demand for the product acts to "pull" the product through the channels. The sport company's promotional methods are designed to target the consumer and create demand. The consumer in turn asks for the product. For example, if a sporting goods retailer does not carry a specific product, a motivated consumer may ask the retailer to carry the product.

Sport product characteristics should guide the sport marketer in selecting the best promotional method for the product.

Laws governing promotion will affect selection of promotional methods. Local, state, and federal government agencies and consumer protection agencies have enacted laws, guidelines, and restrictions that affect a sport company's promotional efforts. Some of these include the Federal Trade Commission, the Food and Drug Administration, the Securities and Exchange Commission, the United States Patent Office, and the Department of Justice. Other organizations and groups also work to control promotions. Some of these are the National Association of Broadcasters and the Better Business Bureau. Further, individual companies exercise ethical decision making in selecting and developing promotional methods.

Sport company resources will impact the promotional methods decision. There are two types of resources within a sport company—material and nonmaterial. Material resources include money, supplies, equipment, and the like. Nonmaterial resources include human resources. Does the sport company have the resources necessary to accomplish the promotional methods it is considering? The critical bottom line may be the ultimate factor affecting the company's decision concerning promotional methods.

As you can see, the sport marketer must consider and analyze many factors in the process of selecting the promotional methods and activities for the company.

Create Promotional Activities

Based on the promotional mix, business enterprises create special activities to promote their programs, products, or purposes. Hiebing and Cooper (1990) indicated that promotions, as marketing tools, provide activities and incentives directly to consumers. One of the most notable names in sport promotion is Veeck. Bill Veeck Jr., one of baseball's most famous (and outrageous) promoters, is perhaps best known for sending a midget to bat in Major League Baseball. More noteworthy contributions included adding names to player uniforms and designing lighted, graphic scoreboards. His son, Mike Veeck seems to have followed in the family tradition as the marketing and promotions director for the MLB Tampa Bay Devil Rays (see side bar for 1999 promotional activities). Perhaps Veeck's (Williams, P., 2000) most disastrous promotion was his 1979 Disco Demolition Night for the Chicago White Sox. The intent was to signal and end to the Disco era. Spectators were asked to bring old disco records to be piled up between the games of a doubleheader to be blown up on the

Sample 1999 Tampa Devil Rays Promotions:

April 21	Office Secretaries' Olympics
May 11	Twin Nights (buy one, get one free)
June 4	Parrot Head Party Night (for Jimmy Buffet fans)
June 22	Conversion Day (trade Yankees hat for Devil Rays hat)
June 27	Raymond's Birthday Bash (the Devil Rays' mascot)
July 5	Blow it up, Blow it out
July 6	Millennium Celebration
July 15	Disco Demolition Night (20 years later)
July 19	Lawyer Appreciation Night (Lawyers pay double)
Sept. 4	Manko Salute to Duct Tape Night
Sept. 6	Labor Day (pregnant women admitted free)

field. However, fans smuggled extra records into the stadium and began a "Frisbee" riot that resulted in the eventual forfeiture of the game.

Intercollegiate athletics and interscholastic sports must likewise engage in promotional activities. From a philosophical viewpoint, some people engaged in athletic programs may prefer to be exempt from promotional activities so that they might devote more of their creativity, time, and energy to the actual conduct of athletic events. Unfortunately, those days have passed, and promotional activities are necessary for survival.

Traditional promotions such as the "hat day," "bat day," and "poster day" events continue to be popular with both fans and sports organizations. The University of Tennessee launched some nontraditional promotions for their women's basketball contests. They have a face-painting night, balloon-making nights and a petting-zoo night. At the petting-zoo promotion, animals are brought into the arena from local animal shelters for fans to pet and possibly adopt (Fechter, 1998.). This type of promotion, which connects the university with a community-based organization, is often referred to as "cause related."

Cause-related promotions can be effective in drawing positive attention to sport programs. The University of Arkansas women's athletic marketing staff created a program called "Read with the Lady 'Backs" for children in grades K–6. The participants earned points, and prizes were awarded in various categories. The event produced significant public goodwill and helped form the image of the women's sport program as one concerned about the academic performance of children ("Athletic Promotions," 1997)

The mid-1990s brought very popular Beanie Baby promotions to many sporting events, including the 1998 Major League Baseball All-Star Game. Research studies into the effectiveness of these activities vary. In some cases, they produced large increases in overall attendance, whereas at other times they produced increases only for those specific events where people attended primarily to obtain the free novelty. Sport marketers should not jump to the conclusion that it is detrimental if a person attended an event for the express purpose of obtaining a free product. Sport can serve an effective (and profitable) role in linking consumers with products from sponsors.

> You must make sure that your marketing practices conform to all regulatory standards and professional ethics.

Promotional activities that involve high school, collegiate, or amateur players require the exercise of considerable caution. Many sport-governing bodies have restrictive guidelines regulating the appearances of athletes in commercial activities. In some instances, if an athlete is associated with a specific product or company, he or she may be declared ineligible for amateur competition.

Some promotional activities seek to draw attention to the team/event/product by awarding prizes to those in attendance. Several sports teams have sponsored contests where spectators' ticket stubs were drawn at random for chances to win prizes by scoring goals (soccer, hockey), kicking field goals, or shooting baskets. These events usually are scheduled prior to the contest or between periods of play. The cost to the sport organization is minimal because the prizes often can be secured from sponsors as a trade-out for name recognition during the event or covered by relatively inexpensive insurance policies. These policies are offered through a myriad of companies that specialize in sport event promotions and contests. However, as with any business decision, you should investigate the company managing the promotion.

Approximately 94.5% of all Americans aged 16 and older participate in some form of outdoor recreation at least once throughout the year.

Source: NSRE

In 1993, what seemed like a typical promotion went horribly wrong. During halftime of a Chicago Bulls NBA game, a 23-year-old office supply worker sank a 73-foot shot to win a million dollars. However, shortly after the event, it was discovered that the contestant had recently played college basketball, a violation of contest rules. With the payout in jeopardy, the Bulls held a press conference the following day and laid blame on the insurer. The insurer noted that the player had signed a waiver (which by the way the Bulls administered after the shot) in which the stipulation was clear. Unfortunately, this promotion did not produce the intended result of positively impacting attendees (Cohen, 1993). Just one year later, a similar controversy erupted in Miami where the Florida Panthers (NHL) conducted a contest in which a fan could win a million dollars by shooting a puck the length of the ice toward a small opening in a template across the goal. The contestant shot the puck into the slot on the template, and an immediate celebration began. However, contest officials began to claim that the puck had not passed "completely through" the opening as required. This promotion generated lengthy litigation rather than the intended promotional benefit. Although the contestant won the initial lawsuit, at the time of this writing, an appeal was still pending.

Some of the many possible promotional activities associated with sport events that have proven successful are presented below:

1. Banquets to honor the participants of various sport teams through tributes to coaches, players, and support staff. These can be effective as award ceremonies where special acknowledgment and honors are accorded either employees or prominent citizens. To obtain the maximum promotional value, you should prepare personal stories, pictures, and awards.

2. Exhibitions of new products, protective sports gear, or the latest in sport and fitness fashion. These have also proven to produce positive media coverage.

3. Team reunions in conjunction with a reception, dinner, and game.

4. Events, including guest days or nights for senior citizens, disadvantaged youth, Boy Scouts, Girl Scouts, and other groups who attend games. Often these programs are enhanced by coordinating the event with a civic or service club where the members of the club provide transportation and supervision.

5. Sports clinics for various age-groups in popular sports. These can expose and profile your staff for the media. Clinics also can be conducted on prevention and care of injuries, new fitness programs, or a myriad of other sport-related subjects.

One of the reasons that promotions are so popular is that they are relatively inexpensive and often do not cost the sport company at all. For example, the Louisville Redbirds, a minor league men's baseball team, planned a Beach Boys concert immediately following one of the games. The promotional event drew three times as many spectators (almost 20,000) as other games, thus easily covering the cost of the promotion and possibly attracting new customers (Branvold and Bowers, 1992). Other examples of successful promotional ideas include the following:

- Hosting a fun-run
- Holding a barbecue for members of the fitness club
- Giving away a car at the halftime of the basketball game as a door prize to someone in attendance
- Hosting a celebrity tennis tournament
- Holding a wellness fair
- Holding an authentic Hawaiian luau
- Holding an open house
- Holding a live-band aerobics evening
- Getting a famous athlete to make an appearance in your store to sign autographs
- Encouraging tailgating for events and contests
- Giving out free-pass coupons
- Hosting a holiday tournament.

A unique aspect of many sport programs is the desire of the public to associate with players, coaches, or employees. This can take many different forms: Colleges and universities offer their coaches, fitness centers provide their instructors, and many corporations offer their leading salespeople for inspirational and informative talks. Many sport organizations circulate lists of speakers available to various organizations that may have the desire for guest speakers, whereas more aggressive organizations actively seek speaking engagements for their employees.

Successful organizations often play on consumers' desire to associate with players, coaches, or employees by making them available through a speakers' bureau.

Develop Promotional Publications

Every sport organization will produce some type of promotional publication at one time or another. The purpose of organizational publications is usually to transmit knowledge or information to the public. A publication also communicates various aspects about the sport organization, style, approach, attitude, and image. For the publication to be effective, it must also be consistent. Herein lies the dilemma for managing promotional publications in many sport organizations. Do you create one single office that is responsible for all publications, or do you allow each department to produce its own publication to fit its individual needs?

Because publications are so crucial in the promotion and marketing of a company's goods and services, most sport organizations have one central unit that is responsible for the organization's publishing. Centralization of this promotional function reduces several publishing problems that have been encountered by sport organizations.

A major problem for many sports organizations is the dreaded desktop publisher. With the popularity of computer-based publishing programs for personal computers, everyone thinks they can be in the publishing business, and they can. According to

Herman (1992), the "freedom of the press belongs to the person who has one" (p. 25). For your organization, this means that you can have untrained people creating and disseminating material to the public about your products and services. The pitfalls here are tremendous. Poorly written, poorly designed, and inaccurate information may be presented to consumers without your knowledge or control.

> Businesses must understand their weaknesses and not undertake projects that they aren't qualified to do—such as publishing their own promotional literature.

Three different methods of addressing this problem have been presented. Herman (1992) suggests that you have a centralized system, a franchise process, or an "official" publications policy. In the centralized system, one office handles all of the printing and publishing for the entire organization. This system affords the greatest amount of control and consistency and is very effective in protecting the organization from unprofessional or inaccurate publications. The limitations with this system are that it requires a relatively large staff and the demands on one unit often fluctuate during different times of the year, which may create ineffective staffing patterns.

The franchising of publication operations can be effective because individual units are allowed to produce their own promotional materials. The franchise allows a representative from each unit to approve any publications from that unit. To qualify as a unit representative, a person has to undertake special training from a publication specialist. Not only do the units often have a better idea of exactly what they need, but they also often have a better idea of the unique benefits of the product or service in which the consumer may be interested. This option retains some of the advantages of having the centralized system in control, yet it decentralizes responsibility and workload.

The official publication method provides the least control of the three options. This policy limits the central publishing unit to the official publications of the organization (catalogs, brochures, advertising copy, etc.). All other units are free to produce their own (unofficial) newsletters or internal releases. This does eliminate the "publications police" that exists in the two previous systems; however, it also allows for the uncontrolled production of promotional literature. There is also a high probability that unofficial publications will find their way into the public eye, creating confusion and occasionally crises.

Regardless of the administrative structure, special brochures about your sport organization are effective in increasing exposure and publicity. Most commercial sport organizations use an annual report for communicating with both internal and external audiences. As a controlled medium, this document can be effective in creating favorable impressions about the organization in the minds of employees, clients, and prospective investors. In sport, these have been used by sporting goods companies, professional and collegiate teams, fitness centers, and commercial recreation enterprises.

Sports teams have, for many years, prepared and distributed game programs as promotional publications. Boeh (1989) indicates that although sports teams have many advertising and promotional opportunities, game programs are still the most popular and reliable.

Irwin and Fleger (1992) found that the game program could be effective as a promotional tool through providing team history and contest information and also as a source of revenue. Data from their research indicate that although attendance figures over the past few years at collegiate events declined, program sales increased signifi-

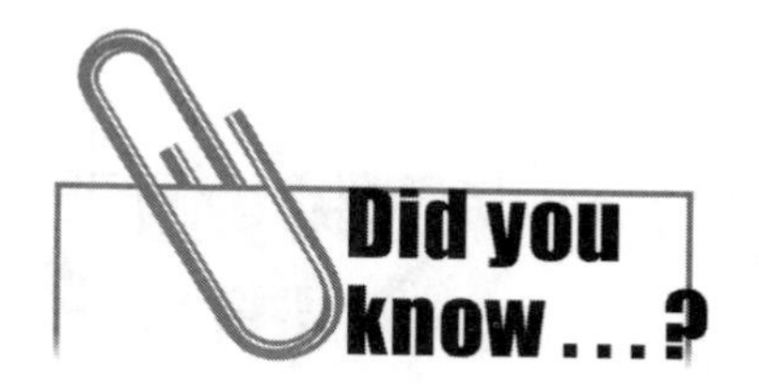

The overall impact of sport fishing on this country's economy in 1996 amounted to $108 billion.

Source: American Sportfishing Association

cantly. The average sales data showed that currently 1 in 10 football fans and 1 in 13 basketball spectators purchased a program.

The philosophy surrounding the production and pricing of ads in the game program is of significant importance. If you are going to be competitive with other advertising media, then you are in the advertising business. If you cannot, you are really asking for philanthropy and contributions. This position/philosophy needs to be established early.

If you decide you are in the philanthropy business, you must recover enough advertising revenue to offset printing costs. These advertisers must know that they will not receive the same exposure for their dollar as they would with other media. This does not, however, automatically mean that they will not purchase an ad. In many small towns, the advertisers are willing to support your organization through the purchase of an ad, irrespective of the cost-benefit ratio. Boeh (1989) advises that

> the sponsor should not be led to believe that he or she will receive the same advertising impact that other mediums offer. Rather, advertising in your game program should be explained as a way for the sponsor to support the athletic program with a donation and receive recognition in the form of an ad. (p. 53)

The way to determine if you are truly in the advertising segment is to calculate a CPM (cost per thousand impressions). In doing so, you present the cost of advertising in your program on the same basis as other media sources such as the local newspaper. Although your ad costs are typically higher, few people keep newspapers as souvenirs.

Irwin and Fleger (1992) presented several ways for sport marketers to manage game programs (see suggested readings). The options they cite for producing profits and exposure provide valuable information in the area.

Evaluate the Promotional Plan

The sport marketer must determine if the promotional plan is effective. The sport marketer must therefore establish a method to determine if the plan or parts of the plan are accomplishing the company objectives. The promotion objectives outlined what the company expects to achieve with the promotional plan. Did the plan accomplish these objectives? To answer that question, the sport marketer must assess the outcomes of the plan. Typically, this is performed through marketing research. Although chapter 5 details marketing research, the following is a brief look at how it can be used for determining promotional effectiveness.

Some types of marketing research are good for determining if the promotional plan is working. If the sport company wants to determine if certain forms of advertising are effective, it can conduct a consumer survey. The survey will provide answers for the sport marketer to analyze. In the analysis, the sport marketer must assess whether or not the advertising is accomplishing its goals. For example, the Blue Ridge Ski Resort wants to determine the effectiveness of the direct mail advertising its special two-for-one ski week. The sport marketer prepares a special skier check-in form that will be used for that week only. Questions on the form ask the skiers to identify where and how they found out about the special. If 50% state that they found out about the special in the direct mail they received, the sport marketer can make a subjective judgment about whether the promotional method was successful. If 12 people came for the special, 50% is 6. Does an increase of six skiers who found out about the special through the direct mail mean that it was an effective method? Before we can answer that question, we must ask, "How many direct-mail pieces were sent to potential buyers?" If the answer is 1,000 pieces, 6 out of 1,000 could be determined unsuccessful. If the answer is 20 pieces, perhaps 6 out of 20, or 30%, may be considered to be a successful method.

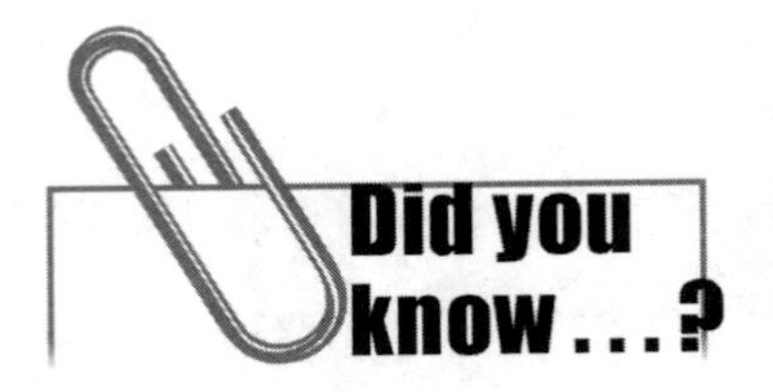

Camping is the number one outdoor vacation activity in America, and one third of U.S. adults say they have gone on a camping vacation in the past 5 years.

Source: Travel Industry Association of America

Study Promotion Laws and Regulations

There are laws, guidelines, regulations, policy, and perception that affect promotion. The primary reason for regulation is consumer protection. The sport marketer must study and understand all of the regulations in order to produce a legal and ethical promotional plan. These areas are discussed in the following sections.

Laws. The sport marketer must know, understand, and apply the laws to the promotional plan. Federal regulation involves two primary laws: the Federal Trade Commission (FTC) Act and the Robinson-Patman Act. The FTC Act prohibits unfair methods of competition. One area of unfair competition is false, misleading, or deceptive advertising. The Robinson-Patman Act outlaws price discrimination and has two sections on promotional allowances. These sections state that promotional allowances must be fair and equal.

Regulation by other organizations. There are many organizations that affect promotional activities. For example, the Better Business Bureau is a nationwide company that works as a consumer advocate and works to control promotion practices.

Industry control. Many industries and individual companies work to affect promotional activities of their counterparts. These controlling mechanisms, although they are not law, are very effective in regulating ethical and tasteful promotional practices of companies.

Promotion and Ethical Issues. Every aspect and function of the sport business must follow ethical guidelines usually determined partially by the company and partially by the public. Ethical consideration should be given serious attention in areas including sociocultural issues and environmental issues. The sport marketer cannot afford to assume that the population of the United States or even other countries is of a similar culture and similar lifestyle. Serious attention to socioeconomic factors, cultural factors, and other such factors will exert a responsible and leadership role for the business. In other words, it is critical that the sport marketer always work to "do the right thing" ethically and in socially responsible ways to position the company as people friendly and earth friendly.

Let us look at an example of how the entire process might work. Management of the Ship Shape Fitness Center has decided to target senior citizens. Their objective is to sell memberships to those senior citizens defined as 60-plus. Some products designed for and to be offered to this group are customized aerobics classes, one-on-one weight training, partner walking, water shaping, and a 60-plus tennis league. T-shirts will be specially designed to give as awards for milestones and league winners. The company develops the following message to be used as its primary promotion slogan: Fitness is good for you no matter how young you are! Management believes that this message is positive and keys on the 60-plus person thinking of her- or himself as young, not old. Promotional activities will include a one-week open house that will include activities designed to educate the 60-plus person about fitness. There will be exhibitions to show how fitness can be fun and an attainable goal. Management decides that the center will get 50, 60, or even 70-year-olds to perform the exhibitions. The objective for this is that the 60-plus person can see someone of his or her age exercising. The target group can relate to this much better than watching a very young and fit person exercising. The methods for communicating the message are selected based on the best method for reaching the audience.

From their marketing research, management learns that this market most likely does not work, they are busy people and are not at home very much, and they do not watch much television or listen to radio. Therefore, management concludes that the best way to reach the audience is through direct-mail advertising. The piece will be informative and simple, and will include information about the open house and the center. Other promotional methods will include coupons for two free days at the center, a special half-price membership fee for the first year, and special membership fee discounts for every year after that.

A successful marketer will identify the target market, select a message, and develop specifically tailored strategies for the market.

The sport marketer in this example has identified a target market, selected a positive message, and developed promotional methods specifically for the market. The products added were designed for the market, and the prices were identified based on the market's income. Communication is the tool used in getting the message to the consumer.

In conclusion, creating and managing promotion as a marketing element are difficult. Therefore, it is essential to unify all of the organization's executives on the role of promotions, the desired results, and the specific strategies to employ. Competition between specialists in various areas of the corporation can defeat the purpose of the promotional mix. For example, the advertising department may claim that it can do more to produce results than can the sales force. On the other hand, the public relations department may assert that its activities are more effective than advertising is. Therefore, a marketing manager must clearly understand the role of each component and be able to integrate promotional functions into the organization's overall business and marketing plan.

Chapter Summary

Promotional systems are central to effective sport marketing because they relate directly to the consumer's decision to purchase. As the various promotional activities described in this chapter indicate, no single approach suits every situation. Promotions are limited only by one's imagination. Sport marketers must carefully analyze a particular setting, become knowledgeable about ideas tried by others, and create a promotional mix that best fits their specific organization and market conditions.

People will not buy a product if they do not know it exists, and promotion is the sport marketer's tool for communicating to the market about the company and its products. Sport promotion is the function of informing people about the sport company's products and influencing their purchase behavior. Promotion can shape a company image, reposition a product, create awareness for a new product, alert the consumer to sales, tell the consumer where the sport company is located, and inform the consumer about where a product can be purchased. The critical steps involved in promotion planning include establishing objectives, determining promotional methods deemed best for achieving those objectives, and developing a promotional mix. The sport marketer must know and understand the many factors that impact the development of the promotional mix. A master plan for all promotional activities should be developed, executed, and evaluated. Finally, the sport marketer must know the laws and the legal and ethical issues surrounding promotion in today's society.

Fundamental to the success of all promotional activities is the confidence of the manager. Oftentimes, those who succeed are the ones who believe they will. Although it is highly unlikely that any sports organization can implement all the promotional methods outlined in the chapter, a complete study should be made of available opportunities. It is hoped that this chapter has provided some basic principles, guidelines, and practices that will improve your confidence and ultimately your chances for success.

Questions for Study

1. What is promotion?
2. What is sport promotion?
3. Why is promotion important to the sport marketer?
4. What is the process of communication?
5. What are promotional methods? Give some examples in the sport industry.
6. What is the promotional mix?
7. What are the factors that affect decisions about the promotional mix?
8. What are legal issues affecting promotion?
9. What are ethics, and what are some ethical issues the sport marketer should use in determining promotion strategies?

Learning Activities

1. Conduct a study of three different sport businesses, organizations, or other enterprises in your city or community. Determine the promotional methods used by each.
2. Collect print advertising of a variety of sport products from numerous sources. Conduct a study of the ads and determine the target market(s) and the promotional message.
3. What are some populations recently objecting to the use of certain promotional messages and logos? In discussion groups, discuss the reasons and the ethical responsibility of the sport marketer.
4. Visit a local media outlet (radio, television station, or newspaper) and producer or editor to talk about their relationships with sports organizations. Prepare a contact sheet for that outlet complete with the names, position titles, and phone numbers of important people.
5. Investigate an advertising purchase for an athletic program or stadium scoreboard sign and determine if it is an equitable media buy compared to other advertising outlets.

Professional Associations and Organizations

National Association of Collegiate Marketing Administrators (NACMA)
24651 Detroit Road, Westlake, OH 44145

Suggested Readings

Helitzer, M. (1995) *The dream job: Sports publicity, promotion, and public relations*, (2 ed.).Athens, OH: University Press.

Irwin, D. L., and Fleger, B. (1992). Reading between the lines. *Athletic Management, 4*,, 15–18.

Chapter 13

Media Relations in Sport

Marketing communication cannot be limited to annual reports, advertising, and brochures. Interaction with the media is both a necessary and a valuable endeavor. Historically, businesses interacted with the public through face-to-face encounters. However, in our mass-mediated society, perceptions of your organization are delivered though multiple communication channels. Media and communication theorists have suggested that the expanded nature of communication in the global community and the speed with which information is transmitted mandate an understanding of media relations (Thompson, 1994).

Media relationships will form a basis from which all marketing and promotional strategies are launched. From the competency standpoint, the sport marketer must be knowledgeable about the specific formats, terminology, and personnel employed by the media.

Media is a broad term when used as a noun. It generally includes two categories, print and electronic. Within these categories, print media refer to newspaper and magazine professionals whereas electronic media typically include television and radio. Although the classification system has worked well for many years, technology is rapidly blurring the lines of distinction. Many television stations are owned by publishers; publishers are producing vignettes for television, and with electronic computer bulletin boards, some newspapers are never printed. Regardless of the labels placed on media professionals, sport marketers must develop sophisticated skills and nurture productive relationships.

> The two most important aspects of media relations are the development of media relationships and media competencies.

Building Media Relationships

The media must be considered as clients. Effective relations with media outlets will provide significant opportunities for communicating marketing concepts and product information with other clients and customers. Radio, television, and newspapers are the traditional media sources with which the sport marketer must become familiar. By providing a high-quality service to the media, all marketing functions can be enhanced.

One example of how not to build positive media relations occurred in 1999 immediately following Michael Jordan's retirement from basketball. Nike offered company chair Phil Knight to ESPN for an interview related to Jordan's announcement. However, Nike demanded that Bob Ley be replaced as the interviewer. Ley had served as the principal reporter on ESPN's documentary critical of Nike's labor practices in Asian shoe factories. ESPN refused, and Nike received additional negative publicity rather than the positive exposure originally sought.

Principles of Good Media Relations

Sport marketers can develop confidence and respect by adhering to some basic principles or guidelines. According to Fox and Levin (1993) and Sports Media Challenge (1991), these include the following:

1. Know the players. A thorough understanding of the titles and responsibilities of media personnel will contribute greatly to your success. In the television environment, you will encounter executive producers, senior producers, talent (on-air hosts and reporters), and other production personnel. With the print media, you will come in contact with editors, reporters, staff writers, and occasionally stringers (those who write for the publication on a part-time basis).

2. Be accessible. Everyone has tight schedules and more work to do than time in which to do it. However, if you want media coverage, you will have to make yourself available on their terms. The only time when the media want you and are willing to wait for you is during a crisis in your organization.

3. Be cooperative and non-combative at all times. You will never win an argument with a reporter or writer. Even stupid questions deserve an answer. Remember, they do the editing and they will always have the last word.

4. Appearance is critical. Although you might think that this aspect of media relations applies only to television, this is not accurate. Your attire projects an image to all reporters. A person in formal business attire is almost always afforded more respect and credibility than a person in shorts and a golf shirt.

Your relationship with the media will affect all your marketing and promotional plans.

Photo reprinted by permission of WVU Photography.

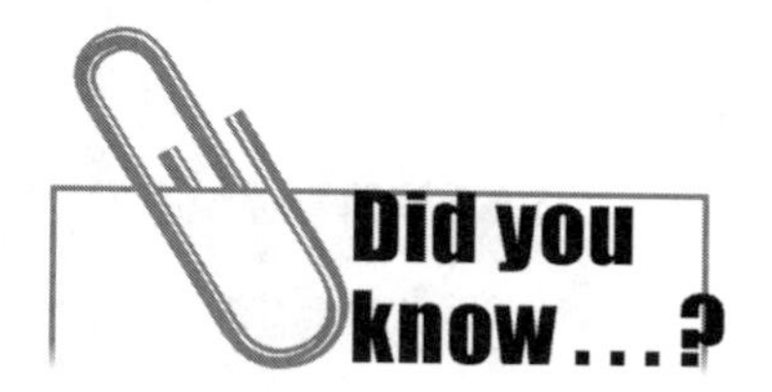

In 1999, one in eight U.S. travelers played golf while on a trip of 100 miles or more. This translates to 17.3 million U.S. adults.

Source: Travel Industry Association of America

5. Don't use jargon. Instead, use words with which the public is familiar. In the sport industry, it is easy for us to use words and phrases that are unique to the field. Although we may believe that everyone should know the meaning of our words, that is not typically the case. Think before you speak, and rehearse the vocabulary that will be most effective with every audience.

6. Use facts, not rumors, and be precise. Gather as many pertinent facts as possible prior to talking to reporters. Although facts in some stories may initially be more detrimental than a rumor, specific examples confine a story whereas rumors tend to remove all boundaries. Good reporters will verify facts through alternate sources prior to airing (printing) a report. Eventually all of the facts will surface, and you do not wanted to be labeled a liar. Honesty and trust are critical to the survival and success of your organization.

7. Don't stress or depend upon off-the-record accounts. If you can see a camera, microphone, or reporter's notebook, assume your words are recorded. Remember, the job of the media is to get facts and report the story; asking a reporter to abide with off-the-record requests is unfair. Never say anything that you would not like to see in the media (i.e., there is no "off the record," and "the microphone is always on").

8. Give as much service to the media as possible. When news occurs, get the story out expeditiously. All reporters desire "hot" news, so you must be willing and able to supply the stories, pictures, and statistics they wish, in the form they need and on time.

9. If a reporter uncovers a story, do not immediately give the same story to other reporters. Treat it as an exclusive right. Many reporters pride themselves on finding sensational news stories and believe that they should have the right to be the first to break the story.

10. Because news is a highly perishable commodity, timing is critical. Breaking stories have a very limited shelf life, and if you want the publicity, you must provide all of the necessary information quickly and in a format that the media outlet needs. Remember that the media need news, not publicity.

Types of Media Outlets

Press Conferences

One essential aspect in providing service to your media clients is identical to the basic concept of marketing: Provide what your client needs. Press conferences can provide that service, but should occur only when circumstances warrant their use. Too often, a media relations director will call press conferences to disseminate information that should have been in a news release. This causes the press to be wary of conferences. A press conference takes up a great deal of a reporter's day; therefore, if the press conference is to be a success, the information must warrant its occurrence.

Press conferences are most appropriate when the information must be distributed to all outlets at the same time.

Helitzer (1995) provides several considerations for planning a successful press conference. He recommends that you assess the value of calling a press conference. The timing of the press conference is also important. You must make sure that the key media people are available at the scheduled time. Although it is not always possible to check everyone's schedule, the media do have some times that are better than others based on the media source (morning paper vs. afternoon, radio vs. television).

If the decision has been made to conduct a press conference, the affected media must receive invitations. The invitation can be delivered to the media sources through the email or in person. The former is the most efficient, with the latter being more effective. The key decision factors often revolve around the number of media invited and the time of the organization to issue the invitations. If the decision was made to send the invitation through the regular mail, it is also advisable to place a reminder call a few hours before the conference.

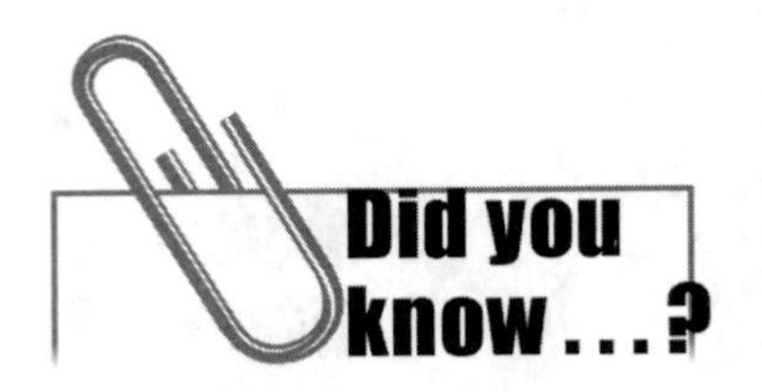

In 1998, the world market for sports equipment at the wholesale level was estimated at about $98 billion, a 2% increase from 1997.

Source: Industry Canada

The preparation and selection of the site are also important considerations. Here, Helitzer (1995) has some specific criteria. Ample space must be assured for the anticipated number of attendees. Parking, seating, telephones, refreshments, and the amount of materials available must also be designed around this factor. Attention should be given to the electrical facilities present at the press conference site. All communication media, including the public address system, the podium height and lighting, projectors, and multimedia equipment, must be checked before the conference. First impressions are critical with the press conference. The agenda or program for the meeting should be distributed along with any particular rules about the process of addressing the speakers.

Too often, sport organizations attempt to use media for free advertising. If you want to serve the media, provide what they need: news. Your task as the sport marketer is to make what you have look like news. This could be a new product being introduced, announcements of new sales records, or even promotions and awards for company personnel. Traditionally, sport marketers provide much of their information to the media in the form of press releases.

Press Releases

Used by commercial, amateur, and collegiate sport organizations for many years, the press release has become a familiar tool for dealing with the media. It has become the most common form of communication in the sport industry. Several authors (Fox and Levin, 1993; Helitzer, 1995; Yudkin, 1994) have presented criteria regarding successful press releases.

The press release must be written in a style that conforms to the style of the particular media even though releases are generally not used exactly as received. The journalist must present the information in a way that attracts audience attention. For electronic media, it is crafted into a usable form by the media, and for newspapers it is redesigned to fit the specific space allotted. In both situations, the release should be written in a style commonly referred to as the "inverted pyramid" (Helitzer, 1995; Yudkin, 1994).

There should be a registration table at the press conference where press kits are available for all attendees.

When scanning a newspaper, people want to see if a story is important to them prior to spending the time to read it. A headline is the first thing the reader will notice. There is some disagreement about whether a press release should have a headline attached. A recommendation would be to supply the headline and allow the reporter to make an editorial decision. In the electronic media, the people listen to the lead-in and make decisions about the relevance of the topic.

A standard element with all press releases is to identify the name of your organization, phone number, and an appropriate contact person in the upper left-hand corner of the first page. The piece must include the essentials of who, what, when, why, where, and how. This should be accomplished in the first paragraph. The media can then decide if the story is worth attention. The first paragraph also may account for all the space the story is allotted in the paper. Thus, the news release must include the details of the story or event in descending order of importance. Writing in this style (inverted pyramid) will more closely match the style of the reporter and will make it more likely that the information will appear in the media.

A good news release has three parts: the significance (headline), the essence (lead), and the details (tail).

It is clear that simply grinding out releases is a costly waste of time and money. Helitzer (1995) reports that only 10% of the information received by daily publications is ever used. These data clearly indicate that most press releases never appear in print, and many are never even read as the news media sort through daily stacks of releases in order to select those stories they believe to be of most interest or benefit to their clients.

The quality of presentation has a bearing upon whether or not a release is used, and competition is intense. One method of improving the chances that a release will be used is to meet the standards expected in preparing and delivering the story. Some of the most critical areas in meeting these standards are the following (Helitzer; Yudkin, 1994):

1. All news releases should be double-spaced on white paper; use $8^1/2$ by 11 inch paper; use only one side of each sheet of paper (Helitzer, 1995; Yudkin, 1994). If the information is sent via electronic transfer, spacing is unimportant as the information will be reformatted upon receipt.

2. Minimum margins of one inch on the sides and two inches at the top and bottom should be provided on each page (Helitzer, 1995).

3. The organization's name, address, and telephone number should appear on the release. Corporate stationary is acceptable, but the information can also be included in the upper left-hand corner of plain paper (Helitzer, 1995; Yudkin, 1994).

4. It is essential that the release contain the name of a "contact" person in the sport organization. This should include full name, position title, address, E-mail address and phone number. News is a 24-hour business, and timely follow-up is an important feature for reporters and editors (Helitzer, 1995; Yudkin, 1994).

5. The words "For Immediate Release" and the date should appear on the upper right-hand corner of the first page on almost all releases. An exception would be stories on future events or quotes from a yet-to-be-presented speech (Helitzer, 1995; Yudkin, 1994).

6. There is considerable debate over whether or not you should write a headline for the story, Helitzer (1995) indicates that a good headline assists the news organization with routing the information and can catch the attention of an editor, spurring more reading. However, both Helitzer (1995) and other authorities (Mullin, Hardy, and Sutton, 2000) indicate that headlines supplied by the sports organization are rarely used.

7. Arrange paragraphs in their descending order of importance. This is known in the trade as the "inverted pyramid." Each succeeding paragraph should contain

information that is less crucial than the preceding one. This style facilitates editorial decisions and enables the newspaper to cut the story to meet its space needs (Helitzer, 1995; Yudkin, 1994).

8. The essential facts and story line must be included in the first paragraph (Yudkin, 1994). According to Helitzer (1995), the editor will only read the first two paragraphs in making preliminary decisions about running or rejecting your release. Therefore, the first paragraph must include the five Ws: who, what, when, where, and why. This is part of the lead for the story and is used to bring the editor (and readers) into the remaining part of the story.
9. Use short sentences because they are more readable and understandable than longer ones. Depending upon the classification of words used, the length of the sentence should seldom exceed 17 words. Sentences that incorporate technical terms, figures, unusual names, or places must be short to ensure clarity and understanding. Paragraphs should be "purposely" short for easier reading (Helitzer, 1995).
10. All pages should be numbered at the top, and at the bottom of every page except the last one, use the word "More." You should also mark the end of the story by the word "End" or a series of encircled ### marks (Helitzer, 1995; Yudkin, 1994).

Other useful tips for getting press releases into the media have been provided by both authors. When mailing press releases to the Sports Editor, the editor's name should also be included so that the person performing those functions will open it. Distribution times are very important because the print/broadcast deadline of the receiver can affect whether the release is available for use. If you personally deliver a news release, avoid the front desk if possible and try to present your release directly to the person who will make the decision on its use. Sports marketers must become familiar with the specific needs of different media outlets. What follows is an examination of the needs of the various media sources that may be used in the sport marketing field.

Media Outlets

Newspapers and Magazines

Although newspapers have continued to be a mainstay of American culture, magazines in sport, health, and fitness and other publications that carry featured sports stories experienced phenomenal growth in the 1980s and 1990s. Almost all segments of the sport industry have specialized publications. Newspapers and magazines are not imposed upon readers; the reader purchases or reads one that someone else has purchased. Thus, at the outset, there is some assurance of readiness to accept or expose oneself to the content. Generally, readers are interested in the content, and most influential citizens make it a practice of reading current newspapers and sport magazines. Because they often are read at leisure, there is time to digest the content of the items read and to formulate at least tentative opinions.

> A file of contacts should be formulated and kept in the media relations office so that essential information can be sent to an appropriate publication at any time.

Sport marketing directors should become acquainted with the publishers, the highest-ranking officer (the executive editor), the editor, the editorial page editor, and finally the managing editor. You want to determine which day or days are best for particular stories. Most authorities suggest that you chart the calendar for appropriate and inappropriate days based on the daily content of a publication and plan accordingly. As a

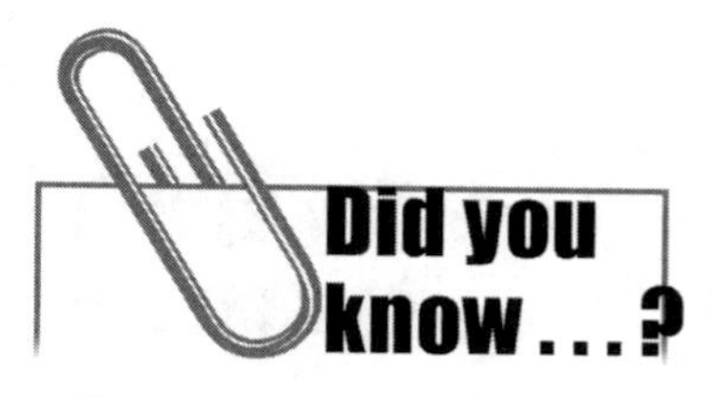

One fourth of Americans picked the Indianapolis 500 as the auto race they would most likely attend. The Daytona 500 followed with 14% of the votes.

Source: Market Facts, Inc.

rule, magazines usually devote more space to stories than do newspapers. Furthermore, magazines provide more specific material for the reader, so the impact of any story may be enhanced. Magazine articles also have a longer life than that of newspaper stories. Most people throw their newspapers away after reading them whereas they tend to keep magazines longer and often pass them on to colleagues and friends, thus prolonging the impact.

A common complaint from newspaper and magazine editors is that the purpose of some sport organizations is to seek free advertising. Experienced media personnel are quick to recognize this tactic, which severely strains relationships. Another familiar complaint is that sport marketers often attempt to color or censor the material, and the editorial personnel rightly believe that it is their duty to the readers to remove any bias that may have been included. Finally, the sport marketer must never attempt to use influence or pressure tactics to get an item in or out of the paper. Although this has been attempted where event sponsors have threatened to withdraw advertising from publications that did not give substantial media coverage to a sponsored event, the practice is considered unethical.

Many sport teams and events utilize the media to enhance their properties. In this process, sport managers often secure media outlets (newspapers and television stations/networks) as sponsors. This allows the sport organization to "leverage" the media for coverage. Because media coverage is vital to sport organizations, sponsorship benefits (i.e., on-site signage, tickets) are often provided to media outlets in exchange for advertising space in their paper or on their network. This exchange (often called "value-in-kind") benefits the sport organization because it offsets the cost of advertising and it benefits the media outlet through preferential access to event or team coverage. In some situations, the sport manager may also extend the advertising options to other sponsors.

Many stories and releases are printed because they include an exciting photograph. Sports are action-packed activities, and high-quality photographs can catch the attention of editors and readers alike. A glossy-finish picture with no more than two or three persons in the picture is preferred. You should identify photographs by typing the information about the event and all people in the picture on the lower half of a standard sheet of paper; then paste the upper half of the paper to the back of the photograph so that the caption material will drop down below the picture when it is withdrawn from the envelope. Although "sticky notes" have become standard office fare, they often fall off photographs and render the information useless.

If possible, provide photographs to accompany press releases.

Yudkin (1994) indicated that the major causes of rejection can be traced to common errors or omissions. She felt that many stories were poorly written and contained "inconsistencies in tense, person and voice" (p. 167). If stories or press releases are continually rejected, arrange to have a conference with the editor, reporter, or others involved to determine any problems that may exist. The stated purpose of this meeting should be to improve your service to the media, and it is hoped that the conference will result in a more positive relationship between your organization and the print media.

Yudkin (1994) continued to point out problems with many press releases. She noted that companies often use meaningless superlatives such as best and newest (p. 166).

These materials cannot be distinguished from advertising and therefore usually conflict with traditional editorial policies. On occasion, some materials are obviously exaggerated or contain apparent inaccuracies.

Of course, newspapers and magazines are also valuable in calling attention to other forms of communication such as forthcoming speeches, event, radio, or television programs. It is through this avenue that many sport marketers encounter the electronic media. Because radio and television are instantaneous communication media, they present special needs to which the sport marketer must attend.

Nearly 40% of auto-racing fans said the Indianapolis 500 was the first auto race they saw on TV or heard on radio, more than twice as many as those who saw or heard the Daytona 500.

Source: Market Facts, Inc.

Radio

Sport marketers can use radio in a variety of ways. Probably the most common is for a team to broadcast its games over an official radio network. These distribution outlets are important in providing the game to fans who cannot attend in person or to those who enjoy the casual atmosphere of listening to sports events without visual cues or while traveling to the event site.

As an example, ESPN Radio Network provides 16 hours of sport programming per week, 7 hours each on Saturday and Sunday evening and 2 hours on Sunday morning. Agreements with affiliates require them to air the Sunday morning segment and 2 hours each on Saturday and Sunday night. The affiliates pay nothing for the program but receive no revenue from commercials. All commercial time is pre-sold by ESPN Radio ("ESPN Radio," 1993). In this situation, the station attracts listeners, but has a reduced capacity to earn revenues. However, the station hopes that the listeners will stay tuned for additional programming and develop loyalty to the outlet.

Television

From the Olympic Games to a local coach's show, sport marketers will encounter television in many aspects of their work. Competition in the television industry increased markedly in the 1990s. From the addition of the Fox Sports Network as a competitor to ESPN to ESPN's addition of ESPN 2, the competition is fierce in the sport broadcast industry. Over 150 new cable networks were established, and 400 new stations came into existence ("ESPN Radio," 1993). Cross-ownership of cable and networks has produced some interesting programming choices. Disney owns the Anaheim Angels, the Mighty Ducks of Anaheim, ESPN (+ ESPN 2), and ABC television. Australia's Rupert Murdock owns the Los Angeles Dodgers and the Fox Sports Network, and he has been purchasing a multitude of European sports properties as well. In this environment, viewers could see the first two rounds of golf's U.S. Open on ESPN and the final two rounds on ABC. Doing some background research in this environment is essential.

Regular network distribution is also changing. Pay-per-view has become available for regional broadcast of sports events. All of the major networks produce and telecast a variety of games on any given day. However, the local affiliates of the network select the contest that they feel will have the broadest appeal in the area. Yet because the other games are also available, the viewer can, for a fee, view other games via cable with a few flips of a switch. The increase in this format has occurred because there few, if any, additional costs to the producer, a limited hassle for the distribution, and the consumer's getting the desired product at a reasonable price.

Sports programming has increased 500% over the past 15 years primarily due to the increase in the available program sources (Stotlar, D. K., 2000). In 1998, over 37,000 hours of sport programming was available to viewers. The types of programming that are traditionally available include regularly scheduled contests (MLB, NBA, college games, motor sports, and horse racing), made-for-TV events (X Games, Goodwill Games, and celebrity sport events), and sport anthology or talk shows (NFL films, ESPN's *Outside the Lines*, etc.). The clear trend in the industry is for media outlets to "develop an equity position" in (read that—own) sporting events ("Steve Risser: The Interview," 1997). ESPN controls all of the details of the X Games and therefore can shape the content to provide the best programming. Companies like the International Management Group own their own television production companies as well as the events so that they can protect the interests of their sponsor and athlete clients.

This has created an interesting situation whereby some experts predict that if television ever stopped its sport coverage, many sport systems would collapse. The dependency of sport on media dollars is exemplified though the following data: NBC purchased the right to the Olympic Games from 1996 to 2008 for $4 billion; CBS spent $1.73 billion for exclusive rights to the NCAA basketball tournament (1995–2002); and BskyB paid almost $1 billion for rights to England's Premier League through 2001 ("Sport and Television," 1996). The professional leagues in the United States also rely heavily on television revenues for income. Fox committed $4.4 billion for its share (NFC) of the NFL contract (1998–2005), with CBS paying $4 billion (AFC). ABC, through corporate owner Disney, secured the rights to *Monday Night Football* for 8 years with a bid of $9.2 billion (ESPN Sportzone, 1998). Thus, sport marketers will associate with television personnel on a regular basis.

If you want to have your event covered on television, the process is quite complicated. However, an overview may be helpful. To obtain coverage, you have to make what you have look like what the networks need. Television stations must pay for all programming, even reruns of *Xena: Warrior Princess* (approximately $150,000 per episode). What you can do is demonstrate to them that your event may be better and cheaper. Remember, your task is to prove it.

> To get your sport event on television, contact the programming director and present a proposal for your event's coverage.

The first step is to contact the programming director, not the sports person. When the contact is made, you will need to present a proposal for the coverage of your event. In general, you will need lead time of approximately 6 to 8 months, 12 if you are trying obtain coverage on a network affiliate. As with most sport marketing areas, the sport marketer must have prepared. Some of the information that you will need to know includes data about television programming. For instance, you must know the difference between *ratings* and *share*.

The Nielsen ratings have long been the benchmark for measuring television-viewing patterns across the United States. The system is based on a selection of 4,000 households equipped with a "people meter." This device records the viewing patterns of the household. The resulting data are transformed into ratings and shares. *Ratings* represent "the percentage of the total television households (approx. 93 million in the United States) that are tuned to a particular program" ("ESPN Radio," 1993, p. 13). *Share*, on the other hand, is "the percentage of those sets in use [at that specific time] which are tuned in to a given program" ("ESPN Radio," p. 13). To be successful, your event must be able to deliver competitive ratings and share for the station.

The outline of your proposal should include the following points:

- Explanation of the event;
- Benefits to the station—-previous rating/share;
- Level of involvement—-production, wild footage, telecast only;
- Your facilities—-camera hookups, knowledge of staff; and
- People and organizations in control—-time/date, during event timing and running.

Although the number of programming and outlet sources has increased, so has the competition across sport. However, with a lot of hard work, it is possible to present your event on television.

Media Relations During a Crisis

Although the scope of this chapter does not allow complete coverage of how to work with the media during a crisis, some attention seems warranted. Sport organizations must manage the flow of information during a crisis to protect the reputation that the company has worked diligently to create. Mangers must direct both the actual crisis and the public's perception of the crisis. The first step in this process entails the establishment of a crisis management team (Young, 1996). This team should have one designated director who will have the ultimate responsibility to control all information provided for the public and serve as the conduit for all information coming in to the organization. In some instances, this person is referred to as the "gatekeeper" (Caywood and Stocker, 1993; Young, 1996). Depending on the team director's public speaking skills and media savvy, this person may or may not be the spokesperson for the group. The crisis management team comprises the top management within the organization. For example, the USOC "Controversy" team for the Atlanta Olympic Games included the USOC president, executive director, *chef de mission* (head of the U.S. delegation), director of public relations, and other staff as specified (United States Olympic Committee, 1996). Essentially, the role of the crisis management team is to "plan, execute, and then evaluate" (Caywood and Stocker, 1993, p. 411).

The crisis management plan should be more than a list of policies, procedures, and actions; it should reflect the full scope of organizational considerations regarding a potential crisis. Once the members of the team have been designated, the team director should select the spokesperson. Depending on the background and experience of this person, some additional training would most likely be appropriate. This training can assist the person in remaining calm, fielding and responding to questions from reporters, and crafting answers that will best serve the organization while simultaneously accommodating the media.

One of the responsibilities of the team director is to prepare and distribute the actual crisis plan. The plan should include the tasks or each member of the team and the sequence of actions required. Implementing the plan depends heavily on the equipment and facilities accessible. For dealing with a crisis in close proximity to corporate headquarters, Caywood and Stocker (1993) have suggested that the following materials be located near a conference room: This "command center should be equipped with computers, modems, fax machines, copier, tape recorder, numerous telephones, pads of paper, pens, pencils, stationary, envelopes and a paper shredder" (p. 416). Other information that would be beneficial would be an organizational chart; a corporate contact sheet with names, addresses, and phone numbers of all key employees; and a copy of the updated database of media contacts. Consideration should also be given to creating a crisis kit that could be carried by key personnel who might be required to travel off-site to handle company problems. In this case, the computers should be portables with E-mail and fax capabilities as well as a small printer.

Once the crisis has been defused, a thorough evaluation should be conducted immediately. "It is critical that all elements of the plan area [be] analyzed to determine the effectiveness of each in resolving the situation" (Caywood and Stocker, 1993, p. 14). These actions have been found to be extremely constructive in preparing for and managing future crises.

Chapter Summary

Media relations should have as a goal the provision of accurate information for all media sources. This information should be disseminated in a professional manner. Sport marketers must develop sophisticated skills and productive media relationships. These can most often be attained by working with the media and providing a high level of service. Quality press conferences and written material are essential in developing the relationships. Radio and television programming are evolving in new directions, and top sport marketers will need to be current with technology and trends. As programming and outlet sources change, so will the competition across sport. Yet, with hard work, your marketing functions can be enhanced through effective media relations.

Questions for Study

1. What are the essential steps in obtaining electronic (television or radio) coverage of your sport event?
2. What are some of the differences between the impact of newspaper and magazine articles that would affect sport marketing?

Learning Activities

1. Contact a sport organization and obtain permission to attend a press conference. Take notes and compare them with material in the text.
2. Working with a local high school and city newspaper, attend a sport event and write a press release after the event. Contact the local newspaper and deliver your release. Go over the content with a local college Sport Information Director and discuss the quality of the release.

Professional Associations and Organizations

College Sports Information Directors of America/ COSIDA
Campus Box 114
Kingsville, TX 78363

Suggested Reading

Young, D. (1996). *Building your company's good name.* New York: AMACOM.

Chapter 14

Marketing Through Endorsements and Sponsorships

Overview

The purpose of this chapter is to describe how sport organizations can enhance their marketing efforts through athlete endorsements and sport sponsorships. Although non-sport companies have long used sport personalities and sports event to sell products, the contents of this chapter will be confined to the use of endorsements and sponsorships by sport organizations.

As explained in the sections of the text on marketing and promotional mix, the sport marketer must incorporate all available resources to satisfy the sport consumer. That process can be expedited through opinion leaders, individuals who have specialized knowledge of your sport product or service and who can influence others in the purchasing process. Pride and Ferrell (1997) noted that opinion leaders are most effective when consumers in the target market share values and attitudes similar to those of the opinion leader. This has been one of the main reasons for the successful use of athlete-endorsers in sport.

Individual athletes have been used to provide sport product endorsements with the hope that their endorsement will result in increased sales. This can be an effective component of sport marketing when matched to target markets and applied appropriately with consumers. Recently, some corporations have begun to tie specific personalities to products and corporate brand-management strategies.

Opinion Leaders and Endorsements

Many sport companies use endorsers and opinion leaders because of their knowledge and power within certain groups. Brooks (1998) indicated that companies could use athletes as endorsers in four fundamental modes:

- The athlete can directly endorse the product (explicit mode).
- The athlete can exhibit product use (implicit mode).
- The athlete can recommend a product (imperative mode).
- The athlete can simply allow his or her image to appear conjointly with the product (co-present mode).

The implicit tactic was employed by sport shoemaker adidas when they signed Kobe Bryant. Bryant was extremely important to Adidas because he played for the Los Angeles Lakers. Adidas Director of Sport Marketing Robert Erb commented that "Los Angeles is the second-biggest market in the United States and of course it's important for us" (qtd. in Mullen, L. 1998, p. 10).

All of the major shoe companies use coaches as opinion leaders. Numerous college coaches have been paid as much as $200,000 per year to outfit their team in specific shoes. Former Florida football coach Steve Spurrier was one of the leaders in coaching endorsements with a $525,000 contract from Nike (Dodd and Pearson, 1997). The considerable economic value generated from the national television coverage of college football and basketball games provides the incentive. Nike's budget for its college basketball coaches runs about $4 million and includes $600,000 in complimentary merchandise as well (Brubaker, 1991). The exposure achieved through this endeavor comes not only in the arena but also through a company's support of the coach's summer sports camps where clothing for the coaching staffs, T-shirts, posters, and related merchandise can influence the impressionable youth market.

Every time they wear them, these cheerleaders provide free advertising for the companies that produce their uniforms and accessories.

Photo reprinted by permission of WVU Photography.

Youth programs represent the grass roots of the sport shoe market. If you want to move shoes, the youth market is the place to be. Establishing the purchasing patterns of customers early in their lives is a powerful tool in marketing. Both Nike and adidas selected this tactic in the late 1990s when they entered into agreements with several high school basketball programs. Basically, each school would receive approximately $2,500 in sport product for players and the coaches would be outfitted in company apparel. The companies' strategy centered on the hope that not only would the players influence their peers, but they would also accessorize with additional company products.

It is not just the coaches and athletes of organized team sports that can be incorporated into endorsement as part of sport marketing plans. In the cheerleading and performance-dance industry, specialty companies often provide free shoes and apparel to the leading groups in the nation in an effort to influence the style selection and purchasing of other participants.

The manufacturer typically put the coaches under contract to guarantee specified actions and to protect the value of the endorsement. A typical contract calls for the following:

1. Give the company use of their name, nickname, initials, autograph, voice, video or film portrayals, facsimile signature, photograph, likeness and image.

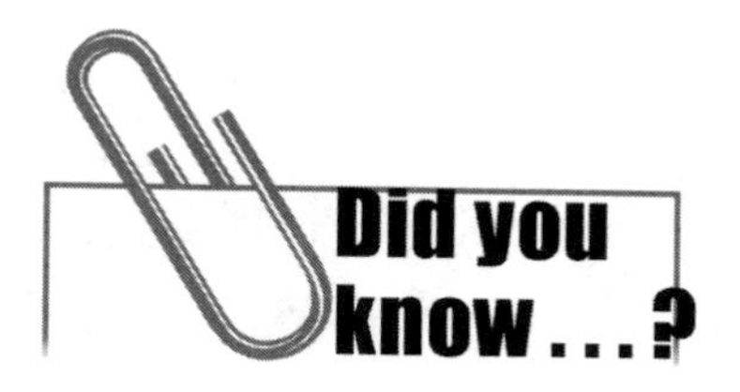

Tiger Woods's financial impact on golf was valued at more than $650 million including more than $100 million in endorsements.

Source: Associated Press

2. Make the company shoes available to players and assistant coaches as well as cheerleaders, game personnel, and the team mascot.
3. Film a TV commercial and participate in two photo sessions the results of which may be exploited by the company throughout the world in any manner determined by the company.
4. Make eight promotional appearances in the United States and one abroad, designated by the company
5. Attend a company party and/or annual retreat.
6. Assist in the production of a promotional video on topics such as basketball fundamentals, physical conditioning, nutrition, academics, drug and alcohol education and preparation for the real world.
7. Comment favorably upon the use of company products whenever possible.
8. Wear a sport jacket, sweater, or shirt bearing the company logo prominently displayed during all college basketball games and at other appropriate . . . public activities.
9. Give the company four complimentary tickets to each game.
10. $5,000 will be deducted from the contract if team members do not achieve a 2.25 mean grade-point average each year. (Brubaker, 1991, p. A1)

Other ways of using opinion leaders in sport have included product sampling and prototype testing as additional ways to receive input. Product sampling always generates a great deal of interest in the product and can be tracked to indicate the overall effect on sales. Often a product new to the market or even a prerelease prototype is distributed to key opinion leaders within an industry. This develops loyalty, and it can provide the company with reliable feedback on its products with minimal costs. For example, Reebok often provides prerelease shoe models to top sales personnel in selected sporting goods stores to seed sales and generate product interest.

Individual Athlete Endorsements

The use of individual athletes to endorse products has been a marketing practice in sport for decades. As early as the 1936 Berlin Olympics, adidas provided track star Jesse Owens with free shoes. Historically, the line between professional and amateur athletes was finely drawn. If an athlete was paid or received money from sport, he or she was a professional; if the athlete received nothing, he or she was an amateur. All of this has changed in Olympic sports, and although the Olympic Games offer no prize money, the athletes certainly collect from their endorsement deals. In 1981, the Olympic rules were modified. The International Olympic Committee (IOC) changed its regulations and allowed each international federation to establish its own standards on the receipt of monies and the effect on eligibility. At this time, the IOC no longer even refers to athletes as amateurs, but as eligible athletes. Many of the shoe companies specify cash incentives tied to medals won at the Olympic Games.

Probably one of the best lessons about individual athlete endorsements for a sports company was the 1992 Dan and Dave campaign initiated by Reebok prior to the Barcelona Olympic Games. Shoe manufacturer Reebok used potential U.S. Olympic decathletes to promote new models of their Pump training shoe. The ad copy ("To be settled in Barcelona") attempted to predict who would win the gold medal. However, Dan (O'Brien) failed to make the U.S. team. With over $30 million in the ad campaign, Reebok parlayed the tragedy into a bonanza of publicity worth several times the advertising costs. Incidentally, a Reebok-sponsored athlete, Robert Zmelik from the Czech Republic, did win the 1992 decathlon gold medal. O'Brien not only made the 1996 Olympic team, but also set several world records in the interim and won the gold medal at the Atlanta Olympic Games. These accomplishments provided Reebok with substantial media exposure and maximized Reebok's marketing campaign with more "authentic" marketing and endorsements.

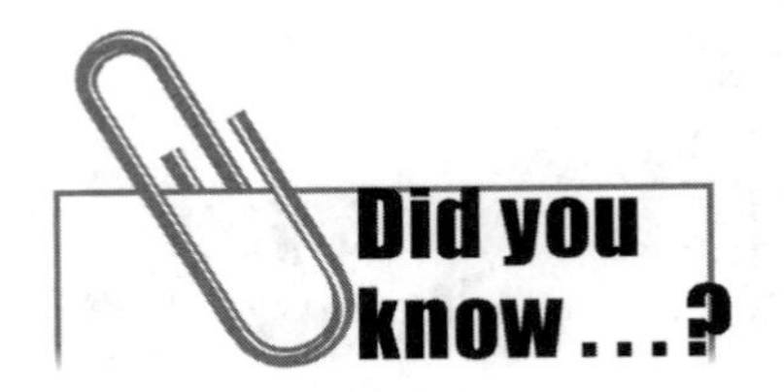

An estimated 250,000 people pour into Augusta, GA, each year to walk the hallowed grounds of the Augusta National Golf Club.

Source: cnnsi.com

For many years, shoe companies engaged in bidding wars in an attempt to secure the next Michael Jordan. As a result, endorsement contracts for some players, particularly those in the NBA, escalated into the millions of dollars. However, weak shoe sales and a change in fashion trends to "brown shoes" (Doc Martins, Vans, Sketchers, etc.) caused a decline in athletic footwear sales in the late 1990s (Hofman, 1999, p. 33–36). In response, many shoe companies substantially curtailed their player endorsements. Reebok went from having over 130 NBA players under contract to having fewer than 10 during the 1999 season. Nike and Fila used similar tactics (Bernstein, 1998).

In some instances, athletes may be able to earn more from endorsements than from salary. Late NASCAR driver Dale Earnhardt won seven Winston Cup Championships and in 1996 accumulated $2.5 million in winnings. However, by licensing his own name and likeness, he was able to generate an additional $8 million in endorsements earnings (Hagstrom, 1998). In a 1998 personal appearance on shopping channel QVC, Earnhardt sold $741,266 in licensed merchandise in a single evening (Spanberg, 1998). Earnhardt's sales accounted for almost 40% of 1998 NASCAR sales (Hagstrom). With his untimely death at the 2001 Daytona 500, Earnhardt merchandise became the sport's most coveted merchandise. NASCAR's youngest champion, Jeff Gordon, was able to generate $5 million in licensing profits after his 1998 Winston Cup Championship (Spiegel, 1998).

Michael Jordan established the benchmark for endorsement earnings. During his last year with the Bulls, Jordan earned $47 million from product endorsements. A cable-based TV channel, the Home Shopping Network, interrupted its programming to air Jordan's retirement from the Chicago Bulls and proceeded to offer Jordan-related merchandise ranging from autographed basketballs to limited-edition trading cards. This event, which immediately followed his press conference, grossed over $1 million. With his reentry into the NBA with the Wizards, Michael Jordan continues to profit from licensed merchandise.

Tiger Woods, arguably the second in class to Jordan, signed a contract with Nike immediately following his final amateur match. The Nike contract (5 year, $40 million) was one of the highest in sport endorsement history (Lombardo, 1998). Tiger Woods renegotiated his Nike contract after the 2000 season (PGA Championship, U.S. Open, British Open, Canadian Open) wins (5 year, $100 million). Other endorsements for Woods included $30 million (5 year) from Buick and additional work for Rolex and American Express. Electronic Arts signed Woods for a video game bearing his name after his victory at the 1997 Masters. In total, Woods's endorsement earnings amount to about $64 million per year ("Fan-Favorite," 2000).

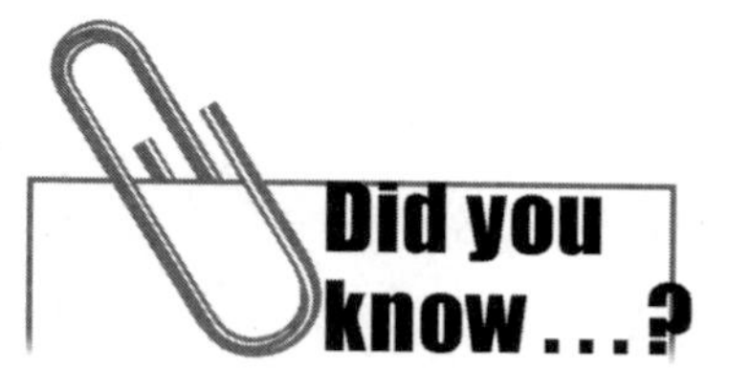

The cities with the highest percentage of sports events visitors in 1999:

Charlotte (19%)
Indianapolis (17%)
Milwaukee (13%)
St. Louis (12%)
Cincinnati (11%)
Kansas City (11%)
Memphis (11%)
Minneapolis (11%)

Source: Travel Industry Association of America

It has been more difficult for women to secure equivalent levels of individual endorsements. Only Reebok's commitment to Venus Williams in 2001 for an estimated $40 million over 5 years has approached the level secured by her male counterparts. The leading female endorsers were Venus Williams ($11 million), Monica Seles ($6 million), Steffi Graf ($5 million), Martina Hingis ($3 million), and Kristi Yamaguchi ($3 million; "Fan-Favorite," 2000; "Top 25," 1998). Seles' deals included Nike, Planet Hollywood, Yonex, and Sportline USA ("Top 25"). Unfortunately, some companies devalue women as athletes and focus on their physical attractiveness. According to Kaufman, "How a woman looks still matters in endorsements and just about everything else. It's not right, but it's reality" (Kaufman, 1998, p. 48)

In 1993, data indicated that over 50% of consumers thought athlete-endorsers did it just for the money (Veltri, 1996). Furthermore, Veltri's research indicated that with the exception of Michael Jordan, few people were able to match an athlete-endorser and the products that she or he endorsed. In general, basketball players were more often accurately recognized than were athletes in other sports, and male endorsers were more likely to be recognized than were female athletes (Veltri).

Another phenomenon that has proven to be successful in the sport marketing industry is cross-promotion. If your sport enterprise sponsors an individual athlete and that athlete obtains other, nonsport endorsements, your company can receive increased exposure. Take for example, Nike's sponsorship of Michael Jordan. When Michael Jordan appeared on a Wheaties box, he was wearing Nike shoes and holding a Wilson basketball. In 1999, *Golf Digest* signed an agreement with Kmart Corporation to establish Golf Digest Accessory and Training Centers in all Kmart stores. Kmart agreed to sell licensed Golf Digest products including instructional videos and training aids, and Kmart agreed to purchase advertising in Golf Digest publications.

Endorsements with individual athletes do not exist without danger and controversy. Who controls the rights? Do team players have the right to select their own shoes, or do coaches have the power to demand that specific shoes be worn? Currently, the rights battle has been going to the player, but it will remain an issue for some time to come.

Another issue relates to organizational control. This has been particularly evident in the Olympic Games. During the 1992 Barcelona games, the U.S. men's basketball team had uniforms sponsored by Champion, and individual players each had their own shoe contracts. However, the United States Olympic Committee had an agreement with Reebok for the medal presentation uniform. Because the players had not signed the USOC agreement (requiring participants to wear the USOC-designated presentation apparel) and because wearing a Reebok logo conflicted with their shoe contracts, a serious problem arose. In the end, the players agreed to wear the Reebok uniforms, but unfolded the collar that covered the manufacturer's logo.

Similarly with Formula One racing, the car owner has the rights to signage on the car and driver's suit, yet the drivers own the rights to the helmet. Many drivers on the circuit earn an average of $500,000 from their helmet sponsorship alone. There are also a variety of personal appearance opportunities arranged with different sponsors that add to the revenues earned by the drivers. In 1999, Ferrari driver Michael Schumacher earned an estimated $80 million in salary and endorsements (East, Ronchin and Smith, 2000, p. 106–123).

Almost all sports organizations (NCAA, the NFL, the NBA, Major League Baseball, and the IOC) have so-called "billboard rules" (Woodward, 1988). These rules limit the size and number of logos that can appear on uniforms and equipment. Even with the tight rules, many sport marketers find loopholes. At the Tour de France, the rules control the riders, but not their equipment cars; as a result, sponsors have literally covered the cars with logos and advertising.

Choosing an Athlete-Endorser

As noted earlier, the principle rationale for selecting an athlete-endorser.is that person's status as an opinion leader. Martin (1996) noted, "The central issue for the manager is to pick an athlete spokesperson with the right set of characteristics who will best be able to produce the most favorable response from consumers" (p. 28). His research found that best endorsement value was generated from situations in which a high level of congruity existed between the image of the athlete and the image of the product. Moreover, for some products, certain sports would be more effective in producing positive consumer response than would others. This determination can only be made through extensive market research.

Martin (1996) suggested several steps needed for marketers to determine the right athlete for a product endorsement:

1. The image of the product must be assessed through market research with customers.
2. Marketers should then measure the image factors associated with a variety of sport activities.
3. Once the images of the product and the sport have been assessed, the marketer should select an athlete(s) from the sport that most closely matches the images of the product.
4. The final step would be to evaluate the athlete's ability to enhance the consumers' perception of the product.

According to Martin's (1996) research, "careful consideration of the perceived degree of fit between images of the product and images of the sport can significantly increase the positive evaluation of the endorsement by an athlete from the chosen sport" (p. 37).

Endorsement Trends

Although sport marketers can still benefit from individual athlete endorsements, the risk is high (e.g., Latrell Sprewell, Mike Tyson). As noted earlier, Veltri (1998) indicated that the power of athletes in endorsing products has faltered. As a safeguard, many endorsement contracts have special clauses to cover instances in which a player or coach is involved in some horrid scandal. Converse's contract has a special termination clause that indicates that Converse can terminate the agreement at any time if the person wears another manufacturer's product, commits any act that "tends to shock, insult or offend" the community, violates any league rule, or becomes "disabled/incapacitated and unable to perform." Thus, Converse terminated its relationship with Latrell Sprewell after he attacked his coach at a practice session.

As a result of the problems and risks associated with individual athlete endorsements, many sport organizations are considering sponsoring more events. Some sport organizations like Nike have encountered difficulty in working with athlete's agents. In response, some of the companies have started their own representation agency. These actions pose a threat of conflict of interest. If Nike is using an athlete to endorse its products, can it truly forward that athlete's best interests in negotiating the best possible deal for product endorsements? Other conflict-of-interest issues arise when companies like Disney own professional sports teams (Mighty Ducks of Anaheim, Anaheim Angels) and the networks (ABC, ESPN, ESPN2) on which the teams may play.

Team and event sponsorships are becoming more common than individual-athlete deals.

Event Sponsorships

The initial question that must be addressed is whether a sport organization should use sponsorship in lieu of traditional advertising. Sponsorship offers a number of distinct advantages over more conventional advertising techniques. Sponsorship spending has grown at a rate three times that of advertising. Although U.S. spending on advertising was about $200 billion in 1998, the growth rate was less than 4% annually (Bonham, 1999). However, advertising delivers a straightforward commercial message, whereas sponsorships get to people through a different source. Within the sport industry, marketers must understand the role of sponsorship as a marketing tool.

> Sponsorship involves a company being prepared to make a commitment and support an activity; it says the company is going to be more people oriented than advertising suggests. In several ways, sponsorship is longer lasting in the terms of its commitment. (International Events Group, 1992c, p. 7)

Sponsorship has been defined as "a cash and/or in-kind fee paid to a property (typically sports, arts, entertainment, or causes) in return for access to the exploitable commercial potential associated with that property" (Ukman, 1995, p. 1). Essentially, the primary goal of sponsorship is to augment marketing communication (Ferrand and Pagés, 1996). The sponsorship of sports activities ranges from local beach volleyball tournaments and fun runs to the Olympic Games. Deals range in scope from the $55-million sponsorship of the Olympic Games to $2,500 sponsorships of youth sport. Collectively, these events can provide sport marketers with an array of opportunities to market their products and services. As outlined at the beginning of this chapter, this discussion of sponsorships will be limited to their use as marketing tools for sport organizations. Although they have been extremely successful and widely used by non-sport companies, that treatment will not be included in this text.

Worldwide, corporate spending on sport sponsorship increased dramatically during the 1980s and 1990s. 2001 U.S. spending on sponsorship was predicted to total $9.5 billion, up 9.6% over 2000 ("IEG Forecast," 2000). Contributing to this total were 61 companies that spent over $10 million each on sponsorship programs ("1999 Sponsors' Spending," 1998). European corporations contributed $7.4 billion, followed by Pacific Rim countries with $4.3 billion, and Central/South America spent an additional $2.1 billion. Various other regional spending accounted for $1.3 billion, bringing the worldwide spending total to $24.6 billion ("IEG Forecast"). This figure represents an increase of 12% above 2000 revenues ("IEG Forecast").

Approximately 5,000 companies that engage in sport marketing activities in almost every sport organization from local fitness centers and high school to the Olympics and professional sport leagues were looking for sponsors. As the number of sports organizations desiring an affiliation with sponsors grew, the leverage in the industry changed.

This created a situation in which the sponsor could weigh the offers from competing organizations seeking sponsors and keep prices down. As a result, during the early part of the decade, the momentum shifted from the sport organizations to the sponsoring corporations. In today's environment it is increasingly important for sport managers to be skilled in the methodologies and techniques of sponsorship as a marketing component. A successful sponsorship arrangement can serve as a positive marketing vehicle for any sport organization.

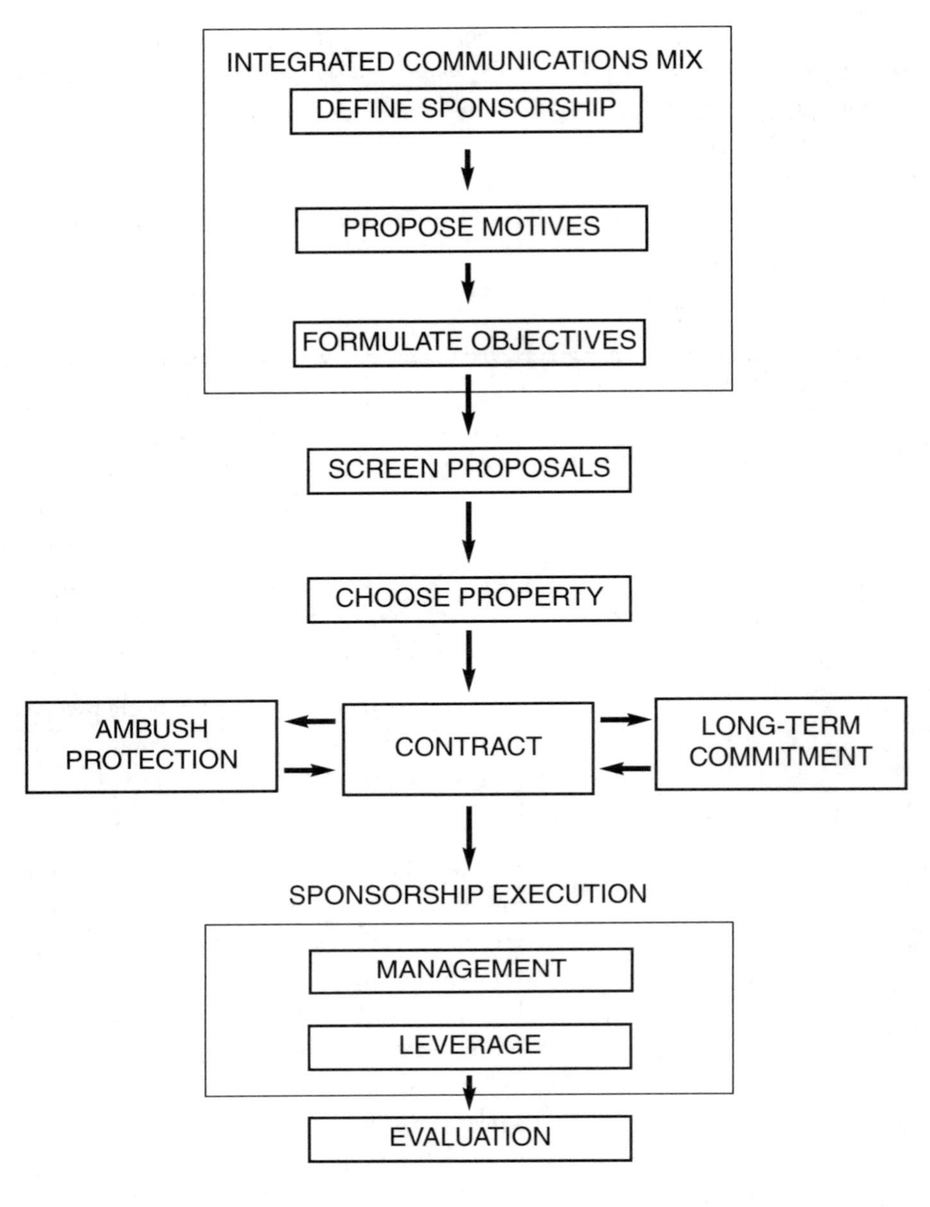

Figure 14.1
The process model of sport sponsorship implementation.

Similar to the research cited with individual athlete endorsements, McDonald (1998) evaluated perceptual fit between the image of a sport and that of a sponsoring company. His research investigated consumer reaction to terms such as sophisticated, rugged, exciting, and wholesome in relation to both companies and the sports considered for sponsorship. His research concluded that creating a good perceptual fit between the sport and a sponsor could contribute to brand equity for the sponsor (McDonald). Thus, the prevailing research (Martin 1996; McDonald) confirms that both sponsorships and endorsements are more effective if there is a high level of congruence between the image of the sport/athlete and the image of the corporation.

Arthur, Scott, Woods, and Booker (1998) provided a model that would serve sport marketers in the evaluation and implementation of sponsorship programs. These authors recommend that the sponsorship be considered as part of the communication mix similar to other promotional activities. As such, sponsorships should be selected with attention to specific criteria.

Rationale for Pursuing Event Sponsorships

Sport organizations can buy into event sponsorship for a variety of marketing reasons. In the past, many organizations were attracted to sport properties to cultivate the social benefits. Sport executives could associate with star players, play in celebrity golf tournaments, and host parties for their friends in conjunction with the event. Although

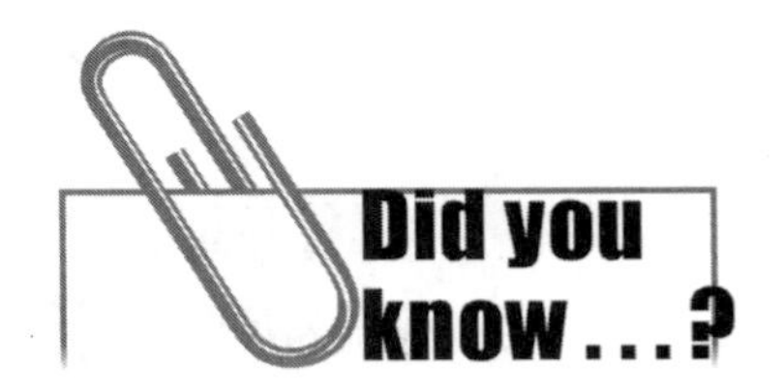

The U.S. Customs Service estimates the knockoffs and counterfeit golf club market to be $4 billion annually.

Source: US Customs Office

these reasons may still exist, their prominence has clearly decreased. In today's business environment, shareholders and boards of directors demand measured return on investment from sponsorship activities.

Thus, decisions to sponsor sport-related properties must be linked to business-related objectives of the company. You must "look at an event to help meet a marketing objective, then make sure it meets sales promotion, PR and internal employee morale needs" (International Events Group, 1992d, p. 4). There must be a match between the organization's target market and the property's audience (or participation base). An obvious example of this can be seen in Reebok's sponsorship of numerous road race events across the nation. These participants clearly represent the core customers for Reebok's products. Sport companies must also look for direct product sales at sponsored events. Thus, Reebok would be more inclined to sponsor a road race if it could access the participants through on-site sales points or obtain the event's database for future marketing initiatives. Sponsorships have also been effective in promoting the image of the sponsor. Continuing the example at hand, Reebok could generate consumer impressions and further position the brand through "authentic" association with national-caliber sporting events.

Ferrand and Pagés (1996) proposed that sponsorship can be effectively used in image management. Companies can use sport sponsorship to (a) establish an image in the consumer's mind, (b) solidify an existing image, or (c) modify the consumer's image of the company. Companies must select rationally the appropriate event or group to sponsor in order to maximize the communication potential. Then, "the sponsor must consider the image of the event, the sponsor's present image, and the desired future image of the sponsor or its brand" (Ferrand and Pagés, 1996. p. 279).

However, recent changes in corporate expectations have mandated more utility from sponsorship association. One company's director of sponsorships stated this point clearly when he said, "We are no longer satisfied with enhanced image; give us opportunities for on-site sales, well-developed hospitality packages and dealer tie-ins and we'll listen" (qtd. in International Events Group, 1992d, p. 5) Sport-related businesses, like most corporations, desire to be seen as community citizens with a responsibility to contribute to the well-being of the communities where they do business. In support of this concept is the message delivered by a special events manager, "Customers want companies that care about them, that give back to the community" (qtd. in International Events Group, 1992d, p. 5). As an example, a local bicycle shop could sponsor a triathlon to influence competitive riders and also could sponsor a child's bike safety class.

A close examination with respect to the reasons your business should become involved in sport sponsorships is essential. Understanding how sponsorship activities can help accomplish your business goals is one of the key elements in selecting successful sponsorship opportunities. These must be specific to each event that the sport marketer intends to approach.

Developing a Winning Strategy

The relationship between your sport entity and event owners involved with sponsorship must include advantages to both parties whereby your product's market value and profits are increased. A key component in the success is the measurement of return on investment (ROI). Sport managers must be fully cognizant of the data with which to demonstrate the accomplishment of specified corporate objectives. For example, data indicate that "73% of NASCAR fans choose products of their sport's sponsors over others" (King, 1998a, p. 9).

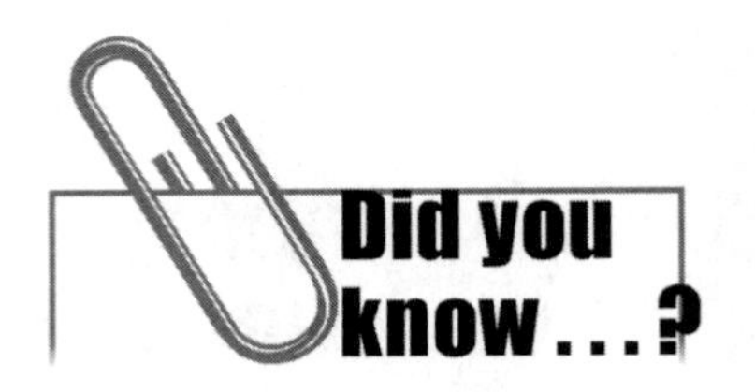

The USTA pays New York City $1.25 million annually to hold the US Open there.

Source: *Tennis Magazine*, September 1999

These data should be provided by the event owner, but are occasionally collected by the sponsor. Sport organizations that use sponsorship as a marketing tool must be prepared to evaluate sponsorship in the same manner as other marketing efforts. You can also have professional market research firms collect the data for you. One such company is Joyce Julius and Associates, which conducts research in sponsor exposure and publishes the results in a publication titled *The Sponsor's Report*. Among the sports analyzed in *The Sponsor's Report* are automobile racing, horse racing, college football and basketball, skiing, tennis, and volleyball. For example, during the 1998 NASCAR season, driver Mark Martin's car sponsor Valvoline generated $43.1 million dollars in exposure through television exposure of its logo for a total of 14 hours, 56 minutes and 10 seconds during races (King, 1998b).

One of the aspects of sponsorship that has attracted sport-related companies has been its ability to reach consumers by breaking through the clutter in advertising. Marketing managers have used sponsorship as an avenue to present their message to consumers in a more relaxed atmosphere and to support their other marketing efforts. Sport events are also attractive because they can provide a cross-sectional exposure when compared to other marketing avenues available to the sport marketer (Stotlar, 1993).

Media attention is another important factor in selecting an event to sponsor. Good events have the potential to generate considerable media coverage. This type of message can be particularly effective because consumers typically see this in a different light than they see traditional advertising. Another related facet of media coverage and sponsorship is that if an event has a media sponsor, you can often obtain discounted or free coverage by tagging their promotional messages. Such a situation exists with the annual Bolder Boulder road race in Boulder, Colorado. The local NBC affiliate and Nike shoes sponsor the event. Not only does Nike get sponsorship of the race, but it also receives logo presentation on all TV spots promoting the race. Similarly, Nike can benefit from the televised coverage of the race, which will of course have several prominent sponsor banners strategically located for the cameras. Media coverage also provides a reliable and measurable method to calculate return on investment.

Although the number of times the sponsor's name was mentioned by the announcers, the column inches of print devoted to the event, and the number of times the corporation's banner was seen on national television are important, the raw data do not always reflect the whole picture. Take for example an announcer who, in the middle of a race, says, "Her Nike shoes have fallen apart, and she'll have to finish this race barefooted." What is the economic value of that? Other sport marketing research firms such as the Denver-based Bonham Group indicated that some of the calculations are based on rate-card advertising costs. Most major corporations purchase advertising at a substantial discount. Thus, some of the reported value assessments may be inflated.

Before undertaking a sponsorship, you should develop criteria for evaluating possible opportunities. This process has been discussed extensively (Irwin and Assimakopoulos, 1992; Mullin, Hardy, and Sutton, 1993; Stotlar, 1993). Irwin, Assimakopoulos, and Sutton (1994) provided an inventory detailing the typical factors to be considered as companies deliberate engaging in sponsorship activities:

- Budget—affordability, cost effectiveness, tax benefits
- Event management—past history, organizing committee
- Image—match to products and services offered
- Target market—demographics, geographical reach
- Communications—media exposure, audience size, and demographics
- Sponsor mix—match with other sponsor's products and image
- Level of involvement—title sponsor, in-kind supplier, exclusivity
- Other Opportunity—wholesaler tie-ins, on-site displays, signage, product sampling, merchandising.

It is critical that all of the components of the sponsorship agreement be detailed in a written contract. Many of the terms and elements provided in a sponsorship lack industry-wide standards, and any confusion must be minimized. Reed (1990) developed an excellent checklist for companies to use when working with an event. If an event owner offers a sponsorship that can meet your criteria, is ethically grounded, and gives you service and data with which to justify continuation, sport sponsorships can be a successful marketing tool for sport organizations.

The Olympic Games and Sponsorship

As with other sports organizations "marketing as a basic function and central dimension of the Olympic enterprise requires specific planning and the performance of distinct activities" (Stauble, 1994, p. 14). Olympic and amateur sport organizations have, over the past several years, become very dependent upon sponsorship income. Stauble views Olympic organizations as resource-conversion machines. These organizations obtain resources from sponsors and convert them into specific products and services that are provided to the public. To accomplish this, Olympic organizations must create an exchange with the sponsor (Stauble). Typically, these have been in the form of signage, logo presentation, hospitality opportunities, and identification with high-level teams and athletes.

There are plenty of opportunities for sale in the five ring circus: television, commercials, product licensing, product exclusivity at the Games, team sponsorships, Olympic movement sponsorships, awards presentations, training center support, product endorsements, and almost anything a marketing [person] could devise. (Marsano, 1987, p. 65)

Sport sponsorships between Olympic organizations and corporations have existed for many years. In 1896, Kodak had an ad in the official program of the first modern Olympics, and by 1928, Coca-Cola had begun its long-standing relationship with the Olympic movement (Pratzmark and Frey, 1989). Sponsorship and the Olympics have a prolonged relationship and one that has increased significantly in complexity.

In 1985, the IOC hired ISL Marketing to create a program to facilitate corporations interested in sponsoring the Olympic Games (Marsano, 1987). The Olympic Programme (TOP) was the creation. According to ISL, TOP "brings together the rights of the IOC as owner of the Olympic Games, the two Games Organizing Committees, and the National Olympic Committees throughout the world as partners in one four year sponsorship programme" (ISL Marketing, 1993, p. 3). This process also accomplished another major goal of any sport marketer—make it easier for consumers to buy your product. Another factor in this formula was the IOC's restructuring of the games so that an Olympic Games (Summer or Winter) would occur every two years instead of both Games occurring in one year with a four-year cycle. This would allow for sponsors to gain more long-term benefits and would spread the payments over an extended period.

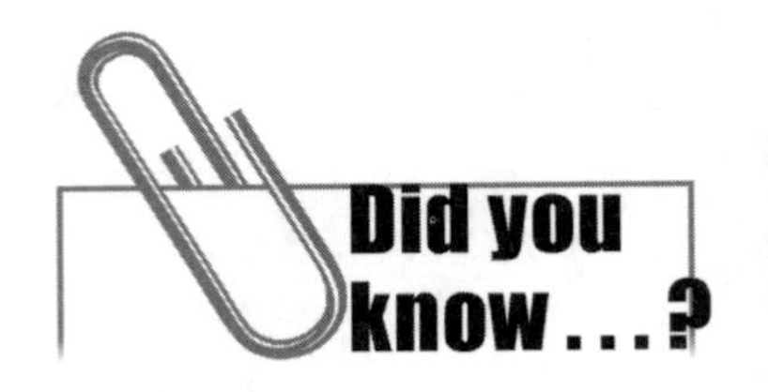

It is estimated that $300 million is generated for New York City businesses from the US Open.

Source: *Tennis Magazine*, September 1999

The system was designed to allow a limited number of sponsors to receive special treatment and benefits on a worldwide basis and achieve exclusivity and protection in their Olympic sponsorship activities (Pratzmark and Frey, 1989). Specifically, TOP Sponsors would receive the following benefits (ISL Marketing, 1993; *Olympic Fact File*, 1998; Pratzmark and Frey, 1989):

1. Product Exclusivity—Only one sponsor would be allowed for any product category. This meant that if Coca-Cola and Visa were members of the TOP, then Pepsi and American Express would not be allowed to become involved with Olympic sponsorship on any level, International, National, or with the Organizing Committee.
2. Use of Marks and Designations—Each participant was granted the right to use the solitary Olympic rings and their use in combination with all NOC designations. This gave them worldwide and local impact. Companies could also use the "Official Sponsor" and "Official Product" designations. All Organizing Committee logos were also available to sponsors.
3. Public Relations and Promotional Opportunities—Sponsors were given special tie-ins and media events to increase their exposure.
4. Access to Olympic Archives—The IOC made articles from its archives in Switzerland available to sponsors for special exhibits and displays. Film and video archives were also available.
5. Olympic Merchandise and Premiums—Clothing and apparel could be used bearing the Olympic logos for sales incentives and marketing activities. Visa had to reorder company shirts five times in 1996.
6. Tickets and Hospitality—Sponsors received priority access to seating at both the Winter and Summer Games.
7. Advertising Options—Each participant in TOP was given first chance at souvenir program ads and the option (where possible) to television commercial purchases.
8. On-Site Participation—Point-of-purchase and product display were included in the package. Companies would also have certain rights to concession areas and space for product sampling. For example, Kodak provides each athlete in the Games with a disposable camera and supplies the 900 photojournalists with 175,000 complimentary rolls of film.
9. Research—Each sponsor would receive a full research report on the public's reception of their participation and an assessment of the valued-added benefits. Research after the 1998 Games showed significant improvements in product image for TOP participants.
10. First Right of Negotiation for the Next Quadrennial—Those who were satisfied with TOP would have the option to continue in their product category. (Pratzmark and Frey, 1989, p. 20–21)

For the 2000 Summer Olympic Games in Sydney, 11 TOP sponsors were secured paying about $55 million each for TOP sponsorship status (*Olympic Fact File*, 1998).

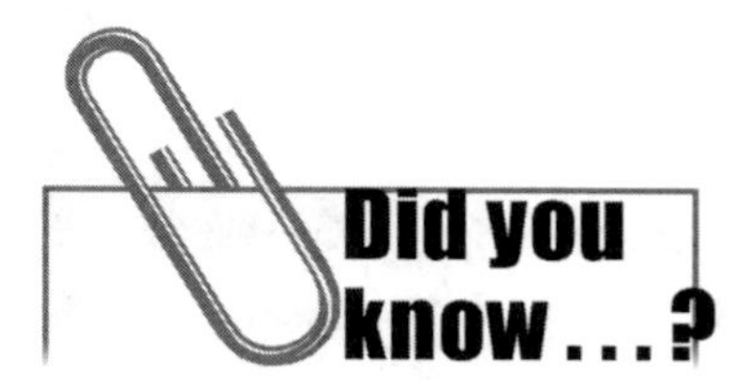

The three counties with the most golf courses:

Maricopa, AZ (168)
Palm Beach, FL (150)
Riverside, CA (145)

Source: (unreadable – a web URL)

Since the 1985 development of TOP, sponsorship has become an integral part of the Olympic movement. Over the last decade, TOP served two major goals of the IOC: It made the IOC less dependent on television revenues, and it assisted all countries in the world with sport development through a shared-revenue system.

Other Olympic Sponsorship Areas

There are a variety of different types of sponsorships that Olympic organizations can offer to corporations. Each entity provides specific sponsor rights associated with participation. Olympic organizing committees normally conduct independent sponsorship programs apart from the IOC. The Sydney 2000 Olympic Organizing Committee together with the Australian Olympic Committee entered into an agreement with Reebok for team apparel and official outfitter status (Koranteng, 1999). National Olympic Committees exist in all of the 170 countries that participate in the Olympic Games. These organizations can authorize the use of the Olympic rings, but only in conjunction with their (NOC) logo. For the 1996 Olympic Quadrennium, the USOC secured sponsorships that amounted to more than 50% of its $400-million operating revenue (Morganthau, Barrett, Dickey, and Talbot, 1992).

Interestingly, for the 1996 Summer Games, the USOC joined forces with the Atlanta Committee for the Olympic Games and created a program similar to TOP with Atlanta Centennial Olympic Properties (ACOP). Following this successful model, the USOC and the Salt Lake Organizing Committee formed OPUS (Olympic Properties of the United States) to manage sponsorship activities for the 2002 Winter Olympics.

National Governing Bodies (NGBs) exist at the base of the Olympic family. They can engage in sponsorship activities separate from those of the IOC and the USOC. Each Olympic sport has an NGB in each country that is a member of the IOC. These organizations can generate sponsorship activities within a single country. The ACOP proposal offered each NGB a package of sponsorships, but also restricted their independent sponsorship activities. The proposal asked the NGBs to

- relinquish 90% of the categories in which they can sell sponsorship
- relinquish all broadcast rights
- refrain from selling cosponsorships, signage, or hospitality rights in unprotected areas
- give ACOP sponsors more rights that NGB sponsors
- give ACOP sponsors the rights to first refusal of NGB events
- allow ACOP sponsors to freely grant to "others"—e.g. competitors of the NGB's own sponsors—marketing rights to the federation. (International Events Group, 1992b, p. 2).

Generally, this proposal received little support from the major sport-governing bodies. Although few of the high-profile NGBs even gave the offer consideration, many of the lesser-known NGBs saw this as a great opportunity. For the 2002 Olympic Winter Games in Salt Lake City, NGBs have been encouraged to join the OPUS (Olympic Properties of the United States) program. This joint venture between the Olympic Organizing Committee and the USOC provided more opportunities than did the program for the Atlanta Games in 1996.

The NGBs with the greatest exposure and public recognition are engaged in their own sponsorship deals. USA Track and Field has signed agreements with several sponsors. Their $1-million deal with Nike provides apparel, official uniforms, and accessories. Another NGB, U.S.A. Swimming, offers ongoing sponsorship packages ranging from $25,000–$500,000. Their sponsors include Murine, Gatorade, Speedo, and Phillips 66. USA Swimming and USA Track and Field have also signed Fuji as their official film supplier, which undermines the IOC and USOC arrangements with Kodak. USA Gymnastics has chosen several sponsors that are already associated with the USOC. Specifically, they have deals with Visa, Reebok, McDonald's, and Hilton.

The USA women's basketball team had a spectacular 1996 Olympic performance and used NBA Properties as its agent for their sponsorship and licensing arrangements. This arrangement helped marketing agreements and reduced conflicts that could have occurred with the formation of the WNBA.

Individual Olympic sports are also involved through their International Federations. International Federations (IFs) are the worldwide organizing bodies for specific Olympic sports. The International Amateur Athletics Federation (IAAF) has signed seven sponsors for the organization and also works to secure sponsors for the IAAF's World Cup Championships in track and field ("Official IAAF Partners," 1999).

The Olympic Organizing Committees have benefited from both sponsorship agreements and from television revenues. The IOC provides the organizing committee with a share of those revenue streams. The organizing committee is free, however, to pursue sponsorships that are not prohibited by the IOC. The Nagano Olympic Organizing Committee secured sponsorship from Mizuno as the "Official Outfitter" and from Kirin Beer as Gold Sponsor for the 1998 Winter Games.

Another strategy associated with sponsorship that has been used during the Olympics is ambush marketing. It has been defined as "a promotional strategy whereby a non-sponsor attempts to capitalize on the popularity/prestige of a property by giving the false impression that it is a sponsor, [and is] often employed by the competitors of a property's official sponsors" (Ukman, 1995, p. 42). Ambushing official sponsors became a successful strategy when Kodak upstaged Fuji in the 1984 Olympic Games by purchasing sponsorships with the USOC and buying numerous television ads touting their association with the USOC. Although Fuji had purchased the right to be an official sponsor from the Los Angeles Olympic Organizing Committee, the U.S. public never really knew that Fuji, not Kodak, was the official sponsor of the 1984 Games (Marsano, 1987). Visa and American Express have also engaged in similar tactics. American Express even took Visa (a TOP sponsor) to court alleging that they mislead the public in their Olympic advertising. Visa made similar allegations about American Express running misleading advertising. Because of tactics like these, each organization must set in place procedures to protect its rights as a sponsor.

As a sport marketer, you will have to decide if you are willing to engage in ambush marketing. Nike has opted for ambush strategies during the Olympic Games and World Cup soccer events. In these instances, Nike marketers have determined that it is in their company's best interest to put marketing dollars into peripheral promotional activities rather than purchasing official rights directly from event owners. During the Atlanta Olympic Games, Nike erected a pavilion near Olympic Park and sponsored a multitude of athletes from around the globe. They felt that these ele-

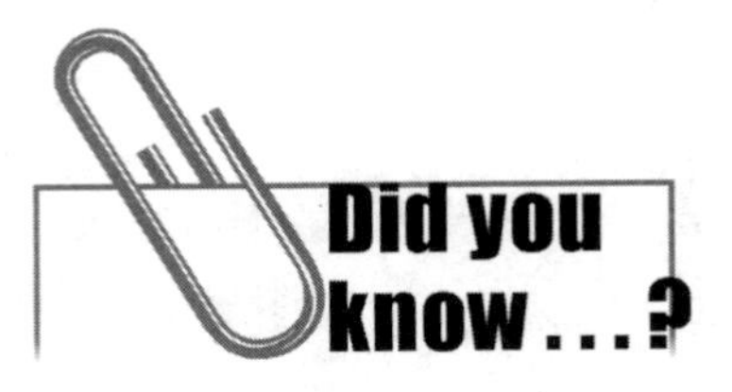

Some of the newest types of corporate sponsors of NASCAR are business-to-business companies that serve contemporary markets like telecommunications and cyberspace:

Cartoon Network, Universal Studios (Cartoons)

Bell South, Trac Fone (Telecommunications)

Philips (Electronics)

Mattel (Toys)

Primestar, *TV Guide*, TBS (Television)

Source: *Sports Business Journal*, August 23–29, 1999, p. 10

ments would be more cost-effective than paying a rights fee to event organizers. At the 1994 World Cup, they cleverly distributed free hats with the Brazilian team colors, country name, and a Nike Swoosh to spectators at specified venues. This tactic gave them an in-stadium presence and generated positive consumer impressions. Their strategy of sponsoring the Brazilian team ($200 million) was not as beneficial as they had hoped when the Brazilians did not qualify for the 1998 World Cup final.

As a sport marketer, one of the most difficult tasks that you will need to perform is evaluating the asking price of available sponsorships. The owner of the event must be able to articulate a fair market price for its sponsorship packages. An article in the sponsorship industry newsletter, *IEG Sponsorship Report*, gave considerable detail on the appropriate considerations and calculations for pricing sponsorships. As with all product pricing, a thorough analysis of the market must be completed. The sport marketer must know what other sport organizations are charging for their sponsorship packages and what the buyers are paying for other promotional/media tools (International Events Group, 1992a).

In all sponsorships there are both tangible and intangible components. The tangible components include media advertising, signage, tickets, programs, and sampling. Each of these activities has a market value. Most organizations include advertising components in their proposals to sponsors. Often the sponsors get tagged to the advertising for the event. In this case, the sponsor simply gets to attach its logo to the promotional ads for the event. The value of these ads for the sponsor certainly does not equate to the full value of the ad. A general guide is about 10% of the value of an identical media buy. If more than one sponsor's logo is included in the media piece, the value should be reduced accordingly (International Events Group, 1992a). Some sponsorship packages offer complimentary media space for the sole use of the sponsor. These "free ads" are typically obtained as a trade-out from a media sponsor of the event. If you are allowed full discretionary use of the space, full value can be applied to that piece of the package based on current advertising rates.

Value calculation for sampling opportunities is more difficult to ascertain. In 1997, Rollerblades teamed with New York City's Parks Department to provide complimentary in-line skates to all park security officers. Through this program, Rollerblades received millions of favorable impressions from park visitors. In addition, Rollerblades was granted an opportunity to stage product demonstrations and skating clinics throughout the NYC park system (A.R.C., 1998). Probably the best approach for value calculation is to investigate the costs of similar activities at area shopping malls and trade shows.

Event tickets and advertising in programs are quite difficult to value for both the organization and for the sponsor. Some organizations simply price all of their sponsor tickets in the VIP section at double the going ticket price. It does not really matter what the organization says they cost because all of the tickets are packaged for sponsors or VIPs. It costs organizers the same to print $50 on a ticket as it does to print $30. The same game is often played with program advertising. To be honest, tickets and program ads should be priced at a competitive rate for both sponsors and non-sponsors.

The intangibles of a sponsorship proposal are often the most important to you as a sponsor, but are extremely difficult to value. Sponsors pay to be associated with an event and typically display the event or property's logo on products or packaging. Can this really help sales? Data collected for the 1994 Soccer World Cup indicated that 63% of consumers were more likely to purchase a product with a World Cup USA logo than one without the logo (International Events Group, 1994). In addition, 73% of NASCAR fans were found to choose a sponsor's product over one from a non-sponsor (Hagstrom, 1998). The desire for sponsors to associate with an event or property is also dependent on its prestige value. Is the sponsored event the "one and only" like the Olympics or the Indianapolis 500, or is it just another softball tournament? Of course, the more prominent and unique the event, the higher the value is that your company can gain through the sponsorship.

Supply and demand are always relevant factors in pricing. In the 1990s, the supply of sponsorship opportunities has been greater than has been the number of companies with the financial capability to sponsor events. Therefore, sport organizations seeking sponsorship opportunities can exert competitive leverage on pricing on property owners. Finally, a major consideration centers on value-in-kind donations from sponsors. Some sponsors like to barter their products with property owners in lieu of cash payments. This situation works well when your company can offer products that are actually used in the event. Take, for example, hurdles for track and field. If the event uses your hurdles during the competition, your company will gain increased exposure through media images of your product. Also important in the barter business is value calculation of in-kind donations. You can often obtain full retail value of your product in trade for advertising or other rights from the event, whereas your true cost for the item was the wholesale price.

> Data shows that the money sponsors pay to display an event or property's logo on their products or packaging is a good investment—consumers are more likely to buy the product with the logo than one without.

Event owners often present sponsorship packages priced approximately 25% lower than the individual package components. However, you may be able to engage in what has been called cherry picking. This practice involves selecting only the most profitable aspects of a package and paying for them separately. Some organizations avoid this by refusing to partition packages or by pricing the individual pieces so high that the package is clearly the best buy. As for payment scheme, most properties require at least 65% at signing, with the remainder due prior to the event (International Events Group, 1994). Most properties will not allow sponsors to negotiate payment plans that postdate the event. However, if it can be arranged, it may be in your best interest in the situation where the results guaranteed in the contract were not achieved. In these instances, final payments to the property holder could be withheld.

As a sponsor, you should also understand that once you have purchased the sponsorship, your company will need to incorporate the event sponsorship into current marketing programs. Some estimates have set the promotional budget to drive the sponsorship recognition to the market at six times the cost of the rights fee. More conservative estimates suggest that an amount equal to your investment in the property can adequately leverage your involvement and produce recognition at the retail level. MasterCard actually uses a 2-to-1 rule. According to their senior vice president of global promotions and sponsorship, "if you're not going to leverage it, don't buy it" (qtd. in "Sponsors Reveal," 1999, p. 7)

Trends in Grassroots Sponsorship

One of the most important issues that sport marketers should look into is how their corporation can benefit from sponsoring at the grassroots level. Many sport-related companies are realizing that speaking to consumers in a local environment may be

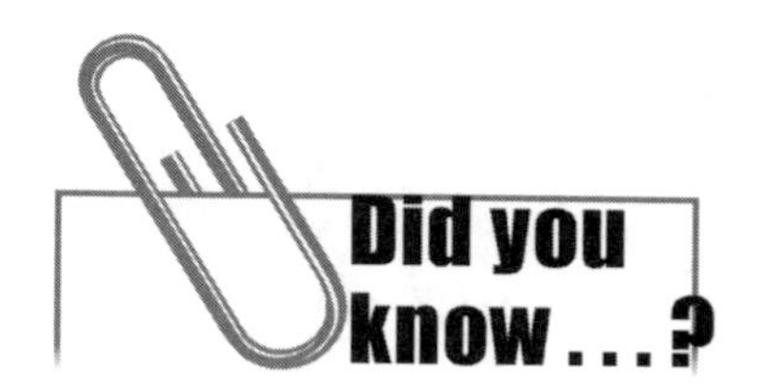

Rodeo is one of the fastest growing participant, spectator, and professional sports in the United States. One part of the rodeo sports industry, the Professional Bull Riders tour, has grown to

- 20 tour events in 1999
- Combined purse of $5.5 million
- 85 million viewers for televised events on TNN.

Source: *Sports Business Journal*, August 23–29, 1999, p. 2

more persuasive than nationwide involvement. However, some caution should be exercised when working with grassroots events. Event personnel are often largely composed of volunteers with unproven success. Thus, when you choose to sponsor their event or property, your corporate reputation is in their hands.

The movement to event sponsorship and away from individual endorsement should continue as consumer data show that the credibility of individual endorsers is low. Events can be successful for the sponsor regardless of who wins, and they are less likely to become entangled in controversy (i.e., Mike Tyson theory). However, the scandal surrounding the Salt Lake City 2002 Olympic bid that surfaced in 1999 showed that events are not immune to controversy that could adversely affect sponsors. The very nature of the event can also cause trouble for sponsors. For instance, animal rights activists have threatened to boycott products from the sponsors associated with the Iditarod dogsled race because of alleged cruelty to animals. The Professional Rodeo Cowboys Association moved to diminish the possibility of controversy through the publication of a brochure detailing the methods employed to safeguard animals used in rodeo events.

Another interesting sponsorship trend appeared when sport computer game manufacturer Electronic Arts began selling sponsorship on outfield walls and other signage in its video games. These proved to be very effective in targeting youth markets.

Sport marketers can certainly look toward including the arts and social issues in their marketing campaigns (Greenwald and Fernandez-Balboa, 1998). Consider these three noteworthy examples. The Denver Nuggets of the NBA had a very successful program exchanging game tickets for handguns. For many years, the United States Sports Academy used various sponsors to support a sport art museum housed on its campus. In relation to social issues, an event was started in 1996 to honor the late college basketball coach Jim Valvano and raise money for cancer research. The college basketball tournament entitled "Coaches vs. Cancer" raises over $1,000,000 annually.

Another notable trend is the sponsorship of women's sport. According to Reynolds (1998), "an increasing number of companies are embracing women's sport with sponsorship dollars. Companies are waking up to the power of marketing to women" (p. 30). Thus, some corporations are turning increasingly to outstanding women athletes for their endorsement options: "Today's crop of women's sports standouts is, for the most part, more accessible than their male counterparts. They will autograph posters and spend time to motivate young fans" (Rodin, 1998, p. 34). In addition, women athletes are also less likely to behave in immoral and unethical ways that might embarrass the sponsor.

The power of the Internet has also made it possible for you to expand your dominion for securing candidates for endorsements and events for sponsor partnering. MCI posted a Request for Proposals (RFP) on its website in order to investigate a wide range of events and properties for sponsorship. Shoe manufacturer Airwalk also used its website to attract potential endorsees through an on-line application form. Airwalk's Internet strategy seemed particularly appropriate given the lifestyles of its primary clientele.

In the dynamic worlds of sport and finance, new trends will certainly emerge. The challenge for sport marketers is to keep abreast of the industry and creatively seek opportunities to use sponsorships and endorsements to market products and services.

Chapter Summary

The purpose of this chapter was to describe how sport organizations could enhance their marketing efforts through athlete endorsements and sport sponsorships. Because of their knowledge and power within certain groups, sport companies can effectively use opinion leaders to increase product sales. Opinion leaders can also be used in product sampling and prototype testing. Endorsement of products by individual athletes has been a marketing practice in sport for decades, yet its popularity has been waning. A credibility problem with individual endorsements exists because many consumers believe that sports celebrities were endorsing products only for the money. The scope of all marketing strategies and tactics must also include attention to the organization's social responsibility and ethical business practices.

A trend that appears to be successful is cross-promotion, whereby several companies band together around an athlete to gain additional exposure. The objectives for sponsorship center on market communication. The company can use sport sponsorship to communicate to the market that it is a successful and socially responsible firm that produces and sells quality products (Ferrand and Pagés, 1996). The concerns for the future are whether the sport sponsorship and endorsement field are saturated and whether sponsors will switch to other areas like the arts and regional festivals to accomplish their objectives.

Chapter Questions for Study

1. Describe the advantages and disadvantages of having an individual athlete as a product endorser.
2. Compare and contrast the sponsorship rights available through each level of Olympic sports: IOC, NOCs, NGBs, IFs.

Learning Activity

Attend a local sport event where sponsors have signage displayed in the venue. After exiting the event, ask patrons which, if any, of the sponsors they can remember.

Professional Associations and Organizations

IEG Sponsorship Report
International Events Group
640 North LaSalle, Suite 600
Chicago, IL 60610-3777
www.sponsorship.com
1-800-834-4850

Sports Market Place
Franklin-Covey
7250 N. 16th Street
Phoenix, AZ 85020
www.sportscareers.com

Suggested Readings

Reed, M. H. (1990). *Legal aspects of promoting and sponsoring events.* Chicago: International Events Group.

Stotlar, D. K. (2001). *Developing successful sport sponsorship plans.* Fitness Information Technologies, Morgantown, WV

Chapter 15

Using Licensing and Logos in the Sport Industry

Overview

Licensing is the act of granting to another party the right to use a protected logo, design, or trademark (Irwin and Stotlar, 1993). Although trademark licensing may be traced back hundreds of years, dramatic growth occurred in the 1980s and 1990s. Comic book heroes, cartoons, schools, professional teams, clubs, causes, characters, and many other subjects became featured designs on clothing. However, sales of sport-related merchandise subsided in the late 1990s due in part to changes in fashion trends. Regardless of fluctuations in market conditions, licensing can be an effective component in branding strategies for many sport entities.

Historically, sport organizations have found it desirable to initiate efforts to protect the investment in their name and marks through trademark licensing (Irwin, 1990). Through such programs, sport organizations could receive name recognition and substantial revenue. In 1963, the National Football League established its licensing program to bring the protection of team names and insignia under central control. On the collegiate scene, the University of California at Los Angeles (UCLA) began its licensing program in 1973 (Irwin and Stotlar, 1993). Other sport organizations such as the International Olympic Committee, Gold's Gym, ABC's *Monday Night Football* and ESPN have also established strong licensing programs.

On the revenue side, the NFL generated over $3 billion in 1998 from licensed product sales. The other professional leagues reported significant revenues as well. The National Basketball Association realized $2.3 billion in sales, followed by Major League Baseball at $1.85 billion and the National Hockey League earning slightly more than $1 billion. The NHL published its own 72-page catalog, *Hot Off the Ice*, which featured over 1,000 items ranging from traditional replica jerseys to a menorah in the shape of a hockey stick. The segment of the industry that showed the most dramatic growth in the late 1990s was the Women's National Basketball Association, where sales tripled from the 1997 to the 1998 season (Bhonslay, 1999a; Rofe, 1999).

Unfortunately, sales of licensed professional sport apparel declined 30–40% in 2000–2001. College-logoed merchandise showed a small, but solid increase of 8% over the same period (Cassidy, 2001). The significant declines in the late 1990s pushed three of the biggest companies producing licensed sports wear into bankruptcy. Pro-Player and Starter went bankrupt in 1999, and in 2000, Logo Athletic also filed for bankruptcy.

The profits generated from licensing are not limited to professional teams completing in league play. NASCAR was able to generate $1.2 billion in licensed product sales ("NASCAR Merchandising," 2001). An analysis of their merchandising indicated that 50% of sales came from apparel, 25% from collectible die-cast cars, 10% from trading cards, and 15% from other products (Bhonslay, 1999b; Hagstrom, 1998). Individual events have also been capable of deriving revenues from licensed products. The Masters golf tournament was successful in increasing its revenues through upgrading its licensing program. Its profits increased from $2 million in 1992 to over $9 million in 1996 (Tarde, 1997). In other events, World Cup France '98 generated $1.4 billion in worldwide sales, the 1999 Women's World Cup was estimated to produce between $50 and $100 million, the 1998 Nagano Olympics brought in $29 million from licensed merchandise, and the 1999 Super Bowl produced $3 million in retail sales (Bhonslay, 1999b; Rofe, 1999).

Thus, the total international sales of licensed sport products are formidable. Worldwide licensed apparel sales were estimated at $10 billion in 1998 (Rofe, 1999), and sales of all licensed merchandise were $110 billion (Goldfisher, 1998). If you think that this effort is not worthwhile for collegiate institutions and amateur sports, consider that sport organizations such as the United States Olympic Committee receive

The large number of college sports fans continues to drive the sales of licensed sports products.
Photo reprinted by permission of WVU Photography.

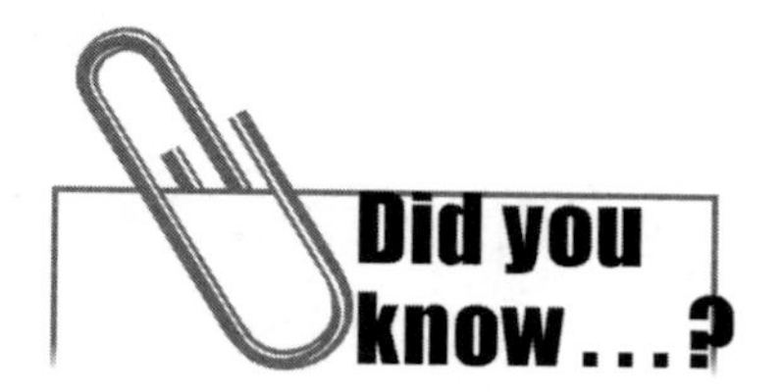

The three largest tennis agent companies:

- International Management Group
- Advantage International
- Pro Serv, Inc.

Source: *Sports Business Journal*, August 23–29, 1999, p. 47

revenues in excess of $5 million per year from their licensing programs. Several collegiate sport entities profit measurably from the sale of licensed products. The University of Michigan ($6 million) and the University of Kentucky ($5 million) are among the more than 20 institutions that make over $1 million per year based on 7 to 10% of gross yearly sales (Blumenstyk, 1996).

In 1999, the National Association of Collegiate Directors of Athletics (NACDA) initiated an organization to provide a forum for information on licensing in the collegiate setting. This organization, the National Collegiate Licensing Association, will assist all interested parties in strengthening the market for licensed apparel through leveraging retailers. Without the organization, it would be difficult for individual institutions to secure shelf space in the market. Furthermore, the organization can work to set more uniform royalty fees and payment schedules.

In sport licensing, four factors led to the development of organized sport licensing (Irwin, 1990). One of those factors was the increased popularity of sport and the resulting media coverage. Successful athletic teams, especially in football and basketball, have, for many years, been a rallying point for the public. Increased popularity led to greater attendance at games, leading to increased media coverage. This, in turn, led to increased popularity, higher attendance figures, and even more media coverage. Stadiums and arenas were enlarged, front pages of major newspapers carried the outcomes of major sports contests, and television magnified sports and multiplied their popularity. Today, sporting events receive headline coverage virtually year round.

Another development during the 1970s was the technology involved with screen printing or silk-screening, which greatly expanded the licensing industry. Blank garments were easily acquired from a number of mills and could be printed to meet any demands. Printed T-shirts became a communications medium during the 1970s. Adults, as well as children, were part of a market that grew dramatically throughout the 1980s.

In sport, the demand for imprinted goods was advanced through fan pride, loyalty, and desire to support the team by wearing team colors and designs. Anyone who has attended major events knows the emotions that fans generate in support of their teams or favorite player. People found themselves extremely attracted to their favorite school, team, or player and desired a means through which they could express their feelings. As the market for imprinted products expanded, fans sought licensed goods as a method of expressing their support.

During the 1980s, the costs of running competitive sport programs increased dramatically. As a result, the sale of imprinted sport merchandise was activated to help build revenues. Parallel with the increases in sales, problems began to occur with logo abuse and counterfeit merchandise. In 1998, losses to counterfeiting were estimated to be $200 billion (Bernstein, 1998). During the Major League Baseball 2000 "subway series," 24 federal marshals confiscated items from 80 bootleggers. After the final World Series Game, the NYPD raided one factory and retrieved $1 million in counterfeit goods and an official MLB logo-disk containing all of the League's protected marks. With these levels of abuse, sport managers quickly decided that they needed greater control over the use of their marks to prevent the obnoxious designs, poor-quality merchandise, and product liability risks that they were beginning to face.

In a sport licensing program, the marketer typically grants a manufacturer the right to use the organization's logo (or indicia) in producing and selling merchandise. The licensee is required to sign a contract, pay royalties, and adhere to strict licensing regulations. Royalties for licensed goods typically run about 6 to 10% of the price for which an item is sold.

As a marketing vehicle, licensing enables sport organizations to generate consumer awareness and interest through logoed products, all with minimal capital outlay (Irwin and Stotlar, 1993). The established protocol for licensing revenues in most professional sport leagues is to engage in profit sharing. All of the major professional leagues collect royalty payments through league subsidiaries normally called "Properties" (e.g., NBA Properties, NFL Properties). These entities collect all licensing revenues and then distribute them equally across all teams in the league. Although teams and events have profited from licensing, sport leagues have also entered the market. The NBA and NASCAR began to open retail outlets to sell not only team and player/driver items but also organizational apparel. These sport organizations believed that they could build strong brands around their own logo (NBA, NASCAR). The USOC also initiated similar brand-building activities in 1998. The market for sport-logoed items is no longer limited to the team's home city, campus, or a local market, but extends around the globe.

Products that carry an organization's logo provide a relatively inexpensive way to increase consumer awareness and interest.

To ensure standardization and quality, many souvenirs such as clothing, mugs, or novelties bearing sport logos are put through rigorous marketing and approval processes. Each item is checked for both quality and design. Products of inferior quality can be rejected, and strict labeling requirements can be enforced so the consumers can identify the merchandise as authentic. In addition, the product manufacturers can be required to carry product liability insurance, which protects the organization if legal action is filed because of an incident involving a licensed product.

Because of the popularity of sport licensing and trademarks on manufactured items and the potential revenue, commercial, professional, intercollegiate, and amateur sports organization marketers must develop a significant knowledge base in this area. There has also been an increasing amount of litigation in this field, and the guidelines governing the use of sports trademarks are still being established in the courts (Wong, 1994). As the national and international markets for merchandise bearing sport logos, names, and indicia develop, sport administrators will be required to seek legal avenues to protect their market, products, and marks. However, most sport organizations know little about how to protect their marks or how to license legally protectable properties to second parties for commercial use (Irwin, 1990).

Licensing is extremely important to the sport organization because it provides control over the way the company name and indicia are portrayed on merchandise.

Another aspect of licensing involves licensing a business name to other businesses. This is similar to a concept with which you may be familiar, franchising. Under licensing agreements, sport organizations such as fitness clubs (e.g., Powerhouse Gyms) purchase the right to use an established name, but are free to operate the business in any manner they wish. However, in a franchise arrangement, the proprietor must purchase the franchise rights and typically agree to relinquish some operational control. Included with the purchase are restrictions on business practices often relating to facility size, mandated equipment, and audits/inspections by corporate officers.

Although many of the benefits associated with franchise and licensing are best suited for start-up businesses, a recent trend has been for existing businesses to switch over to a recognized industry name through this process (Shaffer, 1997).

The Legalities of Trademark Licensing in Sport

The case law governing sport licensing is sparse but has developed rapidly based on traditional trademark law. Sport organizations therefore must develop a firm legal basis for requiring that users of their trademarks obtain permission to use the trademarks and for requiring that the users pay royalties for the privilege. In order to more fully understand trademark licensing, you need to be familiar with the following principles, terms, and definitions surrounding trademark law.

Trademark Principles

The Federal Trademark Act of 1946, Lanham Act 45, 15 U. S. C. 1051–1127 (1946), commonly known as the Lanham Act, governs the law of trademarks, the registration of trademarks, and remedies for the infringement of registered trademarks (Wong, 1994). The Trademarks Law Revision Act, which went into effect in 1989, was Congress's first overall revision of the Lanham Act since 1946. The revised Lanham Act created major changes in federal trademark law that are highly relevant to sport trademark registration and licensing. The most fundamental changes were in the definitions of the use of trademarks (Irwin, 1990):

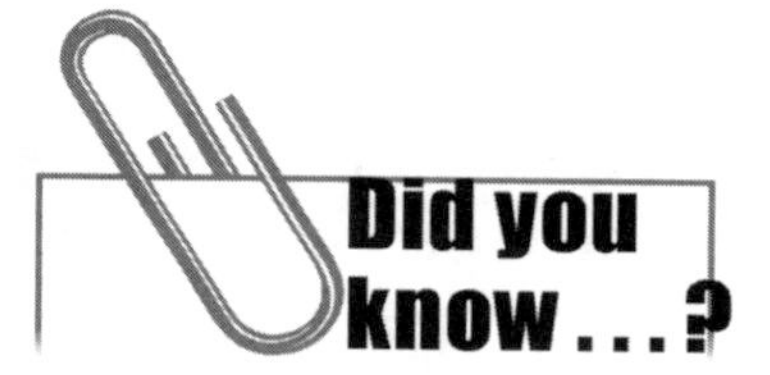

The economic impact of snowmobiling in Pennsylvania in 1996–97 was approximately $95.5 million.

Source: Lebanon Valley College of Pennsylvania and Pennsylvania State Snowmobile Association

1. Trademark: "Any word, name, symbol, or device, or any combination thereof used to identify and distinguish the goods of one person from those manufactured or sold by others."
2. Service mark "Any word, name, symbol, or device, or any combination thereof used to identify and distinguish the services of one person from the service of others."
3. Collective mark: "A trademark or service mark used by members of a cooperative, association, or other collective group or organization."
4. Mark: "A shorthand reference to any type of mark, including trademarks, service mark, and collective marks."
5. Registered mark: "A mark registered in the United States Patent and Trademark Office, as provided under the Act." (United States Department of Commerce, 1993, p. 1)

Infringement of a Trademark

The Act defines trademark infringement as the reproduction, counterfeiting, copying, or imitation, in commerce, of a registered mark "in connection with the sale, offering for sale, distribution, or advertising of any goods or services on or in connection with which such use is likely to cause confusion, or to cause mistake or to deceive without consent of the registrant" (Basic Facts . . . , 1993, p. 7).

Secondary meaning. Secondary meaning is a mental recognition in the buyer's mind, associating symbols, words, colors, and designs with goods from a single source. It tests the connection in the buyer's mind between the product bearing the mark and its source (Wong, 1994). Certain terms that are selected or invented for the express purpose of functioning as trademarks may be classified as inherently distinctive. Such marks are protectable and registerable immediately on use. One such example would be the swoosh created by Nike. However, some potential marks describe products or services, geographic designations, or personal surnames. To qualify for protection as a mark, the courts require evidence that such a term has acquired secondary meaning; that is, consumers associate the products or services under the term with one particular source (Wong). The example here is that one shoe company produced a football shoe called Montana. They claimed that it was a generic reference to a geographical region. Football player Joe Montana, his agent, and eventually the courts disagreed.

Laches. Laches may arise when a party fails to assert a right or claim within a reasonable time, and the other party relies on this inaction to claim use to the other party's mark (Battle, Bailey, and Siegal, 1991). An example of just this case arose when the University of Pittsburgh tried to stop Champion from producing sweatshirts with the Pitt logo. The court in this case said that because Pitt had previously allowed Champion to use its logo, it could not now prevent its use by Champion.

Each of the types of marks described earlier is protected equally under the Lanham Act. Sport organization names, team names, and logos may be described as trademarks, service marks, or collective marks (Wong, 1994). Any of these marks used on items such as clothing and novelties as well as services is entitled to protection. Registered marks are not always confined to team names and indicia. In the not-too-distant past, sports facilities registered their names, including the 1988 Olympic Oval in Calgary, Wrigley Field in Chicago, and the Houston Astrodome.

Because of the complexity of managing a sport-licensing program (integrating financial, promotional, and legal responsibilities), there have been organized efforts to control the use of sport organizations' logos, trademarks, and copyrights. As a result, organizations have been faced with a serious dilemma: internal versus external management (Irwin and Stotlar, 1993). Irwin's (1990) research and subsequent publications shed considerable light on this decision.

Several large companies have entered the business to assist sport organizations in the management of their licensing programs. In these organizations, the licensing agent helps in the protection of an organization's logo or marks. One such company, the Collegiate Licensing Company, developed seven basic goals with short-term and long-term strategies (Battle et al., 1991; Bhonslay, 1999b; Conklin, 1999). The consortium not only affects its members (over 170 in 1999), but it also directly and indirectly affects nonmember schools. Their goals include the following:

1. To attract, maintain, and strengthen a prestigious base of universities, bowls, and athletic conferences.

2. To attract and maintain a base of licensees sufficiently large to cover all potential market segments and distribute all marketable products.

3. To identify retailers that are current or potential carriers of collegiate merchandise and show them the requirements and opportunities of collegiate licensing.

4. To identify consumers of collegiate products and encourage them to buy licensed products.

5. To improve the effectiveness of current methods of enforcement and to develop new methods.

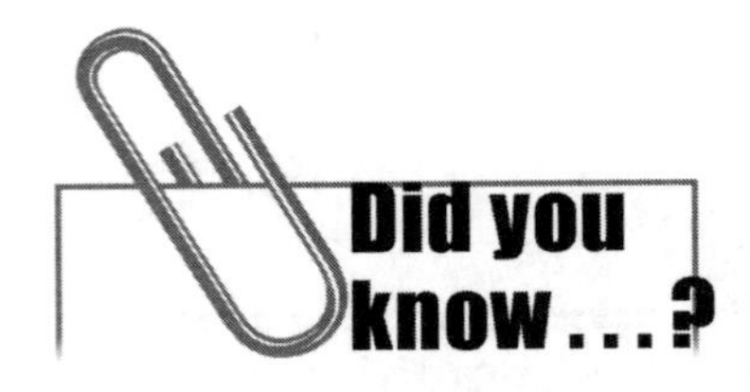

The Superdome was constructed for $163 million in the early 1970s and has had an economic impact of $4.6 billion in its first 20 years of use.

Source: http://www.superdome.com/presskit.htm

6. To establish marketing programs that can expand the market for "Officially Licensed Collegiate Products" and take advantage of synergistic marketing, advertising, and promotional programs.
7. To provide unparalleled services to member institutions and licensees and to develop a database and reports to give management the information needed to analyze, evaluate, and manage progress toward the goals previously listed.

Operational Protocol Factors in Sport Licensing

- Program Governance and Leadership
- Designated internal licensing authority
- Principal licensing assignment full-time
- Direct report to central administrator
- Licensing policy committee assembled
- Professional licensing agency assistance
- Program Protection and Enforcement
- Legal specialist consultation
- Majority of logos registered as trademarks
- Licensee application and screening process
- License issuance and renewal procedures
- Basic agreement nonexclusive
- Execution of joint-use agreements
- Execution of international licenses
- Product sample required for quality control
- "Licensed product" identification required
- Counterfeit logo detection procedures
- Counterfeit logo reduction procedures
- Program Promotions and Public Relations
- Proactive recruitment of licensees
- Proactive recruitment of retailers
- Licensee/retailer public relations program
- Advertising used to promote products/program
- Publicity used to promote products/program
- Licensing program information published
- Revenue Management
- Advance payment required
- Uniform royalty charged on all products
- Written royalty exemption policy
- Royalty verifications routinely conducted
- Royalty verifications conducted by specialist
- Written royalty distribution policy

Although private companies handle some of the nation's large universities, many schools and sport organizations run their own programs. As noted earlier, all of the professional sports leagues (NBA, MLB, NHL) have internal entities that handle their licensed products pioneered by NFL Properties, Inc.

Another twist of the licensing setting occurred in 2000 when Nike signed an arrangement with British football club Manchester United for $432.3 million (10 years beginning in 2002) to manage its licensing program. Not only did Nike obtain exclusive worldwide sales of merchandise, but they also were authorized to run the worldwide merchandising program for the team. Previously, Manchester United had established stores in China, Singapore, Kuala Lumpur, Dubai, Kuwait, Dublin, and Cape Town. Manchester United and Nike formed a joint-venture business with one half of the board of directors from both Manchester United and Nike. The combined entity will split all profits 50-50 (Kaplan, 2001).

Research by Irwin (1990) examined the pros and cons of internal versus external management and found that most organizations are better off handling their own programs. Specific factors in program design were established against which sport organizations could judge their programs. A review of these operational factors seems appropriate (Irwin 1990; Irwin and Stotlar, 1993).

The advantages and disadvantages assignable to internally and externally managed licensing programs must be reviewed within the context of the organization's resources. Generally, internally managed programs are more expensive to run, but they yield higher profits. External or agency-managed programs usually offer easier access to wholesale and retail networks and may have better nationwide success.

Bhonslay (1999b) indicated that many sport organizations utilize agencies to initiate a licensing program. The agencies typically have a higher level of expertise, more manufacturing contacts, and understanding of all of the management factors that must be addressed. Once the licensing program is operating efficiently, the sport organization can bring the program in-house and obtain greater control. Furthermore, profits can be maximized by avoiding the 30% commissions normally charged by agencies.

Sport licensing is a journey, not a single destination. All factors affecting the program must be considered. Irwin's (1990) conclusions prescribed a licensing paradigm. The major components of a licensing system should include

1. An examination of the feasibility of assigning a full-time licensing administrator.
2. An evaluation of the cost-effectiveness of internal versus external management of the program based on internal resources and potential markets and profits.
3. Identification of a single administrative authority for licensing agreements.
4. The development of policy for the issuance of exclusive and nonexclusive license agreements.
5. The design of specific royalty and exemption policies.
6. Application procedures for issuance/renewal of licenses.
7. A process whereby licensees must disclose financial stability, distribution intent, and licensing references.
8. A request for advance payments from licensees as earnest money to be applied to future royalties.
9. The establishment of a uniform royalty rate calculated on the net cost of the licensed item sold.
10. The requirement to furnish finished samples of the licensed merchandise.
11. The requirement to furnish certificates of insurance pertaining to licensed merchandise sold.
12. The federal registration of at least one of the organization's marks.
13. The required use of licensee identification on all merchandise distributed (hang tag, label, etc.).
14. A plan for the allocation of royalties received by the organization.
15. An enforcement policy including the responsibility to police merchandisers and issue cease and desist orders.
16. Consultation with trademark law specialists as needed.
17. The performance of compliance review with licensees.
18. The recruitment and recognition of licensees on a sustained basis.
19. The development of licensing brochures or guidelines for distribution to prospective licensees.
20. The reporting structure for the licensing administrator within the organization (p. 151).

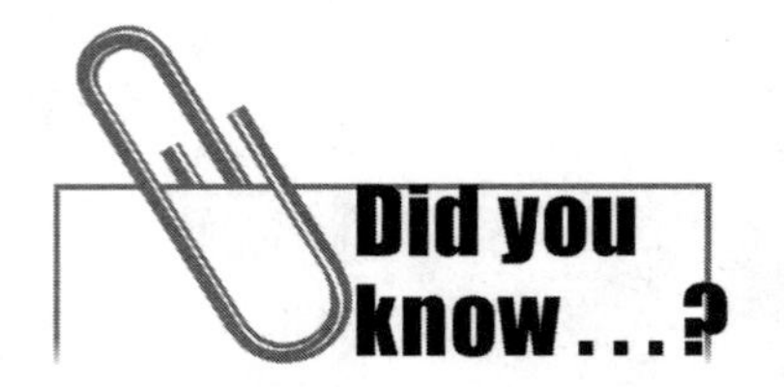

Gay Games V in 1999 in Amsterdam was one of the largest multi-sports events of the 1990s. The number of participants was 14,600.

Source: Pitts & Ayers, NASSM paper, 1999

Many of the professional baseball teams (Chicago Cubs, Atlanta Braves, San Francisco Giants, and New York Yankees, among others) have developed methods that borrowed strengths from both systems. Although MLB administers the licensing program for all baseball clubs, these clubs aggressively began to sell their own merchan-

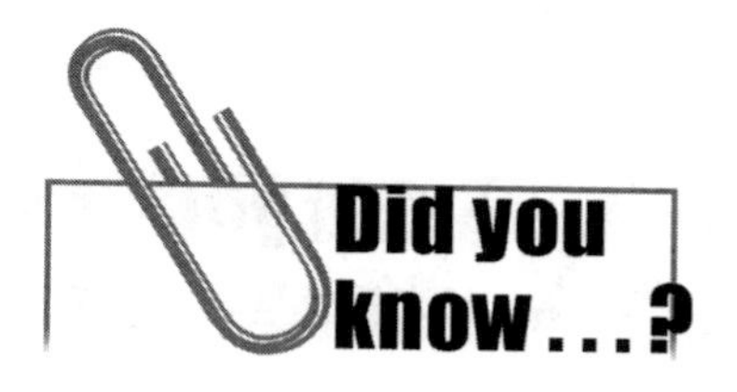

The economic impact of Gay Games V in 1999 in Amsterdam was $350 million.

Source: Pitts & Ayers, NASSM paper, 1999.

dise through specialty catalogs, corporate-owned retail stores, and on-line sales. Not content with collecting only the 10% royalty provided by MLB, these organizations began selling the merchandise directly to their fans to bring retail profit margins to the team. These profit margins averaged 50% after expenses were taken from the typical 350% markup from wholesale cost. By 1999, 40 major professional sport teams operated off-site retail stores. Some teams have opted to establish "single-team stores" like the MLB Colorado Rockies chain of Rockies Dugout stores. Other organizations like the NBA Utah Jazz, began with Jazz-related souvenirs in 4 stores and expanded to 28 full-line shops (Fanzz). In Phoenix, corporately owned shops sell merchandise for all three of their professional franchises, the NBA Suns, the Arizona Diamondbacks, and the Phoenix Coyotes (Bernstein, 1998). The San Francisco Giants opened their first on-line store in 1998 and found that sales quickly grew to equal that of a traditional mall-based shop (Goldfisher, 1998). With the increased use of the Internet by many sport organizations, about 50% of all U.S. licensed product sales in 2000 were accomplished through e-commerce.

Regardless of the system employed, the major objectives of any sport licensing program are threefold: (a) Protection—to protect the trademarks of the organization, (b) Public Relations—to create a favorable image and positive exposure for the organization, and (c) Profit—to maximize revenues (Irwin,1990).

Trademark Licensing Agreements

Program enforcement procedures include all methods of securing and exercising protection of the sport organization's property rights in its name, logo, seals, and symbols. As sport licensing programs are constructed and policy parameters are established, licensing administrators typically develop contractual relationships with licensees as a part of the program enforcement protocol (Irwin, 1990). The primary legal base for this contractual relationship has been the licensing agreement. This agreement should provide for controls, checks, and balances regarding the exclusivity of mark, usage, royalty management, and quality control (Irwin, 1990). Previous empirical data have indicated the authority to grant and execute licensing agreements on behalf of the organization came primarily from upper-level administration. Gaston (1984) found that 42% of respondents identified the financial vice president as the source of authority for executing most licensing agreements.

According to experts in the industry (Baghdikian, 1996; Reed, 1989), the elements that should be examined in a licensing agreement include, first of all, the parties entering into the agreement. The pertinent definitions in the agreement must also be detailed. Service marks and trademarks should be defined with attention to the level of protection through either federal registration or common law use.

The contract should also describe the specific products to be licensed, the duration of the agreement, and terms under which the agreement can be terminated or modified. It is also imperative that the royalty and payment structure be addressed, complete with details providing for audits. Specifically, the contract should define the royalty on net sales without deduction for shipping, advertising, or even returns or uncollectable accounts. The agreement should prescribe the reporting procedures and the payment methods and schedule. Other areas traditionally covered would include the types of products to be licensed, the rights for approval, ownership of artwork and designs, insurance and indemnification, and the territory governed by the agreement. Finally, it is crucial for the organization to restrict the ability of the licensee to assign the license to subcontractors (Baghdikian; Reed).

Although licensing contracts are intended to control the use of registered marks, the situation may be spinning out of control. Battles are continually fought over who has the right to control. This issue has surfaced most frequently in professional sports. The NFL recently instituted a program to capture what seemed to be lost revenues. Although the league obtained royalties from the sale of team-logoed items, the players were attracting sponsorship dollars from corporations for displaying corporate logos on shoes, gloves, and sideline hats. In a move to profit from these images during the game, the NFL established the Pro Line program. This program required companies who wished to have their logo visible during an NFL game to pay a fee to the league. In some instances, depending on the scope of the license, the fees surpassed $50 million per year.

To many, this action seemed like extortion. The league was restricting the rights of player to wear shoes and other items that were not specified as "uniforms" under the collective bargaining agreement. Therefore, if a player wanted to wear a shoe from a company that had not paid the fee to the league, he would have to tape over (spat) the logo. The league even went so far as to hire former players to police the sidelines looking for unauthorized logos. Two Denver Bronco players filed grievances after they were fined for wearing unauthorized logos in a locker room interview after a game. In 2001, the NFL changed its process and contracted with a single company (Reebok) to produce its on-field apparel.

In a similar situation, during the 1998 U.S. Open (tennis), the WTA fined Venus Williams $100 for refusing to wear the Corel WTA Tour patch on her clothing. Williams indicated that the language in her Reebok contract "prohibited any other logo" on her dress (Kaplan, 1998, p. 9). Interestingly, William's attorney discovered that the WTA rules provided an exemption for Nike logos. Williams threatened to sue, but ultimately abandoned her challenge. Saying that Williams could do whatever she wanted to do, Reebok stayed above the fray (Kaplan, 1998). Ultimately, the players in both cases prevailed, but it seems that greed has irreversibly contaminated this aspect of sport.

Sage (1996) has also suggested that many of the professional leagues engage in hypocritical trade practices. Although they have gone to "great lengths" to tie licensed merchandise to an all-American image, the vast majority of merchandise is manufactured by exploited foreign labor. The NFL, MLB, and the NBA all used red, white and blue colors predominantly in their logos and garment hang tags. According to Sage, the leagues are fervently selling the American image and pushing patriotism through these products. Yet, in their quest for profits, it seems that the leagues are increasingly exploiting men and women of color from economically disadvantaged countries. In many cases, these workers labor in unsafe and unhealthy work environments. "It is their low wages and long hours that make manufacturers of licensed merchandise commercially successful, and that provide a significant revenue stream to professional team sports" (Sage, 1996, p. 8). It is imperative that these issues be mitigated and eliminated through the contractual language between sport organizations and licensees.

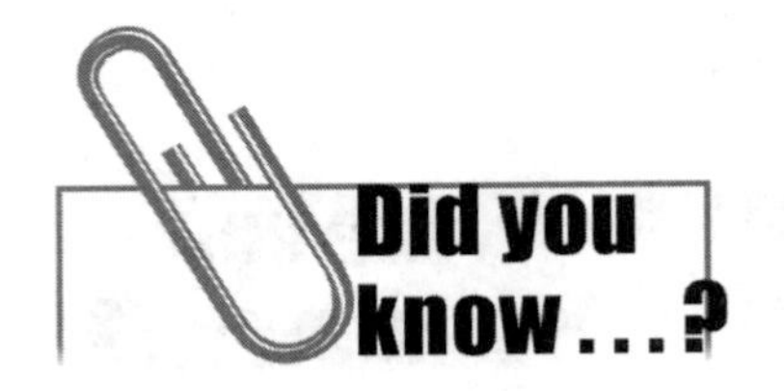

In the WNBA's first year, it had 12 international network partners; it has tripled that number, and in 1999 the WNBA signed a TV agreement with broadcasters in

- Germany
- Haiti
- Ghana
- Italy
- Lithuania
- Uruguay

Source: *Amy Love's Real Sports Magazine*

Chapter Summary

As evidenced by the financial data presented earlier, sport licensing has (since its inception) achieved substantial commercial success. The development of this industry has obviously had a substantial impact on manufacturers, retailers, and consumers. The future of sport licensing seems uncertain but appears to be on solid legal ground. A good foundation has been laid, and the present multi-billion-dollar market should easily expand. However, styles and trends can change as quickly as they evolve. With a clear focus on all three elements of a sound licensing program, Protection, Profit and Public Relations, sport organizations can continue to manage successful licensing programs.

Questions for Study

1. What are the laws that affect licensing and trademarks?
2. What factors led to the development of organized sport licensing?

Learning Activities

1. Investigate the origins of NFL Properties, Inc. Who was their first licensing director?
2. Develop a sport logo and determine the procedures and costs for registering that mark in your state.
3. Contact a sport organization with a registered mark(s) and request a copy of its graphic standards manual.

Chapter 16

Web-Based Sport Marketing

The Importance of Web-Based Sport Marketing

The Internet, particularly the portion known as the world wide web (Web), has been heralded by both marketers and technicians as the most significant new marketing channel introduced in years (Solomon, 1994), and it has the potential to be the greatest marketing tool ever invented (Griffin, 1996). Pope and Forrest (1997) add that not since the advent of television have marketers had an opportunity to develop marketing techniques for a new communications medium. When marketers first began to use television as a tool of advertising, advertising revenue grew from $12.3 million in 1949 to $128 million in 1951. Today, Web advertising revenue, driven by the marketing needs of corporations, is growing at a pace similar to the increases in early television advertising revenue (Foskett, 1996).

As Figure 16.1 depicts, the Internet has grown faster than all other forms of electronic technology and all other mediums of communication (Berthon, Pitt, & Watson, 1996c). So many people are now online that the Internet is mass media. Almost one-quarter of the American adult population, 47 million Americans age 16 and over, used the Internet at least once during the months of November and December 1996 (see Figure 16.2). This was an increase from the 35 million American adults who went online during the months of April and May 1996 (Snider, 1997). At the end of 2000, the online adult population reached 104 million Americans, or 56% of U.S. adults, an increase of 16 million from the numbers in June, 2000. For the first time, the number of females going online equaled the number of males. The average Web user had an income above $50,000 and at least one college degree ("Internet Population Reaches," 2001).

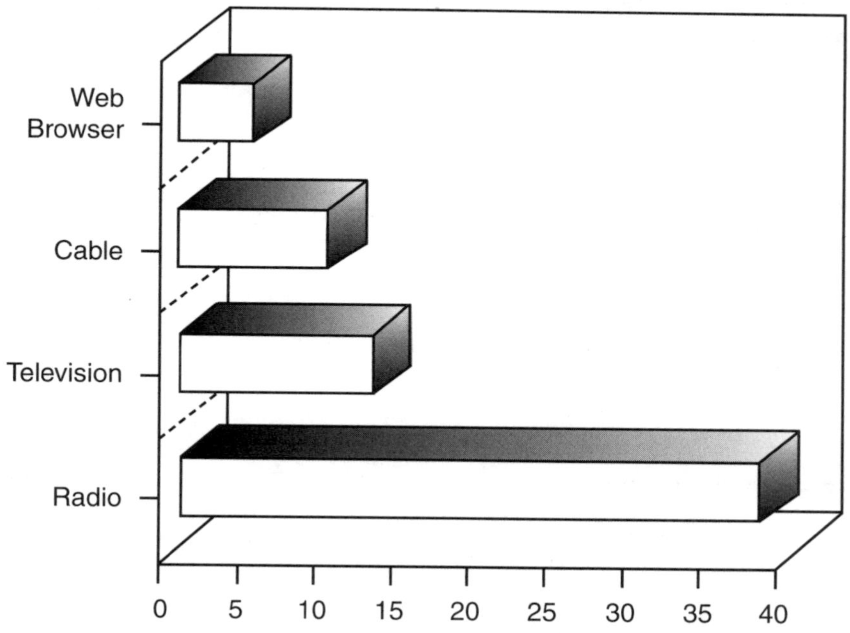

Web
Browser
Cable
Television
Radio
0
5
10
15
20
25
30
35
40

Source: Infoseek Corporation (http://info.infoseek.com)

Figure 16.1
Number of years for various forms of mass media to reach 50 million United States users.

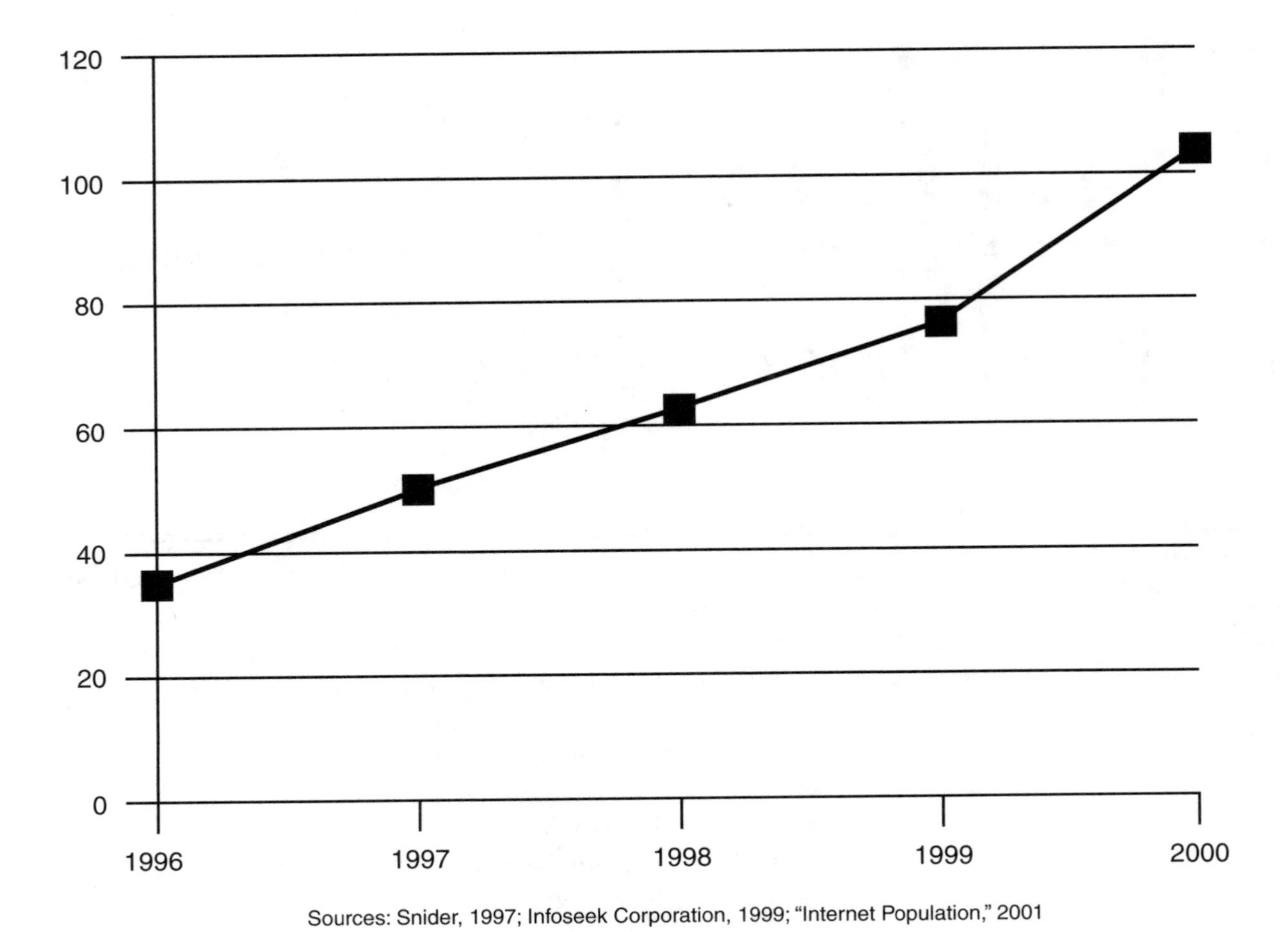

Sources: Snider, 1997; Infoseek Corporation, 1999; "Internet Population," 2001

Figure 16.2
Increase in the number of United States adult citizens online since 1996 (in millions).

With the rapid growth of the number of online users, it is important for sport marketers to understand how to use this technology as a marketing tool. However, as Berthon, Pitt, and Watson (1996a) stated, it is likely that many managers of organizations have not yet tapped into the full marketing potential of the Web. It is the purpose of this chapter to introduce you to this potential. To do so, the following areas will be discussed in depth: (a) the origins of the Internet, (b) the history of the sport industry's use of the Internet, (c) marketing via the Internet, (d) interactive marketing, (e) online sources of revenue, (f) online advertising, and (g) the sport industry and the Internet today.

The Origins of the Internet

The Internet began as a not-for-profit endeavor used to support educational and military communities. Developed in 1968 by the Advanced Research Projects Agency of the Department of Defense, the Internet, or International Electronic Network, connected university computer centers throughout the United States. Originally known as ARPAnet, the Internet was divided into two separate networks in the 1980s. Milnet was used for governmental purposes while NSFnet was used to support educational research (Paul, 1996).

Internet defined:

A global computer network—originally developed by the Defense Department—that enables users to share information. Although service providers sell access to the Internet, it is public property.

World Wide Web (WWW or Web) defined:

The system within the Internet most commonly used by consumers. It connects bodies of information through graphic interface, audio and video capabilities, and point-and-click links.

Browser defined:

A program that navigates the World Wide Web and displays pages. The browser requests a page from a server based on its Internet address. It retrieves the document from the server and displays the contents.

Cyberspace' defined:

Term coined by novelist William Gibson in *Neuromancer*, which now refers to the whole online world of the Internet.

In 1989, the way we view and access data on the Internet was altered when Tim Berners-Lee developed the World Wide Web. The Web was designed as a means to enable an international group of physicists to collaborate online in their research (Semich, 1995). It connected several Internet protocols together including File Transfer Protocol (FTP), Telnet, USENET News, Electronic Mail (Email), HyperText Transfer Protocol (HTTP), and Gopher (Delpy & Bosetti, 1998).

By 1991, more than 3,000 institutions were linked to NSFnet. Since NSFnet was funded by the National Science Foundation, and its charter made it inappropriate for use by private business, private entities had to combine resources to form a commercial network. The creation of the commercial network enabled private business to utilize the resources of the World Wide Web and Internet in a for-profit manner. Today, the Internet is composed of a combination of NSFnet and commercial networks. Communication between networks is governed by Transmission Control Protocol/Internet Protocol (TCP/IP). TCP/IP is used as the standard communications protocol through which data communication is accomplished (Paul, 1996).

The world wide web portion of the Internet began to grow in popularity among Internet users after the web browser was introduced in 1993. The browser let users move from one information source to another with a click of the mouse or stroke of a key. After the browser was introduced, users knew where they were in cyberspace, where they wanted to go, and importantly, how to get there (Semich, 1995).

Prior to 1993, Internet users were limited to viewing text-based information (Noack, 1996) such as the information found on Gopher and Telnet sites (Pfaffenberger, 1996). Now users are able to view website information graphically, hear sound, see video, and link to different websites or web pages (IEG, Inc., 1995). Subsequent to the invention of the web browser, the world wide web has been heralded by both marketers and technicians as the most significant new marketing channel introduced in years (Solomon, 1994).

The History of the Sport Industry's Use of the Internet

Today, the major source of sports news and information is placed on the web by various businesses and organizations such as television networks, professional sports leagues and teams, magazines, newspapers, and dedicated online ventures like ESPN.com and CBS SportsLine. Prior to the advent of the web and the web browser, text-based information was placed on the Internet primarily by sports fans. Sports news and data were posted on the Internet via Telnet, FTP, or Gopher sites. A fan of basketball could find the schedule of his or her favorite NBA team by using Telnet to access culine.colorado.edu 859. Similarly, football fans could Telnet to culine.colorado.edu 863 (Noack, 1996).

Professional Sport Teams and Leagues

After the Mosaic web browser was introduced in 1993, professional sport teams and leagues began developing and launching websites. The earliest sport teams to do so were the Seattle Mariners and the San Jose Sharks (Jensen, 1995). The Mariners launched their site on November 30, 1994. Once launched, the team began to look for a title sponsor for the site. The organization initially sought McDonald's, asking $40,000 with a guarantee of 300 site users a day (IEG, Inc., 1995). The title sponsorship was sold instead to a local Toyota dealership for $17,000 (IEG, Inc., 1996). By the middle of April 1995, the site was attracting an average of 550 visitors per day (IEG, Inc., 1995).

Around the same time, the National Football League (NFL), National Basketball Association (NBA), and National Hockey League (NHL) were all cautiously exploring the possibility of establishing a site on the world wide web. Originally, league sites were created largely to inform team and league officials about the potential of web-based media involvement (Jensen, 1995).

On April 10, 1995, the NFL became the first professional sport league to launch an official website. The league decided to develop the site after determining that the demographic profile of league fans closely resembled that of online users. The league also determined that a website would be valuable in its ability to attract fans in the global marketplace. The NFL planned for their initial website to be temporary, in order to gauge the effectiveness of the new medium. The site existed for only 20 days and was used to cover the 1995 NFL College Football Draft and to promote the re-launching of the World League. The league wanted to eventually add sponsors to a newly designed site and sell licensed merchandise through that site (Jensen, 1995).

Collegiate Sport

College and university athletic departments have also developed organizational websites. Importantly, these sites have led other innovative sport sites. The first audio broadcast of a sporting event via the Internet was of a University of Oregon football game. Also, the first sporting event to be broadcast live over the web in both audio and video was a Christian Brothers University volleyball game (Pickle, 1997). By 1997, almost all—94 percent—National Collegiate Athletic Association (NCAA)-affiliated schools had Internet capabilities. This was an increase from the 84 percent who had Internet capabilities in 1996 ("NCAA Internet," 1998).

Sporting Events

Sporting events were quick to go online as well. At the same time the Mariners launched their website, organizers of events began to use the web for marketing. America's Cup '95 was one of the first sporting events to have an official website. Events On Line was licensed to create and manage the site as well as sell advertising on it. After offering the right of first refusal to official sponsors of the event, an ambush marketing opportunity was created online for those organizations that were not official event sponsors. Advertising prices for the site ranged from $3,000 for six months to $10,000 per month. The first sponsor to purchase advertising was Louis Vuitton Malletier (the title sponsor of the Challenger series). Throughout the six months of the event, an average of 50,000 users visited the site daily (IEG, Inc., 1995).

Sport Media

April 1995 saw the launch of ESPNet SportsZone. Developed jointly by ESPN and Starwave, ESPNet, now ESPN.com, quickly became one of the most popular destinations on the web (Gunther, 1996). One year after its launch, ESPN.com was the most popular content site on the Internet (Tedesco, 1996b).

ABC's *Monday Night Football* (MNF) also developed an online presence, but at a slower pace than that of ESPN.com. Showing a bit of caution, MNF's site was launched during the 1996 football season. The primary purpose for the site was to research Web use and develop an improved site for the 1997 season. ABC did not sell advertising for the MNF site in 1996, but planned to sell ads to current television advertisers when the site was updated for 1997. That first year, the MNF site drew between 80,000 and 100,000 individual users between late Monday afternoon of the broadcast day and the following Tuesday afternoon (Tedesco, 1996d).

Early Online Sponsorship and Advertising Opportunities

As just discussed, early in the creation of websites organizations began to sell online advertising and sponsorship packages. Organizations such as the NFL, ABC, and the Seattle Mariners sought businesses to sponsor or advertise on their sites. Soon, however, sponsors began to insist that professional teams and leagues include website positioning in new sponsorship proposals. For example, Anheiser-Busch began to require advertising space on the official websites of many of the organizations it sponsored.

Marketing Via the Internet

Despite some of the Internet's current marketing problems, many corporations are currently establishing or have already established an online presence. In 1996, 237 thousand new domain names were added by InterNIC (the organization that registers user domain names), and the number of new domain names issued continues to grow rapidly (Sherwin & Avila, 1997). Corporations are establishing websites to create brand positioning, gain Internet-marketing experience while the Web is in its infancy, establish customer loyalty, develop new one-to-one marketing techniques, and reduce organizational costs (Brown, 1998).

E-marketing defined:

Internet or web-based marketing is the pursuit of profit through the exchange process utilizing the Internet as the medium. This type of marketing is also called e-marketing.

Domain Name defined:

The base of a computer's Internet address. For example, a computer with the fully-qualified domain name host.domain.com, host is the host name of the computer and domain.com is its domain name.

Since the demographic profile of the average Internet user closely resembles the demographic profile of the fan base in the NFL, NBA, NHL, and Major League Baseball (MLB) (Delpy & Bosetti, 1998), the web provides a desirable target market for sport organizations that should justify the establishment of an online presence. An ESPN Chilton Sports Poll (InterZine Productions, 1997a) showed that 17 percent of all computer owners and people with access to computers are using them to access sports information online. Additionally, 27 percent of people with a high level of sports interest used the computer to access sports information. A more recent ESPN Chilton Sports Poll of NFL fans showed that 26 percent of fans, age 12 and over, used a personal computer to access sports information online while 41 percent of males, age 18 to 49, with an income above $50,000 used a personal computer to access sports information (see Table 16.1) (InterZine Productions, 1997h). In order to reach this potential market, sport marketers must ensure that their presence online is not merely a source of information but also an effective marketing tool.

Table 16.1
Owners of and People With Access to Computers Getting Sports Information Online.

Level of Sports Interest	% Using PC to Get Sports Information	Average Number of Times Online Per Week
None	4.5	1.72
Light	7.0	1.84
Medium	14.9	1.70
High	27.3	2.31
Total	**17.0**	**2.05**

Source: InterZine Productions, Inc. "ESPN Chilton Sports Poll: Online Sports Information," The Sports Business Daily, May 2, 1997, Vol 3 No 143, p.11.

Benefits to Marketing Via the Internet

Donahue (1998) wrote that there is little doubt the world wide web has an enormous marketing potential. To many marketers, the potential to reach a highly desirable target market justifies the development of a website (Semich, 1995). As stated, all major research organizations have found that Internet users are young, well-educated, and earn high incomes ("Why Internet," 1997).

In addition to access to a desirable target market, marketing via the web also has other benefits. One major benefit is its relative cost. Solomon (1994), Graham (1996), and Semich (1995) stated that web-based marketing will reduce organizational costs, especially those of labor and distribution. Offering an online catalog reduces the number of phone sales representatives needed. The Internet enables a purchaser to order a product and charge it to a credit card without speaking to a representative of the company. The incoming order is also more efficient since it can be sent automatically to a warehouse for instant processing.

Solomon (1994) added that doing business on the web allows for a reduction in costs and the expansion of operations to occur simultaneously. By contrast, when a non-web business expands, the organization must either build a new facility or move to a larger location. For a web-based business to expand, it merely needs to add an additional server, the piece of computer hardware distributing the web content. A server can be purchased for $25,000, substantially less than relocating the company.

Several other benefits of marketing via the web have been identified as well. The web can help establish customer loyalty, especially when an organization establishes its web presence before its competition. Loyal web customers tend to make repeat purchases and refer new customers (Griffen, 1996). Also, marketing on the web can enhance brand positioning by associating it with a particular website (Tedesco, 1996a). Finally, marketing through the web benefits one-to-one marketing (Foskett, 1996) by enabling organizations to easily develop complex databases of user information. Information on previous purchase activity, demographic information, and psychographic information can be tabulated after a user makes a purchase or completes a survey to enter a site contest or promotion. For example, Anheuser-Busch used its Atlanta Olympic Games theme website, budweiser.com, to build a database of customer buying habits during the 1996 Olympics (Warner, 1997). Building a database of consumer information will enable organizations to better understand web customer's needs and buying habits (Griffen, 1996).

Drawbacks of Web-Based Marketing

In spite of the aforementioned benefits, some in the field of marketing have argued that the web is not ready for serious marketing efforts. Though cost has been mentioned as a benefit to marketing online, it is also a detriment. Mainly, there is a high start-up cost for both consumers and sellers (Welz, 1996). Currently, the consumer must purchase a computer and online service to access the web. Organizations must develop their site at an estimated first year start-up cost of between $446 thousand and $1.79 million (Sherwin & Avila, 1997). Additionally, security and privacy issues threaten Internet commerce (Semich, 1995; Graphic, Visualization, & Usability Center, 1997), and some consumers fear that personal information needed for online transactions will be sold to Internet marketers. Therefore, they do not make online purchases. Lastly, Donahue (1998) and Fram and Grady (1997) stated that marketing in cyberspace will not be effective until user-friendly sites are designed that allow fast and easy access to site content.

Characteristics of a Successful Website

Since the web is able to deliver a desirable target market (Jensen, 1995) and the benefits as well as the drawbacks of web-marketing are known, much has been written about the development and management of successful sites. Authors, such as Delpy & Bosetti (1998), Pope & Forrest (1997), Mainardi (1997), Stevens (1996), and Fried-Cassorla (1995), have described the characteristics of a successful site. The following features were common throughout their works: (a) ease of navigation, (b) access to relevant and related information, (c) constant updates with fresh information, (d) entertaining content and site features, and (e) a good web address reflecting the organization's name, such as www.NBA.com. A website was judged most effective when used in conjunction with other marketing communication efforts. See Figure 16.3.

ESPN.com

ESPN's website, ESPN.com, is often hailed as the best example of a successful site and the future of mass media. Since its launch, ESPN.com has been a leader in marketing on the web. In September 2000, ESPN.com had 10.8 million unique users and a 50% market share of page views among the top four sport websites (ESPN.com, CNNSI.com, FoxSports.com, SportsLine.com). The site's advertising rates are some of the highest on the Internet ("ESPN.com Wraps," 2001). In 1998, advertising prices for the site ranged from $15,000 per month for 500,000 guaranteed impressions to $33,000 a month for 1.2 million guaranteed impressions (Starwave Corporation, 1998). That same year, ESPN.com had over 30 monthly advertisers (McMurray, 1998). By providing its users with interactive games, up-to-the-minute scores, game reports, feature stories and statistics, ESPN ensures that users are continually drawn to the site (Gunther, 1996).

ESPN.com's success has resulted from the site's web strategy. First of all, it targets the right customers. Ninety-seven percent of the users were male and 76 percent were

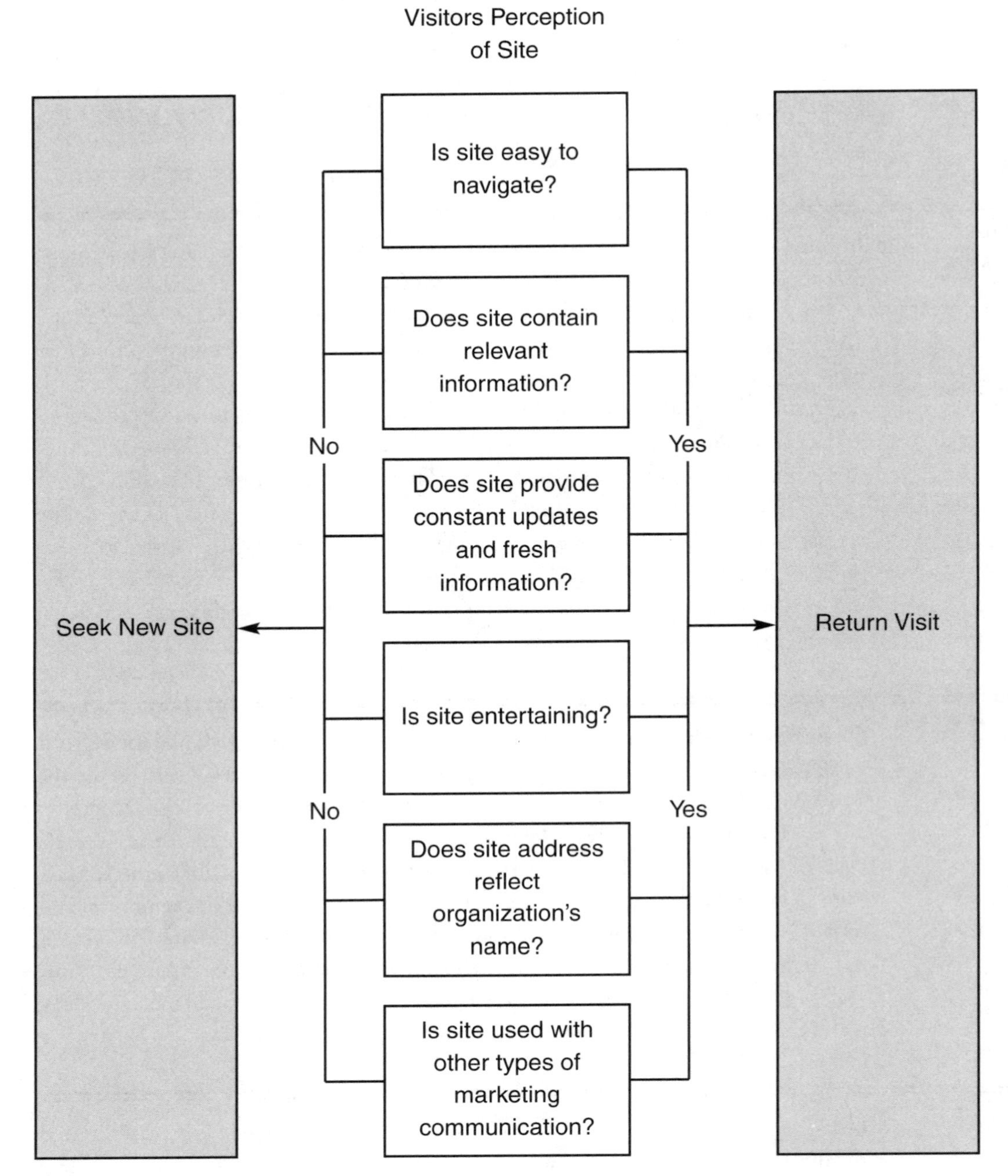

Figure 16.3
Consumer reaction to characteristics of a web site.

between the ages of 18 to 34 in 1998 (Starwave Corporation, 1998). ESPN.com focuses its marketing effort on the 18 to 34-year-old male, especially the displaced sports fan, since 10 percent of ESPN.com users log on from overseas. ESPN also produces an excellent web product. The site has over 18,000 pages of information written and produced by a staff of 80 full-time employees. ESPN.com also effectively uses the ESPN brand name to draw visitors to its site. Those sports fans familiar with the ESPN television product seek out the website. Finally, ESPN.com drives the web market. The site charges for access to premium services. These services include access to interactive features like NBA Live Audio, MLB Batter vs. Pitcher, and Sortable Stats as well as access to ESPN analysts, exclusive feature stories, and special event coverage. Users can gain admittance to premium areas for a $4.95 monthly fee or a $39.95 yearly fee (ESPN, 2000).

Determining a Site's Success

Measurement

Despite all that has been written about web-based marketing, few researchers have considered how to measure the attainment of a site's marketing goals (Berthon et al., 1996a). As Brown (1998) indicated, there is not yet a universal method for measuring a website's success. Some measure success by total site hits or site visits while others consider the number of page views. Some site owners are only concerned with the revenue generated through the site. As Schmetterer (1997) and Bunn (1997b) stated, the future of the web as a advertising medium is uncertain until a means to produce comparable, deliverable, and accurate measurement data is devised.

Hit defined:

A single access of a file on the world wide web.

Visit defined:

A series of transactions performed by a single user at a single web site.

Page View defined:

A unit of measure for web site usage as opposed to a hit. A page may include links to a number of included images that also must be uploaded by a web browser when viewing the HTML file. The HTML file and each of the uploaded, online graphics register as multiple hits, but only one page view.

Message

Marketers have relied on intuition, imitation, and advertising expertise when designing, developing, and implementing their organization's sites (Berthon et al., 1996a). As indicated in traditional marketing theory, marketers must first decide on the desired audience response to the message sent via the web. They must determine whether the response should be cognitive, putting something in someone's mind; affective, changing the consumer's attitude; or behavioral, getting the consumer to undertake a specific action. They also must know how to use the marketing communications mix to transmit the message to targeted customers (Kotler, 1988).

The current belief is that Internet marketing will likely function as a complement to traditional advertising media (Stevens, 1996). Its real power is that it can provide unlimited layers of detailed information about a product or service, interactively, at the request of the user. The primary advantage of utilizing the Internet appears to be the delivery of in-depth, detailed information after traditional advertising creates interest in a product or service. (By contrast, the advantage does not appear to be in attracting attention or transmitting a message (Thomas, 1998).)

Unique Web-Based Marketing Opportunities

Marketing via the web does present unique opportunities. Unlike traditional broadcast media, the web facilitates two-way communication between the seller and the buyer (Berthon et al., 1996c). As such, marketing through the web primarily utilizes two elements of the marketing communications mix: advertising and personal selling (Berthon et al., 1996a). The web enables the marketer to have dialogue with the visitor while creating awareness or providing information about a product or service. Furthermore, two-way communication occurs between the seller and the buyer without concern for distance or time (Berthon, Pitt, & Watson, 1996b).

Since the web can be used as both an advertising medium and a personal selling tool, specific marketing communication objectives for sites may vary. Objectives can range from the traditional advertising objectives of introducing a new product or creating awareness for an existing one to the traditional personal-selling objectives of making a sale and providing feedback on products sold (Berthon et al., 1996c).

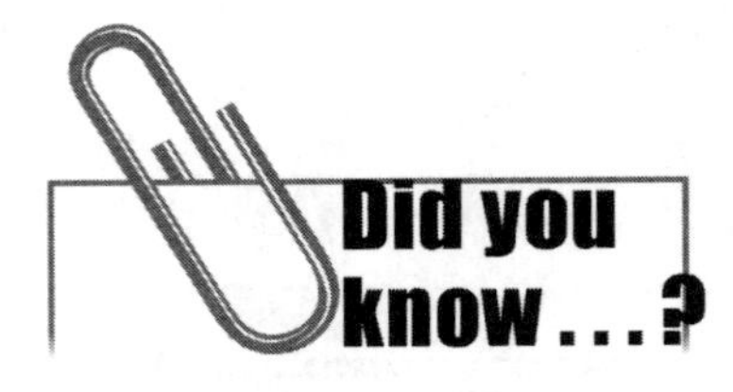

In 1999, 1.1. million girls were playing baseball.

Source: *Amy Love's Real Sports Magazine*

Marketers *must*, however, design the message delivered via the web to meet the goals set forth by their organizations. If the goals are cognitive in nature, an Internet campaign may rely upon the inclusion of the organization's web address in all advertising, publicity, and other corporate communication materials. Also, it may rely upon the creation of a web address that can be easily guessed (i.e. NASCAR.com), the utilization of hyperlinks or advertising banners on related Internet sites, and the registration of the Internet address with web search engines such as Yahoo! and Excite (Berthon et al., 1996c).

If the goals are effective, interesting site content that holds visitors' attention and persuades them to browse the site must be created. The material must be readable and the visual effects should be appealing. Also, the visitor must be able to move about the site and find information quickly and efficiently (Berthon et al., 1996c).

Following behavioral goals would lead site creators to allow the consumer to make a purchase online. To help insure the purchase behavior, the seller must simplify the ordering process, provide a secure means of ordering, and provide alternative ordering methods for those who do not wish to transmit their credit card information via the web (Berthon et al., 1996c).

Interactive Marketing

Berthon et al. (1996c) stated that personal selling and advertising are the two elements of the marketing communications mix used by those marketing online. In their article, the authors use the terms personal selling and direct selling interchangeably. Personal selling, as defined by Kotler (1988), is an "oral presentation in a conversation with one or more prospective purchasers for the purpose of making sales" (p. 588). Since selling via the Internet occurs through electronic means, not orally, personal selling is most likely not the correct term to use when discussing the act of making an electronic transaction between consumers and sellers. As one form of direct marketing is direct selling (Kotler, 1988), the term direct marketing may be plausible for use when discussing Internet transactions. Direct marketing has been defined as "any direct communication to a targeted consumer or business that is designed to generate a response in the form of an order, a request for further information, and/or a visit to a store or other place of business for purchase of a specific product or service" (Bradley, 1996, p. 44). While this term more appropriately describes the activities of the online marketing sales process, a relatively new term, interactive marketing, has been defined to encompass all the aspects of the online seller-consumer relationship. Interactive marketing, as defined by the Direct Marketing Association, is "any interactive communication media that allows the user to request or receive delivery of information, entertainment or marketing materials, products, and/or services (Bradley. 1996, p. 44).

'Interactive Marketing' defined:

Any interactive communication media that allows the user to request or receive delivery of information, entertainment or marketing materials, products, and/or services.

Noack (1998) stated that the web is finally beginning to live up to its potential as an interactive, transactional medium and selling tool. Major advertisers are not just put-

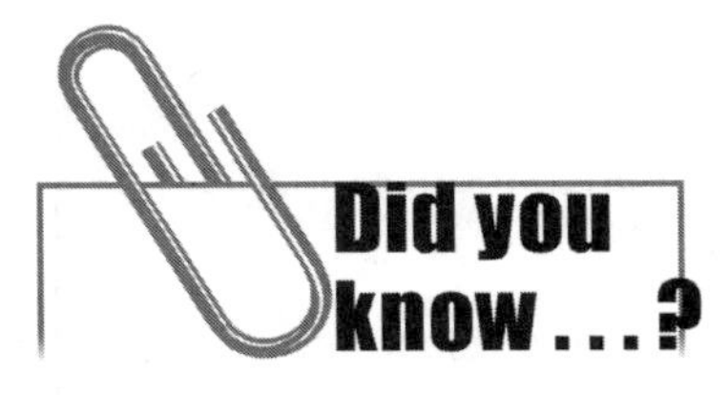

For the first time in its 75-year history, General Mills Wheaties box began showing soccer players. The new cast:

- Michelle Akers
- Mia Hamm
- Brandi Chastain
- Briana Scurry
- Kristine Lilly.

Source: *Amy Love's Real Sports Magazine*

ting up stores; they are creating fully functional businesses. These advertising sites have inventory, cash registers, and customer service centers (Klein, 1997). Organizations are developing these fully functional sites at a time when Internet commerce is growing rapidly. Revenue from the online sales of goods and services is expected to increase by 500 percent between 1998 and 2002 (Forrester Research, 1998b). By 2002, it is expected that 25 percent of all shopping will be conducted via the web (Bunn, 1997a).

The web is ideal for interactive marketing if the advertising message can be targeted to a specific audience (Silverstein, 1996). The web is unique because it is simultaneously mass media and one-to-one media (Godin, 1996). As such, online services are driving marketers from mass marketing to customized one-to-one marketing (Foskett, 1996), which has become the hottest growth area for direct marketers (Schoenbachler, Gordon, Fowley, & Spellman, 1997).

Smith (1998) stated that marketing messages will get lost in the clutter of other marketing messages unless the message can speak to users uniquely. This is especially important as the amount of leisure time available to consumers decreases significantly. Consumers no longer have the time to sift through endless advertising messages prior to making purchases (Schoenbachler et al., 1997).

To be successful in interactive marketing, the marketer must focus on the consumers who have purchased from their organization or are very likely to purchase in the future (Paul, 1997). Also, the marketer must know what information the consumer will want, as well as how and when they want it (Smith, 1998). By knowing the customer and his wants, relationships can be built between the marketer and the consumer enabling the marketer to create customized promotions that will entice the consumer to purchase from his/her organization again (Godin, 1996). The key to success, though, is to control the information collected about the customer and use it immediately to monitor the consumer's buying habits (Bradley, 1996).

A database should be used to monitor and utilize the information collected about the consumer. Databases have become an integral part of the interactive and direct marketing process because of the growth of relationship, or one-to-one, marketing (Schoenbachler et al., 1997). Contained in the database is knowledge that will aid one-to-one marketing (Smith, 1998; Hodges, 1996) and is information is extremely important to the direct marketing process. The information tells the marketer who the customers are, where they live, what items they have purchased from the organization, what television programs they watch, how they are kept as customers, and how they are reached effectively (Millican, 1985). Using a database benefits interactive marketing as it enables the marketer to create a more targeted approach (Schoenbachler et al., 1997).

Benefits of Interactive Marketing

One benefit of interactive marketing is that its results are measurable (Schoenbachler et al., 1997). It is fairly easy for marketers to compare the respondents of the marketing effort to the initial targeted group, thus determining the percentage of customers who reacted to the message (Handel & Forrester, 1997). Also, one-to-one marketing has been greatly aided by recent advances in technology. By combining the functionality of the web, the listserve, and database technology, marketers are now able to communicate with customers on only the topics that interest them (Smith, 1998).

This is especially true as going online has become a normal daily task, and the novelty of the Internet is diminishing (Godin, 1996).

Interactive marketing is a cost-effective method for building relationships with customers, particularly when compared to direct sales. Utilizing the Internet to market one-to-one eliminates direct sales expenses such as long distance or 800 telephone charges, postage, salaries for door-to-door salespeople, and the costs needed to print numerous copies of sales brochures and catalogs (Bean, 1997; Smith, 1998, Noack, 1998). Further, interactive marketing is even more cost effective when the global reach of the marketing efforts are considered (Silverstein, 1996).

Results of marketing efforts are measurable
Ability to communicate with customers on customer-selected topics
Cost-effective means for building relationships with customers
Customer convenience provided

Figure 16.4
Some benefits of interactive marketing.

In addition to the savings to companies, interactive marketing also provides a convenient service to the consumer (Bunn, 1997a). The process of bringing products and services directly to the customer is simplified by the interactive marketing process. Also, when used properly, it allows consumers to eliminate all undesired marketing information prior to receiving it, choosing instead to receive only what interests them. (Bradley, 1996).

Disadvantages of Interactive Marketing

There are also some disadvantages to interactive marketing. The web is still in its early development stage as a marketing medium (Silverstein, 1996), which means that there is little documentation as to what techniques work best. Also, the customer must access the marketer first in order for interactive marketing to begin (Foskett, 1996; Silverstein, 1996). But most importantly, many consumers do not like interactive marketing, specifically direct email (Maddox, 1997). Direct email is an important part of interactive marketing. It enables the marketer to deliver marketing messages to current and potential customers. Direct email may be used to inform web users of new products offered at a company's website or of sales on these products, and it allows the marketer to contact customers in an effort to entice them to visit his or her company's site. Once at the site, interactive marketing can occur (Silverstein, 1996).

Interactive marketing is in its early development stage
Customer must access marketer in order for interactive marketing to begin
Customers do not like direct email

Figure 16.5
Some disadvantages of interactive marketing.

Direct email is free to the sender, and thereby reduces the costs normally associated with direct mail (Godin, 1996). However, since individuals pay for email service, unsolicited email is generally unwelcome (Silverstein, 1996; Godin, 1996). In the online community, it is proper etiquette to ask a consumer that has visited your website if it is allright to communicate with him or her in the future via email. If the consumer replies affirmatively then direct email should be used in the interactive marketing effort. If the consumer replies negatively, direct email must not be sent to the consumer (Silverstein, 1996, Smith, 1998).

A debate over spam, or junk email, has developed between entrepreneurs who wish to use direct email for marketing and Internet pioneers. The marketers feel that direct email is needed to bring products to consumers. Consumers have concerns over privacy issues surrounding direct email (Rosner, 1996). Main privacy concerns involve the use of personal information gathered from the Internet to target potential customers. For example, if an Internet user has subscribed to a health-related bulletin board, a spammer could enter the email address of that consumer into a database and then use the database to send unsolicited health-product email to the consumer (Feigenbaum, 1996).

'Spam' defined:

To indiscriminately post information—often of an irrelevant or commercial nature—to multiple newsgroups or email recipients. Derived from an old Monty Python sketch, "Eggs, spam, spam, spam, bacon, and spam."

Privacy concerns have resulted in a backlash against spammers. Online consumers avoid purchasing products advertised via spam. Further, spammers are being "flamed" by those who receive unsolicited email. Online users reply to the spam, sending a copy of the unwanted message back to the sender. This process, repeated by many of the spam recipients, can result in thousands of email messages filling the online mailboxes of the offending party, thus inundating the organization with junk email. This backlash has begun to hurt legitimate businesses who use email correctly (Greim, 1997).

Attempts have been made to block spamming. Filtering software that detects a possible mass email is available, but soon after release, spammers usually find a way to send messages that avoid software detection. As a result of this lack of protection, legislative help has been sought (Greim, 1997). Many feel that spam should be outlawed as the broadcast-fax advertisement was in 1991. However, no legislation has passed to date (Rosner, 1996). Legislation is unlikely; the Federal Trade Commission (FTC) stated that regulation would hamper the development of the Internet (Feigenbaum, 1996). However, industry experts predict that spam will increase as marketers discover how cheap it is (Feigenbaum, 1996), and with the existing backlash against companies sending unsolicited email, smart organizations should think carefully before using direct email (Rosner, 1996).

Opt-in Marketing

Opt-in marketing enables the consumer to choose if they wish to receive direct email from organizations and has been proposed to end the use of spam. Some see it as the only responsible way a marketer can market via direct email to consumers. During a visit to a website, the site user will be asked whether he or she would like to receive, for example, information on products or updates on sale prices. If the consumer declined the informational or update offer, direct email would not be sent to that consumer (Resnick, 1997).

Online Sources of Revenue

With the emergence of the Internet comes new economic opportunities for businesses (Madsen, 1996). Web-based commerce, or the buying and selling of goods or services via the Internet (Ubois, 1997), has grown rapidly since the 1993 creation of the browser (Sherwin & Avila, 1997). In 1995, two years after the Mosaic browser transformed the way Internet information is transmitted and received, $100 million of Internet commerce was conducted on the web (Stipe, 1996). That same year web advertising revenues were $55 million (Welz, 1996). By 1996, advertising revenue had grown to $301 million (Jupiter Communications, 1998b) and reached $2.7 billion in 1999 (Infoseek Corporation, 1999). In 2000, advertising revenue was $8 billion. It is predicted, though, that online advertising revenue will not grow much beyond the $8 billion mark in 2001 (see Figure 16.6) (Leonard, 2001).

Internet commerce has grown as well. Three-hundred million dollars of Internet commerce occurred in 1996 (see Figure 16.7). Internet commerce reached over $8 billion in 1997 (Forrester Research, 1998b), with $1.1 billion worth of Internet commerce occurring during the months of November and December, 1997 (Mangalindan, 1997; Bunn, 1997a). Since only 52 percent of current web users are searching for products online (Graphic, Visualization, & Usability Center, 1999), there is still potential for rapid growth in Internet commerce. Forrester Research (1998b) predicts that $327 billion of Internet commerce will occur during 2002.

E-commerce defined:

Buying and selling goods or services via the Internet or other electronic means. Also referred to as Internet commerce or web-based commerce.

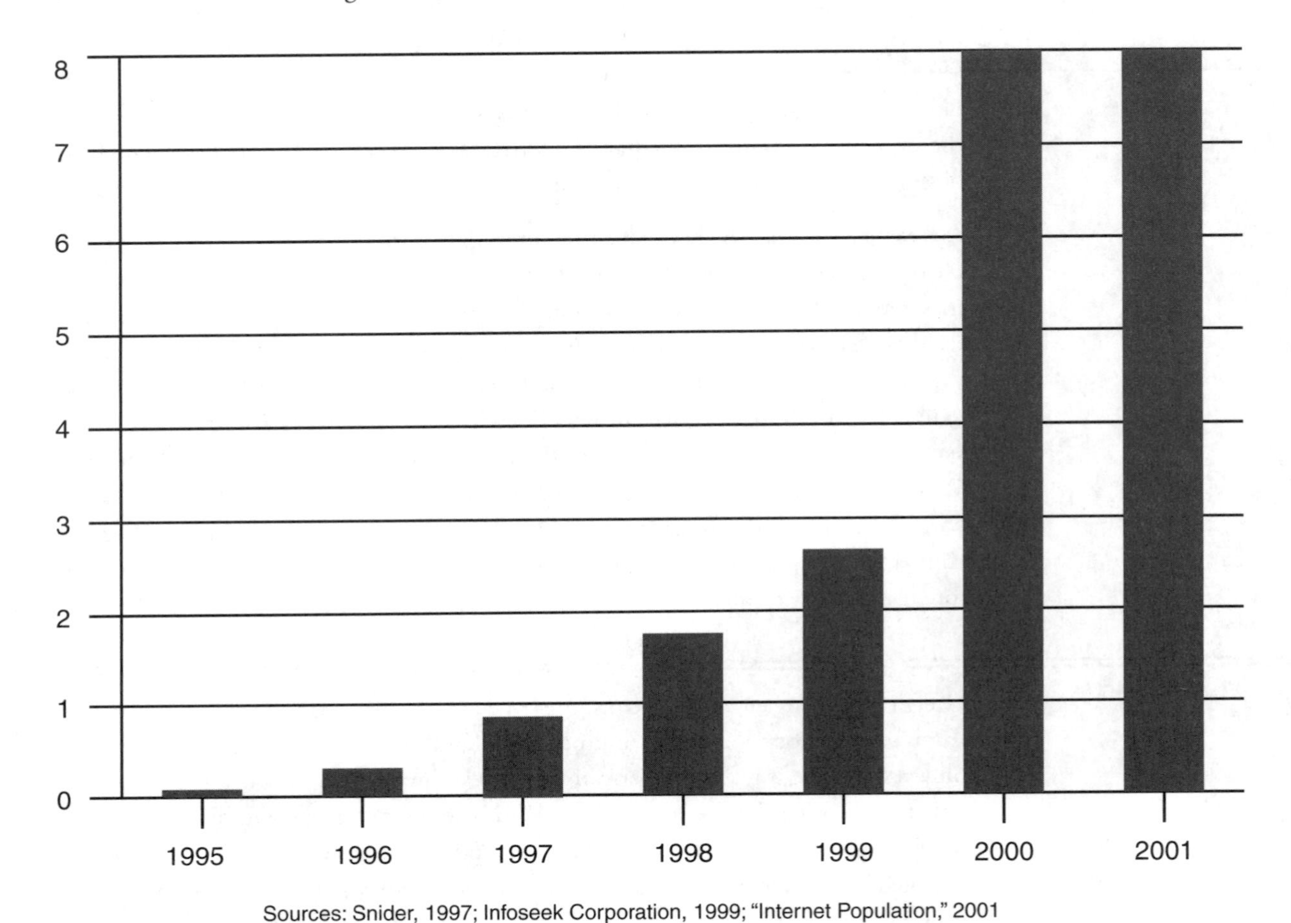

Sources: Snider, 1997; Infoseek Corporation, 1999; "Internet Population," 2001

Figure 16.6
Growth and projected growth of web-based advertising revenue: 1995–2001 (in billions of dollars).

Despite the swift growth in Internet commerce and online advertising revenue that occurred through 2000, sport organizations struggled to make a profit online. The expected halt to the increases in online advertising spending, coupled with the collapse of several sport websites in 2000 (i.e. MVP.com, Ultimatebid.com) and the struggles of Quokka Sports and Broadband Sports early in 2001, has led to caution (Lefton, 2001) in investment practices. Because their sites are currently unprofitable, some organizations are reluctant to invest corporate resources on an Internet venture. For example, a main corporate concern for establishing a website is the cost of initial start-up. Total website development costs were $116.3 million in 1995 with web stor-

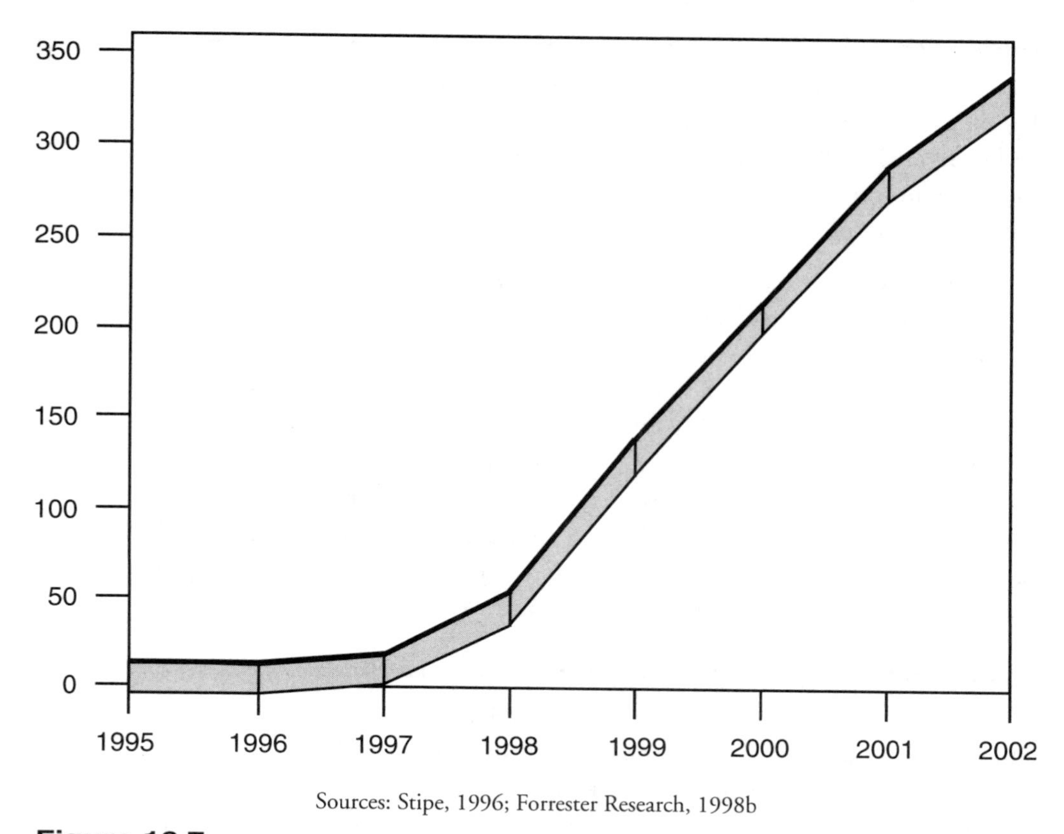

Sources: Stipe, 1996; Forrester Research, 1998b

Figure 16.7
Growth and projected growth of Internet commerce (e-commerce): 1995–2002 (in billions of dollars).

age payments of $15.1 million (Welz, 1996). For many businesses, web advertising revenue did little to cover these costs as 66 percent of total web advertising expenditures in 1996 were concentrated among 10 websites (Welz, 1996). Therefore, of the $301 million spent on advertising in 1996, $199 million was spent on advertising at 10 websites and $102 million was spent advertising on over 237 thousand sites throughout the rest of the web.

Corporations have also been reluctant to engage in Internet commerce because many web users find Internet shopping awkward. To these consumers, items are hard to find, and the shopping interaction isn't user-friendly (Fram & Grady, 1997). Additionally, many consumers avoid online shopping because of privacy concerns. Consumers are reluctant to send credit card information, required for online purchases, via the Internet. Consumers are also afraid that personal information, needed for the online transaction, will be sold to Internet marketers (Graphic, Visualization, & Usability Center, 1999), and thus, many Internet users do not make online purchases. Therefore, until privacy issues are resolved, corporations are reluctant to invest heavily in an online operation.

According to Fitzgerald (1997), web-based profits can be found in entertainment. On sport websites, the most common sources of this revenue are online subscriptions and advertising (Delpy & Bosetti, 1998). Despite revenue from these sources, no major online website has made a profit (McMurray, 1998).

Online Subscriptions

Subscription fees are usually only charged by major content providers like ESPN.com. The average monthly fee for access to premium content is $4.95 while yearly fees are $39.95. While sites such as ESPN.com and CBS SportsLine charge fees for premium access, over 80 percent of the content on the two sites is free (McMurray, 1998; Delpy & Bosetti, 1998).

Another type of fee charged online are fees for entering fantasy leagues and contests. All major sports are represented in fantasy sports leagues. Even sports like stock car racing, golf, bowling, and professional wrestling have fantasy leagues (Berlin, 1996). League entry fees are charged to the user's credit card. These fees range in price from $15 to $70 (Berlin, 1996; Delpy & Bosetti, 1998). Participants' pay, as the grand prize for league winners, can be as high as $10,000 (Berlin, 1996). During the 1997 NFL season, CBS SportsLine had over 23,000 users play one of its two fantasy football games, generating over $1.1 million in revenue for the site. ESPN has also had success generating revenue via fantasy leagues. Revenue from fantasy leagues played on ESPN.com grew 400 percent in 1997 (InterZine Productions, 1998d).

Online Ticketing and Merchandising

Though not mentioned by Delpy and Bosetti (1998) as a major source of revenue, online ticketing and merchandising do have a financial impact on the fiscal success of a website. By offering online merchandising, sites can provide customers with the opportunity to view available merchandise, gather information on sizes and prices, and order the product through the Internet. Through its online merchandising efforts in 1997, CBS SportsLine generated $470,000 in revenue, a 200 percent increase over their 1996 sales figures (InterZine Productions, 1998h).

Possibly more important for sport organizations is online ticket sales. Tickets for almost every sporting event can now be purchased on the Internet (Delpy & Bosetti, 1998). One professional sports franchise even predicted that in three years half of all their tickets would be sold through the Internet. By 2001, online ticketing is expected to grow to a $10 billion marketplace, of which $2 billion in performance tickets will be sold (Forrester Research, 1998a).

Advantages to online ticketing include selling opportunities 24 hours a day, every day, reduced organizational costs, increased customer convenience, access to a global marketplace, and the creation of a new distribution channel (Forrester Research, 1998a; Shatzkin, 1996). Disadvantages include potential difficulties integrating the web with current ticketing systems, consumer security concerns, and the loss of human contact between the seller and the consumer (Forrester Research, 1998a). Forrester, in its 1998 research, concluded that online ticketing is taking root because the benefits outweigh the disadvantages and organizations currently involved with online ticketing are optimistic about opportunities for future growth (1998a).

Online Advertising/ Sponsorship

It appears the greatest current method of generating revenue via online operations is through the sale of secondary site advertising. In total, this form of advertising generated $940 million in 1997 (Jupiter Communications, 1998a) and grew to $8 billion by 2000 (see Figure 16.6) (Leonard, 2001). In 1998, average cost per thousand (CPM) for advertising on websites was $50 with CPM ranging from $5 to $70

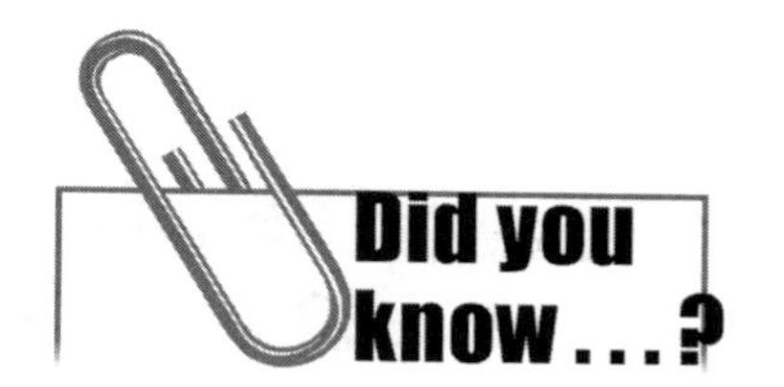

In 1999, the Quaker Oats Company announced a new cereal called Golden Goals exclusively devoted to soccer. The box carries pictures of the Women's World Cup championship USA team. A percentage of the sales will be donated to youth soccer.

Source: *Amy Love's Real Sports Magazine*

(Delpy & Bosetti, 1998). Banner sales accounted for 54 percent of 1997 revenue, while sponsorship of online sites accounted for 41 percent (Maddox, 1997).

League, team, and event websites appear to be an excellent location for the promotion and recruitment of sport sponsors. Sponsorship enables the website owner to offer an alternative to advertising fees while enabling the sponsor to have product exclusivity in a particular area of the site, such as Ford and the auto racing section of the ESPN website (Delpy & Bosetti, 1998).

Currently, the only writings on sponsorship of sport websites cover either major content sites like CNNSI.com, professional league sites, or major event sites like the official Super Bowl site. The number of sponsors and advertisers for the 3 major content sites range from 35 to 100. ESPN has 35 sponsors, CNNSI has 45, and CBS SportsLine has 100 (McMurray, 1998). In 1998, yearly sponsorship on ESPN.com cost between $140,000 and $310,000 for 1.2 million guaranteed impressions a month (Starwave Corporation, 1998). Sponsorship fees for NFL.com, NASCAR.com, and NBA.com averaged approximately $15,000 per month for 400,000 guaranteed impressions. Sponsors for each of the preceding 4 sites receive any or all of the following benefits including full rotation of sponsorship banners or icons throughout each site; promotion, contest, or branded pages; and a listing in the sponsor index (Starwave Corporation, 1998; Starwave Corporation, 1997a; Starwave Corporation, 1997b; Starwave Corporation, 1997c).

Online Advertising

It is important for sport marketers to completely understand online advertising in order to generate revenue for your organization. To begin, television audiences are beginning to fragment as more programming and alternatives to viewing emerge. During the February 1997 television ratings period, it was found that one million fewer people were watching television than were watching during the same ratings period in 1996. At the same time, the online population nearly doubled. Of the online population, 37 percent of web users said they were getting online rather than watching television (see Figure 16.8) ("Why Internet," 1997).

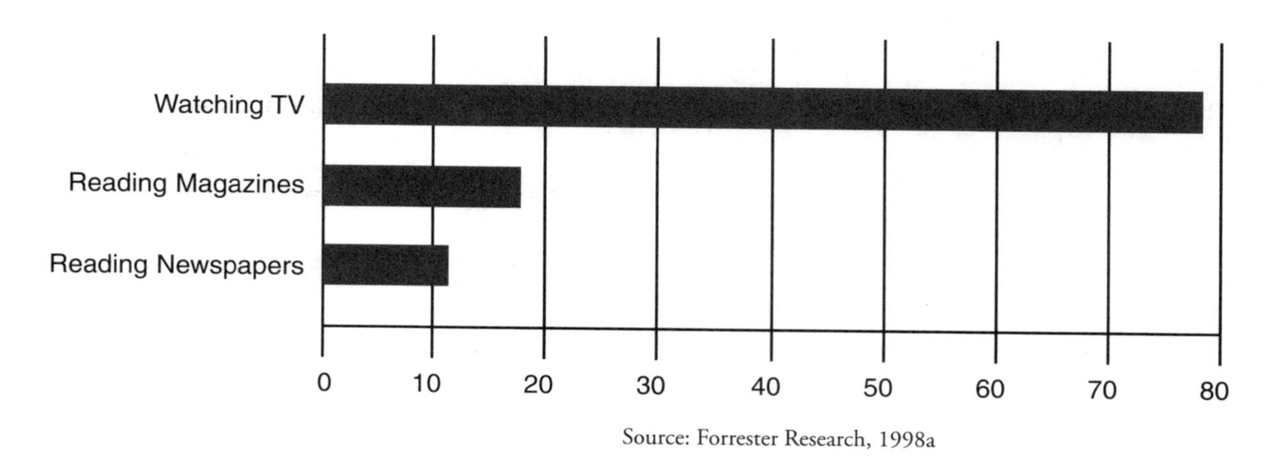

Figure 16.8
Activities consumers are taking time from to spend time on the computer (in percentages).

As the television viewing audience migrated toward the web, so were media plans. Advertisers are beginning to account for the growing number of people who go online instead of using other forms of media ("Why Internet," 1997). It has been found that this audience goes online and seeks particular sites in order to retrieve detailed information on particular products or services (Maddox & Mehta, 1997; Klein, 1997). As this audience is beginning to migrate online, advertisers are moving from cautious, experimental web advertising to committed web advertising (Maddox, 1997). Websites now generate awareness for products, explain or demonstrate products, provide information on products, and allow for consumer feedback on products. The long-term goal of these sites is to sell products through interactive means (Maddox & Mehta, 1997).

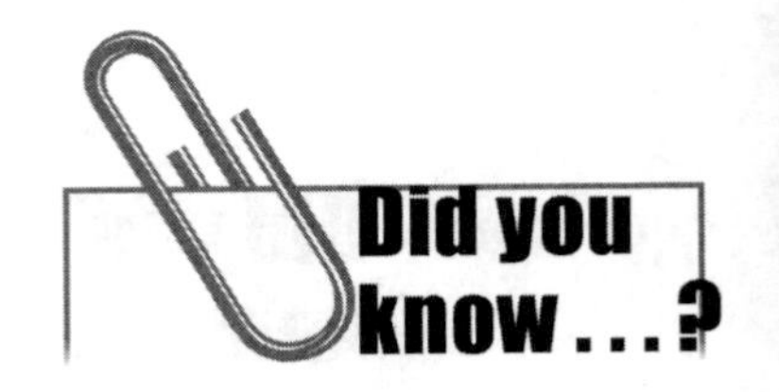

There were a record 268,390 participants in the 1999 ESPN X-Games for 9 days of extreme sports.

Source: *Amy Love's Real Sports Magazine*

Reasons Advertisers Are Going Online

According to Ducoffe (1996), advertisers are turning to the web for a variety of reasons. First, for most consumers, the nature of traditional advertising is not considered worthwhile. Consumers are exposed to numerous ads, making it impossible to give significant attention to most of the advertisements encountered. Also, much of traditional advertising is for low-cost packaged goods with which consumers are familiar. These goods do not require a great deal of thought prior to purchase and therefore advertisements for them are ignored. Finally, customers receive the majority of traditional advertisements when they are not shopping for the product.

To reach consumers while they are shopping for goods or services, web-based advertising should be utilized. Advertising information on the web will be more relevant to consumers as they shop online. Further, web advertising enables customers to access information that is not immediately available through traditional advertising means. The consumer is able to investigate detailed product information through web based advertising. Immediate response to the advertisement can occur in the form of transactions (i.e. purchases made) because of the interactivity of the medium (Hawkins, 1994). Thus, it has been found that web advertising has value to consumers. Additionally, research has shown that consumers also find web advertising to be somewhat valuable (Ducoffe, 1996).

Reasons Web-Based Advertising Is Avoided

Several drawbacks to web advertising have been mentioned by various authors. First, the countless number of sites on the Internet creates clutter. For a site to be effective as an advertising tool, creativity has to be used to differentiate it from other sites (Johns, 1997). Hawkins (1994) added that the limited production quality of sites compounded by users' lack of familiarity with the web makes it difficult to effectively market a product to the online population. Additionally, a major drawback is a lack of standardized measurement for determining the reach of advertisements (Spain, 1996). Without a standard to measure the reach of ads, setting the price for advertising on a secondary website or calculating the return on investment of a stand-alone site becomes difficult.

Methods of Advertising Online

If advertisers were to utilize the resources of the Internet for advertising purposes, the traditional media model would entail static, that is, non-interactive, advertising banners on media content sites such as CNN.com or ESPN.com (Klein, 1997). But, because

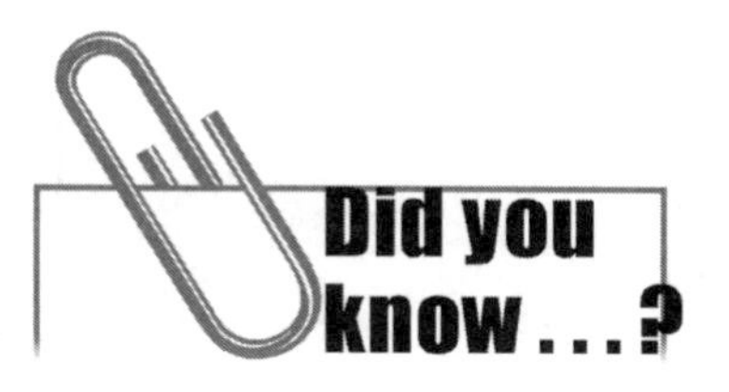

The 1999 World Summer Games of the Special Olympics, held every 2 years, had over 7,000 athletes from around the world.

Source: *Amy Love's Real Sports Magazine*

of its interactivity, the Internet offers the marketer three alternatives for advertising. The marketer can create a destination site, a micro site, or advertise through a banner and/or sponsorship campaign. To determine the best advertising alternative, the marketer must first decide if the product or service advertised can be sold online and if the product or service is a considered purchase (Doyle, Modahl & Abbott, 1997).

Destination and Micro Sites

If a marketer determines that the product or service being marketed can indeed be sold online, and it is a product or service consumers usually collect information on prior to purchase, the marketer should utilize a destination or micro site for his or her online advertising. Destination sites are sites that operate as fully functioning businesses (Klein, 1997). These sites should only be utilized by companies that are able to use the Internet as a dedicated channel for exchanging information between the customer and the seller (Doyle et al., 1997).

Micro sites are similar in use to destination sites. These sites differ only in that they are smaller sites and do not require a large investment. For example, the official sites of the teams in the NBA are micro sites, or smaller websites housed on the larger NBA league site. Micro sites enable advertisers to communicate in-depth product information to the consumer while collecting information from them, without the cost of developing and running a fully functional site (Doyle et al., 1997).

Advertising Banner and/or Sponsorship Campaign

For most marketers though, solely using banner advertising may be adequate. This method of online advertising is usually enough for simple, off-the-shelf products requiring little thought by the consumer prior to purchase (Doyle et al., 1997). For marketers developing destination or micro sites, banner advertising should be used in conjunction with those advertising efforts in order to link the consumer from banner advertisements to the advertising site (Maddox, 1997).

Considering that the first advertising banner was sold only in 1994 ("Why Internet," 1997), there are already several benefits mentioned in the literature for implementing this form of advertising. First, it has been found that online banners are a successful way to extend existing brands into the online marketplace. Examples include the numerous brokerage firms that have opened business on the web. Second, banners have been found to be effective for advertising complex products or services by linking the banner to a destination or micro site containing information on the advertised product ("Tips," 1997). Third, and possibly most important to the interactive marketer, banner advertisements have been found to build brand awareness ("Why Internet," 1998).

A study of online users found that the exposure to a single web banner increased consumers' awareness of the product advertised from between 12 and 200 percent, depending on which product was advertised ("Why Internet," 1997; Rich, 1997). Further, a single exposure to a web banner generated greater awareness than a single exposure to a television or print advertisement ("Why Internet," 1997). Passive product name recognition increased as well (Briggs & Hollis, 1997). Consumers in the study tended to remember the product advertised and even considered purchasing the brand (Rich, 1997). Purchase intent for the brands advertised rose between 5 and 50 percent (Rich, 1997; Briggs & Hollis, 1997).

Drawbacks to banner advertisements have been discussed as well. A major disadvantage to using banners to advertise a product is the existence of either poor or non-existent measuring systems for determining the reach of the advertisement. Additionally, today's modem speeds are not quick enough to allow for rapid transfer of information between the host computer and the consumer's computer; thus, there is currently a limit to the amount of animation that can be used on banners. To insure a banner is loaded quickly onto a site, banner advertisements should be limited to between 10 and 15 kilobytes in size (Rich, 1997).

It has also been mentioned that web banners do not reach across all of the demographic groups that the major advertisers want to target (Rich, 1997). And, diminishing returns on the effectiveness of an advertising banner begin immediately. After seeing the same banner ad three times, there is little likelihood that the consumer will use the banner to link to the destination or micro site for the product advertised (Briggs & Hollis, 1997). Finally, advertising banners are not effective for creating or re-positioning brands online (Rich, 1997).

Measuring Online Return on Investment (ROI)

As mentioned, Rich (1997) stated that a major drawback for advertisers using banner ads is that measuring systems for determining the reach of the advertisement are poor or non-existent. One measurable method does exist—the click-through. The use of click-through is debated by advertisers and content providers. Click-through on advertising banners moves the consumer from a content-focused website to the advertiser's site where interactive marketing can occur. Click-through occurs when a consumer places the cursor over the advertising banner and presses, or clicks, the mouse button. The computer automatically moves the user from the site of the banner advertisement to the advertiser's destination or micro site (Briggs & Hollis, 1997).

It is argued that the click-through is the best method for determining advertising effectiveness, as it is a behavioral response, and it is easy to observe and measure (Briggs & Hollis, 1997). Some have even argued that without click-through, brand building will not occur ("Why Internet, 1997). Those with this view want banners to be considered similar to direct mail, so they feel that click-through is the best measure for gauging response to the advertisement. Some authors, however, feel that the click-through response is affected by surfer traits and habits. These traits include the innate tendency of some web surfers to click on advertisements, the immediate relevance of the product to surfers, and the preexisting allure a brand or company may have on surfers (Briggs & Hollis, 1997).

As it has been shown, basic web banners have value beyond simple click-through (Rich, 1997). Evaluating the effectiveness of advertising based on click-through would be similar to evaluating television commercials for automobiles by measuring the number of people who go to the dealership the very next day (Briggs & Hollis, 1997). Briggs & Hollis further added that since it has been proven that web banners have a sizeable affect on brand loyalty and attitudes toward brands, which is not reflected by the click-through measure, the use of click-through rates alone would undervalue the web as an advertising medium. Finally, the authors stated that as only a small fraction of consumers click-through the banners they see, cost per thousand (CPM) impressions are most often used to determine banner advertising prices.

The Sport Industry and the Internet Today

Sport sites are among the most popular on the Internet ("ESPN.com Wraps Up," 2000). For example, of the top 15 entertainment/information sites on the web at the end of 1997, three were sport sites: ESPN.com, SportsLine.com, and NFL.com (InterZine Productions, 1997c). More people visit sport team sites than visit their respective ballparks and stadiums. On one site, surfers from all 50 states and 35 foreign countries accessed the site during the 1997 baseball season (Zarkowsky, 1997).

Site Content

Three studies have examined the type of information available on sport sites. Farrell and McCann (1997) found that NCAA Division I athletic department sites focused on team schedules, ticketing, press releases, photographs, special events, and player profiles. In his study of Major League Baseball sites, Brown (1998) found that MLB teams focused on team rosters, player information, ticketing, press releases, team schedule, and the team's home ballpark. A study of the use of the Internet by health clubs showed that the primary use of club websites was for communication with members (Tucker, 1997).

However, sport organizations are beginning to change the content of websites. Sites are becoming streamlined, more user friendly, and more interactive (Zarkowsky, 1997). Interactive fantasy games are available to visitors of many professional sport team sites. During the 1997 season, each MLB team featured Cyber Skipper. Cyber Skipper enabled site visitors to manage a team of ballplayers against other teams in the fantasy league (Zarkowsky, 1997). In addition to fantasy games, site visitors can listen to audio broadcasts of many professional sport teams. Over 1,000 NHL games were available via the web during the 1997–1998 season. Additionally, original pre and post game programming was exclusively available to web listeners (InterZine Productions, 1997d). The NBA offered site visitors an opportunity to listen to any game during the 1997–1998 season if they purchased an Audio League Pass for $20 (InterZine Productions, 1997e). These cybercasts are popular on many sites. In fact, of all the visitors to the official site of the Final Four, one-third listened to cybercasts of tournament games ("NCAA to create," 1998).

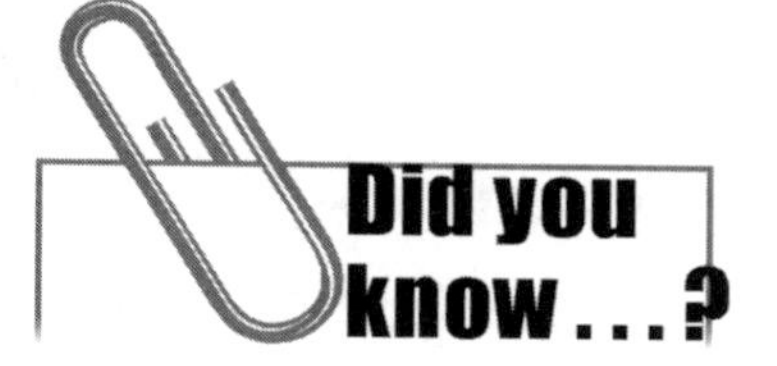

New York State leads in the number of athletes participating in the Special Olympics. They have 40,000 athletes and 30,000 volunteer workers.

Source: *Amy Love's Real Sports Magazine*

Events Attract Site Visitors

Sport sites are visited most frequently when special events related to the sites' owners occur. During game days, the St. Louis Cardinals have found that between 8,000 and 10,000 additional users visit the site to monitor the progress of the game (Zarkowsky, 1997). Site traffic also increases during major events. The Final Four official site saw 9.2 million visitors ("NCAA to create," 1998) while the official site of the 1998 Olympics recorded over 600 million hits (InterZine Productions, 1998d). The amount of traffic on these sites increased as the event neared culmination. This was seen in MLB as well. The official site for the World Series had 840,000 hits for Game 1. On the day of Game 7, the final game of the series, the site had 4.3 million hits (InterZine Productions, 1997e).

Many other events have led to an increase in site traffic and often set records for visits to the site. When the Montreal Canadians relaunched their site, the site logged 500,000 page views in just under 90 minutes, a new record for the site (InterZine

Productions, 1998a). After the pairings for the 1998 NCAA basketball tournament were announced, ESPN had 1.1 million unique visitors log onto the site and became the first site in Internet history to reach 1 million visitors in a day (InterZine Productions, 1998e). Trading deadlines have also brought record activity to websites. The NHL reached a daily high for hits the day of the 1997–1998 season trading deadline (InterZine Productions, 1998f). Finally, the retirement or the loss of a member of an organization can create record site activity. The Chicago Cubs quadrupled their record for page views on opening day 1998, their organization's first official game since the death of team broadcaster Harry Carey. Additionally, a record 25,000 listened to the cybercast of the game (InterZine Productions, 1998g). At the University of North Carolina, a record 83,500 people visited the athletic department's site to read about the retirement of men's basketball coach Dean Smith. The previous high for that site was approximately 16,000 (InterZine Productions, 1997c).

New Ticket Distribution System

To increase ticket sales, sport organizations have moved ticket outlets to suburban malls, sold tickets through Ticketmaster, and developed a means to sell tickets via the Internet. The goal of a ticket distribution system is to facilitate sales by making tickets readily available. Today, online ticket orders are small, but the future has great potential. Online event ticketing generated $274 million in sales in 1999 and is expected to generate $1.8 billion by 2002. Also, more than 75 percent of travel and entertainment companies are planning to sell tickets online, and it was predicted that by the year 2000 over 10 percent of all tickets would be sold via the Internet. To date, sport franchises have had success selling tickets online either directly through their site or indirectly by hyperlinking to Ticketmaster (Williams, 1999).

Benefits to online ticketing include round-the-clock operation, elimination of the middleman, customer convenience, expanding your organization's ticket sales reach, and building a new distribution channel. Disadvantages include the difficulties in integrating the Internet system with existing ones, lack of Internet security, customer apprehension, and loss of human contact with the customer (Forrester Research, 1998a).

Notwithstanding, the impact of online ticketing should have major ramifications in the sport and entertainment industry. First, the bar has been raised for meeting consumer expectations. As online ticketing has developed, consumers now have access to a wealth of information and online assistance. Second, new channels of distribution often mean new pricing. Third, technology alliances will become critical. In order to get people to your site and attract repeat purchasers, alliances will have to be made between sport organizations, web search engines, and web page designers. Finally, new marketing possibilities will erupt everywhere as a result. As discussed, purchasing via the web enables complex databases of consumer information to be developed and compiled by the seller (Forrester Research, 1998a).

In sports, it appears that baseball franchises are most eagerly embracing online ticketing. During the 1998 season, close to 33% of MLB teams offered tickets directly from their site. Teams in smaller leagues like MLS will probably move to online ticketing as well, as these leagues are hungry for new fans, and they often target a suburban, PC-friendly, family audience.

Recent Website Trends in the Sport Industry

Some interesting trends in sport websites have appeared. Almost every athlete now has an official site. Dennis Rodman, John LeClair, and Roger Clemens have official sites (InterZine Productions, 1997c; InterZine Productions, 1998c; InterZine Productions, 1998g). Michael Jordan has an official site. His differs from the rest though, as seven companies have signed agreements to be official sponsors of his site (InterZine Productions, 1997f).

Another trend is the combination of organizational resources to create a website. Major League Baseball combined with television network NBC and cable network MSNBC to create the official site for the 1997 World Series (InterZine Productions, 1997b). The NCAA, because of the popularity of its Final Four site, has created a website separate from its corporate site to be used for its 81 championships ("NCAA to create," 1998). The site will feature news coverage of each championship, ticket information, participating school and athlete information, and cybercasts.

The NFL became the first league to receive rights fees for the production of its site, a fact that may have the greatest ramifications for sport leagues and teams. Until recently, leagues and teams paid organizations to produce their sites. ESPN.com paid the NFL $3 million per year from 1998 to 2001 for the rights to produce the league's official site (InterZine Productions, 1998e).

Chapter Summary

Today's sport sites are among the most popular sites on the Internet (InterZine Productions, 1997c). But, without detailed knowledge of web-based marketing in the sport industry, sport organizations are left to modify their website content and web marketing activities after organizational sites that appear to be successful. Since the future of profitability is uncertain, it is important for sport marketers to understand how to use this technology effectively. Few researchers have focused on this problem and what little is currently known does not necessarily apply to all professional sport leagues (Brown, 1998) and NCAA Division I athletic departments (Farrell & McCann, 1997). Therefore, the phenomenon of website development and usage in the entire sport industry needs to be studied in greater detail.

The evidence that does exist suggests that selling sponsorship might make sites profitable, or at least reduce their debts. This method for revenue acquisition is even more intriguing now as IBM paid a record $1 million—largest sponsorship fee in the brief history of the web—to be the sole sponsor of the 1998 Super Bowl site (InterZine Productions, 1997i). Even more interesting, Insight Enterprises signed a three-year sponsorship agreement with the Arizona Sports Foundation to rename the Copper Bowl the Insight.com bowl in an effort to promote their website and their organization (InterZine Productions, 1997g).

With all the uncertainty surrounding website operations, their usefulness, and their profit potential, you may wonder why it is important for you to understand this relatively new phenomenon. Consider the effect of web-based sport marketing on just one element of the marketing mix. Traditionally, place decisions are some of the most important decisions to the marketer because these decisions have long-range implications and are harder to change than product, price, and promotion decisions, especially in sport, where the basic product is the game form itself. From traditional sport marketing theory, recall that the venue of the game should maximize exposure. Additionally, recall that place can affect the consumption of your product, either positively or negatively. For example, the current problems facing the New York Yankees illustrate the importance of place. In the largest market in the United States, with one of the best teams in baseball, attendance at Yankee games has been disappointing. The Yankees have been considering a move to Long Island, Manhattan, and even New Jersey because people are afraid to go to games at Yankee Stadium, as they perceive crime to be high in the area surrounding the stadium.

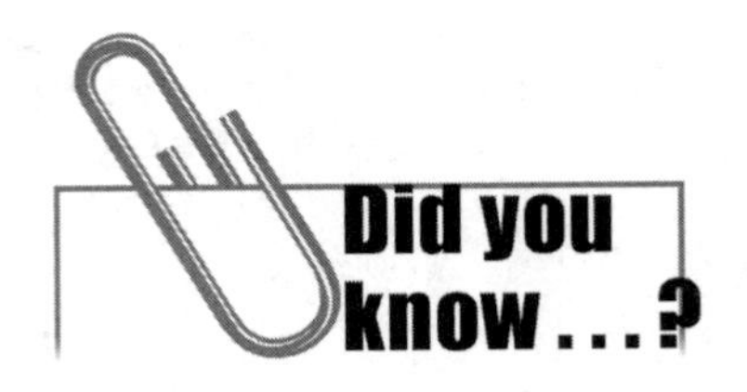

The budget for the Women's World Cup in 1999 was $40 million.

Source: *Amy Love's Real Sports Magazine*

Traditional sport marketing theory states that sport is a unique industry with relation to the marketing mix. Apart from the sporting goods industry, there is little movement of product from the site of production to the site of consumption. The distribution function in sport primarily concerns the facility—its location, layout, access, and amenities—rather than the physical channels of marketing—wholesalers and retailers. But, is the facility the most important consideration with respect to the future?

Through traditional sport marketing theory, we have been told several things about the relevance of place to the sport marketer. Where a high level of impulse buying is involved, a high-traffic location is crucial. But, is this so? Is location important? Remember, it has been said that the three most important factors in marketing are location, location, location. Is location still important? Or is it now more important to have a memorable URL or web address?

With today's technology, do you still have to worry about facility accessibility, parking, the surrounding area, or the geographic location? Or, do baud rates and website navigation now replace location concerns? Do you have to worry about facility layout, or is facility layout still as important as it used to be? We, as sport marketers, must now also worry about website layout. We must know which features of site construction our customers demand. We also must know which elements of site construction make the surfing experience more pleasant for the surfer. Are our customers frustrated because they cannot order tickets online, listen to games online, or order merchandise online? Do we have to worry about the image of our facility? We now must focus our efforts on the image of the company and design the website to reflect that image.

We do still have to worry about marketing channels. To distribute the product, efficient means for the implementation of e-commerce have to be developed. An organization must now be able to process requests and respond to them quickly. We can see this by looking at Movie Phone's online ticketing. Tickets for almost any theater can be purchased at any place at any time as long as you have a laptop computer and a cell phone. Also, we can look at what the St. Louis Cardinals provide their website visitors. Audio broadcasts of all games can be heard through the site. Per cap merchandise items can be ordered while listening to the game. And, when the sport consumer wants to actually go to a game, the site allows the visitor to purchase tickets to any game at any time (www.stlcardinals.com).

By establishing an online presence, almost every traditional cost of doing business can be eliminated (other costs, of course, are created like site design, programming, and online customer service). No longer does a new business have to worry about the storefront, salespeople, and warehouse space. New businesses do not have a concern for displays, lighting, and inventory. Most importantly, location does not matter online. All a customer must know is the company's web address to access the organization from anywhere in the world.

When a customer makes an electronic purchase, the order travels electronically without human contact, going from the purchaser's computer to the company's computer. The company's computer then checks inventory, debits the customer's credit card, and sends the order electronically to a distributor. A confirmation of the purchase is sent to the purchaser vie email, all while the product is on its way.

Graham (1996) stated that there are new challenges facing marketers in a placeless business environment. These challenges must now be considered by all those marketing sport. Place has now become nonexistent or a meaningless blur. We are entering an age of "everything-everywhere." Near and far have no meaning. Information is placeless. The question of how to access a product or information has replaced that of where the information is located. Customers now want careful, continuous, useful information instead of a smiling salesperson. Amazon.com provides an example of this. The question of where the bookstore is located has become, how do I access it?

As place becomes more irrelevant, the marketer must learn more about the cyberworld. To do so, Graham (1996) stated that the marketer must:

1. Think customer—Geography is a meaningless barrier. Without these meaningless barriers, the marketing emphasis changes to defining the customer, not the customer's location.
2. Think communication—Traditionally, sales people think about place or where they are going to sell. Today's salesperson is a gatekeeper, a manager of communication. Communication is now the necessary interaction, and the laptop, cell phone, and modem are what is important.
3. Think access—This is the only significant issue. The customer hates delayed, inconvenient, and inefficient access more than they hate receiving inferior products or services.
4. Think conceptually—Use your visionary skills to look at new ways to reach the customer. Changes must be made constantly. Those who wait to make a change will fall behind.
5. Think seamless—Steps in business planning are now non-existent. Ordering, processing, manufacturing, and shipping are now all a part of a single process. When a new product is developed, it should be released to the market as soon as possible.
6. Think from within—Placelessness means connectivity. Over half of those born after 1971, the year the computer chip was invented, plan to receive their news via the Internet, while only 31 percent will depend on television and the radio, and only 10 percent will receive their news through the print media.

Questions for Study

1. What is the difference between the Internet and the world wide web?
2. Why should sport organizations seriously consider developing a site on the world wide web if they have not done so already?
3. How have sport marketers used the web to market their product thus far?
4. What must a sport marketer consider when developing a website for his or her sport organization?
5. Describe interactive marketing. What are some of its unique features?
6. Will the web alter traditional sport marketing theory, and if so, how?

Learning Activities

1. Visit five official sport sites on the web and compare the features offered on each site. What do you like about the sites? What do you dislike? Do you feel that each of the sites is an effective marketing tool for the organization's creating them?
2. Contact an organization with a site on the web (possibly your school's athletic department). Ask the organization why they created the website and what they hope to accomplish through their site's operation.
3. Conduct a class study and see how many people have purchased a product or products online. How many of these were sport products? For those that have not purchased a product online, why have they not done so? Do they plan to do so in the future?

References

A.R.C. (1998, May). Park and roll. *Athletic Business, 23*, 18.

ABC Evening News. (2000, September 14). Report on ABC Evening News.

ABC Evening News. (2000, September 22). Report on ABC Evening News with Peter Jennings.

Adelman, M. L. (1986). *A sporting time: New York City and the rise of modern athletics, 1820–1870.* Urbana, IL: U of Illinois Press.

Andrew Peck, Pioneer. (1916). *Sporting Goods Dealer, 34*(4), 55–56.

Armstrong, K. L. (1998). Ten strategies to employ when marketing sport to black consumers. *Sport Marketing Quarterly, 7*(3), 11–18.

Arthur, D., Scott, D., Woods, T., and Booker, R. (1998). Sport sponsorships should . . . A process model for the effective implementation of sport sponsorship programs. *Sport Marketing Quarterly, 7*(4), 35–48.

Ashland personnel. (1916). *Sporting Goods Dealer, 34*(1), 78–81.

Athletic Promotions: Ways to generate revenue and increase attendance. (1997, April) *Athletic Administration, 6*, 12–14.

Axtell, R. E. (1991). *Gestures: The do's and taboos of body language around the world.* New York: John Wiley and Sons.

Baghdikian, E. (1996). Building the sports organization's merchandise licensing program: The appropriateness, significance and considerations. *Sport Marketing Quarterly, 5*(1), 35–41.

Ball, A. (1989, November 13). Here's who's living with whom. *Adweek's Marketing Week*, HM 11.

Barlow, R. (1992, March). Relationship marketing: The ultimate in customer service. *Retail Control*, 29–37.

Barney, R. K. (1978). Of rails and red stockings: Episodes in the expansion of the national pastime in the American West. *Sport and Recreation in the West*, 61–70.

Bartels, R. (1988). *The history of marketing thought.* Columbus, OH: Publishing Horizons.

Battle III, W. R., Bailey, B., and Siegal, B. B. (1991). Collegiate trademark licensing. In B. L. Parkhouse (Ed.), *The management of sport: Its foundation and application* (pp. 245–263). St. Louis, MO: Mosby.

Bean, R. B. (1997, December). Business-to-business database marketing: The future is now! *Direct Marketing, 60*(8), 43–45.

Berlin, E. (1996, July). Just a fantasy. *Internet World, 7*(7), 102–104.

Bernstein, A. (1998, August 10–16). Coalition targets $2 billion-a-year counterfeiting trade. *Sports Business Journal, 1*, 29.

Bernstein, A. (1998, November 23–29). Reebok's future not in the stars. *Sports Business Journal, 1*, 7.

Berrett, T., Slack, T., and Whitson, D. (1993). Economics and the pricing of sport and leisure. *Journal of Sport Management, 7*, 199–215.

Berthon, P., Pitt, L., & Watson, R. T. (1996a). Marketing communication and the world wide web. *Business Horizons, 39*(5), 24–32.

Berthon, P., Pitt, L., & Watson, R. T. (1996b). Re-surfing w3: Research perspectives on marketing communication and buyer behavior communications on the world wide web. *International Journal of Advertising, 15*(4), 287–301.

Berthon, P., Pitt, L., & Watson, R. T. (1996c). The world wide web as an advertising medium: Toward an understanding of conversion efficiency. *Journal of Advertising Research, 36*(1), 43–54.

Betts, J. R. (1974). *America's Sporting Heritage, 1850–1950.* Reading, MA: Addison-Wesley Publishing Company.

Bhonslay, M. (1999a, February 8–14). Women's goods don't score with fans. *Sport Business Journal, 2*, 28.

Bhonslay, M. (1999b, February 8–14). You did a great job for us—you're fired. *Sport Business Journal, 2*, 24.

Blumenstyk, G. (1996, April 19). Money-making champs. *Chronicle of Higher Education*, A49–51.

Boeh, T. (1989, October). A program for selling. *Collegiate Athletic Management,3*, 53–55.

Bonham, D. (1999, February). Sport marketing in the new millennium. Presentation at the University of Northern Colorado, Greeley, CO .

Boone, L.E., and Kurtz, D.L. (1989). *Contemporary marketing.* Orlando, FL: The Dryden Press.

Boone, L. E., and Kurtz, D. L. (1992). *Contemporary marketing.* Fort Worth, TX: The Dryden Press.

Borden, N. (1942). *The economic effects of advertising.* Chicago, IL: Irwin, Inc.

Bourdon, S. (2000, December). Glass cutter. *Trailer Boats, 30*, 30–33.

Bradbury, M. (1990). How club life cycles affect strategy. *Club Business International, 11*(7), 16, 35, 37.

Bradley, S. (1996, April 15). D. mail is becoming email: Direct marketers are getting interactive. *Brandweek, 37*(16), 44–45.

Branvold, S. E. (1992). Utilization of fence signage in college baseball. *Sport Marketing Quarterly, 1*(2), 29–32.

Branvold, S. E., and Bowers, R. (1992). The use of promotions in college baseball. *Sport Marketing Quarterly, 1*(1), 19–24.

Briggs, R., & Hollis, N. (1997, March/April). Advertising on the web: Is there response before click-through? *Journal of Advertising Research, 37*(2), 33–45.

Briner, R. A. (1992, April). *European sports business opportunities.* Paper presented at the 1992 International Conference on Sport Business, Columbia, SC.

Brooks, C. M. (1998). Celebrity athlete endorsement: An overview of the key theoretical issues. *Sport Marketing Quarterly, 7*(2), 34–44.

Broughton, D. (2001, January 1–7). Events up for bid. *SportsBusiness Journal, 3*(37), 27.

Brown, M. T. (1998, January). An examination of the content of official major league baseball team sites on the world wide web. *Cyber-Journal of Sport Marketing* [Online], *2*(1). Available: www.cjsm.com/Vol2/brown.htm

Brubaker, B. (1991, March 11). In shoe companies' competition, the coaches are the key players. *Washington Post*, A1.

Brunson, M.W., and Shelby, B. (1993). Recreation substitutability: A research agenda. *Leisure Sciences, 15*(1), 67–74.

Bucklin, L. P. (1972). *Competition and evolution in the distributive trades.* Englewood Cliffs, NJ: Prentice-Hall, Inc.

Bunn, D. (1997a, December 1). Online shopping boon for retailers. *Rocky Mountain News,* 1B, 14B.

Bunn, D. (1997b, December 7). Truecount counts times ad seen on Net. *Rocky Mountain News,* 13G.

Byl, J. (1990). *Organizing successful tournaments.* Champaign, IL: Leisure Press.

Byrd, A. (1999, September 27–October 3). Extreme publications take aim at sport—and lifestyle. *SportsBusiness Journal, 2*(23), 27.

Carpenter, K. (1999, March 8). On edge: The snowsports industry has no need for more challenges these days. *Sporting Goods Business, 32*(5), 30.

Carucci, V. (1994). Touchdown south: Super Bowl XXVIII in Atlanta. *Sky Magazine, 23*(1), 36–40, 43–44, 46.

Caywood, C., and Stocker, K. (1993). The ultimate crisis plan. In J. Gottschal (Ed.), *Crisis response* (pp. 409–427). Detroit: Gale Research Inc.

Chalip, L., and Thoma, J. (1993). *Sport governance in the global community.* Morgantown, WV: Fitness Information Technology, Inc.

Chandler, A. D., Jr. (1977). *The visible hand: The managerial revolution in American business.* Cambridge, MA: Harvard U Press.

Chudacoff, H. P. (1981). *The evolution of American urban society.* Englewood Cliffs, NJ: Prentice-Hall.

Clay, B. (1995). 8 great careers in the sports industry. *Black Enterprise, 25*(12), 158–166.

Coast to Coast. (1998, November 2–8). *Sports Business Journal,* 36.

Cohen, A. (1993, July). How not to run a promotion. *Athletic Business, 17, 14.*

Comte, E., and Stogel, C. (1990, January 1). Sports: A $63.1 billion industry. *The Sporting News, 208*(28), 60–61.

Conklin, A. (1999, April). Licensing Renewal. *Athletic Business, 23,* 32–34.

Cravens, D. W., and Woodruff, R. B. (1986). *Marketing.* Reading, MA: Addison-Wesley Publishing Company.

Danziger, G. (1985). Computer applications in sport. In G. Lewis and H. Appenzeller (Eds.), *Successful sport management* (pp. 215–241). Charlottesville, VA: The Michie Company.

DeBrock, L. (1991). Economics. In B. Parkhouse (Ed.), *The management of sport: Its foundation and application* (56–73). St. Louis: Mosby-Year Book, Inc.

Delpy, L. (2000, January). Winning Contests. *Sports Travel, 4*(1), 8–9.

Delpy, L., & Bosetti, H. (1998). Sport management and marketing via the world wide web. *Sport Marketing Quarterly, 7*(1), 21–27.

Dénes, F., and Misovicz, K. (1993, October). *Changes and contradictions: Sport market in Hungary.* Paper presented at the 4th International Conference on Sport Business, Paris, France.

DePauw, K. P., and Gavron, S. J. (1995). *Disability and sport.* Champaign, IL: Human Kinetics.

Dodd, M., and Pearson, B. (1997, November 21). Big-time matchups underscore the big business of college ball. *USA Today,* 1C, 4C.

Donahue, M. D. (1998, February 2). Adapting the internet to the needs of business. *Advertising Age, 69*(5), 26.

Doyle, B., Modahl, M. A., & Abbott, B. (1997, May 5). What advertising works. *Mediaweek, 7*(18), S38–S41.

Ducoffe, R. H. (1996, September/October). Advertising value and advertising on the web. *Journal of Advertising Research, 36*(5), 21–35.

East, W., Ronchin, F. and Smith, N. (2000, October). The highest earners in European sport. *EuroBusiness,* (24), 106–123.

ESPN Radio Network: One year later, (1993, Winter). *Between the lines: Ernst and Young's financial newsletter for the sports world,* 10–11, 13.

ESPN Sportzone. (1998, January 14). [Online] Available: http://www.espnet.sportzone.com

ESPN. (2000). *ESPN Insider* [Online]. Available: espn.com

ESPN.com wraps up 2000 with record-breaking traffic. (2000, December 29). *Business Wire* [Online]. Available: www.businesswire.com

Evans, J. R., and Berman, B. (1987). *Marketing.* New York: Macmillan Publishing Company.

Fahri, P. (1997, November 4). As women take the field, firms deliver pitches. *Washington Post,* A1.

Falk, H. (1983). *Handbook of computer applications for the small or medium-sized business.* Radnor, PA: Chilton Book Company.

Fan-favorite endorsers. (2000, September 9–15) *Sport Business Journal, 3,* 35.

Farrell, C., and Schiller, Z. (1993, November 15). Stuck! How companies cope when they can't raise prices. *BusinessWeek,* 146–155.

Farrell, P. V., & McCann, D. J. (1997). Computers, the internet, and marketing college athletics. *Sport Marketing Quarterly, 6*(3), 12–13.

Fechter, S. (1998, September). Fun for fans. *Athletic Management, 10,* 48–52.

Feigenbaum, R. (1996, September 9). Garbage in—and in and in. *Business Week, 3492,* 110.

Ferrand, A., and Pagés, M. (1996). Image sponsoring: A methodology to match event and sponsor. *Journal of Sport Management, 10,* 278–291.

Fielding, L. W., Pitts, B. G., and Miller, L. K. (1991). Defining quality: Should educators in sport management programs be concerned about accreditation? *Journal of Sport Management, 5*(1), 1–17.

Fitzgerald, M. (1997, March 8). Web cash lies in entertainment. *Editor & Publisher, 130*(10), 46.

Forrester Research. (1998a). *The forrester report: Entertainment & technology strategies* [Online]. Available: wysiwyg://20/www.forrester.com/cgi-bin/cgi.pl

Forrester Research. (1998b). *Forrester research finds internet business trade to jump to $327 billion by the year 2002* [Online]. Available: www.forrester.com/press/pressrel/970728BT.htm

Foskett, S. (1996, November). Online technology ushers in one-to-one marketing. *Direct Marketing, 59*(7), 38–40.

Fox, J., and Levin, J. (1993). *How to work with the media.* Newbury Park, CA: Sage Publications.

Fram, E. H., & Grady, D. B. (1997, January). Internet shoppers: Is there a surfer gender gap? *Direct Marketing, 59*(9), 46–50.

Freedman, S. (1978). The baseball fad in Chicago. *Journal of Sport History, 5*(1), 42–64.

Frickey, E. (1947). *Production in the United States, 1860–1914.* Cambridge, MA: Harvard University Press.

Fried-Cassorla, A. (1995, March). Successful marketing on the internet: A user's guide. *Direct Marketing, 57*(11), 39–41.

From the Field. (1997, September 17). *Reebok, International,* (12).

Fullerton, R. A. (1988). How modern is modern marketing? Marketing's evolution and the myth of the production era. *Journal of Marketing, 52*(1), 108–125.

Gaston, F. P. (1984). *Administrative decision making: A study of collegiate trademark licensing programs.* Unpublished doctoral dissertation, University of Alabama, Tuscaloosa, AL.

Gauws, J. S. (1997). *Sport management theory and practice.* Pretoria, South Africa: Sigma Press.

Gibson, H., Attle, S. P., and Yiannakis, A. (1998). Segmenting the active sport tourist market: Life-span perspective. *Journal of Vacation Marketing, 4*(1), 51–64.

Godin, S. (1996, December). When stamps are free—using email and the internet for direct response. *Direct Marketing, 59*(8), 46–49.

Goldfisher, A. (1998, August 10–16). Cyberselling delivers global marketplace. *Sport Business Journal, 1*, 25.

Goldstein, W. (1989). *Playing for keeps: A history of early baseball.* Ithaca, NY: Cornell University Press.

Gonzalez, E. (1998, March 9). Marketing ski resorts on Internet a slick idea. *Rocky Mountain News*, 1B.

Gorn, E. J. (1986). *The manly art: bare-knuckle prize fighting in America*. Ithaca, NY: Cornell University Press.

Graham, J. R. (1996, October). How to market and sell in a cyberworld. *Direct Marketing, 59*(6), 26–27.

Grantham, W., Patton, R., York, T., and Winick, M. (1998). *Health fitness management.* Champaign, IL: Human Kinetics.

Graphic, Visualization, & Usability Center. (1997). *GVU's 8th www user survey* [Online]. Available: www.gvu.gatech.edu/user_surveys/survey-1997-10/

Graphic, Visualization, & Usability Center. (1999). *GVU's 10th www user survey* [Online]. Available: www.gvu.gatech.edu/user_surveys/survey-1998-10/

Greenwald, L., and Fernandez-Balboa, J. (1998). Trends in sport marketing industry and in the demographics of the United States: Their effect on the strategic role of grassroots sport sponsorships in corporate America. *Sport Marketing Quarterly, 7*(4), 35–48.

Greim, L. (1997, October 26). Internet users gagging on spam. *Rocky Mountain News,* 1G, 5G.

Griffin, J. (1996, November). The internet's expanding role in building customer loyalty. *Direct Marketing, 59*(7), 50–53.

Gunther, M. (1996, March 4). Web + sports = profit. Right? *Fortune, 133*(4), 197–198.

Hagstrom, R. (1998). *The NASCAR way*. New York: Wiley.

Handel, C., & Forrester, S. (1997, Spring). Database marketing: Increasing participation in recreational sports. *NIRSA Journal, 21*(3), 46–48.

Harada M. (1993, October). *Development and structural changes in sport business in Japan.* Paper presented at the 4th International Conference on Sport Business, Paris.

Hardy, S. (1982). *How Boston played: Sport, recreation, and community, 1865–1915.* Boston: Northeastern University Press.

Hardy, S. (1986). Entrepreneurs, organizations, and the sport marketplace: Subjects in search of historians. *Journal of Sport History, 13*(1), 21.

Hardy, S. (1990). Adopted by all the leading clubs: sporting goods and the shaping of leisure, 1800–1900. In Richard Butsch (Ed.), *For fun and profit: The transformation of leisure into consumption* (pp. 71–101). Philadelphia: Temple University Press.

Hawkins, D. T. (1994). Electronic advertising: On online information systems. *Online,* 15–25.

Helitzer, M. (1995). *The dream job: Sports publicity, promotion, and public relations 2nd ed.* Athens, OH: University Press.

Hendee, J.C., and Burdge, R.W. (1974). The substitutability concept: Implications for recreation research and management. *Journal of Leisure Research, 6*, 157–162.

Herman, J. T. (1992, April). From chaos to control. *Case Currents,* 24–28.

Hiebing, R. C., and Cooper, S. W. (1990). *How to write a successful marketing plan.* Lincolnwood, IL: NTC Business Books.

Higgs, R. (1971). *The transformation of American economy, 1865–1914: An essay in interpretation.* New York: Cambridge University Press.

Himelstein. L. (1997, January 27). The game's the thing at Nike now. *Business Week*, 88.

Hodges, J. (1996, October 28). Direct marketing. *Advertising Age, 67*(42), S1–S2.

Hodgkinson, H. L. (1992, June). *A demographic look at tomorrow.* Washington, DC: Institute for Educational Leadership.

Hofman, M. (1999, December). Searching for the mountain of youth. *Inc.* (21), 18, 33–36.

Holland, M. (1992, May). International opportunities. *Fitness Management*, 39–43.

Holland, S., Pybas, D., and Sanders, A. (1992). Personal watercraft: Fun, speed—and conflict? *Parks and Recreation, 27*(11), 52–56.

Horine, L. (1995). *Administration of Physical Education and Sport Programs 3rd Ed.* Madison, WI: Brown and Benchmark.

Hounshell, D. A. (1984). *From the American system to mass production, 1800–1932.* Baltimore, MD: The John Hopkins University Press.

Howard, D. R., and Crompton, J. L. (1980). *Financing, managing and marketing recreation and park resources.* Dubuque, IA: Wm. C. Brown Company Publishers.

Huang, Y. (1999). *An investigation of the current practices of relationship marketing programs within professional baseball through a content analysis.* Unpublished doctoral dissertation, University of Northern Colorado, Greeley, CO.

IEG Forecast: Sponsorship spending growth will slow in 2001. (2000, December 18). *IEG Sponsorship Report, 19,* 1, 4–5.

IEG, Inc. (1995). *IEG sr briefing: Computer industry sponsorship.* Chicago: Author.

IEG, Inc. (1996). How properties price internet benefits. *IEG Sponsorship Report, 15*(7), 1–3.

Infoseek Corporation. (1999). *Driving the growth of the internet* [Online]. Available: info.infoseek.com/

International Events Group (1992a, September 7). Centerfold. *IEG Sponsorship Report, 11*, 4–5.

International Events Group (1992b, November 2). Assertions. *IEG Sponsorship Report, 11*, 2.

International Events Group (1992c, November 2). Industry news. *IEG Sponsorship Report, 11*, 7.

International Events Group (1992d, December 21). Centerfold: The bottom line on sponsorship. *IEG Sponsorship Report, 11*, 4–6.

International Events Group (1994, December 6). Assertions. *IEG Sponsorship Report 13*, 2.

International Health, Racquet and Sportsclub Association. (1998). *IHRSA: State of the industry report.* Boston: Author.

Internet population reaches 56% of U.S. adults. (2001, February 19). *USA Today* [Online]. Available: www.usatoday.com/

InterZine Productions, Inc. (1997a, May 2). ESPN Chilton sports poll: Online sports information. *The Sports Business Daily, 3*(143), 11.

InterZine Productions, Inc. (1997b, September 30). The daily follows MLB's postseason via the air and web. *The Sports Business Daily, 4*(13), 4.

InterZine Productions, Inc. (1997c, October 22). Online news & notes: One more record for dean at UNC. *The Sports Business Daily, 4*(26), 10.

InterZine Productions, Inc. (1997d, October 23). Online news & notes: NHL puts the puck in audionet. *The Sports Business Daily, 4*(27), 5.

InterZine Productions, Inc. (1997e, October 28). Nba.com included increased game coverage and new sponsors. *The Sports Business Daily, 4*(30), 5,8.

InterZine Productions, Inc. (1997f, October 29). MJ's website takes to the air at jordan.sportsline.com. *The Sports Business Daily, 4*(31), 10.

InterZine Productions, Inc. (1997g, November 7). Throwing copper: Here's some insight on AZ bowl plans. *The Sports Business Daily, 4*(38), 2.

InterZine Productions, Inc. (1997h, November 21). ESPN Chilton sports poll: Internet usage among NFL fans. *The Sports Business Daily, 4*(48), 11.

InterZine Productions, Inc. (1997i, November 24). Big blue connects with NFL for Super Bowl sponsorship. *The Sports Business Daily, 4*(49), 1.

InterZine Productions, Inc. (1998a, January 5). Insight's Copper Bowl sponsorship not a fan favorite. *The Sports Business Daily, 4*(67).

InterZine Productions, Inc. (1998b, January 7). Media notes. *The Sports Business Daily, 4*(69), 8.

InterZine Productions, Inc. (1998c, January 22). Media notes. *The Sports Business Daily, 4*(79), 12.

InterZine Productions, Inc. (1998d, February 12). Online news & notes: Will NFL be shopping internet rights? *The Sports Business Daily, 4*(94), 6.

InterZine Productions, Inc. (1998e, February 25). Nfl.com looks to major players for next online partner. *The Sports Business Daily, 4*(102), 5.

InterZine Productions, Inc. (1998f, March 26). Online news & notes: Is Disney-Starwave deal near? *The Sports Business Daily, 4*(123), 8.

InterZine Productions, Inc. (1998g, April 9). MLB online notes: Yankees sign three-year deal with Audionet. *The Sports Business Daily, 4*(130), 8.

InterZine Productions, Inc. (1998h, April 17). Sportsline USA reports record first quarter performance. *The Sports Business Daily, 4*(134), 20.

Irwin, D. L., and Fleger, B. (1992). Reading between the lines. *Athletic Management,4,* 15–18

Irwin, R. L. (1990). *Development of a collegiate licensing administrative paradigm.* Unpublished doctoral dissertation, University of Northern Colorado, Greeley, CO.

Irwin, R. L., and Stotlar, D. K. (1993). Operational protocol analysis of sport and collegiate licensing programs. *Sport Marketing Quarterly, 2,* 5, 7–16.

Irwin, R. L., Assimakopoulos, M. K., and Sutton, W. A. (1994). A model for screening sport sponsorship opportunities. *Journal of Promotion Management, 2*(3/4), 53–69.

Irwin, R.L., and Asimakopoulos, M. (1992, December). An approach to the evaluation and selection of sport sponsorship proposals. *Sport Marketing Quarterly,1,* 43–51.

Isaacs, G. A. (1931). *The story of the newspaper printing press.* London: Cooperative Printing Society.

ISL Marketing (1993). *The Olympic programme.* New York: Author.

J. Walter Spalding original ledger (1947). *Sporting Goods Dealer, 96*(3), 128–129.

Javalgi, R., and Moberg, C. (1997). Service loyalty: Implications for service providers. *Journal of Services Marketing, 11,* 3, 165–179.

Jensen, J. (1995, April 3). Shooting to score on the 'net. *Advertising Age, 64*(14), 24–25.

Jizhong, W. (1997, June). *The potentiality of sports in the Chinese market.* Paper presented at conference on Marketing of Sports in the 21st Century, Hong Kong.

Johns, R. (1997). Sports promotion & the internet. *Cyber-Journal of Sport Marketing* [Online]. Available: www.cad.gu.edu/market/cjsm/johns.htm

Joyce Julius and Associates. (1991). *The sponsor's report almanac.* Ann Arbor, MI: Joyce Julius and Associates.

Julian W. Curtiss: Master of arts in sporting goods merchandising (1928). *Sporting Goods Dealer, 58*(4), 139.

Jupiter Communications. (1998a). *European online ad markets: Strategic overview* [Online]. Available: www.jup.com/briefs/oa43_02.html

Jupiter Communications. (1998b). *Jupiter model defines online ad/direct marketing convergence* [Online]. Available: www.jup.com/jupiter/release/9708/online.shtml

Kaplan, D. (1998, September 7–13). Venus patches rift with WTA. *Sports Business Journal, 1,* 9.

Kapoor, A., and McKay, R. J. (1971). *Managing international markets.* Princeton, NJ: The Darwin Press.

Kates, S. M. (1998). Consumer research and sport marketing: Starting the conversation between two different academic discourses. *Sport Marketing Quarterly, 7*(2), 24–31.

Kaufman, M. (1998, May 11–17). Women take their place at the table. *Sports Business Journal, 1,* 48.

Kelly, J. R., and Warnick, R. B. (1999). *Recreation trends and markets: The 21st century.* Champaign, IL: Sagamore Publishing.

King, B. (1998a, August 17–23). Earnhardt wants to tune up your engine. *Sports Business Journal, 13,* 9.

King, B. (1998b, May 18–24). NASCAR: It ain't just racin'. *Sports Business Journal, 1, 48.*

King, B. (1998c, October 12–18). Primo premiums: Beanies, beach towels. *Sports Business Journal,* 34–35.

Kirsch, G. B. (1989). *The creation of American team sports: Baseball and cricket, 1838–1872.* Urbana, IL: University of Illinois Press.

Klein, D. (1997, October 27). Advertisers should invest in sites, not just banner ads. *Advertising Age, 68*(43), 52.

Kogan, R. (1985). *Brunswick: The story of an American company from 1845 to 1985.* Skokie, IL: Brunswick Corp.

Koranteng, J. (1998, January). Reebok finds its second wind as it pursues global presence. *Advertising Age,* 18.

Koranteng, M. (1999, May). Huge Response for Olympic Licensing. *The Sydney Spirit,* (10), 4.

Kotler, P. (1988). *Marketing management: Analysis, planning, implementation, and control, 6th Edition.* Englewood Cliffs, NJ: Prentice Hall.

Lamb, C. W., Hair, J. F, and McDaniel, C. (1996). *Marketing.* Cincinnati, OH: South-Western College Publishing.

Lascu, D-N., Geise, T. D., Toolan, C., Guehring, B., and Mercer, J. (1995). Sport involvement: A relevant individual difference factor in spectator sports. *Sport Marketing Quarterly, 4*(4), 41–46.

Lefton, T. (2001, February 18). Fourth and long. *The Industry Standard* [Online]. Available: Lexis-Nexis.

Legergott, S. (1946). *Manpower in economic growth: The American record since 1800.* New York: McGraw-Hill Publishing.

Leonard, D. (2001, February 5). Madison avenue fights back. *Fortune* [Online]. Available: www.fortune.com

Levine, P. (1985). *A. G. Spalding and the rise of baseball: The promise of American sport.* New York: Oxford University Press.

Levitt, T. (1965, Nov.–Dec.). Exploit the product life cycle. *Harvard Business Review, 43,* 81–94.

Liberman, N. (1999, April 19). TV partners provide juice to net sites. *SportsBusiness Journal, 1*(52), 21.

Liberman, N. (1999, September 27–October 3). Publishers cross over to the Web, TV. *SportsBusiness Journal, 2*(23), 27.

Liebert, R. M., and Splegler, M. D. (1970). *Personality.* Homewood, IL: Dorsey Press.

Lombardo, J. (1998, May 4–10). "Team Tiger" takes Woods to the top. *Sports Business Journal, 13,* 22–23.

Lu, D. (2000, October). *Factors affecting spectator attendance in professional baseball: A comparison of Taiwan and USA.* Paper presented at the Florida Association for Health, Physical Education, Recreation, and Dance conference, Orlando, FL.

Lucas, J. A., and Smith, R. A. (1978). *Saga of American sport.* Philadelphia: Lee and Febiger.

Maddox, K. (1997, October 3). Banner quarter for web ad sales, IAB study finds. *Advertising Age, 68*(40), 34.

Maddox, L., & Mehta, D. (1997, March/April). The role and effect of web addresses in advertising. *Journal of Advertising Research,* 47–59.

Madsen, H. (1996, December). Reclaim the deadzone. *Wired, 4*(12), 206–220.

Mainardi, J. (1997, February). Match the media to the message. *Best's Review,* 88–91.

Mangalindan, M. (1997, December 1). Holiday shoppers beat the bustle by booting up pc. *Rocky Mountain News,* 13B.

Marsano, W. (1987, September). A five ring circus. *Northwest, 1,* 64—69.

Martin, J. (1996). Is the athlete's sport important when picking an athlete to endorse a non-sport product? *Journal of Consumer Marketing, 13*(6), 28–43.

Maslow, A. (1954). *Motivation and personality.* New York: Harper and Row.

McCarthy, E. J., and Perreault, W. D., Jr. (1984). *Basic marketing: A managerial approach.* Homewood, IL: Irwin, Inc.

McCarthy, E.J., and Perreault, W.D. (1990). *Basic marketing: A managerial approach,* Homewood, IL: Richard D. Irwin, Inc.

McCarthy, L. M. (1998). Marketing sport to Hispanic consumers. *Sport Marketing Quarterly, 7*(4), 19–24.

McCarville, R. E., Flood, C. M., and Floats, T. A. (1998). *The effectiveness of selected promotions on spectators' assessment of a nonprofit sporting event sponsor.* 15–62.

McCarville, R.E., Crompton, J. L., and Sell, J.A. (1993). The influence of outcome messages on reference prices. *Leisure Sciences, 15,* 115–130.

McDonald, M. (1998). *Sport sponsorship and the role of personality matching.* Buffalo, NY: Conference of the North American Society for Sport Management.

McMasters, L. (1993, March 29). Then there was the time a thrown shoe held up the Derby. *Call to the Post,* 62.

McMurray, S. (1998, January). The web's three-way tug of war. *SportsSense: The Journal of Sports Business, 1*(1), 5.

Meek, A. (1997). An estimate of the size and supported economic activity of the sports industry in the United States. *Sport Marketing Quarterly, 6*(4), 15–21.

Microsoft Corporation. (1996). *Getting started with microsoft frontpage 97: Professional website publishing without programming.* Redmond, WA: Author.

Millar, S. (1999, June 28–July 4). X Marks the Spot—On Center Stage. *Sports Business Journal,* 23–30.

Miller, L., Shaad, S., Burch, D. and Turner, R. (1999). *Sales success in sport marketing.* Wichita, KS: Events Unlimited.

Miller, L. K., Fielding, L. W., and Pitts, B. G. (1993). The impact of the Americans with Disabilities Act of 1990. *Clinical Kinesiology, 47*(3), 63–70.

Miller, L. K., Fielding, L. W. , and Pitts, B. G. (1993). The rise of the Louisville Slugger in the mass market. *Sport Marketing Quarterly, 2*(3), 9–16.

Millican, M. (1985, July). Direct marketing response mail. *Ski Area Management, 24*(4), 52–54.

Milne, G. R., and McDonald, M. A. (1999). *Sport marketing: Managing the exchange process.* Sudbury, MA: Jones and Bartlett.

Moore, M. T. (1993, February 17). Converse makes fast break to rename shoe. *USA Today,* 1B.

Morganthau, T., Barrett, T., Dickey, C., and Talbot, M. (1992, June 22). Piling up the gold. *Newsweek,* 56–58.

Morris, R. (1999, September 27). 3 giants dominate sports publishing. *SportsBusiness Journal.*

Morrison, T., Conaway, W., and Borden, G. (1994). *Kiss, bow, or shake hands.* Holbrook, MA: Bob Adams, Inc.

Mott, F. L. (1957). *A history of American magazines, 1885–1905.* Cambridge, MA: Harvard University Press.

Mrozek, D. J. (1983). *Sport and American mentality, 1880–1910.* Knoxville, TN: The University of Tennessee Press.

Mullen, E. (1998, August 10–16). Asian flu hits sports industry. *Sports Business Journal, 1,* 46.

Mullen, L. (1998, August 31– September 6). Adidas ties up UCLA deal, said to be worth $18 million. *Sports Business Journal,* 10.

Mullin, B. (1985). An information-based approach to marketing sport. In G. Lewis and H. Appenzeller (Eds.), *Successful sport management* (pp. 201–214). Charlottesville, VA: The Michie Company.

Mullin, B., Hardy, S., and Sutton W. A. (1993). *Sport marketing.* Champaign, IL: Human Kinetics.

Murphy, G. G. S. , and Zellner, A. (1959). Sequential growth, the labor safety-valve doctrine, and the development of American unionism. *Journal of Economic History, 19*(3), 402–419.

Nakazawa, M., Mahony, D. F., Funk, D. C., and Hirakawa, S. (1999). Segmenting J. League spectators based on length of time as a fan. *Sport Marketing Quarterly, 8*(4), 55–65.

NASCAR merchandising on a roll. (2001, Feb 20) *Sport Business Daily, 7.*

National Basketball Association. (1998). *NBA international facts.* New York: Author.

National Handicapped Sports. (1993). *Registration pamphlet of the National Handicapped Sports Adaptive Fitness Instructor Workshop.* Rockville, MD: Author.

NBC gets Olympic TV deal. (1993, July 28). *Greeley [CO] Tribune,* B2.

NCAA internet survey. (1998, January 19). *The NCAA News,* 2.

NCAA to create website for all championships. (1998. April 13). *The NCAA News,* 1, 8.

New Gotham headquarters opened by A. G. Spalding and Bros. (1924). *Sporting Goods Dealer, 50*(4), 85–87.

New marketing research definition approved. (1987, Jan. 2). *Marketing News,* 1.

1999 sponsors spending: 7.6 billion. (1998, Dec. 21). *IEG Sponsorship Report, 1,* 4–5.

Noack, D. R., (1996, August). The sporting world. *Internet World, 7*(8), 48–52.

Noack, D. R. (1998, February 21). The secrets of web advertising sales. *Editor & Publisher,* 32–33.

Norris, J. D. (1990). *Advertising and the transformation of American society, 1865–1920.* New York: Greenwood Press.

Ober, E. (1992, August 5). Interview with David Stern, Commissioner NBA. New York: Columbia Broadcasting System.

Official IAAF partners. (1999). [Online]. (Jan. 16, 1999). Available: www.IAAF.org.

Olympic fact file. (1998, Spring) Lausanne: International Olympic Committee.

Oriard, M. (1993). *Reading football: How the popular press created an American spectacle.* Chapel Hill, NC: University of North Carolina Press.

Owens, J. (1999, August 23–29). Strength with retailers powers NASCAR. *SportsBusiness Journal,* 10.

Ozanian, M. K., and Taub, S. (1992, July 7). Big leagues, bad business. *Financial World*, 34–51.

Pajak, M. (1990). Every fly ball is an adventure. *Athletic Business, 14*(3), 26.

Parks, J. B., and Zanger, B. R. K. (1990). *Sport and fitness management: Career strategies and professional content.* Champaign, IL: Human Kinetics Books.

Parks, J.B., and Zanger, B.R.K. and Quarterman, J. (1998). *Contemporary Sport Management.* Champaign, IL: Human Kinetics Books.

Paul, P. (1996). Marketing on the internet. *Journal of Consumer Marketing, 13*(4), 27–39.

Paulin, C. O. (1932). *Atlas of the historical geography of the United States.* Washington, DC: Carnegie Institution.

Peter, J.P., and Donnelly, J.H. (1991). *A preface to marketing management.* Boston: Richard D. Irwin, Inc.

Peter, J. P., and Donnelly, J. H. (1993). *A Preface to marketing management.* Boston, MA: Irwin, Inc.

Pfaffenberger, B. (1996). *Publish it on the web.* London: Academic Press, Inc.

Phelan, M. (1850). *Billiards without a master.* New York: D. D. Winant.

Phoenix Suns. (1996, November 23). Personal correspondence to David Stotlar.

Pickle, D. (1997, October 20). Volleyball video goes on net. *The NCAA News,* 3.

Pitts, B. G. (1997). From leagues of their own to an industry of their own: The emerging lesbian sports industry. *Women in Sport and Physical Activity Journal, 6*(2), 109–139.

Pitts, B. G. (1998). An analysis of sponsorship recall during Gay Games IV. *Sport Marketing Quarterly, 7*(4), 11–18.

Pitts, B. G. (1999a). Sports tourism and niche markets: Identification and analysis of the growing lesbian and gay sports tourism industry. *Journal of Vacation Marketing, 5* (1), 31–50.

Pitts, B. G. (1999b, March). *The $11.8 billion dollar gay and lesbian sports tourism market: Defining, targeting, and competitive advantage strategies for corporate America stakeholders.* Paper presented at the 1999 conference of the Snow Sports Industries of America, Las Vegas.

Pitts, B. G., and Ayers, K. (1999, June). *An economic analysis of Gay Games V.* Paper presented at the annual conference of the North American Society for Sport Management, Vancouver, B.C., Canada.

Pitts, B. G. (1993). [Interviews with soccer players: The Louisville Women's Soccer Association, Inc.]. Unpublished raw data.

Pitts, B. G., and Fielding, L.W. (1987, May). Custom-made bats and baseball players: The relationship between form utility and promotion—J. A. Hillerich's contribution to sporting goods marketing. *North American Society for Sport Management Conference Proceedings.*

Pitts, B. G., Fielding, L. F., and Miller, L. K. (1994). Industry segmentation theory and the sport industry: Developing a sport industry segment model. *Sport Marketing Quarterly, 3*(1), 15–24.

Polsky, N. (1969). *Hustlers, beats, and others.* New York: Anchor Books.

Pope, N. K. L., & Forrest, E. J. (1997, April). A proposed format for the management of sport marketing websites. *Cyber-journal of sport marketing, 1*(2), 43–49.

Porter, G. (1973). *The rise of big business, 1860–1910.* Arlington Heights, IL: Harlan Davidson, Inc.

Porter, M. (1985). *Competitive advantage.* New York: The Free Press.

Porter, M. E. (1985). *Competitive advantage: Creating and sustaining superior performance.* New York: The Free Press.

Pratzmark, R. R., and Frey, N. (1989, January). The winners play a new global game. *Marketing Communications,* 18–27.

Presbrey, F. (1929). *The history and development of advertising.* Garden City, NY: Doubleday, Doran and Company, Inc.

Pride, W. M., and Ferrell, O. C. (1991). *Marketing concepts and strategies.* Boston: Houghton Mifflin Company.

Pride, W. M. and Ferrell, O. C. (1997) *Marketing* (10th ed.). New York: Houghton Mifflin Company.

Quelch, J. A., Buzzell, R. D., and Salama, E. R. (1990). *The marketing challenge of 1992.* New York: Addison-Wesley.

Rader, B. G. (1990). *American sports: from the age of folk games to the age of televised sports.* Englewood Cliffs, NJ: Prentice Hall.

Raju, J. S., Srinivasan, V., and Lal, R. (1990). The effects of brand loyalty on competitive price promotional strategies. *Management Science, 36*(3), 276–305.

Reasons for Spalding success. (1915). *Sporting Goods Dealer, 32*(2), 40–49.

Reed, M. H. (1989). *IEG legal guide to sponsorship.* Chicago, IL: International Events Group.

Reed, M. H. (1990). *Legal aspects of promoting and sponsoring events.* Chicago: International Events Group.

Reiss, S. A. (1989). *City games: The evolution of American urban society and the rise of sports.* Urbana, IL: University of Illinois Press.

Resnick, R. (1997, April). The case for "opt in" marketing on the internet. *Direct Marketing,* 52–53.

Reynolds, M. (1998, June 22–28). Women's sports: A growth industry. *Sports Business Journal,* 30.

Rich, L. (1997. September 22). A brand new game: Does new research prove the branding value of banners? *Brandweek, 38*(35), 55–56.

Ries, A., and Trout, J. (1986). *Positioning: The battle for your mind.* New York: McGraw-Hill.

Rodin, S. (1998, May 11–17). Shrewd marketers can share in boom. *Sports Business Journal,* 34.

Rofe, J. (1999, February 8–14). Winning record makes a sales slump. *Sport Business Journal, 7,* 23.

Rohm, A. (1997) The creation of consumer bonds within Reebok Running. *Sport Marketing Quarterly, 6,* 2, 17–25.

Rosner, H. (1996, March 4). Will email become j-mail? *Brandweek, 37*(10), 30.

Ruff, M. (Ed.). (1992a). The driving force. *AutoWeek, 42*(22), 37.

Ruff, M. (Ed.). (1992b). What's in a name? *AutoWeek, 42*(22), 37.

Ruibal, S. (1998, June 5). Participation grows by leaps and bounds. *USA Today,* 3c.

Sage, G. (1996). Patriotic images and capital profit: Contradictions of professional team sports licensed merchandise. *Sociology of Sport Journal, 13,* 1–11.

Schmetterer, R. (1997, May 5). Meeting the measurement challenge. *Mediaweek, 7*(18), S72–S73.

Schnaars, S. P. (1991). *Marketing strategy: A consumer-driven approach.* New York: The Free Press.

Schoenbachler, D. D., Gordon, G. L., Foley, D., & Spellman, L. (1997). Understanding consumer database marketing. *Journal of Consumer Marketing, 14*(1), 5–17.

Schoenfelt, E. L., Maue, A. E., and Hatcher, E. B. (1999). "We Got Next"—Next what? An evaluation of the effectiveness of the WNBA tag line and a case for sport marketing research. *Sport Marketing Quarterly, 8*(3), 31–38.

Semich, J. W. (1995, January 15). The world wide web: Internet boomtown? *Datamation, 41*(1), 37–41.

Seymour, H. (1989). *Baseball: The early years.* New York: Oxford University Press.

Shaffer, A. (1997, March). What's in a name? *Club Industry, 2,* 17–24.

Shatzkin, C. (1996, September). Opportunity knocks. *Panstadia International, 3*(4), 78–80.

Shaw, R. (1991). *Computer-aided marketing and selling.* London: Reed International Books.

Sherwin, G. R., & Avila, E. N. (1997). *Connecting online: Creating a successful image on the internet.* Grants Pass, WA: The Oasis Press.

Silverstein, B. (1996, January). The internet: It's not a proven direct marketing medium . . . yet. *Direct Marketing, 58*(9), 30–33.

Simmons Market Research Bureau. (1996). *Market report.*

Smith, M. L. (1998, January). One to one: Put the customer in the information driver seat and build better relationships. *Direct Marketing,* 37–39.

Snider, M. (1997, February 19). Growing online population making internet 'mass media.' *USA Today,* D1.

Solomon, S. D. (1994, November 15). Staking a claim on the internet. *Inc. Technology, 16,* 87–92.

Somers, D. A. (1972). *The rise of sports in New Orleans, 1850–1900.* Baton Rouge, LA: Louisiana State University Press.

Spain, W. (1996, October 14). Ad impressions cause headache for web 'zines. *Advertising Age, 67*(42), S2.

Spanberg, E. (1998, June 8–14). The intimidator's empire. *Sports Business Journal, 1,* 17.

Speer, T. (1999, March 16). Avoid gift giving and cultural blunders in Asian locales. *USA Today,* 3E.

Spiegel, P. (1998, December 14). Heir Gordon. *Forbes,* 189–197.

Spoelstra, J. (1997). *Ice to the Eskimos.* New York: Harper Business.

Spoelstra, J. (1997*). Ice to the Eskimos: How to sell a product nobody wants.* New York: Harper Business.

Sponsors reveal how to bring deals to life. (1999, March). *IEG Sponsorship Report, 18,* 7.

Sport and television. (1996, July 20). *The Economist,* 17–19.

Sporting Goods Manufacturers Association. (January 20, 2000). Available: www.sportlink.com/research.

Sports information bulletin. (1992, June). Brussels: Sport for All Clearing House.

Sports Media Challenge (1991). *Pocket guide to media success.* Charlotte, NC: Sports Media Challenge.

Sports participation trends 1999. (1999). *The SGMA Report* [Online]. Available: www.sportlink.com.

Standeven, J., and DeKnop, P. (1999). *Sport tourism.* Champaign, IL: Human Kinetics.

Stanton, W. J., Etzel, M. J. and Walker, B. J. (1991). *Fundamentals of marketing.* New York: McGraw-Hill, Inc.

Starwave Corporation. (1997a). *Nascar online advertising rate card* [Online]. Available: www.starwave.com/saleskit/nascar.html

Starwave Corporation. (1997b). *Nba.com online advertising rate card* [Online]. Available: www.starwave.com/saleskit/nba.html

Starwave Corporation. (1997c). *Nfl.com advertising rate card* [Online]. Available: www.starwave.com/saleskit/nfl.html

Starwave Corporation. (1998). *ESPN sportszone advertising rate card* [Online]. Available: www.starwave.com/saleskit/sz.html

Stauble, V. (1994). The significance of sport marketing and the case of the Olympic Games. In Graham, P. (Ed.), *Sport business* (pp. 14–21). Dubuque, IA: Brown-Benchmark.

Steve Risser: The interview. (1997, April*). Sport Travel, 2,* 30–31.

Stevens, T. (1996, April 1). Increasing net worth. *Industry Week, 245*(7), 54.

Stewart, J. (1999, March 8–14). Formula one finds roar bumpy with EU. *Sports Business Journal,* 34.

Stipe, S. E. (1996, April). Selling on the internet. *Best's Review, 96*(12), 44–48, 96.

Stotlar, D. (2001). *Developing successful sport marketing plans.* Morgantown, WV: Fitness Information Technology, Inc.

Stotlar, D. K. (1987). Managing administrative functions with microcomputers. In J. E. Donnelly (Ed.), *Using microcomputers in physical education and the sport sciences* (pp. 117–132). Champaign, IL: Human Kinetics Pub.

Stotlar, D. K. (1989). *Successful sport marketing and sponsorship plans.* Dubuque, IA: Wm. C. Brown.

Stotlar, D. K. (1989). *Successful sport marketing and sponsorship plans.* Dubuque, IA: Wm. C. Brown.

Stotlar, D. K. (1993). *Successful sport marketing.* Dubuque, IA: Brown-Benchmark.

Stotlar, D. K. and Bronzan, R. T. (1987). *Public relations and promotions in sport.* Daphne, AL: United States Sports Academy.

Stotlar, D. K. and Johnson, D. A. (1989). Assessing the impact and effectiveness of stadium advertising on sport spectators at Division I institutions. *Journal of Sport Management, 3*(1), 90–102.

Swerdlow, Joel L. (1999, August). *National Geographic* [Global Culture issue].

Tarde, J. (1997, August). The PGA's cup overfloweth. *Golf Digest,* 4.

Tarpey, L. X., Donnelly, J. H., and Peter, J. P. (1979). *A preface to marketing management.* Dallas, TX: Business Publications, Inc.

Tedesco, R. (1996a, September 30). Internet panel sees big marketing pull: Full-motion video on 'net could fuel consumer interest. *Broadcasting & Cable, 126*(41), 31–32.

Tedesco, R. (1996b, October 14). Widening the world of sports. *Broadcasting & Cable, 126*(43), 85.

Tedesco, R. (1996c, October 26). Internet business is a waiting game. *Broadcasting & Cable, 126*(45), 36–37.

Tedesco, R. (1996d, December 2). ABC sports scoring with 'Monday night football' site. *Broadcasting & Cable, 126*(50), 60.

10 Steps to build better brands and where sponsorship fits in. (1998, March 30). *IEG Sponsorship Report,* 4–6.

The answer: $213 billion. (1999, December 20–26). *SportsBusiness Journal.*

The herstory of basketball [Advertisement for the Women's Basketball Hall of Fame]. (1999, February 1–7). *Sports Business Journal,* 18.

The new face of America: How immigrants are shaping the face of the world's first multicultural society. (1993). *Time,* 142(21).

Thomas, J. W. (1998, January). The brave new world of internet marketing. *Direct Marketing, 60*(1), 40–41.

Thompson, J. (1994). Social theory and the media. In D. Crowley and D. Mitchell (Eds.), *Communication theory today.* Stanford, CA: Stanford University Press.

Tips to make your internet advertisements more effective. (1997, May 5). *Mediaweek, 7*(18), S46–S49.

Top 25 female athlete endorsements. (1998, May 11–17). *Sports Business Journal, 1,* 25.

Tucker, R. (1997, November). Clubs on the web. *Fitness Management, 13*(12), 29–32.

2001 World Population Data Sheet. (2001). Population Reference Bureau. [Online]. Available: www.prb.org/pubs/wpds2000.

Tucker, R. (1997, November). Clubs on the Web. *Fitness Management, 13,* 29–32.

Tuller, L. W. (1991). *Going global.* Homewood, IL: Business One Irwin.

Ubois, J. (1997, January). Eye on the storm: Marketing guru Geoffrey Moore plumbs the turbulent currents of the internet market. *Internet World, 8*(1), 74–81.

Ukman, L. (1995). *IEG's complete guide to sponsorship*. Chicago: International Events Group.

United States Department of Commerce (1993, September). *Basic facts about registering a trademark*. Washington DC: Patent and Trademark Office.

United States Olympic Committee. (1996). USOC controversy preparedness plan. Colorado Springs, CO: Author.

United States Tennis Association. (1999, June). Spotlight: Women's 60, 70 and 80 National Clay Court Championships. *USTA Magazine*, 30–31.

VALS 2: Your marketing edge for the 1990s. (1990). Menlo Park, CA: SRI International.

van Waterschoot, W., and Van den Bulte, C. (1992, October). The 4P classification of the marketing mix revisited. *Journal of Marketing*, 82–93.

Vavra, T. (1992). *Aftermarketing: How to keep customers for life through relationship marketing*. Homewood, IL: Business One Irwin.

Vavra, T. (1994). The database imperative. *Marketing Management, 2*, 1, 47–57.

Veltri, F. (1996). *Recognition of athlete-endorsed products*. Fredericton, NB: Conference of the North American Society for Sport Management.

Walsh, R. G. (1986). *Recreation economic decisions*. State College, PA: Venture Publishing, Inc.

Walthorn, C. G. (1979). *Consumer behavior*. Homewood, IL: Richard D. Irwin.

Warner, B. (1997, March 3). Brewers tapping the web, at last. *Mediaweek, 7*(9), 38–39.

Webster's II New Riverside Pocket Dictionary. (1978). Boston, MA: Houghton Mifflin Company.

Wells, M. and Oldenburg, A. (1999, July 13). Sports bra's flash could cash in. *USA Today*, 1A.

Welz, G. (1996, July). The ad game: Industry analysts and agencies see the web advertising market exploding. *Internet World, 7*(7), 50–57.

Why internet advertising. (1997, May 5). *Mediaweek, 7*(18), S8–S12.

Williams, P. (1999, April 12). Company's links make it a direct line to virtual ticket window. *SportsBusiness Journal, 1*(52), 33.

Williams, P. (2000). Marketing your dreams: *Business and life lessons from Bill Veeck*. Champaign, IL: Sports Publishing, Inc.

Winer, R. (1988). Behavioral perspective on pricing: Buyer's subjective perceptions of price revisited. In T.M. Devinney (Ed.), *Issues in pricing: Theory and research*. Lexington, MA: Lexington Books, 35–7.

Wong, G. M. (1994). *Essentials of amateur sports law*. Westport, CT: Praeger Publishing Company.

Woodward, S. (1988, May 29). Teams foresee war brewing keeping "billboard rules" in place. *USA Today*, 2C.

Yeh, K. T. and Li, M. (1998, Winter). Globalization of sport: What sport management professional should know. *ICHPER-SD Journal*, 29–32.

Yiannakis, A. (1989). Some contributions of sport sociology to the marketing of sport and leisure organizations. *Journal of Sport Management, 3*, 103–115.

Young, D. (1996). *Building your company's good name*. New York: AMACOM.

Yudkin, M. (1994). *6 steps to free publicity*. New York: Penguin Group.

Zarkowsky, D. (1997, July 21). Cardinals keep score on web, Blues also at bat. *St. Louis Business Journal* [Online]. Available: www.sbj.com

Zhang, J. J., Pease, D. G., Hui, S. C., Michaud, T. J. (1995). Variables affecting the spectator decision to attend NBA games. *Sport Marketing Quarterly, 4*(4), 29–39.

Zhang, J. J., Smith, D. W., Pease, D. G., and Jambor, E. A. (1997). Negative influence of market competitors on the attendance of professional sport games: The case of a minor league hockey team. *Sport Marketing Quarterly, 6*(3), 31–39.

Appendix A

Sport Business Organizations Contact Information

Contents

Age-Related Organizations and Businesses

Amateur Athletic Union
The Walt Disney World Report
PO Box 10000
Lake Buena Vista, FL 32830-1000
407-934-7200
407-934-7242 (Fax)

American Youth Soccer Organization
12501 S. Isis Avenue
Hawthorne, CA 90250
310-643-6455
310-643-5310

AUSSI Masters Swimming
PO Box 835
Campbelltown
Australia NSW 2560
02 4635 9798

Boys & Girls Clubs of America
1230 W. Peachtree Street, NW
Atlanta, GA 30309
404-815-5700
404-815-5789 (Fax)

Charlie Tarricone's American Basketball Consulting Services
1305 Campus Drive
Vestal, NY 13850
607-724-8155

Moreno Valley
14177 Fredrick Street
Moeno Valley, CA 92552
909-413-3000
909-413-3750 (Fax)

National Adult Baseball Association
NABA
3900 E. Mexico, Ste GL-8
Denver, CO 80210
800-621-6479
303-639-6605 (Fax)

National Association of Youth Leagues
2050 Vista Pkwy
West Palm Beach, FL 33411
561-684-1141
561-684-2546 (Fax)

National Senior Games Association
nsga.com
301-217-0960
301-217-0968 (Fax)

PrepUSA
PO Box 97427
Tacoma, WA 98497
253-581-5324
253-756-2900 (Fax)

U.S. Budokai Karate Association
1095 Central Avenue
Albany, NY 12205
518-458-2018

Young American Bowling Alliance (YABA)
5301 S. 76th Street
Greendale, WI 53129
414-421-9000
414-421-4420 (Fax)

Youth Basketball of America, Inc.
10325 Orangewood Blvd
Orlando, FL 32821
407-363-YBOA
407-363-0599 (Fax)

Auto Sports Racing Organizations and Businesses

American Rally Sport Group, Inc.
3650 South Pointe Circle, Suite 205
Laughlin, NV 89028
702-298-8171
413-521-0597 (Fax)

Boston Performance Group, Inc.
18 Fordham Road
Allston, MA 02134
617-787-8035
617-787-6492 (Fax)

Cotter Group
SFX/Cotter Group
6525 Hudspeth
Harrisburg, NC 28075
704-455-3500
704-455-3530 (Fax)

Kelley Racing
9350 Castlegate Drive
Indianapolis, IN 46256

NASCAR/National Association for Stock Car Auto Racing
1801 W. Intl Speedway Blvd
Daytona Beach, FL 32114
904-253-0611
904-252-8804 (Fax)

PacWest Racing Group
4001 Methanol Lane
Indianapolis, IN 46268
317-297-2500
317-297-2100 (Fax)

Pep Boys Indy Racing League
4565 W. 16th Street
Indianapolis, IN 46222
317-484-6526
317-484-6525 (Fax)

Rally School Ireland
Gola Scotstown
Co. Monaghan
047 89098
047 89223 (Fax)

Disabled Sports Organizations and Businesses

American Blind Bowling Association
411 Sheriff Street
Mercer, PA 16137
412-662-5748

Canadian Blind Sports Association
1600 James Naismith Drive
Glouster, ON K1B 5N4
Canada
613-748-5609
613-748-5899 (Fax)

Disabled Sports USA
451 Hungerford Dr., STE 100
Rockville, MD 20850

International Blind Sports Association
ibsa.es

International Paralympic Committee
Adenauerallee 212
D- 53113 Bonn
Germany
Tel: +49-228-2097 200
Fax: +49-228-2097 209

National Foundation of Wheelchair Tennis
940 Calle Amanecer, Ste B
San Clemente, CA 92672
714-361-6811

National Sports Center for the Disabled
PO Box 1290
Winter Park, CO 80482
970-726-1540
303-316-1540
303-293-5446 (Fax)

National Wheelchair Basketball Association
Charlotte Institute of Rehab
1100 Blythe Blvd
Charlotte, NC 28217
704-355-1064

Skating Association for the Blind and Handicapped
1200 East and West Road
West Seneca, NY 14224
716-675-7222

USA Deaf Sports Federation
3607 Washington Blvd, Ste 4
Ogden, UT 84403-1737
801-393-7916
801-393-2263 (Fax)

U.S. Association of Blind Athletes
33 N. Institute Street
Colorado Springs, CO 80903
719-630-0422
719-630-0616

U.S. Cerebral Palsy Athletic Association
200 Harrison Avenue
Newport, RI 02840
401-848-2460
401-848-5280 (Fax)

Wheelchair Sports, USA
3595 E. Fountain Blvd., Ste L-1
Colorado Springs, CO 80910
719-574-1150
719-574-9840 (Fax)

Faith-Based Sports Organizations and Businesses

Fellowship of Christian Athletes
8701 Leeds Road
Kansas City, MO 64129
816-921-0909

Maccabi USA
Maccabi USA/Sports for Israel
1926 Arch Street 4R
Philadelphia, PA 19103

National Christian College Athletic Association
NCCAA National Office
302 West Washington Street
Greenville, SC 29601
864-250-1199
864-250-1141 (Fax)

OC International
PO Box 36900
Colorado Springs, CO 80936-6900
719-592-9292

Fitness Organizations and Businesses

American Council on Exercise
5820 Oberlin Drive, Ste 102
San Diego, CA 92121-3787
800-825-3636
858-535-8227
858-535-1778 (Fax)

American Fitness Professionals & Associates
PO Box 214
Ship Bottom, NJ 08008
609-978-7583

Association of Women's Fitness and Health
273 South Centerville Road
Ashburn, VA 20147

National Gym Association
PO Box 970579
Coconut Creek, FL 33097-0579
954-344-8410
954-344-8412 (Fax)

Nebula Fitness
PO Box 54
1142 North Center St.
Versailles, OH 45380
800-763-2852
937-526-9411 (Fax)

Professional Fitness Instructor Training
PO Box 130258
Houston, TX 77219-0258
800-899-7348
713-868-8086
713-868-2683

The Fitness Zone
2630 6th Avenue South
Birmingham, AL 35233

International Sports Organizations and Businesses

British Athletics
british-athletics.co.uk

Canadian Association for the Advancement of Women and Sport and Physical Activity
1600 James Naismith Drive
Gloucester, ON, Canada, K1B 5N4
613-748-5793
613-748-5775 (Fax)

FIFA
fifa.com
PO Box 85
8030 Zurich, Switzerland

General Association of International Sports Federations
gaisf.org
Villa Le Mas 4, Boulevard
du Jardin Exotique, MC 98000, Monaco
+377 +97 97 65 10
+377 +93 25 28 73 (Fax)

International Amateur Athletic Federation
iaaf.org
Stade Louis II—Avenue Prince Hereditaire Albert
MC 98000 Monaco
377 92 05 70 68
377 92 05 70 69 (Fax)

International Olympic Committee
olympic.org
Chateau de Vidy
Case Postale 356
1007 Lausanne, Switzerland
41.21 621.61.11
41.21 621.62.16

North American Sports Federation
nasf.net
PO Box K
Drifton, PA 18221
570-454-1952

Media Organizations and Businesses

CBS SportsLine
sportsline.com

CNN/SI
sportsillustrated.cnn.com

ESPN
espn.go.com

Fox Sports
foxsports.com

Sports Trend
1115 Northmeadow Parkway
Roswell, GA 30076
800-241-9034
770-569-5105 (Fax)

The Sporting News
sportingnews.com

USA Today
usatoday.com

Minority Sports Organizations and Businesses

African American Sports

African American Golf Association (AAGA)
aaga.com
309-682-1482

Black Coaches Association
c/o Rudy Washington
PO Box J
Des Moines, IA 50311
515-327-1248

Black Entertainment & Sports Lawyers Association
1502 Fairlakes Place
Mitchellville, MD 20721
301-333-0003
301-333-0013 (Fax)

Irish Surf Association
3 Jocelyn Place
Dundalk, Co. Louth
042 32700

Gay and Lesbian Sports

Federation of Gay Games
584 Castro Street Suite 343
San Francisco, CA 94114
415-695-0222
www.gaygames.com

Hotlanta Volleyball Association
PO Box 8144
Highland Station
Atlanta, GA 31106
770-621-5062

International Gay and Lesbian Aquatics
www.igla.org

International Gay and Lesbian Football Association
PO Box 3623
Washington, DC 20007

International Gay and Lesbian Outdoor Organizations
The Chiltern Mountain Club
PO Box 407
Boston, MA 02117-0407
888-831-3100
617-556-7774

Southeast Gay Rodeo Association
PO Box 7881
Atlanta, GA 30357-0881
770-662-9510

Native American Sports

Iroquois Nationals Lacrosse
c/o Stacey Waterman
Ste 250, The Galleries of Syracuse
Syracuse, NY 13210
315-475-2500

National Sports Organizations and Businesses

National Association of Intercollegiate Athletics (NAIA)
6120 S. Yale Avenue, Ste 1450
Tulsa, OK 74136
918-494-8828

National Auto Sport Association
PO Box 21555
Richmond, CA
94820-1555
510-232-NASA
530-884-6435 (Fax)

National Bicycle League
3958 Brown Park Drive, Ste D
Hillard, OH 43026
800-886-BMX1
614-777-1625
614-777-1680 (Fax)

National Collegiate Athletic Association
ncaa.org
PO Box 6222
Indianapolis, IN 46206-6222
317-917-6222

National Golf Foundation
1150 South US Highway One, Ste 401
Jupiter, FL 33477
561-744-6006

National Junior Colleges Athletic Association
PO Box 7305
Colorado Springs, CO 80933-7305
719-590-9788
719-590-7324 (Fax)

National Softball Association
PO Box 7
Nicholasville, KY 40340
859-887-4114
859-887-4874 (Fax)

USA Basketball
5465 Mark Dabling Blvd
Colorado Springs, CO 80918-3842
719-590-4800

U.S. Specialty Sports Association
PO Box 1998
3935 South Crater Rd.
Petersburg, VA 23805
804-732-4099
804-732-1704 (Fax)

Professional Sports Organizations and Businesses

American Bowling Congress
5301 S. 76th Street
Greendale, WI 53129
414-421-6400
414-421-1194 (Fax)

American League of Professional Baseball Clubs, The
350 Park Avenue
New York, NY 10022
212-339-7600
212-593-7138 (Fax)

Association of Surfing Professionals
17942 Sky Park Circle, 4401/HJ
Irvine, CA 92614
949-851-2774
949-851-2773 (Fax)

Association of Tennis Professionals
201 ATP Tour Boulevard
Ponte Vedra Beach, FL 32082
904-285-8000
904-285-5966 (Fax)

Association of Volleyball Professionals (AVP)
330 Washington Blvd, Ste 600
Marina Del Ray, CA 90292
310-577-0775
310-577-0777 (Fax)

Atlantic Basketball Association
PO Box 12727
Wilmington, DE 19850-2727
302-426-9334
302-426-9335 (Fax)

Continental Basketball Association
Two Arizona Center
400 N. 5th Street, Ste 1425
Phoenix, AZ 85004
602-254-6677
602-258-9985 (Fax)

International Korfball Federation
Runnenburg 12
PO Box 1000
3980 DA BUNNIK
The Netherlands

International Shooting Sport Federation
ISSF Headquarters
Bavariaring 21, D-80336
München, Germany
+49-89-5443550
+49-89-5443554 (Fax)

Major League Baseball (MLB)
350 Park Avenue
New York, NY 10022
212-339-7800
212-355-0007 (Fax)

Major League Soccer (MLS)
110 E. 42nd Street, 10th Floor
New York, NY 10017
212-450-1200
212-450-1300 (Fax)

National Basketball Association (NBA)
645 Fifth Avenue
New York, NY 10022
212-407-8000
212-832-3861 (Fax)

National Football League (NFL)
280 Park Avenue
New York, NY 10017
212-450-2000
212-681-7599 (Fax)

National Hockey League (NHL)
1251 Avenue of the Americas
47th Floor
New York, NY 10020-1198
212-789-2000
212-789-2020 (Fax)

National League of Professional Baseball Clubs, The
350 Park Avenue
New York, NY 10022
212-339-7700
212-935-5069 (Fax)

Professional Bicycle League
World Headquarters
853 Broadway, Ste 1516
New York, NY 10003
212-539-6785

Sport Market Research Organizations and Businesses

Joyce Julius & Associates, Inc.
1995 Highland Drive, Ste A
Ann Arbor, MI 48108
734-971-1900
734-791-2059 (Fax)

Simmons Market Research Bureau
530 Fifth Avenue, 10th Floor
New York, NY 10036
212-373-8900
212-373-8918 (Fax)

Society for American Baseball Research
812 Huron Road, Ste 719
Cleveland, OH 44115
216-575-0500
216-575-0502 (Fax)

Sport Advancement and Research Company Limited
Springfield House, Springfield Road
Grantham, Lincolnshire
NG31 7BG
United Kingdom
+44 0 1476 514608
+44 0 1476 514609 (Fax)

Sport Business Research Network
PO Box 1417
Princeton, NJ 08542
609-896-1996
609-896-1903 (Fax)

Sport Marketing Agencies

International Management Group (IMG)
One Erieview Plaza, Ste 1300
Cleveland, OH 44114
216-522-1200
216-522-1145 (Fax)

Proserv, Inc.
1620 L. Street NW, Ste 600
Washington, DC 20036
202-721-7200
202-721-7201 (Fax)

R.L.R. Associates, Ltd.
7 W. 51st Street
New York, NY 10019
212-541-8641
212-262-7084 (Fax)

Sporting Goods and Apparel Manufacturers

Sporting Goods Manufacturers Association
200 Castlewood Drive
North Palm Beach, FL 33408
561-842-4100
561-863-8984 (Fax)

Action & Leisure
45 E. 30th Street
New York, NY 10016
212-684-4470
212-532-6194 (Fax)

Adams USA, Inc.
610 S. Jefferson Avenue
Cookville, TN 38501
800-251-6857
931-526-2109
931-526-8357 (Fax)

Adidas America, Inc.
9605 SW Nimbus Avenue
Beaverton, OR 97008
800-4AD-IDAS
503—972-2300
503-797-4935 (Fax)

Airwalk Footwear
2101 Camino Vida Roble
Carlsbad, CA 92009
800-247-9255
760-931-6868
760-931-6867 (Fax)

Bike Athletic Company
2801 Red Dog Drive
Knoxville, TN 37914
800-251-9230
423-546-4703
423-549-7988

Bolle America
9500 W. 49th Avenue
Wheat Ridge, CO 80033
800-554-6686
303-327-2200
303-327-2300 (Fax)

Discus Athletic
101 Commonwealth Blvd
Martinsville, VA 24112
540-632-6459
800-967-7940 (Fax)

Dolomite America, Inc.
Shore Point
One Selleck Street
Norwalk, CT 06855
203-852-1278
203-855-1360 (Fax)

Hillerich & Bradsby Company, Inc.
800 W. Main Street
Louisville, KY 40202
800-282-2287
502-585-5226
502-585-1179 (Fax)

Nike, Inc.
One Bowerman Drive
Beaverton, OR 97005
800-344-6453
503-671-6453
503-671-6300 (Fax)

Reebok International, Inc.
100 Technology Center Drive
Stoughton, MA 02072
888-898-9028
781-401-5000
781-401-4498 (Fax)

Scott USA
PO Box 2030
Sun Valley, ID 83353
208-622-1000
208-622-1005 (Fax)

Sims Sports, Inc.
8048 Winston Street
Burnaby, BC V5A 2H5
Canada
604-444-3733
604-444-3723 (Fax)

Skis Dynastar Inc.
PO Box 25
Hercules Drive
Colchester, VT 05446-0025
802-655-2400
802-655-4329 (Fax)

Sled Dogs Company, The
212 Third Avenue, North, Ste 420
Minneapolis, MN 55401
612-359-9020
612-359-9017 (Fax)

Spalding Sports Worldwide
425 Meadow Street
Chicopee, MA 01021-0901
413-536-1200
413-536-1404 (Fax)

Tecnica USA Corporation
19 Technology Drive
W. Lebanon, NH 03784
800-258-3897
603-298-8032
603-298-5790 (Fax)

Wilson Sporting Goods Company
8700 W. Bryn Mawr Avenue
Chicago, IL 60631
773-714-6400
773-714-4550 (Fax)

Sports Logo and Licensed Merchandise Organizations and Businesses

Art's Pro Sports Apparel & Things
9879-D Foothill Blvd
Rancho Cucamonga, CA 91730-1608
800-597-5109
909-945-5109
909-989-6375 (Fax)

B&J Collectibles, Inc.
1915 Swarthmore Avenue
Lakewood, NJ 08701
800-388-0912
732-905-5000

BestSportsGifts.com
Summit Bldg.
13575 58th Street N
Clearwater, FL 34620
727-593-8692

eCompanyStore
5945 Cabot Parkway Bldg 200, Ste 150
Alpharetta, GA 30005
800-975-6467
877-588-8932
678-942-3101 (Fax)

InstantPromo.com
1930 Village Center Circle
Suite 3-271
Las Vegas, NV 89134
800-255-1334
888-322-2470 (Fax)

LogoProducts.cc
The Backyard Store
PO Box 14454
San Antonio, TX 78214
888-814-7531
210-829-7531
210-829-1482 (Fax)

Logo Sports Enterprises
PO Box 327
Saratoga Springs, NY 12866
518-581-0331

Nikco Sports
5 Worthington Access Drive
Maryland Heights, MO 63043
800-345-2868
314-469-4770
314-469-1168 (Fax)

Racing USA, Inc.
5968 Chalkville Mountain Road
Birmingham, AL 35235

Rugby Imports
855 Warren Avenue
East Providence, RI 02914
800-431-4514
401-438-2727
401-438-8260 (Fax)

Selinda's
PO Box 1732
Suwanee, GA 30024-0973
678-482-0856
678-482-8239 (Fax)

Twenty-four Seven Incentives, Inc.
5435 S. Gibralter Street
Aurora, CO 80015-3767
303-699-5012
303-699-2931 (Fax)

Wendy Havins Promotions, Inc.
4060 Palm Street, Suite 604
Fullerton, CA 92835
888-556-9010
714-525-3330
714-525-3495 (Fax)

Sports Sponsorship Management Organizations and Businesses

ACC Properties
412 E. Boulevard
Charlotte, NC 28203
704-378-4400
704-378-4465 (Fax)

AJ Sports Inc.
9229 Sunset Blvd, Ste 608
Los Angeles, CA 90069
310-550-5922
310-274-3280 (Fax)

API Sponsorship
1775 Broadway, Rm. 608
New York, NY 10019
212-841-1580
212-841-1598 (Fax)

Barnes Dyer Marketing, Inc.
15510 Rockfield Blvd, Ste C
Irvine, CA 92618
714-768-2942
714-768-0630 (Fax)

Collegiate Advantage, Inc.
313 Congress Street
Boston, MA 02210
617-443-0300
617-443-4545 (Fax)

Empire Management Group, Inc.
415 Minuet Lane, Ste A
Charlotte, NC 28217
704-523-0803
704-523-0998 (Fax)

Event Partners, Inc.
C/o International Sports Plaza
250 Spring Street NW, Ste 3E110
Atlanta, GA 30303
404-522-5101
404-522-4737 (Fax)

Genesco Sports Enterprises, Inc.
4514 Cole Avenue, Ste 600
Dallas, TX 75205
214-826-6565
214-826-6494 (Fax)

Intellectual Properties Group
PO Box 1472
Davidson, NC 28036-1472
704-896-2169
704-896-1641 (Fax)

Miramar Sports & Special Events
PO Box 27
El Granada, CA 94018
650-726-3491
650-726-5181 (Fax)

Premier Management Group
4139 Via Marina, Ste 505
Marina del Rey, CA 90292
310-574-6722
310-574-6727 (Fax)

Strategic Merchandising Associates
1211 Avenue of Americas, 26th Floor
New York, NY 10036
503-645-3199 (Fax)

Vantage Sports Management
222 W. Comstock Avenue, Ste 208
Winter Park, FL 32789
407-628-3131
407-628-3121 (Fax)

Women's Sport Marketing Group, The
5 Bessom Street, Ste 114
Marblehead, MA 01945
781-599-3314
781-593-0338 (Fax)

State Sports Groups

Florida Sports Foundation
2964 Wellington Circle North
Tallahassee, FL 32308
850-488-8347
850-922-0482 (Fax)

Water Sports Organizations and Businesses

American Water Ski Association
799 Overlook Drive, S.E.
Winter Haven, FL 33884-1671
941-324-4341
941-325-8259 (Fax)

American Windsurfing Industries Association
1099 Snowden Road
White Salmon, WA 98672
800-963-7873
509-493-9463
509-493-9464 (Fax)

International Jet Sports Boating Association
27412 Burbank
Foothill Ranch, CA 92610
949-598-5560
949-598-5872 (Fax)

Sail America
850 Aquidneck Avenue, B-4
Middletown, RI 02842-7201
401-841-0900
401-847-2044 (Fax)

Super Boat Racing
1323 20th Terrace
Key West, FL 33040
305-296-8963
305-296-9770 (Fax)

Unlimited Hydroplane Racing Association
19530 Pacific Hwy South, #200
Seattle, WA 98188
206-870-8888
206-878-0866 (Fax)

U.S. Lifesaving Association
425 E. McFetridge Drive
Chicago, IL 60605
312-294-2333

U.S. Offshore Racing Association
18 N. Franklin Blvd
Pleasantville, NJ 08232
609-383-3700
609-383-9501 (Fax)

U.S. Surfing Federation
Kiernan & Angiulo
350 Jericho Turnpike
Jericho, NY 11753
516-935-0400
516-935-0238

U.S. Windsurfing Association
PO Box 978
Hood River, OR 97031
541-386-8708
541-386-2108 (Fax)

Water Polo Canada
1600 James Naismith Drive
Gloucester, ON K1B 5N4
Canada
613-748-5682
613-748-5706 (Fax)

Water-Skiing Federation, International
PO Box 2038
Medellín, Colombia
57-4 277-9783
57-4 281-7788 (Fax)

Women's Sports Organizations and Businesses

Canadian Association for the Advancement of Women and Sport and Physical Activity
caaws.ca
1600 James Naismith Drive
Gloucester, ON, Canada, K1B 5N4
613-748-5793
613-748-5775 (Fax)

International Women's Boardsailing Association
PO Box 116
Hood River, OR 97031
503-427-8566

National Volleyball Association (NVA)
1001 Mission Street
S. Pasadena, CA 91030
800-682-6820
619-669-1141 (Fax)

U.S. Women's Curling Association
c/o Kettle Morain Curling Club
PO Box 244
Hartland, WI 53029

Women's Basketball Coaches Association (WBCA)
4646 B Lawrenceville Hwy
Lilburn, GA 30047-3620
770-279-8027
770-279-8473 (Fax)

Women's Basketball Hall of Fame
118 N. Liberty, Room 202
Jackson, TN 38301
901-423-8349
901-422-9595 (Fax)

Women's International Bowling Congress, Inc. (WIBC)
5301 S. 76th Street
Greendale, WI 53129
414-421-9000
414-421-4420 (Fax)

Women's National Basketball Association (WNBA)
645 Fifth Avenue
New York, NY 10022
212-688-9622
212-750-9622 (Fax)

Women's Ocean Racing Sailing Association
PO Box 2403
Newport Beach, CA 92663
714-840-1869
714-846-1481 (Fax)

Women's Pro Fastpitch (WPF)
90 Madison Street, Ste 200
Denver, CO 80202
303-316-7800
303-316-2779 (Fax)

Women's Professional Volleyball Association (WPVA)
840 Apollo Street, Ste 205
El Segundo, CA 90245
310-726-0700
310-726-0719 (Fax)

Women's Soccer Foundation
PO Box 2097
Norton, MA 02766-0993
508-285-5699
508-285-8856 (Fax)

Women's Sports Foundation
womensportsfoundation.org
Eisenhower Park
East Meadow, NY 11554.
800-227-3988
516-542-4700

Appendix B

Sport Business Trade Organizations

American Association for Leisure & Recreation
Promotes school, community, and national programs of leisure services and recreation education.
703-476-3400
aalr.org

American Sportfishing Association
Ensures a healthy and sustainable resource (more fish), increases participation in sportfishing through promotion and education (more anglers), and helps member sportfishing companies increase their business (more profits).
*Trade shows (ICAST), annual meeting & management conference, Future Fisherman Foundation, Fish America Foundation, American Sportfishing Newsletter
1033 N. Fairfax Street, #200
Alexandria, VA 22314
703-519-9691
703-519-1872 (Fax)
asafishing.org

American Sportscasters Association, Inc.
Promotes professionalism and enhances the image of professional sport broadcasters.
*Sponsors Hall of Fame, Sportscaster of the Year, Sports Personality of the Year
212-227-8080

American Windsurfing Industries Association
Provides information and resources regarding windsurfing to consumers, retailers, media, and manufacturers.
*Surf Expos, exhibits, AWIA/US Windsurfing School Handbook, research & archive information
1099 Snowden Road
White Salmon, WA 98672
800-963-7873
509-493-9463
509-493-9464 (Fax)
awia.org
info@awia.org

Athletic Footwear Association
Promotes the athletic footwear industry.
*Offers generic marketing programs, market research programs, and annual meetings
407-840-1161

Club Managers Association of America

Promotes and advances friendly relations between and among persons connected with management of clubs and other associations of similar nature. Assists club officers and members through their managers to secure the utmost in successful operations.

*Annual Assistant Club Managers conference, managerial openings list, club management forums, premier club services, international staff exchange program, publications

1733 King Street
Alexandria, VA 22314
703-739-9500
703-739-0124 (Fax)
cmaa.org
cmaa@cmaa.org

European Fishing Tackle Trade Association (EFTTEX)

Organizes annual trade show available to anyone involved in the fishing tackle trade.

*Newsline, members website page, annual international business reception (EFTTEX Show Report)

71 St. John Street
London EC1M 4NJ
England
+44 20 7253 0777
+44 20 7253 7779
eftta.com
info@eftta.com

Golf Course Superintendents Association of America

A professional membership organization for golf course superintendents in the U.S., Canada, and throughout the world. Advances the art and science of golf management, collects and disseminates practical knowledge of the problems of golf course management, with a view toward more economical management of golf courses.

*Job listings, seminars, continuing education, certification, *Golf Course Management* magazine, GCSAA News Weekly

1421 Research Park Drive
Lawrence, KS 66049-3859
800-472-7878
785-841-2240
gcsaa.org
infobox@gcsaa.org

Golf Trade

An established resource for the golfing sector.

*Job listing postings, golf sector resource, events calendar, golf chat room

Internet Marketing Services
1500 Shadowridge Drive, Suite 6
Vista, CA 92083
760-599-7001
760-599-7002 (Fax)
golftrade.com

Ice Skating Institute

Provides leadership, education, and services to the ice skating industry.

*Annual World Championship competition, ISI *EDGE* (bimonthly professional journal), *Recreational Ice Skating* (quarterly magazine), education foundation, annual conference and trade show

17120 N. Dallas Pkwy., Ste. 140
Dallas, TX 75248-1187
972-735-8800
972-735-8815 (Fax)
skateisi.com
ISI@SkateISI.com

International Health, Racquet, & Sports Club Association

Exists to enhance the quality of profitability of its member clubs through education, information, networking, and marketing opportunities, group purchasing, legislative support, and public relations.

*Club Business International (CBI) magazine, IHRSA/Boys and Girls Clubs of America Program, passport program, annual trade show, annual conference, annual international convention

263 Summer Street
Boston, MA 02210
800-228-4772
617-951-0055
617-951-0056 (Fax)
ihrsa.org
info@ihrsa.org

International Inline Skating Association

Promotes and encourages inline skating internationally and provides resources and information for its members.
201 North Front Street, #306
Wilmington, NC 28401
910-762-7004
910-762-9477 (Fax)
iisa.com
info@mail.iisa.com

National Association of Charterboat Operators (NACO)

Unifying force for the charterboat industry with over 3,300 members, realizing major successes in combating and challenging government regulation.

*The NACO Report (bimonthly newsletter), Group Rate Liability Insurance Program, drug testing compliance program, government regulation and lobbying, annual conferences and meetings
1600 Duke Street, Suite 220
Alexandria, VA 22314
800-745-6094
703-519-1716 (Fax)
chaterboat.org

National Association of Sports Commissions

Fosters cooperation and sharing of information and professionalism among local and regional sports commissions and authorities.
504-525-5678

National Bicycle Dealers Association

Exists to aid the growth of cycling in America through research, education, and advocacy.

*Bicycle Retail Education Conference (BREC), interbike bicycle trade expos, articles, books, and resources
777 W. 19th Street, Suite O
Costa Mesa, CA 92627
nbda.com
info@nbda.com

National Scholastic Surfing Association (NSSA)

Promotes the sport of amateur surfing, provides top quality, structured events, and encourages the merits of academic achievement for the benefit of its members.

*Eight competitive conferences, National Scholarship Program, rulebook, annual National Championships, current news and news archives
Janice Aragon
PO Box 495
Huntington Beach, CA 92648
714-536-0445
714-960-4380
nssa.org
jaragon@nssa.org

National Skating Suppliers Association

Provides information, merchandise, and resources to skating manufacturers and distributors.
130 Chestnut Street
PO Box 831
N. Attleboro, MA 02760
508-695-4315
508-695-0377 (Fax)
888-543-7868
nssa1@aol.com

National Ski Retailers Association

Develops, improves, and promotes the business of ski retailers, ski shops, ski areas, and other members of the ski industry; improves communication with the ski industry.
708-439-4000

National Sporting Goods Association

Consists of retailers, dealers, wholesalers, suppliers and sales agents in the sporting goods industry. Committed to providing members with up-to-date information.

*Annual management conference, NSGA Newsletter, retail focus articles, industry research and statistics, Team Dealer Summit
1601 Feehanville Drive, Suite 300
Mt. Prospect, IL 60056-6035
847-296-6742
847-391-9827 (Fax)
nsga.org
info@nsga.org

Ontario Association of Sport and Exercise Sciences (OASES)

Provides fitness appraisal certification, training, and national CSEP certification for fitness consultants by offering workshops, which help personal trainers promote safe, effective physical activity.

*Fitness Certification Appraisal, courses and conferences, job opening postings, Vanguard Newsletter, workshops

75 Broadway
Orangeville, Ontario
L9W 1K1
519-942-2620
519-942-2285 (Fax)
oases.on.ca
info@oases.on.ca

Roller Skating Association International

Promotes roller skating and established good business practices for skating rinks. Represents skating center owners and operators, roller skating teachers, coaches, and judges, and manufacturers and suppliers of roller skating equipment.

**Roller Skating Business* magazine, annual convention & trade show, insurance services, advertising and vendor information

6905 Corporate Drive
Indianapolis, IN 46278
317-347-2626
317-347-2636 (Fax)
rollerskating.org

Soccer Industry Council of America

Organization of soccer-related businesses dedicated to the promotion of the sport in the United States.

407-842-1171

Sporting Goods Manufacturers Association

Represents manufacturers of sporting goods equipment, athletic footwear, and sports apparel in the areas of legislation, marketing, market protection and growth, consumer safety, international trade, product liability and program funding.

*Research reports and related studies, annual events, The Super Show, annual conference, advanced management education program, Coalition of Americans to Protect Sports (CAPS), exhibitor manual

200 Castlewood Drive
N. Palm Beach, FL 33418
561-842-4100
561-863-8984 (Fax)
sgma.com
info@sgma.com

Women's Basketball Coaches Association (WBCA)

Promotes women's basketball by unifying coaches at all levels to develop a reputable identity for the sport of women's basketball and to foster and promote the development of the game, in all of its aspects, as an amateur sport for women and girls.

*Annual national convention, WBCA Coaches Poll, publications include: *Women's Basketball Journal*, *Coaching Women's Basketball*, *Fastbreak Alert*, and *At the Buzzer*

4646 Lawrenceville Highway
Lilburn, GA 30047
770-279-8027
770-279-8473 (Fax)
wbca.org
wbca@wbca.org

Women's Sports Foundation

Promotes participation and provides information in the area of sport and fitness to women and young girls.

*Job listings, newsletter, resource center, biennial summit

womenssportsfoundation.org

Appendix C

Sport Business Industry Trade Publications

Agent & Manager
Covers developments, people, and events in the field of athlete management, including representation and marketing.
Frequency: 12 times per year
Circulation: 21,894
212-213-6382

Aquatics International
Focuses on design, management, and programming of public and semi-public swimming pools, waterparks, beaches, and other water-oriented facilities.
Frequency: 6 times per year
Circulation: 30,000
770-955-2500

Archery Business
Archery-related trade publication.
Frequency: 7 times per year
Circulation: 11,000
612-476-8065

Athletic Business
For owners and operators of athletic, recreation, and fitness facilities.
Frequency: 6 times per year
Circulation: 42,000
608-249-0186

Bicycle Retailer & Industry News
Offers news and features about the bicycle industry for retailers, manufacturers, and distributors of equipment, bike-wear, and accessories.
Frequency: 18 times per year
Circulation: 12,000
505-988-5099

Black Belt Books
Martial arts trade publication.
Frequency: 12 times per year
Ohara Publications, Inc.
Palm Coast Data
PO Box 421117
Palm Coast, FL 32142
800-266-4066

Boxing Monthly
Provides worldwide information and current news on the sport of boxing.
Frequency: 12 times per year
Topwave Ltd.
40 Morpeth Road
London E9 7LD
United Kingdom
+44 0 181 986 4141
+44 0 181 896 4145 (Fax)
boxing-monthly.co.uk
bmsubs@mmcltd.co.uk

Club Industry
Business magazine for health club owners and operators.
Frequency: 12 times per year
Circulation: 30,000
215-957-1500

Fitness Management
For owners and managers of athletic and health facilities.
Frequency: 12 times per year
Circulation: 25,000
213-385-3926

Fly Fishing and Fly Tying
Provides practical and technical information in the area of fly fishing and fly tying.
Frequency: 8 times per year
Rolling River Publications Ltd.
Aberfeldy Road, Kenmore Perthshire
Scotland PH15 2HF
+44 0 1887 830526
+44 0 1887 830526 (Fax)
flyfishing-and-flytying.co.uk

Fly Fishing Retailer
Focuses on the health, development, and success of the fly-fishing industry. Covers issues with detailed information and brings them into focus for retailers, manufacturers, and raw-goods suppliers for this marketplace.
Frequency: 5 times per year
Circulation: 4,900
949-376-8135
fly-fishing-retailer.com

Golf Retailer
Business to business publication focusing on off-course golf retailing. Covers in-depth market news and analyzes one of the fastest growing segments of the golf market.
Frequency: 8 times per year
Circulation: 12,000
212-714-1300
golfretailer.com

Health & Fitness Business News
Focuses on bringing industry management late breaking reports on mergers, acquisitions, line extensions, distribution shifts, hiring/firings, financial disclosures, and more.
Frequency: 24 times per year
212-714-1300

Hockey Business News
Covers news and items of interest affecting the ice and inline hockey industries. Audience includes rinks, league members, store owners, industry executives, manufacturers, etc.
Frequency: 8 times per year
310-442-6660

Inside Sporting Goods
A fax or electronic newsletter providing sporting goods industry with current news and information concerning the market.
Frequency: 48 times per year
212-714-1300

NCAA News
Primary means of communication for NCAA with its more than 1,100 member institutions, organizations, and conferences, as well as the news media and other persons interested in staying abreast of developments in college athletics.
Frequency: 52 times per year
Circulation: 25,000
317-917-6222
ncaa.org/news

Outdoor Retailer
Focuses on specialty sports retailers of backpacking, mountaineering, camping, hiking, climbing, cross-country skiing, padding, mountain biking, adventure travel, snowboarding, snowshoeing, and related clothing.
Frequency: 12 times per year
Circulation: 16,100
800-486-2701
outdoorbiz.com

Poundbury Publishing Ltd.
Magazine publishing company that currently publishes six magazines, four of which are sport-related.
Agriculture House
Acland Road
Dorchester, Dorset DT1 1EF
United Kingdom
+44 0 1305 266360
+44 0 1305 262760 (Fax)
football-europe.co.uk
admin@poundbury.co.uk

Procycling
Authoritative, worldwide voice of international professional road racing, distributed in every country where there are English-speaking fans of cycling.
Frequency: 12 times per year
800-428-3003
procycling.com
Nicola.Serjeant@cabalcomm.com

Ski Area Management
Trade publication for the skiing industry conveys event, product, and company information.
45 Main Street North
PO Box 644
Woodbury, CT 06798
203-263-0888
203-266-0462 (Fax)

Sport Business.com
Provides daily on-line information and news concerning sport business.
Frequency: Daily
104 Blackfriars Foundry
156 Blackfriars Road
London, SE1 8EN
+44 0 20 7721 7161
+44 0 20 7721 7162 (Fax)

Sport Business Research Network
Provides a fee-based service, focusing on the sporting goods and sports marketing industry including: sports equipment sales, participation, broadcasting, sponsorship, and marketing.
Frequency: 12 times per year
PO Box 1417
Princeton, NJ 08542
609-896-1996
609-896-1903 (Fax)
sbrnet.com
richard@sbrnet.com

Sporting Goods Business
Over 30 years old, SBG covers and analyzes the sporting goods business.
Frequency: 18 times per year
Circulation: 26,500
212-714-1300
sgblink.com

Street & Smith's Sports Business Journal
Authority on sports spotlights its business journal devoted to news of the industry.
Frequency: 52 times per year
120 West Morehead Street, Suite 310
Charlotte, NC 28202
704-973-1429

Winter Sports Business
Provides product information on ski and snowboard equipment, skiwear, and accessories for owners, managers, sales, and service personnel of ski shops, instructors, and consumers.
Frequency: 10 times per year
Circulation: 15,700
505-988-5099

Appendix D

Sport Business Academic Journals and Associations Directory

Section 1: Sport Management Academic Curriculum Standards

In May 1993 the first NASPE-NASSM Sport Management Curriculum Standards manual was published through a joint task force. Members included scholars and practitioners in sport management representing the National Association for Sport and Physical Education (NASPE) and the North American Society for Sport Management (NASSM). The manual and the review council are listed here, but more information can be found through the NASSM or NASPE web sites.

The Manual:

"NASPE-NASSM Sport Management Curriculum Standards and Program Review"

Published by NASPE, can be purchased through NASPE

The curriculum standards review council:

NASPE-NASSM Sport Management Program Review Council

Made up of six council members, one director, and several reviewers; can be contacted through NASPE or NASSM

Section 2: Sport Business Journals

Entertainment and Sports Law Forum
Entertainment and Sport Lawyer American Bar Association
750 N. Lake Shore Drive
Chicago, IL 60611-4497
312-988-5522

European Sport Management Quarterly of Alberta
Dr. Trevor Slack, Editor
Canada Research Chair in Sport Management
Faculty of Physical Education and Recreation
E-424 Van Vliet Centre
Edmonton, Alberta
Canada, Tb6 249

International Journal of Sport Management
William F. Stier, Jr., Ed. D., Editor
The International Journal of Sport Management
Professor and Graduate Director
Coordinator of Sport Management/Athletic Administration

Physical Education and Sport
State University of New York
Brockport, New York
bstier@brockport.edu
716-395-5331 Office
716-637-8547 Home
716-393-2771 Fax

International Sports Journal
Dr. Thomas Katsaros
University of New Haven Foundation
300 Orange Avenue
West Haven, CT 06516
203-932-7118
203-931-6084 Fax
mharvey@charger.newhaven.edu

Journal of Legal Aspects of Sport and Physical Activity
SSLASPA
5840 South Ernest Street
Terre Haute, IN 47802
Dr. Andy Pittman, Editor
Dept. of HPER
Baylor University
PO Box 97313
Waco, TX 76798-7313
2540710-4002
254-710-3527 Fax
Andy Pittman@baylor.edu

Journal of Sports Economics
Sage Publications
2455 Teller Road
Thousand Oaks, CA 91320-2218
805-499-9774 Fax
805-499-0871
www.sagepub.com

Journal of Sport Management
The journal of the North American Society for Sport Management (NASSM)
www.nassm.org
*Membership includes subscription
Human Kinetics Publishers, Inc.
1607 N. Market Street
Champaign, IL 61820-2200
humankinetics.com

International Journal of Sports Marketing and Sponsorship
Editor: Dr. John Amis
johnamis@memphis.edu
For subscription information:
Gabriel Engelhard
gabriel@winpub.demon.co.uk
www.winthrop-publications.co.uk
+44 0 1234 593440

Marquette Sport Law Journal
National Sports Law Institute
Marquette University Law School
PO Box 1881
Milwaukee, WI 53201-1881
414-288-5815
414-288-5818 Fax
andersonpa@vms.csd.mu.edu
marquette.edu/law/sports

Seton Hall Journal of Sport Law
Seton Hall University School of Law
1111 Raymond Blvd.
Newark, NJ 07102

Southern California Sports & Entertainment Law Journal
PO Box 880542
San Diego, CA 92168
Sport Management Review
Sport Management Association of Australia and New Zealand (SMAANZ)
Sport Management Program
c/o Hans Westerbeek

Deakin University
221 Burwood Hwy
Burwood, Australia 3125
westerbk@deakin.edu.au

Sport Marketing Quarterly
Fitness Information Technology, Inc.
PO Box 4425
University Avenue
Morgantown, WV 26504-4425
fit@fitinfotech.com
fitinfotech.com

The Sport Lawyer Journal
Tulane University School of Law, Editors
Sports Lawyers Association, Publishers
11250-8 Roger Bacon Drive, Ste 8
Reston, VA 20190-5202
703-437-4377
Villanova Sports & Entertainment Law Journal

Section 3: Sport Industry Related Journals

This is a sample listing of the many journals in which you will find sport, recreation, leisure, fitness, and sport tourism related research and material. Additionally, refer to the many journals in the areas of business, such as the *Journal of Marketing*, and law for research and material in foundational and related content areas.

Australian Leisure Management
Karen Sweaney, Editor
Nigel Benton, Publisher
Australian Leisure Management
PO Box 478
Collaroy NSW 2097 Australia
+61 0 2 9984 8588
+61 0 2 9984 8589 (Fax)
leisure@ausleisure.com.au
ausleisure.com.au

Carnegie Research Papers
Carnegie School of PE and Human Movement Studies
Leeds Polytechnic
Beckett Park
Leeds LS6 3QS
Current Issues in Tourism
Channel View Publications
Multilingual Matters Ltd
Frankfurt Lodge
Clevedon Hall
Victoria Road
Clevedon BS21 7HH, UK
Tel: 01275-876519
http://www.multilingual-matters.com

Electronic Journals of Martial Arts and Sciences
PO Box 1694
Lynnwood, WA 98046-1694
ejmas.com

International Review for the Sociology of Sport
R. Oldenbourg Verlag GmbH
PO Box 801360
D-8000 Munchen 80
Germany

Journal of Aging and Physical Activity
Human Kinetics Publishers
PO Box 5076
Champaign, IL 61825-5076

Journal of Applied Sport Psychology
JASP Editor
School of Education and Allied Professions
Phillips Hall
Miami University, OH 45056
513-529-2728
aaasponline.org/journal.html
weinber@muohio.edu

Journal of Hospitality and Leisure Marketing
Haworth Press
10 Alice Street
Binghamton, NY 13904-1580

Journal of International Hospitality, Leisure & Tourism Management
Haworth Press
10 Alice Street
Binghamton, NY 13904-1580

Journal of Leisurability
Leisurability Publications
Box 507, Station Q
Toronto, ON M4T 2M5 Canada

Journal of Leisure Research
National Recreation & Park Association
22355 Belmont Ridge Road
Ashburn, VA 20148-4501

Journal of Park & Recreation Administration
Sagamore Publishing
PO Box 647
Champaign, IL 61824-0647

Journal of Philosophy of Sport
Human Kinetics Publishers
PO Box 5076
Champaign, IL 61325

Journal of Sport and Social Issues
SAGE Publications Ltd.
6 Bonhill Street
London, EC2A 4PU, UK
+ 44 0 171 374 8741 (Fax)
+ 44 0 171 330 1266 (Credit card Hotline)
sagepub.co.uk

Journal of Sport Behavior
Michigan State University Libraries
Electronic resources—Journal of Sport Behavior
lib.msu.edu

Journal of Sport History
Ronald A. Smith, NASSH Secretary-Treasurer
101 White Bldg.
Pennsylvania State University
University Park, PA 16802
nassh.uwo.ca/jounal.

Journal of Sport Tourism
Sports Tourism International Council
PO Box 5580, Station F
Ottawa, Canada K2C 3M1
stic@winning.com
sportquest.com/tourism

Journal of Sustainable Tourism
Channel View Publications
Multilingual Matters Ltd
Frankfurt Lodge
Clevedon Hall
Victoria Road
Clevedon BS21 7HH, UK
Tel: 01275-876519
http://www.multilingual-matters.com

Journal of Vacation Marketing
Henry Stewart Publications
Russell House
28/30 Little Russell Street
London, WC1A 2HN, UK
Tel: +44(0)171-404 3040

Leisure Sciences
Crane Russak & Co. Inc.
3 East 44th Street
New York, NY 10017
NIRSA Journal

National Intramural Recreational Sports Association
Will Holsberry, Executive Secretary
Dixon Recreation Center
Oregon State University
Corvallis, OR 97331

Quest
Human Kinetics Publishers, Inc.
PO Box 5076
Champaign, IL 61825

Parks and Recreation
National Recreation & Park Association
22377 Belmont Ridge Road
Ashburn, VA 20148-4501

Sociology of Sport Journal
Human Kinetics
PO Box 5076
Champaign, IL 61825-5076

Sport Management Global News
Newsletter of NASSM
humankinetics.com

Women in Sport and Physical Activity Journal
Women of Diversity Productions, Inc.
Fay Klein, Business Manager
WSPAJ, 400 Antique Bay Street
Las Vegas, NV 89128
dvrsty@aol.com
lifetimetv.com/WoSport

Section 4: Sport Business/Management Associations

American Alliance for Health Physical Education and Dance (AAHPERD)
Publications: JOPERD, Strategies, Journal of Health Education, Research Quarterly for Exercise & Sport, Update Newsletter
Conference: annual
1900 Association Drive
Reston, VA 20191
800-213-7193
703-476-3400
aahperd.org

Association for the Advancement of Applied Sport Psychology (AAASP)
Publications: Journal of Applied Sport Psychology, Newsletter
Conference: annual
webmaster@aaasponline.org
c/o Cynthia Pemberton
Acting Dean, College of Health and Human Services
Southwest Missouri State University
901 S. National Avenue
Springfield, MO 65804
417-836-4176
417-836-6905 Fax

Division 47 of the American Psychological Association (APA)
Publications: Exercise and Sport Psychology News (ESP-News), Exploring Exercise and Sport Psychology, Graduate Training & Career Possibilities in Exercise and Sport Psychology, Sport Psychology: A Guide to Choosing a Sport Psychology Professional Division Services
American Psychological Association
750 First Street, NE
Washington, DC 20002-4242
202-336-5500
202-218-3599 Fax
psyc.unt.edu
division@apa.org

European Federation of Sport Psychology
Publications: European Yearbook of Sport Psychology, Annual reports, Anxiety in Sport, European Perspectives on Exercise and Sport Psychology, Psychology for Physical Educators
Conference: every 3 years
psychology.lu.se/FEPSAC
International Society for Sport Psychiatry (ISSP)
c/o Daniel Begel, M.D., President
316 North Milwaukee Street, Ste 318
Milwaukee, WI 53202
414-271-2900

International Society for Sport Psychiatry (ISSP)
c/o Daniel Begel. M.D., president
316 N. Milwaulkee St., Ste 318
Milwaulkee, WI 53202

North American Society for the Psychology of Sport and Physical Activity
Publication: Journal of Sport and Exercise Psychology
Human Kinetics Publishers, Inc.
1607 N. Market Street
Champaign, IL 61820-2200

North American Society for Sport Management (NASSM)
Suite 344
106 Main Street
Houlton, ME 04730-9901 USA
nassm.org

National Association for Sport and Physical Education (NASPE)
1900 Association Drive
Reston, VA 20191
703-476-3417
703-476-8316 Fax

National Collegiate Athletic Association (NCAA)
Publication: The NCAA News
Confernce: annual
700 W. Washington Street
PO Box 6222
Indianapolis, IN 46206-6222
317-917-6222
317-917-6888 (Fax)
ncaa.org

European Association for Sport Management (EASM)
Publication: European Journal of Sport Management
Conference: annual
EASM Bureau
ISEF Firenze
Viuzzo di Gattaia 9
50125 Firenze—Italia
+39 055 241799
easm.org
easm@unifi.it

Section 5: Sport Management Conferences

3rd Annual Southwest Sport and Exercise Sport Psychology Conference
Dr. Robert Harmison
Arizona School of Professional Psychology
2301 West Dunlap
Suite 211
Phoenix, AZ 85021
602-216-2600

Conference on Counseling Athletes
Kelly O'Brien, Conference Coordinator
Springfield College
Springfield, MA
413-748-3325

International Society of Sport Psychology
10th World Congress of Sport Psychology
Democritus University of Thrace
Department of Physical Education
69100 Komotini, Greece

North American Society for Sport Management (NASSM)
Conference: annual
nassm.org

National Golf Course Owners Association.
NGCOA Annual Conference and Trade Show
Publications: Marketing research handbooks, marketing manual, annual conference
Conference: annual
1470 Ben Sawyer Blvd., Ste 18
Mt. Pleasant, SC 29464
843-881-9956
843-881-9958
ngcoa.org
info@ngcoa.org

The Center of Sport, Character, & Culture
University of Notre Dame
202 Brownson Hall
Notre Dame, IN 46556
219-631-4445
219-631-8411 (Fax)
cscc@nd.edu

European Association for Sport Management (EASM)
Publication: European Quarterly of Sport Management
Conference: annual
EASM Bureau
ISEF Firenze
Viuzzo di Gattaia 9
50125 Firenze—Italia
+39 055 241799
easm.org
easm@unifi.it

American Alliance for Health, Physical Education, Recreation, and Dance (AAHPERD)
This is the umbrella organization for several organizations, one of which is the National Association for Sport and Physical Education (NASPE). NASPE consists of groups for several different areas, including the Sport Management Council. AAHPERD has an annual conference at which the Sport Management Council hosts 3 to 4 research sessions. Information can be found by contacting NASPE.
www.aahperd.org
AAHPERD
1900 Association Drive
Reston, VA 20191
800/213-7193

Florida State University Sport Management Conference
Education and Sport Administration
Conference: annual
Department of Sport Management and Physical Education
Florida State University
Tully Gym
Tallahassee, FL 32306-4280
850-644-4814
850-644-0975 (Fax)

Georgia Southern University Annual Student Sport Management Conference
Conference: annual
Dr. Ming Li
Department of Recreation and Sport Management
College of Health & Professional Studies
PO Box 8077
Statesboro, GA 30460

Sport Management Association of Australia and New Zealand (SMAANZ)
Sport Management Program
c/o Hans Westerbeek
Deakin University
221 Burwood Hwy
Burwood, Australia 3125
westerbk@deakin.edu.au

National Collegiate Athletic Association (NCAA)
Publication: The NCAA News
Conference: annual
700 W. Washington Street
PO Box 6222
Indianapolis, IN 46206-6222
317-917-6222
317-917-6888 (Fax)
ncaa.org

Appendix E

Sport Marketing Research Briefs

Ten Strategies to Employ When Marketing Sport to Black Consumers

Ketra L. Armstrong

The Black consumer market is a very lucrative market with unique characteristics. It is a widespread belief that Blacks place much emphasis on sport, and sports are salient to their culture. Nonetheless, such salience has not been demonstrated in the rate at which Blacks attend major sport events. This may be a result of Blacks' omission as a viable target market for sports and the lack of concentrated marketing efforts to reach them. This is a trend that the sport industry should not continue, particularly as Blacks increase their economical and sociological power and as marketing continues to be practiced in multicultural environments. The purpose of this paper is to (a) discuss Blacks' interest and involvement in sport, (b) present some key findings about Black consumers, and (c) offer suggestions in which sport organizations may enhance their efforts to market sports to Black consumers.

- *Sport Marketing Quarterly 7(3),* 1998, p. 11.

Sport/Exercise Identity Theory and Participation Marketing: Theory Formation and Theoretical Justification

Christine M. Brooks

Stakeholders in the active lifestyle industry want to understand how people are attracted to specific forms of active lifestyle pursuits. Exploratory research undertaken for the windsurfing and health club industries suggested that a phenomenon labeled as sport/exercise identity holds important marketing strategy clues. A sport/exercise identity appears to be formed from a comparison between an individual's sport/exercise self-concept (which appears to consist of a summary assessment of physique, physical condition, athleticism, socioeconomic status, age, and gender) and the stereotype the individual has of participants and attributes of movement encompassed by the sport or exercise. This paper provides support for the existence of a sport/exercise self-concept and discusses its subsequent use to form an identity with a sport or exercise program. It was concluded that sport/exercise self-concept is supported by the "working self-concept" notion discussed in the self-concept literature. The potential purpose of a sport/exercise self-concept is threefold: (a) It provides a personal history that helps guide behavior; (b) it is a means of efficient information processing; and (c) it serves as a source of motivation. We can explain the variety of reactions among people who appear to lack identity with a sport or exercise program because of possible individual differences in (a) levels of self-consciousness, (b) levels of self-awareness, (c) levels of self-monitoring, and (d) degree of urgency to make changes in one's life, to maintain health, and/or to have psychologically enhancing experiences. These conclusions have an implication of the use of modeling strategies when advertising sport and exercise pursuits to potential participant markets.

- *Sport Marketing Quarterly 7(1),* 1998, p. 38.

Exploring Reader Recognition of Sport/Event Souvenir Program Advertisements

Jacquelyn Cuneen, Bowling Green State University, and Amy J. Sander, Albion College

Souvenir programs represent an important tangible association with sport contests and other events and are often the only enduring evidence of the events themselves. Programs usually contain advertising (Davis, 1998) because production output (viz, lay-out/print costs) is offset by the revenue generated through program ad sales. Sales of program ads can reap large profits for events because local, state, regional, and/or national companies wishing to be linked with particular events are willing to pay large amounts for program ads. But, whether or not readers notice and remember program ads at rates comparable to traditional print ads (e.g., magazines), which are customarily high (Finn, 1988; Beattie & Mitchell, 1985), remains a riddle. The purpose of this study was to determine if souvenir program readers notice ads and can identify them through Recognition Testing (Starch/INRA/Hooper, 1988). An original souvenir program (containing features & ads) was fabricated using combinations of color and black/white full and partial-page ads (N = 45). Subjects (N = 106) perused the program independently (i.e., alone at their own conveniences and paces) and then were asked to identify from a prepared list those advertisers whose ads appeared in the program. Demography indicated that 74% of subjects read programs before (75%), during (75%), and after (45%) events and are motivated to purchase programs because they contain feature stories (69%) and score cards/player rosters (52%). Data (f/%) indicated that subjects correctly recognized ads 1,800 times. Of the top-12 most recognized ads, two were full page, b/w national-level ads (recognition rate = 89%; 81%) and the remaining 10 (79-66% rates) were national-level full-page color except for one local ¼ page color ad. Ads least likely to be recognized (2–19%) were ¼, ⅛, or 1/16 page b/w, local-level ads. No significant relationships emerged between ad recognition and subjects' current/future usage of advertised products (0 = > .001 Bonferroni alpha). Ads placed near feature stories or game cards/rosters yielded highest recognition rates. It was concluded that souvenir program ads provide advertisers with excellent opportunities to reach customers multiple times and ad placement near features or score cards/rosters should be premium priced. Further, a full-page b/w ad constitutes a high intensity medium among full-page color media. Results from this study will be useful in plotting pricing structures for souvenir programs and can encourage a new line of inquiry regarding print media.

- 1999 NASSM Conference Presentation

Celebrity Endorsement: Advertising Agency Managers' Perspective

B. Zafer Erdogan (Dumlupinar University, Turkey) and Michael J. Baker, Professor of Marketing (University of Strathclyde)

This paper explores advertising agency managers' attitudes concerning celebrity endorsement strategy. Although a number of scholars have written about the strategy, their research centers on the characteristics of effective celebrity endorsers. They have usually employed deductive approaches in deriving hypotheses from the communication theory (e.g. Source Effect Theory) and empirically tested with student samples. This study provides another perspective to the celebrity endorsement strategy by using semi-structured in-depth interviews with12 advertising agency managers.

- *Cyber Journal of Sport Marketing, 3(3),* 1999.

Brand Image, Positioning, and Service Quality

Prof Dr. Franz-Rudolf Esch, Director of the Institute for Brand and Communication Research (Institut für Marken-mid Konzni unikationsforschung) at the Justus-Liebig-Universität Gicjen

The concept of service quality partly overlaps with satisfaction. The satisfaction, or rather the degree of satisfaction, of customers is generally shown as a comparison of the actual situation with the target situation, which in a simplified form arises from the customers' expectations of products and services, and the extent to which the consumers subjectively perceive that the service has been fulfilled (see Kaas, Runow, 1984). This definition alone already clearly shows the difficulties in distinguishing service quality from satisfaction (Teas, 1993): In the literature on service quality, fulfilled expectations are seen as an indicator of the perceived quality. In satisfaction research they are considered an influential factor for satisfaction. The degree of (dis)satisfaction is taken from the evaluation of the subjectively perceived degree to which a service has been fulfilled.

Positioning is understood as the separation of a company's own offer from those of rival companies. The positioning characteristics selected must be in keeping with the desires and requirements of the consumers and be relevant for them. This is a necessary condition. Differentiation from the competition means that, in the subjective perception of the consumers, a company gains an independent and distinctive profile (see Kroeber-Ricl. Weinberg, 1996). It can be described as a sufficient measure for successful positioning.

The success or failure of a positioning depends on its realization. Not until the relevant positionings are permanently and uniquely conveyed in a clearly perceivable manner in both sports outlets and other means of communication used by sports shops, can clear images and memory structures for a sports shop be formed by the consumers. These influence how consumers perceive the services to a great extent. This influence on the image can be directly initiated through the positioning if a service positioning is striven for right from the start, e.g. by emphasizing the aspect "empathy." In this case, a clear focus is set on one or two relevant service dimensions that a sports shop must fulfill better than its competitors. All other service dimensions should at the same time not be less well fulfilled than they are by rival companies. However, indirect effects on the perception of service quality can also be targeted, by striving for a non-service-oriented positioning. Profiling occurs here as a result of other important emotional or rational positioning items that are relevant for customers (e.g. competition positioning, self-fulfillment etc.). Through the corresponding halo-effects, a better evaluation of the dimensions of service quality can be counted on when service quality at least fulfills the average expectations. These, in turn, are influenced by what the customer has already experienced in that branch.

- *European Journal for Sport Management,* 82–105.

Volunteer Motivation, Satisfaction, and Management at an Elite Sporting Competition

Jocelyn M. Farrell, Margaret E. Johnston, and G. David Twynam
Lakehead University, Ontario

The purpose of this study was to investigate attributes of satisfaction and motivation for volunteers at an elite sporting competition and the implications of this for effective event management. A survey of 300 volunteers was undertaken immediately following the Scott Tournament of Hearts, the Canadian Women's Curling Championship, held in Thunder Bay in March 1996. The 28-item Special Event Volunteer Motivation Scale was tested in this study. Resulting in four empirically supported factors termed purposive, solitary, external traditions, and commitments. The study measured the level of satisfaction with the general volunteer experience and with specific aspects of the administrative and managerial conditions. This study found that particular attributes of the event organization and competition facility played a role in volunteer satisfaction.

- *Journal of Sport Management, 12,* 1998, 288–300.

Strategy and Competitive Analysis: The Tennis Club Industry in Louisville

Lawrence Fielding, Pamm Kellett, James Brown, and Gary Sailes: Indiana University

Recent studies of the tennis club industry have suggested that tennis participation is in decline (Simmons Market Research Bureau, Inc., 1 985-1996; Warnick & Howard, 1996). Yet the tennis industry in Louisville, Kentucky, is booming. Club managers reported court fill ratios above 85% and in 3 instances court fill ratios exceeded 95%. Tennis clubs supported an average of 8 tennis professionals with a high of 17 and a low of 4. Each club had several tennis pros whose salary was above $30,000 per year. Club managers reported profit margins between 12 and 21 percent.

This study analyzed the tennis club industry in Louisville, Kentucky, to discover why tennis clubs in the area were so successful. The purpose of this research was to answer the following questions: (1) What are the dominant economic traits of the tennis club industry in Louisville? (2) What competitive forces influence the local tennis industry and how powerful are these competitive forces? (3) What key factors determine competitive success or failure in the competitive tennis industry? (4) How do local tennis clubs meet the needs and wants of local tennis players? (5) What are the core competencies necessary for individual tennis club success? (6) How attractive is the local tennis industry in terms of profitability? (In the interest of brevity we have not listed the sub-questions under each of the above categories.)

The answers to the above six questions involved a series of interlocking research approaches. First, economic and demographic data were gathered on Jefferson County

(Socioeconomic Analysis). These data were compared with national data obtained from Simmons Market Research Bureau. They were also used in conjunction with tennis profile survey data to predict market size and market growth rate. Second, focused interviews with club managers and club marketing directors were used to develop a competitive forces model for the tennis club industry in Louisville. Follow-up interviews focused upon financial data, how the club functioned to meet tennis player needs and wants, and the club's approach to marketing. Third, an extensive tennis player survey was used to gather information from tennis players. Tennis club professionals handed out and collected the survey. The survey was divided into five parts as follows: demographic data, sports background, leisure profile, tennis profile, and tennis player needs and wants analysis. Survey results were used to segment the tennis consumer market and to answer questions about core competencies necessary for success and to develop a Key Success Factor list.

The results, discussion, and interpretation of the research are too extensive to place in the abstract (tables, graphs, and data analysis are extensive). At the risk of over simplifying the results there are some general statements that can be used as a summary. First, although the tennis industry in Louisville is highly competitive, tennis club managers cooperate with each other. Second, tennis club marketing directors utilize tennis consumers to promote, advertise, and sell the tennis program. This consumer networking is largely responsible for the current tennis boom in Louisville and is a core competency for successful tennis clubs. Third, successful tennis professionals provide a wide range of services to tennis consumers. This is a key success factor for the tennis club industry in Louisville. Fourth, successful tennis clubs have developed strategies to attract new players and to move low consumption tennis players into higher rates of consumption.

- *1999 NASSM Conference Presentation*

Sport Volunteers: Research Agenda and Application

B. Christine Green and Laurence Chalip

Recruiting and retaining volunteers for sport events and services are fundamentally marketing problems. Successful recruitment of sport volunteers requires that the volunteer experience be constructed and promoted in terms of benefits that differentiate volunteer activities from one another and from alternative leisure pursuits. The present consensus of opinion is that benefits such as insider knowledge, opportunities to earn or display prestigious symbols, and interaction with valued others are possible valued benefits that attract sport volunteers. However, the strength and importance of these benefits appears to vary according to the specific volunteer task. Volunteer retention is essentially a task of relationship marketing, wherein benefits of volunteering are updated, repackaged, and marketed back to volunteers. Research in all these areas lacks the sophistication and detail needed to map the range and impact of benefits sought by various volunteer segments. This paper describes the research status quo, applications of the available knowledge that can be applied to recruitment and retention, and a suggested research agenda that will fill in the major gaps limiting our understanding of volunteer behavior.

- *Sport Marketing Quarterly 7(2),* 1998, 14.

Trends in the Sport Marketing Industry and in the Demographics of the United States: Their Effect on the Strategic Role of Grassroots Sport Sponsorship in Corporate America

Linda Greenwald and Juan-Miguel Fernandez-Balboa

Although few studies exist that focus specifically on corporate sponsorship of grassroots sport, recent statements from sport marketers, and both market and demographic trends, indicate that grassroots sport sponsorship is and will continue to increase. As part of a larger qualitative study investigating the role of grassroots sport sponsorship in corporate America, 14 informants, representing four corporations, four sport-marketing organizations, four grassroots sports organizations, and one publishing company, were interviewed at length to verify these claims and highlight additional trends and issues affecting grassroots sport sponsorship. Informants overwhelmingly stated that corporate attention in this arena has "definitely" increased. In addition to reiterating trends in the literature, informants identified a rise in the number of grassroots sport events broadcast by television cable stations, corporations increasingly pursuing a national reach from their grassroots sponsorships, increased corporate ownership of events, and increased sponsorship measurability. Future implications and cautions based on these trends are discussed.

- *Sport Marketing Quarterly 7(4),* 1998, 35.

Factors Affecting Methods Used by Annual Giving Programs: A Qualitative Study of NCAA Division I Athletic Departments

James S. Hall and Daniel F. Mahony

The importance of having a successful annual giving program has increased for most NCAA Division I schools. The current study focused on (a) the various methods used within annual giving programs, (b) the environmental factors that may influence the annual giving program, and (c) the impact of the environmental factors on the various methods. In order to identify the factors and the methods, interviews were conducted with ten directors of Division I annual giving programs. An effort was made to include directors who worked at both public and private institutions, who were located in various parts of the country, and who were identified as experts at specific fund-raising methods. The researchers then attempted to identify relationships between the factors and the various methods based on the responses by the interviewees. The researchers identified 11 environmental factors, 6 methods, and a variety of relationships between the factors and methods.

- *Sport Marketing Quarterly 6(3),* 21.

Retail Licensing Procedures Used by Selected NCAA Division I Institutions: Implication for Licensees of Collegiate Memorabilia

Mary Elizabeth Mazzeo, Jacquelyn Cuneen, and Cathryn L. Claussen

Because collegiate-logoed merchandise generates significant revenue, many vendors (licensees) are investigating the feasibility of producing collegiate memorabilia. Logo owners (institutions, bowl committees, and so forth) assume minimal commercial risks in collegiate merchandising. Most of the financial risks are assumed by licensees, who may find the collegiate licensing realm to be more imposing than suspected due to diverse licensing procedures and financial expectations of individual institutions. This study described characteristics of selected collegiate retail licensing programs and suggested implications for licensees and vendors to consider before deciding to venture into the collegiate memorabilia business.

- *Sport Marketing Quarterly 6(1),* 1997, 41.

Determining Costs and Forecasting Profits for a Multi-logoed Collegiate Memorabilia Poster: A Profitability Study in New Product Development

Mary Elizabeth Mazzeo, Jacquelyn Cuneen, and Cathryn L. Claussen

This study constitutes a profitability analysis (in abridged form) for an original collegiate memorabilia product (viz., collegiate bowl game poster). Analyses addressed business environmental conditions to determine whether or not it was possible to make a profit by creating, producing, and marketing six individually targeted posters that contained the logos of several different collegiate institutions and three bowl games. This study shows the process of market, (a brief summary of) technical, and (summary) financial analyses commonly used to evaluate market and production conditions and financial projections.

- *Sport Marketing Quarterly 6(3),* 41.

Marketing Sport to Hispanic Consumers

Larry McCarthy and W. Paul Stillman

Hispanic consumers exist in a unique bilingual and bicultural market that allows the consumer to take part in mainstream American society without having to forfeit their Latin culture. Among the numerous demographic changes that will take place in American society as it enters the 21st century is a significant increase in the Hispanic population. This paper examines critical aspects of the rapidly expanding population, and indicates how sport organizations might most effectively tap into this unique market.

- *Sport Marketing Quarterly 7(4),* 1998, p. 19.

Resale Price Maintenance: A Historical View of Its Impact on the Sporting Goods Industry

Lori K. Miller, Wichita State University, and Larry W. Fielding, University of Louisville

Resale price maintenance (RPM) is a system in which the manufacturer of a branded or trademarked product dictates the resale price for the products it sells within the chain of distribution. The practice itself constitutes a vertical restraint of trade since RPM dictates the price at which competing sellers sell a product. Many argue that the vertical pricing restraint represents an agreement, contract, or conspiracy to restrain trade in violation of section 1 of the Sherman Act (15 U.S.C.§ 1). For this reason, the manufacturer's ability to engage in RPM practices has fluctuated over the years as the courts and Congress have vacillated over its legality.

Sporting goods manufacturers have been concerned about resale price maintenance since the late 1800s. Early RPM advocates included Spalding, A. J. Reach; 1. Stevens Arms & Tool Co.; Marlin Firearms Company; Colt; Savage; and Harrington & Richardson (West, 1904). During the 1890s the bicycle industry experienced tremendous growth and competition. When the popularity of the bicycle waned in the late 1890s, competition became even more intense. The bicycle crash that followed forced many companies into bankruptcy. Much of the sporting goods industry concern regarding price control emanated as a result of the bicycle crash in 1899. In the aftermath of the bicycle crash (1899-1900), some manufacturers pointed to the price-cutting tactics of the catalogue and mail order houses as a significant cause of business failure. Sporting goods manufacturers concerned about business profits and industry profitability considered RPM an integral business strategy influencing long-term success.

In response to restraint of trade claims, manufacturers advocating RPM practices argue that RPM has many pro-competitive effects that outweigh the pricing restraint imposed upon the distributor.

This article begins with a discussion of the benefits of RPM from the point of view of the sporting goods manufacturers. It then traces the judicial and legislative history that influences RPM practices in the sporting goods industry. In conclusion, the article comments on the present position of RPM and alternate ways in which sporting goods manufacturers can legally maintain resale prices.

- *Journal of Legal Aspects of Sport 5(1),* 1995, 1-27.

Ticket Distribution Agencies and Professional Sport Franchises: The Successful Partnership

Lori K. Miller and Lawrence W. Fielding

The purpose of this study was to identify the ticket distribution practices of professional sport franchises. NBA, NFL, NHL, and MLB franchises were surveyed (n = 113) regarding the use of ticket agencies, which agencies were used, and the advantages and disadvantages of ticket distribution agencies. The results were used, in combination with existing literature, to ascertain the successful strategies employed by ticket distribution agencies that have created for the ticket industry a sustainable competitive niche. The study also looked at customer discontent emanating from ticket distribution practices and regulatory attempts to control the ticket distribution industry. In conclusion, this paper provides the sport manager with 20 suggestions regarding negotiations with ticket distribution agencies.

- *Sport Marketing Quarterly 6(1),* 1997, 47.

Recent Trends in Sport Consumption in Japan—An Analysis on Household Living Expenditures with Respect to Sports Related Activities

Jun Oga, The University of Electro-communications Tokyo, Japan

A public opinion survey taken by the Prime Minister's Office in Japan indicates that 71.7% of people over age 20 participated in sports related activities in 1997. It shows that sports related activities have been indispensable for enriching the Japanese people's lives.

For enjoying the sports related activities, some expenses are incurred. The expenses are one of the living expenditures taken from family income. The purposes of this study are to grasp changes in household expenditures for sports related activities and to make clear recent trends in sport consumption in Japan.

For that purpose, annual reports on family income and living expenditure surveys taken by the Statistic Bureau of the Management and Coordination Agency were analyzed. The surveys, conducted under the Statistic Law in Japan, aim at providing comprehensive data on incomes and expenditures of consumers. The surveys cover all consumer households expect for those engaged in agriculture, forestry or fishery, and one-person households. About 8,000 households are randomly selected for the survey out of 29 million appropriate households. Family income consists of all income resources of the head of the household and the spouse. Living expenditures include food, housing, fuel, light and water charges, furniture and household goods, clothes and footwear, medical care, education, reading, and other living expenditures. As for expenditures for sports related activities, expenditures for sports shoes, sports outfits, sporting goods, lesson fees for sports related activities, admission fees for sports games and for use of sports facilities are included.

By analyzing annual reports on family income and living expenditure surveys from 1987 to 1997, some findings regarding trends in sport consumption can be found. In 1997, the average number of persons per household was 3.34 and the average age of the heads of those households was 51.6 years of age. The average living expenditure in a year was 33,331 dollars with an exchange rate of 120 Japanese yen per dollar and the average expenditure for sports related activities was $429. The percentage of living expenditures used for sports related activities was 1.3%. During the period of 1987-1997, increases in both average living expenditures and average expenditures for sports related activities have been parallel. The percentages of living expenditure used for sports related activities changed little during that period.

An examination of household income reveals that both average living expenditures and average expenditures for sports related activities increased in parallel as household income increased. The percentages of living expenditure used for sports related activities increased up to the 60,000 dollars income per year, but leveled off or declined for incomes above that.

- 1999 NASSM Conference Presentation

Using Statistical Power Analysis in Sport Management Research

Janet B. Parks and Patricia A. Shewokis, Bowling Green State University, Carla A. Costa, The Ohio State University

Statistical power analysis involves designing and interpreting research with attention to the statistical power (probability) of the study to detect an effect of a specific size. Statistical power analysis, which is based on the interdependence of sample size, alpha, effect size, and power, is acknowledged by scholars of various disciplines as an indispensable component of high quality research. This paper reviews basic principles associated with power analysis and demonstrates its importance by comparing the meaningfulness of significant findings in two studies of job satisfaction. The perspective advanced in this paper is that the use of statistical power analysis will strengthen sport management research and will enable researchers to expand the body of knowledge in a systematic, coherent fashion.

- *Journal of Sport Management, 13,* 1999, 139-147.

An Analysis of Visitor Spending Patterns and the Economic Scale on Amsterdam from the Gay Games V

Brenda Pitts and Kevin Ayers

The Gay Games is an international multi-sport and cultural event and is among the largest multi-sports events in the world. Although many sport event stakeholders, such as host cities, governments, tourism agencies, souvenir vendors, and the hotel and restaurant industries, could benefit from an economic study of the Gay Games, to date there is no such study known. Therefore, the purpose of this study was to measure the economic scale of the Gay Games. Results show that total expenditures from visitor spending and the Gay Games budget on the Amsterdam economy was $350,736, 175 (USD). This represents direct economic impact to the Amsterdam, Netherlands economy. Among the results, there were approximately 208,860 visitors, including participants and spectators, from outside the Amsterdam local economy. Another 55,855 spectators/participants came to Amsterdam for reasons other than the Gay Games but spent an additional five days solely because of the Gay Games. Study participants are from 14 different countries and, among others, spent the following median average dollars: $47.50 on admission fees; $200 on commercial transportation; $300 on food; $50 on Gay Games souvenirs; $550 on lodging; $100 on entertainment; $120 on registration fees; and $90 on retail shopping. Financial implications for potential future sites and sponsors are enormous. Sport management professionals can benefit from this research.

- *International Journal of Sport Management, 2*(2) 2001, 134–151

Inside of the Outside

Robert Rinehart

Despite an ever-increasing number of alternative sports, which have begun encroaching into mainstream sport, the process of commodification of such alternative sports has been little examined. In this article, the author will explore some of the dynamic relationships—the establishment of a "pecking order"—occurring in skateborading and in-line skating as they become commodified in ESPN's 1995 Extreme Games. The author makes the case that an attempt for mass acceptance of a sport articulates with (a) fan identification with the sport's personalities, (b) modeling behavior of younger participants, (c) corporate sponsorship and embracing of certain sports and individuals over others, and (d) an uneasy, contested dynamic between performers' artistic and competitive impulses.

- *Journal of Sport and Social Issues, 22(4),* (1998), 398–415.

"We Got Next"—Next What? An Evaluation of the Effectiveness of the WNBA Tag Line and A Case for Sport Marketing Research

Elizabeth L. Shoenfelt, Allison E. Maue, and Eric B. Hatcher

For its inaugural season the Women's National Basketball Association (WNBA) adopted the tag line "We Got Next." This phrase, commonly heard on playground basketball courts around the country, would appear to be the perfect tag line for the new basketball league. However, anecdotal information suggested that many individuals, even those familiar with the WNBA, did not understand the meaning of "We Got Next." We surveyed two groups, college students and women's basketball fans, to assess their recognition and understanding of the WNBA's tag line. Our findings indicated that the WNBA marketing campaign resulted in a relatively high recognition rate for the tag line, but relatively few understood the meaning of "We Got Next." Our study suggested that the WNBA may have improved the effectiveness of their campaign had they conducted preliminary marketing research to better understand their target audience.

- *Sport Marketing Quarterly 8(3),* 1999, 31.

The Economic Impact of Sports in Flanders (Belgium)

Marijke Taks, Stefan Kesenne, and Eva Dejaegher, KULeuven, Belgium
Willy Laporte and Els Audenaert, UGent, Belgium
Paul De Knop, VUBrussel, Belgium

Belgium is a small, highly developed, and densely populated country (over 10 million inhabitants) at the crossroads of Western Europe. It is recently a federal state, with three relatively autonomous linguistic communities: Flanders in the north, where the language is Dutch ('Flemish'), Wallonia in the south, where the language is French, and a small German-speaking part in the southeast. The centrally located capital, Brussels, is officially bilingual. Culture, and thus also sport, are the responsibility of each of these community governments. The aim of this study, which has been commissioned by BLCSO (the Flemish Sports Administration), is to analyze the economic importance of sport in Flanders. There are three approaches that can be taken when analyzing the economic impact, namely, one can analyze it by looking at expenditures, production, or income. This study has opted for an analysis on the basis of expenditures because it is easier to do so than via production and income analysis. Several types of expenditure patterns are analyzed: 1) private consumption of households, 2) government expenditures (both consumption and investments), 3) private investments, and 4) the trade balance. For the purpose of this study we have chosen a broad definition of sport, and expenditures for active, as well as for passive, practice of sport are included.

Household expenditure is the highest of the above-mentioned types of expenditure in sport. A representative sample of Flemish households ($N = 512$), stratified according to family size and age of the head of the family, has been interviewed by means of a standardized questionnaire. Their answers have been extrapolated and an estimate was made for Flanders. Because of the importance of household expenditure, this paper focuses mainly on the methodology and the results of the household budget questionnaire. Government expenditure in sport is the second in importance. Data are gathered from an analysis of the budgets and bills of 37 representative municipalities and cities. These results are then extrapolated for Flanders. Private investments are estimated on the basis of the presence of sports facilities. The balance of trade results are taken from existing statistics relating to foreign trade. All these expenditures, 17 1.900 million BF (app. 4911 million US $), constitute the Gross Regional Sport Product for Flanders; this equals more than 3% of the Gross Regional Product for Flanders. During the past fifteen years, household expenditure in sport has increased, while government expenditure decreased in real terms. Government contribution, however, still remains necessary because of the legal framework of sport and for the desirable interventions in private expenditure in sport. This study has, in any case, shown the importance of the sports sector for the Flemish economy, mainly through household expenditure.

- 1999 NASSM Conference Presentation

International Relations and Sport—An Australian Perspective

Tracy Taylor, Shayne Quick, and Dimitris Gargalianos University of Technology, Sydney

This paper investigates the place of sport policy in the development and promotion of international relations as it applies to national sports organizations in Australia. The study was designed as a complement to research conducted on Greek national sporting organizations (Gargalianos, 1996), which found that, while sport is often discussed as having the ability to promote international relations, most sports do not have strategies and/or policies in place that relate to achieving this goal.

While recent research has explored the political economy of sport (Guttman, 1993; McKay et al., 1993), globalization of sport relations (Bole & Maguire, 1994; Harvey & Houle, 1994; Harvey et al., 1996) and sport nationalism and identity (Jarvie, 1993; Klein, 1991; Mac quire, 1995), little has been written to further our understanding of the formal processes associated with developing and promoting international relations through sport. The unique contribution of this research is through the examination of issues of national identity, globalization, and discursive practice and the extent to which these issues can be translated into policy and practice within contemporary national sporting agencies.

Primary data were collected from nationally-orientated sporting organizations, which are affiliated sports, associate sports, and recognized sports of the Australian Olympic Committee (AOC). A questionnaire survey of organizations and a content analysis on the policy documents for each of the respondent sports about their formally articulated policies on international relations. The sports surveyed included 31 summer sports, 8 winter sports, 14 associated bodies, and 12 recognized sports.

The results are presented in three main forms: a conceptual model exploring the nexus between sport policy and international relations; an analysis of existing policies on international relations of national sport agencies in Australia; and a narrative of attitudes and opinions of personnel of national sport agencies about the extent to which their sport contributes to international relations.

We conclude that sport can both transcend divisions within society and act as a model for its nation in the international arena, but also reflect and accentuate differences that may be at odds with national politics and undermine international relations. Therefore it is important to distinguish between sport policy contributing to a national identify and the process by which sport is formally used to build an international identity or send a particular message to other nation states.

- 1999 NASSM Conference Presentation

Advertising Banners in Sport Web Sites

Wendy Yu, Chia-Chen, University of Wisconsin-La Crosse

With the fast growth of web users, multimedia capabilities of World Wide Web (WWW), global reach of population, and popularity of sports, sport web sites have been increasing during the past years. Taking advantage of the accessibility of the WWW, sports organizations use WWW where they can reach customers, promote their products, and provide information to others. For example, fans gather in formation about their favorite teams, purchase tickets for sports events, or get the latest sports news and scores on sports web sites.

The increasing number of visitors to sport web sites raises corporations' interest to buy into sports advertising on web sites. There is a common model, the advertising banner, for sponsors to sponsor sports organizations on web sites. Advertising banners online are much like sponsorships in sports events: the hope that users will more closely associate the image of the sport with the sponsors.

Studies of online buying show that the advertising banner is a good way to build brand awareness (Oliver, 1998). Banners have become a significant means of advertising and source of information because they guide people to their web pages. Also, banners have proven to be the most effective direct marketing tool, producing quantifiable units. Moreover, advertising banners remain the predominant advertising vehicle on the Web-accounting for approximately 54% of total online advertising revenues—the increased use of content sponsorships marking a shift towards more creative advertising on the Web (Hyland, 1998).

The purposes of this study were to examine the advertising banners presented on the web pages and also analyze the characteristics of sponsors for sports organizations on WWW. This study focused on the category of sponsors and the content of banners' links to their web pages. In addition, the differences among sports organizations, such as professional sports, amateur sports organizations, and sports events, were also examined by sponsors who put the advertising banners on the sport web pages. The population of this study was randomly selected from Internet search engines.

Based on an analysis of sampling, sponsors valued sports information or news related sites as major places for marketing opportunities on WWW. Results indicated that car, food, and computer product manufacturers, and Internet services are the types of companies most interested in advertising on sports web pages. Advertising banners presented on sports web pages are an apparent symbol/graphic and few words are used to introduce the links under the graphics of sponsors. These findings have important implications that the use of advertising banners will be a trend on sports web sites as another new way of sponsorship for corporations and sports organizations.

- 1999 NASSM Conference Presentation

Appendix F

Examples of Surveys and Questionnaires for Research

Overview: The purpose of Appendix F is to provide examples of research instruments commonly used in sport marketing. The examples are survey instruments. A brief overview of each instrument is provided, offering the topic of study, its purpose, the type of instrument, methodology, and some uses of the information. The survey instruments included are real surveys from actual research in sport marketing.

Activity: Actual studies may be conducted using any of these instruments with appropriate guidance and supervision of the sport marketing course instructor and/or the authors from whom these instruments were derived. (Use of these instruments without the supervision of the instructor is NOT recommended and should not be attempted.)

Topic of Study: Sponsorship and Sports Events

Purpose in Sport Marketing: Sponsors spend money as a method of advertising to increase brand awareness. Sponsors of sports events would like to know if this category of advertising is reaping results, such as brand awareness and increased sales of the company's products. With positive results, sponsor company decision makers will most likely continue to use sponsorship as an advertising form.

Sports event managers desire sponsorship to gain business relationships and as a form of funding the event. Managers would like spectators to support the sponsors as a reward and a show of support for the sponsor's support. This would help in the triangle relationship between the event manager, the sponsor, and the spectator.

Purpose of this study: To measure sponsorship recognition.

Instrument: Survey

Survey 1: Sponsorship Recognition

2001–02 (event)

Directions: Please circle your answer or place an X in the spaces provided. All replies are strictly confidential. Thank you in advance for your assistance!

1. Have you noticed sponsor signs or booths at the (event) stadium or surrounding area for the 2000–2001 season? ❑ Yes ❑ No

Below, answer Yes or No if you think there is a company as a sponsor of the (event). If you answer Yes, identify the *one or more companies* you can remember.

Is there a soft drink sponsor?
a. Pepsi b. Coca-Cola c. RC Cola d. Mountain Dew ❑ Yes ❑ No

Is there a bank sponsor?
a. Capitol City Bank b. Barnett Bank c. Sun Trust
d. Government Employees Credit Union ❑ Yes ❑ No

Is there an American automobile manufacturer sponsor?
a. Chevrolet b. GMC c. Ford d. Dodge ❑ Yes ❑ No

Is there a hotel sponsor?
a. Winn Dixie b. Bruno's c. Albertson's d. Publix ❑ Yes ❑ No

Is there a video rental company sponsor?
a. Blockbuster b. Greg's Video c. Video 21 d. Movie Gallery ❑ Yes ❑ No

Is there a sports magazine sponsor?
a. Sports Illustrated b. ESPN—The Magazine
c. Women's Sport & Fitness d. College Football Weekly ❑ Yes ❑ No

Is there a medical/health facility sponsor?
a. Tallahassee Memorial HealthCare
b. Tallahassee Wellness Center
c. Orlando Orthopedic Clinic
d. Tallahassee Regional Medical Center ❑ Yes ❑ No

Is there an ice cream company sponsor?
a. Ben & Jerry's b. Baskin Robbins c. Edy's d. Haagan-Daas ❑ Yes ❑ No

Is there an internet company sponsor?
a. monster.com b.travelocity.com c. Yahoo! Sports
d. careerbuilders.com ❑ Yes ❑ No

Is there a sports retail sponsor?
a. Jumbo Sports b. Play It Again Sports
c. Champ's d. Finish Line ❑ Yes ❑ No

Is there a local television station sponsor (individual)?
a. WTWC-NBC b. WCTV-CBS
c. WTXL-ABC d. WTLH-FOX ❑ Yes ❑ No

2. Are you more likely to buy the products of sponsor companies of this season because they are sponsors of the (event)? ❑ Yes ❑ No

3. How long have you been a (event) season ticket holder (in years)?

4. Are you a member of the (club) Boosters also? ❑ Yes ❑ No

Please offer some information about yourself (all information is kept confidential).

5. What is your gender? ❑ Female ❑ Male

6. What is your age?

7. What city and state do you live in?

8. Which category below best describes your total, annual household income?

❑ 0–$10,000	❑ $10,000–29,999	❑ $30,000–49,999
❑ $50,000–69,999	❑ $70,000–89,999	❑ $90,000–109,999
❑ $110,000–129,999	❑ $130,000–149,999	❑ $150,000–over

9. What is your highest level of education attained?

❑ grade school	❑ some high school	❑ high school graduate
❑ vocational/technical school	❑ some college	❑ college degree
❑ some post graduate work	❑ master's degree	❑ doctoral degree

When you have completed the survey, please enclose it in the postage-paid, addressed return envelope provided, and drop it in the nearest postal box.

Thank you for participating.

Methodology: As you can see in the example, sponsorship recognition asks the study participant to 'recognize' the sponsor company (or brand) in a particular product category. The typical protocol is multiple choice. (For more specific directions, refer to research methods books and sport marketing literature.)

Surveying takes place during the event away from areas where sponsors' signs would be visible—usually, just outside the arena. The researcher approaches people who attended the event and asks if they would participate in marketing research and complete a survey.

A second surveying technique is to mail the survey to the attendees and ask them to complete it and send it back. This requires gathering a mailing list with names and addresses of people who attended the event. Sometimes, mailing lists are available that contain season ticket-holders, for example.

Sources: (1) Slattery, J., & Pitts, B. G. (2001). Paper presented at the annual conference of the North American Society for Sport Management, Virginia Beach, Virginia, May 29-June 3, 2001. Available from the authors, Florida State University. (2) Cuneen, J., & Hannan, M. (1993). Intermediate measures and recognition testing of sponsorship advertising at an LPGA tournament. *Sport Marketing Quarterly, 2*(1), 47-56.

Topic of Study: Purchase intent; Support of sponsors of sports event

Purpose in Sport Marketing: The purpose of this research is to determine if sports event attendees (spectators) intend to support the sponsors of the event by purchasing the product of that company. Some research is showing that consumers of sports events are more influenced to purchase certain products (of sponsoring companies) and less influenced to purchase others. For example, certain food product companies, such as pizza and sub sandwiches, seem to enjoy more support from attendees than others. The reasons need further investigation. However, if the owner of a more formal restaurant that offers more formal cuisine determines through research that the market (spectators) at certain sports events are less likely to purchase their product, then that owner might decide that advertising (through sponsorship) at this sports event is not producing successful results. This type of research can help answer those questions.

Instrument: Survey

Survey 2: Purchase Intention

Directions: Please circle your answer or place an X in the spaces provided. All replies are strictly confidential. Thank you in advance for your assistance!

Please rate how likely you are to purchase the products of the following sponsors of 2000–01 (event) due to their sponsorship of this organization.

1=definitely will not buy
2=probably will not buy
3=might or might not buy
4=probably will buy
5=definitely will buy

1. Piccadilly Restaurant	1	2	3	4	5
2. Subway	1	2	3	4	5
3. Papa John's	1	2	3	4	5
4. US Airways	1	2	3	4	5
5. U.S. Cellular	1	2	3	4	5
6. Furrin Auto	1	2	3	4	5
7. Comp-U-Wiz	1	2	3	4	5
8. Snookers Billiards Room	1	2	3	4	5
9. Blockbuster	1	2	3	4	5
10. Budweiser	1	2	3	4	5
11. All State Insurance	1	2	3	4	5

Also, please rate your attitude towards these companies as a result of their sponsorship of (event).

1=more favorable attitude due to sponsorship
2=somewhat more favorable attitude
3=doesn't make a difference in opinion about the company
4=somewhat less favorable attitude
5=less favorable attitude due to sponsorship

12. Piccadilly Restaurant	1	2	3	4	5
13. Subway	1	2	3	4	5
14. Papa John's	1	2	3	4	5
15. Airways	1	2	3	4	5
16. Cellular	1	2	3	4	5
17. Furrin Auto	1	2	3	4	5
18. Comp-U-Wiz	1	2	3	4	5
19. Snookers Billiards Room	1	2	3	4	5
20. Blockbuster	1	2	3	4	5
21. Budweiser	1	2	3	4	5
22. All State Insurance	1	2	3	4	5

23. Does the type of signage a person has at an event influence your likelihood to purchase something from that company? ❑ Yes ❑ No
    If yes, why ______________________________________

24. Have you ever purchased the products of any (event) sponsors in the past? ❑ Yes ❑ No

If yes, which companies? And why?

25. Estimate the number of games you attended last season (1999–2000):
❑ 0–10 ❑ 11–20 ❑ 21–over
Estimate the number of games you will attend this season (2000–2001):
❑ 0–10 ❑ 11–20 ❑ 21–over

Please offer some information about yourself (all information is kept confidential).

26. What is your gender? ❑ Female ❑ Male

27. What is your age? _______

28. What city and state do you live in? _______

29. Which category listed below best describes your total, annual HOUSEHOLD income?
❑ 0–$10,000 ❑ $10,001–29,999 ❑ $30,000–49,999
❑ $50,000–69,999 ❑ $70,000–89,999 ❑ $90,000–109,999
❑ $110,000–129,999 ❑ $130,000–149,999 ❑ $150,000–over

What is your highest level of education attained?
❑ grade school ❑ some high school ❑ high school graduate
❑ vocational/technical school ❑ some college ❑ college degree
❑ some post-graduate work ❑ master's degree
❑ doctoral degree ❑ law degree

THANK YOU FOR PARTICIPATING!

Methodology: This instrument attempts to determine the level of purchase intention. As you can see in the example survey, the attendee is asked to rank their level of intention as listed from "definitely will not buy" to "definitely will buy." Surveying takes place during the event. The researcher approaches people attending the event and asks if they would participate in marketing research and complete a survey.

A second surveying technique is to mail the survey to the attendees and ask them to complete it and send it back. This requires gathering a mailing list with names and addresses of people who attended the event. Sometimes, mailing lists are available that contain season ticket-holders, for example.

Sources: (1) Slattery, J., & Pitts, B. G. (2000). Purchase intent of attendees of minor league hockey. Unpublished study. Available from the authors. Florida State University. (2) Shannon, J. R., & Turley, L. W. (1997). The influence of in-arena promotions on purchase behavior and purchase intentions. *Sport Marketing Quarterly, 6*(4), 53-59.

Topic of Study: Market competitors

Purpose in Sport Marketing: The purpose of this research is to determine the level of influence of the competition in the marketplace for your sport business. This information will be used in determining product differentiation and positioning in promotional efforts.

Instrument: Survey

Survey 3: Market Competitor's Influence

Marketing Survey Form

Purpose: This survey is for the purpose of providing better service to the Xxxx (professional team name) audience. The collected information will be solely used for research, and your name will not be identified. Your sincere and honest response is greatly appreciated.

Entertainment Options: Please rate how much you participate in the following activities (5-Always; 4-Often; 3-Sometimes; 2-Occasionally; 1-Never).

1. Attend professional indoor soccer game	5	4	3	2	1
2. Attend a concert	5	4	3	2	1
3. Attend intercollegiate games	5	4	3	2	1
4. Attend professional basketball games	5	4	3	2	1
5. Attend a night club	5	4	3	2	1
6. Attend professional baseball games	5	4	3	2	1
7. Watch sports on TV	5	4	3	2	1
8. Play recreational sports	5	4	3	2	1
9. Attend a movie	5	4	3	2	1
10. Watch non-sport programs on TV	5	4	3	2	1
11. Work out/Exercise	5	4	3	2	1
12. Travel	5	4	3	2	1
13. Attend professional football games	5	4	3	2	1
14. Go to bar/restaurant	5	4	3	2	1
15. Attend other sport shows	5	4	3	2	1

ATTENDANCE INFORMATION. Please fill in the blanks.

How may Xxxxx home games have you attended this season?

How many total Xxxxx home games do you plan to attend this season?

How many Xxxxx games will you attend next season?

DEMOGRAPHIC INFORMATION. Please provide the following information.
Age:
Gender:
Ethnicity (circle one):
a. Caucasian b. Black c. Hispanic d. Asian e. Other

THANK YOU FOR YOUR COOPERATION AND ASSISTANCE!

Methodology: This instrument attempts to determine which competitors in the area are supported by consumers. The attendee (spectator) is asked to rate their involvement in the competitor's products. The attendee is also asked to provide information about their level of involvement in your product (event). This information can be analyzed and the influence of your competitors can be evaluated. Surveying takes place during the event. The researcher approaches people attending the event and asks if they would participate in marketing research and complete a survey.

A second surveying technique is to mail the survey to the attendees and ask them to complete it and send it back. This requires gathering a mailing list with names and addresses of people who attended the event. Sometimes, mailing lists are available that contain season ticket-holders, for example.

Source: Zhang, J. J., Smith, D. W., Pease, D. G., & Jambor, E. A. (1997). Negative influence of market competitors on the attendance of professional sport games: The case of a minor league hockey team. *Sport Marketing Quarterly, 6*(3), 31-39.

Topic of Study: Economic impact, sports event

Purpose in Sport Marketing: The purpose of this research is to determine the financial (economic) impact of a sports event (or business). This information is useful in several ways. It can help the organizers of the event determine how much money the event is responsible for bringing into an area and how much of that money is spent on different areas, such as lodging, food, entertainment, transportation, event admissions (the sports event and other connected events), retail shopping, and event souvenirs. These types of information can help the organizers and local businesses involved (called stakeholders) in decision-making for the future of the event. The information can also be used to garner further support for the event from local government offices, current stakeholders, and potential stakeholders. The information is also used to ascertain the commercial value of the event which is sometimes used to inform prices for advertising and sponsorship fees, broadcasting fees, and other aspects of the event.

Instrument: Survey

Survey 4: Economic Impact, Sports Event

Event Economic Impact Survey

Directions: Simply write your answers or an X in the spaces provided. Thank you in advance!

1. Why are you attending the event?
   ❑ athlete/participant ❑ cultural/participant ❑ exhibitor/sales
   ❑ spectator
   ❑ event worker/staff
   ❑ media with magazine (which one?)
   ❑ media with film crew (which one?) ____________________
   ❑ media with TV (which one?) ____________________
   ❑ media with newspaper (which one?) ____________________
   ❑ media other (which one?) ____________________

2. With whom did you come to the event?
   ❑ family only ❑ partner only ❑ friends only
   ❑ alone ❑ both friends and family/partner

   organization (please fill in): ____________________

3. How many are in your party (including yourself)? ________

4. Would you have come to "city" either now or in the next 3 months if the event were not held? ❑ Yes ❑ No

5. If yes above, how many days longer was your stay (if any) than it would have been if the event had not been taking place? _______

6. How many nights did you spend in city? _______
   In other cities? _______

7. Where (other cities) did you stay? _______

8. If you stayed overnight, where did you stay in city?
   ❑ hotel/motel ❑ with friends/relative ❑ RV
   ❑ camping ❑ hosted housing ❑ hostel
   ❑ apartment ❑ other

9. Have you attended this event previously? ❑ Yes ❑ No
   ❑ 1982 ❑ 1986 ❑ 1990 ❑ 1994

10. Do you plan on attending this event again (Year)? ❑ Yes ❑ No

11. Where do you live?
    Country _______ City ____________ State _____ Postal Code _____

12. What is your source of information about the event?
    ❑ radio ❑ newspaper ❑ TV
    ❑ friends ❑ website ❑ direct mail from the event
    ❑ local (city) sports organization ❑ other

13. How many SPORTS events did you attend/participate in?

14. How many CULTURAL/ARTS events did you attend?

15. Please estimate (in even US dollars) how much you spent on each of the following items during your entire stay for the event in city. Your responses are very important to the study. if you can not covert to US dollars, note what currency you are listing:

    food & beverages (restaurants, concessions, grocery stores, etc.) $ ________
    fees (to participate in the event) $ ________
    admission fees (sports events and other shows) $ ________
    night clubs, lounges, & bars (coverage charges, drinks, etc.) $ ________
    retail shopping (clothing, gifts, etc.) $ ________
    event souvenirs $ ________
    lodging expenses (hotel, motel, etc.) ________
    private auto expenses (gas, oil, repairs, parking fees, etc.) $ ________
    commercial transportation (airlines, bus, train, rental car, etc.) $ ________
    any other expenses (please identify) $ ________

16. What is your age? _______

17. What is your gender?
    ❑ female ❑ male ❑ other

18. What is your sexual orientation?
    ❑ lesbian ❑ gay ❑ bisexual ❑ heterosexual

19. Please describe your household, "I live . . . " (check one and fill in the blanks):

    I am the only adult in my household. I have _______ children.

    I live with my spouse/partner/lover of years. We have _______ children.

    I live with a friend/roommate. I have _______ children.

    Other: Please describe: ____

20. Which category listed below describes your total, annual HOUSEHOLD income in US dollars? (or specify currency)

    ❑ 0–$10,000 ❑ $10,001–29,999 ❑ $30,000–49,999
    ❑ $50,000–69,999 ❑ $70,000–89,999 ❑ $90,000–109,999
    ❑ $110,000–129,999 ❑ $130,000–149,999 ❑ $150,000–plus

21. What is your highest level of education?

    ❑ grade school ❑ some high school ❑ high school graduate
    ❑ vocational/technical school ❑ some college ❑ college degree
    ❑ post-graduate work ❑ doctoral degree

22. What is your occupation? (If retired, please check "retired" and list former occupation.)

    ❑ professional/technical ❑ clerical/office worker ❑ homemaker
    ❑ craftsperson ❑ retired
    ❑ salesperson/buyer/agent ❑ service worker ❑ other: ________

Methodology: This instrument attempts to determine several aspects of economic impact of the event, such as how much money the attendee spends on transportation, lodging, food, and other items by simply asking the attendees to report on the amount of money they spent. Further, the instrument gathers information concerning length of stay, future plans to attend, how many people in the group, how they learned about the event (tells the event marketer which advertising media were effective), in what other activities the attendees participated while in the area, and what other cities were visited by the attendees. Surveying takes place during the event. The researcher approaches people attending the event and asks if they would participate in marketing research and complete a survey.

A second surveying technique is to mail the survey to the attendees and ask them to complete it and send it back. This requires gathering a mailing list with names and addresses of people who attended the event.

Source: (1) Pitts, B. G., & Ayers, K. (2001). An analysis of visitor spending and economic scale on Amsterdam from the Gay Games V, 1998. *International Journal of Sport Management*, in press. (2) Turco, D.M. (1997). Measuring the economic and fiscal impacts of state high school sport championships. *Sport Marketing Quarterly, 6*(3), 49-53.

Topic of Study: Consumer behavior; level of involvement

Purpose in Sport Marketing: The purpose of this research is to study the consumer. The area of research in this study focuses on the influence of an individual's level of involvement with a product as a determinant of level of consumerism. More specifically, how does the consumer's type and frequency of involvement with a particular sport affect their consumption? In this particular study, the authors focused on the spectators at a golf event and attempted to determine if their commitment to play golf, watch golf on TV, attend golf events, money spent on golf, and even use of golf for various activities (such as business and networking) affected their level of involvement as a golf spectator. This type of research can help determine if high level or low level of involvement consumers are more or less likely to attend more similar events. (Typically, research shows that high level involvement consumers of a sport are more likely to attend events.) This information is useful in studying markets, which is then used in making decisions on a number of sport marketing elements concerning the company and product.

Instrument: Survey

Survey 5: Consumer Behavior, Level of Involvement

Personal Involvement Inventory

Place an X in the space that indicates your level of involvement or concern with each item below:

important	___	___	___	___	___	___	___	unimportant*
of no concern	___	___	___	___	___	___	___	of concern to me
irrelevant	___	___	___	___	___	___	___	relevant
means a lot to me	___	___	___	___	___	___	___	means nothing to me*
useless	___	___	___	___	___	___	___	useful
valuable	___	___	___	___	___	___	___	worthless*
trivial	___	___	___	___	___	___	___	fundamental
beneficial	___	___	___	___	___	___	___	not beneficial*
matters to me	___	___	___	___	___	___	___	doesn't matter*
uninterested	___	___	___	___	___	___	___	interested
significant	___	___	___	___	___	___	___	insignificant*
vital	___	___	___	___	___	___	___	superfluous*
boring	___	___	___	___	___	___	___	interesting
unexciting	___	___	___	___	___	___	___	exciting
appealing	___	___	___	___	___	___	___	unappealing**
mundane	___	___	___	___	___	___	___	fascinating
essential	___	___	___	___	___	___	___	nonessential*
undesirable	___	___	___	___	___	___	___	desirable
wanted	___	___	___	___	___	___	___	unwanted*
not needed	___	___	___	___	___	___	___	needed

*Indicates item is reversed scored. Items on the left are scored (1) low involvement to (7) high involvement on the right. Totaling the 20 items gives a score from a low of 20 to a high of 140.

Methodology: Surveying takes place during the event. The researcher approaches people attending the event and asks if they would participate in marketing research and complete a survey.

A second surveying technique is to mail the survey to the attendees and ask them to complete it and send it back. This requires gathering a mailing list with names and addresses of people who attended the event.

Source: Lascu, D. N., Giese, T. D., Toolan, C., Guehring, B., & Mercer, J. (1995). Sport involvement: A relevant individual difference factor in spectator sports. *Sport Marketing Quarterly, 4,* (4), 41-46.

Topic of Study: Consumer behavior, purchase intention, the Internet

Purpose in Sport Marketing: The purpose of this research is to study consumer behavior. More specifically, the purpose of this study was to examine consumer confidence about Internet purchases and purchase intention of sport product on the Internet. The sport company might use this information to design and use the Internet as a distribution channel.

Instrument: Survey

1. In the next 12 months, do you think you are likely to buy XXXXXXX over the Web?

Definitely will buy 1 2 3 4 5 Definitely will not buy

2. Overall, the thought of buying XXXXXXX over the Web causes me to be concerned with experiencing some kind of loss if I went ahead with the purchase.

Strongly Disagree 1 2 3 4 5 Strongly Agree

3. All things considered, I think I would be making a mistake if I bought XXXXXXX over the Web.

Strongly Disagree 1 2 3 4 5 Strongly Agree

4. When all is said and done, I really feel that the purchase of XXXXXXX over the Web poses problems for me that I just don't need.

Strongly Disagree 1 2 3 4 5 Strongly Agree

5. The thought of buying XXXXXXX over the Web causes me concern because some friends would think I was just being showy.

Strongly Disagree 1 2 3 4 5 Strongly Agree

6. Purchasing XXXXXXX over the Web would cause me to be thought of as foolish by some people whose opinion I value.

Strongly Disagree 1 2 3 4 5 Strongly Agree

7. Purchasing XXXXXXX over the Web will adversely affect others' opinion of me.

Strongly Disagree 1 2 3 4 5 Strongly Agree

8. The demands on my schedule are such that purchasing XXXXXXX over the Web would create even more time pressures on me that I don't need.

Strongly Disagree 1 2 3 4 5 Strongly Agree

9. Purchasing XXXXXXX over the Web could lead to an inefficient use of my time.

Strongly Disagree 1 2 3 4 5 Strongly Agree

10. Purchasing XXXXXXX over the Web will take too much time or be a waste of time.

Strongly Disagree 1 2 3 4 5 Strongly Agree

11. Purchasing XXXXXXX over the Web would be a bad way to spend my money.

Strongly Disagree 1 2 3 4 5 Strongly Agree

12. If I bought XXXXXXX over the Web, I would be concerned that the financial investment I would make would not be wise.

Strongly Disagree 1 2 3 4 5 Strongly Agree

13. If I bought XXXXXXX over the Web, I would be concerned that I really would not get my money's worth from the tickets.

Strongly Disagree 1 2 3 4 5 Strongly Agree

14. Purchasing XXXXXXX over the Web would not provide value for the money I spent.

Strongly Disagree 1 2 3 4 5 Strongly Agree

15. As I consider the purchase of XXXXXXX over the Web, I worry about whether they will perform as well as they are supposed to.

Strongly Disagree 1 2 3 4 5 Strongly Agree

16. If I were to purchase XXXXXXX over the Web, I would be concerned that they would not provide the level of benefits that I would be expecting.

Strongly Disagree 1 2 3 4 5 Strongly Agree

17. One concern I have about purchasing XXXXXXX over the Web is that eye-strain could result due from looking at the computer.

Strongly Disagree 1 2 3 4 5 Strongly Agree

18. I am concerned that using the Web may lead to uncomfortable physical side effects such as bad sleeping, backaches, and the like.

Strongly Disagree 1 2 3 4 5 Strongly Agree

19. I am concerned about the potential physical risks associated with purchasing XXXXXXX over the Web.

Strongly Disagree 1 2 3 4 5 Strongly Agree

20. Considering the possible problems associated with an online XXXXXXX vendor's performance, a lot of risk would be involved with purchasing them over the Web.

Strongly Disagree 1 2 3 4 5 Strongly Agree

21. I am confident about the ability of an online XXXXXXX vendor to perform as expected.

Strongly Disagree 1 2 3 4 5 Strongly Agree

22. If you purchase XXXXXXX over the Web, your credit card details are likely to be stolen.

Strongly Disagree 1 2 3 4 5 Strongly Agree

23. I am concerned that if I purchase XXXXXXX over the Web, the vendor will not keep my personal information private.

Strongly Disagree 1 2 3 4 5 Strongly Agree

24. The thought of purchasing XXXXXXX over the Web makes me feel psychologically uncomfortable.

Strongly Disagree 1 2 3 4 5 Strongly Agree

25. The thought of purchasing XXXXXXX over the Web gives me a feeling of unwanted anxiety.

Strongly Disagree 1 2 3 4 5 Strongly Agree

26. The thought of purchasing XXXXXXX over the Web causes me to experience unnecessary tension.

Strongly Disagree 1 2 3 4 5 Strongly Agree

27. To me, the World Wide Web is:

important	1	2	3	4	5	unimportant
of no concern to me	1	2	3	4	5	of concern to me
means a lot to me	1	2	3	4	5	means nothing
matters to me	1	2	3	4	5	doesn't matter
boring	1	2	3	4	5	interesting
unexciting	1	2	3	4	5	exciting
appealing	1	2	3	4	5	unappealing
fun	1	2	3	4	5	not fun
says nothing about me	1	2	3	4	5	says something about me
tells me about a person	1	2	3	4	5	shows nothing about a person

28. In general, I would be one of the last people to buy something over the Web.

Strongly Disagree 1 2 3 4 5 Strongly Agree

29. If I heard that a product I wanted to buy was available over the Web, I would be interested enough to buy it in this manner.

Strongly Disagree 1 2 3 4 5 Strongly Agree

30. Compared to most people, I purchase few, if any, items over the Web.

Strongly Disagree 1 2 3 4 5 Strongly Agree

31. In general, I would be among the last in my circle of friends to buy something over the Web.

Strongly Disagree 1 2 3 4 5 Strongly Agree

32. I would buy something over the Web even if I had not heard of the online vendor before.

Strongly Disagree 1 2 3 4 5 Strongly Agree

33. I like to buy things over the Web before other people do.

Strongly Disagree 1 2 3 4 5 Strongly Agree

34. In selecting from the many XXXXXXX vendors operating on via the Web, would you say that:

I would not care at all as to which one I use 1 2 3 4 5 I would care a great deal as to which one I use

35. Do you think that the various XXXXXXX vendors operating on via the Web are all very alike or very different?

They are all alike 1 2 3 4 5 They are all different

36. How important would it be to you to make the right choice of Web-based XXXXXXX vendor?

Not at all important 1 2 3 4 5 Extremely important

37. In making your choice of Web-based XXXXXXX vendor, how concerned would you be about the outcome of your choice?

Not at all concerned 1 2 3 4 5 Very much concerned

38. What is your age? ______

39. What is your gender? ❑ Male ❑ Female

Methodology: Surveying takes place during the event. The researcher approaches people attending the event and asks if they would participate in marketing research and complete a survey.

A second surveying technique is to mail the survey to the attendees and ask them to complete it and send it back. This requires gathering a mailing list with names and addresses of people who attended the event.

Source: Pope, N., Brown, M., & Forrest, E. (1999). Risk, innovativeness, gender, and involvement factors affecting the intention to purchase sport product online. *Sport Marketing Quarterly, 8*(2), 25–34.

Topic of Study: Consumer behavior, factors influencing attendance

Purpose in Sport Marketing: The purpose of this research is to study consumer behavior. More specifically, the purpose of this is to examine the many factors that influence the consumer's decision to attend a sports event. This information is useful in making decisions concerning several aspects surrounding the event over which the marketer has control, such as, parking fees, ticket prices, seating assignments, cleanliness of the facility, and friendliness of the staff. There are other factors that the marketer has limited or no control, such as parking, weather, competing events or entertainment, and quality or outcome of the event.

Instrument: Survey

Sample 7: Fan Attendance Survey

Part I—Demographics

Directions: The following information is being requested for statistical purposes only. Please answer the following questions by placing a mark or circle on the appropriate box.

1. What is your gender? ❑ Male ❑ Female

2. What is your age?
   ❑ 13–18 ❑ 19–24 ❑ 25–29 ❑ 30–34 ❑ 35–39 ❑ 40–44
   ❑ 45–49 ❑ 50–54 ❑ 55–59 ❑ 60–64 ❑ 65–69 ❑ 70+

3. What is your marital/household status?
   ❑ Single ❑ Married/Partner ❑ Divorced ❑ Widowed ❑ Others

4. What is your highest education level?
   ❑ Elementary ❑ Junior High ❑ High School
   ❑ Undergraduate ❑ Graduate

5. How many children are in your household? (18 yr. old and under)

____

6. What is your annual household income?

❑ Less than $19,999	❑ $20,000–$29,999	❑ $30,000–$39,999
❑ $40,000–$49,999	❑ $50,000–$59,999	❑ $60,000–$69,999
❑ $70,000–$79,999	❑ $80,000–$89,999	❑ $90,000–$99,999
❑ $100,000–$109,000	❑ $110,000–$119,000	❑ $120,000+

7. What is your ethnicity?

❑ African American	❑ Caucasian	❑ Asian
❑ Hispanic	❑ Others:	

8. What is your occupation category?

❑ Blue collar	❑ Clerk	❑ Education
❑ Housewife/husband	❑ Management	❑ Military
❑ Professional	❑ Sales	❑ Student
❑ Technical	❑ Others:	❑ Your title:

9. How many games do you attend each year? ________ games

10. Are you a season ticket holder? ❑ Yes ❑ No

11. What kind of transportation do you use when you come to the stadium?

❑ Driving a car	❑ Bus	❑ Taxi
❑ Motorcycle	❑ Subway	❑ Walk

❑ Others: ________________________________

12. How many miles did you travel to get to the game?
❑ 0–10 ❑ 11–24 ❑ 25–49 ❑ 50–74 ❑ 75–100 ❑ 110+

Part II: Factors

Directions: Please circle the number that best reflects your perspective opinion.
❑ Factor ❑ Influence Rating

How do the following factors influence your attendance at home games?

1= Not at all
2= Very little
3= Somewhat
4= Very much
5= Extremely

1. The price of a ticket. 1 2 3 4 5
2. The price of season ticket. 1 2 3 4 5
3. The price of concessions 1 2 3 4 5
4. TV/Radio coverage of the home game 1 2 3 4 5
in local area

5. TV coverage of another sport event at time of your home game 1 2 3 4 5

6. Other sporting events in the area 1 2 3 4 5

7. Other activities taking place nearby 1 2 3 4 5

8. Other professional franchises in your area 1 2 3 4 5

9. Record (won-loss) of home team 1 2 3 4 5

10. Record (won-loss) of visitor team. 1 2 3 4 5

11. Number of star players on home team 1 2 3 4 5

12. Number of star players on visitor team. 1 2 3 4 5

13. Offensive performance of the home team. 1 2 3 4 5

14. Defensive performance of the home team 1 2 3 4 5

15. Offensive performance of the visitor team 1 2 3 4 5

16. Defensive performance of the visitor team 1 2 3 4 5

17. Closeness of competition 1 2 3 4 5

18. Games with rival teams 1 2 3 4 5

19. A chance to see a record breaking performance by a team or athlete 1 2 3 4 5

20. Special promotion (hat day, poster day, etc.) 1 2 3 4 5

21. Home team's place in the division standings. 1 2 3 4 5

22. Home team's place in the league standings 1 2 3 4 5

23. Home team's involvement in race for a playoff spot 1 2 3 4 5

24. Media advertising (TV, radio, newspaper, Internet, etc.) 1 2 3 4 5

25. Day games during the weekdays. 1 2 3 4 5

26. Night games during the weekdays 1 2 3 4 5

27. Weekend day games. 1 2 3 4 5

28. Weekend night games 1 2 3 4 5

29. Weather conditions 1 2 3 4 5

30. Cleanliness of the facility 1 2 3 4 5

31. Easy and/or multiple access to your facility (via subway, highway, transit, etc.) 1 2 3 4 5

32. Availability of parking at or near facility	1	2	3	4	5
33. Size of the facility (seating capacity)	1	2	3	4	5
34. Crowd behavior at the game	1	2	3	4	5
35. New stadium or arena	1	2	3	4	5
36. Number of years the team has been in the area	1	2	3	4	5
37. The variety of concessions available	1	2	3	4	5
38. Violence in the game	1	2	3	4	5
39. The design and color of uniform	1	2	3	4	5

Methodology: The people to be studied include any group of potential consumers. The sport business might determine to target any group of consumers in order to assess general attitudes toward purchasing their product via the Internet.

Sources: (1) Lu, D. (2000). Factors affecting attendance in professional baseball: A comparison of Taiwan and USA. Paper presented at the Florida Association for Health, Physical Education, Recreation, & Dance annual conference, October, 2000. Paper available from the author, Florida State University. (2) Zhang, J.J., Pease, D.G., Hui, S.C., & Michaud, T.J. (1995). Variables affecting spectator decision to attend NBA games. *Sport Marketing Quarterly, 4*(4), 29-39.

Index

S

T

U

V

W

X

Y

Z

About the Authors

Brenda G. Pitts, Ed.D.

Professor, Sport Marketing

Dr. Pitts is currently professor in sport marketing and program director of sport management at Georgia State University in Atlanta, Georgia, after having spent 6 years at Florida State University and 12 years at the University of Louisville. Dr. Pitts is author/coauthor of three sport marketing textbooks and numerous publications and presentations, primarily in sport marketing and published in several scholarly journals such as the *International Journal of Sport Management*, *Journal of Sport Management*, *Journal of Vacation Marketing*, and the *Sport Marketing Quarterly*. She has helped and consulted in sport marketing for various sport businesses, has reviewed materials in sport management, and has spoken at conferences. Her international stops have included South Africa, Hong Kong, Singapore, Malaysia, France, Australia, Germany, Hungary, England, The Netherlands, Scotland, and France. In recognition of her scholarly achievements, Dr. Pitts was the recipient of the Dr. Earle F. Zeigler Scholar Award in 2000 and became one of the first Research Fellows of the North American Society for Sport Management in 2001. Some of Dr. Pitts's service accomplishments have included being a member of the committee that wrote the Sport Management Curriculum Standards (first published in 1993), serving on the first Sport Management Program Review Council, acting as Program Chair of 2 NASSM conferences, hosting the 1990 NASSM Conference, and fulfilling the roles of Council Member, President-Elect, President, and Past-President of NASSM 1990–1995. In addition, she was an Editorial Board Member (1991–1998) and later Co-Editor-in-Chief of The Sport Management Library (1998–00), a project that has produced 11 textbooks in sport management and has another 6 in development. On a more fun note, Dr. Pitts is always playing sports, most recently soccer, golf, boating, volleyball, jogging, and softball. Finally, Dr. Pitts says that her only claim to fame is that once she rode in an elevator with Michael Jordan and Scottie Pippin.

David K. Stotlar, Ed.D.

Professor, School of KPE, University of Northern Colorado

Dr. David K. Stotlar teaches sport marketing and sport law. He has had over fifty articles published in professional journals and has written several textbooks and book chapters in sport marketing, fitness risk management, and sport law. He has made numerous presentations at international and national professional conferences. On several occasions, he has served as a consultant in sport management and to fitness and sport professionals, and in sport law, to attorneys and international sport managers. David was selected by the USOC as a delegate to the International Olympic Academy in Greece and the World University Games Forum in Italy. He has conducted international seminars in sport management and marketing for the Shanghai Sports Council, the Hong Kong Olympic Committee, the National Sports Council of

Malaysia, Mauritius National Sports Council, the National Sports Council of Zimbabwe, the Singapore Sports Council, the Chinese Taipei University Sport Federation, the Bahrain Sport Institute, the government of Saudi Arabia, the South African National Sports Congress, and the Association of Sport Sciences in South Africa. Dr. Stotlar's contribution to the profession includes an appointment as Coordinator of the Sport Management Program Review Council (NASPE/NASSM) from 1999–2001. He previously served as Chair of the Council on Facilities and Equipment of the American Alliance for Health, Physical Education, Recreation and Dance and as a Board Member and later as President of the North American Society for Sport Management.

Contributing Author Bios

Lori Miller, co-author of Chapter 2, "Historical Eras in Sport Marketing," is a professor in sport administration and the Chair of the Kinesiology and Sport Studies Department at Wichita State University. Lori has an Ed.D. in physical education, a Masters of Business Administration, a Master of Education, and a BA in business. Lori has published over 40 refereed journal articles, five book chapters, and three books. Lori's current research emphasis focuses on legal issues in the sport industry.

Lawrence W. Fielding is a professor and Director of the Sport Marketing/Management Graduate Program in the Department of Kinesiology at Indiana University. He received his Ph.D. from the University of Maryland in sport history in 1974. Dr. Fielding has integrated his interest in sport history with his interest in sport management. He has published more than 50 articles in sport history and sport management and has presented more than 75 papers at research meetings. He has served on the editorial review boards of the *Journal of Sport History* and the *Journal of Sport Management*. He delivered the Stewart C. Staley Address at the North American Society of Sport History Annual Meeting in 1985 and became a North American Society for Sport Management Research Fellow in 2002. His major research interests are the history of the sporting goods industry and the history of commercialized spectator sports. He teaches sport business strategy, sport history, management theory, and sport marketing.

Matt Brown, author of Chapter 16, "Web-Based Sport Marketing," is an assistant professor of sports administration and facility management at Ohio University. He received a B.A. in political science from Truman State University, an M.S. in sport management from Western Illinois University, and an Ed.D. from the University of Northern Colorado in sport administration. Prior to pursuing his doctorate, Dr. Brown worked in campus recreation, collegiate athletics, and tennis club management. At Ohio, he teaches risk management in sport, sport sponsorship, and sport finance. Dr. Brown is currently conducting research on sport management curriculum standards and financial issues in professional sport.